D1584684

Time Out

Buenos Aires

timeout.com/buenosaires

Penguin Books

PENGUIN BOOKS

Published by the Penguin Group
Penguin Books Ltd, 80 Strand, London WC2R ORL, England
Penguin Books USA Inc., 375 Hudson Street, New York, New York 10014, USA
Penguin Books Australia Ltd, 250 Camberwell Road, Camberwell, Victoria 3124, Australia
Penguin Books Canada Ltd, 10 Alcorn Avenue, Toronto, Ontario, Canada M4V 3B2
Penguin Books (NZ) Ltd, cnr Rosedale and Airborne Roads, Albany, Auckland, New Zealand

Penguin Books Ltd, Registered Offices: 80 Strand, London WC2R 0RL, England

First published 2001

Second edition 2004

10 9 8 7 6 5 4 3 2 1

Copyright © Time Out Group Ltd 2001, 2004
All rights reserved

Colour reprographics by Icon, Crowne House, 56-58 Southwark Street, London SE1 1UN
Printed and bound by Cayfosa-Quebecor, Ctra. de Caldes, Km 3 08 130 Sta, Perpètua de Mogoda, Barcelona, Spain

Except in the United States of America, this book is sold subject to the condition that it shall not, by way of trade or
otherwise, be lent, re-sold, hired out, or otherwise circulated without the publisher's prior consent in any form of binding
or cover other than that in which it is published and without a similar condition including this condition being imposed
on the subsequent purchaser.

Edited and designed by
Time Out Guides Limited
Universal House
251 Tottenham Court Road
London W1T 7AB
Tel +44 (0)20 7813 3000
Fax +44 (0)20 7813 6001
Email guides@timeout.com
www.timeout.com

Editorial

Editor Cathy Runciman
Deputy Editor Joshua Goodman
Consultant Editor Chris Moss
Listings Editor Agustina Saubidet
Proofreader John Pym

Editorial/Managing Director Peter Fiennes
Series Editor Ruth Jarvis
Deputy Series Editor Lesley McCave
Guides Co-ordinator Anna Norman
Accountant Sarah Bostock

Design

Art Director Buenos Aires Gonzalo Gil
Designers Georgina Gil, Andrés Castro

Art Director Mandy Martin
Acting Art Director Scott Moore
Digital Imaging Dan Conway
Picture Editor Jael Marschner

Advertising

Sales Director Mark Phillips
International Sales Manager Ross Canadé
Project Co-ordinator (Buenos Aires) Agustina Saubidet

Marketing

Marketing Manager Mandy Martinez
US Publicity & Marketing Associate Rosella Albanese

Production

Guides Production Director Mark Lamond
Production Controller Samantha Furniss

Time Out Group

Chairman Tony Elliott
Managing Director Mike Hardwick
Group Financial Director Richard Waterlow
Group Commercial Director Lesley Gill
Group Marketing Director Christine Cort
Group General Manager Nichola Coulthard
Group Art Director John Oakey
Online Managing Director David Pepper
Group Production Director Steve Proctor
Group IT Director Simon Chappell

Contributors

Introduction Chris Moss, Cathy Runciman. **History** Peter Hudson, Chris Moss. **BA Today** Joshua Goodman. **Literary BA** Chris Moss. **Where to Stay** Eric Amsler, Joaquin Cruise, Sean McAlister. **Sightseeing: Introduction** Chris Moss (*Guided tours* Declan McGarvey). **The Centre** Nicolás Kugler, Chris Moss; **South of the Centre** Joshua Goodman, Chris Moss; **North of the Centre** Chris Moss (*Saint Evita?* Tomás Eloy Martínez). **West of the Centre** Declan McGarvey, Chris Moss. **Along the River** Declan McGarvey, Chris Moss. **Further Afield** Declan McGarvey, Chris Moss. **Restaurants** Joshua Goodman; *additional reviews* Chris Moss, Mark Rebindaine, Mariana Rapoport, Cathy Runciman (*The wine box* Chris Moss; *Mi BA Querido: Germán Martitegui* Cathy Runciman). **Cafés, Bars & Pubs** Joaquin Cruise, Sean McAlister. **Shops & Services** Alicia Peyrano, Mariana Rapoport; *additional reviews* Cathy Runciman, Agustina Saubidet. **Festivals & Events** Joshua Goodman, Nicolás Kugler. **Children** Kristin James Henley. **Clubs** Pola Caracciolo (*Mi BA Querido: Hernán Cattáneo* Cathy Runciman). **Film** Pablo Suárez (*Mi BA Querido: Cecilia Roth* Chris Moss). **Galleries** Christine Castro Gache (*Mi BA Querido: Guillermo Kuitca* Cathy Runciman). **Gay & Lesbian** Pablo Suárez. **Music: Classical & Opera** Julio Nakamurakare. **Music: Rock, Folk & Jazz** Chris Moss, Silvio Najt. **Sport & Fitness** Mark Rebindaine. **Tango** Chris Moss. **Theatre & Dance** Julio Nakamurakare (*Mi BA Querido: Diqui James* Cathy Runciman). **Trips Out of Town: Getting Started** Joshua Goodman. **Upriver** Chris Moss, Mark Rebindaine; *additional research* Declan McGarvey, Nicola Price. **Country** Joshua Goodman; *additional reviews* Mariana Rapoport (*A bird's eye view* Chris Moss). **Beach** Mark Rebindaine. **Uruguay** Joshua Goodman, Mariana Rapoport, Mark Rebindaine, Cathy Runciman. **Directory** Joshua Goodman, Carolina Gryngarten, Declan McGarvey, Chris Moss, Mark Rebindaine.

Maps Nexo Servicios Gráficos, Luis Sáenz Peña 20, Piso 7 'B', Buenos Aires, Argentina (www.nexolaser.com.ar).

Photography Gonzalo Gil, except: pages 6, 9, 10, 11, 16, 26, 82, 208 Archivo General de la Nación, Departamento de Documentos Fotográficos; pages 10, 11, 20, 74, 234 Clarín Contenidos; pages 19, 76, 83, 191 Joshua Goodman; page 74 Ernesto di Pietro; pages 92, 237, 239, 241, 242 Derek Thompson; page 164 Secretaría de Cultura, G.C.B.A.; page 173 Carlos Ibarra; pages 186, 187 César Cigliutti/Marcelo Suntheim; page 190 Martín Bonetto; p209 Piazzolla Tango; page 226 Chris Moss; pages 228, 231 estanciasargentinas.com. The following images were provided by the featured artists/establishments: pages 33, 45, 130, 167, 171, 175, 177, 180, 182, 214, 215, 224.

The Editor would like to thank: Tribalwerks, Valeria Puopolo, Mercedes Jáuregui, José & Estela Pais, Leticia Saharrea, Ian Barnett, Charlie Luxton, Jason Murphy, Andrew Graham Yooll, Dhyana Levy, Tomás Eloy Martínez, Sofía Vaccaro, Federico Andahazi, Martín Gontad, María Luisa Monti, José de Santis, and all contributors to the previous edition of *Time Out Buenos Aires*, whose work forms the basis for parts of this book.

© Copyright Time Out Group Ltd
All rights reserved

Contents

Introduction

It's often remarked that Buenos Aires' passionate residents – the *porteños* – love their psychoanalysts. Like good Freudians, they transfer their identity crises on to their city, comparing it unfavourably to Paris, Rome, New York and Madrid, yet bursting into tears upon hearing a tango abroad. Secretly, they love the place and ask every foreign visitor: 'Do you like *my* city?'

Right now, your answer is likely to be an unequivocal '*Sí*'. Following the economic debacle of 2002, BA has managed not only to rehabilitate its battered ego, but to put energy into all it does best. This means a roaring trade in steaks, tango and football, but also includes a thriving contemporary design scene and lots of new talent in the arts, especially film and theatre. Even icons are getting a marketing makeover. Evita, Gardel and Maradona, ingrained in the Argentinian psyche as mother, father and rebellious son, have been given new museums. In the more mundane sphere of commerce, leather has been taken off the pampas and reworked into designer furniture and undies, and Mendozan wine is being drunk in beautiful wine bars as well as exported to every corner of the planet.

Bearers of hard currency can indulge in all these local luxuries at bargain prices. There are also booms in gastronomy and property, and festivals year-round celebrate the myriad rebirths. Trying to keep up with all this, and the ever-swelling nightlife scenes in Palermo Viejo, Madero Este and San Telmo, is an enjoyable challenge. Restaurants open weekly, and a serious bar crawl would take a long night – something that BA specialises in. It's all a measure of the energy and resourcefulness of *porteños*, especially the younger generation, who, deprived of the opportunity to travel by the enfeebled peso, are spending vast amounts of creativity and sizeable wads of cash picking the place up.

Some things don't change. BA can be occasionally bad-tempered, crumbling and chaotic, but this is part of the package. In fact, it is from the slums that a punky new cumbia music, recycling campaigns and refreshingly radical politics are emerging.

It all makes for a hectic, edgy lifestyle for *porteños* and tourists alike. Far from more obvious traveller hubs, stranded on the edge of the strangely beautiful pampas and only as European as you want it to be, this is a capital for seasoned hedonists and educated escape artists. Glamorous, gorgeous, gritty and always glad to welcome foreigners, BA is addictive, suited to those who thrive on raw passion and the unpredictable. Buenos Aires has been called many things over the years – Queen of the Plate, Paris of South America, city of fury, secret city, eternal city, and, of course, a city of shrinks and couches – but it's not taking its current crisis lying down.

ABOUT TIME OUT GUIDES

This is the second edition of the *Time Out Buenos Aires Guide*, one of an expanding series of Time Out guides produced by the people behind London and New York's successful listings magazines. Our guides are all written and updated by resident experts, who have striven to provide you with all the most up-to-date information you'll need to explore the city or read up on its background, whether you're a local or a first-time visitor. The guide contains practical information, plus features that focus on unique aspects of the city.

THE LOWDOWN ON THE LISTINGS

Above all, we've tried to make this book as useful as possible. Addresses, telephone numbers, websites, transport information, opening times, admission prices and credit card details are all included in our listings.

And, as far as possible, we've given details of facilities, services and events, all checked and correct as we went to press. However, venues can change their arrangements and some places in BA opening and close their doors according to the level of trade. Likewise, during holiday periods, some businesses and attractions have variable hours. Before you go out of your way, we'd advise you whenever possible to phone and check opening times, ticket prices and other particulars.

While every effort has been made to ensure the accuracy of information contained in this guide, the publishers cannot accept responsibility for any errors it may contain.

There is an online version of this guide, along with guides to 45 international cities, at **www.timeout.com**.

THE LIE OF THE LAND

Buenos Aires' grid system makes getting around the city relatively easy, although there are differences between 'official' area names and those commonly in use. We have divided the city into overall areas (the Centre, North of the Centre, South of the Centre, and so on), and then barrios or neighbourhoods within those (Recoleta, San Telmo, La Boca, Congreso, and so on). For more details, *see p53*. As the city is huge and many streets cover more than 30 blocks, every place is listed with its exact address, the barrio it is in and the nearest two cross streets or intersection – written in Spanish, to help you tell a taxi driver or ask a local.

PRICES AND PAYMENT

The prices we have supplied should be treated as guidelines; volatile economic conditions can cause prices to change. We have published prices as they were quoted to us – in either Argentinian pesos (AR$) or US dollars (US$). As a two-tier pricing system seems to be creeping into use, this allows you to identify the places that are charging tourists dollar rates for their services (and often charging lower peso prices to locals). At the time of going to press, one US dollar was worth about AR$2.90 and the value of £1 hovered around AR$5.

We have noted whether venues such as shops, hotels and restaurants accept the following credit cards: American Express (**AmEx**), Diners Club (**DC**), MasterCard (**MC**) and Visa (**V**). A few businesses may take travellers' cheques. If prices vary wildly from those we've quoted, ask whether there's good reason. If not, go elsewhere. We aim to give the best and most up-to-date advice, so we always want to know if you've been badly treated or overcharged.

TELEPHONE NUMBERS

To phone Buenos Aires from outside Argentina, dial your country's international code, then 54 (for Argentina) then 11 (for Buenos Aires) and finally the local eight-digit number, which we have given in all listings. If you are calling from within Argentina, but outside the city, you will need to add 011 before the eight-digit number. Within the city just dial the eight digits.

ESSENTIAL INFORMATION

For all the practical information you might need for visiting the city, including emergency phone numbers and details of local transport, turn to the **Directory** chapter at the back of the guide. It starts on page 243.

MAPS

Map references indicate the page and square on the street maps at the back of the book for all places in central Buenos Aires. The map section, which begins on page 269, also includes useful overview maps of the capital, northern suburbs, and a map for planning trips out of town. To make the maps easier to navigate there is a street index (pages 282-284).

LET US KNOW WHAT YOU THINK

We hope you enjoy the *Time Out Buenos Aires Guide*, and we'd like to know what you think of it. We welcome tips for places that you consider we should include in future editions and take note of your criticism of our choices. There's a reader's reply card at the back of this book for your feedback – or you can email us at **buenosairesguide@timeout.com**.

Advertisers

We would like to stress that no establishment has been included in this guide because it has advertised in any of our publications and no payment of any kind has influenced any review. The opinions given in this book are those of *Time Out* writers and entirely independent.

IRISH CHARM EXPLODES
IN BUENOS AIRES

THE KILKENNY

Enjoy the best fun,
where the perfect pint lives

Happy Hour
6,00 p.m. to 8,00 p.m.

Whiskey club
with more than 80 brands

♣

♣

Promotions
8,00 p.m. to 10,00 p.m.

Live bands or DJ's
playing everyday
11,30 p.m. to 6,00 a.m.

♣

♣

Best Irish food
in town

Major credit cards
accepted

THE
KILKENNY
Irish Pub & Restaurant
BUENOS AIRES

M.T. de Alvear 399 • Downtown Buenos Aires
• Tel. (54-11) 4312-7291
E-mail: thekilkenny@redynet3.com.ar

In Context

Evita and Juan Domingo Perón.

History

From rags to riches, and revolution to ruin: the Queen of the River Plate's biography is never boring.

CONQUEST AND CONTRABAND

Thousands of years before Europeans arrived in the Americas, peoples from northeastern Asia migrated south from the Bering Strait, then a frozen bridge between present-day Siberia and Alaska. The area stretching inland from the southern shore of the estuary of the Río de la Plata (River Plate), far from the Inca empire, was populated by bands of hunter-gatherer Querandí, who eked out an existence killing the llama-like guanacos, flightless rheas and small deer that inhabited the vast grassy plains that are the pampas.

For most *porteños* – as Buenos Aires residents are known – the city's history began when the European conquistadors arrived in the 16th century. It was an inauspicious start. Juan Díaz de Solís, a Portuguese navigator employed by the Spanish crown, landed in 1516, 24 years after Columbus reached the Americas. He and the rest of the landing party were killed and eaten by the indigenous tribes on the eastern bank of the Plate. Nevertheless, successive waves of Spanish and Portuguese explorers sparked a race to colonise the area, sailors returning home with

tales of rich civilisations and great wealth – to which the Río de la Plata's name (*plata* means silver) bears testimony. The silver was elsewhere though – notably, in Potosí in Bolivia – and subsequent attempts at settlement fared little better than the first landing.

Prestigious Spaniard Pedro de Mendoza arrived with between 1,200 and 2,000 soldiers and settlers in February 1536. The Ciudad y Puerto Santa María de los Buenos Ayres that he founded was probably located near what is now Parque Lezama. But after initial friendly contact, conflicts with the indigenous inhabitants further upriver grew. Some settlers resisted, but the main force of Spanish colonisation switched northwards and, in 1541, Domingo Martínez de Irala, commander of the garrison in Asunción (later to become the Paraguayan capital), ordered the abandonment of Buenos Aires.

Settlement of what is today Argentina continued with the foundation of three regional capitals in the interior: Santiago del Estero, Tucumán and Córdoba. But it became clear that a port would be necessary to service the vast area to the south of the silver deposits of Potosí, and on 11 June 1580, Lieutenant Juan de Garay replanted the Spanish flag in the soil of Buenos Aires. However, Spanish interest in South America was largely restricted to plundering gold and silver, and scant attention was paid to the new settlement – which had neither.

Until 1610, Buenos Aires had scarcely 500 inhabitants, few of whom cared to venture into the as yet unsettled and uncultivated pampas, making them dependent on supply ships for survival. Unfortunately, these were infrequent; Spain sent virtually all its goods on a circuitous route, allowing voyages to Buenos Aires only every one or two years in an attempt to avoid pirates and control trade. Despite Spain's best efforts, this policy had the opposite effect. Goods were smuggled in, mainly from Brazil, and contraband trade became rife.

From these humble beginnings, Buenos Aires gradually grew in importance, sparking jealous rivalries: first with the Viceroyalty of Peru, power centre of Spain's South American empire, which resented the city's attempts to usurp its place; then with neighbouring provinces, which coveted the cattle that had proliferated on the pampas; and later with nearby Montevideo (capital of present-day Uruguay), which claimed advantages over Buenos Aires as the region's principal port. Furthermore, the city's refusal to send men to help fight hostile indigenous groups in the north provoked much ill-feeling – a resentment between Buenos Aires and the surrounding provinces that has bubbled up throughout Argentinian history.

By the 18th century, the process of taming the pampas was under way. Hardy settlers ventured out into the fertile plains and established what would become the vast *estancias* (cattle ranches) of the province, and the resultant trade in leather and dried beef continued to flow through Buenos Aires. In 1776, in recognition of the port's strategic position and in a bid to regain commercial control, Spain created the Virreinato del Rio de la Plata (Viceroyalty of the River Plate). It comprised a vast administrative area the size of the US, comprising what are today Bolivia, Paraguay, Argentina and Uruguay – and was finally separated from the command of Peru.

The new authorities immediately set up free trade agreements with Chile, Peru and Spain, and during the last two decades of the 18th century, the port boomed. The first of many waves of immigrants arrived from Europe (*see p16* **Peopling the pampas**). Buenos Aires became a bustling commercial centre, free from the strict social hierarchy that characterised its rivals in the interior. Its growing wealth funded an orphanage, a women's hospital, a shelter for the homeless and street lighting.

But the rapid growth also brought tensions. The new pro-free trade merchant class, mainly *criollos* (American-born Spanish) began to face off against the Spanish-born traditionalists, who favoured Spain's monopoly. The creation of the city's first newspapers and the prospect of revolution and war in Europe also inspired heated debate about the country's future.

'The *porteños* bombarded the British with every imaginable projectile – including boiling oil – as they tried to advance along the city's narrow streets.'

The empire-building British had ideas of their own. Having annihilated the Spanish and French fleets at the Battle of Trafalgar in 1805, they began to cast a covetous eye on Spain's colonies. A year later, under the command of General William Carr Beresford, some 1,500 British troops entered Buenos Aires. Although they won a degree of local support with attractive promises of free trade and reduced tariffs, the majority sided with the garrison commander Santiago de Liniers and his forces.

When the invaders were overwhelmed and expelled within six weeks, Liniers was made viceroy by popular acclaim. He proved his worth by heading off a second invasion attempt in 1807, backed by determined resistance from the *porteños*, who bombarded the British with every imaginable projectile – including boiling oil – as they tried to advance along the city's narrow streets. Retouched bullet holes from this battle can still be seen on one of the towers of the Santo Domingo church on the corner of Defensa and Avenida Belgrano in San Telmo, which British troops used as a base.

BREAKING WITH SPAIN

Simmering tensions in the city were heightened by news that Napoleonic forces had triumphed in Spain. The *criollos* demanded that Santiago de Liniers' successor, Viceroy Baltasar Hidalgo de Cisneros, convene an open meeting of the city's governing body to consider the situation. Despite attempts by Spanish loyalists to restrict the size of the meeting, the vote was conclusive. The *criollos* declared the viceroy's reign to have expired and an elected junta (council), presided over by Cornelio Saavedra and consisting of such revolutionary thinkers as Mariano Moreno and Manuel Belgrano, was formed to replace him. This marked a revolutionary transfer of power from the Spanish elite to the *criollos*. The loyalists made a last-ditch attempt at resistance, but a massive public protest backed by the *criollo* militia units on 25 May 1810 – in the square later to be named Plaza de Mayo in honour of the events that took place there – convinced them of the inevitable.

This conflict, known as the Revolución de Mayo, sparked a rise in anti-Spanish feeling. With the opening of the economy, the English began to dominate trade and transport, but proposals for a stronger alliance with Britain were resisted by various factions. They finally foundered when the country formally declared its independence under the name of the United Provinces of the River Plate in the northern province of Tucumán on 9 July 1816. On this day, celebrated annually as Argentina's independence day and commemorated in the name of the city's major avenue (Avenida 9 de Julio), the new nation announced its opposition to 'any other form of foreign domination'.

Emboldened by having crushed the English invaders in the previous decade, *criollos* in Buenos Aires subsequently led the movement for independence from Spain, promising to consult the provinces later. But the city had scarcely 40,000 inhabitants, and the provinces, jealous of its power, were not easily convinced. The province of Córdoba staged a counter-revolution, led by Liniers, who the junta executed for his trouble. Opposition was also fierce in Montevideo, Asunción and what is now Bolivia, all of which eventually separated from the former Viceroyalty of the River Plate.

The conflict between provinces and capital was further stirred up by the vested interests of those who stood to gain or lose from the transfer of political power, particularly over the port's customs house, principal source of state funds.

The resulting civil war lasted 10 years, during which the government, constituted in various guises in Buenos Aires, sought to assume all the rights and privileges of the former Spanish colonial authorities.

This period saw the establishment of professional armed forces led by General José de San Martín and the rise of the *caudillos*, provincial strongmen who brutally defended regional autonomy. In the name of Federalism, these opposed centralised Unitarian rule. San Martín, the son of Spanish officials, ensured his place in Argentina's list of national heroes by joining the revolutionary cause and leading a daring advance across the Andes to liberate Chile. But he refused to intervene in Argentina's civil war and, after defeating the Spanish again in Peru, eventually retired to Europe.

In 1820, provincial forces defeated the nationalist army at Cepeda, outside Buenos Aires, and the centralist intentions of the city were scuppered. Thereafter, the city suffered a period of turmoil. But by the end of 1820, order had been restored under Bernardino Rivadavia, a centralist leader during the early years of the revolutionary government in Buenos Aires. With the provinces rejecting rule from Buenos Aires, Rivadavia was free to dedicate the income from its customs house to improving the city, reorganising its government and justice system. His government saw the founding of the agricultural college with its botanical garden, the natural history museum and the University of Buenos Aires.

The intellectual, architectural and economic growth of the city, which now had over 55,000 inhabitants, contrasted with underdevelopment in the provinces. Nevertheless, relations with the rest of the country improved temporarily and Buenos Aires took on the responsibility for international relations as the new nation was recognised by the major foreign powers.

Rivadavia became the first president of a united and independent Argentina in 1826, but a year later the provinces were again up in arms. Rivadavia's constitution was rejected by most of the provincial *caudillos*, led by Juan Manuel de Rosas and Juan Facundo Quiroga.

Rosas, who served a first term as governor of Buenos Aires between 1829 and 1832, was the ultimate land- and cattle-owning *caudillo* with a strong following in the countryside. He consolidated his standing in 1833 by organising an expedition to exterminate the indigenous Araucano, who competed with the wealthy ranch owners for the region's cattle.

Two years later, Rosas again became governor of Buenos Aires. Although a self-

The Liberator: **General José de San Martín.**

The English Invasions.

Despite further uprisings, the national army successfully defended the republic, but were further battle-hardened during a pointless war with Paraguay, from 1865 to 1870. The 'desert campaign' of 1879, on the other hand, led by General Julio Roca, was deemed a success. The campaign resolved the long-running conflict with indigenous groups – by the simple but brutal measure of exterminating the majority of them – and in the process opened up 605,000 square kilometres (233,500 square miles) for cattle- and sheep-farming.

Agricultural output was not restricted to livestock. New technology boosted wheat exports, begun in 1878, and the following year saw the first shipment of refrigerated meat. Both developments would have a major economic impact. The bulk of the profits went to the large landowners, however, or were spent on British imports. The British also reaped handsome rewards from the construction of the railways, which grew by 2,516 kilometres (1,563 miles) from 1862 to 1880.

proclaimed federalist, his rule was absolutely centralist and he steadily amassed the powers of national government. During his 17-year reign, he consolidated the power of the port and province of Buenos Aires. But he also imposed rigid censorship and ruled by murder and repression. All citizens were compelled to make public their support for Rosas by wearing a red Federalist ribbon (the Unitarian colours were sky blue and/or white) and public documents, newspapers and personal letters were required to start with the forceful slogan 'Long live the Federation and death to the savage Unitarians!'

At the end of his second governorship, Rosas left a country that was isolated and economically backward. But he had also, albeit forcibly, encouraged national unity and paved the way for the federal constitution drafted in 1853, which established a republic with a strong central government and autonomous provinces.

A NATION TAKES SHAPE
The next two decades saw the forging of the new nation, as successive presidents worked to create a unified state. Democracy, even imperfectly administered, represented an advance over the earlier despotism. Bartolomé Mitre, governor of Buenos Aires and the founder of *La Nación* newspaper, was succeeded by Domingo Faustino Sarmiento. Sarmiento is widely remembered for improvements to the education system, the pink paintwork of the presidential palace and for penning *Facundo*, a denunciation of Rosas, written as a biography of Quiroga, his tyrannical lieutenant – described by some as the most important book written in Spanish America.

'Yellow fever killed more than one-tenth of the city's population and encouraged its wealthiest inhabitants to relocate to Barrio Norte.'

Characteristically, the city benefited the most from these economic advances, developing a cosmopolitan look and feel. Nevertheless, the absence of water and sewerage systems led to outbreaks of cholera in 1867 and yellow fever in 1871. The latter killed more than one-tenth of the city's population and encouraged its wealthiest inhabitants to relocate from the hard-hit southern sections to Barrio Norte.

In 1880, the city of Buenos Aires suffered its final assault at the hands of the provinces. Roca, like Rosas before him, used his slaughter of indigenous groups as a springboard for the presidency. Although backed by the provinces, he was resisted by Buenos Aires. The fighting that ensued killed more than 2,000, most of them *porteños*, before the national government was able to prevail. The city was then placed under central government control and separated from the province, which adopted as its capital La Plata, 60 kilometres (37 miles) to the east.

BOOM AND BUST
Roca was the figurehead for an oligarchy, represented by the Partido Autonomista Nacional (PAN), which held power for the next three decades, during which Buenos Aires mushroomed. Immigration, especially from

The historical hall of infamy

In Context

Pedro de Mendoza

BA's founder is, depending on your point of view, a nemesis or a flop. But even upbeat versions of Hispanic history cannot hide the fact that the founding mission of this court aristocrat, arriving in 1536 with 16 ships carrying around 1,600 men (three times the number Cortés had in Mexico) was a blundering disaster. He failed to win over the native Querandí, ended up fighting a war with them, and lost hundreds of soldiers through starvation and disease. Mendoza died at sea on his way back to Spain, saving him from further embarrassment.

William Carr Beresford & John Whitelock

The failed English Invasions of 1806 and 1807, led, respectively, by Beresford and Whitelock, proved the *criollos'* capacity for fierce resistance. A few Anglophiles wonder 'what if' their campaign had succeeded and Argentina had become part of the British Empire – but the episode is more than anything a classic case of eccentric English captains in the corsair tradition, getting thrashed by canny locals. The English will be forever known as '*piratas*' in Buenos Aires.

Juan Manuel de Rosas

'Each morning, we'd whisper about who and how many had been beheaded' – so wrote Víctor Gálvez of the regime of Rosas, twice governor of BA province (1829-32, 1835-52). Recognised by some historians as a clever nationalist politician with a finger on the gaucho pulse and despised by liberal president Sarmiento for the atrocities carried out by his henchmen – known as La Mazorca – Rosas is an early prototype of the Latin American dictator. Crushed by Justo José de Urquiza at the battle of Monte Caseros in 1852, Rosas finally fled to England.

María Estela Isabel Martínez de Perón

Evita would always be a hard act to follow, but Perón's third wife's unsuitability for rule was matched only by the weakness of the economy and the nest of vipers she inherited on coming to power after Perón's death in 1974. Known as Isabelita (a term of endearment that would become risible), this

Spain and Italy, had already swollen the city's population from 90,000 in 1854 to 526,000 by 1890. By 1914, it was the largest city on the continent, with 1,575,000 inhabitants.

Inspired by Haussmann's Parisian project, Buenos Aires was remodelled under Torcuato de Alvear, municipal chief from 1883-87 and considered the father of the modern city. The grand public buildings, parks and plazas date mainly from this time. British companies built tramways, gas and electricity networks, and a modern sewerage system was created. Meanwhile, Argentina established its place as the world's leading grain exporter and was second only to the US as a frozen meat exporter, creating a second boom for the port city.

But booms were fragile. A rise in British interest rates led the British Baring Brothers bank – which had funnelled vast sums into the republic – to cut off its cash supply and demand repayment. In 1890, Argentina was plunged into a sudden, massive economic crisis.

If emergency measures and the general conditions at the time – including devaluation and further credit from Britain – allowed Argentina to recover, the shaky economy sparked dissent from the more vulnerable sections of society. The growing urban working class enjoyed little protection from social and economic problems. Discontent made them a ready audience for revolutionary ideas imported with European immigrants, and there was a series of strikes and armed uprisings. The government controlled these with police repression and the threat of deportation.

In 1912, Roque Sáenz Peña, leader of the PAN's liberal faction, enacted compulsory universal male suffrage. Electoral fraud had kept the party in government for three decades, but now the law signalled its own demise. Hipólito Yrigoyen, leader of the newly formed Unión Cívica Radical (the Radicals), was elected president in 1916, marking the advent of popular politics after a century of elite rule.

former cabaret dancer had only the support of her husband's Rasputin-like former advisor José López Rega. Together they led Argentina to the brink of all-out civil war and heralded the darkness of the 1976-83 dictatorship.

Leopoldo Fortunato Galtieri

The last of the military dictators in the 1976-83 period was also perhaps the most clueless. Nonetheless, the Plaza de Mayo filled with supporters when he sent a force to recover the Falkland/Malvinas in April 1982 in a cynical attempt to deflect attention from a rising tide of anti-government protest. When British troops forced an Argentinian surrender, Galtieri's rule – and the regime that he represented – was moribund; he was later tried for 'incompetence'. Sentenced but granted an amnesty by Menem in 1990, Galtieri spent his last days drinking whisky under house arrest for human rights abuses and died while awaiting trial in January 2003.

Domingo Cavallo

This Harvard-trained Finance Minister who pegged Argentina's roller-coaster currency to the dollar in 1991 once enjoyed demi-god status. He gave middle-class Argentinians mortgages, holidays abroad and all the luxuries of the 'first world' and the people smiled upon him. Recession ensued as the 'strong peso' was shown to be a superficial cure – but Cavallo defended his baby with blind faith. Kicked out of Menem's cabinet in 1996, Cavallo ran for the presidency in 1999, but was beaten by Fernando de la Rúa. Returned to a ministerial position by de la Rúa in 2001, he finally proved all too human and quit in the face of massive protests demanding his resignation.

Fernando de la Rúa

Sweeping to presidential victory in 1999 on an anti-corruption ticket (and the motto 'They say I'm boring'), de la Rúa was the calm-headed Radical politician who would turn around the Babylonian excesses of the Menem years and return Argentina to its standing as a major member of the world economy. Before anyone could yawn, there was a bribery scandal, his Vice President resigned, the economy collapsed, unemployment rocketed, IMF loans went unpaid and the peso's pegging to the dollar was coming unstuck. Following riots and heavy-handed police repression, de la Rúa stood down in December 2001 and handed the reins to five presidents inside two weeks. Boredom, Argentina-style.

RADICALS ON THE RISE

The Radicals were to rule Argentina for the next 14 years. During this period, 10 per cent of the rural population migrated to the cities, keen to join a vibrant, upwardly mobile middle class. Yrigoyen was equal to the party's promise of order, but did nothing to alter conservative political and economic structures. From 1914, international prices for Argentina's produce declined and growth was curtailed.

After initial conciliatory overtures to the unions, causing heated conservative protests, the government subsequently permitted their brutal repression. In Buenos Aires, the terror reached its height during La Semana Trágica (Tragic Week) in 1919, when the government put down a metalworkers' strike with the aid of gangs organised by the employers, who also attacked Jewish immigrants. The body count, although numerous, was never established.

Nevertheless, Yrigoyen, in typical *caudillo* style, enjoyed almost reverential support as a populist demagogue who displayed a paternal interest in his supporters – especially students, for whom he opened up free university education. He also made nationalist gestures by creating the state-owned petroleum company Yacimientos Petrolíferas Fiscales to exploit the country's new oil wealth (oil had been discovered in 1907), and opposing US colonialism. But when Yrigoyen was re-elected in 1928, he was in his twilight years. The worldwide Great Depression, which started in 1929, limited his ability to buy support by dipping into the state coffers. His government was overthrown in 1930 by an army that he himself had helped politicise, heralding a period of military intervention in state affairs after half a century in which the army had kept out of politics.

The coup was backed by the rural oligarchy, who were hardest hit by the global crisis and resented their removal from power in 1916. But it also owed much to the rise of fascist ideologies imported from Europe, which saw little use for democracy. General José Félix Uriburu's decision to dissolve Congress, censor the media and imprison political opponents in 1930 and the subsequent election of his military rival General Agustín Justo in 1931 inaugurated a period of what some termed 'patriotic fraud' – a populist ploy to prevent the Radicals from taking power.

With the economy in crisis, the government halted immigration and intervened massively in the markets to favour large producers. Little attention was given to the working or middle classes and many of the latter were forced to sell their grand family homes (now used as embassies or government offices). But import controls and migration of cheap labour from the countryside helped foster an industrial sector that employed around 1,200,000.

When the British announced in 1932 that they would favour imports from their colonies, the government negotiated the Roca-Runciman Treaty, proudly declaring that it made the the country another British colony. The deal guaranteed continued purchases of Argentinian beef in return for a British monopoly over transport and meat packing plants – and was deeply unpopular with the public.

Justo invested heavily in public works, including trunk roads from Buenos Aires to the provinces. Three new Subte (subway) lines – B, C and E – were inaugurated between 1930 and 1936, to supplement line A, the continent's oldest, which opened in 1913. Avenida 9 de Julio was also widened to its current size and the city's administration decided to broaden every third or fourth street between Avenidas Caseros and Santa Fe, replacing the narrow colonial streets with today's busy transport arteries.

Production flourished with the start of World War II, which stemmed the tide of European imports. Argentina stayed neutral until late in the war, while maintaining its traditional alignment with Britain, but by 1943, the conservative government had lost much of its lustre and the army again intervened.

MEET THE PERONS

The military was now installed as a de facto political party, running government for much of the rest of the century. But it had little idea what to do once in power. The issue was resolved with the emergence of another modern-day *caudillo*, army colonel Juan Domingo Perón, head of the then obscure labour department. He had a very keen understanding of the power of the masses, picked up during his time as a military attaché in late-1930s Italy, where he was impressed by Europe's burgeoning fascist movements.

Perón's genius was to recognise the growing importance of the Argentinian working class and win the support of the union movement,

which remains under his spell to this day. He was soon named vice-president and war minister and eventually presidential candidate. With Argentina's produce fetching bonanza prices, the healthy state of the economy allowed Perón considerable leeway with welfare projects, including housing and health schemes and the introduction of universal pensions.

Between 1936 and 1947, Buenos Aires' population swelled from 3,430,000 to 4,724,000. Most of the new inhabitants were poor migrants from the provinces – they increased from 12 to 29 per cent of the city's population – and they formed the bedrock of Perón's support. When the oligarchy decided, in 1945, that Perón had gone too far and arrested him, it was this underclass (known in Peronist lore as the *'descamisados'* or 'shirtless ones') that came to his rescue. On 17 October – still celebrated by Peronists as Día de la Lealtad (Loyalty Day) – workers massed in the Plaza de Mayo to defend Perón. When he appeared around midnight on the balcony of the Casa Rosada, to the cheers of 300,000 supporters, it became evident that he was too powerful to be stopped, at least for the time being.

In February 1946, Perón won the first democratic election since Yrigoyen, launching propaganda and state welfare campaigns that converted him and his young, ambitious wife, Evita (born Eva Duarte; *see p82* **Saint Evita?**), into legends. While Perón fulfilled his duties, Evita dispensed the government's welfare budget, mixing easily with the poor, while enjoying her new wealth. As leader of the women's wing of Peronism, she took up the campaign that enacted women's suffrage in 1947.

Massive state intervention in the economy, however, was poorly handled. The railways, which were bought from the British to popular rejoicing, cost four times their official valuation. Mismanagement of the transport, gas and phone services damaged their efficiency. Nonetheless, in 1949, a new constitution was approved, guaranteeing social rights and allowing for Perón's re-election.

Perón was elected to a second term in 1951, but less than two months after retaking office, Evita died from cancer, aged 33. Although Perón remained a crucial figure until his death in 1974, the heart had gone from Peronism. Moreover, Argentina had exhausted most of its reserves of gold and foreign exchange, and two bad harvests exposed the fragility of his welfare drive. He promptly abandoned the more radical economic policies and passed a law protecting foreign investment. Yet even as the economy recovered, Perón inexplicably launched a series of barbed attacks on the church, which had previously backed him. The move fuelled a growing opposition. In 1955, the Plaza de Mayo was bombed by naval planes during an attempted military uprising, killing more than 200 government supporters. In response, Peronists torched city churches. Argentina had begun to spin out of control.

STATE OF FEAR

The next two decades saw a fragmentation of Argentinian society that gave rise to a period of unparalleled barbarism. In December 1955, Perón was overthrown by the military – with wide support from the upper and middle classes – and went into exile. His Partido Justicialista, or PJ, was banned and persecuted.

The Radicals split, too, and Arturo Frondizi, leader of their more combatative wing, was elected president in 1958. Once in power, however, Frondizi alienated those who had voted for him by reneging on campaign promises, though he won friends in the oligarchy with free-market policies. Despite repeatedly yielding to military demands, the generals eventually tired of him. Angered by news that the president had held a secret meeting in Buenos Aires with Ernesto 'Che' Guevara, Argentinian-born hero of the Cuban revolution, the army forced his resignation in 1962.

With the Peronists outlawed and harried, Arturo Illia, leader of the Radicals' more conservative wing, was elected president the

Almost three decades of dignified protest: the **Madres de Plaza de Mayo**.

following year, with just 25 per cent of the vote. Although his brief rule restored economic growth, the military was once again dissatisfied and retook power in 1966, under Juan Carlos Onganía. It seized control of the political parties, the press and the universities, infamously assaulting unarmed students and staff of the University of Buenos Aires in La Noche de los Bastones Largos (Night of the Long Batons). The country continued its descent into chaos with the growth of guerrilla movements, led by the Montoneros, who had Peronist origins, and, later, the Trotskyite People's Revolutionary Army (ERP).

'When Perón returned from exile to Argentina in 1973, the tension erupted into bloodshed at a massive rally to welcome him.'

Eventually even his opponents accepted that Perón was the only viable alternative to military rule, even though his movement was split between left-wing nationalists and conservatives. When Perón returned to Argentina in 1973, the tension erupted into bloodshed at a massive rally to welcome him. The violent conflict between the two factions left scores dead and the party split.

After his election as president the same year, Perón sided with the right, forcing the Montoneros to abandon the movement after haranguing them at the May Day rally in 1974. He died two months later at the age of 74, leaving the country in the incapable hands of his third wife, Isabel. She in turn was dominated by José López Rega, who Perón had promoted to minister of social welfare. López Rega is famous as the founder of the Triple A, a shadowy paramilitary organisation dedicated to the murder of political opponents. As the violence spiralled and the economy collapsed, much of the population breathed a sigh of relief when Isabel was replaced in 1976 by a military junta, led by General Jorge Rafael Videla.

DIRTY WARS

The satisfaction was short-lived. The Proceso de Reorganización Nacional (known as 'El Proceso'), presided over by Videla, imposed order by eliminating the regime's opponents. Although the exact number is still disputed, it may have been as great as 30,000, according to human rights groups. A minority of those killed had taken part in the armed struggle, but most were trade unionists, political activists, rebellious priests and student leaders. Most

Power to the *pueblo*

Despots have come and gone during two centuries of independence, and a stereotype of Argentina's image since the 1970s has been the tyrannical military leader. But there have always been popular rebellions led – and sometimes won – by republicans, anarchists and union militants.

The Peróns were masters at unleashing the passions of the *pueblo*, and it was a public protest that forced Juan Perón's release from prison in October 1945.

But the roots run deeper. A united civilian force resisted the English Invasions of 1806-7 and three years later a mass gathering underpinned the ousting of the Spanish colonial powers.

A key form of demonstration is the *escrache* – noisy, public humiliation of high-profile figures. Regular *escraches* – many organised by HIJOS, a group of children of the 'disappeared' – denounce those who sanctioned torture and murder during the 1976-83 dictatorship.

These same generals assassinated hundreds of radicals and intellectuals, bereaving Argentina of an entire political class. Nonetheless, the Madres de Plaza de Mayo kept up the voice of dissent and became a global icon of peaceful protest.

Since the return of democracy, there have been growing signs of discord – from union and student protests, to massive marches and full-scale riots, as at the end of 2001 when economic depression began to affect the middle classes.

Marching in Argentina is not always deadly serious; at times slogans are chanted football-style to terrace anthems. Music has a close relationship with mass movements, and a near-carnival atmosphere can spill on to the streets on key dates such as May 1 – Labour Day.

Porteño protest often takes the form of *cacerolazos*, men, women and children taking to the streets to beat cooking pots. Such protests brought down both economy minister Cavallo and president de la Rúa at the end of 2001. Today, the *piqueteros* (picketers), who block roads to make their point, keep up the tradition of improvising organised chaos to force a public or political reaction (*see chapter* **BA Today**).

were kidnapped, taken to torture centres and then 'disappeared': buried in unmarked graves or heavily sedated and thrown from planes over the River Plate. In the face of such horrors, many Argentinians emigrated – although many more stayed and feigned ignorance.

The military government introduced radical free-market policies, reducing state intervention and allowing a flood of imports, much to the detriment of local industry. The deregulation of financial markets created a speculative boom, while spiralling national debt left a legacy from which Argentina has yet to recover. Inflation soared again and the regime sought ways to distract the population. The 1978 World Cup, staged in Argentina, was one such distraction.

The tournament was turned into a major propaganda event. But although Argentina eventually triumphed on the football field (after what many consider a rigged match against Peru), growing opposition off it encouraged political parties and the church to raise their voices. The greatest courage was displayed by human rights groups, particularly the Madres de Plaza de Mayo, who, in the face of terrible repression, marched in front of the Casa Rosada on a weekly basis to demand information on their missing children.

On 2 April 1982, under the leadership of General Leopoldo Galtieri, the military made one last desperate attempt to flame popular support, invading the Falkland Islands/Islas Malvinas, occupied by the British since 1833. The action unleashed a flood of nationalist fervour, but the generals had misjudged the reactions of friends and enemies alike.

Britain had earlier shown little interest in preserving the Falklands, even downgrading the British citizenship of the islands' 1,800 inhabitants. But the British prime minister Margaret Thatcher's unpopularity at home meant a tide of patriotic passion was as much in her interests as the junta's. On 1 May, a British submarine attacked and sank the Argentinian cruiser *General Belgrano*, killing almost 400 crew members. The ship was outside the 200-mile 'exclusion zone' that the British had imposed around the islands and was steaming away from them, although the Admiralty claimed that it might have intercepted British ships on their way to join the conflict. In retaliation, the Argentinians sank the British destroyer HMS *Sheffield* three days later, killing 20 of its crew.

A peaceful settlement was now impossible. Galtieri had trusted in US support, which never materialised; Washington eventually backed the British. The junta had an equally poor understanding of the military side of the conflict. After the sinking of the *Belgrano*, the navy sat out the rest of the conflict, and Argentinian forces, badly led and composed largely of ill-equipped conscripts, were no match for a professional British task force. The defeat was the final nail in the regime's coffin. It was also a huge shock to a society that had been convinced by its press that Argentina was winning the war until the very moment of surrender.

Defeat brought the population back to its senses, although the issue has by no means gone away. Most Argentinians believe that *'las Malvinas son argentinas'* and the 1994 constitution ratified Argentina's claim to the islands, specifying that the recovery of sovereignty is an unwaivable goal of the Argentinian people. The islands appear on all Argentinian maps as Argentinian territory, and a memorial to the 655 Argentinian servicemen killed stands in Plaza San Martín.

A FEAST OF DEMOCRACY

Free at last, democracy returned in 1983 with the election of Radical leader Raúl Alfonsín, one of the few political leaders to have maintained his distance from the military and opposed the Falklands War. The momentous changes afoot were described at the time as *'una fiesta de democracia'* and a party atmosphere prevailed.

But the new president lacked a majority in Congress and faced a range of vested corporate interests. He also faced stiff military opposition to the investigation of abuses committed during the Proceso – although he was helped by the publication in 1984 of *Nunca Más* (*Never Again*), a harrowing report of human rights abuses during the military government, identifying 9,000 victims. In the ensuing public outcry, the three juntas that presided over the Guerra Sucia (Dirty War) were tried in 1985 and stiff sentences handed down, including life for Videla – one of very few cases of Latin American military leaders being imprisoned for their crimes. But in the face of military pressure, the government passed the Punto Final (Full Stop) law in 1986, limiting the trials.

Another military uprising during Easter Week in 1987 was met by impressive public demonstrations in support of democracy. But after persuading the rebels to lay down their arms, Alfonsín then caved in to the military's demands, passing the Obediencia Debida (Due Obedience) law, which excused the vast majority of the accused officers on the ground that they were only following orders.

Among the trade unions Alfonsín initially attracted hostility with a failed attempt to introduce new labour laws. But 13 general strikes later, he capitulated and appointed a senior union leader as labour minister. He did

little better with the economy. After initial economic stabilisation as a result of the Plan Austral in 1985, the government's nerve again failed when faced with serious restructuring.

With the Peronist opposition gaining strength, Alfonsín finished his term in rout. His successor, Carlos Menem, was forced to take office five months early as the economy spun out of control, monthly inflation hit 197 per cent and looters raided supermarkets. Once in office, Menem abandoned his electoral promises and embraced neo-liberalism.

Under convertibility, introduced by Finance Minister Domingo Cavallo in 1991, the peso was pegged to the dollar at one-to-one. Privatisation resolved the problem of a bloated state sector, with handsome rewards for the business oligarchy. International capital was appreciative, too; the brisk opening of the economy left virtually all leading companies and financial institutions in foreign hands. But the measures also won Menem the backing of the electorate. After 10 years of negative growth, Menem's decade in office saw total growth of around 35 per cent, and inflation was vanquished.

> **'Menem modelled himself on the brutal 19th-century *caudillo* Facundo Quiroga, from whom he borrowed his characteristic sideburns.'**

Politically, too, Menem was unassailable. He modelled himself on the brutal 19th-century *caudillo* Facundo Quiroga, from whom he borrowed his characteristic sideburns. Menem's ex-wife, Zulema, claimed that he would wander on to the patio with his arms raised, imploring Quiroga's spirit to enter his body.

He ruled largely by decree and with little regard for constitutional niceties. But he finally dominated the military, and the mutiny by army rebels in December 1990 was the last of its kind. Although he dismayed human rights campaigners by granting an amnesty to the jailed junta leaders, he also starved the armed forces of funds, leaving them operationally incapable of another coup. He negotiated a constitutional amendment allowing him to win re-election in 1995, although the opposition extracted some changes in return, including elected authorities for Buenos Aires city.

But Menem's second term could not sustain the impetus of his first. Local industry largely collapsed under foreign competition, turning the industrial belt around Buenos Aires into a wasteland, populated by an increasingly bitter and impoverished underclass. Real wages

Peopling the pampas

Porteños love to refer to their city as a 'crisol de razas' ('pot of races'). This self-image is largely nostalgic, referring to a boom migration period that ended before World War II. Nevertheless, immigration has given Buenos Aires tango, pizza, football and lots of shrinks to talk the population through its identity crisis.

Furthering government policy ('to govern is to populate') adopted in the mid-19th century to attract new European settlers, steps to whiten Argentina and make space for the new population were taken in the 1870s. President Julio A Roca led a campaign to rid the interior of its native population. Buenos Aires' black population – present since the late 16th century and constituting about one third of the city's population shortly after

independence – was either wiped out in battles against the natives, or in later wars against Brazil and Paraguay. Since the black community lived in the poorest parts of the city, it also suffered disproportionately from the yellow fever epidemic of 1871.

Around six million people arrived by ship between 1870 and 1914. Despite hopes that industrious immigrants would flock from northern Europe, most came from Italy (around half of the total) and Spain. Significant numbers of Ottomans, Eastern Europeans and Russians also arrived, as well as British, French and Portuguese. The city was equipped with a special hotel for newcomers, as well as a social welfare system and employment service.

Large numbers of Jewish immigrants settled in Buenos Aires, many fleeing pogroms in Russia and its satellites. Armenians fled to Argentina after the Turkish massacres of 1895-1918. The city also became the world capital of the white slave trade when the Mafia-like organisation Zvi Migdal began to traffic in Polish Jewish prostitutes to service the burgeoning male population.

Though the immigration boom ended in the 1930s, Spaniards continued to arrive well into the '50s, fleeing Franco's regime, though Perón's secret scheme to grant

dropped and the gulf between the rich and poor steadily widened. Menem's flamboyant style and love of showbiz glitter – la farándula, as Argentinians call it – went hand in hand with numerous high-profile corruption scandals.

In the 1991 'Yomagate' or 'Narcogate' scandal, various Menem officials were accused of links to money laundering and the illegal drugs trade. The case centred on the appointment of Syrian colonel (and Menem in-law) Ibrahim al Ibrahim as special advisor to the customs service – despite having no expertise and only a limited grasp of Spanish.

Menem's association with Alfredo Yabrán (a shadowy businessman implicated in the murder of journalist José Luis Cabezas in 1997), and allegations that his Middle Eastern connections (he is of Syrian descent) had hampered official investigations into the terrorist attacks on the city's Jewish communities in 1992 and again in 1994 were sufficient to give Argentinians the impression that every injustice led back to the presidential palace.

DEBT AND DISORDER
Tired of such excesses, the population turned to Fernando de la Rúa, head of Buenos Aires' city council and self-styled antithesis of Menem. Running at the head of the Alliance, formed by the Radicals and Frepaso, a smaller left-wing party, de la Rúa promised little in the way of policies, but benefited from a slick PR and marketing campaign.

He was elected president in December 1999. For some, the rise of such an unexceptional man to the head of a coalition government marked the death of the caudillo and a new period in Argentinian politics. In retrospect, the de la Rúa years can be seen as little more than a period in which international financiers demanded payback for investing in Menem's chimerical new economy. Throughout his term, de la Rúa maintained an image of calm – soporific even – government, but the manner with which the Alliance led the country to economic meltdown was dramatic for all Argentinian society and devastating for the economy.

asylum to high-ranking Nazi officials gave Argentina its own fascists.

For all this mixing and matching, some groups have been victims of overt racism; native and mixed race people, many of whom come to the capital from poor interior provinces are known as *cabecitas negras* (little black heads). In contrast, British, Syrian, Japanese and French populations have a positive presence disproportionate to their numbers, producing new cultural and linguistic habits. Italian restaurants, French-style mansions, Levantine belly dancing shows and British schools are visible vestiges of a city that was once a veritable New York of the River Plate.

Immigrants have tricked in during the 1990s, including small numbers from Korea, Russia, the former Eastern Bloc and poorer South American countries. But Buenos Aires is anything but a promised land these days – and many Bolivians, Peruvians and Paraguayans, from maids and construction workers to prostitutes, have returned home since the 2001 economic meltdown. The same is true for many third-generation Spaniards and Italians, often to be seen queueing at their respective embassies to apply for work visas in the Old World.

The beginning of the end was a scandal over alleged vote-buying in the Senate, which dominated the media throughout the spring of 2000. The subsequent resignation of his popular vice president Carlos 'Chacho' Alvarez, left de la Rúa weak and isolated. By this time, Brazil's decision to devalue its currency by 30 per cent the year before had caused Argentinian exports, still pegged to the dollar, to plummet. The ensuing crisis was met by severe austerity measures, but recession worsened and the beleaguered president turned, in early 2001, to former Peronist financial guru Domingo Cavallo to turn the economy round. But this time, Cavallo was unable to rescue the country, and eight billion dollars of emergency aid was sought from the International Monetary Fund.

It was not enough. The economic situation atrophied as unemployment rose to 20 per cent in Buenos Aires and far higher levels in many provinces. Argentina's credit rating fell to a historic low, its national bonds designated as junk stock, and the dithering, quiet-mannered

president was ill-equipped to reverse the inevitable economic disaster. In October 2001, the Peronist opposition took control of both houses and began to lead a takeover.

'De la Rúa declared a state of emergency when protests segued into full-scale riots and looting, prompting heavy-handed police repression.'

Cavallo's last crisis measure – the *corralito* or 'little fence' limiting access to cash to prevent further runs on bank deposits by worried savers – incensed the middle class. But the banking sector was in tatters and, in a final, critical blow to Argentina's battered society, bank accounts were sequestered by the state.

On 19 December, protests segued into full-scale riots and looting, prompting heavy-handed police repression; de la Rúa declared a state of emergency. On 20 December, Cavallo resigned, followed next day by de la Rúa after massive rallies took to the streets and over 20 people were killed when police (and some shopkeepers) opened fire on looters, protesters and bystanders. For some, de la Rúa was the classic fall guy, his personal and political debacle little more than a leftover legacy of the Menem years; but others point to his inability to be anything greater than 'not Menem'.

For Christmas 2001, Argentinians were gifted four presidents in just 11 days, the largest ever default in history – around US$150 billion – and the contempt of the IMF. When de la Rúa stood down, Ramón Puerta took over as caretaker between December 20 and 23; Adolfo Rodríguez Sáa ruled between December 23 and December 30 but was ousted by fellow Peronists when he made it clear that he wanted more than an interim role; Puerta became caretaker again for December 30 and Eduardo Camano stood in between December 31 and January 1.

The man then chosen by Congress to run Argentina until the next elections, Eduardo Duhalde, was a populist Peronist known for his opposition to neo-liberal ideology. A classic *caudillo* type, he had served as Menem's vice president and as governor of Buenos Aires province, where he built up his power base. For 15 months, he managed, with the aid of his appointed finance minister, Roberto Lavagna, to contain the crisis, further exacerbated by the January 2003 devaluation of the peso, and, slowly, a semblance of calm and order was restored in Buenos Aires and across the country.

BACK TO REALITY?

When Néstor Kirchner took office on 25 May 2003, while not entirely a shift away from *caudillo*-style politics, his presidency was welcomed as a change of atmosphere and a break with the Duhalde-Menem-Cavallo dynasty. But his mandate is by no means universal. Menem opted out of presidential run-offs when he looked likely to lose, allowing Kirchner to come to power with just 22 per cent of the vote.

Porteños view Kirchner with a healthy mix of optimism and scepticism, the latter borne of decades of disillusion. The future, like the new president, is unknown, as the now shrunken peso economy must provide jobs and justice as well as repaying the massive debt. Few, indeed, would any more risk predicting the coming century than Solís, Mendoza or Garay would have when they sailed up the nameless brown river at the bottom of the world.

Key events

1516 Spanish settlers reach the River Plate and are killed by Querandí natives.
1536 First settlement of Buenos Aires.
1541 City abandoned.
1580 Juan de Garay resettles the city.
1620 Diocese of Buenos Aires created
1776 Spain creates the Viceroyalty of the River Plate.
1806-07 British troops make two unsuccessful attempts to occupy Buenos Aires.
1810 Argentinian-born leaders replace the Spanish viceroy with an elected junta.
1816 Argentina formally declares independence in Tucumán on 9 July.
1821 The University of Buenos Aires is established.
1826 Bernadino Rivadavia assumes the national presidency, declaring Buenos Aires the capital.
1853 Federal constitution drafted.
1862 Bartolomé Mitre elected first president of the new Republic of Argentina.
1871 Outbreak of yellow fever kills over 7,000 city residents, mostly in the south.
1880 Buenos Aires becomes federal capital.
1898 New docks at Puerto Madero finished.
1913 First South American underground railway – or Subte – is operated on Line A.
1912 President Roque Sáenz Peña enacts compulsory universal male suffrage.
1919 During 'Tragic Week', gangs organised by employers help the government of Hipólito Yrigoyen brutally repress strikers.
1930 Yrigoyen government overthrown by an army coup.
1931 General Agustín P Justo elected president, heralding period of 'patriotic fraud'.
1937 Offical opening of Avenida 9 de Julio, at 140m (459ft) the widest avenue in the world.
1943 Army overthrows conservative regime.
1945 Workers mass on 17 October to force liberation of Juan Domingo Perón.
1946 Perón wins presidential elections by 1,487,886 votes to 1,207,080.

1951 Perón is re-elected, beating Radical leader Ricardo Balbín 2:1.
1952 Perón's wife, Evita, dies aged 33.
1955 Perón is overthrown by a military coup.
1963 Radical, Arturo Illia, is elected president with just 25 per cent of the vote.
1966 Military takes power.
1973 Perón elected president for a third term, defeating the Radical slate of Balbín and Fernando de la Rúa by more than 2:1.
1974 Perón dies.
1976 General Jorge Rafael Videla leads military coup against Isabel Perón.
1978 Buenos Aires hosts World Cup final, won by Argentina.
1982 Under the leadership of General Leopoldo Galtieri, the junta occupies the Falklands/Malvinas, but is defeated by a British task force.
1983 Radical leader Raúl Alfonsín democratically elected president.
1985 Leaders of the three juntas that presided over the 'Dirty War' are tried and sentenced.
1987 Rebel army leaders revolt. In response, the government halts trials of most officers.
1989 Peronist President Carlos Menem is forced to take office five months early as Alfonsín finishes his term in chaos.
1990 Menem amnesties junta leaders.
1992 Bomb attack on Israeli embassy kills 29 and wounds more than 200.
1994 Bomb attack on AMIA Jewish welfare centre kills 86 and wounds more than 250.
1995 Menem elected for second term.
1999 Fernando de la Rúa elected president for the Alliance.
2001 De la Rúa resigns when the economy collapses, prompting widespread rioting and violent police repression.
2002 Peronist Eduardo Duhalde is chosen as president by Congress on January 1.
2003 Peronist Néstor Kirchner elected president in run-offs with 22 per cent of vote.

BA Today

After the crash and the chaos, Buenos Aires is reborn (again).

The traffic is gridlocked on the corner of Honduras and Fitz Roy streets, in the heart of Palermo Hollywood – it's 1am. At the trendy bars and restaurants you have to fight to get a table. As you squeeze through the crowds of glamorous women and goatee'd executives a camera-mounted car rolls by – another film crew at work. The crumbling brick house you spotted last week has been replaced by a shiny boutique whose only item is designer soap – the ultimate shrine to conspicuous consumption. Wait – isn't this Buenos Aires? Where's the chaos and angry protestors? The Depression-like soup lines?

The last time the city made international headlines it was up in flames. But if that's your only lingering image of the 11.5 million-person metropolis you're in for a shock. Since Argentina's cataclysmic meltdown in late 2001, the city has undergone a dramatic, phoenix-like revival... on the surface, at least.

If you'd been asleep for three years and woke up – as a visitor – in Buenos Aires you might never know that the city had recently survived its worst economic crisis in a century. Instead of sitting around licking their wounds, industrious *porteños* are getting back to work. Everywhere you look – from teeming restaurants and fully-booked hotels to a construction boom and the

dusting off of cobwebbed assembly lines – the image is one of a city on the move. Even normally pessimistic taxi drivers begrudgingly admit that *'vamos todavía'* (something like 'we're still kicking') – the closest thing to a confession you'll get that things are improving.

How did it happen? When Argentina scrapped its rigid exchange rate in January 2002, after a decade's parity with the dollar, Buenos Aires went overnight from South America's most expensive capital, on a par with Paris or New York, to its cheapest. As imported goods became hugely expensive, factories reopened and Argentinians resumed manufacturing goods once judged too costly to compete. Meanwhile on the pampas, farmers got fat selling their soya and beef abroad for dollars.

When a fragile stability was achieved under interim President Eduardo Duhalde, upper middle-class *porteños* began to spend some of the US$20 billion in greenbacks that they had been lucky enough to snatch from banks before the crisis peaked. They spent the windfall fixing up their homes, starting new businesses or holidaying in Patagonia (instead of Miami).

Though erratic inflation eventually tempered the buying spree, the jolt was enough to lead to an eight per cent surge in GDP in 2003, the fastest rate in Latin America. It helped, of course, that the economy had shrunk by over 20 per cent in the preceding five years to levels unseen since 1980, a dubious feat matched by very few countries. Still, even die-hard sceptics like the International Monetary Fund were forced to admit that the bottled-up potential unleashed by the devaluation was amazing.

Perhaps the most dynamic impact has been on tourism. The old rap against Buenos Aires – that it's a great place to visit but too costly to stay very long – is no longer true, as evidenced by the arrival of three million tourists in 2003, a record. What's more this growth is predicted to continue at a torrid rate of 20 per cent per year. As the city becomes more polyglot than ever, especially in areas like Palermo Soho and San Telmo, services have become more sophisticated. Instead of benignly ignoring tourists as before, entrepreneurial *porteños* now outcompete themselves for king dollar or euro. New tourist services – English-language brochures, walking tours and menus, short-term rentals and football tour guides – now abound.

Attitudes have also improved. Though the sight of grinning foreigners devouring an

Righting past wrongs

It's too early to tell if Argentina is turning over a new leaf or not. But in at least one sensitive area President Néstor Kirchner is already making history. 'We're all children of the Mothers and Grandmothers of the Plaza de Mayo,' a visibly emotional Kirchner told the UN General Assembly in 2003, in reference to the human rights activists who for the past three decades have fought a long and lonely struggle to force Argentina to confront its 'Dirty War' past.

So far he's remained true to his word. Since taking office, Kirchner has made human rights the idée fixe of his government. In July 2003, he stripped military officers of immunity from extradition for human rights abuses committed against foreign nationals during the 1976-83 dictatorship. Then he lobbied the Senate to annul its own controversial Full Stop and Due Obedience Laws, which had let walk thousands of human rights violators who claimed to be 'just following orders' when charged in 1987. As a result several hundred officers could face jail terms anew – indeed, several dozen are already under arrest. Finally, in a forceful move to weed out apologist sentiment, he purged the military of its top brass.

It's hard to overstate how important Kirchner's campaign for justice is, although cynics might argue that it's also politically convenient for a president desperate to consolidate popular support after being elected by a slim margin. During the 'Process', as the dictatorship liked to call its policies, the Obelisco was draped with a large banner containing the Orwellian phrase 'Silence is health', and ever since, politicians, along with much of society have gone to great lengths to sweep the entire issue under the carpet.

Kirchner – who was jailed twice briefly during the dictatorship for activism – marks a generational shift in Argentinian politics. He's the first president to have come of age during the 1960s and '70s, when revolution was in vogue and the price one paid for ideals was life. Among his advisors are the noted human rights campaigners Estela de Carlotta, director of Grandmothers of Plaza de Mayo, and Horacio Verbitsky, investigative journalist at the left-wing newspaper *Página/12*.

Nonetheless, his critics say he may be opening a Pandora's box. Currently before the Supreme Court is a controversial case, put forward by the Mothers and Grandmothers, to make DNA testing compulsory for those believed kidnapped as babies during the dictatorship, even when those whose identity is in question don't give their consent. Kirchner has so far been silent on the issue, though some say his high-profile rebuke of the Menem-stacked Supreme Court signals his implicit support for obligatory testing.

No matter how the case is resolved, though, no one expects the military to be marching back into power anytime soon. Although in the end the public are more likely to judge Kirchner's performance for the jobs he creates than the assassins and torturers he puts behind bars, it's an auspicious sign for Argentina's still young democracy that such gross impunity will probably never again go unchecked.

In Context

enormous AR$5 tenderloin steak is jarring to some penniless *porteños*, grudges are rarely held. Instead as soon they can cobble together a few bills, many will go out and do the same, eschewing at all costs the nation's still despised banks. As any affable local will tell you, hard times are no excuse for staying at home.

Another constant is BA's prestige as one of the world's great cultural capitals. The huge variety of round-the-clock offerings has barely suffered. If anything, the arts flourished during the crisis as a shell-shocked, middle class clung tightly to the one thing it had left – intellectual stimulation. Theatre and film attendance has increased during the past few years, and the *electrónica* dance music scene has exploded.

At the same time, the crisis inspired creative expression among the city's young artists, eager to talk, write and sing about their new reality – often on a shoestring budget and for little or no pay. If, in the past, folk-rock and theatre were the most politicised artistic expressions, these days it's tango (*see p206*), cumbia music (*see p194*) and cinema (*see p174*).

A TALE OF TWO CITIES

Of course, not all that glitters is gold. Dig a little deeper and you'll find Buenos Aires ridden with scars. In many ways it has become a Dickensian city. Although unemployment has waned (to 16 per cent at the end of 2003), it's likely to remain stubbornly high for some time yet. Meanwhile poverty, already widespread, has reached epidemic proportions, with the numbers unable to buy basic goods or services rocketing from 24 per cent of the metropolitan population to 52 per cent in five years – and the figures are more desperate still in the northern provinces. To cut poverty by half Argentina needs to create one million jobs a year for the next 12 years. For a nation with the means of feeding its population many times over, the sight of street kids competing with street dogs to feed themselves is a harrowing reminder of how far their country has fallen.

> **'BA's alternative political groupings were the toast of the anti-globalisation movement worldwide.'**

Much of the task of coping with this social emergency is being managed at street level. More out of desperation than political conviction, *porteños* have banded together to form a host of do-it-yourself collectives. *Cartoneros* (collectors of cardboard for recycling), *fábricas tomadas* (factories 'squatted' – and made productive – by boss-less employees), and *clubes de trueque*

(barter associations) are among the new political groupings to emerge. Many *porteños* attend barrio-based gatherings, known as *asambleas populares*, which seek to devolve democratic power to a neighbourhood level.

By the end of Duhalde's presidency, though, many of the solidarity groupings were co-opted by fringe, leftist parties, who tried to reinvent them as quasi-revolutionary cells to assail the IMF, foreign debt and the entire capitalist system. At their prime, however, these collectives were the toast of the anti-globalisation movement worldwide, drawing attention from such high-profile activists as *No Logo* author Naomi Klein, who spent six months in 2002 filming a documentary here.

For its part, the BA city government pitched in for a while, slowly putting into place a number of social welfare and urban improvement schemes. But the damage done by Argentina's economic paralysis – boarded-up banks, graffiti-strewn monuments, falling masonry, potholed roads and broken pavements – so far exceeds the reach of any clean-up effort. And no amount of state solidarity can cover up the fact that so many Argentinians now live at the limit of destitution.

More agonising still, is a sharp rise in crime in what was long considered one of the world's safest cities. Increasingly *porteños* live in fear of being caught in a *secuestro express* (express kidnapping), in which victims are held, often for just a few hours for relatively modest sums. In one gruesome, month-long saga, parents of student Pablo Belluscio were sent their son's severed finger by captors demanding a AR$100,000 ransom. The case sparked the return of the pot-banging protests that had brought down Fernando de la Rúa. In the end, President Kirchner blamed the corruption-ridden Bonaerense – the BA Province police force – for colluding with the kidnappers, a belief confirmed in the eyes of many by Pablo's release soon after. Although the crime wave dominates the media, the good news is that such extreme violence remains far from the norm, especially for tourists (*see p255* **Staying safe**).

For *porteños*, police involvement in such savagery is further proof of their city's moral and physical decay. The biggest object of their scorn, though, is reserved for the *piqueteros*, a catchall term for the dozens of 'picketer' armies who invade the centre on an almost daily basis from the poor outer suburbs, blocking traffic and decamping in the city's plazas. Strikers' demands – and tactics – range considerably, from desperate pleas by impoverished mothers for basic sanitation to the blockading of government ministries by masked, crowbar-wielding gangs in search of welfare subsidies.

While *piqueteros* take to the streets in protest... on Florida's shopping strip, life goes on.

Although protests rarely turn violent, incidents such as the explosion of a homemade bomb during a march in December 2003 do sporadically take place. Despite controversial support from some leftist groups, most view the *piqueteros*, especially the most hardline groups like Quebracho (named after a local hardwood), as common thugs. There's more than just a hint of hypocrisy in this view – most middle-class professionals didn't think twice about forming mobs to boot out a constitutionally-elected de la Rúa when their savings accounts were confiscated. Yet when it comes to those striking for more modest goals of *pan y trabajo* (bread and work), their compassion for direct democracy runs out.

SPECIAL K

The man in the middle of the maelstrom is President Kirchner. A barely known governor from Patagonia when elected, he's so far surprised sceptics by adeptly handling an irate public's demand for social justice and an end to the official impunity that brought on the crisis in the first place. Since taking office, he's doggedly taken on some of the country's most mistrusted institutions – the Supreme Court, police and even labour unions, traditionally a staunch ally of his Peronist party. He's also bargained hard with the IMF, securing a fresh, US$6.6 billion lifeline to the country in 2003. The biggest target of Kirchner's crusade against the old model has been the military (*see p20* **Righting past wrongs**).

Add everything up and it's easy to see why *porteños* are applauding what they call Estilo K (or K Style), as much a sobriquet for Kirchner's tongue-twisting (for Argentinians) last name as a description of his scrappy, confrontational

style. By the end of 2003, Néstor Kirchner's approval rating had soared to almost 80 per cent – an impressive feat after being elected with just 22 per cent of the vote.

Piggybacking on Kirchner's popularity, Buenos Aires' agile mayor Aníbal Ibarra has pinned his political fate to that of the new president, ditching his affiliation with the Alliance that backed de la Rúa's successful candidacy. In line with national trends, he plans to spend lavishly on labour-intensive public works like the extension of subway lines (line H is due to open in 2005) and the sprucing up of major thoroughfares in the capital.

Nonetheless there are signs the honeymoon could be ending. Estilo K may be popular with voters, but don't expect a sympathetic ear from foreign creditors, who were left holding US$90 billion in worthless bonds after the default. Although resource-rich Argentina has huge potential, most foreign investors and banks are hedging their bets until longstanding problems like tax evasion, wasteful spending, corruption and lax legal protection are dealt with.

OLD HABITS DIE HARD

In a sense, the challenges facing Argentina after devaluation are the same as before. Only now it has to meet them without the benefit of the free-spending foreign investment and international prestige that Menem flaunted in the booming 1990s. It's also hamstrung by the loss of many of its best and brightest professionals, part of an invisible but unprecedented brain drain whose consequences will sting for decades. An estimated 255,000 Argentinians have emigrated since 2000, three times more than fled the 1976-83 dictatorship. Although queues outside foreign embassies for visas and passports have disappeared and enterprising *porteños* – along with bargain-hunting foreigners – began trickling back in 2003 to open businesses they could scarcely afford in Europe or the US, polls indicate that 20 per cent still want to leave.

> **'Even as glitzy real estate projects offer enviable lifestyles to the monied few, much of BA's sizable middle class have joined the ranks of the "new poor".'**

That's just one of many jarring contradictions *porteños* reluctantly shrug their shoulders at. Another is the huge disparity caused by recovering property values – still cheap for outsiders, unmanageably expensive for most locals. However, in dollar terms, values are only slightly more those in Asunción, Paraguay, traditionally a much poorer city. Even as glitzy real estate projects, in Palermo and the dockside Madero Este development, or in private gated communities outside the city limits, offer enviable lifestyles to the monied few, much of Buenos Aires' sizable middle class – once the envy of South America – have free-fallen into the ranks of the so-called 'new poor'. For an immigrant country built on the promise of upward mobility, that's a bitter pill.

Still, an optimist might conclude there's reason for hope. By all accounts, the events surrounding 19 and 20 December 2001 were burned into the collective consciousness in a way that was comparable – in the eyes of locals – with the disorienting impact the terrorist attacks of 9/11 had in the US. In the intense soul-searching that followed, a number of taboos have been confronted. Perhaps the most important is the now untenable view that Argentina's problems can be solved by magic or a bit of *viveza criolla* (native Creole wit).

In a fundamental psychological shift, proud *porteños*, who long considered themselves a satellite European state, now humbly accept that their future is tied to Latin America's. Kirchner has gone to great lengths to revitalise Mercosur, the Southern Cone trade bloc. Instead of kowtowing to the US or Europe as every president in recent memory has done, he chose Brazil for his first presidential trip abroad.

Argentina, and specifically Buenos Aires, has been down this road before, only to see its illusion of a better future end in exasperation. When it emerged from the dictatorship in 1983, the city revelled in its newfound freedom with an explosion of the arts and mass-based

BA by numbers

38 million population of Argentina in 2002.
11.5 million population metropolitan Buenos Aires (2.8 million in the capital).
1:30 ratio of psychoanalysts to population in Argentina
1:100 same ratio in developed nations.
1 in 30 number of Argentinians who have undergone plastic surgery since 1970.
50,000 estimated number of tangos ever composed.
220,000 people who went to BA's international tango festival, 2003.
53 number of Argentinian-made feature films released in 2003.
41st Argentina's ranking on most corrupt nation index 2002 (out of 133 countries).
3 number of presidents since 1914 to complete a full term and hand power to elected successor.
1 in 3 *porteños* who believe that democracy is still at risk in Argentina.
US$3,800 Argentina's GDP per capita in 2003 (in 1900 it was US$2,756).
US$850 value per square metre of used apartment in Recoleta.
US$300 average monthly salary of secondary school teacher in the capital.
50 percentage of homes in Argentina with cable or satellite TV.
95 percentage literacy rate for Argentina.
4th Buenos Aires' ranking among the world's nosiest cities (Corrientes and Madero is the loudest street corner).
2 million number of weeping mourners who waited in the rain to file past Evita's coffin after her death in 1952.
35 percentage of *porteños* who rate Carlos Gardel as the city's most representative personality.
38 percentage of *porteños* who consider soccer star Maradona to be their idol.
1/5 fraction of city streets still cobbled.
60 percentage of *porteños* who see themselves as show-offs.
29 percentage of *porteños* who see themselves as charitable.

political participation. Recently, though, a TV documentary on the last 20 years of democratic rule was titled *Blood, Sweat and Tears*. For now, it's still too early to tell whether the current ethical re-awakening will flourish into real and permanent change. If it doesn't, then yet another crisis down the road is inevitable. As you read this book the battle is being waged.

Literary BA

Track down the ghosts haunting the city's fictional landscape.

Buenos Aires is a very bookish place. For all the perennial protests from educators about bibliophobic youth, there are bookshops and literary newspapers galore. Café culture gives rise to literary circles, public readings and lone poets scribbling over their *cortado* coffees (an old adage has it that there are more writers than people in Buenos Aires). And, as proven by Jason Wilson's *Cities of the Imagination* guide to BA, the ghosts of writers and their creations are to be found on every street corner. Cerebral guides now offer tours exploring the life and works of great authors such as Jorge Luis Borges, Julio Cortázar or some of the tango poets. Literature matters: in a society where politicians and bureaucrats are mistrusted, *porteños* idolise their literary forebears.

There are just a handful of world-renowned authors working from the Argentinian capital these days – but then again, there is no Latin American literary boom like that of the 1960s. Yet new authors emerge all the time, penning novels, books on Argentinian identity, self-help manuals and poetry (you may be offered a rustic collection of verse while travelling on the Subte).

You can get into the city's seminal texts whatever your chosen genre. The earliest works were letters and travelogues: Ulderico Schmidt (1525-81), a sailor on Pedro de Mendoza's

El Ateneo Grand Splendid. *See p142.*

landmark 1536 voyage penned the first accounts of 'a new town… Bonas Aeres, that is, in German, Guter Wind'. Since then, travellers have been regular contributors to the foreign idea of what Buenos Aires and Argentina mean – with Charles Darwin, Graham Greene, VS Naipaul, Bruce Chatwin, Paul Theroux and Colm Tóibín passing through (*see p28* **The things people say**). But it is in the homespun poems, plays and narratives that a vividly colourful and far more complex story is to be found.

TOWN AND COUNTRY

Three authors in particular are considered to have laid Argentina's literary foundations. The first is José Hernández, who wrote *Martín Fierro* (1872), an epic poem about a persecuted gaucho which was the culmination of a 19th-century tradition of *gauchesco* writing. The second, Esteban Echeverría (1805-51), was the refined author of long Romantic poem *La Cautiva*, the blood-soaked short story *The Slaughterhouse* – titles are given here in English where translations are widely available – and other books with rural settings that were strongly critical of authoritarian regimes. The third is Domingo Faustino Sarmiento (1811-88), writer, educationalist and Argentinian president, who wrote *Facundo*, widely considered to be the first Argentinian novel, but more like a treatise in fictional trappings.

The 1880s are famous for a generation of authors who stressed the European texture of the capital. Miguel Cané's stories and Pedro Bonifacio Palacios aka Almafuerte's lyrical poetry respond to the first waves of immigration and the growth of Buenos Aires from a backwater into the Gran Aldea (Grand Village). But it was Nicaraguan modernist Rubén Darío and Argentinian Leopoldo Lugones who introduced Symbolism and Spanish *modernismo* to *porteño* readers, preparing the way for the emergence of local movements such as *criollismo* and *simplismo*, both a celebration of the popular.

During the 1920s, a group of writers, including Jorge Luis Borges (*see p26* **Enter the labyrinth**), published a magazine called *Martín Fierro* which explored the poetic and critical potential of a native Argentinian cultural ideal. Borges was part of the elegant Florida Set, which defended the cultured and refined, in part imported from and influenced by Europe. The group also included Leopoldo Marechal, author of the vast, *Ulysses*-like novel *Adán Buenosayres*, and poet Oliverio Girondo, author of *Veinte poemas para ser leídos en el tranvía*. More left-leaning writers, such as Leonidas Barletta and Elías Castelnuovo, took part in the Boedo gatherings – named after a humdrum street in southside Buenos Aires.

Standing apart was Roberto Arlt (1900-42), journalist and the highly original author of *The Seven Madmen*, about the efforts of a marginal group of conspirators to organise an anarchist revolution. A *porteño* to his bones, Arlt – like his inspiration, Dostoevski – was a tormented soul, whose complex and explosive style was considered clumsy by some critics. But his works have stood the test of time: they reveal a period marked by the downfall of a supposedly harmonious world and the birth of a chaotic and violent era.

20TH-CENTURY GIANTS

Jorge Luis Borges (1899-1986) and Julio Cortázar (1914-84) are the two giants of Argentinian literature, known throughout the world for their complex portrayals of Buenos Aires and its inhabitants. The first went blind and the second exiled himself to Paris, yet both recounted the mysteries of the city better than any of their contemporaries. Utterly distinct in tone, vision and ideology, Borges and Cortázar are the two mainstream masters of prose.

Borges is considered one of the greatest writers of the 20th century, and despite his apparent nonchalance about the subject, most people are surprised to discover he was never awarded the Nobel Prize for Literature. He was a prolific writer of poetry, fiction and non-fiction. Key works include *The Book of Sand* and *The Aleph* and many of the early poems. Not only have the vast majority of his writings been widely translated, but Borges himself was a professor of English literature in BA, and considered the best Spanish translator of works by Walt Whitman and Virginia Woolf. In fact, his love for English-language literature and all things European, as well as some of his political views, made him a polemical figure in Argentina. He chose to be buried not in the city he so intimately portrayed, but in Geneva.

Cortázar caused an upheaval in the literary world with his highly intelligent, imaginative style, known as *lo fantástico*, where the borders between the ordinary and the unreal take on a new dimension. His most famous novel, *Hopscotch*, with its fragmentary structure, is a milestone of contemporary storytelling. For him, words not only had meaning and sound, but colour and weight. He wrote in the language of the streets of Buenos Aires, and remains the hero of left-leaning university students.

The pantheon of consecrated 20th-century *porteño* writers includes Adolfo Bioy Casares (1914-99), whose most celebrated and personal work was *The Invention of Morel*. Leaning also towards the fantastic and towards thriller-writing, Bioy Casares wrote with Borges under the joint pseudonym Bustos Domecq. His wife, the aristocratic Silvina Ocampo (1909-1993), wrote short stories and poems. Silvina's sister, Victoria Ocampo, was not as successful a writer as her sibling, but she was the founder of the magazine *Sur*, the most significant periodical in Argentinian literature, which was published regularly from 1931 until 1970.

Such was the range and ambition of their lyrics, major tango poets like Homero Manzi,

Washington Cucurto at the **Eloisa Cartonera** book launch. *See p28*.

Enrique Cadicamo and Enrique Santos Discépolo should also be included in a list of literary luminaries from Buenos Aires' belle époque. If the dance hall scene was a popular, low-brow affair at the beginning, both Borges and Cortázar would attempt to compose tangos during their careers – and neither could match the skilful economy of Manzi's *Sur* or the sardonic bite of Discépolo's 'Cambalache'.

Manuel Puig (1932-90), along with Borges and Cortázar, is one of the Argentinian authors most widely translated into English. His 1976 novel, *The Kiss of the Spider Woman* – a dialogue between a Marxist and an apolitical homosexual in a South American prison – was turned into an Oscar-winning Hollywood movie in 1985, and is the reason most visitors will have heard of him, even if they don't realise he's Argentinian. Puig was born in a remote town in BA province, but his acclaimed detective novel, *The Buenos Aires Affair*, attests to the effect the city had on his work, and there's a famous film and a BA hotel and bar named after his novel *Boquitas Pintadas*.

The surviving giant is Ernesto Sábato. The multi-prize-winning 92-year-old author of the ambitious novel *On Heroes and Tombs* is the best-known and respected living Argentinian writer. His publications range from dictionaries of philosophical aphorisms, through literary criticism, to *Never Again*, the definitive account of the tortures and murder perpetrated by the 1976-83 dictatorship. But it is an existentialist novella after the French school, *The Tunnel*, published in 1948, which features on every school and college reading list – its spare prose unfurls into a dark, psychological thriller about jealousy, obsession and urban alienation. The scenes in the Parque Lezama and Recoleta have given those leafy refuges a mysterious quality for anyone who has read the book.

CONTEMPORARY CURRENTS

There is also a whole set of young and not-so-young writers, who together describe a very different city to that visualised and dreamed of by many of the above. Children of the military dictatorship, they reflect the authoritarian past and the ideological transformations of the city, not merely the physical changes. They harbour no nostalgia for the era of tango, and are more cynical, using acidic and corrosive humour. One such exponent is Ricardo Piglia (born 1940). His works include the critically acclaimed *Artificial Respiration* and, more recently, *Money to Burn*, which won the 1998 Premio Planeta – an important national literary prize. The film adaptation was a big hit in 2000.

Enter the labyrinth

Alongside Kafka, Dickens and Graham Greene, Jorge Luis Borges belongs to that select group of writers who transform a sense of place into a powerful poetic trope. Using deceptively simple language, the *universo borgeano* he created is a beguiling realm of mirrors, libraries, labyrinthine corridors and streets, patios, bars and tigers in zoos – all culled from a childhood in early-20th-century Buenos Aires.

Best known to a global audience for fantastic stories set in exotic locations and filled with strange cabalistic codes, he started his literary career in 1923 with a thin volume of avant-garde poems about Buenos Aires. This first literary effort, *Fervor de Buenos Aires*, was, in his words, a book about the 'Buenos Aires of low houses', its outer barrios. With time, Borges would, literally, move downtown and his interests would shift from the blood-red sunsets of Palermo that disturbed him so much to 'mornings, the centre and serenity'.

For those who want to emulate Borges – he loved to walk aimlessly round the backstreets of the city – highlights of a Borges stroll include the author's childhood home at Serrano 2129 (though the street has now been rechristened JL Borges in his honour). Note the plaque at the corner of Borges and Guatemala alluding to the 'mythical foundation of Buenos Aires', one of his best poems. Nearby are the house of Evaristo Carriego, one of Borges' earliest influences, at Honduras 3784, and the **Jardín Zoológico** (*see p166*), where Borges discovered the motif of the tiger.

Though he rejected the tag 'bibliophile', Borges was happiest when working in libraries. The **Biblioteca Miguel Cané** at Carlos Calvo 4319, was his first post as a librarian – he was moved on in 1946 when his arch-enemy, Perón gave him the highly unsuitable job of Inspector of Poultry and Rabbits – and the former **Biblioteca Nacional** at Mexico

Many of the outstanding writers of the 1970s have been greatly influenced by rock culture and postmodern cultural trends. Some remain faithful to the traditions of their predecessors, while others question the idea of literature as storytelling and lean more towards fragmentation and the combination of different styles. Exemplars are writers/journalists Rodrigo Fresán, Juan Forn and Carlos Gamerro.

A bright new star is Federico Andahazi (born 1963), whose 1997 novel *The Anatomist*, about the discovery of the clitoris, was well received by critics and readers (although a prize awarded was then snatched away due to the book's erotic content). Since then he has published *Merciful Women* and *El secreto de los flamencos*, highly readable novels which, like *The Anatomist*, are set in the European past. He is currently working on a novel about tango, in which the characters sing their dialogue.

Another major literary figure is Tucumán-born Tomás Eloy Martínez, author of bestsellers *Santa Evita* (*see p82* **Saint Evita?**) and *The Perón Novel*. The first book tells of the odyssey of Eva Perón's embalmed corpse and the odd characters who accompanied it on its journey: soldiers, hairdressers, frustrated actors, politicians. Both books have been translated into English.

Eloy Martínez has been commissioned by UK *Harry Potter* publisher Bloomsbury to write a book inspired by Buenos Aires – he has also chosen tango as the theme of this work.

'Whether exploring Buenos Aires' backstreets, bars, genteel mannerisms or genitalia, there's a text to take you through the multiple layers of meaning.'

The same author has also produced a 'national identity' book, *Requiem para un país perdido*. This is part of a general boom in journalistic, political and philosophical essays (as writers seek to rework genre forged by Sarmiento in *Facundo*). For a long time, Argentina viewed itself critically as *un país sin memoria* (a country without memory), and the popularity of this genre reflects a desire to recover the country's lost political and social collective memory. Journalists like Jorge Lanata and José Pablo Feinmann are authoritative commentators on the Menem years and Martín Caparrós is one of several left-leaning authors

564, was his main place of work between 1955-73. In middle age, he also taught Anglo-Saxon and English literature at the University of Buenos Aires' Facultad de Filosofía y Letras located at Viamonte 430.

A corner of the Galerías Pacífico shopping mall is occupied by the **Centro Cultural Borges** – which occasionally includes Borges-related themes in its busy repertoire – and the scholarly world's HQ is the **Fundación Internacional Jorge Luis Borges** at Anchorena 1660. For Borges-obsessed pilgrims only, there are other Borges houses, including his birthplace at Tucumán 840 (now a dull museum to his memory), as well as a flat at Pueyrredón 2190, his home from 1929 to '39, and a posher pad at Avenida Quintana 222 where he lived between 1943 and '46.

But Borges' Buenos Aires extends way beyond biographical loci. The early poems of *Fervor...* and *Luna de enfrente* and the stories contained in *The Universal History of Infamy*, in particular, somehow plumbed the soul of the city and rendered it anew in a crisp, economic style. While there are detractors in

his home city – in 1999, the centenary year, a group of scholars published a collection of essays titled *Anti-Borges* to register their fatigue with his fame and influence – the Borges universe continues to seduce readers and inspire writers from Andahazi to Piglia at home, and such major international authors as Martin Amis and Thomas Pynchon abroad.

exploring the implications of the dictatorship. Caparrós's *La Voluntad* records invaluable testimony of political militancy in Argentina.

If the novel has never quite attained the status that it merits in Europe and the US – and the 19th-century-style 'generational novel' is notably absent from the back catalogue – wonderful poems, essays and short prose works reflecting the frenzied, fragmentary character of contemporary life in Argentina enjoy wide appeal. Squeezed into these small spaces are an enthusisam for experiment and edgy themes galore – whether exploring the Buenos Aires backstreets, bars, genteel mannerisms or genitalia, there's a text to take you through the multiple layers of meaning.

LITERARY CIRCUITS

As well as Jason Wilson's literary guide, local authors have been exploring the literary psychogeography of the city. The best such works are *Buenos Aires Ciudad Secreta* by TV journalist Germinal Nogués and *Al Pie de la Letra* by Alvaro Abós, the author of several anthologies and literary guides to Buenos Aires.

Many visitors are struck by the number of bookshops in the city. The grander ones, especially Gandhi and the Ateneo, also organise literary gatherings, and are a good source of information on readings. For more details, check the 'Cultura' and 'Espectáculos' sections of daily newspapers. Admission to readings

is usually free, although in bars you may have to buy at least one drink. Buenos Aires is also recognised as a great place to pick up antiquarian books at competitive prices.

All keen readers head to the **Feria del Libro** (Book Fair – *see p165*) every April, attracting around a million visitors and, over the years, celebrated authors such as Isabel Allende, Paul Auster and Doris Lessing, as well as local luminaries. There is a popular Children's Book Fair in July/August too.

Argentina is one of the strongest publishing markets in the Spanish-speaking world. But though book sales remain encouragingly high, many bookshops have been forced to close due to a drop in real income following devaluation. The weak peso has also affected production costs, forcing up the retail price.

One new project to emerge from the crisis is the Eloisa Cartonera imprint. Respected authors – from Piglia to supermarket shelf-stacker turned poet and writer Washington Cucurto – are participating in this venture, which publishes short works inside covers made from the waste cardboard collected by *cartoneros* on the city streets.

▶ For more on **tango poets and composers**, see chapter **Tango**.
▶ For **bookshops**, see p142.

The things people say

'On Sundays in Buenos Aires, options are few and exact: the church and raviolis, football and racing, cycling and bathing, a picnic and a family visit, cinema and a dance, a drink or tango.' Julio Cortâzar, *Buenos Aires, Buenos Aires*

'Hard to believe Buenos Aires had any beginning/I feel it to be as eternal as air and water.' Jorge Luis Borges, 'Mythical Foundation of Buenos Aires'

'[Buenos Aires] has all the elegance of the old world in its buildings and streets, and in its people all the vulgarity and frank good health of the new world. All the news-stands and book shops – what a literate place, one thinks; what wealth, what good looks.' Paul Theroux, *The Old Patagonian Express*

'The city kept reminding me of Russia – the cars of the secret police bristling with aerials; women with splayed haunches licking ice-cream in dusty parks; the same bullying statues, the pie-crust architecture, the same avenues that were not quite straight, giving the illusion of endless space and leading out to nowhere.' Bruce Chatwin, *In Patagonia*

'I arrived in a city that seemed fascinated by the possibility of its own collapse... The grand European architecture that had given Buenos Aires its cherished nickname, "Paris of the South", was in places relaxing into a dilapidation from which it might never be roused.' Miranda France, *Bad Times in Buenos Aires*

'Argentina is a simple materialist society, a simple colonial society created in the most rapacious and decadent phase of colonialism. It has diminished and stultified the men whom it attracted by the promise of ease and to whom it offered no other ideals and no new idea of human association.' VS Naipaul, *The Return of Eva Perón*

FEDERICO GARCIA LORCA
(1898 ~ 1936)
EN ESTE HOTEL VIVIÓ DURANTE SU VISITA A BUENOS AIRES
EN EL SEPTUAGÉSIMO ANIVERSARIO DE SU LLEGADA AL PAÍS.
HOMENAJE DE LA
LEGISLATURA DE LA CIUDAD AUTONOMA DE BUENOS AIRES
1933 ~ 13 de OCTUBRE ~ 2003

Where to Stay

Buenos Aires
Doubly great !

dazzlerhotel.com

syasuites.com

Libertad 902
Buenos Aires Argentina
+54 11 4816 5005

Suipacha 1359
Buenos Aires Argentina
+54 11 4325 8200

Where to Stay

French palaces, tango academies and designer B&Bs – oh, and hotels.

The unprecedented tourism boom sparked by devaluation turned BA's hotel industry on its head. Mid-range hotels have been spruced up, and though dull four-star properties aimed at domestic business visitors remain, there are now some great value hotels in this sector. A hostel boom has also multiplied choices for budget travellers, though it remains to be seen how many will stay the course. In the five-star bracket, Sofitel opened an impressive hotel in 2003, while the Hyatt's plans for Palacio Duhau on grand Avenida Alvear and the ambitious Faena Hotel venture (*see p44* **The Faena things in life**) are exciting works in progress. As Argentinians say, when commenting on the construction boom: 'Buenos Aires will be beautiful when it's finished.'

The corporate Centre and leafy Recoleta are traditionally the most popular accommodation areas, thanks to their proximity to shops and monuments. The Centre has obvious advantages for business travellers, but noise and traffic may be a problem once the city rolls into gear at 8am. In historic San Telmo in the south, or north in hip Palermo Viejo, options are generally limited to hostels or B&Bs, though there are some funky choices. Constitución and Barracas have dirt-cheap accommodation, but aimed more at immigrant families than holiday-makers.

Geographically and demographically at the other end of the spectrum, Zona Norte is starting to attract tourists keen to stay in the smart suburbs and commute in for sightseeing. The 19th-century **Hotel del Casco** (Avenida del Libertador 16170, 4723 3993, www.hoteldel casco.com, double room US$95) in San Isidro offers modern comforts in a historic house, while **Patio Inn** (Labardén 466, 4743 2981, www.patioinn.com.ar, double room US$30-$45) is a delightful three-bedroomed guest house close to Acasusso train station. Converting your home into a hotel is a new trend and ensures guests get an intimate service, though it may not be ideal for business travellers. In Palermo, **Posada Palermo** (Salguero 1655, 4826 8792, www.posadapalermo.com.ar, double room US$40) has two spacious rooms and a lovely private garden.

PRICES, BOOKINGS AND SERVICES

The star rating system is not the best guide to quality in BA – except with five-star hotels. It's also in this category that prices have held up, and you'll still pay anything from US$300 per night. Yet several excellent mid range hotels have rooms for as little as US$70. Note that many hotels charge dollars to foreign tourists and a much lower rate in pesos to Argentinians to soften the blow, though this is not an official industry-wide policy and all hotels must, in theory, display their rack rate. Those that stick to charging only in pesos are often better value. Hotels will negotiate significantly, especially when not full – from corporate rates with hefty discounts, to reductions for long-stays or cash payments. Many places also have triple and quadruple rooms or apartments, to share the load if travelling with a group or family. Prices given in this chapter include VAT (here called IVA, a whopping 21 per cent) and breakfast – but always check when booking what is included in the rate quoted.

Our listings follow the following categories: **Luxury** (over US$200 – around AR$580 – for a double); **Expensive** (US$100-$200/AR$290-$580); **Moderate** (US$50-$100/AR$145-$290); **Budget** (under US$50/AR$145); **Hostels**. For rental options, *see p50* **A home from home**.

Hotels are busiest in July, August and November when local businessmen compete with tourists for rooms. Traditionally BA's low season is January and February when *porteños* are on their summer hols, but this is now offset by a huge influx of foreigners on their way to Patagonia, Iguazú and elsewhere in the provinces. Booking in advance is increasingly necessary and usually ensures better rates.

All hotels have concierges, air conditioning, in room telephones and safes. Hostels have neither air-con nor phones in rooms unless stated, but usually provide lockers or some sort of safe deposit. Other services are listed below.

Luxury

The Centre

Marriott Plaza Hotel

Florida 1005, y Marcelo T de Alvear, Retiro (4318 3000/reservations 4318 3069/fax 4318 3008/www.marriottplaza.com.ar). Subte C, San Martín/61, 93, 130, 152 bus. **Rates** US$363 single/double; US$484 suite. **Credit** AmEx, DC, MC, V. **Map** p277 F8.
For over 100 years, this regal hotel (taken over by Marriott in 1994) opposite the flowering Plaza San Martín has provided a white-gloved service fit for royalty. Guests have a choice of three sumptuous

Buenos Aires, Argentina.

Hilton Buenos Aires stands out for its contemporary architecture, its functional rooms and its great variety of services, especially created for guests' comfort and pleasure.

- *Privileged location in Puerto Madero's heart, close to malls, restaurants, movie theatres and the roomy green spaces of the Ecological Reservoir.*
- *418 rooms including 13 suites.*
- *A 6623 sq. Mts convention centre, cutting edge IT equipment to carry out product launchings, conferences and business meetings.*
- *Business Center Service with personalized assistance for those executives travelling on business.*
- *Hilton Health Club with fitness center, body building room, heated outdoor swimming pool and body treatments.*
- *Terrazas al Río, the best place to enjoy a typical Argentinian barbecue with an outstanding city view.*
- *Innovative Services: Express Check-In during the transfer in a private car from the airport to the hotel, bicycle rental and agreements with Puerto Madero restaurants, through which guests can charge their bills to their room account.*

It happens at the Hilton

Av. Macacha Güemes 351, Puerto Madero C1106BKG - Buenos Aires - Argentina - Tel. (5411) 4891-0000 Fax: (5411) 4891-0001
reservations.buenosaires@hilton.com - **hilton.com** - South Convention Center S.A.

restaurants, including the Plaza Hotel Grill, with its Dutch porcelain tiles and fabulous open grill. Cascading chandeliers light the ballrooms and corridors, and the rooms are, as you would expect, top-notch. The sophisticated bar is open to the public (*see p127*), and a small pool overlooks the plaza.
Hotel services *Babysitting. Bar. Beauty salon. Business services. Disabled: adapted rooms. Gym. Laundry service. No-smoking rooms/floors. Parking. Pool (outdoor). Restaurants (3).* **Room services** *Bathrobe. Dataport. Free newspaper. Iron. Minibar. Room service (24hr). Turndown. TV: cable.*

Sheraton Buenos Aires Hotel & Convention Centre

San Martín 1225, entre LN Alem y Madero, Retiro (4318 9000/reservations 4875 4669/fax 4875 9395/www.sheraton.com). Subte C, Retiro/26, 93, 130, 152 bus. **Rates** US$338 single/double; US$459 suite. **Credit** AmEx, DC, MC, V. **Map** p277 F8.
Towering high over Retiro, the Sheraton's top floors offer an awe-inspiring view of the River Plate. Newer and bigger than the other Sheraton on Córdoba, it was built for corporate entertainment and has vast convention facilities, and not much individual charm. Still, the 742 rooms are sizeable, staff efficient and its well-equipped, butler-serviced suites popular with visiting boy bands, Latino pop stars and the IMF. Decent recreational facilities include a gym, tennis court and two pools.
Hotel services *Babysitting. Bar. Beauty salon. Business services. Gym. Laundry service. No-smoking rooms/floors. Parking. Pools (indoor & outdoor). Restaurants (2).* **Room services** *Dataport. Minibar. Room service (24hr). Turndown. TV: cable/VCR.*
Other locations: Sheraton Libertador Hotel Avenida Córdoba 680, Microcentro (4322 6622).

Sofitel Buenos Aires

Arroyo 841, entre Suipacha y Esmeralda, Retiro (4131 0000/reservations 4131 0125/fax 4131 0001/www.sofitel.com). Bus 61, 92, 93, 130. **Rates** US$290-$350 double; US$411 suite. **Credit** AmEx, DC, MC, V. **Map** p277 F8.
Opened in 2003 by French hotel group Accor, Sofitel – the latest five-star addition to the city – has been constructed in the Torre Bencich, an emblematic 20-floor building erected in the 1930s. The impressive glass-roofed lobby, with its black and white floor and huge chandelier sets the tone. It's located on a street, which has an atmosphere reminiscent of Paris, with cafés, galleries and elegant women parading their Louis Vuitton purchases. Rooms are on the small side, though offer great views of the river or city and modern furnishings have a French twist. City socialites congregate in its library, café or revered French/Med eaterie, Le Sud.
Hotel services *Babysitting. Bar. Business services. Disabled: adapted rooms. Gym. Internet (free). Laundry service. Limousine service. No-smoking floors/rooms. Parking. Pool (indoor). Reading room. Restaurant.* **Room services** *Bathrobe. Dataport. Minibar. Newspaper. Room service (24hr). Turndown. TV: cable.*

North of the Centre

Alvear Palace Hotel

Avenida Alvear 1891, entre Callao y Ayacucho, Recoleta (4808 2100/reservations 4804 7777/fax 4804 0034/www.alvearpalace.com). Bus 17, 67, 93, 124, 130. **Rates** US$349-$380 single/double; US$503-$3,630 suite. **Credit** AmEx, DC, MC, V. **Map** p278 G7.
Since the 1930s, this has been BA's grandest hotel by a long stretch and was recently the residence of choice for the King and Queen of Spain. The current clean up of the façade (scheduled to end in January 2005) will completely restore its original Parisian elegance. Filling half a block of the lavish Avenida Alvear, it shares a glitzy pavement with the likes of Armani, Ralph Lauren and Cartier. The 210 rooms – among the largest in the city – are an ocean of opulence: rich burgundies, silks, antique French furniture and Hermès bathroom goodies. They also come with butler service. Such resplendence is not withheld completely from the hoi polloi; the bar and restaurants are open to the public. The cream of the crop is La Bourgogne, overseen by French superchef Jean-Paul Bondoux.
Hotel services *Bar. Beauty salon. Business services. Butler service. Disabled: adapted rooms. Gym. Limousine service. No-smoking rooms/floors. Parking. Pool (indoor). Restaurants (2).* **Room services** *Bathrobe. Dataport. Minibar. Newspaper. Room service (24hr). Turndown. TV: cable/VCR (some rooms).*

Caesar Park

Posadas 1232, entre Montevideo y Libertad, Recoleta (4819 1100/fax 4819 1299/www.caesar-park.com). Bus 61, 67, 92, 93, 130. **Rates** US$428 double; US$539-$2,727 suite . **Credit** AmEx, DC, MC, V. **Map** p278 G8.

Gallic chic at **Sofitel Buenos Aires.**

LoiSuiteS
HOTELES

THE BEST MEETING POINT IN BUENOS AIRES

RECOLETA

LoiSuiteS
RECOLETA HOTEL

Vicente López 1955 • C1128ACC • Cdad. de Buenos Aires, Argentina
Telephone: (54 11) 5777-8950 • Fax: (54 11) 5777-8999
E-mail: recoleta@loisuites.com.ar • http://www.loisuites.com.ar

Directly behind plush Patio Bullrich shopping centre, the 170 suites and rooms of Caesar Park make ideal closets for your latest acquisitions. Step inside the reception and survey the marble floors, towering pillars and gleaming stairways. Tapestries and paintings by local artists adorn the corridors that lead to the suites, decadently furnished with lavish gold trimmings and dark woods. A communal lounge for waltzing and schmaltzing has a resident classical pianist tinkling the ivories. Shops, Agraz restaurant – featuring acclaimed chef Germán Martitegui's inventive menus – and a small swimming pool area add to the lavish experience.

Hotel services *Babysitting. Bar. Beauty salon. Business services. Disabled: adapted rooms. Garden. Internet (free). Laundry service. Limousine service. No-smoking floors/rooms. Parking (free). Pool (indoor). Restaurant.* **Room services** *Bathrobe. Dataport. Iron. Minibar. Newspaper. Room service (24hr). Turndown. TV: cable/satellite.*

Four Seasons Hotel

Posadas 1086, y Cerrito, Recoleta (4321 1200/fax 4321 1201/www.fourseasons.com). Bus 17, 59, 67, 102, 130. **Rates** US$363 single/double; US$423 Club Floor; US$527 suite; US$545-$4,235 mansion suites. **Credit** AmEx, DC, MC, V. **Map** p278 G8.

Towering over sloping Posadas and Libertad streets is the Four Seasons (formerly Park Hyatt), one of the most popular choices for business visitors (and Fidel Castro). It's a 13-floor, 165-room luxury hotel, with marble walls, capacious rooms and impressive artworks. Behind the tower, an attractive outdoor pool and a seven-suite mansion with 24-hour butler service, styled like a mini French château and frequently booked by visiting celebs. All guests are privileged with a personalised check-in and allotted a service tailored to their needs. It's rare to find an establishment that orchestrates such a classy blend of modern facilities and old-fashioned values.

Hotel services *Babysitting. Bar. Business services. Disabled: adapted rooms. Garden. Gym. No-smoking rooms/floors. Parking. Pool (outdoor). Restaurant.* **Room services** *Bathrobe. Dataport. Minibar. Newspaper. Room service (24hr). Turndown. TV: cable/satellite.*

Along the River (Puerto Madero)

Hilton Buenos Aires

Avenida Macacha Güemes 351, Dique 3, Madero Este, Puerto Madero (4891 0000/fax 4891 0001/ www.hilton.com). Bus 2, 130, 152. **Rates** US$200-$260 single/double; US$484 suite. **Credit** AmEx, DC, MC, V. **Map** p277 D8.

The Hilton, designed by Argentinian architect Mario Roberto Alvarez, was built with prominent executives and affluent couples in mind. The vast glass-roof atrium/lobby is embellished with chrome sofas, a marble reception, dazzling carpets and a pair of glass elevators at the back of the foyer. Spread over seven floors, the 418 modern rooms share similar features – deluxe amenities and king-size bathrooms

– but differ in that not all peer over the picturesque docks. It's worth the extra for a superior room with a view. This is a fine hotel, deserving of its popular acclaim; cool location, professionally run and with the killer advantage of the best hotel pool in town.

Hotel services *Babysitting. Bar. Beauty salon. Business services. Disabled: adapted rooms. Garden. Internet (free). Limousine service. No-smoking floors/rooms. Parking. Pool (outdoor). Restaurants (2).* **Room services** *Bathrobe. Dataport. Iron. Minibar. Newspaper. Room service (24hr). Turndown. TV: cable/VCR (on request).*

Expensive

The Centre

Crowne Plaza Panamericano

Carlos Pellegrini 551, entre Lavalle y Tucumán, Microcentro (4348 5000/reservations 4348 5100-200/fax 4348 5250/www.buenosaires.crowne plaza.com). Subte B, Carlos Pellegrini or C, Diagonal Norte or D, 9 de Julio/6,17, 24, 59, 67 bus. **Rates** AR$363-$484 single/double; AR$690 suite. **Credit** AmEx, DC, MC, V. **Map** p277 E7.

Opened in 1981, the Panamericano's two imposing towers sit bang opposite the Obelisco. A large, deluxe hotel, the best of the 396 rooms are in the modern Torre Norte – they are bigger, homelier and better-designed. But it's the additional services that give the hotel an edge: haute cuisine in award-winning Tomo 1 restaurant, and Le Mirage – the rooftop swimming pool and spa, with sushi bar, sun loungers and mind-blowing views.

Hotel services *Babysitting. Bars (2). Beauty salon. Business services. Disabled: adapted rooms. Gym. No-smoking rooms/floors. Parking (free). Pool (indoor). Restaurants (2). Spa.* **Room services** *Dataport. Iron. Minibar. Room service (24hr). Turndown. TV: cable.*

Howard Johnson

Florida 944, entre Paraguay y Marcelo T de Alvear, Retiro (4891 9200/fax 4891 9208/www.hojoar.com). Subte C, San Martín/10, 106, 109, 132, 152 bus. **Rates** US$91-$139 single/double; US$115-$163 triple. **Credit** AmEx, DC, MC. V. **Map** p277 E8.

High living at **Crowne Plaza Panamericano.**

1555 MALABIA HOUSE

Design Bed & Breakfast

- · Historic Building
- · 15 Rooms
- · Safety Box
- · Gardens
- · Meeting Rooms
- · Executive room

- · Air Conditioning
- · Consierge 24hs.
- · Continental Breakfast
- · Room Service 24hs.
- · Laundry Service
- · Parking

Malabia 1555 · Palermo Viejo · Soho Buenos Aires, Argentina
(54-11) 4832-3345 / 4833-2410 · e-mail: info@malabiahouse.com.ar · www.malabiahouse.com.ar

Luxury Apartments for Rent
daily or weekly
In the heart of Recoleta
Buenos Aires Finest Neighbourhood

(swimming pool, gym,
free internet, laundry, sauna,
jacuzzi, lounge and meeting room)

BUENOSAYRES

J.E. URIBURU 1756 • BUENOS AIRES • C1114AAT • ARGENTINA • TEL.: 54 11 4805 6063
www.ayresderecoleta.com • info@ayresderecoleta.com

AyresdeRecoleta

Hidden on the first floor of a mall, the Howard Johnson works hard to ensure visitors find it: location markers on street signs, brochure hand-outs, and a gigantic sign out front. Designed for corporate tourism, the 77 rooms are thoughtfully designed, if slightly unmemorable, but with high-tech amenities, the ideal downtown location and cordial staff, it's a guaranteed success. The king size rooms are particularly spacious with generous beds.
Hotel services *Bar(s). Business services. Disabled: adapted rooms. Gym. Internet (free). Laundry service. Limousine service. No-smoking rooms/floors. Parking. Pool (indoor). Restaurant.* **Room services** *Dataport. Hairdryer. Iron. Minibar. Newspaper. Room service (24hr). Turndown. TV: cable.*
Other locations: Inn Classic Bartolomé Mitre 2241, Once (4952 6010); **Da Vinci** Tucumán 857, Microcentro (4326 6607); **Express Inn** Vuelta de Obligado 2727, Belgrano (4789 9383).

Meliá Buenos Aires Boutique Hotel
Reconquista 945, entre Paraguay y Marcelo T de Alvear, Retiro (4891 3800/fax 4891 3834/www.solmelia.com). Subte C, San Martín/26, 93, 152 bus. **Rates** US$85 single/double; US$168-$195 suite. **Credit** AmEx, DC, MC, V. **Map** p277 E8.
Spanish chain Melia has over 350 hotels around the world. This nine-floor 'boutique' (by their standards) version, opened in 1999, is both chic and formal, as epitomised by the brass and wood reception area. Particular attention is paid to disabled guests, with electric chairlifts and specially designed rooms. Executive suites on the higher floors, with king-size beds and river view, are worth the added cost. Building work on the adjacent 90-room extension is due for completion by March 2005, with the welcome inclusion of a pool, spa and additional restaurant. A wise choice for a pleasant downtown stay.
Hotel services *Babysitting. Bar. Business services. Disabled: adapted rooms. Gym. Limousine service. No-smoking rooms/floors. Restaurant.* **Room services** *Dataport. Minibar. Room service (24hr). Turndown. TV: cable.*

Murano
Carlos Pellegrini 877, entre Córdoba y Paraguay, Retiro (5239 1000/fax 5239 1000/www.murano hotel.com). Subte C, San Martín/10, 59, 132, 152 bus. **Rates** US$109-$120 single/double; US$162-$218 suite. **Credit** AmEx, DC, MC, V. **Map** p277 F7.
Opened in February 2003, the gleaming Murano is the baby of the strip of hotels that line the massive Avenida 9 de Julio. Beyond the shining, glass exterior lie 133 spacious and soundproofed rooms, whose pale walls contrast with the dark wood furnishings. Junior executive suites are designed to double as offices and have enough dataports to start a small internet café (including one in the bathroom – bringing new meaning to the word 'multi-tasking'). Suites at the front of the hotel, with balconies facing the historic Teatro Colón are the best of the bunch. Staff are both friendly and informative and there are plenty of recreational facilities as extras, including an indoor pool, spa, sauna and gym.

Hotel services *Babysitting. Bar. Beauty salon. Business services. Disabled: adapted rooms. Gym. Internet (free). Laundry service. Limousine service. No-smoking floors/rooms. Parking. Payphone. Pool (indoor). Restaurant. Spa. TV room: satellite.* **Room services** *Bathrobe (suites). Dataport. Minibar. Room service (6am-2am). Turndown. TV: cable.*

Suipacha y Arroyo Suites
Suipacha 1359, entre Arroyo y Juncal, Retiro (4325 8200/reservations 4325 4545/fax 4325 1886/ www.syasuites.com). Bus 61, 92, 93, 130, 152. **Rates** US$97-$120 suite. **Credit** AmEx, DC, MC, V. **Map** p277 F8.
Inside this soothing, stylish hotel you will find a heated pool, tennis court, and international restaurant decorated with pebbled floors, bamboo plants and modern furniture. The 78 suites are enthusiastically decorated and cosied up with candles and flower arrangements to compensate for the lack of views. Despite its central location, noise is minimal – the hotel lies on one of BA's quieter streets, close to the Museo de Arte Hispanoamericano.
Hotel services *Babysitting. Bar. Business services. Garden. Gym. Internet (free). Laundry service. Limousine service. No-smoking rooms/floors. Parking*

The best # Hotels

For a view
Sheraton (*p33*); **Plaza Francia** (*p43*).

For a classy corporate act
NH Jousten. See *p41*.

For rock stars
The mansion at **Four Seasons**. See *p35*.

For royalty
Alvear Palace Hotel. See *p33*.

For a poolside paradise
Hilton. See *p35*.

For chic charm
1555 Malabia House (*p43*); **Bel Air** (*p43*).

For total tango immersion
Mansion Dandi Royal. See *p38*.

For a Martini moment
Marriott Plaza. See *p31*.

For quirky design
Boquitas Pintadas. See *p41*.

For a bargain
Gran Hotel Hispano (*p44*); **Che Lulu** (*p45*).

For backpacker bonding
Milhouse (*p47*); **Casa Jardín** (*p49*).

(free). Pool (outdoor). Restaurant. **Room services** *Iron (upon request). Kitchenette. Minibar. Room service (7am-midnight). TV: cable.*

South of the Centre

Mansion Dandi Royal

Piedras 922, entre Estados Unidos y Carlos Calvo, San Telmo (4361 3537/fax 4307 7623/www.dandi royal.com.ar). Bus 10, 24, 29. **Rates** US$180-$230 single/double; US$300 suite. **Credit** AmEx, DC, MC, V. **Map** p277 D6.

Tango is synonymous with San Telmo and this self-styled 'Residential Tango Academy' – created by Héctor Villalba, globe-trotting entrepreneur and tango teacher – fuses five-star service with the spirit of this sensual dance. The 15 rooms of this lovingly converted early-20th-century mansion are sumptuously appointed, with lush bedspreads and stately wooden furnishings. The best rooms are higher up, and there's one suite named after Astor Piazzolla. The tango theme is carried to its maximum conclusion throughout, with murals, paintings and ambient music. Round the clock butler service is standard and facilities include a small heated rooftop pool, exercise machines and two pretty tiled patios. But it's all about dancing: two-hour classes in the hotel's adjoining salon are available daily to guests, and if you book a week's package, additional excursions including *milongas* and tango tours, are included. **Hotel services** *Babysitting. Bar(s). Beauty salon. Business services. Garden. Internet (free). Laundry service. Limousine service. No-smoking floors/rooms. Parking. Payphone. Pool (outdoor).* **Room services** *Bathrobe. Dataport. Newspaper. Room service (24hr). Turndown. TV: cable/VCR.*

NH City

Bolívar 160, entre Alsina y Hipólito Yrigoyen, Monserrat (4121 6464/fax 4121 6450/www.nh-hoteles.com). Subte E, Bolívar or A, Plaza de Mayo, 10, 17, 22, 29, 64 bus. **Rates** AR$271-$296 single/double; AR$323-$545 suite. **Credit** AmEx, DC, MC, V. **Map** p277 D7.

The NH City, part of the excellent Spanish hotel chain, is one of the few five-star boutique hotels in the country. It's located in the heart of the historic centre, steps from the Plaza de Mayo. A restored 1931 art deco building, the 303-room City is endowed with contemporary chic – marble floors, works by Argentinian artists and armchairs with curving contours. For passionate stays, the red and black suites raise the temperature – cool off in the rooftop pool with its view of the domes of the old quarter of the city. A highly regarded restaurant serves Spanish cuisine in the hotel's basement. Ask for one of the front-facing rooms as high up as possible, to avoid a view of a neighbouring brick wall. The hotel is popular with huge tour groups, making the reception area impossibly busy at peak times. **Hotel services** *Babysitting. Bar. Business services. Disabled: adapted rooms. Gym. Laundry service. Limousine service. No-smoking rooms. Payphone.*

Mansion Dandi Royal: you know when you've been tangoed.

Pool (outdoor). Restaurant. Spa. **Room services** *Bathrobe. Dataport. Minibar. Newspaper. Room service (7am-2am). TV: cable.* **Other locations:** NH Florida San Martin 839, Retiro (4321 9850); **NH Latino** Suipacha 309, Microcentro (4321 6700).

North of the Centre

Design Suites & Towers

Marcelo T de Alvear 1683, entre Rodríguez Peña y Montevideo, Recoleta (tel/fax 4814 8700/www. designsuites.com). Subte D, Callao/12, 37, 39, 52, 111 bus. **Rates** US$97-$145 suite. **Credit** AmEx, DC, MC, V. **Map** p277 F6.

Granted, ultra-cool Design Suites is a specialist in chic accommodation and a big hit with media types, but parts of the hotel are starting to need of a lick of paint. The standard suites are minimalist in style – with a white, pine and steel decor combo – flooded with light, excellently equipped and deceptively big. Larger suites sleep up to four (five if agreed in advance), but if you are a couple, ask for a room with a view of Plaza Rodríguez Peña. The lobby area typifies the avant-garde feel; glossy magazines, stylish staff, and tables and chairs flanking a decorative lobby pool (it's not for swimming in – free access is provided to a nearby gym and pool). Some rooms have whirlpool baths. **Hotel services** *Bar. Laundry service. Limousine service. No-smoking rooms/floors. Parking. Restaurant.* **Room services** *Bathrobe. Dataport. Kitchenette. Minibar. Newspaper. Room service (24hr). Turndown. TV: cable.*

LoiSuites Recoleta

Vicente López 1955, entre Junín y Ayacucho, Recoleta (5777 8950/fax 5777 8999/www.loisuites. com.ar). Bus 59, 60, 101, 102, 110. **Rates** US$150-$175 single/double; US$224 suite. **Credit** AmEx, DC, MC, V. **Map** p278 G7.

Part of a small chain of well-run local hotels, this LoiSuites – in the bosom of Recoleta, across from the cemetery and Village Recoleta complex – is the flagship. The 112 decent-sized suites in the 13-floor building are chic and contemporary in style with double-glazing and soundproofed walls to muffle snuffles and grunts. Below in the spacious white lobby, large pastel sofas and potted plants sit in front of the Jardin de Invierno, a two-tiered patio with a retractable roof and a Roman-style pool. Extremely popular, you'll need to book early or settle for one of the other LoiSuites downtown.

Hotel services *Babysitting. Bar. Beauty salon. Business services. Disabled: adapted rooms. Garden. Gym. Limousine service. Parking. Patio. Pool (indoor). Restaurant. Spa.* **Room services** *Dataport. Microwave. Minibar. Refrigerator. Room service (7am-2am). Turndown. TV: cable.*

Other locations: LoiSuites Arenales Arenales 855, Retiro (4324 9400); **LoiSuites Esmeralda** Marcelo T de Alvear 842, Retiro (4131 6800).

West of the Centre

Abasto Plaza

Avenida Corrientes 3190, entre Anchorena y Jean Jaurès, Abasto (6311 4466/reservations 6311 4433-55/fax 6311 4465/www.abastoplaza.com). Bus 24, 26, 124, 168. **Rates** US$200 single/double; US$242 suite. **Credit** AmEx, DC, MC, V. **Map** p278 G4.

Across the road from the Abasto mega-mall, this 20-floor hotel – formerly the Holiday Inn – sits in the barrio synonymous with tango legend Carlos Gardel. In keeping with the spirit, the hotel has all the trappings and trimmings you might expect: a gallery dedicated to tango painters, conference rooms named after singers and free tango classes for guests. The rooms are large if unimaginatively decorated with dark wooden furnishings and comfortable amenities. It looks far on the map, but by taxi or Subte, it's just a few minutes from downtown.

Hotel services *Babysitting. Bar. Business services. Disabled: adapted rooms. Gym. No-smoking rooms/ floors. Parking. Pool (outdoor). Restaurant.* **Room services** *Dataport. Iron. Minibar. Room service (6.30am-2am). Turndown. TV: cable/satellite.*

Moderate

The Centre

Castelar Hotel

Avenida de Mayo 1152, entre Salta y Lima, Congreso (4383 5000-9/fax 4383 8388/www.castelarhotel. com.ar). Subte A, Lima/39, 64, 86 bus. **Rates** AR$140-$160 single/double. **Credit** AmEx, DC, MC, V. **Map** p277 E6.

In the middle of Avenida de Mayo, this historic hotel is where Spanish writer Federico Garcia Lorca resided for over a year – his room has been restored and is open to the public. Interior rooms have limited light and are slightly melancholic – choose one of

the 44 rooms facing the Avenida instead – but if you prefer a sense of history over mod cons, this is ideal. Staff display a tangible sense of pride about the place. In the lobby, there's an attractive cocktail bar, while an elegant old-fashioned Turkish spa is hidden in the basement, with steam rooms, sauna and massage facilities for men and women (open to the general public as well as hotel guests).

Hotel services *Bar. Beauty salon. Gym. Laundry service. Limousine service. No-smoking rooms/floors. Restaurant. Turkish baths (men & women).* **Room services** *Dataport. Minibar. Newspaper. Room service (7am-11pm). Turndown. TV: cable.*

Dazzler

Paraguay 902, y Libertad, Tribunales (4816 5005/ reservations 4815 7383/fax 4816 5005/www.dazzler hotel.com). Subte D, Tribunales/29, 39, 111, 152 bus. **Rates** US$58 single/double; US$78 apartment for 4. **Credit** AmEx, DC, MC, V. **Map** p277 F7.

The Dazzler hotel sits on the edge of Plaza Libertad, and some of the 88 rooms offer a tree-top view of the picturesque square. This 11-floor block was built in the 1980s, an era recalled by the geometric decor of the reception area and breakfast room where a generous buffet is served, though the hotel was completely refurbished when it took on its current incarnation in 2002. In the bedrooms, the furnishings combine vintage and contemporary styling. Staff are friendly, verging on laid back.

Hotel services *Babysitting. Bar. Business services. Internet (free). Laundry service. Limousine service. No-smoking floors/rooms. Parking (free). Restaurant.* **Room services** *Bathrobe. Minibar. Newspaper. Room service (24hr). TV: cable.*

Golden Tulip Savoy Hotel

Avenida Callao 181, entre Perón y Bartolomé Mitre, Congreso (4370 8000/reservations 4370 8010/fax 4370 8020/www.gtsavoyhotel.com.ar). Subte A, Congreso/24, 37, 60 bus. **Rates** US$70 single/ double; US$130 suite. **Credit** AmEx, DC, MC, V. **Map** p277 F5.

Literary lair: the **Castelar Hotel**.

Posada Palermo
Bed and Breakfast

A new way to stay in Buenos Aires

BAHOUSE
Buenos Aires House Temporary Rentals

tel/fax (5411) 48 15 76 02
info@bahouse.com.ar • www.bahouse.com.ar

www.posadapalermo.com
e-mail: info@posadapalermo.com
Salguero1655 between Soler and Paraguay

Mansion
Dandi
Royal
Tango Residential Academy

An Elegant
Petit Hotel
in the heart
of San Telmo

Style & Elegance

Comfort and
personalized attention

Welcome reception
at airport and transfers

Tango "A la Carte"
(lessons, shows, Milongas)

Argentina

Piedras 922/936 - San Telmo C1070AAT - Buenos Aires Town
Phone.: (+54-11) 4361-3537 - Phone/Fax: (+54-11) 4307-7623
www.dandiroyal.com.ar e-mail:reservas@dandiroyal.com.ar

This extremely popular choice, built at the turn of the 20th century, may no longer compete with the very best, but it still has all the hallmarks of a classy hotel – high ceilings, green-jacketed valets, crystal chandeliers. A recent redecoration has buffed up the 174 generously sized rooms, with a lick of paint and essential double-glazing (Callao streams with traffic and the odd demonstration). As well as white-collar extras – business centres, conference rooms – there is even free mud therapy beauty treatments. **Hotel services** *Babysitting. Bar. Business services. Disabled: adapted rooms.Internet (free). Laundry service. Limousine service. Parking. Restaurant.* **Room services** *Dataport. Minibar. Room service (24hr). Turndown. TV: cable.*

Hotel Colon

Carlos Pellegrini 507, entre Lavalle y Tucumán, Tribunales (4320 3500/reservations 4320 3511/fax 4320 3516/www.colon-hotel.com.ar). Subte B, Carlos Pellegrini or C, Diagonal Norte or D, 9 de Julio/6, 59, 106, 109, 132 bus. **Rates** *US$75 single; US$80 double; US$105-$115 suite.* **Credit** AmEx, MC, V. **Map** p277 E7.

Located on the main artery to the city's heart, and facing its namesake – the Teatro Colón – is this good value mid range hotel. The marble reception is brightened up with greenery and the 173 bedrooms are simply but attractively kitted out, with good size beds. Front facing rooms – especially the 'Obelisco' double rooms with panoramic views of that famous monument – have good light (avoid the ones at the back). Up above, there's a rooftop swimming pool for a dip with a view. **Hotel services** *Babysitting. Bar (24hr). Business services. Gym. Internet (free). Laundry service. Limousine service. No-smoking floors/rooms. Parking (free). Payphone. Pool (outdoor). Restaurant. TV room: cable/VCR.* **Room services** *Dataport. Dressing gown. Minibar. Newspaper. Room service (24hr). Turndown. TV: cable.*

Hotel Lancaster

Avenida Córdoba 405, y Reconquista, Retiro (4311 3021-6/fax 4312 4068/www.lancasterhotel-page.com.). Subte B, LN Alem/26, 93, 99, 152 bus. **Rates** AR$135 single; AR$145 double; AR$185 suite. **Credit** AmEx, DC, MC, V. **Map** p277 E8.

Opened in 1945, the red-brick Lancaster Hotel – a sensible mid range, downtown option – is as British-looking as its name suggests. The reception area is fairly discreet, but take the lift up and you'll be greeted by wooden corridors bathed in a soothing creamy hue. Dainty antique touches adorn the slightly small but perfectly well-equipped rooms. Avoid those which overlook noisy Avenida Córdoba; instead, reserve on the higher floors above quiet Tres Sargentos street or be a devil and treat yourself – for just a few extra bucks – to one of the suites. Annexed to the hotel is the White Rose, a cosy corner pub full of hotel guests and passers-by. **Hotel services** *Bar. Laundry service. Restaurant.* **Room services** *Dataport. Minibar. Room service (24hr). TV: cable.*

NH Jousten

Avenida Corrientes 280, entre 25 de Mayo y Leandro N Alem, Microcentro (4321 6750/reservations 4328 4852/fax 4321 6775/www.nh-hoteles.com). Subte B, LN Alem/26, 93, 99, 152 bus. **Rates** AR$271 single/double; AR$408 suite. **Credit** AmEx, DC, MC, V. **Map** p277 E7.

Constructed in 1928, the Jousten oozes style, its stunning façade fronting a neo-Hispanic interior. During its illustrious years, Argentinian icons such as boxer Carlos Monzón, President Hipólito Yrigoyen and Juan and Evita Perón slipped through its imposing doors. It then shut for 20 years before NH invested US$10 million in its resurrection. The results are splendid – the Jousten has become the boutique business hotel of downtown BA. Long wooden corridors lead to stylish rooms furnished with huge beds and minimalist furniture; suites have large terraces. The Spanish restaurant is one of the best in town. **Hotel services** *Babysitting. Bar. No-smoking rooms. Restaurant.* **Room services** *Dataport. Dressing gown. Minibar. Newspaper. Room service (24hr). TV: cable.*

South of the Centre

Boquitas Pintadas

Estados Unidos 1393, y San José, Constitución (4381 6064/fax 4384 5548/www.boquitas-pintadas. com.ar). Subte E, San José/39, 53, 60, 102, 168 bus. **Rates** AR$135-$285 single/double. **No credit cards.** **Map** p277 D5.

A walk around 'Painted Mouths' (named after Manuel Puig's famous novel) is like clambering around a Pedro Almodóvar film set. Mixing 1950s antiques with colourful paintwork, this funky pop art hotel is redecorated every two months and then 're-opened' with a lavish party (any excuse for a knees-up). The five rooms, in which kitsch rules, vary considerably in standard – rooms 102 and 201 are the most recommended – although everyone gets to jump around in the mini pool or lounge on the decadent porches. The bar is a mass of silver and gold, where a blend of pumping music and generous measures should rock you to sleep. Only three of the rooms have air-conditioning. **Hotel services** *Bar. Internet access. Library. Patios (3). Pool (outdoor). Restaurant.* **Room services** *Room service (7am-10pm). TV: cable/VCR.*

North of the Centre

Americas Towers

Libertad 1070, entre Avenida Santa Fe y Marcelo T de Alvear, Recoleta (4815 7900/fax 4816 3982/ www.grupoamericas.com.ar). Bus 10, 39, 102, 152. **Rates** AR$190 single; AR$205 double; AR$304 suite. **Credit** AmEx, DC, MC, V. **Map** p277 F7.

Excellent value Americas Towers is the newest of two hotels that lie side by side. If the older sibling appeals to nostalgic Europeans, this version is designed for artistic types – check out the Miró Bar,

PATIO INN

A C A S S U S O
BED AND BREAKFAST

Labarden 466 | Acassuso | San Isidro
TEL/FAX (5411)4743-2981 Cel. (5411)1549163848

w w w . p a t i o i n n . c o m . a r

MIDTOWN
BUENOS AIRES

Temporary apartment rental
Fully equipped
Day - week - month

Belgrano R
Argentina

Tel./Fax: (54 11) 4552-4903 / 5852
www.midtownba.com.ar
info@midtownba.com.ar

Como en Casa
Bed and Breakfast

STYLE • WARMTH • HOSPITALITY

Gurruchaga 2155 • (1425) • Palermo Viejo
Buenos Aires • Argentina
Tel. (54 11) 4831-0517 • Fax: (54 11) 4831-2664
www.bandb.com.ar • info@bandb.com.ar

BAYRES
GAY BED & BREAKFAST

Av Córdoba 5842 Tel: (54-11) 4772-3877
Palermo Viejo
bayres@fibertel.com.ar

www.bayresbnb.com

1555 Malabia House – delightful designer B&B in the heart of Palermo Viejo.

Dalí Restaurant and Picasso Ballroom. From the outside, it looks rather like a classy office block – all marble and glass. The good-sized rooms at the back catch glimpses of the garden patio while on the top floors there's easy access to the roof terrace fitted with pool, sauna and fitness centre.

Hotel services *Bar. Business services. Disabled: adapted rooms. Garden. Gym. Internet (free). Laundry service. No-smoking floors/rooms. Payphone. Pool (outdoor). Restaurant.* **Room services** *Dataport (some rooms). Minibar. Room service (24hr). Turndown. TV: cable.*

Cristóforo Colombo

Justo Santa María de Oro 2747, entre Juncal y Cerviño, Palermo (4778 4900/reservations 4778 4944 /fax 4778 4944/www.torrecc.com.ar). Subte D, Palermo/15, 29, 39, 64, 152 bus. **Rates** *AR$142 single; AR$183 double; AR$224 suite.* **Credit** *AmEx, DC, MC, V.* **Map** p279 J6.

Popular with Europeans, this hotel – dedicated to the great explorer – is sandwiched between the parks of Palermo and its cafés and bars. The 160 rooms are more like middle-class apartments, with one, two or three bedrooms, a pull-out sofa, kitchenette, washing machine and balcony. For primping and preening there's a circular swimming pool, an in-house masseur, sauna and hairdresser.

Hotel services *Babysitting. Bar. Beauty salon. Garden. Gym. Internet access. Limousine service. Parking. Pool (outdoor). Restaurant. Spa.* **Room services** *Dataport. Kitchenette. Minibar. Room service (7am-11pm). Turndown. TV: cable.*

Hotel Bel Air

Arenales 1462, entre Uruguay y Paraná, Recoleta (4021 4000/fax 4021 4070/www.hotelbelair.com.ar). Bus 10, 17, 39, 11, 152. **Rates** *AR$140-$160 single; AR$150-$170 double; AR$190-$260 suite.* **Credit** AmEx, DC, MC, V. **Map** p278 G7.

With a 1920s decorative façade, a funky bar and restaurant off the lobby, and a location just steps from Plaza Vicente López in leafy Recoleta, the Bel

Air is a real find, and unbeatable value. The service is poised and helpful and rooms are pale and fresh – a blend of avant-garde furnishings and stripped pine, with double-glazing to hush up any barking dogs or revving engines. Perfect for a few days in town, and ideally situated for a Santa Fe shopping spree or Recoleta's sights, as more people discover its delights, it's getting harder to get a room – make sure you book early.

Hotel services *Babysitting. Bar. Business services. Gym. Internet access (free, 24hr). No-smoking rooms/floors. Patio. Restaurant.* **Room services** *Bathrobe. Dataport. Mini-bar. Room service (7am-midnight). Turndown. TV: cable.*

Hotel Plaza Francia

Eduardo Schiaffino 2189, y Libertador, Recoleta (tel/fax 4804 9631-7/www.hotelplazafrancia.com). Bus 61, 67, 93, 130. **Rates** *US$80-$90 single/double; US$115 suite.* **Credit** AmEx, DC, MC, V. **Map** p278 G8.

In the heart of Recoleta, Hotel Plaza Francia offers style and elegance at affordable rates. The 54 cosy rooms mix contemporary comforts with old-fashioned touches, but the most attractive feature of the front-facing rooms (some with balcony) are the park views that form a tableau through the floor length windows. Even better are the top-floor suites with picture-perfect views of the Río de la Plata and northern suburbs. Popular with Europeans, its singular, intimate atmosphere is a far cry from the impersonality of some of the luxury hotels in the area. Free access is provided to a nearby gym.

Hotel services *Babysitting. Bar. Business services. Internet (free). Laundry service. Parking (free).* **Room services** *Dataport. Minibar. Newspaper. Room service (24hrs). Turndown. TV: cable.*

1555 Malabia House Design B&B

Malabia 1555, entre Gorriti y Honduras, Palermo Viejo (tel & fax 4833 2410/www.malabiahouse.com. ar). Bus 15, 39, 55, 168. **Rates** *US$50-$60 single; US$70-$90 double; US$110 suite.* **Credit** AmEx, DC, MC, V. **Map** p279 J4.

The Faena things in life

When French design guru Philippe Starck signed up to convert a derelict building in BA's docklands – called El Porteño – into a luxury hotel and apartment complex, some thought he'd agreed to one urban redevelopment project too many. But Starck the man who turned both the lemon squeezer and the Elysée Palace upside down, loves a challenge, and the Porteño – a US$100 million dollar investment – is just that.

It is being built from the shell of an eye-catching, English-style red brick silo in the heart of Madero Este – BA's latest dockside development and home to the Hilton and several other futuristic building projects. When finished – completion is scheduled for mid/late 2004 – the complex will consist of an 85-room hotel and 85 privately-owned apartments. The man who charmed Starck to join the project was Alan Faena, who made his name and money in high street fashion. Faena's self-consciously aesthetic vision is to create a total concept – touted as an experience where 'dreams are transformed into reality'. He's christened the project Faena Hotel + Universe, the 'Universe' being the value-added amenities that the complex will have, all open to the public as well as hotel guests. They will include bistro, beauty corner, cabaret, hamam, spa, boutiques, business centre, an outdoor gourmet food market and even a 'School of Good Living'.

Hotel rooms will be along classic boutique lines, with Starck's unmistakable hand in the decor and furnishings. Apartments and rooms face either the downtown skyline or the ecological reserve and River Plate.

Hype and expectations are high, but Faena is confident – so confident that the same group of investors are even planning further projects in Madero Este. The Porteño will be BA's first genuine designer hotel and while visitors are bound to love the chic Starck look and state-of-the-art facilities, the challenge will be to seduce *porteños* into embracing this shrine to the high life.

Faena Hotel + Universe

Martha Salotti 445, Dique 2, Madero Este (4021 5555/www.faenaexperience.com). **Rates** US$363 double; US$605-$1,452 suite. **Credit** AmEx, DC, MC, V. **Map** p276 C7.

With 15 well-appointed rooms, just a hop and skip from the heart of the Palermo bars and boutiques, this chic and comfortable bed and breakfast is the best accommodation option in the area. Constructed from two attractive, late-19th-century *casas chorizos* (sausage houses), the owner has baptised the decor 'faux Australian Country House' (lots of wood, daylight and nods to nature). There are mini interior winter gardens, but most of the daytime lounging takes place in the cream-coloured front living rooms or communal breakfast area. The guest book, full of glowing praise and promises to return, is proof that visitors leave here content.
Hotel services *Babysitting. Bar. Business services. No-smoking rooms. Parking.* **Room services** *Bathrobe. Dataport. Minibar. Room service (24hr). Turndown. TV: cable.*

Budget

The Centre

Facón Grande Hotel

Reconquista 645, entre Viamonte y Tucumán, Microcentro (4312 6360/fax 4312 6361 ext 14/www. hotelfacongrande.com) Subte B, Florida/61, 92, 99, 106, 132 bus. **Rates** AR$100 single; AR$120 double. **Credit** AmEx, DC, MC, V. **Map** p277 E7.

Dolled up in 2002, the decor of this decent mid range hotel leans heavily on a folkloric theme – inspired by the heroic gaucho José Font (aka Facón Grande or Big Dagger). Downstairs the lounge area is scattered with indigenous weavings, wooden sofas and poncho covered armchairs, while the 97 dimly lit bedrooms are decorated with gaucho photos and farming tools tacked on to the walls. You'd expect there to be a stable at the rear, though in fact the views are limited to the back of the neighbouring building. Most guests gather in the hotel's restaurant, which, appropriately, serves up a fine steak.
Hotel services *Babysitting. Bar. Business services. Internet (free). Laundry service. No-smoking floors/rooms. Parking. Pool (outdoor). Restaurant.* **Room services** *Dataport. Minibar. Room service (11pm-7am). Turndown. TV: cable.*

Gran Hotel Hispano

Avenida de Mayo 861, entre Piedras y Tacuarí, Monserrat (4345 2020/fax 4331 5266/www.hhispano. com.ar). Subte A, Piedras or C, Avenida de Mayo/10, 17, 64, 86 bus. **Rates** US$21 single; US$25 double. **Credit** AmEx, DC, MC, V. **Map** p277 E6.
Since the early 20th century, a family of proud Iberian origins has run this wonderful, good-value hotel in the heart of the Spanish barrio. Built in 1870, the building is anchored by a splendid indoor patio, where all rooms converge under an iron and glass

roof. Most guests prefer to drift around the communal areas, rather than stick to the hotel's basic, but decent, rooms (note that interior rooms have no windows, so if you prefer natural light to silence take a room higher up overlooking the avenue).
Hotel services *Babysitting. Bar. Garden. Internet access (free). No smoking rooms/floors. TV room: cable.* **Room services** *Minibar (some rooms). Room service (7am-10pm). Turndown.*

North of the Centre

Che Lulu Guest House

Pasaje Emilio Zola 5185, entre Justo Santa María de Oro y Godoy Cruz, Palermo Viejo (4772 0289/www. luluguesthouse.com). Subte D, Palermo/39, 55, 111 bus. **Rates** US$10 per person dorm; US$25-$30 double. **No credit cards. Map** p279 J5.

Hidden down an inconspicuous side-street, close to Palermo's red light transvestite zone, lies this diamond in the rough: with bright red paintwork, antique staircase and stone pathways leading to a roof terrace or patio, it's a litle gem. All areas, including the eight bedrooms, are air-conditioned and benefit from abundant light. They are given extra splashes of colour by local artists and abundant plant life. The dining area with TV is a good spot to plan the day's activities; nearby excursions include Palermo parks, zoo, golf course and race track.

Hotel services *Cooking facilities. Internet access. Laundry service. Library. No-smoking rooms/floors. Payphone.*

Como en Casa B&B

Gurruchaga 2155, entre Paraguay y Guatemala, Palermo Viejo (4831 0517/fax 4831 2664/www. bandb.com.ar). Subte D, Plaza Italia/ 29, 39, 60, 152 bus. **Rates** US$15-$35 single; US$25-$45 double. **Credit** AmEx, MC, V. **Map** p279 J5.

Como en Casa was a Palermo pioneer – establishing itself as a reliable option when everyone was visiting the area, but few stayed. Long and narrow, most of the 11 rooms sit on the ground floor along a corridor leading to the outside patio. They tend to be a little spartan but the rest of the building is dressed up in the old colonial style – lots of rugs and heavy wood, making it a lovely winter option. With little going on in the rooms (no TV or telephone), the socialising takes place in the kitchen and lounge or, in summer, in the delightful little garden.

Hotel services *Garden. Internet access. Laundry service. Terrace. TV room: cable.* **Room services** *Bathrobe.*

Guido Palace Hotel

Guido 1780, y Callao, Recoleta (4812 0674/fax 4812 0341/www.guidopalace.com.ar). Bus 60, 102, 124. **Rates** (not incl breakfast) AR$80 single; AR$100 double. **Credit** AmEx, MC, V. **Map** p278 G7.

Your best choice in Buenos Aires.

- 173 Rooms.
- 8 Meeting Rooms.
- Coffee shop 24 hs.
- Indoor Parking.
- Restaurant International Food.
- Fitness Center.
- Business Center.
- Outdoor Swimming Pool.

The Hotel Colon is a first-class hotel located in the "Heart Of Downtown". Hotel Colon is a few steps from the opera house the city's most elegant shopping and tourist centers.

Location Summary
Ezeiza Int'l Airport - EZE - 30 km / Opera House - nearby
Domestic Airport - AEP - 5 km

HOTEL COLON
★★★★

Carlos Pellegrini 507
(C1009ABK) Buenos Aires - Argentina
Tel: 54-11-4320-3500 - Fax: 54-11-4320-3507/3516
E-mail: reservas@colon-hotel.com.ar
http//: www.colon-hotel.com.ar

GOLDEN TULIP
SAVOY HOTEL

*O*PTIMUM LOCATION SITUATED IN THE HISTORICAL CENTRE OF BUENOS AIRES. JUST FIVE MINUTES FROM RECOLETA, THE OBELISCO AND A FEW METRES FROM PARLIAMENT.

- 174 SOUND-PROOFED ROOMS AND SUITES WITH RECEPTION HALL, TELEPHONE, ELECTRONIC SAFE, INTERNET, MINIBAR, CABLE TV, AIR CONDITIONING AND HEATING.
- BUSINESS CENTRE.
- 9 CONVENTION ROOMS.
- RESTAURANT WITH MEDITERRANEAN CUISINE AND ORIGINAL DISHES CREATED BY OUR CHEF.
- POOL AND FITNESS CENTRE 100 METRES AWAY.

Av Callao 181 • C1022AAB Buenos Aires
Telephone: (05411) 4370 8000
República Argentina • www.gtsavoy.com.ar
info@hotel-savoy.com.ar
reservas@hotel-savoy.com.ar

Buenos Aires

U T E L L Amadeus (OTSURSAV) • Worldspan (OT60157)
SABRE (OT15021) • Apollo (OT95966)

Gran Hotel Hispano. *See p44.*

For two-star lodging, they don't come much better than this. Perfectly located, this French-style hotel attracts budget travellers looking for something a little better. It's not a palace, but the rooms are clean, nicely decorated, well lit and most have balconies. On the fourth floor, there's a patio with seating, so you can enjoy a cold beer under the sinking sun.
Hotel services *Bar.* **Room services** *Room service (24hr). TV: cable.*

Hostels

The Centre

Aventura Inn

3rd Floor, Sarmiento 669, entre Florida y Maipú, Microcentro (5199 0831/fax 5199 0830/www. aventurainn.com). Subte B, Florida/10, 24, 29 bus. **Rates** AR$12 per person dorm. **Credit** MC. **Map** p277 E7.
At the moment 86 beds occupy one floor, but by mid 2004, this will be a three floor 300 bed mega-hostel. Extension plans include adding a roof terrace, kitchen and jacuzzi, plus table tennis and pool tables, though it may prove tricky to gloss over the fact that this was a once a police station. Still, it's cheap, central, sociable and a night's stay includes breakfast, and a drink in the footy themed Bar de Boca below.
Hotel services *Bar. Internet access (free). Restaurant. TV room: cable.*

BA Stop

Rivadavia 1194, entre Lima y Salta, Congreso (4382 7406/www.bastop.com). Subte A, Lima/29, 59, 64, 67, 86 bus. **Rates** AR$18 per person dorm; AR$52 double. **No credit cards. Map** p277 E6.
This 'recycled' hotel dates back to 1860 – the high ceilings and tall windows are hallmarks, but it's been funked up with colourful walls and artwork. Two common rooms, offering table tennis, pool, TV, or an

old-fashioned bar to siddle up to, make it popular with young travellers. The buses streaming past means noise can be a problem as the bedrooms (one double, four dorms) overlook the street. In-house activity includes tango shows (request in advance), and a chef is available on some weeknights.
Hotel services *Bar. Cooking facilities. Internet access (free). Laundry service. No-smoking rooms. TV room: cable.*

Hostel Estoril

2nd floor, Avenida de Mayo 1385, entre San José y Santiago del Estero, Congreso (tel/fax 4381 0377/www.hostelestoril.com.ar). Subte A, Sáenz Peña/29, 64, 86, 102 bus. **Rates** AR$17 per person dorm; AR$37 double; AR$50 triple. **No credit cards. Map** p277 E6.
Sister act Isabela and Tomasa run this clean, back to basics hostel, suited to couples and those that enjoy a quieter life. The living room has balcony views of Palacio Barolo and Plaza del Congreso, while all but one of the rooms are located at the rear (away from street noise) alongside a secluded reading nook. The owners prepare breakfast daily and give good advice on *estancia* trips. The best double room has en suite bathroom and TV for a few pesos more.
Hotel services *Cooking facilities. Laundry service. Internet. Payphone. TV room: cable/VCR.*

Milhouse

Hipólito Yrigoyen 959, entre Tacuarí y Bernardo de Irigoyen, Monserrat (tel/fax 4345 9604/4343 5038/www.milhousehostel.com). Subte A, Piedras or C, Avenida de Mayo/39, 64, 86 bus. **Rates** AR$20 per person dorm; AR$66 double. **No credit cards. Map** p277 E6.
Tucked between the centre and San Telmo, this three-tiered 1890 colonial house was built from materials shipped from Europe. Nowadays it's the city's liveliest and, arguably, most ambitious hostel – they have recently added new rooms on the top floor, fridges, a laundry room and an in-bound travel agency. From top to toe a good vibe hums, inspiring tango sessions, walking tours and barbecues – though some groups prefer simply to huddle round the television. Popular, so book in advance.
Hotel services *Bar. Cooking facilities. Internet access (free). Laundry service. No-smoking rooms/ floors. Patio. Payphone. TV room: cable/VCR.* **Room services** *Iron. TV: cable (some doubles/triples).*

North of the Centre

Casa Esmeralda

Honduras 5765, entre Bonpland y Carranza, Palermo Viejo (4772 2446/www.casaesmeralda.com.ar). Bus 39, 93, 111. **Rates** US$7 per person dorm; US$20-$22 double. **No credit cards. Map** p279 K4.
Mora, the resident pooch, guides you to the patio scattered with picnic tables, *parrilla* and a hammock, and Sebas, the amiable Franco/Argentinian owner, follows close behind. This is a small hostel in the epicentre of the barrio everyone wants to be in. The two

Where to Stay

boquitas pintadas
haute cuisine, dj club,
raumkunst, royal suites,
business-center, terrazas, pool

rubén zertzuela

ee uu 1393 (c1101 aba), buenos aires, argentina
ph: (54 11) 4381 6064
pop-hotel@boquitas-pintadas.com.ar
www.boquitas-pintadas.com.ar

AROUND THE WORLD EVT - LEG: 11.690 / DISP: 0657

The Independent Traveller Agency

- Flights, Accommodation,
  Transfers and Tours in
  Argentina and All Around
  South America
- Visit Buenos Aires,
  Ushuaia, El Calafate &
  Iguazu
- Book Before You Travel

Florida 971. Shop # 59. First Floor.
Buenos Aires (1005). Argentina.
(+54 11) 4312-7276 / 4313-5503
tours@tangol.com
http://www.tangol.com

The hotel is located in the heart of Buenos Aires. Situated on the
famous Florida pedestrian Street and surrounded
by elegant boutiques and art galleries.

Howard Johnson®
Plaza
Florida Street

FREE LOCAL CALLS - WIDE BAND FREE INTERNET ACCESS - ROOM SERVICE 24 HS
COMPLIMENTARY NEWS PAPER DELIVERED TO EACH ROOM
GYM AND SPA - MULTILINGUAL STAFF - CABLE TV - GIFT SHOPS

Florida 944 · Buenos Aires (C1005AAU)
Phone: (54-11) 4891-9200 · Fax:(54-11) 4891-9208
reservas@hjflorida.com.ar · www.hjflorida.com.ar

Ciudad de Buenos Aires-Defensa 1120
Tel./Fax: (5411) 4300-4747
thefirstgay@infovia.com.ar
www.lugargay.org

doubles (with private bath) and three dorms are a tad dim, so guests tend to chill on the roof terrace, or in the TV room complete with bar. Plants cover as decor, though work is going on to spruce up the aging building. Relaxed and recommended.
Hotel services *Bar. Cooking facilities. Garden. Internet access. Laundry service. No-smoking rooms/floors. Payphone. TV room: cable/VCR.*

Casa Jardín

Charcas 4416, entre Thames y Uriarte, Palermo Viejo (4774 8783/www.casajardinba.com.ar). Subte D, Plaza Italia/29, 39, 41, 60, 93 bus. **Rates** AR$30 per person dorm; AR$45 single; AR$70 double. **No credit cards.** **Map** p279 J5.
So, it's not the first hostel to open in Palermo, and yes, this one is also in a converted town house, but journalists-cum-owners Nerina Sturgeon and Laura Eiranova's genuine enthusiasm sets this one apart. Aimed at the thinking traveller, it's all books and art exhibitions and a huge, green roof terrace where regular gatherings include guitar recitals, barbecues and free-form conversation. The rooms are clean, airy and very fairly priced. All in all, a sound choice.
Hotel services *Bar. Cooking facilities. Internet access. Garden. Laundry service. No-smoking rooms. Parking (free). Payphone. TV room: cable/VCR.*

El Firulete

Güemes 4499, y Thames, Palermo Viejo (4770 9259/www.el-firulete.com.ar). Subte D, Plaza Italia/12, 29, 39, 41, 59, 118 bus. **Rates** US$8 per person dorm; US$22 single/double. **No credit cards.** **Map** p279 J5.
This two-storey hostel is located right above a grocery store, close to the bustling transport hub of Plaza Italia. The four dorms and one double share communal bathrooms, but are a good size and have comfortable beds. Most of the mingling takes place in the air-conditioned communal areas like the pool room or the second-floor terrace where sun-loving carnivores feast on impromptu barbecues.
Hotel services *Bar. Cooking facilities. Internet access. Payphone. TV room: cable/VCR. Terrace.*

Milonga

Ayacucho 921, entre Paraguay y Marcelo T de Alvear, Barrio Norte (4815 1827/fax 4822 9117/www.milongahostel.com.ar). Subte D, Callao/37, 39, 106, 109, 132. **Rates** (per person) AR$18-$22 dorm; AR$26 doubles. **Credit** (5% surcharge) AmEx, DC, MC, V. **Map** p278 G6.
Young travellers can't really go wrong in this converted mansion as it's brimming with extras for a low price. Centre of the action is Los Mareados (the Tipsy) bar, with happy hours, live music and flowing drinks. Milonga can be loud, but the six bedrooms (all with shared bathrooms) are on the second floor, far enough away from the buzz downstairs, and you can always cosy up in the TV room or head to the flower-draped roof terrace for some peace.
Hotel services *Bar. Cooking facilities. Internet access. Laundry service. Garden. No-smoking rooms. TV room: cable/VCR.*

The Recoleta Hostel

Libertad 1216, entre Arenales y Juncal, Recoleta (4812 4419/www.trhostel.com.ar). Subte C, San Martín/10, 17, 39, 152 bus. **Rates** AR$24 per person dorm; AR$45 double. **No credit cards.** **Map** p277 F7.
Two spacious patios and a roof terrace are the highlights of this simple hostel. All 22 rooms can best be described as basic, providing only the bare necessities: bed, locker and nightlight, but if you just want a place to crash before exploring the city, you could do worse. It's also very well located, equidistant between the Teatro Colón and Recoleta Cemetery.
Hotel services *Cooking facilities. Internet access. Laundry service. Payphone. Terrace. TV room: satellite/VCR.*

South of the Centre

Garden House

Avenida San Juan 1271, entre Santiago del Estero y Salta, Constitución (4304 1824/www.gardenhouse ba.com.ar). Subte C, San Juan/29, 39, 59, 60, 102 bus. **Rates** AR$18-$21 per person dorm; AR$36-$45 double. **No credit cards. Map** p277 D5.
The barrio may not be the most pleasant nor the hostel's façade the most attractive but despite its limitations, you're liable to bump into a more interesting sort of backpacker here. The first floor has a book-stacked library and a great couch for reading or watching films. Up above, there's a kitchen and a chill-out area where guests swap stories and write letters. As for sleeping, the shared and double rooms are smallish and plain, but overall this is a recommendable budget choice.
Hotel services *Cooking facilities. Internet access (free). Laundry service. Terrace. TV room: cable/VCR.*

Charming **Che Lulú Guest House.** *See p45.*

A home from home

Almost overnight, following the currency devaluation, Buenos Aires' flagging property market became the stuff of foreigners' dreams. Now if you want a second home in a glamorous destination or just a place to take a sunny sabbatical, BA merits consideration.

In the rental market, an increasing number of properties are available to tourists on a daily, weekly or monthly basis as an alternative to hotels – many equipped with terrace, barbecue and fully fitted kitchen, for entertaining your new *porteño* friends. Prices for foreigners are slightly higher, but agencies in this market save you the hassle of contractual negotiations or guarantees.

For short-term rentals in the northern barrio of Belgrano, **Midtown** (www.midtownba. com.ar) has several bright, well-appointed flats. For a double bedroom and a pull-out sofa in the living room, the cost is US$600 per month, with discounts for longer stays. **BA House** (www.bahouse.com.ar) is an Internet-based lettings agency with scores of apartments on its books. Monthly prices range from US$380 for two rooms in Barrio Norte to US$2,500 for an ostentatious five-room residence on chic Avenida del Libertador (add 15 per cent commission). In leafy, tourist-friendly Recoleta, **Art Suites** (www. artsuites.com) has lovely minimalist lodgings with parquet floors, white linen and chrome kitchens. Also look out for new-kid-on-the-block **Ayres de Recoleta** – a luxury apartment complex with swimming pool in the heart of Recoleta due for completion in mid 2004.

For the real long-term bargains, do as locals do and check the *clasificados* (classifieds) in *Clarín* or *La Nación* newspapers. Rents start at about AR$300 (excluding service charges) for a two room apartment; as a ball-park figure, estimate between AR$10-$20 per square metre. However, you'll have to deal with local bureaucracy. Once you're ready to sign, you'll need a local guarantor (usually a property owner), two months deposit and a trustworthy *escribano* (notary) – contracts are normally for 12 months minimum.

For those with spare cash or a desire to leave their overvalued studios back home, the temptation to buy is huge. In a 2003 study, prices per square metre ranged from US$450-$1,000 dollars. Put simply, you could pick up a 50 square metre (538 square foot) apartment in Recoleta for US$100,000 and less than half that in San Telmo.

Nevertheless, you'll need to be on your guard: red tape is thick, the jargon complicated and there are plenty of sharks. So, expect to bargain, take an Argentinian friend, and make sure the legal paperwork is in order. For extra security, use an estate agent. **JR Reynolds** (www.homes.com.ar) is a reputable English-speaking agency, or check multi-agency website www.argenprop.com.ar – also with a section in English. Remember, too, that while property looks like a bargain now, there's no such thing as risk-free investment in BA. The economic and political situation tends to be depressingly cyclical, and what goes up, may well have to come down.

Hostel Inn – Tango City

Piedras 680, entre Chile y México, Monserrat (4300 5764/fax 361 5846/www.hostel-inn.com). Subte E or C, Independencia/2, 17, 59 bus. **Rates** AR$15-$26 per person dorm; AR$33 double. **Credit** MC, V. **Map** p277 D6.

A link in the popular chain of hostels that stretches across Argentina from Iguazú to Patagonia, the fiery red interior walls of this Hostel Inn are in marked contrast to the uniform greyness of the surrounding buildings. Hand-carved furniture and diverse artwork are standout features of this eclectic, boisterous lodging, with capacity for 100 backpackers. It comes complete with its own Irish themed tavern, pool table and multi-language library. The 18 rooms have a homely feel and capture the mood of the area's tango roots. If you're tempted to dance, lessons are offered each Sunday.

Hotel services *Air-conditioning. Cooking facilities. Internet access (free). TV room: satellite/VCR.*

Sandanzas Cultural Hostel

Balcarce 1351, entre Cochabamba y Juan de Garay, San Telmo (4300 7375/fax 4362 1816/www. sandanzas.com.ar). Bus 10, 29, 93, 152. **Rates** AR$17-$38 per person dorm; AR$45 double. **No credit cards. Map** p276 C6.

The multi-coloured walls of this San Telmo hostel are adorned with eye-catching artwork, photo exhibits and a host of other oddball creations by the multi-talented staff. Owners Verónica and Nicolás are a likeable duo, who will offer you *mate*, a 'who, what, where' lowdown on the other guests and tips to help with expedition planning (both are experienced travellers). Good-sized rooms are standard and an inner patio with a hammock allows guests to indulge in a little hard-earned laziness – albeit one at a time. There's a *parrilla* and free use of bicycles.

Hotel services *Cooking facilities. Internet access. Laundry service. Payphone. Terrace. TV room: cable/VCR.*

Sightseeing

Features

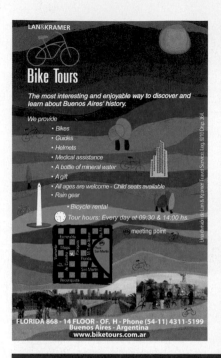

LAN&KRAMER

Bike Tours

The most interesting and enjoyable way to discover and learn about Buenos Aires' history.

We provide
- Bikes
- Guides
- Helmets
- Medical assistance
- A bottle of mineral water
- A gift
- All ages are welcome - Child seats available
- Rain gear
  - Bicycle rental
  - Tour hours: Every day at 09:30 & 14:00 hs.
    meeting point

FLORIDA 868 - 14 FLOOR - OF. H - Phone (54-11) 4311-5199
Buenos Aires - Argentina
www.biketours.com.ar

SPANISH School _ ARGENTINA

Borges

Learn Spanish in the sprawling environment of Buenos Aires.

Data: (+54 11) 4393·1975
spanish@jorgeluisborges.com.ar
www.jorgeluisborges.com.ar

PROA
FUNDACION

Fundación Proa is a contemporary art space located in the historical barrio of La Boca, beside Caminito and opposite the Riachuelo. Artists to have been exhibited include, among others:

LUCIO FONTANA
ANSELM KIEFER
FRIDA KAHLO
JENNY HOLZER
DAN FLAVIN
MARIO MERZ
RUFINO TAMAYO
SOL LEWITT
SEBASTIAO SALGADO
ANDRES SERRANO
FRANCESCO CLEMENTE
JOHN HEJDUK

AV. PEDRO DE MENDOZA 1929, LA BOCA, BUENOS AIRES
TEL (54-11) 4303-0909 | info@proa org
TUESDAY TO SUNDAY 11AM - 7PM. CLOSED MONDAY

www.proa.org

SPONSORS: Tenaris TECHINT

Introduction

Sprawling, chaotic, diverse – but mercifully easy to explore.

Argentina's capital – the Ciudad Autónoma de Buenos Aires – covers some 200 square kilometres (77 square mile), and sprawls out into a vast perimeter of suburbs and slums. Luckily for the visitor, however, most of BA's culture and hedonism can be found in a manageable corridor from La Boca in the south through the centre and in a north-westerly direction up the coast along the River Plate.

Immigration and growth in the late 19th century and a need for self-improvement in the 20th have left a cornucopia of European styles. You will also see a lot of Latin America in most barrios, whether in the mad commercial mess that is Once or simply in the general decay, the dizzying traffic chaos and frenetic street life.

PRACTICALITIES

The city is largely laid out on the standard Spanish colonial-style grid pattern of wide *avenidas* and narrower *calles* in regular blocks – called *cuadras* or *manzanas* – with a regular numbering system that makes navigation relatively easy. Maps (ours included) are rarely oriented north, instead flipping the city to show the river to the south. In fact, Avenida 9 de Julio, the city's main thoroughfare runs north–south. Traffic is one-way; to orient yourself, remember that on Avenidas Santa Fe and Corrientes traffic heads towards downtown, and away from it on Avenida Córdoba. The names of the north–south streets change at Avenida Rivadavia.

We've provided detailed street maps covering the barrios you'll spend most time in. Maps start on page 270 and the street index on page 282.

The best way to get intimate with the barrios is to accept the expense of shoe leather and, in summer, a fair amount of sweat. If you want a quick overall view of the city, take a *colectivo* (public bus) – the most useful routes are detailed on page 86 – or, if you're in a hurry, one of the many guided air-con buses that leave from the hotels. The Subte (subway) system is useful for the central areas. For details of all transport options, *see chapter* **Getting around**.

Note that many museums and government-run sights are closed on Monday. A lot of museums close for a break in the Austral summer (January and February) too, though market demand from the ever-increasing influx of tourists is shortening closed periods. Take cash when visiting museums: those that aren't free charge at most a few pesos, and rarely

Palacio del Congreso.

accept credit cards. You may be asked for some form of photo ID (a photocopy is sometimes acceptable) in certain public buildings. Most museums and historical sites offer scheduled guided tours in Spanish. If you phone ahead, many larger museums will try to arrange a guided visit with an English-speaker – alternatively talk to a tour specialist (*see p55*).

Barrio guide

Not all *porteños* use the city government's barrio denominations, although you'll see them on many maps. For instance, Once is not a barrio, but everyone uses the term for the commercial zone around Once de Septiembre train station, and hardly anyone uses the barrio names Balvanera or San Nicolás, preferring to highlight major buildings, such as the Abasto shopping mall and Congreso. Thus we have divided the city in a way that incorporates both officialdom and common usage.

The Centre's focal point is Plaza de Mayo – the city's original main square and site of many important public buildings. Elegant Avenida de Mayo runs from the plaza across gaping Avenida 9 de Julio to the Plaza del Congreso, in the barrio of Congreso. Next door is Tribunales, the legal quarter, and to the north the railway termini of Retiro. The Microcentro is the capital's downtown, a heaving commercial and financial hub. East of *calle* Florida – one of only three pedestrianised streets – is the Bajo, with its banks, bars and skyscrapers.

MUSEO
DE LA PASION
BOQUENSE

The most important soccer
museum in America

CABJ

* Audiovisuals
* 360° exhibition
* Touch-screens
* Trophies
* Tour around the heart of Boca Juniors Stadium
* Official merchandising

Open daily from 10 am to 7 pm
Brandsen 805 (under the Stadium stands)
La Boca - Buenos Aires
www.museoboquense.com

THE TRAVEL AGENCY
FOR BUDGET TRAVELLERS

SAY HUEQUE

BUDGET
IGUAZU &
PATAGONIA

Fun & cheap
Journeys in
Argentina.

you can book and pay
for your trip from the u.k.

Viamonte 749 6th floor of.1
Tel.: (+5411) 5199-2517/18/19/20
Buenos Aires - Argentina
sayhueque@mayerymayer.com.ar

MAYER & MAYER TURISMO

SPANISH
IN BUENOS AIRES

- Intensive Spanish Courses
- In the heart of Buenos Aires:
  on our unique pedestrian street
- 5 students per class
- Free Tango class every Friday
- Accommodation upon request

DOWNTOWN
LANGUAGE STUDIO

FLORIDA 378 | Galería Central | 3rd Floor
Buenos Aires | Argentina | Tel.: 4325 - 8092
www.downtown-studio.com.ar — info@downtown-studio.com.ar

Guided tours

As well as panels around the city to help you on self-guided walks, the Tourist Board supports **Cicerones** (4330 0800/4431 9892, www.cicerones.org.ar), an organisation offering free, tailor-made tours. Fill in the online form detailing your topic of interest, allow 72 hours, and a guide will be chosen from among 50 multilingual volunteers. Bus tours can be organised by most hotels and **Argentina Adventures** (4326 6907, www.aaye.com.ar) offers private, English-speaking guided tours. Below are other recommended options.

History & culture

Fundación Konex (4816 0500, www.fundacion konex.org) organises tours of Museo Nacional de Bellas Artes and Malba. **Eternautas** (4384 7874, www.eternautas.com) have a team of university teachers and historians who lead visits to different barrios, exploring tango, politics and history. Stimulating literary tours are run by **Lihue Expeditions** (5031 0070).

Immigration & communities

To understand the history of Argentina's immigrant communities, join a walking tour with an architecture specialist (4374 2222, www.espacioverde.com.ar, AR$20). Explore Jewish Buenos Aires on a private tour with Deb Miller of **Travel Jewish** (4257 5977, www.traveljewish.com, US$30 per hour).

Active tours

To stretch your legs, see the city and get some air, see BA by bike. **Bike Tours** (4311 5199, www.biketours.com.ar, US$25-$35) arrange a variety of city rides with English-speaking guides, leaving twice daily from Plaza San Martín in Retiro. **Urban Biking** (4855 5103, www.urbanbiking.com, AR$55-$85) tours the city's southern and northern barrios, and can arrange night-time rides. Both firms provide safety equipment and bike hire. For less effort and more thrills, see the city from the air. **Tangol** (4312 7276, www.tangol.com) has 15-minute helicopter rides over the city for US$50. To arrange extreme sports, golf or sailing, speak to Dicky at **Salidas Deportivas** (mobile 15 4444 3499, prices US$70-$170), which organises a range of outings for sports enthusiasts. For accompanied football outings, *see p198*.

Out of town

Most agencies run trips to Zona Norte, Tigre and the delta. For cowboys and countryside, choose between a gaucho fiesta at an *estancia* (**Lan y Kramer Travel**, 4312 2355, www.estanciastravel.com, AR$97) with an *asado*, *folklore* music and plenty of wine, or a trip to a working ranch, via the gaucho town of San Antonio de Areco (**Tore Savino**, 4815 9853, www.toresavino.com, US$59).

The **South of the Centre** chapter includes Monserrat, the historical district south of the Plaza de Mayo. San Telmo follows, drawing visitors to its antiques, tango and bustling Plaza Dorrego. Lying on the Riachuelo – the little river that empties into the River Plate – is La Boca, a working-class barrio famous for its football team and colourful street, Caminito. Run-down Constitución contains the railway terminal for the south. Barracas, historically a factory zone, is starting to enjoy the fruits of long overdue redevelopment.

North of the Centre, beyond Retiro, is Recoleta, where the rich live and the famous are buried. Its cemetery, plazas, shops and museums make it a tourist magnet. Barrio Norte is a neighbouring residential district. Further north is Palermo. It has three distinct sub-areas around the huge Parque Tres de Febrero: expansive Palermo proper, a middle-class residential area with gardens, the zoo and well-kept plazas; opulent, tranquil Palermo Chico; and trendy Palermo Viejo (divided into sub-barrios Palermo

Soho and Palermo Hollywood), full of hip restaurants and boutiques. The dining quarter of Las Cañitas is in Palermo too.

Just to the **West of the Centre** are Once and Abasto, rich in immigration, history, tango and commerce. Other western barrios for visitors willing to wander are Caballito, Villa Crespo and, slightly north, Chacarita, home to a vast proletarian necropolis.

Along the River is the Costanera Norte, north of the city airport, a popular place for weekend promenades. Next to the southern bank of the river is Puerto Madero – BA's yuppie dockland complex – and Costanera Sur, skirting the coastal eco-reserve.

Heading **Further Afield** to the north is Belgrano, with its plazas, museums and shops; nearby are Nuñez and Saavedra. Further still, beyond the limits of the capital, are the wealthier suburbs of Zona Norte: Olivos, Martínez and San Isidro. On the city's western edge are Liniers and Mataderos, both associated with cowboys, cattle-dealing and meatpacking.

The Centre

The city's historic heart is also the centre of national power and protest.

Sightseeing

The compact, historic city centre is where the noble idealism of the nation's founding fathers has repeatedly clashed with Argentina's complex realities. Born as the northern half of the original Spanish settlement, el Centro gained power and prestige as the political and commercial heart of the entire country.

Its central square, Plaza de Mayo, is where independence was first conceived, where the Peróns wooed the masses, where human rights group the Madres de Plaza de Mayo continue to protest the freedom of their children's killers and where any other public claim has at least a slim chance of being heard among the noisiest streets in the city. The centre was the platform for city mayor Torcuato de Alvear's vision of a great capital in the late 19th-century – a city of French-style palaces, wide avenues, green plazas and imposing architecture better suited to Argentina's prosperity.

Buenos Aires was once the face of a rich nation, and the centre its showcase. Mansions became the seats of power and two main thoroughfares, Avenida de Mayo and Roque Sáenz Peña (better known as Diagonal Norte), were opened to link the three key republican palaces: Congreso, Justicia and the Casa Rosada.

Spread over several barrios, the centre is daytime home to millions. Renowned landmarks lend their names to some of its sectors, but otherwise the zones that compose it converge under the 'el Centro' label. On weekdays, the combination of modern life and pre-independence town planning makes the central business district a sometimes claustrophobic experience. Commuter traffic pours into the narrow roads, shoppers throng pedestrianised Florida and Lavalle streets and workers head for offices in the bajo (low place). A mass evacuation takes place around 6-8pm, after which the show is stolen by entertainment venues and cabarets along Corrientes.

The centre has also become the main stage for picketers' protests, and after dusk, hordes of cartoneros (cardboard collectors) descend, hauling their carts around before heading back to Retiro station or shanty town Villa 31. Just a stone's throw from such poverty is the affluence surrounding lush, stunning Plaza San Martín. Startling to outsiders, such contrast is taken for granted by porteños accustomed to the centre's competing visions of past and present.

Plaza de Mayo

The **Plaza de Mayo**, the original *plaza mayor* (main square), was laid out by Juan de Garay in the 1580s, shortly after the successful foundation of Buenos Aires. Garay still stands as a bronze statue in a tiny square just metres north-east of the plaza, beside an oak tree from his Basque motherland. Though much changed, the plaza is still the city's focal point and a logical starting point for an exploration of the places, people and events that created it.

The colonial plaza became Plaza de Mayo to commemorate 25 May 1810, when the masses assembled there to celebrate the deposition of the Spanish viceroy and the swearing in of the Primera Junta (First Council). Ever since, the plaza has been centre stage in the dramatic political life of the nation. Famously, it was the site of the great gatherings of the *descamisados* or 'shirtless ones' under Perón and was bombed by the military in 1955 (to oust Perón); bullet holes are still visible in the **Ministerio de Economía** building on Hipólito Yrigoyen next to Avenida Paseo Colón. Today, the Madres de Plaza de Mayo still march here every Thursday at 3.30pm to protest the 'disappearance' of their loved ones during the last military government and the official impunity granted to the perpetrators. The Plaza was also the epicentre of the protests that led to the downfall of de la Rúa (*see p14* **Power to the *pueblo***). To defend against disturbances, heavily policed barricades are now a permanent presence.

At the plaza's centre is the **Pirámide de Mayo**, an obelisk raised in 1811 for the anniversary of the May revolution. The Madres' famous symbol – a headscarf that alludes to motherhood and to the nappies of their lost children – is painted on the tiles circling the pyramid. To the east is a statue of independence patriot Manuel Belgrano – the only national hero to be honoured with a statue in the plaza.

Glowing like a vermilion psychedelic fantasy, especially at sunset, the **Casa Rosada** (Pink House) is the presidential palace (not the residence, which is out in the sticks in Olivos). Built between 1862 and 1885, it stands where Buenos Aires' 17th-century fort, later the viceroy's palace, used to be. The splendour of its European Renaissance-style façade came together in several stages. The emblematic

Governmental grandeur: the colonial town hall, or **Cabildo**, and the **Banco de la Nación**.

rosy hue originated during Sarmiento's 1868-74
presidency, when it was traditional to add ox
blood to whitewash to provide colour and
thicken the mix. Some also argue that liberal
Sarmiento also wanted to incorporate the red
of the Federalists to keep the peace with Rosas'
followers. Today the front is pinker than the
rest because a project to doll it up during the
Menem years ran out of funds when only one
side had been finished.

The central balcony has been the soapbox of
diverse demagogues and dictators, although the
Peróns used the lower balcony, above the doors
on the Rivadavia side, presumably to be 'closer
to the people'. This was also used by Madonna
in the filming of Alan Parker's *Evita*, despite
protests by Peronists who felt that she was
tarnishing the memory of Saint Evita.

The **Museo de la Casa Rosada** (*see p58*)
displays, predictably, portraits, hats, *mate*
gourds and carriages that once belonged to
Argentinian presidents. There are more curious
items, including a black doll given to poor kids
by Evita's charity. Downstairs, a dungeon-like
arcade gives access to a moat from which there
is an imposing view of the eastern façade of the
Casa Rosada. Guided tours visit the palace's
opulent halls and inner patios. Outside, the
changing of the guards takes place every
two hours between 7am and 7pm.

Surrounding the Plaza de Mayo are several
important buildings. On the corner of Avenida
Rivadavia and 25 de Mayo is the **Banco de la
Nación**, the country's biggest state bank. The
present building, constructed between 1940 and
1955, is topped by an enormous, neo-classical

dome. It's still a functioning bank, and as such
tourists aren't welcome. Instead, to peek inside
the bank's splendid marble corridors, walk
through to the rather dry **Museo Histórico
y Numismático** (*see p58*), at the back of the
building. There's a collection of rare coins and
notes as well as a cheque book for a never
opened branch in the Falklands/Malvinas.

Heading west on Avenida Rivadavia is the
neo-classical **Catedral Metropolitana** (*see
p58*). The plan for the present cream-coloured
building, the sixth cathedral on this site, was
hatched in 1753; the first façade was blessed in
1791 and the final touches were added in 1910.
The high baroque interior arches create a sombre
atmosphere and one of the side chapels contains
a popular statue of Christ donated in 1981 by
two local football players. The rococo main altar
stands out, as does a life-sized Christ to its left
made from the wood of the native *algarrobo*
(carob) tree in 1671. The right-hand nave houses
the mausoleum containing – since 1880 – the
repatriated remains of the Liberator José de San
Martín (who died in France in 1850). An eternal
flame outside the cathedral burns in his memory.

The Plaza's other main building, the
Cabildo, was HQ of the city council from 1580
to 1821, and the place where revolutionaries
took the first steps towards independence.
Seemingly the oldest building on the plaza, it
recovered its colonial style only in the 1940s,
a few decades after six of the original 11 arches
on the façade were lopped off to make room
for Avenida de Mayo and Avenida Julio A Roca
(known as Diagonal Sur). Today it houses the
Museo Histórico Nacional del Cabildo y

de la Revolución de Mayo (*listings below*). Austere rooms preserve valuable items such as a magnificent gold and silver piece from Oruro (Bolivia), one of the first printing presses in the country and objects related to the English Invasions. A first-floor balcony provides fine views of the Avenida de Mayo. Behind the Cabildo is a shaded colonial patio around a beautiful well. Accessible from Avenida de Mayo and Hipolito Yrigoyen, it hosts a handicrafts fair on Thursdays and Fridays.

Behind the Casa Rosada, Avenida de la Rábida follows the shape of the Customs building that stood here in the late 19th century, now a green space called **Parque Colón**, where a monument of Columbus (Cristóbal Colón in Spanish) looks out to sea. A massive Argentinian flag – which Graham Greene likened to the steam from a ship cutting into the blue of the heavens – waves dramatically against the sky.

Catedral Metropolitana

Avenida Rivadavia, y San Martín (4331 2845/4345 3369). Subte A, Plaza de Mayo or D, Catedral or E, Bolívar/24, 29, 64, 86, 111, 130 bus. **Open** *Jan, Feb* 9am-7pm Mon-Fri, Sun; 3-7pm Sat. *Mar-Dec* 8am-7pm Mon-Fri; 9am-7.30pm Sat, Sun. **Guided tours** (Spanish) *Temple* 11.30am, 4pm Mon-Fri. *Crypt* 1.15pm Mon-Fri. *Temple & crypt* 4pm Sat, Sun. **Admission** free. **Map** p277 D7.

Museo de la Casa Rosada

Hipólito Yrigoyen 219, entre Balcarce y Paseo Colón (4344 3804/www.museo.gov.ar). Subte A, Plaza de Mayo or D, Catedral or E, Bolívar/24, 64, 86, 152 bus. **Open** 10am-6pm Mon-Fri; 2-6pm Sun. **Guided tours** *Museum* (Spanish) 11am, 4pm Mon-Fri; 3pm, 4.30pm Sun. *Casa Rosada* (Spanish) 4pm Mon-Thur; (Spanish & English) 4pm Fri. **Admission** free. **Map** p277 D7.

Museo Histórico Nacional del Cabildo y de la Revolución de Mayo

Bolívar 65, entre Avenida de Mayo y Hipólito Yrigoyen (4334 1782/4342 6729). Subte A, Plaza de Mayo or D, Catedral or E, Bolívar/24, 29, 64, 86, 111, 130 bus. **Open** 10.30am-5pm Tue-Fri; 11.30am-6pm Sun. **Guided tours** (Spanish) 3pm, 4.30pm Sun. **Admission** *Museum* contribution AR$1. *Tours* AR$2. **No credit cards**. **Map** p277 D7.

Museo Histórico y Numismático del Banco de la Nación Argentina

1st Floor, Bartolomé Mitre 326, entre 25 de Mayo y Reconquista (4347 6277/6267). Subte A, Plaza de Mayo or D, Catedral or E, Bolívar/24, 29, 64, 130 bus. **Open** 10am-3pm Mon-Fri. **Admission** free. **Map** p277 D7.

Avenida de Mayo

Opened in 1894, the grand **Avenida de Mayo**, its spacious pavements dotted with plane trees, is the most obvious example of Buenos Aires trying to emulate the wide boulevards of Paris. In reality, though, it's more closely associated with Spain, due to the large numbers of Spanish immigrants who settled in – and still live in – the neighbourhood and its resemblance to Madrid's Gran Via and La Rambla in Barcelona.

Newly elected presidents make their way down this avenue to the Casa Rosada after being sworn in at the Palacio del Congreso. Common folk travel below, on Latin America's oldest underground railway, opened in 1913, just nine years after New York's. Although the Subte's *linea* A has lost much of its old lustre to modernisation, the retro posters and fittings at Perú station (Avenida de Mayo between Bolivar and Perú) recalls the Argentina that used to be.

Divine inspiration

Convinced of imminent war in Europe, Italian-born textile magnate Luigi Barolo combined his wealth with compatriot architect Mario Palanti's genius to create the Palacio Barolo – at Avenida de Mayo 1370 in the barrio of Congreso – in 1923 as a neo-gothic shrine to the author of the *Divine Comedy*. Dante Alighieri's ashes were to be brought here for safekeeping, though in the end they never left Ravena. All the same, even if Buenos Aires didn't get the poet's dust, it did get one of its most emblematic, and, until the construction of the Edificio Kavanagh (*see p64*) in 1935, tallest buildings.

The palace was conceived along the lines of Dante's masterpiece. Mirroring the work's

100 cantos, the 22-floor building, with its Gaudi-esque curves and lumps, reaches a height of 100 metres (328 feet). Hell is on the ground-floor (where, ironically, the Argentinian secret service have offices). In the entrance hall, in the nine vaults above the passageway, are engraved Latin inscriptions taken from nine different literary works from the nine infernal hierarchies. The first 14 floors comprise Purgatory, eventually giving way to Paradise in the upper reaches. The very top, inspired by the Hindu temple Rajarani Bhubaneshvar, is reserved for God and represented by a domed lighthouse.

Each floor contains 11 or 22 offices, corresponding to the number of stanzas that

Despite run-down sections, modern towers and some of the more faded-looking Spanish restaurants along and around its ten blocks, fine European-style buildings with exquisite architectural details still abound. The best example of art nouveau, richly decorated with elements from the natural world, is the **Hotel Chile**, on the corner of Santiago del Estero.

Heading west from Plaza de Mayo, the first highlight is the Gallic *La Prensa* newspaper building, from 1896, crowned by a Pallas Athena statue and now the city government's **Casa de la Cultura** (*listings below*). The French feel goes beyond the façades – the impressive Salón Dorado, inspired by the Palace of Versailles, hosts regular classical concerts; ask inside for the programme. A siren on top, sounded during crucial moments in the city's history, was last heard in 1983 when democracy was restored. Guided tours also take in the city government headquarters on the Plaza de Mayo.

The **Café Tortoni** (*see p125*) is a legendary place for coffee, tango and the arts, visited by Federico García Lorca, Borges and feminist poet Alfonsina Storni in the days of its famous *peñas* (literary gatherings) in the 1930s. More recent guests include Hillary Clinton. Above is the **Academia Nacional del Tango** (*see p212*) where courses and a library attract tango researchers. The **Castelar Hotel** (*see p39*) further up the avenue at No.1152 is where Lorca lived between 1933 and 1934, a block from the **Teatro Avenida** where some of his plays were performed. Another surviving café from his era is **Los 36 Billares** (*see p203*) where Lorca had coffee; it's not known if he played billiards on any of the original tables. The run-down building at No.1317 was once

a classy hotel where the Kiev-born ballet dancer Vaslav Nijinsky spent his wedding night.

The avenue's outstanding edifice and one of the city's notable buildings is the **Palacio Barolo**. It was built as, and remains, office space, but you can enter its ground floor passageway with gargoyles, Latin inscriptions and a film setting-like kiosk. It's got a great story too, linking the architecture to Dante's *Divine Comedy* (*see p58* **Divine inspiration**).

Another stunning building marks the avenue's west end. With its two slender domes the **Edificio de la Inmobiliaria**, built in 1910 for an insurance company, is a nattily eclectic celebration of several styles including Italianate balconies and Eastern motifs. From here it's a few steps to the Plaza del Congreso.

Casa de la Cultura

Avenida de Mayo 575, entre Perú y Bolívar (4323 9669). Subte A, Perú or D, Catedral or E, Bolívar/ 24, 29, 64, 86, 111, 130 bus. **Open** *Feb-Dec* 8am-8pm Mon-Fri; by tour Sat, Sun. **Closed** Jan. **Guided tours** (Spanish & English) 4pm, 5pm Sat; hourly 11am-4pm Sun. **Admission** free. **Map** p277 D7.

Congreso & Tribunales

Plaza del Congreso is the popular name for the three squares filling the three blocks east of the Palacio del Congreso. Run down in recent years by protestors, vagrants and metal thieves who hijack commemorative plaques, all that's left of its once stately elegance are the shady jacarandas, *tipa* and *ceibo* trees (whose red blossom is the national flower) that colour the plaza in spring. It contains a version of Rodin's *Thinker* and a statue of Mariano Moreno, one of the May revolutionaries. The plaza is also at

Sightseeing

most of the cantos contain. The cryptic style is also reflected in the predominance of Latin-inscribed vaults and circular shapes, for Dante the perfect synthesis of his closed-loop view of a universe ordered by God. Although shadowed by BA's overbuilt contemporary skyline, the Barolo's dome, with its 300,000 light bulbs, once lit up the night sky. The idea was that its beam would meet halfway above the River Plate with the beam from the Palacio Salvo – the equally impressive twin building that Palanti later built

in Montevideo. Despite the international fame Barolo brought Palanti, his esoteric flare didn't last long. Shortly afterwards he left for Mussolini's Italy, where he designed cold, fascist-inspired buildings for Il Duce.

Although the building was a landmark edifice even before construction began, much of its allure remains a mystery since the original plans have never been found. But those familiar with its secrets say that in early June, at 7.30 pm, the Southern Cross constellation moves into perfect alignment with the building's axis.

'kilometre zero', from which all distances in Argentina are measured. There's a small flea market on the Hipólito Yrigoyen side.

The western section of the plaza is dominated by the **Monumento a los Dos Congresos**, in remembrance of the first constitutional assembly held in 1813 and the Declaration of Independence three years later in Tucumán. The monument's centrepiece is the statue of the republic, propped up by a plough and waving a victorious laurel branch. Lower down, two female figures, one bearing the national flag and shield, the other breaking the chains of colonial rule, complete the liberation allegory.

Like Argentina's federal constitution, which was inspired by the US model, the Greco-Roman **Palacio del Congreso** (*see p61*) is a dome-and-column affair resembling Washington's bicameral legislature. Finished in 1906, its extravagant interior (including the Salón Rosado frequented by Evita), can be visited with a guided tour (no access when in session). Note that the 72 Senate desks all have a button for direct calls to the cafeteria.

On the corner to the right of the palace is a historical *confitería* (closed since 1996) where politicians used to sip their espressos between sessions. It's called **El Molino**, a rerference to the windmill above its entrance. Currently under refurbishment, the small **Teatro Liceo**, on the corner of Rivadavia and Paraná, is one of the oldest playhouses in BA. It opened in 1876 and has been the stage for many of the country's greatest thespians. It's also where a struggling young actress named Eva Perón once performed.

Worth visiting a block north of Avenida de Mayo at Bartolomé Mitre and Paraná is the **Pasaje de la Piedad**. The aristocratic veneer and carriage entrance of this residential block have made it a star of film and TV. **Pasaje Rivarola**, connecting the 1300s blocks of Mitre and Perón, is curious for its twin façades.

To visit the rest of civic Buenos Aires, a good starting point is **Diagonal Norte**, running north-west from Plaza de Mayo. The avenue is a masterpiece of urban harmony; every building is ten-storeys-tall with a second-floor balcony, though a rigidly monumental style dominates many of its edifices. Empty on weekends, the Diagonal's finest architecture is on the corner of Florida where Bank Boston shows off its decorative façade and heavily decorated gilt ceiling of the inner hall (visible during bank opening hours only). The style of the exterior is known as *plateresque*; popular in the 16th century, the name (*plata* means silver) refers to the ornamental complexity, comparable to the work of a master silversmith. Competing for visual attention is graffiti adorning its walls or door, attacking the bank's behaviour during the

2001-02 financial collapse. At night, the upper reaches of the building are lit up, highlighting details rarely visible during the midday rush.

Diagonal Norte links the Plaza de Mayo with the barrio of Tribunales, where the law courts are surrounded by solicitors' offices, law firms and kiosks selling legal pamphlets. At the end of 2003 the block between Cerrito and Libertad was pedestrianised. The avenue's disappointing dead-end is the grubby-looking **Palacio de Justicia**, seat of the scandal-ridden Supreme Court, and another popular venue for public protest. Stretching out in front as far as Avenida Córdoba is the **Plaza Lavalle**, an attractive green spot rich in history and sprawling *ceibo* trees. Its focal point is a monument to Juan Lavalle, one of the military heroes who crossed the Andes with San Martín. Across the Plaza, and filling a whole block, is the **Teatro Colón**. With its regular lines and tempered classicism, it's a key landmark and an internationally renowned venue for opera and classical music. A one-hour tour, available in English, visits the Colón's elegant salons and workshops. *See p189* **Opera magnifica**.

A block away on Libertad 785, behind concrete barricades, is the **Templo Libertad**, the city's oldest functioning synagogue serving the sizeable local Jewish population (*see p89* **Shalom, Buenos Aires**). If you have photo ID you can visit the small **Museo Judío** (*listings below*), where among collections of Judaica is an exhibit recounting the story of the Jewish gauchos and a letter from Einstein.

On the corner of Avenida Córdoba and Libertad, is the **Teatro Cervantes** (*see p217*), the capital's grand old lyric theatre. Unveiled in 1921, its façade is a near replica of the university at Alcalá de Henares in Spain, where Don Quixote's creator was born. It's another fine example of *plateresque* style. Equally impressive inside, the building also houses the **Museo del Teatro** (*listings below*), a tribute to Argentina's thespian history. It's just a short walk from here to the wide asphalt canyon of Avenida 9 de Julio and its iconic central monument, the **Obelisco** (*see p65* **A superlative city**).

Museo del Instituto Nacional de Estudios de Teatro

Avenida Córdoba 1199, y Libertad (4815 8881/8882 ext 156). Subte D, Tribunales/29, 39, 109 bus. **Open** 10am-6pm Mon-Fri. **Admission** free. **Map** p277 F7.

Museo Judío de Buenos Aires Dr Salvador Kibrick

Libertad 769, entre Viamonte y Córdoba (4123 0834). Subte D, Tribunales/29, 39, 109 bus. **Open** 3-5.30pm Tue, Thur. **Admission** US$5; free under-18s. **Guided tours** (Spanish, English, French & German). **No credit cards. Map** p277 F7.

Palacio del Congreso

Hipólito Yrigoyen 1849, entre Entre Ríos y Combate de los Pozos (4959 3000/6310 7100/www.senate. gov.ar). Subte A, Congreso/12, 37, 64, 86 bus. **Closed** sometimes Jan. **Guided tours** *Spanish & English* 11am Mon-Wed. *Spanish only* 5pm, 7pm Mon, Tue, Fri. *English only* 4pm Mon, Tue, Fri. **Admission** free. **Map** p277 E5/F5.

Microcentro

Weekdays during business hours the whole downtown district is a frenzy of frantic *porteños* shopping, working, running, shouting and generally fulfilling their big-city stereotype. In reality, they're the only ones adroit (or mad?) enough to breeze through the Microcentro's obstacle course of potholed narrow sidewalks, roaring motorcycles and poison-spewing buses.

The district is nicknamed La City – and was once known as 'the 20 blocks that rule the country' – for its early association with British commerce. It has the largest concentration of financial institutions in the country, extending almost the entire length of Florida, San Martín and Reconquista (named after the reconquest, when Buenos Aires repelled the English in 1806-07). Many of the banks were built during the first half of the 20th century, at a time when affluent Argentinians had money to put in them, and stand out for their architectural refinement. A good example is the former **Banco Tornquist**, at Bartolomé Mitre 559, on the first section of street to be paved in BA. Scale models of what the district looked like during the 19th century and how it is now are on display in the **Museo del Banco de la Provincia** (Sarmiento 362, 4331 1775). Another financially-themed museum, the excellent **Museo Numismático** (First Floor, San Martín 216, 4348 3882) exhibits early bank notes featuring dogs, goats, sheep, cows and even a kangaroo, plus rare coins minted in Tierra del Fuego and those of the French-claimed Patagonian Kingdom of Araucanía. Both museums are closed at weekends.

To see how affluent *porteños* lived during the economic boom of the late 19th century, step into the **Museo Mitre** (*see p62*) – home of former president and founder of *La Nación* newspaper, Bartolomé Mitre. It contains his rich library specialising in American history and open to the public. On the seventh floor of San Martín 353, you can check out the little visited **Museo de la Policía Federal** (4394 6857), an unintendedly kitsch tribute to crime fighting. Together with a stuffed police dog, there are some gory photos and wax models illustrating sex crimes. The cover of Perón's coffin is kept here, its glass broken from when his hands were cut off and stolen by vandals.

Pedestrianised **Florida** street.

At the corner of Reconquista and Perón, protected by wonderful wrought iron gates is the 18th-century **Basílica Nuestra Señora de la Merced**, the richly decorative façade of which was restored in 1905. Next door, the **Convento de San Ramón**'s patio contains small attractive shops and a hidden lunchtime eaterie overlooking an attractive garden. There's an antiques market here every Sunday. The more humble **Catedral Anglicana de San Juan Bautista**, at 25 de Mayo 282, where meals are given to the homeless, was the first non-Catholic temple in South America. The church's wooden altar features images of birds and flora from the Chaco region.

Along the west side of Avenida Leandro N Alem, more commonly called *el bajo* – meaning the low place – runs an almost uninterrupted arcade packed with banks, cafés, the stock exchange and, on its east side, the colossal **Correo Central**, located at Sarmiento 151. Inaugurated after 41 years of construction in 1928, the Central Post Office is one of BA's best examples of French-inspired classical architecture. Philatelists will want to check out the little museum inside. Diagonally opposite the post office's northeast corner is **Luna Park**, where Carlos Gardel's funeral was held in 1935 and where in 1944 Perón met Eva. It's now a music venue; *see p193*. North of Plaza Roma, the area officially called Catalinas Norte is a proliferation of glass skyscrapers and suited executives. Renowned Argentinian-born architect César Pelli designed the striking **Edificio República** on Avenida Madero.

Though once an elegant thoroughfare, Florida, the only remaining pedestrianised street in BA, is now unashamedly commercial. However, amid the cybercafé promo girls, money changers and other hawkers, you can find a trace of the refined past by browsing at **El Ateneo** bookshop at No.340, taking tea at **Confitería Richmond** (*see p125*) or joining the beef-baron-only **Sociedad Rural** at No.460 (a modestly priced meal at the restaurant is available to underlings; 4322 5837). **Galería Güemes** at No.165 was the city's first shopping arcade. Though more interesting for its decor than shops, it is now home to the impressive multi-faceted **Piazzolla Tango** museum and tango salon, opened in October 2003; *see p214*.

As Florida's old glamour wanes, more modern variations on retail sophistication spring up. **Galerías Pacífico** (*see p139*) is the city's most aesthetically inspired mall. In its south-east corner (with an entrance at the corner of Viamonte and San Martín) is the **Centro Cultural Borges** (5555 5359, www.ccborges.org.ar), built in memory of the writer, and a thriving venue for the arts. Behind it on the corner of San Martín and Viamonte is the 18th-century church of **Santa Catalina**. To the left of the altar, by a Portuguese tiled wall, is a tiny door leading to the convent used to quarter British troops during the 1806-07 invasion.

A few steps further on at Florida 887 the Buenos Aires branch of **Harrods** department store, built in 1914, was for many years the pride and joy of Anglophiles and Anglo-Argentinians. The London firm sold its shares in the 1960s and after a long closure the seven-storey megashop finally reopens in late 2004.

Lavalle, for pedestrians only between San Martín and Carlos Pellegrini, is even brasher than Florida, packed with blockbuster and B-movie cinemas, fast-food outlets, advertising boards and neon lights, plus a Bible-bashing, liberal-lashing evangelical church.

Close by, but extending beyond the Microcentro, is Corrientes. Though it's been an *avenida* since 1936, people still fondly call it a *calle*. Until the 1970s it was the mecca for tango artists, BA's Broadway and a coffee-drinking, literature-loving nocturnal scene, where bohos would meet to talk revolution and rock 'n' roll.

Despite being a shadow of its former self, not all is lost on Corrientes, which remains a hub of Buenos Aires' cultural life. West of Avenida 9 de Julio are several small venues presenting some of the best theatre found anywhere in the Spanish-speaking world. The main theatre complex is the city-run **Teatro San Martín** (*see p217*), plus there are art house cinemas, the **Centro Cultural General San Martín** (Sarmiento 1551, 4373 1252), and other cultural hotspots such as the **Centro Cultural de la Cooperación** at No.1543, (5077 8000, www.cculturalcoop.org.ar), which organises seminars on a topics ranging from politics to modern dance, and **Gandhi** bookshop (*see p142*), with its first-floor music venue. Student coffee houses compete for space with pizzerias and 24-hour second-hand book and CD stores.

The chocolate shop **Lion D'Or** at No.1469 and the fragrant spices and coffee shop **El Gato Negro** (*see p155*), whose logo was taken long ago from the Trans-Siberian Express menu, are reminders of Corrientes' former splendour, as is creaking **Confitería Ideal**, just off Corrientes at Suipacha 384.

Museo Mitre

San Martín 336, entre Corrientes y Sarmiento (4394 8240/7659/www.museomitre.gov.ar). Subte B, Florida/93, 99, 109, 132 bus. **Open** *Museum* 1-6.30pm Mon-Fri. *Library* 12.30-6pm Mon-Fri. **Admission** AR$1 suggested contribution; free under-12s, concessions. **No credit cards. Map** p277 E7.

Retiro

For centuries this area – a natural point on the river – was the northern edge of the town, and was once the refuge of a hermit known as 'la ermita de San Sebastián'. When a late-17th-century Spanish governor built a country house in the area for his retirement, and called it El Retiro – *retiro* means retreat – the district took its name. But the peace was shattered soon after when slave pens were erected here, followed by a military fort, then a bullring and finally, in the early 19th century, a training ground for independence fighters. Today the area's main attraction is it's open space – the well-shaded green swath that is the lovely **Plaza San Martín**, the city's second most important plaza.

This natural bluff stretches down to three railway terminals, beyond which lie a jumble of official buildings and the docks. It's named after José de San Martín, who trained his troops here. The Liberator is still revered. According to protocol, all visiting dignitaries must lay a wreath at the **Monumento al Libertador General San Martín**, the city's most important monument. It's a heroic marble and bronze equestrian affair created in 1862 by French sculptor Louis Joseph Daumas.

Sun-worshipping office workers lunch in the plaza, while an inordinate number of couples locked in marathon kissing sessions loll underneath overhanging branches or lie exposed to the sun on the windy vantage point of the green slopes. Borges, who lived nearby, used to stroll along its winding pathways decorated with some 300 trees of 37 different species, many of them exotic.

The captivating **Kavanagh**
building. *See p64.*

The first block of Florida leading off the plaza was called *'la manzana loca'* (the crazy block) in the 1960s for the avant-garde art experiments held at the Instituto Di Tella at Florida 940 (now a multi-brand shop with a small art space). The district is still arty – with numerous galleries and regular gatherings among the creative set at trad cafés such as **Florida Garden** (*see p126*) and funky bars like **Dadá** (*see p125*). Pubs catering to the happy-hour crowd – as well as escort bars – keep the area busy after dark.

Several impressive buildings surround Plaza San Martín. South-west is the gargantuan Palacio Paz, the largest private residence in the country and formerly the home of José C Paz, founder of the once important (but now derided) *La Prensa* newspaper. Since 1938, by which time the Paz empire had shrunk to insignificance, military officers have luxuriated in part of the palace renamed the **Círculo Militar** (to see inside, you have to join a 90-minute Spanish guided tour; 4311 1071, www.circulomilitar.org). One wing now houses the **Museo de Armas de la Nación** (*see p66*), a sizeable collection of arms and military uniforms, some dating from medieval times, plus a room of ancient Oriental weapons.

At the edge of the plaza, the **Palacio San Martín** (Arenales 761, 4819 8092) – until recently home of the Argentinian foreign ministry – was built between 1909 and 1912 for the mega-rich Anchorena family. Nowadays,

Flowering jacarandas create a purple haze over **Plaza San Martín**.

it's mostly used for official galas, although it opens for guided tours in Spanish most Thursdays and Fridays, which include a view of the garden containing a section of the Berlin Wall and an excellent collection of pre-Columbian Argentinian art, including rare stone masks from the north-west.

On the opposite side of the plaza, the **Basílica del Santísimo Sacramento**, at San Martín 1039, regularly plays host to society weddings. Also built with Anchorena money (before they lost it all in the Depression) and consecrated in 1916, the French exterior hides an inner sanctum combining Flemish and Italian handiwork with French and North African raw materials. Mercedes Castellanos de Anchorena, the woman who used some of her savings to build the church and lived at the Palacio San Martín, rests in expensive peace in an ornate marble vault in the crypt. The **Edificio Kavanagh** next door also points heavenward – at 120 metres (394 feet) it was South America's tallest building when completed in 1935. At the time of its construction, this apartment block was admired by rationalist architects all over the world and is still considered an art deco landmark. Next door the luxurious **Plaza Hotel** (now part of the Marriott chain – *see p31*) was built, in 1908, by Alfred Zucker, architect of Saint Patrick's Cathedral in New York. Even if you can't afford to stay here, a Martini in its wood-panelled cocktail lounge (*see p127*) is recommended.

At the very foot of the plaza is a black marble cenotaph to those who fell in the Falklands/Malvinas War, watched over by two soldiers in traditional uniforms who perform a stiff changing of the guard several times a day. Every 10 June veterans gather to commemorate the dead and to protest the denial of pensions and other support by the authorities.

Across the road from this sombre memorial, in an ironic twists of history, stands a Big Ben lookalike. The British-designed and built clock tower used to be known as the **Torre de los Ingleses** – it was presented as a gift to Argentina by local Anglo-Argentinians for the 1910 centennial celebrations. Since war with the UK in 1982, though, the authorities have insisted on using its official name, Torre Monumental, though most locals are too stubborn to hop on the patriotic bandwagon. Likewise, the land around it, formerly called the Plaza Británica, was renamed **Plaza Fuerza Aérea Argentina**. For a panoramic view of the plaza and the English-built railway stations, you can take a lift to the sixth floor – 35 metres (115 feet) up (though opening hours are irregular). There are occasional exhibits in the small photo gallery inside.

A superlative city

If size matters, then *porteños* have a fair amount to boast about. Starting with height, there's the Obelisco, star of so many postcards. Its architect, Alberto Prebisch, confessed that his 1936 creation was meaningless, but there was a space to fill where what would be Avenida 9 de Julio and Avenida Corrientes intersect. The remembrance of not one, but four historical events was the official motive for raising this monument: the first attempt and final foundation of Buenos Aires; the declaration of the city as federal capital in 1880; and to mark the site of the demolished church of San Nicolás, where the national flag was flown for the first time. Each event is inscribed on one of the four sides of the white needle.

The 68-metre (223-foot) Obelisco was built in concrete. A box at its peak is said to have been put there by the head of the construction firm that built it; it contains a photo of him and his wife and a letter addressed to anyone who would dare demolish the fruit of his labour.

As soon as the obelisk was finished, the critics spoke out. They said it was an undignified, phallic, cement spike; radical feminist groups suggested lopping it in half. Just three years after its erection the city's parliament voted for its demolition, yet the decision was ignored and the Obelisco became, over time, the city's emblem and a symbol of its self-conscious monumentalism.

When bragging about dimension, *porteños* always mention the avenue that flows around the Obelisco, which they claim is the widest

in the world. Avenida 9 de Julio was widened to its current 140 metres (460 feet) in the late 1930s. It doesn't feel much like a proper avenue, however. A 20-lane gash, it's basically a motorway for traffic moving from one end of the city to the other. Moreover, the smaller streets that run parallel on its two sides are actually called by other names (Lima, Cerrito, Bernardo de Irigoyen and Carlos Pellegrini), though the whole strip is always referred to as 9 de Julio.

A focal point for football celebrations, political rallies and open-air concerts, the avenue also offers an adrenaline-pumping experience on a daily basis – the death-defying challenge of crossing it; you'll need to do it carefully, in two stages.

But never mind the width – look at the length. Locals are wont to tell visitors that Rivadavia is the 'longest street in the world'. This doubtful claim is based on the fact that it runs for 18 kilometres (11 miles) with the same name. Along the way it changes into an avenue and accompanies a railway line before petering out in an ugly suburb.

By Roman standards, it's a mere cul-de-sac, but it is the only road to get so far out of the capital without changing name. Every 5 October, pilgrims use Rivadavia to traipse to the religious centre of Luján, 68 kilometres (42 miles) outside the city. More importantly, Rivadavia is also the point where all of Buenos Aires' streets that run north–south (except Avenida 9 de Julio) change their names, as well as being the symbolic border between the richer *norte* and poorer *sur*.

Shattering the peace is the endless din of traffic on Avenida del Libertador leading to the railway stations. Though everyone says they are going 'to Retiro' to get a train or bus, there are, in fact, three separate train terminals plus a bus station along Avenida JM Ramos Mejia. The largest, English-built terminal, the Mitre, dates from 1915, and stands out as one of South America's best examples of Crystal Palace-inspired architecture. A plaque on an arch of its

iron structure reads 'Francis Morton & Co Ltd – Liverpool'. Although recently renovated it still retains a hue of the golden age of railways in objects such as a tobacco-stained map of Argentina's once 45,000-kilometre (27,000-mile) network, by far the largest in South America.

Surrounding the terminals, food stands and market stalls add to the general noise and chaos, making for a colourful though stressful walk, especially in rush hours. The **Paseo del**

...ro handicrafts fair, created to give some
... to the uninviting wasteland opposite the
...us station, runs every weekend.

Just north of the bus terminal is Villa 31, the
capital's best-known shanty town. The reason
for the slum's notoriety is the community's
refusal to move from this potentially prime
real estate until the city offers them something
better. The adjacent badlands consist of run-
down military and other buildings. Avoid
this area, especially after dusk.

A couple of blocks up Libertador in an old
railway building is the **Museo Nacional
Ferroviario** (*listings below*). The two floors
are an intriguing hotchpotch from a railway era
that puts recent car-obsessed governments to
shame. Beside the museum is the workshop of
Carlos Regazzoni, an internationally respected
sculptor whose creations are made from the
scrap he finds in the railway yards. A small
theatre, the **Teatro del Gato Viejo**, also
operates from this spot. Telephone 4315 3663
for information on the workshop and theatre.

Just a hop across the road and up the incline
at Suipacha 1422 is one of BA's cultural gems,
the **Museo de Arte Hispanoamericano
Isaac Fernández Blanco** (*listings below*)
in a beautiful Peruvian-style mansion, with
gorgeous Andalucian gardens. The white
baroque building – also known as the Palacio
Noel, for its architect – houses Spanish
American paintings, religious objects and
silverware. The ghost of a lady in white is said
to inhabit the house. Cultural events and
high-quality art exhibitions are staged here.

The **Plaza Embajada de Israel** lies on
the corner of Suipacha and Arroyo streets.
A bomb destroyed a previous Israeli
embassy on this site in 1992. Each of the
29 trees represents a victim of the blast.
The surrounding area has recovered
from this dramatic episode and the
secluded *calle* Arroyo is now the
heart of a gallery circuit, attracting
affluent tourists from five-star
Sofitel (*see p33*), opened in late
2002 in the architecturally
impressive Torre Bencich.

At Suipacha 1333,
Argentina's main English-
language teaching organisation
runs the **British Arts Centre**
(BAC; *listings below*). It puts
on loads of free events such as
plays and films in English as
well as jazz, Celtic and classical
concerts, and photo and art
exhibits and workshops.

Torre de los Ingleses (*p64*).

Don't miss Sights

Dramatic deathvilles
History is written on the tombs of **Recoleta**
(*p77*) and **Chacarita** cemeteries (*p88*).

Family fun
Temaikén free range zoo (*p167*) and **Abasto**
mall (*p139*), with its kids' museum and
fairground, keep the little monsters happy.

Football fanaticism
Make a pilgrimage to **La Bonbonera** (*p73*)
and pay homage at the Boca Jrs museum.

Gorgeous greenery
Parque Tres de Febrero (*p84* has acres
of it and floral delights, while picturesque
Plaza San Martín (*p62*) and palm-lined
Parque Lezama (*p71*) offer airy urban relief.

Monumental magnificence
The heroic eligy of **Canto al Trabajo** (*p69*) or
the glorious gift from **Los Españoles** (*p84*).

British Arts Centre
*Suipacha 1333, entre Juncal y Arroyo, Retiro (4393
0275/www.britishartscentre.org.ar). Bus 59, 61, 93,
130, 152.* **Open** *Feb* 12.30pm-6.30pm Mon-Fri. *Mar-
Dec* 3-9pm Mon Fri. **Closed** Jan. **Admission** free.
Map p277 F8.

Museo de Armas de la Nación
*Avenida Santa Fe 702, y Maipú (4311 1071/
1072 ext 179). Subte C, San Martín/10, 17,
70, 152 bus.* **Open** *Mar-Dec* 11am-7pm
Tue-Fri; 2-6pm Sat, Sun. **Closed** Jan,
Feb. **Admission** AR$2; free under-5s,
concessions. **No credit cards.**
Map p277 F7.

Museo de Arte Hispanoamericano Isaac Fernández Blanco
*Suipacha 1422, entre Arroyo y
Libertador (4327 0272/0228).
Bus 59, 61, 93, 130, 152.*
Open 2-7pm Tue-Sun. **Guided
tours** (Spanish) 3pm Tue; 3pm,
5pm Sat, Sun. **Admission** AR$3.
Free Thur. **No credit cards.**
Map p277 F8.

Museo Nacional Ferroviario
*Avenida del Libertador 405,
y Suipacha (4318 3343/3538).
Subte C, Retiro/59, 61, 93,
130, 152 bus.* **Open** *Feb-Dec*
10am-4pm Mon-Fri. **Closed** Jan.
Admission free. **Map** p277 F8.

South of the Centre

The city's scenic founding quarter is a timeless Eden, where tourists wander the cobbled streets and linger in atmospheric bars in search of the ghosts of tango.

Peel away Buenos Aires' thin veneer of order and progress and what's left is *el Sur* – the South – the maternal womb of the city. Just a stone's throw from the centre, the low-lying barrios south of Plaza de Mayo – Monserrat, San Telmo, La Boca and Barracas – are stuck in the past, and exhibit little of the Centro's flare for commerce. A nostalgic daydreamer if there ever was one, the young Borges wrote that 'the Sur is the original substance from which Buenos Aires is made.'

Although seriously spruced up for tourists in recent years, its crumbling façades, narrow passageways and sepia-toned cafés still breathe history, and for all the welcome progress, the south has shed little of its lyrical melancholy. At least for a while longer, el Sur remains a magnet for owl-eyed bohemians and anyone searching for the city's primordial soul.

Monserrat

It may garner little of the limelight enjoyed by more touristy San Telmo, but when it comes to history Monserrat is in a class of its own. At the time of independence, when Buenos Aires was still a Gran Aldea ('big village'), the sector known as Catedral al Sur was an affluent area of patrician families and merchants. A rivulet running down Chile street was the city limit and artisans from the suburb of San Telmo had to cross a bridge to sell their goods. Over time, a building spree would make the dividing line all but illusory. Indeed, today the two barrios share a common identity as an enclave of tranquillity just a few steps from the downtown bedlam.

What distinguishes them from one another is Monserrat's pivotal role in the country's independence struggle, still apparent in the district's colonial-era churches. Bounded by Alsina, Bolívar, Moreno and Perú streets is a complex of historical buildings filling the whole city block and known as the **Manzana de las Luces** (Block of Enlightenment; *see p68*). The illumination moniker was coined in the early 19th century in reference to the wisdom garnered by the leading lights who were educated here. A church and school have their own entrances, the former open for Mass, the latter only for those going to classes. The main attractions are the Jesuit and early political institutions, entered

on Perú. The courtyard is sometimes used in the evenings for cultural events and by day a small café serves drinks and sandwiches.

The block's **Iglesia de San Ignacio**, on the corner of Alsina and Bolívar, dates from 1734 and is the oldest church in the city. Despite its importance, it almost collapsed in 2003 when the gaping fissures caused by neglect started to rupture. After frocked priests took to the streets in protest, the city closed the block and erected scaffolding to prop up the edifice.

Hidden behind the church is the brick-walled patio of the **Procuraduría de las Misiones**, accessed on Avenida Julio A Roca (also known as Diagonal Sur), which cuts into the block, via a small handicrafts market. This was the headquarters of the top Jesuits who ran the conversion programme in the New World in the 18th century. The Jesuits, who worked closely and sympathetically with indigenous groups, were evicted from their HQ in 1767 when the colonial authorities began to fear their power.

Next door, at Perú 272, is the **Sala de Representantes** (Representatives' Chamber), from which BA province was governed until

Marketing history at **Manzana de las Luces**.

1880, when the federal district was created and provincial capital moved to La Plata. You can take a guided tour of the semicircular chamber, the patios and a series of 18th-century tunnels – whose purpose remains a mystery – which once linked the building to the coast behind what is now Plaza de Mayo, several hundred metres away. Another law-makers' edifice, the belle époque **Legislatura de la Ciudad**, is at Perú 130 (www.legislatura.gov.ar).

The last building on this block, on the corner of Bolívar and Moreno, was once the location of the Jesuits' school. Today, the **Colegio Nacional de Buenos Aires** is considered the best state school in the country – among its alumni are two Nobel Prize winners and countless authors and heads of state.

On the opposite corner of Alsina and Bolívar from the church is the **Librería de Avila** (4331 8989), the city's oldest bookshop, dating from 1785. There's another bookish haunt a few blocks south; the old Biblioteca Nacional building on Mexico 564, now a research centre for musicologists, is where Jorge Luis Borges served as library director for 17 years.

On the corner of Alsina and Defensa is the charming 1894 chemist La Estrella, whose mahogany interior has barely been touched. At lunchtime office workers file in to test its two-metre (seven-foot) Toledo, Ohio-made iron weighing scale, reputed to be the most accurate in the city. Directly above is the **Museo de la Ciudad** (*listings below*), created as a labour of love in 1968 by José María Peña, a leading authority on Buenos Aires' architecture. In addition to displays of antiques, photos and junk collected by Peña, there's a re-creation of the living quarters of a well-heeled, 19th-century family. Around the corner on Alsina a row of crumbling houses saved from the wrecking ball gives testament to Monserrat's successive facelifts. In an attempt to link Monserrat with more vibrant San Telmo, free walking tours of this historic area, in Spanish, set out from the museum on Sundays at 3pm.

Opposite the chemist's is the **Iglesia de San Francisco**, begun in 1730 by Jesuit architect Andrés Blanqui, who also worked on the Pilar church in Recoleta and the Cabildo. Inside, there is a 20th-century tapestry of St Francis by Argentinian artist Horacio Butler, evidently a fan of psychedelic flowers and cartoon animals.

Adjacent to this church is the smaller **Parroquia San Roque** (Roque parish church), built in the 1750s. Opposite, the **Plazoleta San Francisco** contains four statues, moved here from the Plaza de Mayo in 1972. They depict geography, sailing, astronomy and industry – all the sciences that have tested belief in the God worshipped across the road.

In the middle of all these Roman Catholic ramparts and monuments to post-colonial ambition, the **Museo Etnográfico** (*listings below*) is a much-needed reminder that before the arrival of the Europeans, Argentina had such a thing as an indigenous population. The small but eye-opening collection contains headdresses, masks, cutting and cooking implements and panels describing the different tribes region by region. However, a wood-carved, gold-speckled Buddhist altar from Japan is the museum's most valuable object. The sad stories of the Fuegian Yamana tribe are part of the display, including that of Jemmy Button, a young man shipped to England in 1830 as a living example of the 'noble savage'.

The **Basílica de Santo Domingo** and the adjoining **Basílica Nuestra Señora del Rosario**, at Defensa and Belgrano, are two other important 18th-century centres of worship. One of the towers of the former was punctured by bullets during the English Invasions of 1806-07. The flags seized from the vanquished invaders are on display in the far corner left of the altar and even the street name Defensa pays homage to this first popular local resistance against foreign forces. In the forecourt is Italian sculptor Errore Ximenes' monument to Manuel Belgrano, the Argentinian independence hero and the man behind the sky-blue-and-white national flag.

Another sort of church, this one to industry, is the old Hirsch hardware store at Perú 535 built in 1908 by Gustave Eiffel. Crowned with a bronze statue, the three-floor iron arcade is now a party venue called **Museum**.

Comisión Nacional Manzana de las Luces

Perú 272, entre Moreno y Alsina (4342 3964). Subte A, Plaza de Mayo or D, Catedral or E, Bolívar/24, 29, 86, 126 bus. **Open** 10am-midnight Mon-Sat. **Guided tours** (Spanish) 3pm Mon-Fri; 3pm, 4.30pm, 6pm Sat, Sun. **Admission** *Manzana* free. *Guided tours* AR$3; free under-6s. **No credit cards. Map** p277 D6.

Museo de la Ciudad

Defensa 219, entre Alsina y Moreno (4331 9855/ 4343 2123). Subte A, Plaza de Mayo or D, Catedral or E, Bolívar/24, 29, 64, 86, 130 bus. **Open** *Museum* 11am-7pm Mon-Fri; 3-7pm Sun. *Library* 1-6pm Mon-Fri. **Admission** AR$3; free under-12s. Free Wed. **No credit cards. Map** p277 D7.

Museo Etnográfico Juan Bautista Ambrosetti

Moreno 350, entre Balcarce y Defensa (4331 7788/ 4345 8196). Subte A, Plaza de Mayo or D, Catedral or E, Bolívar/24, 29, 64, 152 bus. **Open** Feb-Dec 2.30-6.30pm Wed-Sun. **Closed** Jan. **Admission** AR$1. **Guided tours** (Spanish) during opening hours Sat, Sun. **No credit cards. Map** p277 D7.

San Telmo

It's hard to imagine Buenos Aires without San Telmo. But as recently as the 1950s, the city's most emblematic barrio was in jeopardy of being razed by short-sighted city planners with no appreciation for its faded, historic architecture. Indeed, until strict zoning laws were passed in the 1970s, much of San Telmo's patrimony was demolished anyway. But plenty more survived, and thanks to a regeneration spurred by the arrival of antique dealers and restaurateurs – and more recently hostel owners – the area is faring better than ever.

Heading to San Telmo from the Plaza de Mayo, Defensa and Balcarce are the most pleasant streets to walk along. The former is full of antique shops and the latter a quiet street with tango venues (even though San Telmo is not historically linked to the dance). While walking you will pass several crumbling mansions that give San Telmo its unmistakable appearance. Most were occupied by grand families until a mass exodus from cholera and yellow fever took place over a century ago.

Subsequently the old houses were turned into tenements – called *conventillos* – with poor immigrant families occupying what were formerly single rooms round the main patio. As these humble abodes are still very much lived in, no matter how open the doors look, the

general public are not welcome. To see the inside of an 1880 house, visit the lovely **Pasaje de la Defensa** (at Defensa 1179), a refurbished two-storey building originally owned by the Ezeiza family, and now hectic with souvenir and bric-a-brac shops.

The adjacent streets are also of interest, with a myriad of bars and restaurants punctuating the houses. The quaint Pasaje San Lorenzo and Pasaje Giuffra – their cobbles harking back to a more attractive city from the 1930s and '40s – were formerly streams running down to the river where Avenida Paseo Colón now pullulates. At San Lorenzo 380 is the ultra-thin colonial house **Casa Mínima**, which is part of the same conservation initiative that has rescued **El Zanjón**, a tastefully restored colonial mansion round the corner where San Lorenzo butts against Defensa (*see p72* **Digging up the past**).

Down on Avenida Paseo Colón is Rogelio Trutia's intriguing bronze monument **Canto al Trabajo** (Song to Work) on the plaza of the same name (at Avenida Independencia). Another five blocks south there's a different, less exalting monument. Beneath the motorway flyover, a grim sculpture of climbing bodies stands guard over an unearthed pit where Argentina's long-buried, 'Dirty War' past is literally being resurrected. In 2002, a team of archaeologists discovered intact the basement torture centre of the former Club Atlético, where some 1,800 prisoners 'disappeared' before the military government demolished the building to build the highway in 1978.

The rest of Avenida Paseo Colón is dominated by a series of serious-looking public buildings, three of them – the army's **Edificio del Libertador**, the **Aduana** (headquarters of the customs service) and the **Secretaría de Agricultura** (Ministry of Agriculture) – built along French Academic lines. The Libertador is fronted by tanks, cannons and a Soviet-looking statue of an Unknown Soldier. The soldier has a hole in his chest, a symbol of those who died in the Falklands/Malvinas, but, while not buried on the islands, left their hearts there.

The fourth public building is the University of Buenos Aires' **Facultad de Ingeniería** (Faculty of Engineering), a harsh classical building that wouldn't have gone amiss in Hitler's Berlin. It originally housed the the Fundación Eva Perón, the charity created by Evita. Far more attractive is the tall, slim red-brick **Iglesia Dinamarquesa** at Carlos Calvo 257. A Lutheran church built in 1931, its modern gothic style is jovially at odds with everything else in San Telmo.

On Sundays, **Plaza Dorrego**, one of BA's few Spanish-style plazas where you can drink

Nuestra Señora del Belén. *See p71.*

beer and coffee in the open air, is taken over by traders, tango and tourists. Although it's a genuine, fully functional antiques market (*see p141*), it also provides one of BA's most popular days out for visitors and locals alike, especially when the sun is shining. To avoid the, at times, overwhelming crowds, arrive before noon.

Half a block from the square's busy **Bar Plaza Dorrego** (*see p127*) at Humberto I° 378 is the **Museo Penitenciario Nacional** (open Sundays only; 4362 0099) tracing penal life from the city's foundation to the present. On the same block, at Humberto I° 340, stands the **Iglesia Nuestra Señora de Belén**, an architecturally eclectic church crowned by blue and white Andalucian-style tiled towers. Nine altars, and assorted virgins and saints adorn the busy interior, among them San Pedro Telmo, the patron saint of the barrio and guardian of sailors. The church's role as a place of asylum for those injured in the so-called English Invasions (*see p7*) is recorded in a thank-you message from the 71st Regiment of the Scottish Rifles.

Another authentic bastion of barrio life – and one you can visit – is the traditional produce market on the corner of Carlos Calvo and Defensa and open Monday to Saturday. The Crystal Palace-like arcade was built in 1897 and is still going strong, though antiques stalls are creeping in beside the fruit 'n' veg.

For fashion victims only, there's an enjoyable small museum – **Museo del Traje** (Museum of Suits – Chile 832, 4343 8427, www.funmuseo deltraje.com.ar) – tracing Argentinian fads and fashions from 1850 to the present. Art lovers should head for the under-appreciated **Museo de Arte Moderno** (*listings below*). It's no Tate Modern or MOMA, but is an important proving ground for contemporary Argentinian artists working in a variety of media. The museum, housed in a recycled tobacco warehouse, has an extensive collection, but no permanent exhibit. Instead, it hosts excellent temporary shows, as well as music and video events.

Next door, with an entrance on Defensa, the dank and smallish **Museo del Cine** (*listings below*) contains relics and movie posters from almost a century's worth of Argentinian film-making, though it is otherwise a poor tribute to the country's luminous auteurs (*see chapter* **Film**). The projection room shows Argentinian movies for free on Wednesdays; Tuesday's documentary screenings cost AR$1.

At the southern end of San Telmo, **Parque Lezama** is a dramatic patch of greenery on the bluff of the old city. A monument at the Brasil and Defensa corner commemorates Pedro de

Mendoza's hypothetical landfall at this spot in 1536 and on the south side is an impressive Monument to Brotherhood – **Monumento a la Confraternidad** – expressed as a neo-industrial boat. It was presented to the city on its fourth centenary by the Uruguayan capital Montevideo.

A beautiful terracotta-coloured colonial mansion houses the **Museo Histórico Nacional** (*listings below*), one of Buenos Aires' best museums and a very useful introduction to the city's history (the entrance is on Defensa, rather than via the park). The collection includes exhibits from pre-Columbian, Conquest and, especially, Argentinian periods, with maps, household artefacts and artworks. There is also extensive material on Rosas and San Martín.

Outside the museum, the park is a dramatic cliff, awash with majestic palms and yellow-flowered *tipa* trees. Larger and greener than most plazas, it's a popular spot with local families. Musicians and second-rate market stalls populate the park at weekends and a wonderfully out-of-place **Iglesia Ortodoxa Rusa**, topped with blue onions in the Muscovite style, adds further colour to the Lezama scene.

Until recently San Telmo was busiest during the day, but new bars and restaurants are making it a dinner and dancing destination. Some touristy eateries around Plaza Dorrego are richer in history than in food and service, and thus better for a drink than meal. Tango supper shows at the venues on Balcarce are another option. The best-known is **El Viejo Almacén** (*see p214*), while the **Viejo Hotel** (Balcarce 1053), no longer a hotel, is a pleasant spot for a coffee on the patio amid artists' studios and artisans' workshops. **Espacio Ecléctico** (Humberto I° 730, 4307 1966, closed Jan, Feb), an artist-run co-operative comprising a theatre and art exhibition space, also has a cute café.

Museo de Arte Moderno

Avenida San Juan 350, entre Defensa y Balcarce (4361 1121/www.aamamba.com.ar). Bus 29, 64, 86, 130, 152. **Open** Mar-Jan 10am-8pm Tue-Fri; 11am-8pm Sat, Sun. **Closed** Feb. **Guided tours** (Spanish) 5pm Tue, Wed, Fri, Sun. **Admission** AR$3. **No credit cards. Map** p276 C6.

Museo del Cine

Defensa 1220, entre San Juan y Cochabamba (4361 2462/www.museos.buenosaires.gov.ar). Bus 29, 64, 86, 130, 152. **Open** 10am-7pm Tue-Fri; 11.30am-6.30pm Sat, Sun. **Admission** free. **Map** p276 C6.

Museo Histórico Nacional

Defensa 1600, y Caseros (4307 1182/4457). Bus 10, 24, 29, 39, 64, 130, 152. **Open** Feb-Dec 11am-5pm Tue-Fri; 3-6pm Sat; 2-6pm Sun. **Closed** Jan. **Guided tours** (Spanish) 3pm Sat, Sun. **Admission** AR$2. **No credit cards. Map** p276 B5/C5.

Scenes of San Telmo street life, including the Sunday antiques fair in **Plaza Dorrego.**

Digging up the past

Although *porteños* pride themselves on size, be it in their steaks or wide boulevards, not everything in the city is so grandiose. Especially in San Telmo, the city's flare for cosmopolitan greatness and neo-classical monumentality cede to the modest beauty of narrow cobbled streets and tiny, brick and adobe (mud and straw) residences.

The very smallest example is the **Casa Mínima** – the narrowest house in the city. It's an extreme version of the *casa chorizo* (sausage house) style common throughout the city – dwellings with narrow street frontage that stretch back a whole block inside. Legend holds that this one, just two metres (six feet) wide – but 50 metres (165 feet) long – was built by freed slaves in 1800 on a sliver of land bestowed by their master next door. In death master and slave have been joined – an impossibility in life – by the partial removal of the wall that separated the dependency from the main house.

In 2003 Casa Mínima threw open its teeny door. History and architecture buffs can now take an unforgettable voyage to the past, on a guided tour of both this house and

El Zanjón. Part archaeological museum, part event space, El Zanjón is a beautifully restored residence encapsulating three centuries of urban living. Although the façade dates from 1830, traces from an earlier patrician home – an open-air cistern, a lookout tower and a 1740 wall comprised of seashell mortaring – magically transport you to the era of Spanish settlement.

The name derives from El Zanjón de Granados, a rivulet bisecting San Telmo, which in the days before proper sewage removal was a natural dump. It was bricked over following the yellow fever epidemic, burying with it rubbish containing clues to life in the young city. In 1985, the crumbling wreck was rescued by amateur historian Jorge Eckstein, who started dredging the 166 metres (545 feet) of tunnels beneath his property. Seventeen years and 139 truckloads of debris later, he unearthed a treasure chest of everyday objects – French tiles, African pipes, English china.

Within the marginal world of architectural conservationists, Eckstein's garbage-heap archaeology has drawn as much flack as it

La Boca

With its seedy *cantinas* and crowded tenements, the waterfront quarter of La Boca still feels like the melting pot where tango flourished a century ago. The working-class barrio derives its name from its location at the mouth of the Riachuelo, until the late 19th century the obligatory entry point to the city. But when the docks moved north to Puerto Madero, decline set in. Today, all that's left of the once bustling port are a few abandoned hulks and rusting warehouses.

Although La Boca can and certainly should be enjoyed, keep your loitering to the area closest to Caminito and the adjacent promenade running along the edge of Riachuelo – Avenida Pedro de Mendoza. If you do go further afield, leave the Nikon at the hotel, as not all residents relish their status as tourist attractions. For all its charm, La Boca is one of the city's crime hot spots.

The barrio stretches from the river right up to the roundabout where Avenida Paseo Colón becomes Avenida Martín García, and where a mast and a 3-D frieze announce that you are entering the 'República de la Boca'. The lively artwork, made from the scrap left behind when one of the tin tenements was torn down, is a collage of all the icons and sights of Boca. Buses

enter the neighbourhood here, heading down Avenida Almirante Brown, named after the Irishman who created the Argentinian navy. A 1983 reconstruction of his house, the **Casa Amarilla**, stands out in bright yellow, against the Soviet-style high-rises. Still used by the navy, its library is only of interest to historians.

There is a curious, castle-like tower, known locally as the **Torre Fantasma** (Ghost Tower), at the entrance to the main residential area, at the intersection of Almirante Brown, Wenceslao Villafañe and B Peréz Galdos. This turreted, quaintly gothic building is like nothing else in the area.

Set back from the river, on Brandsen, is the reason why people who have never been to Buenos Aires have heard of La Boca. The port a thing of the past, the communal heart now beats at the Estadio Alberto J Armando, aka **La Bombonera** (Chocolate Box – *see p198*), where top-flight football team Club Atlético Boca Juniors have held court for nearly a century. The blue and yellow of the team strip are ubiquitous on walls and balconies throughout the neighbourhood. Boca's most famous ex-player and fan, Diego Armando Maradona, is still idolised by the club's ardent supporters (*see p74* **Fallen hero worship**).

has praise. Although grounded in history, El Zanjón and Casa Mínima are more myth then faithful re-creation of the past. Coexisting with the ghosts of yesteryear is a modern scheme of sparse, post-industrial details. It's tastefully done, but it can be easy to confuse what's original from the merely picturesque.

El Zanjón

Defensa 755, entre Chile y Independencia (4361 3002). Bus 24, 29, 130, 152. **Tours** (English) Mon-Fri on the hr 11am-6pm. **Admission** AR$20; AR$13 Mon; AR$8 under-12s. **No credit cards. Map** p277 D6. Tours visit Casa Mínima as well. Weekend tours due to start late 2004.

You can't miss the stadium from Avenida Almirante Brown, as the sheer walls rise high above the wasteland where community events take place. Murals on the stadium walls by Argentinian painter Pérez Celis and others tell the story of the port. Football motifs record how the workers embraced the beautiful game as an escape from hardship. It's best to avoid the area surrounding the stadium on game days.

The team's exploits have spurned an empire controlled by its politically ambitious president Mauricio Macri, who finished a close second in Buenos Aires' 2003 mayoral race. In addition to a Boca theme bar and cable TV channel, Macri is responsible for what's bound to become a mecca for football-worshipping tourists: the **Museo de la Pasión Boquense** (Museum of Boca Passion – *see p75*), located at the stadium's entrance. Much of the museum and gift shop consists of ephemera appealing to the already devout Boca fan, such as an exhibit of a century's worth of shirts or Boca Juniors deodorant. But tourists will appreciate the exhibit that puts the club's successes in their larger, national context. Football-as-opiate conspiracy theorists will note that Boca's on-field performance seems to improve the more Argentina unravels. The entrance fee to the

museum includes a tour of the stadium, the only way to see inside if not attending a game.

From the Museo's entrance a disused railway track runs down Garibaldi (where Nazi Adolf Eichmann once lived), which comes out two blocks later at the back end of **Caminito**, a short, banana-shaped pedestrianised theme street recognised as Argentina's only open-air museum. The better way to arrive is via the riverside promenade. Its name – which means 'little walkway' – comes from a 1926 tango by legendary composers Gabino Coria Peñaloza and Juan de Dios Filiberto, the melancholic lyrics of which are inscribed on a wall plaque.

One of several barrios claiming to be the birthplace of tango, La Boca is the kind of place where you can imagine sailors, hustlers, drinkers and wide-boys from all over Europe rubbing shoulders and flashing blades in the early 1900s. The corrugated zinc shacks on Caminito owe their vivid colours to the imaginative but impoverished locals, who begged incoming ships for excess tins of paint so that they could doll up their houses. These days, the street is overcrowded with stalls hawking artwork of typical tango scenes. Many *porteños* view the area as a picturesque slum, but Argentinian and foreign tourists alike appreciate the lack of traffic and absence of any bourgeois posing. The dancers who strut their stuff are certainly aiming at the tourist trade, but the overall chaos of Caminito is pleasant rather than overbearingly commercial.

At Magallanes 861, a former *conventillo* slum dwelling has been transformed into crafts studios (many unoccupied) and souvenir shops, called **Centro Cultural de los Artistas**. There's not much to see, but it's interesting to peek into an old slum dwelling. Papier-mâché models of famous Boca figures lean from the balconies. At Del Valle Iberlucea 1261 is the tiny **Museo Histórico de Cera de La Boca** (4301 1497, www.museodecera.com.ar), an old-fashioned museum housing a slightly spooky waxwork collection of indigenous people, mummies, national figures and native fauna.

La Vuelta de Rocha, the road that follows the bend in the river at the opening to Caminito, is marked by a mast and rigging. A painting at the Museo Nacional de Bellas Artes in Recoleta bears the same name, and its stylised portrayal of this corner is an acknowledgement of the near-mythical status the area has for *porteños*.

However, it's not all nostalgia in La Boca. **Fundación Proa** (*see p181*), in a recycled waterfront mansion just south of Caminito, is one of the city's premier art spaces and a great reason to visit the area. At B Perez Galdos 93, **Grupo de Teatro Catalinas Sur** (www.catalinasur.com.ar) is a theatre staging *El Fulgor*

Sightseeing

The city's mosy colourful street: **Caminito**, La Boca. *See p73.*

Argentino, a slapstick musical comedy where 100 Boca residents-cum-performers, in an act of ritual catharsis, recount Argentina's turbulent history from 1930 to 2030; performances at 10pm every Friday and Saturday.

You can climb aboard a moored ferryboat that has been turned into a floating souvenir mall, café and so-so art gallery, but the real art is in the buildings donated to La Boca by painter Benito Quinquela Martín (1890-1977), close friend of tango composer Juan de Dios Filiberto. It was Quinquela Martín who suggested that the main street be named Caminito when the musician fell ill. The **Museo de Bellas Artes de La Boca** (*see p75*) contains works by

Quinquela Martín and other Argentinian artists, as well as a collection of bowsprits, relics of the neighbourhood's nautical past. This is also the site of the **Teatro de la Ribera**, part of Buenos Aires' main state-run theatre complex (*see p217*).

In the 1930s, local critics compared Quinquela Martín's canvases, with their characteristic spatula marks, to those of Van Gogh's. The vibrant collection is grouped into three themes: fire (a constant risk for La Boca's wood-framed buildings), port workers and ships' graveyards. Quinquela Martín also had a wacky sense of humour, creating a parodic masonic organisation called the Orden del Tornillo (Order of the Screw). He welcomed artists and assorted nobles

Fallen hero worship

Mohammed Ali, Michael Jordan, Tiger Woods – all are sports legends for the ages. But only one sports personality can claim to have his own church with around 20,000 'worshippers' spread as far as Vietnam and Iceland.

Diego Maradona may not be Buenos Aires' noblest emissary to the world but he's definitely its most prolific. So much a part of Buenos Aires' psyche is his rags-to-riches story, turbulent lifestyle and fall from grace, that no visit to BA can be considered complete without a basic understanding of the city's most famous son.

Diego was born to be a star, on a football Sunday at the Eva Perón Hospital in the poor southern suburb of Lanús. According to legend, on entering the hospital his mother discovered a star-shaped brooch on the floor,

which she clutched while giving birth. His first magical touch with a football came on a dusty pitch in the Villa Fiorito shanty town where he grew up. Age the tender age of 10 he was plucked to play for Cebollitas (Little Onions), the youth team of Argentinos Juniors. Five years later he debuted for Argentinos in the equivalent of the British Premier League; he was the youngest player ever to do so.

But the club closest to Diego's heart is Boca Juniors, where he played in the early '80s and again from 1995-97.

If New York's Yankees stadium is the house that Ruth built, then Boca's La Bombonera will forever be linked to Diego. Even when not there in person, showing his Che tattoo and waving his shirt in the air from his private box, his presence is still invoked by fans shouting 'Diego, Diego, Diego.'

by presenting them with a ribbon decorated with a screw as a reminder that they were only in this elite club by virtue of having a screw loose.

There is a real sense of being on the edge of a city in La Boca. Three bridges at the northern end of Avenida Pedro de Mendoza connect the capital with the province and symbolise the changes that have taken place as La Boca has dwindled as a maritime and commercial centre. The oldest is the **Puente Trasbordador** (transporter bridge), a massive iron contraption that ferried trains, animals and people across to crime-ridden Isla Maciel in the industrial suburb of Avellaneda from 1914 to 1940. These days, a small rowing boat plies a service to and from the dangerous wasteland.

The Riachuelo, which for over a century was a repository of cattle carcasses, oil, oxidised metals and assorted toxins, is nearer black than brown and still stinks, but some progress has been made in cleaning it up. During the Menem years, María Julia Alsogaray – an unpopular, fur coat-wearing environment minister, now in jail awaiting trial for malfeasance – promised to swim in the Riachuelo when it was clean. NASA would have to design a nuke-proof bikini if anyone was planning to do it soon. The only real change has been to remove most of the beached oxidised barges and wrecked ships that gave La Boca some character. A complete emptying of the river would strip the area of some of its most important ghosts.

Museo de Bellas Artes de La Boca Benito Quinquela Martín

Avenida Pedro de Mendoza 1835, entre Palos y Del Valle Iberlucea (4301 1080). Bus 29, 53, 64, 152. **Open** *Feb-Dec* 10am-5.30pm Tue-Fri; 11am-5.30pm Sat, Sun. **Closed** Jan. **Admission** suggested contribution AR$1. **No credit cards. Map** p276 A5.

Museo de la Pasión Boquense

Brandsen 805, y la Vía (4362 1100/www.museo boquense.com). Bus 10, 24, 29, 53, 64. **Open** 10am-6pm daily. **Guided tours** (of stadium) hourly 11am-5pm. **Admission** *Museum or tour only* AR$7.90; AR$4 under-12s. *Museum & tour* AR$12.90; AR$8 under-12s . **Credit** AmEx, DC, MC, V. **Map** p276 A5.

Constitución & Barracas

Constitución and Barracas are run-down barrios that most *porteños* prefer to avoid. But without the former's railway station and the latter's warehouses, Buenos Aires would never have reached its late-19th-century economic splendour. Although close to the centre, these areas are rarely explored due to their desolate streets and dodgy after-dark reputation. A mini-renaissance, however, is under way in Barracas, and with so many pyramids to the golden age of industry for the taking, it's possible that the area could yet regain some of its former glory.

At Plaza Constitución, the **Estación Constitución** was the terminal for all railway lines coming in from the coast, the southern

Sightseeing

At the peak of his career, Maradona was a national idol. His supreme moment of triumph came after winning (with one of the world's greatest goals and the divine intervention of the 'Hand of God') the 1986 Mexico World Cup, for which he was fêted on the balcony of the Casa Rosada. Three years later he was married before 11,000 guests at Luna Park. The 1937 Dodge convertible used during the ceremony can still be seen at the Museo del Automóvil out on the city's western limits (www.museodel automovil.org.ar).

Since his emergency admission to hospital in Uruguay in 2000, he spends most of his time as a guest of Fidel Castro. When he leaves Cuba, it's usually to shore up his shaky finances by lending his name to sometimes shrewd, occasionally wacky business ventures. But even when forced to work, Diego still courts controversy. On promotional tour to China in 2003, a local paper ran a headline 'Prima Maradona' after he stiffed the organisers, spending the week holed up in a hotel eating roast chicken and watching TV.

Despite his roguish behaviour, and polemical taking of Cuban citizenship, his name remains as good as gold in Buenos Aires, gracing everything from wine bottles to cologne. There is even a musical based on his life, called *No 10: Between Heaven and Hell*. His most ambitious venture is the Diego Armando Maradona Museum, or M10, an exhibition now touring the world but eventually to settle in Buenos Aires. The museum contains more than 600 personal objects, including a replica of the ramshackle bungalow he grew up in and photographs taken alongside personalities as diverse as Castro, Pope John Paul II and Freddy Mercury.

pampas and northern Patagonia. Since Menem privatised the railways in the mid 1990s, the station is basically for the suburbs only. The forecourt is a mad whirl of vagrants, vendors and commuters, with numerous bus lines terminating here too, just to add to the chaos.

Apart from the shell of the station – an imposing 1880s construction, recently restored – which dominates the whole area, the only point of interest, aside from a few Spanish restaurants, is the **Santa Casa de Ejercicios Espirituales** (House of Spiritual Exercises – Avenida de Independencia 1190). In 1795, Sister María Antonia de la Paz Figueroa walked 1,000 kilometres (620 miles) along the Camino Real (Royal Highway) to Buenos Aires from her hometown in northern Argentina. On arrival, she approached the authorities for permission to open a Jesuit-style retreat. The tenacious nun got her way and the interior of her temple houses a wealth of old relics and religious paraphernalia. There's a guided tour for AR$5 on the third Sunday of each month; call 4305 4285 for details.

The name Barracas refers to the warehouses that clustered here from the late 18th century onwards; cheap housing and brothels completed the picture by the early 1900s. The eastern limit of Barracas, Avenida Regimiento de Patricios, is the extension of Defensa, but instead of bars and antique shops, the keynote building is the large factory built in 1885 by the Alpargatas firm, famous for its espadrilles.

A gentrification effort is converting many of the crumbling warehouses and grand relics of capitalism into affordable housing and offices for young artists and professionals. Indeed, with its quiet, sun-soaked streets and panoramic views, Barracas feels like a post-industrial urban oasis, similar to East Berlin, just five minutes from the city centre. An early anchor of the renewal is the **Centro Metropolitano de Diseño** (*listings below*), a city-run incubator for young designers that set up shop in 2001 in a remodelled facility that

Street art on *calle* Lanín.

Top five Museums

Malba
The new cultural heavyweight – LatAm art, cinema and edgy events. *See p85.*

Museo Casa Carlos Gardel
See where the tango star with the famous smile and the voice of angels lived with his mum. *See p87.*

Museo de Arte Hispanoamericano
Great collection from across the continent – worth a visit for the building alone. *See p66.*

Museo de la Pasión Boquense
A victorious century of footy memorabilia at Maradona's old soccer club. *See p73.*

Museo Evita
The lowdown – from the pro-Evita angle – on Argentina's leading lady. *See p83.*

long ago housed the city's fish market. One block away along Villarino, underneath the elevated, art-deco Yrigoyen train station, the recently restored **Arcos de Barracas** are a fine example of English-built, exposed brick arches. The entire block surrounding the arches looks straight out of the 1920s, which is why the city promotes it as a film location.

Among the artists breathing new life into Barracas is Marino Santa María. Since 2001, on the dead-end *calle* Lanín, Santa María has been spearheading an imaginative public-art project he calls the post-modern version of La Boca's Caminito. Every house on the curved two-block street is painted with colourful, abstract streaks resembling psychedelic tiger stripes. Santa María's studio can be visited at Lanín 33. On weekends, he transforms a solid brick viaduct into an installation of mirrors and baroque-framed cloudscapes that reflect the timeless aura of low-lying Barracas.

Despite revival efforts, most *porteños* still associate Barracas with illness and death as the barrio is home to several hospices and two massive psychiatric hospitals. The male section, **El Borda** at Ramón Carrillo 375, has a cultural centre showcasing art and bonsai by patients – donations of art materials welcome.

Centro Metropolitano de Diseño
Villarino 2498, y Santa María del Buen Ayre (4126 2950/www.cmd.org.ar). Train to Hipólito Yrigóyen/12, 37, 45 bus. **Open** 10am-6pm Mon-Fri. **Admission** free.

North of the Centre

Live it up (and die in style) in BA's greenest, grandest neighbourhoods.

In 1871, when the rich fled yellow fever in the southern barrios, they gravitated north to Barrio Norte. Mansions and palaces soon spread to Recoleta and Palermo and together these are the most exclusive, expensive and European of all the city's districts.

The area is bordered by Avenida Córdoba and a string of plazas and parks along busy Avenidas del Libertador and Figueroa Alcorta. The city is monumental and notably French in style in these parts, the wide boulevards and open spaces exploited as sites for statues honouring national heroes, immigrant communities and assorted international bigwigs. Many of Argentina's late greats are buried in the Cementerio de la Recoleta, one of South America's most important necropolises.

The greenery is in no small part due to the vision of French botanist and landscaper Charles Thays (1849-1934), who travelled to Argentina in the 1880s to study trees and ended up staying and designing the zoo, the Jardín Botánico, Plaza San Martín, Parque 3 de Febrero and numerous private gardens.

Recoleta

In & around the Cementerio

One of the world's great necropolises, the **Cementerio de la Recoleta** (*see p79*), proposed by Rivadavia and designed by Frenchman Próspero Catelin, was opened in 1822. The narrow passages and high walls make comparisons with the real city outside inevitable. Yews and cypresses line the main thoroughfares, creating refuges of shade. Entrance to the cemetery is through a grand Doric-columned portico designed in 1886 by Juan Buschiazzo, one of Argentina's most important architects. A useful plan is available in the doorway.

The cemetary is home to hundreds of illustrious corpses (*see p78* **Death becomes them**), laid out in a compact maze of granite, marble and bronze mausoleums – most of the materials came from Paris and Milan – and a slow walk down its avenues and alleyways is one of BA's undisputed delights. Originally a public cemetery on the fringes of the city – nearby Avenida Callao marked the limit of Buenos Aires until the 1880s – it is now even

harder to get into than the posh flats that surround it. Seafarers and freed slaves were once given their final berths in Recoleta, but now ordinary folk can only get in alive. Numerous Argentinian presidents are entombed here, though most visitors come to see the final resting place – an architecturally uninspired family vault – of María Eva Duarte de Perón, aka Evita. Her husband, Juan Domingo Perón, is buried alongside Gardel at the commoners' cemetery in Chacarita (*see p88*).

There are also impressive collective tombs (housing fallen soldiers), great pantheons and cenotaphs, inches away from one another. Assorted architectural styles are arranged side by side, from distinguished chemist Dr Pedro Arata's diminutive Egyptian pyramid to aristocrat Dorrego Ortiz Basualdo's monumental sepulchre, decorated with 'prudent virgins' and topped by a great candelabra. Among the patrician families here, residing in a style befitting one-time mansion dwellers, are the Alvears, the Estradas, the Balcarces and the Alzagas, together with members of the Paz clan.

The plazas outside the cemetery walls were once on the banks of the river, like the cliffs in *el bajo* (downtown). Though barely a bump in its present landscaped form, the mount was of sufficient size to serve as a hiding place for bandits and other undesirables in the 17th century. Between 1716 and 1730, a French chapter of the Franciscans, known as the Padres Recoletos, chose the area to build a chapel and convent as a place of retreat. At the same time, the Jesuits, already established as missionaries and merchants in northern Argentina, Paraguay and Brazil, settled in the

New Age seers in **Plaza Francia**.

Death becomes them

Almost every major hero, villain and capitalist is buried in Recoleta's glorious necropolis.

Along with Evita are several high-profile presidents including the two 19th-century arch-enemies – educator Domingo Sarmiento and tyrant Juan Manuel de Rosas – and Julio A Roca. National personages include San Martín sidekick Tomás Guido's grotto-like pile of stones and La Rioja *caudillo* Juan Facundo Quiroga's mausoleum. Quiroga, assassinated during the bloody civil war in the 1830s, is buried standing up – a sign of courage, or as the cemetery's subdirector puts it, 'so he can get his sabre out quickly if need be.'

Irish freedom fighter and naval hero William Brown spends his afterlife beside a green mast bearing a frigate. His daughter Elisa is also buried here. She was found drowned in her wedding dress in the Riachuelo. Legend has it she killed herself out of grief for her Scottish lover, who died helping her father foil Brazil's imperial ambitions.

Another sad story is that of Rufina Cambaceres, a rich kid buried alive after a cataleptic attack. When she woke up, she managed to prise the coffin open but

died during the night from a heart attack. She is buried in an art nouveau tomb stylishly decorated with much-admired wrought iron.

Someone who could have punched his way out is Luis Angel Firpo, heavyweight boxer, who nearly beat Jack Dempsey in 1923. A statue of the boxer by the eminent sculptor Luis Perlotti stands on Firpo's granite tomb.

Look out also for:

Stylish patricians: Carlos de Alvear, Familia Dorrego – Ortiz Basualdo, Familia Leloir.
Noble-looking leaders and politicans: Manuel Dorrego, Lucio Lopez/Juan Lavalle, Pantheon of the Fallen in the Revolution – Leonardo M Alem, Hipólito Yrigoyen and Aturo Illia.
Key artists and writers: José Hernández, Vicente López y Planes, Miguel Cané, Eduardo Mallea, Adolfo Bioy Casares, Victoria Ocampo.

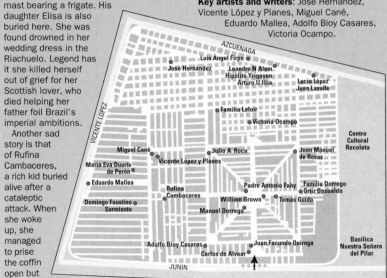

Recoleta. Building of their **Basílica Nuestra Señora del Pilar** (Junín 1904, 4803 6793) began in 1716 and the church site was consecrated in 1732. Today the city's elite hold lavish weddings here.

The plain-looking façade, the whiteness barely interrupted but for the sky-blue Pas-de-Calais ceramic tiles that decorate its upper reaches, is reminiscent of many colonial churches found in remote northern provinces. Inside, is a superlative baroque altar, featuring Inca and other pre-Hispanic motifs. The altar was brought

along the mule trails from Peru, the heart of colonial South America, and given a wrought-silver frontal in Jujuy in north-west Argentina. You can visit the cloisters, with a mini-museum of religious art, the crypt beneath the church and adjoining tunnels, thought to connect with tunnels in Monserrat, on regular guided tours (AR$1) in Spanish and English.

To the north of the Pilar church, on the site of the Franciscan convent, is the **Centro Cultural Recoleta** (*see p79* and *p180*). It promotes contemporary visual arts and contains several performance rooms – including a new space opened in 2001 for De La Guarda's *Villa Villa* show. There is also a film projection room and an interactive science museum for kids (*see p168*). From the roof terrace, you can view the surrounding plazas and other sights.

It's not all high culture and high church: a specialised mall, **Buenos Aires Design**, occupies two floors showcasing the latest in designer furniture and interiors. To complete the incongruous picture of a city of the dead encircled by outer suburbs full of fun and frivolity, the terraces of Buenos Aires Design are lined with cafés and restaurants. South-west of the cemetery on Vicente López, the **Village Recoleta** shopping and leisure centre has a multiplex cinema (*see p176*), bars, restaurants and a good bookshop, and its large courtyard is a bustling scene of family life.

In the attractive grassy spaces in front of the Centro Cultural stretching down to Avenida Libertador are three giant *gomero* trees that provide shade for strollers, loungers and dog walkers. **Plaza Francia**, directly north-east of the cultural centre is taken over on weekends and bank holidays by a handicraft fair, which draws tourists, stragglers and neo-hippies.

Across Posadas is the belle époque **Palais de Glace** (*listings below*), which was an ice-rink, a ballroom and an important tango salon in the 1920s, run by aristocrat Baron de Marchi. It was in this circular building that tango was officially embraced by the bourgeoisie. Now it has been adopted by the city for trade expos, high-profile art exhibitions and fashion displays.

In front of the Palais de Glace stands a monument to Carlos María de Alvear, an officer who created the horseguards regiment in 1812 with San Martín, and was the first in a line of Alvears to become key figures in the city's history. Opposite are the monument and plaza dedicated to Carlos María's son, Torcuato de Alvear, the first governor of the city of Buenos Aires and an important urban planner.

The pedestrian walkway **RM Ortíz**, which runs from the corner of Junín and Vicente López to Avenida Quintana, is one of BA's most popular strips for the time-honoured evening stroll known as *el paseo* – though the new trend of restaurant staff hustling passers-by to come and eat is annoying. At the corner of Avenida Quintana is traditional, classy café **La Biela** (*see p130*). Opposite the café, its tentacle-like bowers casting a great shadow over the outdoor terrace, is a magnificent tree known as the Gran Gomero. Planted in 1878, it's 20 metres (65 feet) high and a staggering 50 metres (164 feet) wide.

Of all the streets in the area, **Avenida Alvear** is the most palatial and rents here hit New York levels. It's all super smart, but

walking south-east from the Recoleta plazas towards downtown, the first really grand building is the **Alvear Palace Hotel** (*see p33*), at No.1891, a 1932 French-style construction. Further along are some early-20th-century palaces, once the homes of the *porteño* gentry, including the art nouveau **Palacio Duhau** (No.1683 – destined for a new life as a five-star Hyatt hotel) and two neo-classical mansions, the sober **Residencia Duhau** (No.1671) and the **Nunciatura Apostólica** (No.1637). The latter once belonged to the mega-rich Anchorena family and was used in the 1920s by president Marcelo T de Alvear; the last big name to sleep there was Pope John Paul II on visits in 1982 and 1987. The palaces are not open to the public, but you can visit the restaurants and shops off the lobby of the Alvear Palace Hotel.

Cementerio de la Recoleta

Junín 1760, entre Guido y Vicente López (4803 1594). Bus 10, 17, 60, 67, 92, 110. **Open** 7am-6pm daily. **Guided tours** *Apr-Oct* by arrangement. **Admission** free. **Map** p278 H7.

Centro Cultural Recoleta

Junín 1930, y Quintana (4803 9799/tours 4803 1040/www.centroculturalrecoleta.org). Bus 10, 17, 60, 67, 92, 110. **Open** 2-9pm Tue-Fri; 10am-9pm Sat, Sun. **Admission** *Exhibitions* suggested contribution AR$1. *Shows* AR$3-$10. **No credit cards. Map** p278 H7.

Palais de Glace

Posadas 1725, y Schiaffino (4804 1163). Bus 17, 61, 67, 92, 93. **Open** 2-8pm Tue-Sun. **Admission** suggested contribution AR$1. **Map** p278 G7.

Avenida del Libertador

Beyond the cluster of life, leisure and style that has sprung up around the necropolis, Recoleta has other public spaces and venues along Avenida del Libertador. At the centre of Plaza Francia, at Libertador and Pueyrredón, is a baroque marble monument to Liberty, which was presented to Argentina by France as part of the 1910 centenary celebrations.

Across the avenue from the Palais de Glace is the newest patch of urban landscaping, **Parque Carlos Thays**, boasting a heroic bronze *Torso Masculino* by Colombian sculptor Fernando Botero. At Libertador and Callao is the **Museo de Arquitectura** (4800 1888), located in a former railway water tower dating from 1915. Exhibitions trace the evolution of Buenos Aires and more general issues of design and architecture. It's open afternoons only from March to December; phone for more details.

A few blocks north-west stands the dusty orange-coloured, quietly neo-classical **Museo Nacional de Bellas Artes** (*see p80*). Not vast

Sightseeing

by international standards, the MNBA is nonetheless home to 32 rooms, sculpture patios, an architecture display, studios, library and auditorium. Though it has no indigenous and little colonial art, it does hold the country's most extensive collection (11,000 pieces) of 19th- and 20th-century Argentinian art and some important European works. The Argentinian collection includes outstanding works from Ernesto de la Cárcova (*Sin pan y sin trabajo*) and Cándido López (*Soldados paraguayos heridos*). Twentieth-century pieces feature all the major names in Argentinian art, including Eduardo Sivori, Antonio Berni, Xul Solar, Jorge de la Vega and current star Guillermo Kuitca (*see chapter* **Galleries**).

The international collection on the ground floor contains works by El Greco, Rubens, Rembrandt, Goya, Van Gogh, Monet, Chagall, Picasso and Pollock among other big names. In the main, there is only one work by each major artist, but all in all, it's an impressive grouping. The MBNA is compact enough to visit in a few hours. It also has an excellent bookshop, free guided tours and makes imaginative use of its space to hold other cultural events.

Behind the museum, on Avenida Figueroa Alcorta, is the **Facultad de Derecho** (Law Faculty), thronged all year round by thousands of students. In 2003, Fidel Castro made a classically lengthy public speech from its steps. Plazas Urquiza, Uruguay and Naciones Unidas are plain public spaces that have been saved from development by virtue of their location and the lobby-potential of local residents. The shiny new steel and aluminium *Floralis Genérica* by Eduardo Catalano is a popular sculpture, its six huge petals opening each day as the sun rises and closing again at dusk.

Occasionally, a building or two gets in the way of the greenery – such as the Bauhaus-style, state-owned ATC Channel 7 TV studios, built in 1978 to broadcast the World Cup – but there are open spaces all the way to Palermo and beyond on the river side of Libertador.

Back across the road, the plazas don't last as long but they are more dramatic. At the top of **Plaza Mitre** a great red granite pedestal is adorned with lively allegorical and lyrical figures in marble, above which rides a stern bronze of Bartolomé Mitre, president from 1862-88 and founder of *La Nación* newspaper .

The next patch of grass, the **Plaza Rubén Darío** – named after the Nicaraguan poet and philosopher – is brooded over by the jutting upper half of the functional-looking **Biblioteca Nacional** (*listings below*), designed in the 1960s (when its straight lines were probably sci-fi avant-garde) by three prominent architects, Clorindo Testa, Alicia Cazzaniga de Bullrich

and Francisco Bullrich. Building dragged on for years and the library only opened to the public in 1992. Most of the two million books and manuscripts are kept underground, so there's not much to see except for occasional exhibits catering to history buffs. Current and back issues of periodicals and newspapers are available, however – go to the Hemeroteca in the basement, with photo ID, and be ready for some bureaucratic form-filling.

Before the concrete block of the library was conceived, this was the land of the Unzué family and for a time the site of the presidential residence, where the Peróns lived and Evita died at 8.25pm on 26 July 1952. The military tore down the mansion to erase the memory of Peronism, unswayed by the fact that Juan Domingo had risen from its very own ranks.

A monolithic monument of a stylised, skinny, athletic-looking Evita was erected on the plaza in 1999 after years of wrangling about shifting the existing statue of Darío, who now sits across the road. There's also a statue of a smirking Pope John Paul II in front of the library. To the rear of the library is the attractive, if unshaded, **Plaza del Lector**, with benches for reading. It is also home to a small fountain, art gallery and restaurant.

At the Palermo end of Recoleta, at Avenida del Libertador 1902, is the beautiful French-style mansion Palacio Errázuriz, which houses the **Museo de Arte Decorativo** (*listings below*). French architect René Sergent, who built the mansion in 1911, gave the building a complex façade containing French, Corinthian and Tuscan elements. The building became a museum in 1937 and its stunning ballrooms, sumptuous bedrooms and hallways today display over 4,000 pieces of decorative art – plus works by El Greco and Manet – collected by Chilean aristocrat-diplomat Matías Errázuriz and his wife, Josefina de Alvear.

Biblioteca Nacional

Agüero 2502, entre Libertador y Las Heras (4806 4721 ext 1140/www.bibnal.edu.ar). Bus 59, 60, 93, 102. **Open** 9am-9pm Mon-Fri; noon-8pm Sat, Sun. **Admission** free. **Map** p278 H7.

Museo Nacional de Arte Decorativo

Avenida del Libertador 1902, y Pereyra Lucena (4806 8306/4802 6606/www.mnad.org). Bus 10, 59, 60, 67, 130. **Open** 2-7pm daily. **Closed** 1st 2wks Jan. **Admission** AR$2 Mon, Wed-Sun; AR$1 concessions. Free Tue. **No credit cards.** Map p278 I7.

Museo Nacional de Bellas Artes

Avenida del Libertador 1473, y Pueyrredón (4803 8814/4691/www.mnba.org.ar). Bus 17, 62, 67, 93, 130. **Open** 12.30-7.30pm Tue-Fri; 9.30am-7.30pm Sat, Sun. **Guided tours** (Spanish) 5pm Tue-Sun. **Admission** free. **Map** p278 H7.

Barrio Norte

When alluding to the overcrowded, middle-class residential area between Avenida Las Heras and Avenida Córdoba, though still officially Recoleta, most *porteños* – and estate agents – use the term Barrio Norte. The nickname is often associated with the *chetos* (social-climbing, nouveau riche poseurs) and *paquetes* (also poseurs, but with the confidence of older money) who live here. Evita, in one of her many fiery speeches to seduce the working classes, declared her ambition to 'bomb Barrio Norte'. The neighbourhood's main consumer corridor and a Barrio Norte symbol par excellence is **Avenida Santa Fe**, a gauntlet of big-name brand shops and boutiques.

If you do take a stroll down Santa Fe, spend some time in the converted cinema at No.1860 that now houses the **Ateneo** bookshop (*see p142*). It's a pity the movie theatre closed, but the bookshop is at least a nod to a continuing cultural presence in the area. Just few blocks from here (between Callao and Pueyrredón), is one of Buenos Aires' most openly gay scenes, especially on weekend evenings.

The rest of the area is taken up by the **Universidad de Buenos Aires**, including the dental and medical faculties with their respective state hospitals, and lots of private clinics. Barrio Norte is also littered with language schools, where *mamá* and *papá* expect their little ones to learn fluent *inglés*.

Literary pilgrims should wander into the **Museo Casa de Ricardo Rojas** (*see p83*). Rojas (1882-1957) was an influential writer and one of Argentina's most important educators, teaching Argentinian literature at the state university before becoming its rector in 1926. His ascetic house, with its original furnishings and household objects and Rojas' personal library of 20,000 volumes, is the quintessential writer's refuge – a guide will escort you through the rooms. It's also of note for the mixture of Spanish and Incaic styles in the patio, tiles and ornamental motifs.

Barrio Norte's other creative oasis is the **Museo Xul Solar** (*see p83*), two blocks from Santa Fe. This museum – installed in an award-winning modern space – contains a wondrous collection of esoteric objects, weird instruments and artworks by the city's most eccentric visionary: sailor turned painter, astrologer, musician, inventor, mathematician, writer and philologist Oscar Agustín Alejandro Schulz Solari (1887-1963) – Xul Solar, as he chose to be called, or Shulze, as Borges, whose writings he depicted, called him. Look out for the game of Pan-Chess and skim the books on Solar's invented language, also called Pan.

Sightseeing

Museo de Arte Decorativo (top; *p80*) and the **Museo Nacional de Bellas Artes** (*p79*).

Saint Evita?

Eva Perón always wanted to be an actress but she never made the grade – any kind of performance required an effort beyond her abilities. The only role in which she truly shone was her own: the standard-bearer of the underclass addressing the masses in Buenos Aires' Plaza de Mayo from the balconies of the Casa Rosada.

She was born on 7 May 1919 in Los Toldos, a former native reservation some 300 kilometres (186 miles) from the capital. She was the fifth illegitimate daughter of farmhand Juana Ibarguren and ranch-owner Juan Duarte. An acute consciousness of her illegitimacy and the poverty in which she was reared left its mark on Evita. Her biography is less of a Cinderella story, as some have suggested, and more a female version of *The Count of Monte Cristo*. Her vilification of the landed gentry and her crazed handing out of gifts and money to the downtrodden were more acts of belated revenge than mere signs of resentment.

Aged 15, she fled Junín, the city where she was living, and moved to Buenos Aires. She seemed condemned to be a bit part film and theatre actress when she met Colonel Juan Perón at a charity performance. Following that January night in 1944, they were inseparable. Theirs was a union sealed more by power than love – or, rather, by the love of power.

Of all Latin American women, none have been listened to – or read – like Evita. Her best-known book, *La razón de mi vida* (1951), was ghostwritten by Valencian journalist Manuel Penella da Silva, who met Evita when she was on a tour of hospitals and poor neighbourhoods in Spain in 1947.

Four years later, at the height of her glory, Eva sought to become Argentina's vice president. She orchestrated a massive rally to cheer on her acceptance speech, but was forced to resign by Perón on 31 August 1951. In September, she was diagnosed with cancer. While undergoing a series of treatments, multitudinous marches and Masses to pray for her health took place, and she was awarded numerous honours: in January 1952, the province of La Pampa was renamed Eva Perón; on 7 May, on her 33rd birthday, parliament made her the Spiritual Leader of the Nation.

Eva tried to mitigate her enforced convalescence by speaking out. From March to June 1952, between relapses, she wrote *Mi mensaje*. This book's 30 short chapters put forward three basic themes: fanaticism as a profession of faith; condemnation of the armed forces for abusing its powers; condemnation of the Catholic hierarchy for its 'indifference to the real suffering of the people'. Perón banned *Mi mensaje* and the manuscript remained unavailable until 1986, when it resurfaced at a bric-a-brac auction. The only occasion on which Evita wrote, the only time she tried to build her own mythical status in writing, she failed.

The real Evita mythology was created posthumously. Eva died on 26 June 1952, and that same night Spanish embalmer Pedro Ara began working on the corpse. He wanted to suspend the body in an illusion of eternal life. Before Ara could complete the task, the mummy was kidnapped by the military authorities that overthrew Perón in 1955, locked away in a cupboard, driven in trucks through the streets of Buenos Aires, mutilated and profaned, until it was given a secret burial in a Milan cemetery. In 1971, another military government decided to exhume the body and return it to Perón. When he died, Eva was laid to rest in the Duarte family mausoleum in Recoleta cemetery where she remains.

Evita Perón was intolerant, illiterate, fanatical, desperate for love and the admiration of the masses. She liked jewels, furs, Dior dresses, and she could have anything she wanted without needing to steal. She fell far short of being a saint, though millions of Argentinians see her as such. But nor was she a villain. Human beings are contradictory – they are rarely as presented in Hollywood musicals.

Tomás Eloy Martínez, author of *Santa Evita*.

Museo Casa de Ricardo Rojas

Charcas 2837, entre Anchorena y Laprida (4824 4039). Subte D, Agüero/12, 39, 152 bus. **Open** 10am-6pm Mon-Fri. **Admission** free. **Map** p278 H5.

Museo Xul Solar

Laprida 1212, entre Mansilla y Charcas (4824 3302/ www.xulsolar.org.ar). Subte D, Agüero/12, 39, 64, 152 bus. **Open** *Mar-Dec* noon-8pm Tue-Fri. **Closed** Jan, Feb. **Admission** AR\$3; AR\$1 concessions. **No credit cards**. Map p278 H5.

Palermo

Palermo has the lot: museums and monuments galore, parks, lakes, a zoo, a transvestite strip, polo and cricket clubs, an airport, a botanic gardens, a Japanese gardens, a rose garden. In some ways, it's the capital's most representative barrio, identified with the typical *porteño* family, neither rich nor poor, neither ultra-conservative nor ultra-cool, though within its extensive borders there are pockets of extremity. Numerous sub-divisions exist within Palermo, but everyone accepts three basic areas: tiny Palermo Chico (bordering Recoleta) for the filthy rich; atmospheric Palermo Viejo (comprising Palermo Hollywood and Palermo Soho) for global cuisine, funky boutiques and smart lofts; and plain Palermo for the rest, including all the greenery.

From the little street called Cavia to Monroe in Belgrano (the next barrio along), there is a patchwork of plazas and parks congregating round the Parque Tres de Febrero, formerly a flood plain drained in the late 16th century by the barrio's namesake, Italian farmer Giovanni Domenico Palermo. At the northern limit of the park is the **Hipódromo Argentino** racecourse (*see p199*), but keen walkers and cyclists (there's a bike path all the way) can skirt this by heading towards the river and continue on to Nuñez and the River Plate football stadium.

Although you may stroll into Palermo as a continuation of your wanderings through Recoleta, the point of access to the peaceful green heart of the park that has the most public transport options is **Plaza Italia**. It's one of the noisiest junctions in the city and a far cry from the lawned delights that punctuate most of the area. Buses and the Subte empty out shoppers, visitors to the exhibition centre – which hosts motor shows, commercial events and, most famously, the Exposición Agrícola, Ganadera e Industrial, aka **La Rural** (*see p165*), in mid winter – and anyone heading for the parks. The grandiose monument to Italian hero Giuseppe Garibaldi at the centre of the plaza is the only static figure in this hectic scene.

The **Jardín Botánico Carlos Thays**, created in 1902 in between Avenida Santa Fe,

Las Heras and Gurruchaga, is quieter. Thousands of species (and feral cats) flourish here, and there is a sizeable greenhouse brought back from the Argentinian pavilion at the 1900 Paris Exhibition. Fountains, orchids, cacti, ferns and spectacular trees and bushes make this a paradise for anyone who likes to potter around the garden. There are plans to convert Thays' former park dwelling into a café and exhibition space. Monuments include a Venus, a Saturnalia and a Romulus and Remus, and there's a botanical library (open from 8am to 3pm on weekdays), but the main attraction is the calm offered by this small hedged-in triangle.

The **Jardín Zoológico** (*see p166*) across the road is one of those interesting but somewhat discomfiting attractions many animal lovers will shun, although serious zoological work takes place here. This small city zoo houses big cats, a polar bear and native species – such as rheas, penguins and the four camelids (llama, guanaco, vicuña and alpaca). In late 2003, a sextuplet of white Bengal tiger cubs was born. Of more general interest are the buildings, designed mainly by Eduardo Holmberg (the zoo's first director) between 1888 and 1904, and finished off by Charles Thays in 1905. Holmberg's idea was to house each animal in a building that aped the architecture of its native country, resulting in a landscape of scaled-down monumental follies that make the zoo look rather like 'Animal Town'. Wildlife watchers with more time may prefer the newer Parque Temaikén, outside the city; *see p167*.

In 2001, a small new museum – the **Museo Evita** (*see p86*) – opened its doors on one of Palermo's quieter back streets. It is housed in an aristocratic, neo-gothic residence that Perón expropriated to convert into a women's shelter for his wife's quasi-statal welfare agency. It's worth a visit to see the range of myths her person has inspired in Argentina. Paintings, propaganda posters and busts are displayed alongside clothes she wore on her regal tours of Europe. As HQ of an Evita Foundation, the exhibitions tend to be positive, but the most earnest of curators can't hide the words of her ghost written autobiography or the ironies in

Eva Perón mythologised at **Museo Evita**.

Sightseeing

Palermo's great outdoors: the lakes, rose garden and greenery of **Parque Tres de Febrero**.

Sightseeing

many depictions of the eternal First Lady of Argentina. *See p82* **Saint Evita?**

South of the zoo, at the junction of Avenidas Sarmiento and del Libertador is the bleached-white **Monumento de los Españoles** – a convenient spot for entering the main parkland. A centenary gift from the Spanish, the four bronzes represent Argentina's four main geographical regions: the Pampas, the Andes, the Chaco and the River Plate. Allegorical sculptures in Carrara marble further embellish this striking symbol of Hispanic union.

Designed and overseen by Thays, the **Parque Tres de Febrero** – which locals call Parque Palermo or Los Bosques de Palermo (the Palermo Woods) – was finally opened at the close of the 19th century. In addition to well-kept lawns, beautiful jacarandas and palms and a lake, there are cafés and a good art gallery, the **Museo de Artes Plásticas Eduardo Sívori** (*see p85*). Once a chic restaurant, it now houses a major collection of Argentinian paintings and sculpture, with a café on the grass patio inside.

The park is named after the date in 1852 when pro-Urquiza forces defeated the despotic General Rosas at the Battle of Monte Caseros. Using land formerly owned by Rosas, Sarmiento – who razed Rosas' mansion – envisaged the park as a way for Buenos Aires to resemble more closely the capitals of Europe. Statues of a dashing Rosas and a stern Sarmiento face off diagonally at the Libertador–Sarmiento crossroads, the latter's monument (by Auguste Rodin) on the site of the flattened house.

A statue of Urquiza stands one block north at Avenidas Sarmiento and Figueroa Alcorta.

The backdrop to the statue is the large sci-fi orb of the city's planetarium, **Planetario Galileo Galilei** (*see p168*). Armies of children and star-gazing adults are treated to film, light and sound shows exploring the Argentinian night sky, black holes and other cosmic spectacles.

Within and around the park, highlights include the delightfully pretty **Rosedal** (Rose Garden – entered at Avenidas Iraola and Puerto Montt), the **Jardín de los Poetas** with its peaceful fountains surrounded by busts of literary giants, a lovely, tiled **Patio Andaluz** and a shaded pergola by the lake. A map at the entrance to the Rosedal helps with orientation. In these well-planted spaces, look out for native bird life, such as the *hornero* (oven bird – it has an oven-shaped nest) and the yellow and black *cabecita negra*, not to mention the common-or-garden sparrow, introduced from Europe by Sarmiento as yet another 'civilising' presence. Non-botanists and kids can spend the afternoon on the lake (pedalos and boats are for hire opposite the Museo Sívori), or cycling through the park.

The other glorious spot for greenfingered visitors is the **Jardín Japonés** (*see p85*). The garden is awash with artificial lakes brimming with weirdly anthropomorphic giant koi carp, ornate bridges and – in the pagoda – an attractive all-day tearoom serving green teas and cakes, and a fine Japanese restaurant open in the evenings. Botanic species include black pines, sakura and ginkgo and there are regular exhibitions of bonsai. The entrance is at the corner of Avenidas Berro and Casares.

Along Avenida Figueroa Alcorta are a number of facilities, including **Paseo Alcorta** shopping centre (*see p139*), to further enhance the lifestyles of Palermo residents. But the area's most important addition is a cultural space, described by newspaper *Página/12* as 'about the only good thing to happen to Buenos Aires in 2001'. Paid for and stocked by art collector Eduardo Costantini, the Museo Latinoamericano de Buenos Aires (**Malba** – *listings below*) is an impressive contemporary gallery containing works by some of the very best Latin American artists of the past century. Frida Kahlo and Diego Rivera, Tarsila do Amaral and other groundbreaking painters share the walls with wonderful but not internationally famous Argentinian modern masters such as Antonio Berni and Jorge de la Vega. There is also an excellent café, plus a cinema specialising in cult and art-house retrospectives. The space is used for interesting alternative events as well. It's an essential visit for anyone interested in culture and the arts.

Back on Libertador, heading towards the centre, is the refurbished **Museo de Motivos Argentinos José Hernández** (*see p86*), so-named because of the gaucho motifs and other decorative elements of Argentina's rural past that constitute the main collection. It's named after the author of Argentina's national epic, *Martín Fierro* (1873). Two buildings off a patio are hung with *mate* gourds, spurs, weapons (especially knives) and other gaucho paraphernalia. There's also a reconstruction of a *pulpería*, the inn-cum-grocer's shop that was the focal point of 19th-century country life. Photos and models of real *pulperías* do more to conjure up these rural oases than the small replica. The museum also features temporary exhibits of modern arts and crafts inspired by issues of identity and Argentinian history.

Heading back to Recoleta from the park, or vice versa, you can detour off Avenida del Libertador into **Palermo Chico** (aka Barrio Parque). This tiny, upscale patch of suburbia

is where TV stars like Susana Gimenez and diplomats park their bulletproof jeeps.There are no shops or even *kioscos* to spoil the views, just plenty of grand architecture to admire. One exception: at the roundabout where Bustamante hits Rufino de Elizalde is the **Monumento San Martín Abuelo**, a rare effigy of the general without his horse. *Abuelo* means 'grandfather' and this likeable likeness of the Liberator shows him in his later years, dispensing advice to his granddaughters (how to garden, how to walk along the Seine, how to clean guns). Arranged south of the monument are statues of those who aided San Martín in his independence campaign. The **Instituto Sanmartiniano** research centre nearby is an over scale replica of Grand Bourg, the house where he lived in exile in France.

Jardín Japonés

Avenida Casares y Berro (4804 4922/9141/www. jardinjapones.com.ar). Bus 37, 67, 102, 130. **Open** 10am-6pm daily. **Guided tours** (Spanish) 3pm Sat. **Admission** AR$4; AR$1 6-10s, concessions; free under-6s. **No credit cards**. **Map** p279 J7.

Malba: Colección Costantini

Avenida Figueroa Alcorta 3415, entre Salguero y San Martín de Tours (4808 6500/www.malba. org.ar). Bus 67, 102, 130. **Open** noon-8pm Mon, Thur-Sun; noon-9pm Wed. **Guided tours** (Spanish). **Admission** AR$5; AR$2.50 concessions. Free Wed. **Credit** AmEx (AR$20 minimum). **Map** p278 I7. Tours in English by prearrangement for groups of 15 or more (AR$12 per person, including entry).

Museo de Artes Plásticas Eduardo Sívori

Avenida Infanta Isabel 555, y Libertador (4774 9452/ 4778 3899). Bus 10, 34, 37, 67, 130. **Open** *Dec-Apr* noon-8pm Tue-Fri; 10am-8pm Sat, Sun. *May-Nov* noon-6pm Tue-Fri; 10am-6pm Sat, Sun. **Guided tours** *Mar-Dec* twice daily Sat, Sun; call for times. *Jan, Feb* 4pm Sat, Sun. **Admission** AR$3; AR$1 residents Tue, Thur-Sun; free students, under-12s. Free Wed. **No credit cards**. **Map** p279 K7.

Thoroughly modern **Malba**.

Museo Evita

Lafinur 2988, entre Gutiérrez y Las Heras (4807 9433/0306). Subte D, Plaza Italia/37, 59, 60, 102 bus. **Open** 2-7.30pm Tue-Sun. **Admission** AR$5; AR$2 residents. **No credit cards. Map** p279 J6.

Museo de Motivos Argentinos José Hernández

Avenida del Libertador 2373, entre San Martín de Tours y Coronel Díaz (4802 9967/4803 2384/www. museohernandez.org.ar). Bus 10, 37, 59, 60, 92, 102. **Open** 1-7pm Wed-Sun. **Admission** AR$3; AR$1 residents; free under-12s, concessions. Free Sun. **No credit cards. Map** p278 I7.

Palermo Viejo

Away from the high rises, open spaces and views of the river, Old Palermo clusters. Most of the homes here are just one or two storeys high, and the town houses, many of them revamped into urban lofts, come with terraces or trees and long dark entrance ways. There's a literary/boho past here as evidenced by the street called Borges (*see p26* **Entering the labyrinth**) and the Plazoleta Cortázar (at the junction of Borges and Honduras – sometimes referred to by a former name, Plaza Serrano), but these days there's more emphasis on house music and cocktails than Latin American literature.

Run down and romantic until the early 1990s, it's since been thoroughly brightened up by restaurants, fashion and design outlets marking up smelly candles, oversized cushions, art books and fancy writing paper.

East European and Armenian communities made Palermo Viejo their home in the early 20th century and while there has been no significant recent immigration, cuisines from all over the world are served in its many restaurants. For open air drinks, Plazoleta Cortázar has long been popular, and those who find the pseudo-bohemian bars too expensive lounge beneath the lime trees with a bottle of Quilmes beer.

Such has been the impact of new money on Old Palermo that the food and lifestyle boom has expanded across the barrio's limit at Avenida Juan B Justo – famous as the north-western limit of BA's *zona roja*, a transvestite meat market – and now the sub-barrio once known as Pacífico is being give a face-lift too. It's been renamed Palermo Hollywood by employees of a TV station there, a nickname happily adopted by eager estate agents.

In the southern corner of Palermo Viejo, inside restaurant-theatre-wineshop **Club del Vino** (*see p193*) is a small wine museum. It falls short of a complete history of Argentinian wine, but a series of maps, labels and presses tell part of the story and when you've finished you can pop upstairs for a tasting session in the bar.

The best Bus routes

37: From Congreso to the Costanera Norte through Plaza Italia, the Botanic Gardens, Avenida Sarmiento and the city airport.
60: The most popular bus route here links Constitución, Callao, Plaza Italia and Belgrano with the Delta way north at Tigre.
152: From *sur* to *norte* – runs between La Boca and Zona Norte's Olivos, via Parque Lezama in San Telmo, Plaza San Martín in Retiro and the Palermo zoo.
130: The only bus going through Palermo's park – connecting San Isidro with Belgrano, Recoleta's museum strip and the Customs building behind Plaza de Mayo.
188: Cruise the untouristy areas (stay on board): the route travels Hipódromo-Zoo-Abasto-Once-Pompeya-Puente Uriburu.

Elsewhere in Palermo

Fringed by the polo ground and racecourse is a buzzing residential and dining district known as **Las Cañitas** (there were once sugar canes growing wild here). A popular focal point for the monied socialites of Palermo and Belgrano, there is little historical interest by day, though the **Cañitas Creativa** street fair on Fridays and Saturdays at 6pm brings in visitors. The area made the news big time when former president Carlos Menem gave the Saudis land to build BA's mega-mosque and religious centre, the **Centro Islámico Ray Fahd** at Avenidas Bullrich and del Libertador. For information on Spanish guided tours call 4899 1144.

One of Palermo's most curious unofficial sub-barrios just south of Plaza Italia, is called **Villa Freud**, in reference to the number of psychoanalysts working there. Sharing the area with the shrinks are several spiritual centres, including a Buddhist cemetery, a mosque and the **Basílica del Espíritu Santo** on Plaza Güemes (at the corner of Mansilla and Medrano). This sturdy church, built between 1901 and 1907, is known by locals as Guadalupe – after the local parish, which was named in honour of the saint that Pope Pius X appointed as Empress of the Americas in 1945. The saint appeared to worshippers in Mexico in 1531 and inside the nave is a painting of Mexico's Mount Tepeyac. A church run by the monastic Order of the Divine Word and a chapel complete the religious nucleus: Jesus, Guadalupe and gang vying with the secular scripts of the Lacanian analysts for the souls of the locals.

West of the Centre

Real world Buenos Aires.

The city's western districts are where to go for a dose of reality – it's where ordinary *porteños* live, work and die. Yet the area has its own vibe. Once is a riotous commercial hub, while neighbouring Abasto is being spruced up and given back some of its tango heritage. Chacarita's cemetery is a built-up, brick and mortar version of Recoleta's glamorous deathville, and Caballito and Villa Crespo offer highlights for the fringe-friendly tourist.

Once & Abasto

Once (pronounced 'on-say'), about 20 blocks west along Corrientes, is the city's most hectic commercial district – a maze of wholesale and retail outlets. Visitors who find Buenos Aires almost a touch too European, should head here – Once is as loud, bustling and brash as a Guatemalan bus station. Historically associated with the city's large Jewish population (*see p89* **Shalom, Buenos Aires**), it now contains sizeable Korean and Peruvian communities.

Named after the ugly 11 (Once) de Septiembre railway station – which in turn commemorates an 1852 battle between the provinces and the capital – on **Plaza Miserere** (usually called Plaza Once), the barrio wakes up early as arriving vans unload the reels of fabric that constitute the area's traditional trade. Avenidas Rivadavia and Pueyrredón are the main streets, but Once's pulse is found in the blocks to the south and west of their intersection.

Here, the selling of tack and trash spills on to the streets and Latin dance beats blast out from every other store. Visual pollution is taken to extremes as shops and street vendors compete for attention. If you like sterile shopping malls forget Once, although it certainly deserves a quick jaunt just to experience what local author Alvaro Abós calls a 'branch of hell'.

Once is, in fact, part of a barrio officially known as Balvanera, with its northern limit at Avenida Córdoba. At Córdoba 1950 is the striking **Palacio de Aguas Corrientes** (Palace of Running Waters) occupying a whole block. It's home to the capital's water works, run by private company, Aguas Argentinas. Constructed between 1887 and 1895, this flamboyantly decorated building, with its vivid colours and jigsaw of architectural styles, is a real one-off among the city's civic piles.

Just up from Once, at Avenida Corrientes and Anchorena, is the beautiful Mercado de Abasto building, an art deco masterpiece built between 1930 and 1934 as a central wholesale market for the city. Neglected for decades thereafter, the building's powerful, but empty, decaying presence became symbolic of the Abasto neighbourhood's own downward spiral into a seedy scene of blues, booze and cocaine.

In 1998 the market building was the first to see rejuvenation, converted into a shopping mall (known simply as **El Abasto** – *see p139*). Inside the mall is the **Museo de los Niños Abasto** (Abasto's Children's Museum – *see p168*), three floors of educationally minded displays about the commercial and industrial activities of Buenos Aires.

A subsequent transformation of the area has taken shape, its fortunes linked to those of its famous landmark. Completion of the ambitious 'Cultura Abasto' initiative, currently under way, will see El Abasto's surrounding ten blocks benefit from a full, 1930s style make-over, transporting the curious back to the barrio's heyday. Tango will be a central theme, and the small but neat **Museo Casa Carlos Gardel**, offering a peep into the house of the legendary crooner, has already opened (*see p88*). For more on Abasto's tango heritage, *see chapter* **Tango**.

Centre stage in Abasto's redevelopment plan, is the multi-purpose **Ciudad Cultural Konex**, a vast arts complex under construction at the intersection of Sarmiento and Jean Jaurès, to be opened in stages starting in 2005; until then, the foundation behind it runs events from

Textile shops add local colour to **Once**.

Childhood home of a legend: the **Museo Casa Carlos Gardel**.

its current cultural centre at Avenida Córdoba 1235 (4813 1100, www.fundacionkonex.com.ar). The new building's exterior will echo the geometric design of the Abasto's art deco style, and the inside will include an opera house, convention centres, theatres, museums, art galleries and a hotel. Inspired by Paris' Pompidou Centre, the government hopes this prestigious new site will have a similarly revitalising effect on its neighbourhood.

Museo Casa Carlos Gardel

Jean Jaurès 735, entre Zelaya y Tucumán (4964 2071). Subte B, Pueyrredón or Carlos Gardel/ 19, 92, 124 bus. **Open** 11am-6pm Mon, Wed-Sun. **Guided tours** (Spanish) 3pm Mon, Wed-Fri; 1pm, 3pm, 5pm Sat, Sun. **Admission** AR$3; free under-10s. Free Wed. **No credit cards. Map** p278 G5.

Almagro, Caballito & Villa Crespo

West of Abasto, Almagro, Caballito and Villa Crespo are districts with particularly proud residents and a real neighbourhood air. **Parque Centenario**, in Caballito, serves as the sole public park for these densely populated barrios and is as local and mundane as you'd expect.

The main crowd-puller, and great for kids, is the **Museo Argentino de Ciencias Naturales Bernadino Rivadavia** (*see p167*), a sizeable collection of stuffed fauna from all over the continent, with plenty of rocks, fossils and botanical exhibits. Highlights include one of the most important vertebrate palaeontology collections in Latin America, featuring several enormous Patagonian dinosaurs.

Another museum, the **Museo de Esculturas Luis Perlotti** (*listings below*), brings together some 900 wooden, bronze, plaster and stone sculptures by one of Argentina's foremost artists. American themes are central to Perlotti's art, from busts of indigenous people to statues of independence heroes, and many of his largest creations adorn the parks and plazas of the city.

Caballito is also a reminder of a gentler era in Buenos Aires, when the tram was king. Now, this is the only barrio that keeps the soothing clankety-clank alive, with a 25-minute service departing from Emilio Mitre and José Bonifacio every 15 minutes on Saturday afternoons and Sunday mornings and afternoons. Call the **Asociación Amigos del Tranvía** (4431 1073, www.tranvia.org.ar) to check exact times. Trips are free and very popular with families.

Almagro and Villa Crespo are traditional neighbourhoods and even more ordinary than Caballito, but worth a stroll to check out a true barrio vibe. Life in both revolves around the main Avenidas Corrientes and Rivadavia; off these streets, the pace is about as stressful as a *mate*-drinking session after a heavy siesta.

Museo de Esculturas Luis Perlotti

Pujol 644, entre Felipe Vallese y Méndez de Andes (4431 2825/4433 3396). Subte A, Primera Junta/ 92, 99, 106 bus. **Open** 11am-7pm Tue-Fri; 10am-1pm, 2-8pm Sat, Sun. **Admission** AR$1. Free Wed. **No credit cards. Map** p274 F1.

Chacarita

Like many one-time outlying barrios, Chacarita developed around a railway station, Federico Lacroze. The terminus, opened in 1880, is now little more than a run-down shed for suburban trains. Equally gloomy but far more interesting is the **Cementerio de la Chacarita** (*see p89*) on the other side of Avenida Guzmán. Avenida Corrientes, untold bus lines and the Subte's *línea* B also end their journeys here, creating a tumultuous traffic terminal in front of the cemetery's Doric-columned entrance, the crossing of which could easily mean delaying your visit until you've been embalmed.

The cemetery owes its existence – and size – to the yellow fever outbreak of 1871. A funeral train was set up that year, with an Englishman, Mr Allen, piloting the steam engine (until he too caught the plague and died). Every day more than 500 bodies – dead and nearly dead – were carried to the cemetery. Coffin-makers couldn't keep up and many were buried without so much as a shroud to cover their dignity.

Unlike the upper-class Recoleta cemetery, this more expansive necropolis, with numbered streets and car access to its thousands of vaults, is largely for common folk. Still, a number of popular heroes have also made Chacarita their choice of charnel house. The most famous is tango legend Carlos Gardel, while coming a close second would be ex-political strongman and demigod, Juan Domingo Perón, buried in a plain family crypt at the intersection of streets 3 and 34. At the corner of 113 and 14, the daring feats of aviation pioneer Jorge Newbery are dramatically captured by a sepulchre showing a fallen Icarus lying battered beneath some rocks.

Many other stars are grouped together at the Recinto para Personalidades (Celebrity Corner), roughly at the cemetery's centre. Here, the poet Alfonsina Storni is entombed in a rock-like cavern, sculpted at the rear into a female form, while La Boca painter Benito Quinquela Martín

is fittingly commemorated by a handful of colourful blocks. Most of these tombs are less morbid than the institutional pantheons and aristocratic mausoleums near the cemetery's entrance, but the cartoonish appearance of comedy actor Luis Sandrini's tomb is perhaps just a little too jolly for its own good.

Until 1939, Chacarita also held the cemeteries of the Jewish, British and German communities. With Hitler affecting relations even in far-off Argentina, the Jews left for a new site west of the city, and the Brits and Germans built walls to separate their dead. The German cemetery has its own entrance on Avenida Elcano, just past the intersection with Girardot, while the British cemetery is located next door. Here, the tombs, and the (English) epitaphs inscribed on them, offer reminders of a past maritime era.

Cementerio de la Chacarita
Guzmán 630, y Federico Lacroze (4553 9034/9038/ tours 4553 0041). Subte B, Federico Lacroze/42, 93, 111 bus. **Open** 7am-6pm daily. **Admission** free. **Map** p275 L2.

Shalom, Buenos Aires

Buenos Aires is home to the vast majority of Argentina's 200,000 Jews – the largest Jewish community in Latin America and the seventh largest in the world.

To see the heart of Jewish BA, head to Once – a real melting pot of Jewish cultures – think London's East End or New York's Lower East Side. Today, it's densely populated with Jewish-owned textile businesses, but it was once the centre of the white slave trade, with Jewish prostitutes working in brothels along Lavalle street, between Ayacucho and Callao.

For synagogues, **Templo Libertad** (*see p60*), located in Tribunales, is the city's biggest synagogue, and also has a small museum of Judaica. Back in Once, the **Congregación Sefardí**, a domed Moorish-style Sephardic synagogue on Lavalle 2400, is well worth a visit and two blocks from here, on Paso 400, is the elegant, **Ashkenazi Templo de Paso**, squeezed in among the rag traders. All the city's synagogues are best visited with a tour (*see p55* **Guided Tours**), as access has been severely restricted since the Jewish-targeted terrorist attacks of the 1990s.

The **Plaza Embajada de Israel** (*see p66*), a memorial to the victims of the first of these attacks, the 1992 Israeli Embassy bombing, can be visited in Recoleta at Arroyo 910, while those who fell victim to the subsequent

1994 attack on Once's AMIA Jewish Welfare Centre are remembered by the **Monumento de Homenaje y Recordación a las Víctimas del Atentado al AMIA**. This poignant work of multiple meanings and images by Israeli kinetic artist Yaacov Agaam is housed in the courtyard of the reconstructed building, at Pasteur 633. Tour agencies require 48 hours' notice to arrange a visit here. The city's small **Museo Memoria del Holocausto**, meanwhile, is located on Montevideo 919.

Away from the centre, several outlying barrios offer glimpses of Jewish life today. The northern neighbourhood of Belgrano has a large German-Jewish presence and is home to the only non-Orthodox seminary in Latin America – the **Seminario Rabinico Latin Americano**, open to the public at José Hernández 1750. It also ordains female rabbis – no mean feat in the overwhelmingly macho Argentinian society. Also in Belgrano, is **La Galería del Ángel** at Cuba 1937 (First Floor), where the genial owner and artist, Ariel Levin, welcomes those with an interest in contemporary Jewish art.

To the west, Abasto – long home to a large Sephardic community – boasts the only kosher McDonald's outside Israel, in Jewish-owned El Abasto mall, and many city ice-cream parlours offer kosher flavours.

Along the River

Beside the big, brown river there are eating, strolling and nature-watching opportunities… plus a chance to visit Jerusalem, *porteño*-style.

The River Plate was fundamental to the early development of Buenos Aires – yet the city's back is turned on its lifeblood. Chances to enjoy the coast can seem rare, but you should make time for the reinvigorated riverside. Both the designer docks of Puerto Madero and the unpretentious Costanera Sur nearby allow you to escape the clutches of the city, with long promenades, riverside restaurants and the latter's nature reserve. On the Costanera Norte, the Tierra Santa religious theme park attracts hordes of visitors, while the sobering Parque de la Memoria is an important site of remembrance.

Puerto Madero & Costanera Sur

The appearance of Puerto Madero – the dockland area to the east of Plaza de Mayo – is a reflection of Buenos Aires' self-image as a grand European-style city. The red-brick port buildings and grain warehouses, built between 1889 and 1898, were the first view of BA seen by incoming immigrants and the city fathers wanted to impress with a modern skyline.

Yet as early as 1911 a new harbour was being built, the narrow rectangular wharves having proved hopelessly inadequate. Puerto Nuevo, as it is known, is still loading up container ships north of Retiro. Meanwhile, Puerto Madero went into decline and the dream docks became rat-infested husks. It was only in the late '80s that the area was upgraded, along the lines of London and Baltimore. When the new-look Puerto Madero was opened in 1994, many locals would have liked to see a more civic, cultural slant. Instead, they got exclusive restaurants with high-rent flats on top.

Puerto Madero, however, is nothing if not open to change, and new projects with history and the arts are springing up. Aware that BA needed a monument to its early-20th-century settlers, the **Museo de la Inmigración** (*see p91*) was inaugurated by the city government in 2001. The museum is housed in the former Hotel de Inmigrantes, the first entry point for thousands of Europeans arriving in Argentina. The museum's collection of film, photos and objects – with information panels in Spanish – shows how it all started for many *porteños*.

Just south of here is Dársena Norte (North Harbour), where naval vessels are stationed. They can sometimes be visited for free at weekends, but admission is at the discretion of on-duty officers. When not at sea the impressive training ship, the **Fragata *Libertad***, and the towering icebreaker *Irízar*, used for Antarctic expeditions, also dock here intermittently.

A short distance south are the promenades of Puerto Madero's ever expanding dockland complex, a world created for the rich and beautiful. While unabashed in celebrating the finer things in life, much of Puerto Madero is, curiously, also dedicated to struggle, as all its streets are named after women who fought for female emancipation within Argentina. Strange, as the rest of BA is unwaveringly macho when it comes to baptising its thoroughfares.

At the entrance to the quays, on the eastern side of Dique (Dock) 4, is a building modelled on the Sydney Opera House, but in fact home to **Opera Bay**, a glitzy if pretty cheesy night club. Next door, among the steel and glass of Madero Este (as the Eastern side of the docks – now the focus of all the big investment bucks – is called), an art museum to house the collection of Amalia Fortabat, Argentina's richest woman, is being built. Just opposite, on Dique 4's western side is the local tourist office.

For evidence of the area's maritime history visit the impeccable **Corbeta *Uruguay***, moored further down on Dique 4 at Alicia Moreau de Justo and Corrientes. A museum vessel of Argentina's Naval Academy dating back to 1874, regular warfare would appear to have been beneath the 'glorious' *Uruguay* which distinguished itself in revolutions, expeditions and search-and-rescue missions. At Dique 3 is the even more impressive **Fragata *Presidente Sarmiento*** (Alicia Moreau de Justo y Belgrano). This frigate, built in Birkenhead, was used as a training ship from 1899 to 1961 and is now a wonderful museum full of photos, maps and domestic objects, with cabins of original oak and teak.

Stretching in front of the Sarmiento is the elegant **Puente de La Mujer**, an asymmetrical pedestrian bridge, designed by the renowned Spanish engineer Santiago Calatrava. Opened to acclaim in December 2001, the bridge's US$6 million construction costs were covered by

Alberto R González, late owner of much of Madero Este and its **Hilton Hotel** (*see p35*). The Hilton is soon to face competition from the Philippe Starck-designed hotel complex opening late 2004 (*see p44* **The Faena things in life**). Also for the smart set, on this side of the docks is Puerto Madero Yacht Club with its chic lunch restaurant. A small boat will ferry you from the other side.

Down on Dique 1, **Water Tour** (4342 4849, www.navegandobuenosaires.com) runs river trips for those who fancy seeing Puerto Madero from the water. Trips take just over an hour and cost AR$25 for adults, AR$12 for under-12s. Check website for departure times.

Beyond Madero Este is an altogether earthier experience, the River Plate's other urban jungle; the **Reserva Ecológica Costanera Sur** (*listings below*), BA's biggest – free – wilderness on the edge of the city. Within its boundaries, four lakes, giant *cortaderas* (foxtail pampas grass), willows and shrubs provide natural habitats for more than 200 bird species. Iguanas can be spotted scuttling across the hard earth, but on weekends you're more likely to see joggers, cyclists and picnickers as up to 15,000 visitors descend on the reserve. Moonlight tours are arranged one night per month closest to the full moon; phone ahead to book your place.

The long esplanade skirting the reserve is one of the city's most pleasant spaces for walking, sunbathing and seeing sky. A lavish 1927 beer keller, the **Cervecería Munich** houses the Centro de Museos, from where all the city's museums are administered. A guided tour of the picturesque pub gives an insight into how good life used to be for wealthy weekenders.

Slightly south, at the centre of a roundabout near the reserve's entrance (Avenida Tristán Achaval Rodríguez and Padre ML Migone), is

an eye-catching fountain, executed in 1902, by Tucumán-born artist Lola Mora. The **Fuente de las Nereidas** is a marble allegory set in a clam shell, depicting erotic fishy female forms.

One block south is the **Museo de Calcos y Escultura Comparada**, an outpost of the city's main public art college, with a collection of sculpted and moulded replicas of ancient and Renaissance masterpieces. Around the museum, the land is occupied by cheap *parillas* making this a popular weekend lunch spot.

The open-air grills continue down Rawson de Dellepiane, where, by a side road, the extravagantly decked out steamboat *Estrella de la Fortuna* is docked, housing the **Casino Buenos Aires** (4363 3100, ext 2100) – the only gaming hall in the capital, located on a boat rather than on land, as gambling is illegal in the city. It boasts 100 roulette tables, 650 slots, several bars and a restaurant and is open 24 hours a day. Be cautious arriving or leaving with cash. A free shuttle bus runs to/from LN Alem and Avenida Córdoba every 15 minutes.

If heading for La Boca or San Telmo, Rawson de Dellepiane is the best exit from Costanera Sur. Otherwise, aim north and use one of the bridges crossing to Puerto Madero.

Museo de la Inmigración

Antiguo Hotel de Inmigrantes, Avenida Antártida Argentina 1355, y Avenida de los Inmigrantes (4317 0285). Bus 6, 20. **Open** 10am-5pm Mon-Fri; 11am-6pm Sat, Sun. **Admission** free; suggested contribution AR$1. **Map** p277 E8.

Reserva Ecológica Costanera Sur

Avenida Tristán Achaval Rodríguez 1550, entre Brasil y Estados Unidos (4893 1588/0800 444 5343 freephone). Bus 2,4. **Open** *April-Oct* 8am-6pm Tue-Sun; *Nov-March* 8am-7pm Tue-Sun. **Guided tours** (Spanish) 10.30am, 3.30pm Sat, Sun. **Admission** free. **Map** p276 B8/C8.

Puerto Madero: BA's posh postcard to the world. *See p90*.

Costanera Norte

North of town, skirting the Aeroparque Jorge Newbery – the city airport that runs the length of Palermo – is a traditional promenade. One of the few places where the mud-coloured river laps close to the land, the paved thoroughfare contains numerous restaurants and is thronged on Sundays with anglers, walkers and *mate*-supping, picnic-eating day-trippers. Cyclists slalom through the crowds, though a new bike path should ease congestion. The main road – Avenida Costanera Rafael Obligado – hums with traffic heading out of the city, but at least you can turn your head and watch yachts gliding across the water. The city's beach clubs, where thousands go to melt during the hot months, dot the avenue. The Boeings zooming overhead make the noise pollution almost comic, but it's dramatic in an urban jetsetter kind of way.

At the southern end of the airport is the chalet-style **Club de Pescadores**, a private fishing club of which Carlos Gardel was once a member. The pier is for the club's anglers, but visitors can dine in the airy restaurant, accessed via the oak and marble entrance hall. North of the airport is wacky religious theme park **Tierra Santa** (*see* **The belief business**).

On the final northern curve of the Costanera Norte, near the Ciudad Universitaria, the **Parque de la Memoria** is being developed in remembrance of Argentinian victims of human rights violations. Due for completion in 2005, the park's central work will be the Monumento a las Víctimas del Terrorismo de Estado. Designed as an open wound on a barren hill, the monument will contain stone tablets bearing the names of Argentina's 'disappeared', many of whom were thrown to their deaths in the adjacent river. The first stage, the Plaza de Acceso, including works by American sculptors Dennis Oppenheim and William Tucker, is open to the public from 10am to 8pm daily. The information centre and website (www.parque delamemoria.org.ar) have progress updates.

For a boat trip along this part of the river, head to Puerto Madero's Dársena Norte (Northern Harbour), from where the **Galileo** (www.galileobuenosaires.com.ar) makes a two-hour tour on weekends; tickets AR$10-$25.

The belief business

Heralded by its creators as the world's 'first religious theme park', and a chance 'to visit Jerusalem all year round', Tierra Santa has become one of BA's most popular attractions since opening at the turn of the millennium.

Taking Argentinians' affinity for kitsch to a whole new, celestial level, this Holy Land experience begins with a son-et-lumière extravaganza celebrating the Nativity. As the Angel of the Annunciation descends from a neon-lit sky, locals in Middle Eastern drag shepherd visitors into the 'world's largest manger'. The narrator's voice booms as the drama unfolds on stage. A series of triumphant 'hallelujahs' hail down from the heavens as the act ends and the light show goes into overdrive.

A brief stroll from Bethlehem to Jerusalem follows; thankfully this Holy Land offers a more comfortable pilgrimage than the real thing. Within its confines you can sip a Coke in Baghdad Café, have your photo taken in a mock-up mosque or take in a belly-dancing show. Visit the Wailing Wall, where the faithful slip notes in between the polystyrene bricks or witness the Last Supper, 'the most famous dinner in history'.

Alternatively, be led by a guide in robe and sandals, loudspeaker in hand, down suitably baptised streets on tours detailing the life and teachings of Jesus. See Lazarus brought back from the dead on Carpenter Street and watch out for the plotting Pharisees and scribes seated beneath the fibreglass palms on Gentile Street and Ark Passage.

The park's pièce de résistance is the Resurrection – every half hour! A giant Christ rises from the bowels of Mount Golgotha to choral music, more jazzy lighting effects and the earnest gaze of believers below. It's all as tacky as hell, but the local faithful love it.

Tierra Santa

Avenida Costanera Rafael Obligado 5790 (4784 9551/www.tierrasanta-bsas.com.ar). Bus 33, 37, 42, 160. **Open** *May-Nov* 9am-9pm Fri; 11am-10.30pm Sat, Sun. *Dec-Apr* 5.30-11.30pm Fri; 3-11.30pm Sat, Sun. **Guided tours** (Spanish) every 20mins. **Admission** AR$7-$8; AR$4-$5 3-11s. **Credit** MC, V. **Map** p281 N7/N8.
Last entry to the park is two hours before closing time.

Further Afield

Wild west or tamed north – take your pick.

Though a journey beyond the centre takes you through barrio after barrio of unchanging urban sprawl, one or two attractions tempt visitors further afield. The northern neighbourhood of Belgrano hides historical and art museums, while Zona Norte offers you the chance to rub shoulders with Buenos Aires high society while enjoying a spot of aquatic diversion; and out in the west by the cattle market, an urban rodeo draws in the tourists every Sunday.

Belgrano & Núñez

From the north–south downtown axis, all roads initially lead west, but Avenidas Santa Fe, Córdoba and Corrientes eventually fan out to the smarter north-western neighbourhoods in the conurbation of Belgrano. Those who live there rave about it, but it's essentially a residential and commercial district. Named after independence hero General Manuel Belgrano, it was originally a city in its own right, but its incorporation into the capital in 1887 turned the area into a des res option for affluent *porteños*. Though the Subte from town gets you there in a matter of minutes, it still feels like a separate town and its main thoroughfare, Avenida Cabildo, is as important and as horribly busy as any downtown.

The best bits of Belgrano are a block from the commercial epicentre; the two museums on Plaza General Belgrano are definitely worth a visit. The **Museo de Arte Español** (*see p94*) is housed in the neo-colonial mansion that once belonged to wealthy Uruguayan exile Enrique Larreta. His varied, valuable collection, including Renaissance and modern Spanish art, is set among stunning furniture, tapestries and silverware. Equally attractive are the gardens, a riot of flowering and climbing plants skirting a large native *ombú* tree.

Across the road is the **Museo Histórico Sarmiento** (*see p94*), dedicated to one of America's greatest educators, Domingo Sarmiento, Argentinian president from 1868 to 1874. He was also a writer; his major work, *Facundo*, was a treatise on the need for Argentinians to stop being gauchos. The museum, housed in a neo-classical building that once served as Belgrano's city hall, contains documents, old books and household objects gathered by the liberal thinker in his travels.

Juramento Street runs north to the *barrancas* (cliffs) bordering the Belgrano C railway station (on the Mitre line from Retiro). On and around Arribeños, running parallel to the northbound railway line, is BA's diminutive Chinatown, populated by mainland Chinese and especially Taiwanese immigrants, who arrived in several waves after World War II. Restaurants and specialist supermarkets add a hint of Asian exoticism to this very European-style city. At Chinese New Year (*see p164*), the community takes its celebrations on to the streets in style.

Nearby, at O'Higgins 2390, is the **Museo Casa de Yrurtia** (*see p94*), the home of sculptor Rogelio Yrurtia (1879-1950) and a joy to visit as much for the beautiful white house and lush garden as for the small sculptures and casts of major works. You'll see many of his notable creations dotted around the city.

Avenida Cabildo runs on into Núñez, which borders BA province. Again, this is largely a residential district, with the smartest houses encircling the huge 100,000-spectator **Estadio Monumental** (*see p199*), home to River Plate Football Club and used in the '78 World Cup – which Argentina won amid rumours of bribery and protests about atrocities being committed under military dictator Videla. Nearby, at

Top five Churches

Basílica de Santo Domingo
Shelled by the English invaders, and later a hospital for the defeated. See p68.

Catedral de San Isidro
Neo-Gothic glory in the upscale suburbia of Zona Norte. See p96.

Catedral Metropolitana
Worship central, where the Liberator rests in peace. See p57.

Nuestra Señora de Pilar
Simple, elegant church on Spanish colonial lines for the Recoleta gentry. See p78.

Iglesia Ortodoxa Rusa
Gloriously, garishly incongruous onion domes at Parque Lezama. See p71.

Avenida del Libertador 8000-8500, is the Escuela Mecánica de la Armada, the country's most notorious torture centre and death camp of the 1970s. Proposals to raze the building have been blocked since 2001, when the Supreme Court ruled that its demolition would be illegal on the grounds that evidence might get 'lost' among the ruins.

Flanking Nuñez is Saavedra, where Parque Saavedra and Parque Sarmiento provide urban dwellers with cleaner air and greenery. The **Museo Histórico Cornelio de Saavedra** (*listings below*) at the western limit of Crisólogo Larralde, located in the former residence of Luis María Saavedra (descendant of the museum's namesake, one of the heroes of Argentinian independence), is surrounded by a park that used to be the family *chacra* (smallholding). In addition to 18th- and 19th-century furniture, silverware and arms, the museum records daily life and highlights the fashions used in the old city, including the oversized *peinetones* (decorative combs) worn by well-to-do ladies in the early 19th century to remind admirers, including a young Darwin, that they were every bit as voguish as their Spanish peers.

Avenida General Paz is the throbbing highway that divides the the capital from Buenos Aires province. It runs from the river's edge at Núñez in a huge loop round the city to Villa Riachuelo in the far west. Designated as the city limit in 1887, it has since been invoked by non-*porteños* as a symbolic divide and provincial protesters have regularly reminded the higher-earning, easier-living urbanites that 'Argentina doesn't end at General Paz.'

Museo de Arte Español Enrique Larreta

Juramento 2291, y Vuelta de Obligado (4783 2640/ 4784 4040). Subte D, Juramento/60, 152 bus. **Open** *Jan* 3-8pm Wed-Sun. *Feb-Dec* 2-8pm Mon, Wed-Sun. **Guided tours** (Spanish) 4pm, 5.30pm Sun. **Admission** AR$1. Free Thur. **No credit cards. Map** p281 N5.
On the first Sat of the month there are guided tours of the gardens, at 3.30pm and 5.30pm.

Museo Casa de Yrurtia

O'Higgins 2390, y Blanco Encalada (4781 0385). Bus 29, 59, 60, 152. **Open** 1-7pm Tue-Fri; 3-7pm Sun. **Admission** AR$1; free concessions. Free Tue. **No credit cards. Map** p281 O5.

Museo Histórico Cornelio de Saavedra

Crisólogo Larralde 6309, y Constituyentes (4572 0746). Train to Villa Urquiza, then bus 176/28, 110, 111, 176 bus. **Open** 10am-6pm Tue-Fri; 10am-8pm Sat, Sun. **Guided tours** (Spanish & English) by arrangement Sat, Sun. **Admission** AR$1; free under-12s. Free Wed. **No credit cards.**

Museo Histórico Sarmiento

Juramento 2180, entre Cuba y Arcos (4783 7555). Subte D, Juramento/60, 68, 152 bus. **Open** *Museum* Apr-Dec 2-7pm Tue-Fri; 3-7pm Sun. Jan-Mar 2-7pm Mon-Fri. *Library* Feb-Dec 2-6pm Mon-Fri. **Guided tours** (Spanish) *Apr-Dec* 4pm Sun. **Admission** AR$1. Free Thur. **No credit cards. Map** p281 N5

Mataderos & Liniers

In the far west, the barrios get noticeably poorer, with occasional shanty towns dotting the gloomscape of high-rise 'mono-blocks'. People tend to be friendlier and calmer in the outer reaches, but some streets are dodgy and night strolls are not recommended. This is definitely the case at the outer city limits in the barrio of Mataderos, named after its slaughterhouses and formerly known as Nueva Chicago for the cattle carnage theme it shares with the Windy City.

On Sundays (Saturday evenings in summer), the place is brightened up by a rural-style fête, the **Feria de Mataderos** (*see p95*). Gauchos show off their skills with guitars and horses, and day trippers indulge in country food and browse round the predominantly gaucho-themed flea market, set up at the junction of Avenida de los Corrales and Lisandro de la Torre. Examples of *fileteada*, the colourful Argentinian lettering craft, are visible on the walls around the market and one stall sells examples. Restaurants lay out tables under the arcade of the 100-year-old administration building of the **Mercado Nacional de Hacienda** (www.mercadode liniers.com.ar), a massive livestock market where cows and sheep are corralled for auction (the market is still very much alive, but there are no auctions on Sundays, so you can eat a steak without feeling too guilty). Folk bands perform on a small central stage and locals join in the *chacareras* country dance. On the southern spoke of Lisandro de la Torre, brilliant horsemen take each other on at spearing the *sortija* – a small ring dangling on a ribbon – while standing high on galloping *criollo*-breed horses.

The excellent **Museo Criollo de los Corrales** (*see p95*) – the entrance is beneath the same arcade as the market – exhibits farming implements and country artefacts, along with cartoons by Argentina's most famous painter of gaucho life, Florencio Molina Campos and a reconstruction of a *pulpería* (rural bar/grocer's store). It's only open on Sundays.

In nearby Liniers, another barrio associated with the meat trade, the country's second most important saint (after the Virgin of Luján) has his shrine. San Cayetano, a 15th-century Venetian priest, is the patron of bread and work, to whom proletarian pilgrims flock each month (*see p163* **Waiting for a miracle**).

Feria de Mataderos

*Lisandro de la Torre y Avenida de Los Corrales
(information Mon-Fri 4374 9664/Sun 4687 5602).
Bus 55, 80, 92, 126.* **Open** *Jan-Mar* 6pm-1am Sat.
Apr-Dec 10am-9pm Sun. **Admission** free.

Museo Criollo de los Corrales

*Avenida de los Corrales 6436, y Lisandro de la Torre
(4687 1949). Bus 55, 80, 92, 126.* **Open** *Mar-Dec*
noon-6.30pm Sun. **Closed** Jan, Feb. **Guided tours**
(Spanish) by arrangement. **Admission** AR$1; free
concessions. **No credit cards**.

Zona Norte

Originally home to the grand *quintas* (or
summer houses) of BA's 19th-century
aristocracy, the riverside neighbourhoods
of Zona Norte, stretching from Olivos to San
Isidro, still exude exclusivity – elegant abodes,
private country clubs and a wealthy minority
renowned for it's love of the 'upper class'
sports of rugby, windsurfing and yachting.

To lord it with the privileged or simply to
enjoy the river life, take the **Tren de la Costa**
(*see p168*), which skirts the River Plate all the
way up to Tigre. The train departs from Olivos'
Maipú station, and three blocks from here is La
Quinta Presidencial, the presidential residence.
The *quinta's* main entrance is at the intersection
of Maipú and Libertador, but its grounds cover
nine blocks; it's so big that ex-President Carlos
Menem kept a private zoo here. Views of the
residence are obscured by tall perimeter walls.

For dramatic vistas head towards the river,
to **Puerto Olivos**, situated between Corrientes
and Alberdi streets. This private yacht club's
200-metre-long (656-foot) public pier offers a
stunning panorama spanning the River Plate
and BA's city skyline to the south.

Windsurfers and kiteboarders should hop
off at Barrancas Station – serving the barrios of
both Martínez and Acassuso – five minutes up
the line from Olivos. The **Perú Beach** complex
opposite the station (*see p202*) has numerous
wet and dry sports activities and along with
Club Social bar and restaurant next door are
popular places to hang out. These areas are
favourites with kite-flyers and rollerbladers
too. For a swampy alternative to the trendy
vibe, try Acassuso's **Reserva Ecológica**

Sightseeing

Urban cowboys:
the **Feria de
Mataderos**.
See p94.

Catedral de San Isidro.

(*listings below*) – habitat to over 200 animal species – including snakes and iguanas.

Far removed from nature, but perfect for shopaholics, is Martínez's **Unicenter** shopping mall (Paraná y Panamericana, Martínez, 4733 1130, www.unicenter.com.ar), Argentina's biggest. For dining, check out the riverside bars or Acassuso's strip on Avenida del Libertador, between Roque Saénz Peña and Almafuerte.

Another eating strip, whose restaurants include Mexican eaterie María Felix (*see p119*), traditional Almacén Popular Argentino (*see p102*) and numerous *purrillas*, is developing on Dardo Rocha, which runs inland alongside the grassy expanses of the **Hipódromo de San Isidro** racetrack (*see p199*) and the Jockey Club. Funky menswear boutique Etiqueta Negra (*see p149*) is also upping this strip's hip factor.

Sticking to the coastal train, the next stop is San Isidro, the most exclusive, and enchanting, of all the riverside neighbourhoods. Highlights are dotted around the main square, Plaza Mitre, located in front of the station and home to an artisans' fair every Sunday. At the square's far end is the towering, neo-Gothic **Catedral de San Isidro**, home to excellent programmes of classical music (*see p188*). Situated opposite are the area's tourist office and the **Museo del Rugby** (*listings below*), where the toothless and cauliflower-eared, but wonderfully humorous, Horacio Cufre shows visitors around. Located on the same corner is the **Museo Biblioteca y Archivo Histórico Municipal** (*listings below*), a colonial-era building housing exhibits relating to the area's rich history.

Beccar Varela, one of several cobbled streets wending from Plaza Mitre, leads visitors to the **Mirador de los Tres Ombúes**, which offers breathtaking views across the Rio de la Plata to the lush islands of Tigre's delta. This hidden lookout point is surrounded by some of the most sumptuous summer abodes of Argentina's upper-class. Hummingbirds, flowering jasmine and fragrant orange groves complete an idyllic scene.

Three blocks east is the **Museo Histórico Municipal Juan Martín de Pueyrredón** (*listings below*), the Spanish-colonial style *quinta* of one of the heroes of Argentinian independence. Its glorious gardens include the carob tree under which Generals Pueyrredón and San Martín sat and compared battle scars while they plotted the defeat of the Spanish.

Another mansion where ghosts of the past linger is the masterfully eclectic **Villa Ocampo** (Elortondo 1811, y Uriburu), former residence of literary luminary and arts patron Victoria Ocampo. The guest list at Ocampo's parties here read like a who's who of the literary world, and included the likes of Borges, Albert Camus, Aldous Huxley and Grahame Greene. Partially destroyed by fire in 2003, after three decades of neglect, this national monument and UNESCO protected site is finally being restored as a museum and cultural centre (to open late 2004).

Museo Biblioteca y Archivo Histórico Municipal

Avenida del Libertador 16362, San Isidro (4512 3282). Train Mitre or de la Costa to San Isidro/ 60, 168 bus. **Open** *Museum* Feb 8am-3pm Tue, Thur; 2-6pm Sat, Sun. Mar-Dec 8am-noon, 2-6pm Tue, Thur; 2-6pm Sat, Sun. *Library* Feb 10am-3pm Mon-Fri. Mar-Dec 10am-6pm Mon-Fri. **Closed** Jan. **Admission** free.

Museo Histórico Municipal Juan Martín de Pueyrredón

Rivera Indarte 48, y Roque Saéz Peña, San Isidro (4512 3131). Train Mitre or de la Costa to San Isidro/60, 168 bus. **Open** *Feb-Dec* 8am-6pm Tue, Thu; 2-6pm Sat, Sun. **Closed** Jan. **Guided tours** (Spanish) *Garden* 3pm 2nd Sun of mth. *Museum* 4pm Sat, Sun. **Admission** free.

Museo del Rugby

Ituzaigó 608, y Libertador, San Isidro (information 4512 3209/www.museodelrugby.com). Train Mitre or de la Costa to San Isidro/60, 168 bus. **Open** 10am-6pm Tue, Sat, Sun. **Admission** free.

Reserva Ecológica Municipal

Camino de la Ribera, entre López y Planes y Almafuerte, Acassuso (4747 6179/ www.geo cities.com/riberan). Train Mitre or de la Costa to Acassuso/168 bus. **Open** *Jan-Mar, Nov* 9am-7pm daily. *Apr-Oct* 9am-6pm daily. **Guided tours** (Spanish) *Jan-Mar, Nov* 5pm Sat, Sun. *Mar-Oct* 4pm Sat, Sun. **Admission** free.
The reserve closes in heavy rains or high tides.

Eat, Drink, Shop

GRAN BAR
DANZON

RESTAURANT
WINE BAR
COCKTAILS
SUSHI
HAPPY HOUR EVERY DAY
LIVE JAZZ WEDNESDAYS & FRIDAYS

RESERVATIONS 4811- 1108
LIBERTAD 1161

DANZON@GRANBARDANZON.COM.AR
WWW.GRANBARDANZON.COM.AR

OPEN 7 DAYS A WEEK

MONDAY THRU FRIDAY FROM 7 PM
SATURDAY AND SUNDAY FROM 8 PM

WE CLOSE LATE

BAR URIARTE

Almuerce, meriende y cene

Restaurant
Bar
Lunch, afternoon tea & dinner

Happy Hour from 6 pm to 9 pm
Open 7 days a week from 12 pm

Till late

Uriarte 1572   Reservations 4834-6004

uriarte@baruriarte.com.ar   www.baruriarte.com.ar

Restaurants

Meat rules, but only just. BA's food scene is going global.

What's a typical *porteño* meal? Considering the city's immigrant past, it could well consist of a plate of Italian gnocchi served with kosher paella in Arabian seasoning and accompanied by a carafe of French claret – hardly the most appetising prospect. Thank heaven (or the pampas) that when settlers came to Argentina, they brought cows with them, and out of the melting pot came *carne* (steak).

Porteños rank among the world's greatest carnivores and beef plays an important role in the national cuisine and culture (*see p230* **Holy cow**). As succulent as the steaks can be, for too long they were served on chequered tablecloths with metallic cups of rough wine at drab eateries. But thanks to a creative cadre of chefs and restaurateurs returning from abroad over the last decade, the Buenos Aires dining scene is today more diverse than ever.

Consequently, the ubiquitous *parrillas* (steakhouses) have been joined by restaurants, bars and bistros cooking up exotica from Russia, Morocco and Vietnam. Meanwhile, since its appearance in the 1990s, sushi has become almost as commonplace as empanadas, the traditional pastries stuffed with meat, cheese or other fillings. While the bar scene has grown, many places turning out good cocktails and beers also serve great creative food accompanied by a diverse wine list: Milión, Dadá, Lelé de Troya and Via Via are among the best (for all, *see chapter* **Bars, Cafés & Pubs**).

Another encouraging sign: Latin American cuisine is moving out of the Peruvian and Bolivian diners in Abasto to crop up in pan-Latin menus at upscale places like **Sucre** (*see p113*) or **María Fulô** (*see p119*). Although less authentic and costlier than traditional eateries, the proliferation of modern fusion restaurants is staggering, proof that *porteños* are becoming more sophisticated eaters. For the most part, though, dead cow (a *lomo* – tenderloin – in its quintessential form), pizza, pasta and empanadas still dominate a carb-heavy diet.

If the previous decade was about *porteños* opening their palates to the world, the current one is definitely about a rediscovery of their own, long-neglected taste buds. Taking their cue from hordes of foreign tourists, *porteños* are going native. At new thematic restaurants like **Almacén Popular Argentino** (*see p102*) and **Aires de Patagonia** (*see p101*) it's now

possible to indulge in such previously rare – in BA – regional delicacies as Patagonian *ciervo* (venison), smoked *jabalí* (wild boar) and sweetish, white Torrontés wine from Salta.

Mirroring BA's northward development, the bulk of serious dining takes place in Palermo, at gourmet ghettos Palermo Viejo and Las Cañitas. In the past five years they've been transmogrified – often to the dismay of old-time neighbours – from leafy barrios into bustling corridors of fast cars and fusion gastronomy. Still, a few relics of its soon-to-be-bygone past, such as **El Preferido de Palermo** (*see p121*) and **La Casa Polaca** (*see p114*), are thriving on Palermo's newfound popularity.

While each trendy restaurant is busier and more glamorous then the last, quality varies considerably. Another problem is service, which inattentive owners often let slip in their rush for cool informality. Given the huge gap between style and substance, we've selected restaurants based on cuisine, location and price. Our choices reflect where growth has been strongest – in modern and traditional Argentinian cuisine.

If Palermo is where BA's culinary renaissance is taking place, downtown Buenos Aires sticks to tradition. Although many of the Centro's older restaurants have all but given up the ghost – food is overcooked, menus are identical and

Almacén Popular Argentino. *See p102.*

LOMO a sacred word in argentina

avant garde argentine cuisine • special meats • fine wines

4661 costa rica st. - palermo viejo, b.a., argentina - (5411) 4833 3200
e-mail:reservas@restaurantlomo.com.ar / restaurantlomo@arnet.com.ar

SUCRE

Restaurant
Bar
Grill

Open
Monday thru
Sunday

Lunch from
12 pm to
4 pm

Evenings
from 8 pm
till late

Sucre 676   Reservations: 4782-9082
sucre@sucrerestaurant.com.ar   www.sucrerestaurant.com.ar

wines as warm as tea – a few classic venues survive, relying on such staid qualities as good cooking and well-mannered service instead of a flashy decor or belly-button-pierced waitresses. In response to the night-time exodus some of the very best, like the authentically *porteño* **Sabot** (*see p105*), the **Club Danés** (10th Floor, Avenida LN Alem 1074, Retiro, 4312 9266) and **Club Sueco** (5th Floor, Tacuarí 147, Monserrat, 4334 7813) only open at midday. Others, such as the **Restaurant del Círculo Italiano** (Libertad 1264, Recoleta, 4811 1160), **Club del Progreso** (Sarmiento 1334, Tribunales, 4371 5053) or **Club Español** (Bernardo de Irigoyen 180, Monserrat, 4344 4876), have the added attraction of their palatial setting and link to the past as one-time immigrant social clubs.

Helping to revitalise downtown dining are several haute cuisine restaurants in the area's top hotels. Classiest is the Alvear Palace's **La Bourgogne**, one of two Relais Gourmand venues run by chef Jean Paul Bondoux, though elegant **Le Sud**, at Sofitel, is challenging its predominance. Another rival is **Agraz** at Caesar Park (for all, *see p33*). Agraz is chef Germán Martitegui's French fusion compliment to his Nordic-inspired menu at Olsen (*p111; see p115* **Mi Buenos Aires Querido**). Gourmet grandma Ada Concaro is routinely voted BA's best chef, her three-decade old **Tomo I** at the Crowne Plaza Panamericano (*see p35*) the progenitor of the current *cocina de autor* craze.

TIMINGS, PRICES & TIPS

By the standards of London or New York, even BA's most expensive restaurants are a steal. A typical three-course meal costs around AR$40, AR$20-$40 more for a decent Malbec, the crown jewel of Argentina's increasingly prestigious wine selection (*see p102* **The wine box**).

Even if a Palermo dinner is beyond your budget you can enjoy fixed-lunch specials at many stylish bistros for a bargain AR$12-$16 – Bar 6, Central, Social Paraiso and Abril are among the best. If you do max out your credit card there are still plenty of cheap-eat alternatives, from no-frills *parrillas*, where a *bife* goes for about AR$5, to all-you-can-eat buffets known as *tenedor libre* ('free fork') restaurants.

Porteños eat late, uncorking the *vino* around 10pm or later – finding a restaurant open before 8pm is a challenge. A ten per cent *propina* (tip) is the norm and will be gratefully pocketed by underpaid waiters, who are known as *mozos* (male) and *mozas* (female). If you need service just raise your hand; for the *cuenta* (bill) scribble a cheque in the air. To order, it's worth knowing a few words of Spanish, though many restaurants now offer English menus. For restaurant vocabulary, *see p108* **The menu**.

The best Restaurants

... for a fashionable feast
Central (*p108*), **La Corte** (*p109*), **Dashi** (*p118*), **Filo** (*p117*), **Sucre** (*p113*).

... for a romantic rendezvous
Abril (*p107*), **Thymus** (p113).

... for a starlit supper
Giulia (*p117*), **Lomo** (*p111*), **Olsen** (*p111*).

... for a taste of the old country
La Casa Polaca (*p114*), **El Preferido de Palermo** (*p121*).

... for bargain basement *bife*
Manolo (*p105*), El Obrero (*p105*).

... for border crossing
Al Andaluz (*p120*), **Green Bamboo** (*p120*), **El Kozako** (*p114*), **Sudestada** (*p120*).

... for *haute* cow
La Cabaña (*p102*), **Cabaña Las Lilas** (*p102*).

Argentinian

Traditional

Traditional meateries are *parrillas* or *asadores*. The former grill meats and the latter crucify them around a fire. As well as barbecued meat and offal, battered hake, breaded veal *milanesas* and chicken are staples, with stuffed tomatoes, salads, chips and grilled provolone cheese (*provoleta*) for vegetarians. Other restaurants specialise in empanadas, corn and pork-based *locro* stew and smoked meats from the interior.

Aires de Patagonia

Alicia Moreau de Justo 1798, entre Humberto 1° y Carlos Calvo, Puerto Madero (4315 2151). Bus 4, 130, 152. **Open** noon-2am daily. **Main courses** AR$17-$30. **Credit** AmEx, DC, MC, V. **Map** p276 C6.
Profiting from the craze for all things Patagonian, rustic tables made of *lenga* wood, volcanic stones and Mapuche handicrafts (all for sale) decorate this huge chalet-style restaurant. Martin Repetto, executive chef at Bariloche's famed Llao-Llao Hotel, has designed an exquisite menu full of regional delicacies largely unknown in BA, including grilled quail breast, venison and stuffed rabbit. Better known plates like *cordero patagónico* (lamb), Tierra del Fuego king crab and meaty rainbow trout also appear. After the kitchen has closed, a *tabla* of smoked meats, organic wild musrooms and cheeses can be ordered until 2am to enjoy with rich microbrewed El Bolsón beer or a bottle of Río Negro red.

Eat, Drink, Shop

The wine box

Wine comes pouring into Buenos Aires from the Andean regions, especially Mendoza and the North-west, but also from as far south as Patagonia. There has been viticulture since colonial times but as recently as the '80s wine was well below export quality (hence Chile's high profile) and the old-fashioned woody Malbecs were only drunk at home, over dinner with a shot of soda to calm it down.

Over the last decade, quality has soared and volume has risen to meet national and international demand. Major winemakers like Catena, Weinert, Bianchi and Trapiche have brought in top experts from France, Spain and New World regions to refit their vineyards, enabling them to enter – and win– international competitions. On the back of the culinary revolution in the capital, restaurants began to stock better bottles and wine bars, or *vinotecas*, sprung up in several barrios.

The story of Malbec – as the definitive beef accompaniment – mirrors the radical change in local wine culture. Originally from Bordeaux, but a grape that wine critics agree takes best to Mendoza's dry, high-desert terrain, ten years ago it was mixed to produce plonk *vino tinto* (red wine) for *damajuanas* (jugs). When you were lucky enough to find a stand-alone variety it was usually heavy with oak and an obese amount of body. As you can't visit BA without indulging in this pungent red, you'll be glad to discover that even AR$30 bottles – the San Telmos, Nortons, Santa Julias, Trapiches and Graffignas – are now very, very palatable. The Catena Zapata 1999 Malbec is princely – but expect to blow around AR$200 for the pleasure. In wine annals, 1999 was a good year across the board so keep an eye open for the odd, overlooked bottle.

There are also several fine Tempranillos and Cabernet Sauvignons. While most of the old whites (*blancos*) were only a tad better than German mass-market offerings and have yet to attain Aussie standards, the Sauvignon Blancs (try Rutini) are often light and crisp and the Chardonnays are improving all the time. Argentina is an acclaimed producer of the sweetish Torrontés – an acquired taste, with lemon and pepper in the better varietals. There are many subtler, plumier wines around. Bodegas Benegas is a boutique winery that is a model for the revolution in

Almacén Popular Argentino

Dardo Rocha 1402, y Pringles, Martínez (4793 9222). Train to San Isidro & taxi/60 bus. **Open** 9am-2am daily. **Main courses** AR$17-$24. **Set menu** (lunch only) AR$10-$12 Mon-Fri; AR$20 Sat-Sun. **Credit** AmEx, DC, MC, V.

If you want traditional Argentinian cuisine, but are all barbecued-out, then this attractively converted stud building is your place. A compact menu changes every two months, but always offers *criollo* standards like ravioli, risotto, chicken and – if you must – steak. The speciality is meat and cheese platters (ideal as a shared starter) designed around Argentina's regions: *norteño*, *porteño*, Patagónico, the house special (Almacén Popular) or create your own. A real *almacén* (general store) sells Argentinian delicacies to go.

La Brigada

Estados Unidos 465, entre Bolívar y Defensa, San Telmo (4361 4685). Bus 22, 24, 29, 126. **Open** noon-3pm, 8pm-midnight Tue-Sun. **Main courses** AR$30-$35. **Credit** AmEx, DC, MC, V. **Map** p276 C6.

Parrillas of the cheap and cheerful variety are a plague in San Telmo, but this one is a cut above most for steak, offal, wine and general ambience. For about AR$35 per person you get grilled cheese and a rump to share, loads of salad, some sausage and black pudding, a fair bottle of red, and a fruit salad with ice-cream. Elegant in an old-fashioned way, this split-level meat house is sober and serene. If you prefer a livelier (and cheekier) scene follow the herds of tourists to El Desnivel at Defensa 855 (4300 9081). **Other locations:** Peña 2475, Recoleta (4800 1110); Demaria 4701, Palermo (4777 1414).

La Cabaña

Rodríguez Peña 1967, entre Posadas y Alvear, Recoleta (4814 0001/www.lacabanabuenosaires. com.ar). Bus 17, 61, 67, 92, 93. **Open** 9am-12.30am daily. **Main courses** AR$38-$45. **Credit** AmEx, DC, MC, V. **Map** p278 G7.

After a US$6 million investment, the legendary supper club of BA's oligarchy reopened its doors in 2003 in a restored Recoleta mansion. Although management and clientele are mostly foreign, the stuffed cows, rustic decor, and elaborate woodwork on its four floors were rescued from the original location. Also left in tact was the famed Grand Baby Beef, at 1.5kg (3.3lbs) and 10cm (4in), it's a fitting tribute to beef bravado. More museum than mere steakhouse, the steep prices reflect the privilege of admission.

Cabaña Las Lilas

Alicia Moreau de Justo 516, entre Corrientes y Perón, Puerto Madero (reservations 4313 1336/ 4343 6404/www.laslilas.com.ar). Subte B, LN Alem/ 62, 93, 130, 152 bus. **Open** noon-3.30pm, 7.30pm-midnight daily. **Main courses** AR$34-$53. **Credit** AmEx, V. **Map** p277 D8.

vino argentino. Look out also for Carmelo Patti, Estancia Ancón and Finca Los Leiva.

Far from the wine-growing regions, wine tasting in BA means a mix of bar hopping, visiting smarter restaurants and, before leaving, hitting one of the wine shops to get a top-value case of your fave. For the true Dionysian, there are sommelier courses – the Club del Vino is a lovely place to learn. All the best hotel restaurants have expansive wine lists – check out the Alvear Palace's lovely basement bodega – as do Gran Bar Danzón (*see p109*) and Cavas y Cuevas (*see p133*).

Even ordinary-looking *parrillas* now boast intelligent wine lists. If length is proof of clientele, then **Cabaña Las Lilas** (*see p102*) epic viticultural poem wins the prize. If you want to try the new breed of Patagonian wines from Río Negro province, restaurant **Aires de Patagonia** (*see p101*) stocks brands Infinitus and Marcus.

Be careful when scanning wine lists. Mid range wines like those by Finca La Anita, Weinert and Felipe Rutini that cost, say AR$35 in a store, can go for AR$100 or more at a restaurant. Although Nicolás Catena's name is gold in international wine circles, he markets his lush Malbecs and blends under several brands, including Angélica Zapata, Saint Felicien, Alamos and Escorihuela Gascón.

Shopping for wine is a cinch. The **Winery** and **Ligier** are two highly professional wine chains, and a number of smaller shops (often with a few tables, such as **La Finca** – *see p134*) are spread throughout the city (*see chapter **Shopping**). For just AR$6, you can sample a glass of quality wine unlikely to be on sale anywhere else in the world. Just learn some basic wine words – *vaso* is glass, *botella* is bottle, *seco* is dry, *dulce* is sweet and *más* is more – and indulge.

Argentina's premier steakhouse got a full-page kiss-up from *New York Times* roving gourmet Johnny Apple – 'nuff said. But it's not just the melt-in-your-mouth, slow-cooked steaks from beef baron and owner Octavio Caraballo's prize-winning Angus and Hereford farm that keep the reservation-less masses salivating at the bar for an hour on Mondays. Outstanding service, rare for a restaurant in Puerto Madero, and two sommeliers on hand to help sift through the encyclopaedic wine list, also help justify the high prices (AR$36 for a *bife de chorizo*). If the wait is too long, next door's La Caballeriza (4514 4444) is a more affordable, but still classy alternative, dressed up as a gaucho's barn.

La Cabrera

Cabrera 5099, y Thames, Palermo Viejo (4831 7002). Bus 39, 55. **Open** 7pm-1am Mon; 9am-1am Tue-Sun. **Main courses** AR$14-$18. **Credit** AmEx, DC, MC, V. **Map** p279 J4.

Although located in Palermo Viejo, this modern take on the traditional *parrilla* hasn't completely succumbed to the barrio's Soho-style pretensions. In an attractive corner site, which used to be a general store, professional staff serve extra large portions of expertly prepared beef, grilled with a dash of rosemary or sage. Unconventional but still all-natural items like goat's cheese and roasted almonds make great accompaniments. Outside tables are a plus.

Cumaná

Rodriguez Pena 1149, entre Santa Fe y Arrenales, Recoleta (4813 9207). Bus 10, 37, 39, 101, 124, 152. **Open** noon-1am daily. **Main courses** AR$5-$11. **No credit cards. Map** p278 G6.

Pizzas, calzones, *locro*, *cazuelas* (casseroles) and empanadas – all come served piping hot out of this lively joint's trademark *horno al barro*, the domed adobe oven used in the north. Despite the rustic tinge, Cumaná's public is pure Recoleta and there's an unmistakable girls-night-out feel to the place. The mince and pumpkin *pastel* (soufflé) is unforgettable, and at AR$6, an incredible bargain. Kids of all ages are invited to scribble with crayons on their paper placemats. Expect to wait for a table.

El Estanciero

Báez 202, y Argibel, Las Cañitas (4899 0951). Bus 15, 29, 59, 60, 64. **Open** noon-4pm, 8.30pm-2am daily. **Main courses** AR$12-$15. **Credit** AmEx, MC, V. **Map** p279 K6.

Not your typical gaucho grill. Large groups keep returning to this chic, mod *parrilla* because of its airy, covered terrace and its simple but sure-footed grill, arguably the best in Las Cañitas. A gentle Bob Marley soundtrack keeps the mood laid-back, but the AR$18 *bife de chorizo* is of the same, export quality found at formal Puerto Madero steakhouses. If nouveau barbecue isn't your style, walk a few blocks

SUDESTADA

SUDESTE ASIATICO RESTAURANT

FINEST ASIAN FOOD IN TOWN
MON-SAT DAY+NIGHT
GUATEMALA+FITZROY BUENOSAIRES
47763777 SUDESTADA@FIBERTEL.COM.AR

bar

comedor 6

armenia 1676. 48 33 68 07
buenosaires (1414)
barseis@hotmail.com

FILO   10 years of pleasure and folly
"*filo* is one big party"

San Martín 975 | Buenos Aires | Reservations: (5411) 4311-0312 / 1871
provision@filo-ristorante.com | www.filo-ristorante.com

to Bastián (Arévalo 3056, 4771 5555), where master *parrillero* Martín Milesi cooks up quality steak, over smokier *quebracho* ironwood, for a better price.

El Establo

Paraguay 489, y San Martín, Retiro (4311 1639).
Subte C, San Martín/62, 93, 106, 132, 152 bus.
Open 7am-2am daily. **Main courses** AR$18-$25.
Credit AmEx, DC, MC, V. **Map** p277 E8.
Happy diners throng to this brightly lit Ibero-Argentinian classic: locals come back again and again, mixing with tables of tourists from nearby hotels. It's also a very comfortable spot for eating solo, with a cheerful band of old-time waiters for company. Vast steaks come off the *parrilla* perfectly, and there's a wide range of pizzas, salads, fish and pasta too, plus classic Spanish tapas of *jamón*, peppers and tortilla. Desserts are sinfully big.

Manolo

Bolívar 1502, y Brasil, San Telmo (4307 8743). Bus
10, 24, 29, 39. **Open** 7am-1am daily. **Main courses**
AR$3.50-AR$30. **No credit cards.** Map p276 C5.
The strip lighting, propeller-size fans and football memorabilia tell only half the story. If this old world *bodegón* lacks finesse, it more than makes up for it with the best value menu in town: the half portion of rump steak costs AR$3, the *platos del día* start at AR$4, and the delicious *flan con dulce de leche y crema*, all of AR$2.50. Fellow clients might be sellers of *Hecho en Buenos Aires* (BA's version of the *Big Issue*) or neighbourhood families who have realised that eating here is as cheap as cooking at home. Amid the action, owner Manolo shuffles around, badgering waiters and bantering with diners.

Miramar

Avenida San Juan 1999, y Sarandí, San Cristóbal
(4304 4261). Subte E, Entre Ríos/12, 37, 53, 126 bus.
Open noon-11pm Mon, Wed-Sun. **Main courses**
AR$12-$25. **Credit** AmEx, MC, V. **Map** p277 D4.
Beloved by its barrio, Miramar boasts a well-stocked wine store and an unpretentious – but serious – eaterie with super-amiable waiters. For lunch, try rabbit in white wine, a perfect Spanish tortilla, frogs' legs, or Spanish-style oysters and shrimps in garlic while listening to the crackly tangos. On Sundays, at 10pm, *bandoneón* virtuoso Julio Pane plays live.

El Obrero

Agustín Caffarena 64, y Pedro de Mendoza, La Boca
(4362 9912). Bus 25, 29, 68, 130. **Open** 9am-3am
Mon-Sat. **Main courses** AR$5-$19. **No credit**
cards. Map p276 A6.
Everyone – from U2's Bono to Wim Wenders – has discovered this museum piece in the heart of the old port (best to come by taxi and with company). The decor is busy with boxing and soccer legends, the paint is peeling, the toilet is a glorified outhouse, but it's still a classic place for long lunches or dinners with a gang of friends. Most people choose from the *parrilla* items listed on the chalkboard, but there are also fair pastas and fish dishes, and a selection of old-style desserts such as *sopa inglesa* (like trifle).

La Paila

Costa Rica 4848, entre Thames y Borges, Palermo
Viejo (4833-3599/www.lapaila.folkloreclub.com.ar).
Bus 39, 55. **Open** 4pm-1am Tue-Fri; from 12.30pm
Sat-Sun. **Closed** Jan. **Main courses** AR$4-$12.
Credit AmEx, MC, V. **Map** p279 J4.
A friendly young couple from Catamarca, in north-west Argentina, opened this rustic restaurant in late 2002 to give BA's trendy, global gourmet scene a home-baked option. Andean high plains standards, – spicy *locro*, *humita* corn wraps and empanadas – are filling anytime, but particularly satisfying on Fridays and Saturdays, when La Paila becomes a folk music venue. The legendary Mercedes Sosa was spotted here in 2003, so it must be authentic.

Sabot

25 de Mayo 756, entre Córdoba y Viamonte,
Microcentro (4313 6587). Subte A, Alem/62,
93, 106, 132, 152 bus. **Open** noon-4pm Mon-Fri.
Main course AR$20-$25. **Credit** AmEx, MC, V.
Map p277 E8.
The favourite of Derek Foster, the *Buenos Aires Herald* newspaper's portly food critic, is the closest it gets to an authentic *porteño* cuisine that doesn't simply follow the tried-and-tested formula of the neighbourhood steakhouse. The congenial hospitality comes from Spanish-born owner Ramón Couñago, the menu of delicately prepared meat and fish classics (including baked kid and a perfect salmon kebab) the work of Italian partner Francesco de Nicola, and the restaurant's name is Dutch for clog. From its staid white-cloth interior, barely changed since its 1970 opening, you'd never know this is one of the most sought-after tables by BA's top suits. Open for lunch only.

El Sanjuanino

Posadas 1515, y Callao, Recoleta (4804 2909/4805
2683). Bus 10, 17, 124, 130. **Open** noon-1am daily.
Main courses AR$5-$30. **Credit** AmEx, MC, V.
Map p278 G7.
This four-decades-old establishment is a must if you want to try empanadas (AR$1.60 each), the semicircular pies that formed the backbone of Argentinian fast food, until burger chains arrived. The *locro* is a

Old world charm aplenty at **Miramar**.

LA MEJOR CARNE DEL MUNDO

LA CABAÑA

Steak out

The legendary steakhouse famous since the early 30´s
re-opened by Orient Express Hotels.
Monday to Sunday 9:00 to 12:30 am

ORIENT-EXPRESS
HOTELS

Rodriguez Peña 1967 . Buenos Aires . Argentina . Tel/Fax: +5411 4814 0001
www.lacabanabuenosaires.com . info@lacabanabuenosaires.com.ar

A pizza the action

Beef may be every *porteño*'s preferred chow, but thanks to Argentina's Italian heritage, pizza is the daily staple for most. Walk ten minutes in any direction and you'll find a bland and basic Ugi's or Zapi's franchise advertising the inflation-proof, AR$3.90 Grande Muzzarella. Although it tastes more like cardboard, it's probably the city's most effective barricade against all-out hunger.

Not that pizza is strictly working-class fare. A flamboyant Carlos Menem took pizza eating to a new, tasteless level when, as president, he served slices of *muzza* over a bit of bubbly to the likes of Madonna and Claudia Schiffer. In contrast to those famed '*pizza con champán*' parties – symbolic of the frivolity of the '90s – junk food was becomng the mainstay of a lost 'pizza, beer and smokes' generation, as described in the 1997 film of the same name.

Though less famous than Chicago-style deep-dish or stuffed Sicilian, the *porteño* slice is just as authentic – and tasty – a local creation. In general, pizzas are light on sauce but drooping in greasy layers of cheese and toppings – to avoid a big dry cleaning bill make like the locals and use a knife and fork.

The three main types of pizzas are the crispy, thin *a la piedra* (heated directly on the floor of a stone oven), the middleweight *media masa* and doughy *al molde*. A myriad of toppings, everything from ketchup and mayo-based *salsa golf* and palm hearts to jalapeños and shrimp, reflects the city's multicultural flavour. Two pizza by-products are the *fugazza*, a white pizza base topped only with oregano and browned onions, and *fugazetta*, the same but with cheese. Another specialty is *faina*, a baked, chickpea pizza accessory usually eaten over a slice.

Pizza is to Buenos Aires what the baguette is to Paris and finding a slice is easy, though connoisseurs prefer traditional parlours. One of the most historic, from the barrio where pizza was introduced, is **Banchero** (Suárez 396, La Boca, 4301 1406, and branches), opened in 1932 by Genovese Juan Banchero, credited with inventing the *fugazetta*. At **Pizzeria Guerrín** (Corrientes 1368, Tribunales, 4371 8141) you can lean against the 1927 counter and enjoy a slice of heaven for AR$1.30. Brave souls wash it down with a glass of *moscato*, a sweet wine immortalised in band Memphis's tribute to pizza culture 'Moscato, pizza y faina.' Two other late-night haunts are **Las Cuartetas** (Corrientes 838, Microcentro, 4326 0171) and **El Cuartito** (Talcahuano 937, Tribunales, 4816 1758).

Even if the venues haven't evolved that much, pizza making has. Amid the hip bars of Las Cañitas, pizzeria **Morelia** (Báez 260, 4772 0329, and branches) attracts an equally fashionable crowd with its house speciality: *pizza a la parrilla*, a mouth-watering creation achieved by slowly melting cheese and thin crust over a barbecue. Two other exceptions are **Pizza Piola** (Libertad 1078, Barrio Norte, 4812 0690) and **Filo** (*see* p117), two lively joints with endless combinations of toppings and bases as waif-like as the hip diners they attract in droves.

Eat, Drink, Shop

perfect winter dish, and has a refreshing bite to it in a *criollo* culture where spices are frowned upon. This branch serves deer and antelope specials, regional fruit-based desserts and fruity sangria.
Other locations: Sánchez de Bustamante 1788, Barrio Norte (4822 8080).

El Trapiche
Paraguay 5599, y Humboldt, Palermo Viejo (4772 7343). Subte D, Palermo/29, 60, 111, 152 bus. **Open** noon-4pm, 8pm-1.30am daily. **Main courses** AR$7-$20. **Credit** AmEx, DC, MC, V. **Map** p279 K5. Surrounded on all sides by fashionably foreign food haunts, El Trapiche is unstintingly Argentinian, unfailingly reliable and always full. The grilled meat is magnificent, from the fillet steaks to what is prob-ably the best pork flank (*matambrito de cerdo*) in town, and the bill reasonable. There's an interesting mid range wine list and the mountainous desserts include the classic Don Pedro (whisky and ice-cream) and hot *sambayón*. The maître d' and waiters are friendly and extremely efficient.

Modern

Abril
Balcarce 722, entre Chile y Pasaje San Lorenzo, San Telmo (4342 8000). Bus 29, 86, 93, 130, 152. **Open** noon-4pm, 8.30pm-midnight Mon-Fri, Sun; noon-4pm, 9pm-2am Sat. **Main courses** AR$10-$20. **Set menus** AR$10 lunch; AR$18 dinner. **Credit** AmEx, DC, MC, V. **Map** p276 C6.

Asian and Argentinian crossover cooking in what is easily San Telmo's swankiest, gourmet destination. A short menu and three-course fixed menu changes daily, but everything is prepared with art and attention to detail. Service is amiable, but the waiters have to wait for master chef Leandro Paino (who trained at Michelin three-starred restaurants in Europe) to deliver, so be patient. A planned 2004 expansion is likely to alter its hideaway setting, ideal for clandestine couples, but prices are to remain affordable. Save room for dessert.

Bar 6

Armenia 1676, entre El Salvador y Honduras, Palermo Viejo (4833 6807). Bus 15, 39, 151, 168. **Open** 8am-3am Mon-Sat. **Main courses** AR$15-$22. **Set menu** (lunch only) AR$14. **Credit** AmEx, MC, V. **Map** p279 J4.

A curved Scandinavian ceiling, cement and brick walls, velvet couches, and a tiny patio create a modern coffee house feel for one of Palermo's most loved hangouts. Brimming most hours of the day and night, a menu of vegetable wok dishes, fusion *bifes* and daily, chalkboard specials is solid and slightly less expensive than nearby bistros of half the quality or funk. By day, browse the newspapers and mags over coffee or juice, while on Thursday to Saturday evenings a DJ spins some tunes.

Bar Uriarte

Uriarte 1572, entre Honduras y Gorriti, Palermo Viejo (4834 6004/www.baruriarte.com.ar). Bus 33, 55, 111. **Open** noon-2.30am daily. **Main courses** AR$16-$23. **Set menu** (lunch only) AR$9 Mon-Fri; AR$18 Sat-Sun. **Credit** AmEx, DC, MC, V. **Map** p279 J4.

From part of the same team behind Sucre comes this less pretentious but still visually and gastronomically impacting eatery. As you walk into the superbly designed interior, past the open kitchen, you'll catch a whiff of chef Paula de Felice's Med-inspired creations. Grab a sofa upfront, or a table past the long bar towards the back patio, and start with a mini *bondiola* (pork sausage) and asparagus pizza cooked in an adobe oven. Sophisticated main dishes include a tender *matambrito* (pork flank) with mango and apple chutney and baked chicken in a thyme, garlic and dry Martini marinade. The happy hour champagne offer is an added treat.

Central

Costa Rica 5644, entre Fitz Roy y Bonpland, Palermo Viejo (4776 7374/www.centralgourmet.com.ar). Bus 39, 93, 111. **Open** 12.30pm-3am Mon-Fri; 10.30am-3am Sat-Sun. **Main courses** $11-$15. **Set menus** (lunch only) AR$12-$16 Mon-Fri; AR$20 Sat-Sun. **Credit** AmEx, DC, MC, V. **Map** p279 J4.

The menu

Basics

Menú/carta menu; **desayuno** breakfast; **almuerzo** lunch; **merienda** afternoon tea/snack (often *mate* and *medialunas*); **cena** dinner; **entrada** entrée; **minutas** short-orders; **plato principal** main course; **postre** dessert; **aceite y vinagre** oil and vinegar; **ajo** garlic; **casero** home-made; **pan** bread; **sopa** soup; **agua** water (**con gas** fizzy, **sin gas** still); **mate/yerba** local herb tea; **te** tea; **vino** wine (**tinto** red, **blanco** white, **de la casa** house).

Cooking styles & techniques

A la parrilla grilled; **al horno** baked; **al vapor** steamed; **asado** grilled; **frito** fried; **hervido** boiled; **picante** spicy/hot; **salteado** sautéed; **jugoso** rare; **a punto** medium rare; **bien cocido** medium to well done; **muy bien cocido** between well done and shoe leather.

Carne y aves (Meat & poultry)

Albóndigas meatballs; **asado** barbecue(d); **asado de tira** or **tira de asado** rack of ribs; **bife de chorizo** rump/sirloin; **bife de costilla** rib; **bife de lomo** tenderloin; **cerdo** pork; **chimi churri** spicy sauce for meat; **chivito** kid; **choripan** spicy sausage sandwich; **chorizo** sausage; **chinchulín** chitterling/intestine; **chuleta** chop; **conejo** rabbit; **cordero** lamb; **entraña** entrail; **hígado** liver; **jamón** ham (**cocido** boiled, **crudo** Parma-style); **lechón** suckling pig; **lengua** tongue; **lomo** tenderloin; **milanesa** breaded cutlet; **mondongo** tripe; **morcilla** blood sausage/black pudding; **molleja** sweetbread; **pancho** hotdog; **parrillada** small table grill; **pato** duck; **pollo** chicken; **riñones** kidneys; **ternera** veal; **vacío** flank.

Pescados & mariscos (Fish & seafood)

Anchoa anchovy; **almeja** clam; **atún** tuna; **calamar** squid; **camarón** prawn; **cangrejo** crab; **centolla** king crab; **langosta** lobster; **langostino** king prawn; **lenguado** sole; **mejillón** mussel; **merluza** hake; **ostra** oyster; **pulpo** octopus; **rabas** squid rings; **trucha** trout.

Verduras, arroz y legumbres (Vegetables, rice & pulses)

Apio celery; **arroz** rice; **arveja** green pea; **batata** sweet potato; **berenjena** aubergine/egg plant; **berro** watercress; **calabaza** pumpkin/squash; **cebolla** onion; **chaucha**

Beautiful food, beautiful people, beautiful **Bar Uriarte**. *See p108.*

Even the bathrooms are slick at Central, a pioneering Palermo Hollywood lounge/restaurant/deli. Still bustling with beautiful people, this marble and concrete hangar's crossover cuisine is superb – though service is occasionally more about glamour than efficiency. Relax on the long, low, hide-covered couch (go for a high table with back-supporting chairs if you are more than two) and sample chef Rodrigo Tosso's deer pâté with herbs, and for a main dish, grilled sea bass in a black olive sauce. Or mosey on down to the open-air terrace for BBQ. For lazy solo lunches, there's a great magazine selection – it's scary how easily a chilled afternoon passes by here.

green beans; **choclo** corn; **espinaca** spinach; **garbanzo** chickpea; **humita** grated, cooked sweetcorn; **lechuga** lettuce; **lenteja** lentil; **palmito** palm heart; **palta** avocado; **papa** potato; **pepino** cucumber; **puerro** leek; **remolacha** beetroot; **repollo** cabbage; **soja** soya; **zanahoria** carrot; **zapallito** courgette/zucchini.

Fruta (Fruit)

Ananá pineapple; **cereza** cherry; **ciruela** plum; **durazno** peach; **frambuesa** raspberry; **frutilla** strawberry; **manzana** apple; **naranja** orange; **pera** pear; **pomelo** grapefruit.

Postres (Desserts)

Budín de pan bread pudding; **flan** crème caramel; **helado** ice-cream; **miel** honey; **queso** cheese.

Local specialities

Alfajor cornflower biscuits; **carbonada** thick local stew of corn, meat, rice and veg; **dulce de leche** milk jam (tastes like caramel); **locro** stew of pork, beans, spices; **medialunas** croissants (**de manteca** sweet and buttery, **de grasa** saltier, made with oil).

La Corte

Arévalo 2977, entre Arce y Báez, Las Cañitas (4775 0999). Bus 15, 29, 59, 60, 64. **Open** *Jan, Feb* 6pm-1am daily. *Mar-Dec* 6pm-1am Mon-Fri; from 10am Sat-Sun. **Main courses** AR$14-$24. **Credit** AmEx, DC, MC, V. **Map** p279 K6.

The epitome of Las Cañitas' anti-intellectual cool, this three-floored, minimalist *multiespacio* boasts a DJ-decked sushi lounge, large-screen TV, homeware boutique and tables close enough to share the fun with the gorgeous groups of diners leaving Sartre at home with the boyfriend. Oh, they also serve food – fab fusion plates and daily fish and pasta specials. From the service to the *cortados* served with funky mini-whisks for stirring, the attention is in the detail.

Dominga

Honduras 5618, entre Fitz Roy y Bonpland, Palermo Viejo (4771 4443/www.domingarestaurant.com). Bus 39, 93, 111. **Open** 12.30-4pm, 8pm-1am Mon-Fri; 8pm-1am Sat. **Main courses** AR$13-$25. **Set menu** AR$12-$16. **Credit** AmEx, MC, V. **Map** p279 K4.

Adorned in the now standard Feng Shui style of the district, Dominga is also graced with an ivy-clad patio for intimate chitchat. Half the menu is expertly rolled sushis and sashimis, the other a random hotchpotch of tasty dishes, including semolina gnocchi and grilled goat's cheese with sweet tomato-based jam. Original starters include a pâté spiked with Malbec – only desserts lack inspiration.

Gran Bar Danzón

Libertad 1161, entre Santa Fe y Arrenales, Recoleta (4811 1108/www.granbardanzon.com.ar). Subte D, Tribunales/17, 39, 67, 102, 152 bus. **Open** from 7pm Mon-Fri; from 8pm Sat-Sun. **Main courses** AR$17-22. **Credit** AmEx, DC, MC, V. **Map** p277 F7.

Frequently pigeon-holed as a great wine bar, which it is, upscale lounge Danzón dishes it up as good as it decants. Like sister bistros Sucre and Uriarte, the focus is on sexy modern design – right from the entrance via the candlelit and incense-scented stairs – and even sexier pan-LatAm cuisine, such as *ceviche* salmon salad and prawns in red *mole* sauce. Sushi (not served on Mondays) is also superb. A 200-bottle wine list, happy-hour promotions and live jazz on Wednesdays and Fridays keep the crowds happy. Noise levels soar through the night (especially on jazz evenings), so dine early if you like it tranquil.

Eat, Drink, Shop

GReeN BamBOO
BAR RESTÓ VIETNAMITA
COSTA RICA 5802 PALERMO Bs As te: 4775·7050
greenbamboo@dmmdg.com.ar

LA CORTE
restó arévalo 2977
las cañitas, buenos aires
T.47 75 09 99
lacortecanitas@arnet.com.ar

EMPIRE
thai

An American bar
& Thai food restaurant in
the heart of downtown
Buenos Aires.

Tres Sargentos 427 Retiro
Tel. (5411) 4312-5706
empire_bar@hotmail.com

PAPPA DEUS
RESTAURANT
PUBLIC BAR

Mediterranean cuisine with subtle Asian
flavours, homemade pastas
and a specially selected wine list

Bethlem 423 - Plaza Dorrego - San Telmo -
Bs. As. Argentina | Te: (5411) 4361-2110 / 4362-6300
pappadeus@tutopia.com | www.pappadeus.com.ar

Gran Bar Danzón: designer dining and one of the best wine bars in town. *See p109.*

Lola

RM Ortiz 1805, y Guido, Recoleta (4804 5959). Bus 17, 60, 101, 102. **Open** noon-4pm, 7pm-1.30am daily. **Main courses** AR$30. **Set menus** AR$29 lunch; AR$38 dinner. **Credit** AmEx, DC, MC, V. **Map** p278 G7.

An icon of the upper classes and one of the only sure bets in a Recoleta swamped by tourist traps, white-tableclothed Lola has been combining classic dishes like steak tartare with more artful creations like shrimp and almond-stuffed trout for two decades. The menu changes with the seasons, but the homemade pastas and fresh fish are always strong.

Lomo

Costa Rica 4661, entre Gurruchaga y Armenia, Palermo Viejo (4833 3200/www.restaurantlomo. com.ar). Bus 15, 39, 55. **Open** 8.30pm-2am Mon; from 9am Tue-Sun. **Main courses** AR$15-$27. **Set menu** (lunch only) AR$14-$16 Mon-Fri; AR$16-$18 Sat-Sun. **Credit** AmEx, DC, MC, V. **Map** p279 J4.

Lomo is Argentina's prime cut, but it's also slang to describe a great bod. At this hip *multiespacio*, with its art gallery and leather sofas, beauty and *bife* co-exist. A Zen-like roof terrace is gorgeous for a drink even if you not staying for dinner. A jokey menu – the Mata Hambre ('kill hunger') *matambre, mollejas santas* ('holy sweetbread') – showcases the myriad ways chef Guillermo Gonzalez uses regional flavours to prepare the mother of all meats. Great wines too.

Museo Renault

Avenida Figueroa Alcorta 3900, y San Martín de Tours, Palermo (4802 9767/9626/www.mrenault. com.ar). Bus 67, 102, 130. **Open** 7am-3am daily. **Main courses** AR$16-$30. **Set menu** (lunch only) AR$36. **Credit** AmEx, DC, MC, V. **Map** p278 I7.

Museo Renault is a classy café-restaurant where the only cars on show are likely to be of the chauffeur-driven variety. A great breakfast or lunch spot, the evening menu stretches from French fusion to sushi. It boasts a wine list of over 3,000 labels as well as the only Cordon Bleu-trained chef in the country.

Nacional

Balcarce 907, y Estados Unidos, San Telmo (4361 5539). Bus 22, 24, 29, 93, 152. **Open** 9am-2am daily. **Main courses** AR$12-$18. **Set menu** (lunch only) AR$9 Mon-Fri. **Credit** AmEx, DC, MC, V. **Map** p276 C6.

With its art deco bar and long windows overlooking one of BA's moodiest streetscapes, this dimly-lit bistro exudes San Telmo's melancholy charm better than any. The menu and wine list are less ambitious than would be true in a similar place in Palermo, but even so, dishes like the chicken breast marinated in sesame oil, mustard and honey are pleasingly light and fairly priced.

Novecento

Báez 199, y Argüibel, Las Cañitas (4778 1900/www. bistronovecento.com). Bus 5, 29, 59, 60, 64. **Open** 10am-2am Mon-Fri; 12.30-4pm, 8pm-1.30am Sat-Sun. **Main courses** AR$13-$24 lunch. **Set menu** (lunch only) AR$9 Mon-Fri. **Credit** AmEx, DC, MC, V. **Map** p279 K6.

A thriving, self-styled American bistro, which manages to be bustling, smart and intimate enough for a candlelit smooch. The outdoor tables are often full, too. It has branches in Manhattan, Miami and Punta del Este but here at the flagship, the menu is classic mod Argentinian, with great meat dishes like the pepper steak or booze-soaked sweetbreads. Its strength is in the simplicity of its menu, which transcends typical *parrilla* fare without being too exotic.

Olsen

Gorriti 5870, entre Carranza y Ravignani, Palermo Viejo (4776 7677). Bus 39, 93, 111. **Open** noon-1.30am Tue-Sun. **Main courses** AR$16-$28. **Set menu** (lunch only) AR$14 Tue-Fri. **Credit** AmEx, V. **Map** p279 K4.

Soon after opening in 2001, this tall, blonde, handsome Scandinavian-inspired restaurant became one of Palermo Hollywood's biggest draws and solidified the reputation of Germán Martitegui as one of the city's most daring young chefs. It's hard to say

Eat, Drink, Shop

Sensual Jazz
Teatro Erótico

design : info@we-multimedia.com.ar

Aphrodisiac Dishes - Erotic Show - Sensual Jazz

PALERMO
Paraguay 4062
reservas: 48 31 91 56

Te Mataré Ramirez
RESTAURANTE AFRODISIACO
Buenos Aires - Argentina

SAN ISIDRO
Primera Junta 702
reservas: 47 47 86 18

WWW.TEMATARERAMIREZ.COM

DELI
COFFEE &
HOUSE

MARKS
DELI & COFFEE HOUSE

el salvador 4701 tel.48.32.62.44

info@markscoffee.com | www.markscoffe.com

mon to sat 8.30 am - 9.30 pm | sun 10.30 am - 9.00 pm

which stands out more – the wooden sculptures and verdant garden or the fresh oysters and piled-up smörgåsbords, which go down great with a sampler of ice-cold vodka and aquavit shots. Desserts are worth leaving space for. Olsen is classy, cool and suited to just about any kind of clientele.

Sifones y Dragones

Ciudad de la Paz 174, y Santos Dumont, Colegiales (15 4413 9871/www.sifonesydragones.com.ar). Bus 68, 152. **Open** 9pm-2am Tue-Sat. **Main courses** AR$16-$18. **No credit cards. Map** p275 L5.
Argentinian couple Mariana and Favio are quick to point out that 'this is not a restaurant, but a kitchen with tables'. And so it is; just 16 spots, dotted around a flame-throwing hob, where the delightful pair drum up made-on-the-spot wonders from near and far. With such limited space and a location near the upper reaches of Palermo, you'll need to reserve in advance.

Social Paraiso

Honduras 5182, entre Thames y Uriarte, Palermo Viejo (4831 4556). **Open** 12.30-4pm, 8.30pm-midnight Tue-Sat; 12.30-4pm Sun. **Main courses** AR$11-$17. **Set menu** (lunch only) AR$10 Mon-Fri; AR$12-$14 Sat-Sun. **Credit** AmEx, V. **Map** p279 J4.
Youngsters and seniors, New World and Old, mix freely in this sober, high-ceilinged bistro that helped pioneer Palermo Viejo's gourmet explosion. Chef-owner Federico Simoes was raised on Syrian-Lebanese cuisine brought by his immigrant father overland from Brazil, and although purposefully non-exotic, his small, constantly changing menu reflects his polyglot roots, though Mediterranean flourishes predominate. One refreshing item his loyal clients won't let him change is the *maracuyá*

Enjoy your **Lomo** alfresco. *See p111.*

(passion fruit) mousse and Szechwan pepper ice-cream wedged between caramelised apple slices. The AR$10 fixed lunch menu is a gift.

Sucre

Sucre 676, entre Figueroa Alcorta y Castañeda, Belgrano (4782 9082/www.sucrerestaurant.com.ar). Train to Scalabrini Ortiz/37, 130 bus. **Open** noon-5pm, 8pm-1am daily. **Main courses** AR$16-$24. **Credit** AmEx, DC, MC, V. **Map** p281 N7.
If you have just one night in the city, this is the modern Argentinian restaurant to visit… if you can get a table. Sucre is the pinnacle of neo-industrial design, the centrepiece of which is a bunker wine cellar and kaleidoscopically coloured ceiling-high bar. There's a real showtime feel to the entire dining experience, although there's only one star: celebrity chef Fernando Trocca, who brightens up local classics with pan-Latin flavours like diced mango, papaya dressings and jalapeños. Grab a high table near the open kitchen and watch the artist at work. An exciting 18-page wine list roams from Mendoza to Bordeaux and barman Tato is BA's best.

Thymus

Lerma 525, entre Acevedo y Malabia, Villa Crespo (4772 1936/www.restaurant-thymus.com). Bus 55, 106, 110. **Open** 8.30pm-12.30am Tue-Sat. **Main courses** AR$16-$24. **Set menu** AR$32-$65. **Credit** AmEx, MC, V. **Map** p275 J4.
As romantic as it is aromatic, Thymus deserves all the praise it gets from discriminating gourmets. Sculptor Martín Vegara's skilful copies of classical antiquities decorate his former house and studio, converted into a restaurant made for all five senses. Chef Fernando Mayoral, who trained in France with Michel Bras, uses freshly garnered garnishes of rosemary, thyme and pineapple mint from a rooftop herb garden to layer exotic-sounding dishes like tandoori sweetbread and grilled *cordoniz* (quail), seasoned with edible flowers and foie gras.

Basque

Burzako

México 345, entre Defensa y Balcarce, Monserrat (4334 0721). Bus 29, 93, 130, 152. **Open** 12.30-4pm Mon-Wed; 12.30-4pm, 8.30pm-1am Thur, Fri; 8.30pm-1am Sat. **Closed** dinner Jan. **Main courses** AR$8-$16. **Set menu** (lunch only) AR$7-$12. **Credit** AmEx, DC, MC, V. **Map** p277 D6.
A bar-restaurant with touches of a traditional Spanish tavern, but that also tries to show that Basque cuisine can be young and cool. The fish specialities and the ice-creams with strawberries are highlights, and a fine bottle of La Rural Cepa Trad 97 at AR$14 makes this a strong candidate for a classy but not wallet-draining meal.

Laurak Bat

Avenida Belgrano 1144, entre Salta y Lima, Congreso (4381 0682). Subte C, Moreno/39, 59, 98 bus. **Open** from 10am Mon-Sat. **Main courses** AR$8-$16. **Credit** AmEx, DC, MC, V. **Map** p277 E6.

Eat, Drink, Shop

Pride and joy of the Centro Vasco since 1877, serving reasonably priced soups (the leek is lovely), tapas, fish and hearty meat dishes. *Natillas* – the Spanish version of custard – is the classic closer. A grand old oak tree, said to have sprouted from a seedling of the Guérnica Tree (which the Basques consider divine), stands in the centre of this dingy but authentic Basque restaurant

Chinese

Several inexpensive, inoffensive Chinese restaurants are dotted around town, as well as Chinese options at many of the all-you-can-eat *tenedor libre* buffets, but aficionados will find the fare disappointing. For more authentic eats, head to Belgrano's miniature Chinatown on the calle Arribeños, next to the Belgrano C train station, where kitschy **Todos Contentos** at No.2177 (4780 3437) is the best of the bunch.

Chino Cantón
Avenida Córdoba 4015, y Gascón, Palermo Viejo (4863 2333). Bus 26, 106, 109, 140, 168. **Open** noon-3pm, 8.30pm-midnight daily. **Main courses** AR$7-$20. **No credit cards. Map** p278 I4.
If you want cheap, tasty duck, rice dishes, chow mein and prawns, this plain-verging-on-dingy canteen delivers the goods fast and fresh. The typical order-by-number menu is dizzyingly long (fittingly the last item, #1807, is tea), but clients from the local Chinese community keep returning, so authenticity is assured. A block away, Ricos (Córdoba 4122, 4864 4693) is a Chinese tearoom serving vegetarian meals for under AR$5. On Fridays and Saturdays there are free Koto (Japanese floor harp) recitals.

Eastern European

La Casa Polaca
Jorge Luis Borges 2076, entre Soler y Guatemala, Palermo Viejo (4899 0514/4774 7621). Subte D, Plaza Italia/15, 39 bus. **Open** 8pm-12.30am Tue-Sat. **Closed** Jan **Main courses** AR$7-$14. **Credit** AmEx, DC, MC, V. **Map** p279 J1.
This basement restaurant in the Dom Polski cultural centre for Polish immigrants is poles apart from anything else in Palermo Viejo, but don't let the crusty decor put you off. Ultra-friendly, wildly camp chef Antos Yaskowiak and his trusty staff serve delicious rollmops, stews and goulash, each course punctuated by a sharp vodka and informative chat

El Kozako
Junín 1460, entre Pacheco de Melo y Peña, Recoleta (4804 3527). Bus 10, 37, 59, 60. **Open** 8pm-1.30am Tue-Thur; noon-3pm, 8pm-1.30am Fri-Sun. **Main courses** AR$11-$19. **Credit** AmEx, DC, MC, V. **Map** p278 H7.
With its terracotta interior filled with samovars and Slavic waitresses in pastoral costume, El Kozako's atmosphere combines an exotic journey east with

authentic Russian cooking. If you don't splurge on the AR$300-peso caviar blinis, a few eggs are smattered for show with the Zakuscki de Pescado, a sampler of cold, fish-based appetisers. Main dishes like the cream and dill herring are fit for the czar.

Fish

Azul Profundo
Avenida del Libertador 310, entre Suipacha y Esmeralda, Retiro (4393 4747). Train to Retiro/ 67, 92, 93, 130 bus. **Open** noon-4pm, 8pm-1am Mon-Fri; 8pm-1am Sat-Sun. **Main courses** AR$14-$21. **Credit** AmEx, MC, V. **Map** p277 F8.
Dim lighting, turquoise-painted walls and fish tanks create the Atlantis effect in this elegant, 'deep blue' restaurant. Although it's fallen somewhat out of fashion with the hip, sushi crowd, Mediterranean-inspired classics like the algae and filo-wrapped salmon or tuna steak (unusual in Buenos Aires) keep its fish-loving, loyal clientele coming back.

Coyar de Buitres
Honduras 5702, y Bonpland, Palermo Viejo (4774 5154). Bus 39, 93, 111. **Open** from 6pm daily. **Closed** Sun in Jan and Feb. **Main courses** AR$12-$28. **Credit** AmEx, DC, V. **Map** p279 K4.
Succulent oysters are the signature of this young, happening spot, with a small pavement terrace and pub-style wooden tables. There's also flavoursome clam, mussel, octopus and squid dishes. The menu is divided into main courses and tapas, so you can call in for a drink and a bite or make a night of it.

French

Au Bec Fin
Vicente López 1827, entre Ayacucho y Callao, Recoleta (4805 0861/www.aubecfin.com.ar). Bus 10, 37, 59, 60, 102. **Open** noon-4pm, from 8pm daily. **Main courses** AR$14-$36. **Set menu** (lunch only) AR$17. **Credit** AmEx, DC, MC, V. **Map** p278 G7.
Awkwardly aristocratic in the century-old *petit hôtel* that's been its home since 1979, Au Bec Fin prides itself on its Gallic classics, which have matured gracefully here. Start with a crock of French onion soup or stuffed *au gratin* mushrooms before indulging in a duck with apricots magret or an oyster and spinach fondue. The cobalt-blue porcelain and musty red wallpaper have seen better days.

Christophe
Fitz Roy 1994, y Nicaragua, Palermo Viejo (4771 1155). Bus 93, 111. **Open** 12.30-4pm, 8.30pm-midnight Mon-Thur, Sun; 12.30-4pm, 8.30pm-1am Fri, Sat. **Closed** lunch Mon-Thur in Jan and Feb. **Main courses** AR$16-$24. **Credit** V. **Map** p279 K4.
A charming chalkboard bistro, which does a mean camembert appetiser, superb basil-brushed liver salad and more elaborate items like rabbit tarragon. The daily menu is king, adapted to both what's best in the local market as well as in the mind of owner-gastronome Christophe Krywonis.

Mi Buenos Aires Querido
Germán Martitegui

My beloved Buenos Aires

Buenos Aires is a city in constant movement. When I came from Necochea – a town of 100,000 – it was the rhythm of the people that struck me most.
I adore BA when it empties out in January, when you've got the whole city for yourself. I never go on holiday then.
The Reserva Ecológica is fantastic. It's the first place I would take a visitor, along with San Telmo and Palermo Viejo.
A good night out should end at Pachá. Visitors must go clubbing in order to see the full spectrum of the city's people.
The art deco architecture along Diagonal Norte is stunning. It's my favourite zone. It's also where I live – in the dome of one of the office buildings there. I have the best views in the city.
You can live in the centre if you don't work there, as the time you spend in the area is really quiet: evenings and weekends.
At last, what's Argentinian is in vogue here. I never thought it would happen. We have always looked outwards.
Native cuisine is fashionable too. The crisis forced local growers to improve quality for the domestic market – now you can get good Argentinian olive oil.

We are over-exploiting exportable produce: if we keep hunting wild hares to send to Europe there won't be any left.
The organic movement here is getting stronger all the time – it's a huge opportunity for us.
Buenos Aires is only now becoming more open to new cuisines. *Porteños* don't have naturally adventurous palates.
Flavours need to be subtle, as very few people like spicy food.
My work doesn't leave me much time to go out – but I enjoy eating at Danzón and Sudestada, as well as at the simple *parrillas* on the Costanera Sur.
There's a tendency for everything to become like a football match in Argentina, and people behave with the same overexcitement, especially when places become fashionable.
There's a lot of touching in Buenos Aires – and not much respect for personal space. People are very tactile, even in the street.
Buenos Aires is friendly, melancholy and sophisticated. It's a contradictory city.
● Germán Martitegui is one of the leading chefs in BA. He has worked in France, California and Australia, and is now executive chef at Agraz, in the Caesar Park Hotel, as well as chef and co-founder of Olsen (pictured).

Eat, Drink, Shop

Greek

Dafni
Armenia 1231, entre Córdoba y Niceto Vega, Palermo Viejo (4899 0770). Bus 106, 110. **Open** *Jan, Feb* from 4pm Mon-Sat. *Mar-Dec* 11am-1am Mon-Sat; 11am-4pm Sun. **Set menu** AR$17 lunch; AR$30 dinner with show Fri, Sat. **Credit** AmEx, MC, V. **Map** p279 J4.
Epicurean to the very core, in 2003 Olympia-born Lambis Charalambopoulos abandoned a 40-year medical career to pursue his life's passion for food. Using goat's cheese, olives, filo pastry and aubergine, he livens up traditional Greek dishes as well as original creations like Tsagonaki, a cross between a pizza and omelette. The *picada del chef* selection of nibbles makes a great starter, although the overly bright salon is a turn off.

Mykonos
Olleros 1752, entre Soldado de la Independencia y Migueletes, Belgrano (4779 9000/4777 4357/www. mykonostaso.com.ar). Subte D, Olleros/29, 60, 118 bus. **Open** from 8pm daily. **Main courses** AR$10-$28. **Credit** AmEx, DC, MC, V. **Map** p281 M6.
This would be just another 'Zorba the Greek' theme restaurant if all the festive plate-breaking and pastiche Acropolis ambience weren't backed up by an

RESTAURA

LOUN

WINE B

FINE DINI

DANCE FLO

DORREGO

Av. Dorrego s/n entre Av. del Libertador y Cerviño. Buenos Aires. Argentina
www.dorregobuenosaires.com.ar

authentic Mediterranean kitchen. Fresh feta and olives make the Greek salad a perfect start for a meal of moussaka or souvlaki (kebab), rounded off with baklava and a bitingly strong coffee.

Italian

Cantina Pierino

Lavalle 3499, y Billinghurst, Abasto (4864 5715). Subte B, Carlos Gardel/24, 26, 168 bus. **Open** 8pm-1am daily. **Main courses** AR$9-$16. **Credit** V. **Map** p278 H4.

Way off the tourist track, Pierino has been serving authentic Italian food since 1907. Tango legends Astor Piazzolla and Anibal Troilo were regulars in the 1960s. Pedro, grandson of the original owners, is liable to suggest what he regards as best for you, but the delicious starters – *friatta* (mozzarella tortillas) and *chiambotta* (baked aubergine with onion, courgettes, celery and mushrooms) – home-made pasta dishes and value for money don't disappoint.

Filo

San Martín 975, entre Marcelo T de Alvear y Paraguay, Retiro (4311 0312/www.filo-ristorante.com). Subte C, San Martín/10, 93, 130, 152 bus. **Open** from noon daily. **Main courses** AR$12-$18. **Credit** AmEx, DC, MC, V. **Map** p277 E8.

Despite its popularity with the pizza and champagne crowd, there's nothing pretentious about the modern Italian menu at this swinging 'art restaurant' and bar. Garrulous groups are kept happy by stylish waitresses doling out imaginative salads, delicious pastas and panini, superb steaks and, most popularly, over 100 slimline pizzas. Or order a cocktail and check out 180 Grados art gallery in the basement (*see p180*).

Giulia

Sucre 632, y Figueroa Alcorta, Belgrano (4780 3603). Train to Scalabrini Ortiz/37, 130 bus. **Open** 8pm-midnight Mon; noon-3pm, 8pm-midnight Tue-Fri; 1-4pm, 8pm-12.30am Sat, Sun. **Main courses** AR$18-$28. **Set menu** (lunch only) AR$16. **Credit** AmEx, MC, V. **Map** p281 N7.

Frank Sinatra would feel at home in this Vegas-styled joint located in a slender *casa chorizo* with a divine rooftop terrace facing the park. Owned by the children of Boca Juniors coach Carlos Bianchi, the football player-sized plates of pasta and risotto are traditional and home-made. The revered 'viceroy' of Argentinian footy frequently drops in after practice.

Guido's Bar

República de la India, entre Cabello y Gutiérrez, Palermo (4802 2391). Subte D, Plaza Italia/29, 39, 152 bus. **Open** 7pm-1am Mon-Fri. **Main courses** AR$20-$25. **No credit cards.** Map p279 J6.

Every millimetre of this pea-sized trattoria is covered in kitsch, from a Humphrey Bogart necktie to pin-ups of Marilyn Monroe. But there's nothing jokey about owner Carlos' passion for Italian cooking. For AR$25 smirking waiters will force-feed you a parade of colourful appetisers followed by home-made pastas and desert made from whatever is on

hand. A kitchen radio turned purposefully too loud is the epitome of the Italian nonchalance this neighbourhood landmark is after.

Il Gran Caruso

Olga Cossentini 791, y Macacha Güemes, Madero Este (4515 0707). Bus 2, 130, 152. **Open** noon-2am daily. **Main courses** AR$20-$35. **Set menu** (lunch only) AR$15-$19. **Credit** AmEx, DC, MC, V. **Map** p277 D8.

A classy corporate joint that also welcomes strolling sightseers and weary birders coming back from the nature reserve. For AR$15 you can feast on lunch specials like a yummy zucchini soufflé and pastas or a melon-and-ham starter with main of simple grilled hake, with a glass of wine. A dockside terrace with lovely views of the Puente de la Mujer bridge is a major plus. Come dusk, splash out on spider crab and caviar agnolottis or lamb pizza.

Il Matterello

Martín Rodríguez 517, y Villafañe, La Boca (4307 0529). Bus 29, 64, 86, 152. **Open** Feb-Dec 12.30-3pm, 8.30pm-midnight Tue-Sat; 12.30-3pm Sun. **Closed** Jan. **Main courses** AR$10-$18. **Credit** AmEx, DC, MC, V. **Map** p276 A5.

This attractive, rich restaurant in a poor quarter is still faithful to the barrio's Italian roots and an ideal stop if you want to follow the Italo-Argentinian family tradition of Sunday lunch pasta after a stroll round the port. Fantastic pastas include a Cima Rellena (cold pork roll with peas, cheese, carrot, egg) and a rocket tagliatelle with sundried tomatoes and onion. Desserts include Postre de la Nonna ('grandma's sweet'), a trifle-like calorie-bomb.

Pappa Deus

Pasaje Bethlem 423, y Defensa, San Telmo (4361 2110/www.pappadeus.com.ar). Subte C, San Juan/22, 24, 29 bus. **Open** 9am-6pm Mon; from 9am Tue-Sun. **Main courses** AR$8-$21. **Set menu** (lunch only) AR$10. **Credit** AmEx, DC, MC, V. **Map** p276 C6.

Inexpensive home-made pastas, like lip-smacking lamb raviolis and pumpkin-stuffed triangles, are the main draw, but the Mediterranean salads are its undiscovered gem. At lunchtime, this bright little restaurant in a spruced-up, antique-laden 1890 townhouse sets out tables on the tourist-cramped Plaza Dorrego – and it's by far the best of the bunch.

Japanese

Although trad Argentinian food is largely fish-free, despite a 5,000-kilometre (3,106-mile) coastline, *porteños* have fallen big time for the raw stuff. Mundo Bizarro (*see p134*) bar hosts sushi nights, while Gran Bar Danzón and Dominga (for both *see p109*) make it a major – and excellent – feature. Las Cañitas and Palermo Viejo are teeming with (often uninspired) options and there's even a Sushi Club chain (three locations thus far) churning it out. Many sushi joints will deliver. These are the best:

Eat, Drink, Shop

Ab fab **Filo**. *See p117*.

Bokoto

Huergo 261, entre Clay y Arevalo, Las Cañitas (4776 6505/www.bokotoresto.com.ar). Bus 41, 60, 92, 118. **Open** *Jan, Feb* 8pm-2am Tue-Sun. *Mar-Dec* noon-4pm, 8pm-2am Tue-Sun. **Main courses** AR$10-$16. **Set menu** (unlimited sushi) AR$33. **Credit** AmEx, MC, V. **Map** p279 K5.

Located in a long, narrow house, with a red and black colour-scheme that stretches from the tableware to the uniforms, Bokoto has over three years' experience, and is already a survivor and a safe bet to outlast further pruning of the area's multiple sushi options. A lengthy menu includes classic as well as special items like the Crazy Roll with shrimp, avocado, philadelphia and salmon. Cooked options include the Yaki Guy, a speared lomo kebab with white rice and teriyaki sauce and wok specials.

Comedor Nikkai

Avenida Independencia, entre Chacabuco y Piedras, San Telmo (4300 1182). Bus 10, 22, 24, 29, 86. **Open** noon-3pm, 7.30-11pm Mon-Thur, 8pm-midnight Fri-Sat. **Main courses** AR$10-$27. **Set menu** (lunch only) AR$15. **Credit** AmEx, MC, V. **Map** p277 D6.

It may be ubiquitous in leafier areas, but finding sushi in San Telmo is about as hard as getting a steak in Calcutta. This informal yet traditional diner inside the Asociación Japonesa is a real gem – the sushi is top notch and the beamed-in Japanese TV for local clients adds an element of uncontrived authenticity.

Dashi

Fitz Roy 1613, y Gorriti, Palermo Viejo (4776 3500/www.dashi.com.ar). Bus 93, 111. **Open** 12.30-3pm, 8.30pm-1am Mon-Fri; 8.30pm-1am Sat. **Main courses** AR$16-$44. **Set menu** AR$26-$36. **Credit** AmEx, DC, MC, V. **Map** p279 K4.

Humongous windows on a prime corner site reveal the elegant nature of Buenos Aires' classiest sushi restaurant, artfully directed by Jorge, its gregarious, globetrotting gourmet owner. The chic, dusky rose and grey interior and zero-calorie (but surprisingly satisfying) salad court the Palermo crowd, but sushi man Pablo Nohara's creative rolls and superb sashimi slivers are second to none. Non-sushi eaters should try the hot seafood platter or share a sublime *salmón a la rueda*. The home-made ice-creams are unmissable. This is sushi with style.

Other locations Salguero 2643, Palermo (4805 5575); Aguilar 2395, Palermo (4782 2666/3666)

Irifune

Paraguay 412, y Reconquista, Retiro (4312 8787). Subte C, San Martín/61, 93, 130, 152 bus. **Open** noon-3pm, 8pm-12.30am Mon-Fri; 8pm-12.30am Sat. **Main courses** AR$15-$30. **Main courses** (lunch only) AR$20-$23. **Credit** AmEx, MC, V. **Map** p277 E8.

This cute little split-level restaurant is building a solid Japanese clientele – an endorsement trendier sushi bars can only dream of. Strong wasabi and fresh ginger garnish complement well made, if slightly pricy, classic items and less common fare like the huge Gunkan Seafood rolls of tuna, king prawn and Japanese cucumber. If small and subdued isn't your taste, try flashier Morizono on the corner of Reconquista and Paraguay (4314 4443).

Yuki

Pasco 740, entre Independencia y Chile, San Cristóbal (4942 7510). Bus 95, 98. **Open** 7.30pm-midnight Mon-Sat. **Main courses** AR$10-$25. **Credit** AmEx, MC, V. **Map** p277 E4.

Trust those who know – the crème de la crème of the BA's Japanese community eats at Yuki, a true oriental paradise tucked discreetly behind a bland façade on a gloomy street. Choose between the Zen-style dining room, private side rooms or sushi bar. There's a wide range of traditional dishes, or put yourself in the expert hands of the sushi man and let him create you the perfect sushi/sashimi combo.

Latin American

Cielito Lindo

El Salvador 4999, y Thames, Palermo Viejo (4832 8054). Bus 39, 55. **Open** 8pm-midnight Mon-Thur, Sun; 8pm-1am Fri, Sat. **Main courses** AR$5-$15. **No credit cards. Map** p279 J4.

Down and out with Argentina's economy went the imported *mole*, once the house special. But there's still plenty of hot stuff to lace your tacos, chicken and fish dishes with. Rightly priced and colourfully decorated with Mayan textiles, sombreros and Day-of-the-Dead skeletons, this cheerful little box of a restaurant is so popular on weekends that queues form around the outdoor tables. If there's no room, try Xalapa at El Salvador 4800 (4833 6102).

María Felix

Dardo Rocha 1680, entre Fleming y Corvalán, San Isidro (4717 1864/www.mariafelix.com.ar). Bus 60. **Open** noon-3.30pm, 8pm-1am daily. **Main courses** AR$13-$29. **Set menu** (lunch only) AR$14-$16. **Credit** AmEx, DC, MC, V.
BA is a long way from the Rio Grande and spice pho-bic *porteño* tastebuds are an obstacle to authentic Aztec cuisine. But charming María Felix gets close. The chilli-scattered *nueva cocina mexicana* menu of regional faves, from *mole poblano* to *acapulqueño* grilled prawns, reads like a culinary tour of the country. Decor is suggestive of a hacienda without being too pastiche. A mariachi group serenades diners on Friday and Saturday nights. Service, however, can be outstripped by its popularity.
Other locations: Soldado de Independencia 1150, Belgrano (4775 0380).

María Fulô

Honduras 4795, y Armenia, Palermo Viejo (4833 4051). Bus 15, 39, 151, 168. **Open** 8pm-midnight Tue-Fri; noon-4pm, 8pm-1am Sat-Sun. **Main courses** AR$12-$25. **Credit** AmEx, MC, V. **Map** p279 J4.
After decades of disregard, *porteños* are warming to Brazil's undeniably seductive charm. At María Fulô it's easy to see why. Even the dreariest of winter days brighten up inside this carnival of colours, soulful samba and hip-swaying Brazilian waitresses. Just as vivid are the exquisitely prepared *feijoada*, fish *moqueca* and pork recipes owner Edoardo Pinheiro collects during his frequent travels to the Bahia region. You haven't lived until you've tried the passion fruit caipirinha – one of a kind in BA.

Status

Virrey Ceballos 178, entre Alsina y Yrigoyen, Congreso (4382 8531/www.restaurantstatus.com.ar). Subte A, Saenz Peña/37, 60, 168 bus. **Open** noon-5pm, 8pm-1am Mon-Thu; noon-1am Fri-Sun. **Main courses** AR$5-$20. **Credit** AmEx, MC, V. **Map** p277 E5.

Although Argentinians tend to shun most things indigenous to their own continent, one day soon they're going to wake up to the potential of Peruvian cuisine, which is tasty, cheap and different from *criollo* beef and wine culture. This canteen owned by the friendly Valenzuela family from Trujillo serves abundant platters of *ceviche* (marinated raw fish) and lamb, as well as spicy starters such as the must-order *papas a la Huancain*, an exotic highland spud cooked in cheese and chilli.

Middle Eastern

Bereber

Armenia 1880, entre Costa Rica y Nicaragua, Palermo Viejo (4833 5662). Bus 39, 55. **Open** 8pm-1am daily. **Main courses** AR$17-$23. **Credit** AmEx, DC, MC, V. **Map** p279 J4/5.
A modern Moroccan restaurant – a rarity in Buenos Aires – of low tables and divans and home-made *merguez* (spicy lamb sausage) guarantee an authentic experience. Besides a full range of couscous and tagines, Bereber douses Argentina's tender meats in a slew of marinades to make exquisite dishes like Habra, lamb in a coriander pesto sauce. This, like most of the dishes, can be pepped up with *harissa* (a spicy sauce). Cool off afterwards with tasty desserts like a Bloody Labne – ice-cream topped with red fruits. Staff are efficient and charming and there's a lovely rooftop terrace up above.

Garbis

Scalabrini Ortiz 3190, y Cerviño, Palermo (4511 6600/www.garbis.com.ar). Bus 10, 37, 41, 59, 60. **Open** noon-3.30pm, 8pm-12.30am Mon-Thur, Sun; noon-3.30pm, 8pm-1.30am Fri-Sat. **Main courses** AR$9-$17. **Set menus** AR$13 lunch; AR$18 dinner. **Credit** AmEx, MC, V. **Map** p278 I6.
Unlike the other designer digs of Palermo, this chain restaurant focuses on a simple goal of delivering authentic ethnic eats to a mass audience at an affordable price. For AR$13 at lunchtime (AR$18 at dinner) gourmet chowhounds can feast on a tasty buffet of hummous, baclava and other Arabic and Armenian delights. If you prefer to order something from the menu, try the Ensalada Belen (marinated aubergine with cashews and raisins) or *boio de verdura* (a filo-wrapped spinach pie).
Other locations: Monroe 1799, Belgrano (4789 9300); Lerma 1, Villa Crespo (4866 4000); La Pampa 2379, Belgrano (4781 0900).

Eat, Drink, Shop

Dashing **Dashi**. *See p118.*

Sarkis

Thames 1101, y Jufre, Villa Crespo (4772 4911).
Bus 34, 55, 168. **Open** noon-3pm, from 8pm daily.
Main courses AR$5-$15. **No credit cards.**
Map p275 J3.

The fluorescent-lit atmosphere is wanting and the Monday belly-rippler could be your grandma, but Sarkis' food means it's packed at weekends. Choose dips, snacks, soufflés, raw mince and kebabs, or ask for a miscellany of biggish starters, which will have you jumping straight to dessert. Great for groups.

South-east Asian

Bi Won

Junín 548, entre Lavalle y Tucumán, Once (4372 1146). Subte B, Pasteur or D, Facultad de Medicina/ 24, 26, 60, 124 bus. **Open** noon-3pm, 7pm-midnight Mon-Sat. **Main courses** AR$10-$20. **No credit cards.** **Map** p277 F5.

Ignore the Korean tourist board posters and hammy backing track at this authentic community restaurant down a dark Once street, because the food is delightful and inexpensive. Two should share, as meals come with ten side dishes of turnip, anchovies, corn, seaweed, spinach, kimchi (a Korean plant), cucumber and beans, most of them doused in chilli and garlic. The meat is cooked at the table.

Empire Thai

Tres Sargentos 427, entre San Martín y Reconquista, Retiro (4312 5706/www.empirethai.com). Subte C, San Martín/26, 93, 152 bus. **Open** noon-1am Mon-Fri; 7pm-1am Sat. **Main courses** AR$16-$33. **Credit** AmEx, MC, V. **Map** p277 E8.

This groovy, dimly lit grotto of a restaurant offers the gamut of heat from tongue-frazzling red and green curries to milder, Argentinian-friendly noodle and veg dishes. Coconut and tropical fruits sweeten much of the menu, and there are chilli-free seafood options for the puritanical palate. The mixed satays make for mean starters, especially with a cocktail – the house drink, which changes daily, is half-price.

Green Bamboo

Costa Rica 5802, y Carranza, Palermo Viejo (4775 7050). Bus 93, 111. **Open** 8.30pm-2.30am daily. **Main courses** AR$17-$25. **Credit** AmEx, DC, MC, V. **Map** p279 K4.

Busily, but charmingly, decked out to convincing oriental effect, Green Bamboo is a touch of class on a picturesque Palermo corner. The look is elegant, green and moody with candle-lit floor-level or regular tables, a long L-shaped bar, and a red Ho Chi Minh peering down from above – ask for a cute matchbox with his picture. The menu, too, is spot on, with pork in a minty sauce and refreshing fruit gazpacho, and the cocktail list is wonderfully inventive.

Sudestada

Guatemala 5602, y Fitz Roy, Palermo Viejo (4776 3777). Bus 15, 55, 111. **Open** noon-3.30pm, 8pm-midnight Mon-Sat. **Main courses** AR$8-$20. **Set menu** (lunch only) AR$12. **Credit** AmEx, V. **Map** p279 K5.

Vietnamese chef Tien Duic dishes up ideas from Laos, Thailand, Burma and his homeland in this coolly minimalist corner restaurant. The best starters are the ones eaten by hand like the spring rolls that you wrap in lettuce and dip into an aromatic herb sauce. Main dishes can get seriously spicy by local standards, but foreign palates will eagerly devour sophisticated items like the Kaw Moo Daeng, a charcoal grilled pork in spicy peanut sauce. Fruit crumble and coconut ice cream deserts are excellent complements to a classic Vietnamese coffee.

Spanish

Al Andaluz

Godoy Cruz 1823, entre Honduras y El Salvador, Palermo Viejo (4832 9286). Bus 39, 55, 111. **Open** 8.30pm-midnight Tue-Sat. **Main courses** AR$12-$18. **Set menu** AR$15. **Credit** AmEx, DC, MC, V. **Map** p279 J4.

Dizzying tapestries and Muslim spice scales are among the exotic delights decorating Al Andaluz's *Arabian Nights*-style dining room. Even more alien are the medieval recipes personable chef-owner Ricardo Araujo has culled from his frequent pilgrimages to Southern Spain. Don't miss the decadent *cordero de konga*, a lamb meatball cooked over seven hours and served with spicy yoghurt and pilaf, and start with salmon marinated in *jerez* vinegar, honey and herbs. One of a kind.

Avila

Avenida de Mayo 1384, entre Santiago del Estero y San José, Congreso (4383 6974). Subt A, Sáenz Peña/29, 64, 86, 102 bus. **Open** noon-5pm, from 8pm Mon-Sat. **Main courses** (average spend) AR$15-$25 lunch; AR$40-$75 dinner & show. **No credit cards. Map** p277 E6.

Avila is dark and atmospheric with a set-up as quirky as owner Miguel, whose family have been on the premises since the '40s. Once you're settled, a glass of *jerez* and steaming dishes of stew, paella and squid and other seafood tapas, are dumped on your table. They keep on coming until the flamenco troupe – of local *gitanos* – leap up and the clapping, stomping and strumming begins. Bag a table close to the stage (though you'll likely be invited to join in, especially the girls). When it's all over, Miguel strolls over and conjures up a price for your pleasure. Cheeky, perhaps, but considering the show and the quantity consumed, spot on. Reservations are a must – the liveliest nights are Thursday to Saturday.

El Preferido de Palermo
Guatemala 4801, y Borges, Palermo Viejo (4774 6585). Bus 39, 55, 111. **Open** from 8am-midnight Mon-Sat. **Main courses** AR$5-$80. **Credit** AmEx, DC, MC, V. **Map** p279 J5.
A century-old general store, straight out of a Borges story, occupies the corner of the block where the writer grew up. Converted into an excellent Spanish restaurant, its dusty bar decorated with regional crests of Spain, it's the last of a dying breed. Family-owned since 1952, head honcho Arturo attends the till, nephew Martín the customers and Arturo's wife María del Carmen churns out traditional Asturian dishes like paella, a near-perfect grilled salmon and, on Saturdays, *fabada* (stewed black pudding, chorizo, bacon, beans and parma ham).

Museo del Jamón
Cerrito 8, y Rivadavia, Congreso (4382 7648). Subte A, Lima/29, 59, 64, 67, 86. **Open** noon-4pm, 7.30pm-midnight daily. **Main courses** AR$18-$68. **Credit** AmEx, DC, MC, V. **Map** p277 E6.
Classier than many Spanish restaurants in BA, though still decorated with the traditional legs of ham and wreaths of garlic, the Museo packs out most nights with tourists from nearby hotels. Food is solid even if some plates could be better prepared. Delicious aromas rise up from the pans of steaming *cazuelas* and sizzling *paellas*; the Iberian black leg ham is a house speciality and even standard tapas include cockles in an intricate leek-based sauce.

Oviedo
Beruti 2602, y Ecuador, Barrio Norte (4822 5415). Subte D, Pueyrredón/ 12, 64, 152 bus. **Open** noon-4pm, 8pm-1am daily. **Main courses** AR$25-$65. **Set menu** AR$48-$60. **Credit** AmEx, DC, MC, V. **Map** p278 H6.
Outstanding *alta cocina* from the motherland, taking the standards of the Iberian kitchen – sole, sea bass, cod – and a netful of freshly caught seafood to forge good-looking, tantalising dishes. Beef, rabbit and lamb appear, too, the latter dressed in traditional *setas* (wild mushrooms). The wine list pays homage to Galicia and La Rioja, with nods to France, Argentina and Portugal (including quality port).

Rodi Bar
Vicente López 1900, y Ayacucho, Recoleta (4801 5230). Bus 59, 60, 101, 102, 110. **Open** 6am-2am Mon-Sat. **Main courses** AR$5-$15. **Set menu** (lunch only) AR$6-$8. **Credit** AmEx, DC, MC, V. **Map** p278 G7.

¡Olé! **Avila.** See p120.

Rodi's is great for a Recoleta lunch. The roots are Galician, with old-time waiters, bright lighting and a menu of Spanish-sounding dishes, such as Merluza a la Catalana (hake in seafood sauce) and Pulpo a la Gallega (octopus in tomato and pepper sauce). Winter offerings include lentil and *mondongo* (tripe) stews, and, from the Argentinian half of the kitchen, *locro*. A local lady has been creating the desserts for years, among them a tantalising tiramisu and a soft meringue in sambayón, known as Isla Flotante.

Tancat
Paraguay 645, entre Maipú y Florida, Retiro (4312 6106). Subte C, San Martín/10, 132, 152 bus. **Open** noon-1am Mon-Sat. **Main courses** AR$10-$25. **Credit** AmEx, MC, V. **Map** p277 E7.
You'll find tapas, tortillas and baby squid at this modern Catalan kitchen, which has come to stir up and add style to BA's dilapidated Spanish scene. It's pricier than the home-grown tapas bars, but regulars keep returning to sample the seafood pastas and casseroles and sherry consommé, and the imported hams and Manchego cheese. Great for small groups.

La Tasca de Plaza Mayor
Posadas 1052, entre Cerrito y Carlos Pellegrini, Recoleta (4393 5671/www.grupoplazamayor.com). Bus 62, 92, 93, 130. **Open** 9am-1am daily. **Main courses** AR$9-$60. **Credit** AmEx, DC, MC, V. **Map** p278 G8.
Situated under the flyover on 9 de Julio, this classy eaterie draws prominent businessmen and the odd president – fish-loving Néstor 'the penguin' Kirchner is a fan – with its offering of distinguished, Iberian fare, including Valencian paellas and the pick of local catches. Permanently popular; opposite is a less formal outlet that specialises in beers and tapas.

Meaty marvels at **El Establo** (*see p105*). If you don't fancy this, try one of the vegetarian options opposite.

Vegetarian

Tenedor libre buffet restaurants have veggie options and plenty of salads: **Los Sabios** is a 100 per cent vegetarian version at Avenida Corrientes 3733 in Abasto. The city is also splattered with *dieteticas* (healthfood stores); two serving sit-down meals on Avenida Córdoba in Tribunales are **La Esquina de las Flores** at No.1587 (4811 4729) and **Lotos** at No.1577 (4814 4552). **Senutre** (République Arabe Siria 3090, Palermo, 4800 1300) is a chic organic deli with take away vegetarian dishes and a couple of tiny tables.

Bio

Humboldt 2199, y Guatemala, Palermo Viejo (4774 3880/www.biorestaurant.com). Train or Subte D to Palermo/93, 111 bus. **Open** 10am-3pm Mon; 10am-1am Tue-Sun. **Main courses** AR$9-$15. **Set menu** (lunch only) AR$10. **No credit cards.** **Map** p279 K5.

Even hardened carnivores will consider going green after vegging at this utterly organic gourmet corner bistro. A fish- and meat-free menu reflects what is seasonally available – in summer there's gazpacho or aubergine *milanesa*, while in winter pumpkins are carved open and filled with sweetcorn stew. Veg juices and refreshing ginger lemonade are available throughout the year. Great salads too.

Krishna

Malabia 1844, y Costa Rica, Palermo Viejo (4833 4618). Bus 39, 55. **Open** noon-6pm Tue; noon-midnight Tue-Sun. **Main courses** AR$7-$12. **No credit cards.** **Map** p279 J4.

In an ideal Palermo Viejo location, in purplish haze of esoteric Gaias, Vishnus and an out-of-place Jimi Hendrix, an all-Krishna kitchen staff say a mantra before offering their protector – and New Age hippie guests – Indian delights like kofta dumplings and a thali platter with pakoras, raita, and other spicy vegetarian meals. Ideal for a quick, cheap and divinely nutritious lunch.

Restaurants by area

Eat, Drink, Shop

Cafés, Bars & Pubs

Where coffee evenings segue into cocktail mornings.

The strict definitions that distinguish a pub from a bar from a café in other places hold little sway in Buenos Aires. Cafés have always played an important role in the artistic and political life of the city, but in recent years a more socially frivolous bar and pub scene has flourished. In the *porteño* tradition of maximising return from a single space, some venues serve multiple purposes, and boundaries are blurred as a result; you can even quench your thirst in music shops, hairdressers and clothes stores (*see p154* **Multiespacios**).

In this chapter we've listed a selection of the best cafés, bars and pubs in each area – for our top recommendations, *see p129* **The best hangouts**. For places serving a predominantly gay clientele, *see pp183-87* **Gay & Lesbian**. Many restaurants also make fine spots for a drink, especially early evening or after the main dinner rush. Funky Italian eaterie Filo (*see p117*) is fun for a cocktail, stylish Gran Bar Danzón (*see p109*) mixes some of the best drinks in the city and has great happy hour deals (including on sushi). In Palermo Viejo, Central (*see p108*) and Bar 6 (*see p108*) are lovely for a daytime coffee or an early drink while browsing their magazine selections, and the terrace of Lomo (*see p111*) is spectacular at sundown. Alternatively try the lemon-grass laced drink, Green Bamboo, at the restaurant of the same name (*see p120*), or head to Scandinavian-inspired Olsen (*see p111*) for a fruity vodka cocktail in the designer garden.

CAFE CULTURE

Cafés are busiest around midday and often stay open into the evening; some stay open around the clock. Alcohol is usually available and it's not uncommon for a quiet daytime spot to morph into a livelier bar at a certain time of night (Bella Italia). Styles of café vary: the traditional neighbourhood hubs of yesteryear (Florida Garden) sit beside Starbucks-style coffee shops and trendy delis (Marks).

For daytime snacking, typical café favourites include the *tostado* (a crustless, triple layered toasted sandwich, usually with ham and cheese), *picadas* (literally little 'bites' of food – olives, cheese, ham and the like) and *medialunas* (small, sweet, croissant-shaped pastries). Many cafés have extensive food menus.

Little wonder, considering the Italian heritage, that coffee is so popular. And even if it

sometimes fails to meet Italian flavour standards, there are numerous ways to drink it. The most common caffeine kicks are a *café* (a single espresso) and a *cortado* (a single espresso with a drop of hot milk). Other options include *café con leche*, *cappuccino* and a light option, the *lágrima* (warm milk with a 'teardrop' of coffee). Unfortunately it's practically impossible to find a decaf. Tea drinking is growing in popularity too, with an expanding range of designer Argentinian brews on offer. A sweet speciality for winter is a *submarino* – a glass of hot milk with a bar of chocolate submerged in it. Try one accompanied with *churros* (sticky cucumber shaped doughnuts) in a classic caff (La Giralda).

BARS & BOOZE

Despite the hugely increased options for going out for a session, Argentinians are not big boozers – non-drinkers can choose from soft drinks, milkshakes (*licuados*) and juices. Wine, especially red, is many people's tipple of choice – unsurprising, considering the quality of the local grape harvest (*see p102* **The wine box**). There are other local alcoholic specialities to get to grips with, along with the rules of BA bar life; *see p131* **Getting them in**.

Many bars and pubs may also have a varied food menu – *porteños* have a penchant for eating whenever they drink. Shrewd tourists will take advantage of long happy hours (a six-hour stretch at The Shamrock), and the lack of licensing laws, to lengthen their night.

An explosion of contemporary places, which began in the late '90s, has transformed areas like Palermo Viejo, and its sub-barrio, Palermo Hollywood, into the city's most happening 'hood. New bars seem to pop up by the week – sample as many as you can (*see p132* **Pub crawling through Palermo**). Town houses have been converted into late-night art bars (Sonoridad Amarilla) and classy cocktail joints (Mundo Bizarro). Architectural innovation stretches to other areas too – in Recoleta a grand old mansion has become a lush drinking hole (Milión), while downtown, Reconquista Street is the main drinking drag, with busy Irish pubs (Kilkenny), pool bars (Deep Blue) and a bustling atmosphere. If you like things more low-key, head to the bohemian bars in historic San Telmo (Gibraltar), or, for the flash factor, visit the area around the Palermo polo ground (Dorrego, Voodoo Lounge).

The Centre

Avenida de Mayo

Café Tortoni
Avenida de Mayo 829, entre Piedras y Tacuarí (4342 4328/www.cafetortoni.com.ar). Subte A, Piedras/10, 17, 64, 86 bus. **Open** 8am-3am Mon-Sat; 9am-1am Sun. **Credit** AmEx, MC, V. **Map** p277 E6.
Since it opened in 1858, the splendid Tortoni – Argentina's oldest traditional café – has played host to a stellar cast, from the depths of bohemia to the heights of the literati and across the political spectrum. Today its reputation attracts bus-loads of camera-swinging tourists – but don't be put off, the Tortoni is one of a kind. Beyond the wooden tables and marble floor, there's a popular salon that hosts jazz and tango shows, while in the back room pool tables await. Service is less than snappy.

Tribunales

La Giralda
Avenida Corrientes 1453, entre Paraná y Uruguay (4371 3846). Subte B, Uruguay/24, 26, 102 bus. **Open** from 8am Mon-Sat; 3-11pm Sun. **No credit cards. Map** p277 F6.
Pre- and post-theatre crowds come for La Giralda's famous *chocolate y churros*, and bleary night owls drop in for a last drink. Brightly lit, with white-tiled walls and ashen-faced waiters, this quirky little café remains a Corrientes classic.

Microcentro

Le Caravelle
Lavalle 726, entre Esmeralda y Maipú (4322 1673). Subte B, Florida or C, Lavalle/10, 17, 99, 111 bus. **Open** 7.30am-10.30pm Mon-Fri; 7.30am-11.30pm Sat; 9.30am-9pm Sun. **No credit cards. Map** p277 E7.
Despite its location – on tacky Lavalle – Le Caravelle maintains a timeless aura. It is also one of BA's few cafés that still knows how to make a *ristretto* – Italians' favourite caffeine shot. Check out the coffee percolators for sale, the clocks and some of the local oddballs reminiscing over their steaming cups.

La Cigale
25 de Mayo 722, entre Viamonte y Córdoba (4312 8275). Subte B, LN Alem/26, 93, 130, 152 bus. **Open** from 6pm Mon-Fri; from 8pm Sat. **Credit** AmEx, MC, V. **Map** p277 E8.
A huge bar counter, booth seating, fairy lights and big moon lamps – this is not your classic French café. Nevertheless, La Cigale, a forerunner among late-night drinking dens, does very well, with a crowd that leans towards music mag readers and the odd French expat. Big nights include Tuesday's Soirée Française – when Ricard drops to a bargain two pesos – and DJs spin *electrónica*, and the weekends, when a party atmosphere prevails later on.

Cosy, colourful **Dadá**.

Confitería Richmond
Florida 468, entre Lavalle y Corrientes (4322 1653/ 1341/www.restaurant.com.ar/richmond). Subte B, Florida/10, 26, 93 bus. **Open** 8am-10pm Mon-Sat. **Credit** AmEx, DC, MC, V. **Map** p277 E7.
The *New York Times* once ran an article on this 1917 classic, claiming that the food and service were among the best in BA. The owners' boast of 1,400 visitors a day seems to prove such accolades. Offering a touch of class and respite from mad Florida street, the Richmond pulls a mix of weary tourists and stately, cigarette-smoking gents. Settle into a red leather chair and enjoy a whisky upstairs or a game of chess below. Tango shows on Saturdays (7-10pm).

Retiro

Dadá
San Martín 941, entre Marcelo T de Alvear y Paraguay (4314 4787). Subte C, San Martín/61, 93, 130, 152 bus. **Open** noon-2am Mon-Sat. **Credit** AmEx, MC, V. **Map** p277 E8.
Drenched in colour with Mondrian glass, Pop art walls and a mosaic bar, Dadá is a bar-restaurant with serious sex appeal. It draws in an engaging mix of intellectuals, artists and tourists who come for Paolo and Julián's classy cocktails and the modern bistro cuisine, featuring established classics such as the *lomo Dadá* steak, *cordero al romero* (Patagonian lamb) or the wild mushroom and grilled polenta special. The bar itself is quite small, and the secret is definitely out, but you should be able to find a stool and a friendly ear to help you unwind.

Eat, Drink, Shop

Deep Blue

Reconquista 920, entre Paraguay y Marcelo T de Alvear (4312 3377/www.deep-blue.com.ar). Subte C, San Martín/7, 26, 93, 152 bus. **Open** 11am-4am Mon-Fri; 8pm-4am Sat, Sun. **Credit** AmEx, MC, V. **Map** p277 E8.

With booth seating upstairs and a funky white basement below, Deep Blue is where fashion-conscious pool-heads come to play (AR$4 per game). Although the place is awash with friendly staff, some tables are equipped with their own self-service beer tap – keep count though, it's not free. If you're peckish there are very palatable burgers and other US-style comfort food on offer till late. The formula is obviously a hit, as new branches are being planned. **Other locations:** Ayacucho 1204, Recoleta (4827 4415).

Druid Inn

Reconquista 1040, entre Rojas y Marcelo T de Alvear (4312 3688). Subte C, San Martín/26, 93, 152 bus. **Open** from noon Mon-Fri; from 8pm Sat. **Credit** AmEx, MC, V. **Map** p277 E8.

An Irish pub that flies the flag of tradition: beer towels on the beams, tankards hung up on the bar, old maps of Ireland and a TV in the corner. Dim lighting and mahogany partitions add to the cosy feel, while the chatty staff are quick to take orders. Everything costs a little more than it possibly should, but it's on a par with the surrounding area.

Florida Garden

Florida 899, y Paraguay (4312 7902/4311 6878). Subte C, San Martín/6, 26, 93, 130, 152 bus. **Open** 6.30am-midnight Mon-Fri; 8am-11pm Sat, Sun. **Credit** AmEx, V. **Map** p277 E8.

Many of the clients of this exalted two-tier establishment – a leader in literary café culture – are the same as when it came to eminence in the 1960s. Prominent local artists have been gathering here on Saturday mornings for decades. These days, they are joined by business people and tourists, sitting between the handsome copper columns or leaning on the glass- or

Florida Garden: a charmingly cultured café.

marble-topped bars. Courteous service accompanies the excellent coffees, teas and pastries, or old-school cocktails with a generous snack selection. There's a lengthy food menu too, for lunch or dinner.

The Kilkenny

Marcelo T de Alvear 399, y Reconquista (4312 7291). Subte C, San Martín/26, 93, 152 bus. **Open** from 5.30pm-6am Mon-Fri; 8pm-6am Sat, Sun. **Admission** AR$10 minimum spend (men only) Thur-Sat. **Credit** AmEx, DC, MC, V. **Map** p277 E8.

Four suits walk in, with nods to the left and winks to the right and make for the circular bar; a table of giggling girls juggle popcorn, and check their mobile phones; meanwhile, a live band is thrashing out Joe Cocker covers. Welcome to the most popular pub in BA. Unabashedly thematic, the Kilkenny is a loud, low-lit venue, dressed up in Gaelic maps, railway signals and the usual Irish paraphernalia, with a whisky lounge up on the first floor. Bustling during the week, by Saturday it's all out mayhem: hefty bouncers on the door, runners staggering under the weight of glasses and strong wafts of cologne. In summer, the Kilkenny puts on fun parties on a small island in the delta near Tigre – ask staff at the bar for details about where and when.

Marriott Plaza

Basement, Florida 1005, y Santa Fe (4318 3000 ext 873/www.marriott.com). Subte C, San Martín/61, 93, 130, 152 bus. **Open** 11am-1am daily. **Credit** AmEx, DC, MC, V. **Map** p277 F8.

You can easily imagine heads of government, company chairmen or Argentina's literary greats slipping down to this beautiful art deco bar. The service accessorises perfectly with the leather furnishings, background classical music and artwork synonymous with the city's heyday. It's expensive in local terms – AR$20 for a Bloody Mary – though the quality of the cocktails helps justify the price tag, and the (free) platter of tasty canapés is another plus.

650

San Martín 650, entre Tucumán y Viamonte (4313 9650/www.seis50.com.ar). Subte B, Florida/93, 99, 109, 132 bus. **Open** 10am-11pm Mon-Fri. **Credit** AmEx, MC, V. **Map** p277 E7.

Box seating, cheap happy-hour deals (two beers and a *picada*, AR$6.50) and a central location make this a popular spot for a post-work downtown drink. The flickering TV screens and optimistic attempts at minimalist chic are at best distracting, but it hardly matters – most of the execs and secs are too busy eyeing each other up to care. Manic early on, by 10pm almost every one has either copped out or copped off.

South of Centre

San Telmo

Bar Plaza Dorrego

Defensa 1098, y Humberto 1º (4361 0141). Bus 24, 29, 126, 130, 152. **Open** 8am-3am daily. **No credit cards**. **Map** p276 C6.

With outdoor seating on the picturesque Plaza Dorrego, this century-old watering hole perfectly embodies the *tanguero* spirit of San Telmo. Inside, a pale lemon hue is cast over the dusty bottles and etched walls, while tango crackles over black-and-

white images of Gardel. It's an ideal spot from which to watch the Sunday market goings-on or on a warm evening for a *chopp* and a plate of monkey nuts.

Bar Seddón

Defensa 695, y Chile (4342 3700). Bus 24, 29, 126, 130, 152. **Open** 6pm-4am Tue-Fri; 9pm-6am Sat; 5pm-2am Sun. **No credit cards**. **Map** p277 D6.

When a government rescue package never arrived and the Seddón was forced to change location – the original was perhaps BA's best looking bar – many feared the worst. But thankfully, the owners found themselves an attractive San Telmo corner site and threw in much of the same from before: yellow and blue spot-lighting, black and white floors, wooden tables and a fine array of well worn antiques. Like many bars in the barrio, weekdays are tranquil, but then the space packs out on weekends, especially for Sunday's live tango evenings.

El Británico

Avenida Brasil 399, y Defensa (4300 6894). Bus 10, 29, 39, 93, 152. **Open** 24hrs daily. **No credit cards**. **Map** p276 C5.

There's a real Jim Jarmusch feel to this creaking relic. During the Falklands/Malvinas War, the bar diplomatically changed its name, but the decor remained – and the waiters, too, it seems, who totter around in a stoic manner. Open round the clock, it's handy for that final 'one for the road'.

La Farmacia

Bolívar 899, y Estados Unidos (4300 6151). Bus 10, 24, 29, 86. **Open** 9am-1.30am Tue-Thur, Sun; 9am-2.30am Sat, Sun. **No credit cards**. **Map** p276 C6.

This former pharmacy (hence the name and array of medicine bottles) is an amalgam of lots of little spaces spread around a three-tiered corner spot. Upstairs is a popular restaurant, with a roof terrace above, while the drinking area is on the red-hued ground floor. Sadly the bar is too small to sit at – settle into a cosy sofa instead and wash down the cheese platter with a glass of *tinto*.

Eat, Drink, Shop

Deep Blue has 'em cue-ing round the block.

IN ALCOHOL WE TRUST

MUNDO **BIZARRO**

19 97

COCKTAIL LOUNGE & GRILL

THE HOTTEST SPOT IN BUENOS AIRES

GUATEMALA 4802 - PALERMO

4773-1967

LOCAL
LAGERS–ALES–STOUT AND CIDER
ON DRAUGHT

1999

GIBRALTAR DESDE 1999

SAN TELMO

EVERYDAY FROM 6. 00PM TIL LATE

BEST PINT
&
BEST PRICE IN TOWN

THAI–INDIAN–CHINESE
AND
CONTINENTAL FOOD

Calle Peru 895 Capital Federal Buenos Aires Argentina
tel. 4362-5310

THEGIBRALTAR@HOTMAIL. COM

Milion **M** LA CASA

Restaurant - Bar - Happy Hour - Art - Events - Animations

Paraná 1048 - Buenos Aires - Argentina - Tel. (54-11) 4815-9925
milion@fibertel.com.ar - www.milion.com.ar

El Federal

Carlos Calvo 599, y Perú (4300 4313). Bus 10, 22, 24, 29, 86. **Open** 7.30am-2am Mon-Thur, Sun; 7.30-4am Fri, Sat. **Credit** MC, V. **Map** p276 C6.

El Federal is one of BA's historical listed bars (built in 1864), and also one of the best kept – check out the magnificent cash registers. It's pretty original too; bar staff work from a lowered floor while the bar itself is thigh-high. There's a standard offering of beers and spirits and a long menu of sandwiches and other snacks (though not the best *picadas*). With the faded, yellow lamps hanging overhead and the old advertising posters, it captures that elusive spirit of the Buenos Aires of a bygone era. Occasional tango events add to the ambience.

Fin del Mundo

Defensa 700, y Chile (15 5314 4729 mobile). Bus 24, 29, 126, 130, 152. **Open** from 6pm Mon-Sat; from 3pm Sun. **No credit cards. Map** p277 D6.

Pull up a pin-head stool and try and not to fall off as the dreadlocked DJ (and owner) spins his silky repertoire of classics. A corner bar with a large terrace, the musical theme continues from the live sets in the basement room (Thursdays to Saturdays) to the stacks of on-sale vinyl on the shelves. The decor and lighting are kind of haphazard, but it's lively and refreshingly unpretentious.

Gibraltar

Perú 895, y Estados Unidos (4362 5310). Bus 10, 22, 24, 29, 86. **Open** from 6pm daily. **No credit cards. Map** p276 C6.

A brave name, in a brave location, Gibraltar is as authentically English as you'll find in BA – and naturally attracts a lot of expats. The owners are good fun and have employed bar staff with similar spirit – check out Beaver the barman's bad taste jokes. Following the trend of some British pubs, a combination of English classics (huge burgers, fish 'n' chips) and Thai and Indian dishes is served up. There's a fine choice of drinks, and it all comes at extremely reasonable prices. At the rear, there's a pool table, while up front, a TV broadcasts Premier League football and other sporting events. When the mood is right, Gibraltar can rock until sunrise; at other times, there's a real *Cheers* feel.

Via Via

Chile 324, entre Bolívar y Defensa (4300 7259). Bus 24, 29, 126, 130, 152. **Open** 8am-2am Mon-Thur, Sun; 8am-6.30am Fri, Sat. **No credit cards. Map** p277 D6.

Part of the flourishing dining and drinking scene springing up around *calle* Chile, Belgian-owned Via Via is one of the most popular (and affordable) – Friday nights are rammed. The 'world cuisine' is the tastiest on the block (and the good old Argentinian *bife de chorizo* is especially succulent), which is more than can be said for the misspelt and mis-made 'froozen Margarita'. Even if you're just after a cheap beer on the terrace, or the chance to mix with some fellow tourists, it's not a bad place to be.

The best Hangouts

Bar Plaza Dorrego
The *tanguero* spirit hangs over the checkered floor of San Telmo's coolest old-style bar. *See p127.*

Dadá
Slick, good-looking and fun. *See p125.*

Lelé de Troya
A colour for every mood plus a sizzling, summer terrace. *See p134.*

Florida Garden
Classic '50s styling and old-fashioned manners in the Microcentro. *See p126.*

Gibraltar
Beers, burgers and pool in Brit pub style.

Marks
A designer café with deli treats. *See p134.*

Milión
Where the opulent and the avant-garde meet to get drunk on al fresco aperitifs. *See p130.*

Mundo Bizarro
Crazy, sexy, cool – and just a tad decadent. *See p134.*

Omm
Small, but perfectly formed. *See p135.*

The Shamrock
A boozer's drinking hole, a clubber's club and a haven for foreigners. *See p130.*

Voodoo Lounge
Sleek 'n' chic with a thumping Wednesday club night. *See p135.*

La Boca

La Perla
Avenida Pedro de Mendoza 1895, y Del Valle Iberlucea (4301 2985). Bus 29, 53, 64, 152. **Open** 7am-7pm Mon-Fri; from 7am Sat, Sun. **No credit cards. Map** p276 A5.

Just metres from Caminito and the less-than-fragrant waters of the Riochuelo, this former brothel (although you'd never guess it), opened nearly a century ago. The special promotions are generous and the *picadas de mariscos* (seafood nibbles) popular with regulars – it's less of a tourist trap than first impressions suggest. Bill Clinton stopped by on a presidential tour; he'd be impressed to see that his photo takes pride of place, next to one of Maradona and friends.

Eat, Drink, Shop

Constitución

Boquitas Pintadas

Estados Unidos 1393, y San José (4381 6064/
www.boquitas-pintadas.com.ar). Subte E, San José/
39, 53, 60, 102, 168 bus. **Open** noon-3am Mon-Fri;
7pm-3am Sat. **No credit cards. Map** p277 D5.
Boquita's bar adds a bit of much needed colour and
kitsch to a dark street corner. It's also a bit odd; with
gold and silver painted walls, quirky lighting and
high angular bar – and the decor is regularly
rethought and retouched. Drawing guests from the
hotel above (*see p41*) and those familiar with the
scene, it's busiest on party nights when DJs drop by
or the basement is opened up; details from the bar.

Make beer buddies at **The Shamrock**.

North of the Centre

Recoleta

La Biela

Avenida Quintana 596, y RM Ortiz (4804 0449/
www.labiela.com). Bus 59, 60, 101, 102, 110. **Open**
7am-3am Mon-Thur; 7am-4am Fri, Sat; 8am-3am
Sun. **Credit** V. **Map** p278 G7.
La Biela is Recoleta's most prominent café and former stomping ground of Argentinian writer Adolfo
Bioy Casares. It's named after the 'connecting rod'
in car engines, testimony to the the fact that motor
racing drivers hung out here in the 1950s. A couple
of decades later, at the height of the dictatorship,
guerrilla groups targeted La Biela and its bourgeois
clientele. Nowadays, the massive rubber tree shelters
a terrace full of tourists and Recoleta's most monied
residents. The fixed-price lunches are good value.

Henry J Beans

Junín 1749, entre Guido y Vicente López (4801
8477/www.henryjbeans.net). Bus 59, 60, 101, 102,
110. **Open** from 6pm Mon-Fri; from 12.30pm Sat,
Sun. **Credit** AmEx, DC, MC, V. **Map** p278 G7.
As with all branches of the Beans chain, you'll find
bog-standard Tex-Mex food, televised sport, star-
studded memorabilia, jugs of beer and the odd
British tourist. Thursdays are especially popular,
when queues for happy hour spill into the streets;
admission is AR$5, but includes two beers or soft
drinks. A DJ cranks out tunes on Friday nights. If
you want to try a different theme bar on the same
strip, Buller Brewing Company (RM Ortiz 1827, 4808
9061) offers excellent micro-brewed beers.
Other locations: Arce 904, Belgrano (4776 4192).

Locos x el Fútbol

Village Recoleta, Vicente López 2098, y Uriburu
(4807 3777/www.locosxelfutbol.com). Bus 59, 60,
101, 102, 110. **Open** from 11am daily. **Credit**
AmEx, MC, V. **Map** p278 G7.
The 'x' means 'for', and Crazy for Football lives up
to its name. This multi-screened bar displays a non-
stop bonanza of previews, *partidos* (matches) and
highlights. Mini-skirted waitresses serve beers and
snacks, nourishing a fickle crowd whose mood
sways with the game. For big matches, book in
advance; a variable minimum charge applies. You
can also pick up a wide range of footy memorabilia
from their shop next door. At 2am on Friday and
Saturday nights, the tables are pushed back to make
room for dancing to cheesy pop; admission AR$7 for
women and AR$10-$13 for men, one drink included
– it's free if you're dining.

Milión

Paraná 1048, entre Marcelo T de Alvear y Santa Fe
(4815 9925/www.milion.com.ar). Bus 29, 39, 102,
152. **Open** noon-2am Mon-Wed; noon-3am Thur;
noon-4am Fri; 7.30pm-4am Sat; 8pm-2am Sun.
Credit AmEx, V. **Map** p277 F7.
For 79 years, this French-style mansion belonged to
a smart German family. Lovingly restored, it was
reborn in 1999 as Milión – a stylish bar and restaurant. It's huge, but consistently filled by the young
and cool, drawn in by its blend of serenity and stunning aesthetics. Upstairs is the bar and main eating
area, while outside visitors are spoilt for choice; a
first-floor terrace, sweeping marble staircase and a
gorgeous garden, with a sheltered back area lit with
candles and projected visuals. Food is mainly variations on the tapas theme, the music ambient and
service friendly, if at times a touch slow.

The Shamrock

Rodríguez Peña 1220, entre Juncal y Arenales (4812
3584/www.theshamrockbar.com). Bus 10, 37, 39,
101, 124, 152. **Open** from 6pm Mon-Fri; from 8pm
Sat, Sun. **Credit** AmEx, MC, V. **Map** p278 G7.
A few years back, this type of boisterous drinking
establishment was almost unheard of. It's not your
average Irish pub – open-plan and modern – but its
fun, friendly and perennially busy, so that even early
in the week, you're guaranteed a scene. It's also good
value, with a generous happy hour (from opening
time until midnight). The tunes and jokey bar staff
– many are ex-clients who hopped over the bar –
keep the down-to-earth crowd of twenty- to thirty-
somethings on their toes, while some older, and
odder, regulars stick close to the bar. The heavy
drapes lead down to the heaving Basement Club (*see
p170*), open from Thursday to Saturday.

Eat, Drink, Shop

Barrio Norte

Clásica y Moderna

Avenida Callao 892, entre Paraguay y Córdoba
(4812 8707/4811 3670/www.clasicaymoderna.com).
Subte D, Callao/12, 29, 37, 124 bus. **Open** 8am-2am
Mon-Thur; 8am-4am Fri, Sat; 5pm-2am Sun.
Admission (shows) AR\$8-\$20 plus minimum spend
AR\$5-\$7. **Credit** AmEx, DC, MC, V. **Map** p277 F6.
A pioneer in the library-bar-café model, its brick
walls, wooden tables, soft lighting and classic jazz
attract a middle-aged intellectual crowd. Food is
served all day, including a solid breakfast in winter.
Live shows on Wednesdays to Sundays range from
tango performances to poetry readings.

The Spot

Ayacucho 1261, entre Arenales y Juncal (4811 8955).
Bus 12, 39, 60, 152. **Open** from 8pm Mon-Fri; from
10pm Sat. **Credit** AmEx, MC. **Map** p278 G6.
Beyond the dramatic, velvet-curtained entrance, lies
a cosy relief from shopping and sightseeing. A 'local'
away from home, The Spot offers cheap beers, a dart
board and friendly banter in a pub-like setting. A
late haunt for overworked bar staff, it thrives when
most other establishments close. The usual world-
weary barflies linger at quieter times.

Palermo

Good options for daytime in Palermo are the
area's museums and gardens (you have to pay
entrance): the **Jardín Japonés** has a lovely
tea room; the café in the **Museo de Artes
Plásticas Eduardo Sívori** has attractive
views of the park; and **Malba's** airy café-
restaurant offers fine cuisine. For all, *see pp84-5.*

Bella Italia

República Arabe Siria 3330, entre Segui y Libertador
(4807 5120). Bus 10, 67, 102, 130. **Open** 8am-1am
daily. **No credit cards**. **Map** p279 J7.
Bella Italia is *bella* indeed. This relaxed and airy side-
street café positively whiffs of the Mediterranean.
The dappled yellow interior is designed for whiling
away the hours. Pick up a magazine, indulge in a
thick wedge of lemon pie and idle at a wooden table
inside, or head to the patio. A sister restaurant of the
same name is one block up the street at No.3285.

Dorrego

Avenida Dorrego, entre Libertador y Cerviño (6775
2222/www.dorregobuenosaires.com.ar). Bus 15, 29,
55, 60, 64. **Open** 8pm-6am Wed-Sat. **Credit** AmEx,
MC, V. **Map** p279 K6.

Getting them in

Undeniably, drinking in Buenos Aires is a real
pleasure. It's cheap, it's fun and it boasts the
world's most generous licensing laws: none.
Moreover, bar designs are slick, staff are sexy
and they mix great cocktails with a smile.

So, what's the problem? Arguably, getting
served is the first. If you want to prop up the
bar for the night, you'll need to order directly
from whoever is behind it. If you sit at a table,
someone will come to take your order. Drinks
that look easy to order often deceive; JB is
pronounced *hotter bay*, vodka is *bodka*, and
tougher yet, a whisky cola requires a pinch of
the nose to come out right as *wiscola*.

Argentinians also enjoy some
very strange drinks. Check out the
herbal-tasting, Fernet Branca liqueur
(usually mixed with Coke) or the
sweet and sickly Gancia
Batido (using Gancia
vermouth) that looks
like the bathwater you
probably just got out
of. As for champagne and
red wine, they often add ice
and to the latter, a dash of
soda. Of course you may
just fancy a beer. Quilmes

– decorated in the national colours – is the
most ubiquitous, but Brazilian Brahma is
becoming more common. Isenbeck and
especially Warsteiner are tastier and less
chemical. Beer is generally consumed in small
bottles, called a *porrón*, or for draught, ask for
a *chopp*. In cheaper bars or restaurants, go
for larger bottles called *tres-cuatros*.

Boozers be warned: this is not a hard-
drinking town. Women tend to sip a Coke or
at a push, or the local best-seller – strawberry
daiquiri (Daiquiri de Frutilla) – while men are
usually content with a couple of beers or
whiskies. Pulling is a far more serious
business. People dress up and scent up
and the lucky ones will think nothing of
snogging over their drinks for hours on
end – which is why some bars impose
a minimum spend.

Thankfully, you're unlikely to
get an overly flash, juggling
barman behind the bar, and
service is generally friendly
and good – so remember to
leave a tip (at least ten per
cent). It won't be expected but
it will definitely be appreciated
– bar staff earn a pittance.

Eat, Drink, Shop

Short on space, but big on style: **Omm**. *See p135.*

Located in the exclusive neighbourhood close to the Palermo polo ground, first it was a railway station, then a nightclub, and now it's potentially BA's most designer-conscious drinking spot. The bars are a tad '*histérico*' (a local expression for 'hectic, heated and horny') but, luckily, quality mod Argentinian cuisine is also on offer for more serious punters. Opened in late 2003, it was immediately chosen as the venue for several glam fashion and food magazine parties, packed wall-to-wall with the city's beautiful people. It's a huge space, intelligently divided and perfectly suited to the well-heeled crowd. The central bar dominates, while the principal eating area is out back – you can watch the clamour from a calmer vantage point. Lighting is soft and chill-out areas plentiful – snag a white sofa behind the main bar, with mohair cushions and matching retro chairs, or sneak upstairs to the sinister land of the black beds.

Pub crawling in Palermo

While the Buenos Aires pub scene may be blossoming, it doesn't take the keenest eye to realise that this is not a hard-drinking town. For the thirsty traveller who doesn't mind standing out from a sober crowd, Palermo Viejo – BA's principal drinking destination – boasts a large number of daytime spots and late-night joints to keep your chops thoroughly lubricated. It's the perfect barrio for an old-fashioned pub crawl.

Start at **Lomo** restaurant (No.1; *see p111*) at around 6pm. The beach-style terrace, pebbled floors and native plant life are a great backdrop for a medicinal loosener, while catching some late afternoon rays. If the cocktail man's arrived, Daiquiri de los Dioses, an icy mix of rum, lime, grenadine and mango will cool your parched palate. The sun-lounges of **Lelé De Troya** (No.2; *see p134*) are the second stop on the tour. Gancia Batidos and two-litre bottles of Bud are served under the sun, as you look out at the Palermo Viejo skyline, before moving on to the early-evening decadence of happy hour.

An essential cocktail stop is **Mundo Bizarro** (No.3; *see p134*), with daily special promotions. Its dark and sultry interior, provides ample cover in which to sample its devilish daiquiris. Try to retain some composure for stylish **Bar Uriarte** (No.4; *see p108*). Among the happy hour bargains (which runs to 10pm Monday to Saturday and until 11pm Sunday) are two-for-one glasses of champagne – ideal for toasting a night of revelry.

Next, cross the tracks, where there's more fizz on offer at **Cavas y Cuevas** (No.5; *see p133*) – 80 different kinds, to be precise. A cheeky champagne cocktail is the perfect order for keeping your spirits up. Then to **Dubliners** (No.6; *see p133*), where half-price beers (until 9pm) and an easy atmosphere

Rond Point

Avenida Figueroa Alcorta 3009, y Tagle (4802 0790). Bus 67, 102, 130 bus. **Open** 6am-3am daily. **Credit** AmEx, DC, MC, V. **Map** p278 H7.

The two-tiered Rond Point is one of the city's more serious cafés. It sits on busy Figueroa Alcorta, beneath Uruguayan painter Carlos Páez Vilaró's cheerful mural of Carlos Gardel. A former darling of the barrio's preppie set, it recently replaced the classic 1970's Parisian coffee house decor with a more modern concept. It's a great place to take a breather after a Sunday stroll in the nearby parks.

Palermo Viejo

Acabar

Honduras 5733, entre Bonpland y Carranza (4772 0845/4776 3634). Bus 39, 93, 111. **Open** from 8pm daily. **Credit** MC, V. **Map** p279 K4.

Neon lights, coloured corrugated-iron sheets, canteen-style food and games galore. This bar of odds and sods is a circus-like frenzy of junkyard proportions. Note the Afro-wigged mannequin and childish faux-classic art as you charge your glasses long into the night. A bustling place to eat, drink and play – it's good, down-to-earth fun at generous prices.

Blur

El Salvador 5729, entre Bonpland y Carranza (4771 4844). Bus 39, 93, 111. **Open** from 8pm Tue-Sat. **No credit cards. Map** p279 K4.

Large, sparse and echoey, Blur is the zenith of BA minimalism. With mouth-watering tapas and brave new cocktails to boot – try Se Dice De Mi (frozen

apple, pineapple, orange, mint and vodka) – the menu is as modern and chic as the bar itself. Unrepentantly exclusive, the spacious decor leaves ample room for small talk and insincere flattery.

Cavas y Cuevas

Guatemala 5650, entre Fitz Roy y Bonpland (4773 0598). Subte D or train to Palermo/39, 93, 111 bus. **Open** from 6.30pm Tue-Sat. **Credit** AmEx, MC, V. **Map** p279 K5.

If champers is your thing, or even if you're just partial to the odd drop, then specialist bar Cavas y Cuevas is a definite must-try. More than 80 varieties of regional and imported bottles hang above the bar of this classy Palermo joint. The delectable Cavas Cooler (fresh ginger, lemon and champagne) is just one of the sparkling drinks on offer. If that's still not enough bubbly, order one of the tasty meals, laced with sauces made of – yep, you guessed it – champagne. One of the venues on BA's Jazz Route (*see p194*), Friday nights are when live bands play.

Dubliners

Humboldt 2000, y Niceto Vega (4771 6178/www. dublinersirishpub.com.ar). Bus 39, 93, 111, 168. **Open** from noon Mon-Sat. **Credit** AmEx, MC, V. **Map** p279 K4.

While this is one of the city's more authentic-looking Irish pubs, the table service and the incense burning at the bar asuggest something other than a snug on O'Connell Street. That said, the huge Guinness posters, green ceilings and stained glass windows assist a gratifying night of make-believe. With imported beers at up to AR$30 a bottle (for Chimay), only the desperate or foolish veer from local brews.

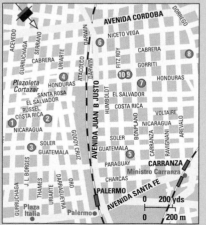

will help you recharge, before heading round the corner to self-styled gamesville, **Acabar** (No.7; *see p133*). By now, with the darker setting in, you may feel a slight itch in your two left feet and the dance floor of **Genoma** (No.8; *see p134*) is as good a place as any to strut your stuff. The chill-out room downstairs caters for a cooler crowd, as well as the incapably inebriated.

En route to your last stop, take a breather on the terrace of chic, petite **Omm** (No.9; *see p135*) for a mouth-watering Mojito. Almost next door, at the end of the trawl, **Unico** (No.10; *see p135*) offers late night tipples to the merry. Its all-night bustle make it a good last stop for beer and banter. It's bound to be busy, but you can sit on the floor at the edges of the terrace. You may even find yourself deep in conversation with a national celebrity – though by this time you're unlikely to know, or care.

La Finca

*Costa Rica 4615, entre Armenia y Gurruchaga
(4832 3004). Bus 15, 39, 55.* **Open** 11am-midnight
daily. **Credit** MC, V. **Map** p279 J4.
A charming outlet for lesser-known Mendoza micro-
wineries, the micro-bar La Finca is a rustic pleasure.
Wine buffs will blush at the array of vintage and lim-
ited-edition bottles. The rest of us can chin wag at
one of the four, small tables, while sampling a glass
of the hand-picked wine of the week. Tastings that
include tapas of goat's cheese, pâté and olives for six
people can be arranged for AR$40 per person.

Genoma

*Avenida Dorrego 1735, entre Cabrera y Gorriti
(4776 6300/www.genomabar.com.ar). Bus 39, 93,
111, 168.* **Open** from 8pm Wed-Sat. **No credit
cards. Map** p279 K4.
Ignore the lantern-lit, Halloween feel in the front room
of this multi-faceted bar and sidle through to the attractive hidden garden. Outside, a thirsty crowd refuel on
long cocktails, in between treks upstairs to the dancefloor, where black and white umbrellas glow under the
UV lights. As the night boils on, kick back on the leop-
ard-print chaises longues in the chill-out lounge and
unwind to the down-tempo beats.

Janio

*Malabia 1805, y Costa Rica (4833 6540/www.janio
restaurant.com). Bus 15, 39, 55.* **Open** 8am-4am
daily. **Credit** AmEx, MC, V. **Map** p279 J4.
A stroke of architectural opportunism converted a
three-storey house overlooking Plaza Palermo Viejo
into a café-bar. It's not the hippest joint, but the
padded benches and parasols on the roof terrace
make it an ideal sunspot. The fusion menu is seasonal, the presentation nouvelle cuisine. Open late,
Janio attracts an eclectic crowd, varying in age and
eminence according to the hour of your visit.

Lelé De Troya

*Costa Rica 4901, y Thames (4832 2726). Bus 39,
55.* **Open** from 8pm daily. **Credit** AmEx, MC, V.
Map p279 J4.
Unlike her namesake Helen of Troy, proprietress
Lelé's take on beauty is this vivid restaurant/bar.
Colour-coded rooms vary as much as the tasty, world-
themed menu. If you're in the mood for passion, try
the boudoir chic of the red room, with its low-lying
chaises and tousled, gypsy lampshades. In summer
the terrace offers a panoramic view of the area, while
sun loungers for kicking back on with bottles of
chilled white wine satisfy the posturing vainglorious.

Malas Artes

*Honduras 4999, y Borges (4831 0743/www.malas
artes.com). Bus 34, 39, 55, 168.* **Open** from 8am
daily. **No credit cards. Map** p279 J4.
This boho bar, on the corner of Plazoleta Cortázar, is
the best of the bunch around the square, though traditionalists prefer older El Taller across the street.
Sheltered under a mulberry tree, it's a café for all
seasons. Enjoy a cold beer outside in summer or, in
winter, a *cortado* and *tostado* in the brick interior.

Mark's Deli

*El Salvador 4701, y Armenia (4832 6244). Bus 15,
39, 55.* **Open** 8.30am-9.30pm Mon-Sat; 10.30am-9pm
Sun. **No credit cards. Map** p279 J4.
Mark's is modelled along the lines of a hip New York
deli. This bright, orange-hued café is favoured by
trendsetting Palermo folk. Take time out of your day
to sip an icy lemonade and sink your teeth into a
large smoked salmon sandwich, or go for giant
chocolate-chip cookies and a café latte, while watching the fashion identicats play with their time. Cheap
lunchtime menus are available on weekdays.

Mundo Bizarro

*Guatemala 4802, y Borges (4773 1967). Subte D,
Plaza Italia/34, 55, 93 bus.* **Open** from 7pm Mon-Fri;
from 8pm Sat, Sun. **No credit cards. Map** p279 J5.
Mundo Bizarro is a kitsch, dimly lit cocktail lounge
with a nocturnal, underground vibe. A mixture of
'50s artwork, cool graphics, funky photographs and
a giant fly sculpture suspended over the bar, give
this space a totally original vibe. Above the black
leather booths, where revellers repose, red lanterns
hang like smouldering torches as a single beam projects random images that flicker to electronic beats.
The cocktail list is imaginative and extensive – try
a spicy Holiday in Cambodia, a peachy Fuzzy Navel
or a peerless Cosmopolitan. Every night has a special angle or offer: sushi and jazz, varying happy-
hour promotions and DJs spinning tunes into the
early hours on weekends.

Mark's the spot for Palermo fashionistas.

The sublimely strange world of **Mundo Bizarro**. *See p134.*

Omm

Honduras 5656, entre Fitz Roy y Bonpland (4774 4224). Bus 39, 93, 111. **Open** from 6pm Mon; from 11.30am Tue-Sun. **Credit** AmEx, MC, V. **Map** p279 K4.

The owners of Central (*see p108*) tested their minimalist chic when they opened Omm. Within its tiny space they've jammed chrome tables, a long bar and enough waitresses to keep your glass permanently filled. The all-white decor is softened by candles and down-to-earth service, a combination that entices a fashion-conscious crowd. The bar staff mix a fantastic Mojito, to accompany selections of tapas. Upstairs is a wine attic with a single table for an intimate dinner or wine-tasting sessions, while the outside terrace is great for Palermo people-watching.

Sonoridad Amarilla

Fitz Roy 1983, y Nicaragua (4777 7931). Bus 39, 93, 111. **Open** 2-8pm Tue; 2pm-2am Wed-Sat. **Closed** Jan. **No credit cards**. **Map** p279 K4.

Inspired by Kandinsky, this quirky, arty bar attracts a beatnik crowd who lounge on pillows beside tiny tables. A small but reasonable menu includes Middle Eastern bites and regional Argentinian beers. The bar doubles as a daytime gallery and the off-beat, contemporary collections add to the mood of improvised eccentricity. You have to ring first to reserve.

Unico Bar Bistro

Fitz Roy 1892, y Honduras (4775 6693). Bus 39, 93, 111. **Open** 8.30am-6am Mon-Fri; 8.30pm-6am Sat, Sun. **Credit** MC. **Map** p279 K4.

Meeting place for Palermo hipsters, this corner bar sets a precedent in the area's popularity stakes (the 4,000 party people that turned out for its fourth anniversary speak for themselves) and the nearby TV studios make it a prime spot for avid stargazers. Unico is a sound bet for a night of mayhem, while catering for even the most unfashionably late. The kitchen, serving bistro fare, is open till 2am.

Las Cañitas

Supersoul

Báez 252, entre Arévalo y Arguibel (4776 3905). Bus 15, 29, 59, 60, 64. **Open** from 5pm Mon-Fri; from 6.30pm Sat; from 6pm Sun. **Credit** V. **Map** p279 K5.

The '70s-feel, sister bar of larger, redder Soul Café next door, Supersoul's retro glam is bound to get your mojo working. Disco balls, psychedelic swirls, funky DJs and, strangely enough, a small sweet shop, breathe life into this dinky space. Pull up a seat at the tangerine-coloured bar, where the gorgeous staff will attend to your thirst with a smile. In both of the Soul venues, there are regular live music happenings directed by owner/rock musician Fabián 'El Zorrito' Von Quinteiro.

Van Koning

Báez 325, entre Arévalo y Chenaut (4772 9909). Bus 15, 29, 59, 60, 64. **Open** from 8pm Tue-Sun. **No credit cards**. **Map** p279 L5.

An anti-fashion bar in the heart of flashy *calle* Báez, Van Koning's archaic interior resembles a medieval tavern. Gigantic tankards and strangely named, strangely made shots ('Shit on the Grass') fuel a feisty crowd cheesed off with the surrounding glam. A roof terrace provides airy relief.

Voodoo Lounge

Báez 340, entre Arévalo y Chenaut (4772 2453/ www.voodoorama.com). Bus 15, 29, 59, 60, 64. **Open** from 8pm Tue-Sat. **Admission** minimum spend AR$10 after midnight. **Credit** MC. **Map** p279 L5.

This funky cocktail bar shines, with its fluorescent panelling, plucky waitresses, and cool Cañitas crowd. Aloof but hip, it has assorted live performances, late-night dancing and an electronic vibe that gets the crowd up on its feet: Wednesday nights are one of the city's essential club dates. Open late, it's a good spot to finish a classy binge.

Much-loved **Las Violetas**: worth the trip out west.

West of the Centre

Abasto

El Banderín

*Guardia Vieja 3601, y Billinghurst (4862 7757/www.
elbanderin.com.ar). Subte B, Carlos Gardel/24, 26,
92, 99 bus.* **Open** 8am-7pm Mon-Fri; 9am-1pm Sat.
No credit cards. Map p278 H4.

An antiquated Abasto café, built in 1929, with more
than 400 dusty football flags hanging on the cracked
walls, and good old barrio boys reminiscing over coffee. El Banderín is the latest addition to the official
list of notable cafés/bars in BA, an honour that has
delayed planned extensions to the building. Ask for
a tour of the aged bottles of booze that line the shelves;
some are over 70 years old, so drink at your peril.

Almagro

Confitería Las Violetas

*Rivadavia 3899, y Medrano (4958 7387). Subte A,
Castro Barros/26, 52, 86, 132 bus.* **Open** 6am-2am
Mon-Thur; 6am-4am Fri; 6am Sat-2am Mon. **No
credit cards. Map** p274 D4.

When Las Violetas (established 1884) closed in 1998,
8,000 distressed customers signed a petition, successfully forcing a reopening three years later. Since
then, it's been business as usual. Around the circular bar, white-jacketed waiters zigzag between the
columns, delivering coffees and tempting cakes from
the in-house patisserie. It may be off the beaten
track, but the exquisite stained glass windows, old-
fashioned atmosphere and impeccable service make
this huge corner relic worth a visit.

Shops & Services

Designer togs, gaucho gear and boutique wines – and all of it dirt cheap.

There's never been such a great time to shop in this city. Devaluation of the peso forced local manufacturers into action, and 'Industria Argentina' is back on its feet, big time. Just about anything worth splashing out on is locally produced; imports are still noticeably expensive and all but non-existent. Even Levi's jeans or Puma trainers are made in Argentina or neighbouring Brazil – which can mean that quality is variable, so check finishings carefully.

Though dollars, sterling and euros stretch far, some purchases are better value than others. Just as anywhere, you get what you pay for here. For absurdly cheap, in quids and quality, head to the Once barrio, but the best shopping is in and around Florida Street, and in Recoleta and Palermo Viejo – it's still affordable and definitely worth the price difference.

Some streets are known for purveying certain goods. Downtown, Libertad is cluttered with gold, watch and used-camera shops, Azcuénaga has numerous textile stores, Talcahuano is known for musical instruments, Arenales for interior design and Avenida Corrientes for its bookshops. Avenida Santa Fe is a shop-till-you-drop experience from top to bottom, Avenida Córdoba between numbers 4000 and 5000 is lined with factory outlets selling discounted clothing lines, while Avenida Alvear (and Rodríguez Peña and Posadas nearby) is the Rodeo Drive/Fifth Avenue/New Bond Street of Buenos Aires. Arroyo is dotted with art galleries and antique stores, and the other major antiques area is San Telmo, whose weekly highlight is Sunday's fair in Plaza Dorrego.

The easy option is to head straight for one of the major shopping centres (simply called 'shoppings') – Galerías Pacífico, Patio Bullrich or Abasto have the best choice – for clothes, food, books and beauty treatments. But it's boutiques, rather than big brands, making an impact, and it's fun to hunt out the individual shops and designers creating the scene.

Palermo Viejo/Hollywood is retail bliss – over 300 businesses (bars, shops and restaurants) have opened over the last two years. It's vast – around 15 by 15 city blocks, impossible to trawl in one day – so best to dip in and out. Start in the zone between Gorriti, Uriarte, Costa Rica and Malabia. For menswear – finally making gallant strides – Gurruchaga between Costa Rica and Honduras is especially

fruitful. Some places double up as a shop/bar/gallery or service business (*see p154* **Multiespacios**). In most areas there are free maps to orient you, though some of the best shops are off the beaten track, so a wrong turn can only enhance your own discovery route.

Antiques, CDs and wine all make great buys, and Argentinian designers are busy producing stylish furnishings, household goods and decorative items. You'll also find excellent leather shoes, handbags and luggage, some beautifully created crafts, as well as slim-fitting clothes. Low hipster trousers have been fashionable in Buenos Aires since before Britney was born, and clothes are shaped to show off that quintessential Argentinian focal point – the arse. Another note of caution, Argentinian women tend to be thin, naturally or otherwise, and more petite than many Europeans or North Americans. So, shopping for larger sizes (above a women's UK size 14 or US size 10) can be frustrating, and even shoes are made for little feet (you'll have difficulty if your feet are larger than a European size 40, US size 9). Sizes for men are less problematic.

For more practical requirements, on nearly every street in the city you'll find a *kiosko*. These conveniently manned windows look out on to the street and stock snacks, refreshments and something for all your gum-chewing, soft drink-swilling and ciggie-smoking needs.

Note that esteemed old Buenos Aires department store Harrods – once an outpost of the famous London shop, now independently run – is due to reopen permanently in 2004 after a 15-year closure. Judging by the offer during a temporary opening in 2003, it will be a shopping hotspot when it does.

HOURS, CREDIT CARDS AND TAX

Shopping centres open from 10am to 10pm (with cinema access until later), and are among the few places trading on Sundays. Hours at other shops vary – but 10am to 7pm is standard; bookstores, especially on Corrientes, stay open as late as 11pm or midnight. In Palermo Viejo, some shops get going a little later (11am or noon). Some places close for summer holidays in January or February (usually two weeks).

Major credit cards are accepted in larger shops. The price on the tag is the price you pay (21 per cent value added tax included). The price should be in Argentinian pesos unless

Eat, Drink, Shop

ETIQUETA NEGRA

HOMBRES

DARDO ROCHA 1366   SAN ISIDRO   ·   www.etiqueta-negra.com.ar

indicated (dollars are shown as US$ or USD). Be wary of being charged dollars for a product priced in pesos – a Consumer Association (*see p249*) can help with complaints.

Most shops have clear-out sales at the end of each season, but there are no fixed sales periods. When you buy Argentinian-made products worth at least AR$70 in a shop displaying a Global Refund/Tax Free Shopping sticker, ask for the *factura* (bill) and the *cheque de reintegro*. When you leave the country, present both at Customs, which will send you to a *puesto de pago* where you are given back 10 to 16 per cent of the 21 per cent sales tax.

Shopping centres

All the shoppings are strategically located, have cinemas (*see p176*), numerous fashion outlets, food courts, at least one bookshop, souvenir/crafts shop, toy shop, music shop, sports store and a hair or beauty salon. Some have travel agents, solariums, opticians and even plastic surgery consultants.

Abasto de Buenos Aires
Avenida Corrientes 3247, entre Agüero y Anchorena, Almagro (4959 3400/www.altopalermo.com.ar). Subte B, Carlos Gardel/24, 26, 124, 146, 168 bus. **Open** 10am-10pm daily. **Credit** AmEx, DC, MC, V. **Map** p278 G4.

Elegant **Galerías Pacífico**.

The newest of the big malls (opened in 1998) in a former produce market is a local landmark. It houses more than 200 shops, including Prenatal for maternity and baby gear, Tascani for menswear and Akiabara for the girls. A children's museum – El Museo de los Niños – is on the second floor; *see p168*.

Alto Palermo
Avenida Santa Fe 3253, entre Coronel Díaz y Bulnes, Palermo (5777 8000/www.altopalermo.com.ar). Subte D, Bulnes/12, 15, 39, 64, 152 bus. **Open** 10am-10pm daily. **Credit** varies. **Map** p279 I6.
One of the oldest and most typical of the shoppings, but with one of the youngest crowds. Popular with families and gaggles of giggling mall rats, it contains most of the Argentinian chains from fashion outlets such as Chocolate, Maria Vazquez, Zara and Bensimon to electrical appliance shops.

Galerías Pacífico
Florida 737, entre Viamonte y Córdoba, Centro (5555 5100/www.galeriaspacifico.com.ar). Subte B, Florida/6, 93, 130, 152 bus. **Open** 10am-9pm Mon-Sat; noon-9pm Sun. **Credit** varies. **Map** p277 E7.
In an elegant turn-of-the-century building, the exquisite frescos in this downtown mall were painted by five great muralists: Berni, Spilimbergo, Urruchúa, Colmeiro and Castagnino. Among the famous brand names are Christian Dior and Ralph Lauren, while Espacio Para Ti groups together shops like Etnia (accessories), Serena Tais (bedlinen) and Class Life (swimwear). Look out, too, for Fin de Mundo, selling Patagonian products. An entrance to the Centro Cultural Borges is on the third floor.

Paseo Alcorta
Salguero 3172, y Figueroa Alcorta, Palermo (5777 6500/www.altopalermo.com.ar). Bus 67, 102, 130. **Open** 10am-10pm daily. **Credit** varies. **Map** p278 I7.
Paseo Alcorta is home to the gigantic Carrefour hypermarket and four cinemas. Also catch the latest Argentinian designer wears and wares from children's shops (Cheeky, Mimo & Co) to Sibyl Vane (shoes) to womenswear from Ayres and Awada and well known brands like Lacoste and Cacharel.

Patio Bullrich
Avenida del Libertador 750, entre Montevideo y Libertad, Recoleta (4814 7400/7500/www.altopalermo.com.ar). Bus 67, 92, 102, 130. **Open** *Shops* 10am-9pm daily. *Restaurants* 10am-midnight daily. **Credit** varies. **Map** p278 G8.
The most luxurious and oldest of them all (opened in 1988) was once the city's meat auction house. The elegance extends from the marble floors to the uniformed lift operators, and top-end boutiques include Trosman, Ricky Sarkany (shoes) and Jazmin Chebar as well as Versace and Maxmara.

Solar de la Abadía
Arce 940, entre Maure y Gorostiaga, Palermo (4778 5000/www.elsolarshopping.com.ar). Bus 15, 29, 59, 60, 64. **Open** 10am-10pm daily. **Credit** varies. **Map** p279 L5.

Eat, Drink, Shop

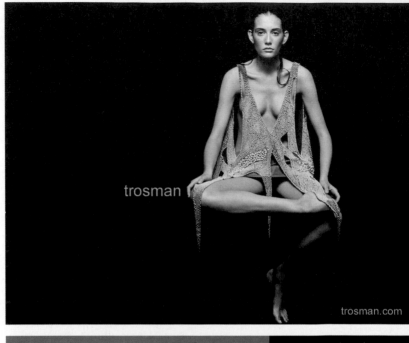

trosman

trosman.com

ONA SAEZ

www.onasaez.com

This shopping centre, housed in what was once a paper factory, exemplifies the same spirit of boutique-love found elsewhere in trendy Las Cañitas. It attracts mostly families from the surrounding barrio, who go to shop, eat and catch a film.

Antiques & collectibles

San Telmo – particularly Defensa street between Independencia and San Juan – has the biggest concentration of quality antiques dealers in the city. Serious collectors should go on weekdays (though many close on Monday), but for a light hearted browse go to the area's central square, Plaza Dorrego, on Sundays between 10am and 5pm. Officially known as **Feria San Pedro Telmo**, 270 stalls sell antique dolls, soda syphons, jewellery, tango memorabilia, toys and other collectibles, though much of what's on offer is usually more picturesque than valuable. Around the plaza are the larger dealers, and cafés and street performers. Request a certificate for anything over 100 years old to ensure its authenticity.

International auction houses **Christie's** (4393 4222) and **Sotheby's** (4814 4454) have representation in Buenos Aires. Local auctioneers **Breuer Moreno** (Libertad 1650, 4815 8523, www.breuermoreno.com.ar) has weekly Wednesday evening sales and **Bullrich Gaona Wernicke** (Maipú 932, 4311 4527, www.bullrichgaonawernicke.com) holds four major arts and antiques auctions per year.

There are numerous shops selling collectibles. For armoury, **Armería La Veneziana** in Tribunales (Libertad 1033, 4812 5522) will trigger your fancy, and for antiquarian books, the **Antique Book Shop** (Libertad 1236, Recoleta, 4815 0658, www.antique.servisur.com) specialises in European and Latin American history and art, maps and artworks. These specialists are recommended:

El Churrinche

Defensa 1031, entre Humberto 1º y Carlos Calvo, San Telmo (4362 7612/www.churrinche.com.ar). Bus 24, 29, 126, 130, 152. **Open** 11am-7pm Tue-Sun. **Credit** AmEx, MC, V. **Map** p276 C6.
It's rare to find so many lamps under one roof. El Churrinche's stock includes 300 European examples that work with gas, oil, candles or kerosene from the late 1700s to the early 1900s.

Club de Tango

5th Floor, Office 114, Paraná 123, entre Bartolomé Mitre y Perón (4372 7251/www.clubdetango.com.ar). **Open** 10am-6pm Mon-Fri. **No credit cards**. **Map** p277 E6.
Over 2,000 tango CDs, plus rare cassette recordings, and a massive selection of tango memorabilia, publications, artworks, videos, books and more. A total treat for tango fanatics.

Gil Antigüedades

Humberto 1º 412, entre Defensa y Bolívar, San Telmo (4361 5019). Bus 24, 29, 126, 130, 152. **Open** 11am-1pm, 3-7pm daily. **Credit** AmEx, V. **Map** p276 C6.
The sheer volume will dazzle vintage fashion victims. The speciality is Victorian clothing (exquisite handbags bordered with gems), but there are also German-made *mates* from 1880-90. Christophe Lambert and Catherine Deneuve have fallen for items here.

Guevara Art Gallery

Defensa 982, entre Carlos Calvo y Estados Unidos, San Telmo (4362 2418/www.guevaragallery.com). Bus 24, 29, 126, 130, 152. **Open** 2-7pm daily. **No credit cards**. **Map** p276 C6.
For lovers of art deco and nouveau, this gallery has around 2,000 WMF collector's items from 1850-1930, as well as Daum, Lalique and Müller Frères pieces.

Silvia Petroccia

Defensa 1002, y Carlos Calvo, San Telmo (4362 0156). Bus 24, 29, 126, 130, 152. **Open** 10am-7pm daily. **No credit cards**. **Map** p276 C6.
Michael Jackson and Donna Karan have had their wallets out in this super-cool store. It's atypical – the furniture is more old than antique, and has been touched up by Petroccia, but you can find amazing items rescued from old *porteño* palaces, as well as extra large mirrors and candelabra.

Te Acordás Hermano

Units 14 & 15, Florida 971, entre Paraguay y Marcelo T De Alvear, Retiro (4894 1215). Subte C, San Martín/6, 26, 93, 130, 152 bus. **Open** 10am-7pm Mon-Fri; 10am-6pm Sat. **No credit cards**. **Map** p277 E8.
A wonderful and well-arranged treasure trove of collectibles and old tack, all from Argentina – toys, matchboxes, coins, comics, newspapers, old photos and posters. The array of tango, gaucho and football paraphernalia is huge.
Other locations: Unit 23 and 25, Pasaje Obelisco Norte, Microcentro (4384 8624).

Second-hand

There are two contenders for second-hand items in Nueva Pompeya: **Ejército de Salvación** (Avenida Sáenz 580, 4911 0781) and **Cotolengo** (Cachí, entre Avenida Perito Moreno y Ventana). Both are packed warehouses frequented by savvy bargain hunters, but it's a dodgy barrio, so go by taxi or with a local, and get there early.

El Mercado de las Pulgas

Niceto Vega y Dorrego, Palermo Viejo (no phone). Bus 140, 151, 161, 168. **Open** 10am-5pm daily. **No credit cards**. **Map** p275 K4/L4.
This flea market (*pulga* means flea) offers junk piled high in a chaotic warehouse. Unearth small worthwhile oddities, such as wooden shoe moulds or vintage lamps, and there are tons of old vinyl, as well as glassware and restored furniture.

Bookshops

Porteños are well-read and BA boasts more than 1,000 bookshops. Avenida Corrientes is home to numerous new and second-hand bookstores, and most shopping centres and main shopping streets have something for avid readers. Look for **Cuspide**, **Distal** and **Yenny** book chains and also **Zival's** (*p159*). For used or second-hand books (and music), you can try the weekend outdoor markets at Plaza Italia, Parque Rivadavia and Parque Centenario.

Asunto Impreso

Centro Cultural Recoleta, Junín 1930, y Quintana, Recoleta (4805 5585/www.asuntoimpreso.com). Bus 17, 60, 67, 92, 110. **Open** 2-9pm Tue-Fri; 10am-9pm Sat, Sun. **Credit** AmEx, MC, V. **Map** p278 H7.
Flipping though art books at this crammed store inside the Centro Cultural Recoleta is a most agreeable way to spend an afternoon.
Other locations: Pasaje Rivarola 169, Congreso (4383 6262).

Ateneo Grand Splendid

Avenida Santa Fe 1860, entre Callao y Riobamba, Barrio Norte (4811 6104/4813 6052/www.tematika.com). Subte D, Callao/12, 39, 152 bus. **Open** 9am-10pm Mon-Thur; 9am-midnight Fri, Sat; noon-10pm Sun. **Credit** AmEx, DC, MC, V. **Map** p278 G6.
A gloriously renovated cinema now contains the largest bookstore in South America, with an ample choice of English and French books. Founded in 1912, the original Ateneo on Florida is in what was once Carlos Gardel's recording studio. Look for flyers for details of book launches and author talks held in its auditorium. Ateneo is part of the same group as Yenny, a chain with branches across town.
Other locations: Florida 340, Microcentro (4325 6801).

El Club del Comic

Marcelo T de Alvear 2002, y Ayacucho, Barrio Norte (4375 2323/www.clubdelcomic.com.ar). Subte D, Facultad de Medicina/39, 101, 111, 132, 152 bus. **Open** 10am-8.30pm Mon-Sat. **Credit** AmEx, DC, MC, V. **Map** p278 G6.
Comics galore from Europe, the US and Argentina.
Other locations: Montevideo 355, Tribunales (4375 2323).

El Faro

Gorriti 5204, y Uriarte, Palermo (4831 2239). Bus 39, 55. **Open** 10.30am-8.30pm Mon-Sat. **Credit** AmEx, DC, MC, V. **Map** p279 J4.
A hidden gem specialising in literature and philosophy, but also carrying a strong children's section.

Gandhi Galerna

Avenida Corrientes 1743, entre Callao y Rodríguez Peña, Tribunales (4374 7501). Subte B, Callao/12, 24, 37, 60 bus. **Open** 10am-10pm Mon-Thur; 10am-midnight Fri, Sat; 4-10pm Sun. **Credit** AmEx, DC, MC, V. **Map** p277 F6.

Gandhi has long been the place where Buenos Aires' thinkers and talkers gather. It has a noteworthy music selection and the best choice of local journals and mags. Staff are friendly and helpful. Live music venue/restaurant Notorious (*see p195*) is installed on the first floor.
Other locations: throughout the city.

KEL Ediciones

Marcelo T de Alvear 1369, entre Uruguay y Talcahuano, Recoleta (4814 0143/www.kel-ediciones.com). Bus 39, 102, 111, 152. **Open** Feb-Mar 9am-7pm Mon-Fri; 9.30am-1.30pm Sat. **Closed** Jan. **Credit** MC, V. **Map** p277 F7.
KEL stocks English-language fiction, non-fiction, travel books and teaching materials.

Librerías ABC

Avenida Córdoba 685, entre Florida y Maipú, Centro (4314 7887/www.libreriasabc.com.ar). Subte B, Florida/6, 26, 93, 130, 152 bus. **Open** 9am-8pm Mon-Fri; 10am-1.30pm Sat. **Credit** AmEx, DC, MC, V. **Map** p277 E7.
Specialises in books published in English and German, both old and new.
Other locations: Galería Larreta, Florida 971, Retiro (4515 0202).

Design & home accessories

For one-stop designer shopping for the home, head to **Buenos Aires Design** (Pueyrredón 2501, y Azcuénaga, 5777 6000). Located next to the Recoleta Cultural Centre, it has two floors with more than 60 shops of interior design, among them **Morph** (4806 3226, www.morph.com.ar) for fun, affordable home accessories. **Puro Diseño Argentino** on the roof terrace (Unit 1004, 5777 6104, www.purodiseno.com.ar) stocks pieces by 100 of the most talented emerging local designers – but prices are set for foreign pockets. There's clothes, candles, shoes, and furniture – look for Paula Levy's silver jewellery and sheepskin handbags from Cima. It's the perfect one-stop gift shop.

Arte Etnico Argentino

El Salvador 4600, y Malabia, Palermo Viejo (4833 6661). Bus 15, 39, 55. **Open** *Jan, Feb* 3pm-8pm Mon-Fri; noon-4pm. *Mar-Dec* 10.30am-7.30pm Mon-Fri; 11am-6pm Sat. Credit AmEx,V. **Map** p279 J4.
Even the window display at this corner shop is a must-see. Goods hail from the north-western province of Santiago del Estero and include rugs (from AR$500) in brilliant fuchsias, bloody reds, screaming greens and deep browns, and chairs made of leather and wood (starting at AR$200).

Calma Chicha

Honduras 4925, entre Gurruchaga y Serrano, Palermo Viejo (4831 1818/www.calmachicha.com). Bus 39, 55, 151, 168. **Open** 10am-8pm Mon-Sat; 2pm-8pm Sun. **Credit** AmEx, DC, MC, V. **Map** p279 J4.

Eat, Drink, Shop

Funky home decor and fun such as Argentinian-produced game sets (dominos and chess) and design books. Cowhide, leather, denim and woven textiles are fashioned on the premises into big bean bags, purses, cushions and more.

Gropius
Honduras 6027, entre Arevalo y Dorrego, Palermo Viejo (4774 2094/4776 4420/www.gropiusdesign-1920-2000.com). Bus 39, 93, 111. **Open** 10am-8pm Mon-Sat. **No credit cards. Map** p279 K4.
In this slickly produced showroom you'll find one of the finest selections of classic furniture replicas: pieces or entire ranges from George Nelson, Charles Eames, Gropius, Le Corbusier, Mies van der Rohe, Saarinen. The similarities are uncanny and the prices about one-fifth of the originals.

Materia Urbana
Defensa 707, entre Chile e Independencia, San Telmo (4361 5265/www.materiaurbana.com). Bus 24, 29, 126, 130, 152. **Open** 11am-7pm Tue-Thur; 11am-8pm Fri-Sun. **Credit** AmEx, DC, V. **Map** p277 D6.
Take an enjoyable meander through this grand, second-floor apartment where each of the three rooms is dedicated to small-format art and designer objects from around 70 local artists.

Milagros
Gorriti 5417, y las vías, Palermo Viejo (4899 0991/ www.milagrosresta.com.ar). Bus 39, 111.
Open 10 am-9pm Mon-Sat; 1pm-7pm Sun.
Credit AmEx, MC, V. **Map** p279 J4.
Interior designer Milagros Resta's warehouse is crammed with objects, from recycled antiques and patchwork bedcovers to embroidered pillows and velvet-covered boxes. The style is romantic shabby chic-meets-Laura Ashley. There's also a small bar and clothes from model-turned-vedette Ginette Reynal.

Oda – Objetos de Artistas
Costa Rica 4670, entre Armenia y Gurruchaga, Palermo Viejo (4831 7403). Bus 15, 39. **Open** 11am-8pm Mon-Sat. **Credit** AmEx, MC. **Map** p279 J4.
Discerning *objetos* by respected Argentinian artists are arranged at this shop by curator Valeria Fiterman of Fundación Klemm (*see p181*). Boyo Quintana's sweet and sullen sculptures (AR$350-$450) are a worthy investment for any collector.

La Pasionaria
Godoy Cruz 1541, entre Cabrera y Niceto Vega, Palermo Viejo (4773 0563). Bus 39, 55, 111. **Open** 4pm-8pm Mon-Fri; 11am-8pm Sat. **No credit cards. Map** p279 J4.
In a huge warehouse, Pancho Salomón stores hundreds of items from the 1920 to '50s. It's disorganised, though almost poetically so, and worth a visit just to see the hundreds of gems he's accumlated.

Rajatabla
Balcarce 1068, entre Humberto 1° y Carlos Calvo, San Telmo (no phone). Bus 24, 29, 64, 86. **Open** noon-7pm Tue-Sun. **No credit cards. Map** p276 C6.
Baby-sized straw chairs, hardwood worktables and colourful textiles are among the rustic finds restored by anthropologist Dolores Spangenberg following her research trips to Argentina's interior provinces.

30quarenta
Arroyo 890, entre Esmeralda y Suipacha, Retiro (4326 1065). Bus 59, 61, 93, 130, 152. **Open** Feb-Dec 11am-1.30pm, 2.30-7.30pm Mon-Fri; 10am-1pm Sat. **Closed** Jan. **Credit** AmEx. **Map** p277 F8.
Dolled-up junk at this chic design shop will charm any drab corner of your home. Carlos Gardel's face is painted on to bowling pins, clown faces turned into collages and chairs refurbished with *Alice in Wonderland*-like polka-dot fabrics.

Eat, Drink, Shop

Puro Diseño, on the terraces of Buenos Aires Design. *See p142.*

By appointment

Some of the city's most talented designers – of clothes, accessories or furniture – will create unique pieces by appointment. It's a great chance to peek behind the scenes as well as ensuring you have a piece of cutting-edge Argentinian design. Phone or email for your slot and to check location.

Pablo Ramírez (4826 8713, www.pablo ramirez.com.ar), the hot designer celebrated by Isabella Blow, creates custom-made gowns and ultra-elegant menswear, in his statement black and white palette. His haute clientele includes such local celebrities as the musician Gustavo Cerati and TV superstar Susana Giménez. Though his collection will be open to the public in a new location in Recoleta by mid 2004, you can secure an interview with the main man himself by prearrangement – so call ahead to get a piece of him while you can.

To accessorise, make a date with **Sylvie Geronimi** (4774 5408, www.sylviegeronimi. com.ar), doyenne of made-to-measure shoes, and loved by tango dancers. Her personal touch shows in daring styles and colour combinations – orders take about one month. Then book in with **Celedonio Lohidoy** (4803 7292, www.celedonio.net), a former architect now designing glam jewellery and watches for the likes of Princess Máxima Zorreguieta of Holland and Sarah Jessica Parker.

If you want to take home a bit of Argentina, **Ricardo Paz** and his wife **Belén Carbello** – whose gorgeous shop Arte Etnico Argentino (see p142) sells to the public – also have a delightful gallery of magical objects, including rustic furniture and tapestries, that you can see by appointment (4832 0516, arteetnico argentino@sion.com). Now with showrooms in Milan and London, their business has caught the eyes of international collectors.

For original pieces in leather and cowhide – including a great backpack and a reworking of the BKF (or butterfly) chair – go and see **Humawaca**'s showroom (4552 2354, www. humawaca.com). It's the creation of two architects who know a lot about proportion. Some of their models are available at Puro Diseño (see p142).

The most exquisite hand-crafted silverware – eagerly snapped up by every celeb to visit BA – is the work of **Juan Carlos Pallarols** (4361 7360, www.juancarlospallarols.com), a sixth-generation silversmith. Call ahead to see his amazing workshop or pick up ready-to-go pieces at Defensa 1039 in San Telmo.

Finally, to add an original touch to a simple pair of jeans, go see **Jeans Makers** (Malabia 1784, 4831 4914) for an appointment with Teresa Castagnino. They call it a jeans kitchen and Teresa is the cook. Have a pair made from scratch, buy one on display, or bring one of your faves, then choose from embroidery, studs, vintage buttons, diamante and appliqués and Teresa will make jeans that are all about you, signed and stamped. The shops is open to the public, and the ready-to-wear skirts are unmissable.

Fashion

Many international designer boutiques are present in the capital, among them Giorgio Armani, Louis Vuitton, Ralph Lauren, Hermès, Burberry and Versace – but imported luxury brands sell for top dollar prices. Most are in Recoleta, on Posadas or Avenida Alvear, or in Patio Bullrich shopping centre. Apart from **Zara** – even better value here than elsewhere – with several branches around town including a major one at Florida 651 (4312 8170), few of the major high-street names have set up here. Other international brands like Levi's, Nike and Adidas have several outlets, though most of the goods sold are manufactured locally.

Some of the best local designers have showrooms you can visit only by calling ahead; see **By appointment**. Many places with multiple branches (listed as 'throughout the city' in this chapter) will be present in the shopping centres. The shops listed below concentrate on more local and unique names.

Designer

Cora Groppo

El Salvador 4696, y Armenia, Palermo Viejo (4833 7474/www.coragroppo.com). Bus 15, 39, 55, 151, 168. **Open** 11am-8pm Mon-Sat. **Credit** AmEx, MC, V. **Map** p279 J4.

Famed for making beautiful wedding dresses, Cora's designs are now available for non-matrimonial celebrations. Her shop is full of sexy, wearable clothes with unique details.

María Martha Facchinelli

El Salvador 4741, entre Armenia y Gurruchaga, Palermo Viejo (4831 8424/www.facchinelli.com). Bus 15, 39, 55, 151, 168. **Open** 10.30am-8pm Mon-Sat. **Credit** AmEx, DC, MC, V. **Map** p279 J4.

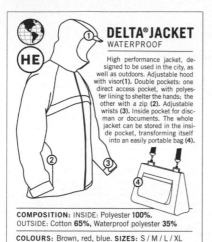

DELTA®JACKET
WATERPROOF

High performance jacket, designed to be used in the city, as well as outdoors. Adjustable hood with visor(1). Double pockets: one direct access pocket, with polyester lining to shelter the hands; the other with a zip (2). Adjustable wrists (3). Inside pocket for discman or documents. The whole jacket can be stored in the inside pocket, transforming itself into an easily portable bag (4).

COMPOSITION: INSIDE: Polyester **100%**.
OUTSIDE: Cotton **65%**, Waterproof polyester **35%**

COLOURS: Brown, red, blue. **SIZES:** S / M / L / XL

HE hermanos estebecorena
MENSWEAR

SHIRTS / JACKETS / LEATHER JACKETS / T-SHIRTS / SWEATERS / TROUSERS / SHOES / ACCESSORIES / UNDERWEAR / AND MORE

El Salvador 5960, Bs.As. (54 11) 4772 2145
OPEN FROM MONDAY TO SATURDAY / 11 to 13 / 13:30 to 21
www.hermanosestebecorena.com / info@hebue.com

coragroppo

urban clothes
el salvador 4696, palermo viejo.
argentina.
www.coragroppo.com

timeout.com

The online guide to the world's greatest cities

This young designer – praised by *Bazaar* and *Nylon* – has finally opened a boutique in Palermo Viejo. Her creations stand out for a refinement rare among her contemporaries. Star pieces are dresses in gauze and natural silk and cashmere coats.

Nadine Zlotogora
El Salvador 4638, entre Malabia y Armenia, Palermo Viejo (4831 4203/www.nadinez.com). Bus 15, 39, 55. **Open** 11am-8pm Mon-Sat. **Credit** AmEx, DC, MC, V. **Map** p279 J4.
Zlotogora's mens- and womenswear combines fantasy and contemporary styles, floaty fabrics, knots, zips, cut-outs and radical shapes – both beautifully made and far out.

Tramando, Martín Churba
Rodríguez Peña 1973, entre Posadas y Alvear, Recoleta (4811 0465/www.tramando.com). Bus 17, 61, 67, 92, 93. **Open** 10.30am-8.30pm Mon-Sat. **Credit** AmEx, DC, MC, V. **Map** p278 G7.
Martín Churba, a textile phenomenon, innovates printing and weaving techniques by applying plastic and paint. The clothes are basic in shape but extraordinarily constructed. Homeware goods like rugs, bowls and chairs are also made out of this peculiar combination of pop and craft.

Trosman
Patio Bullrich, Avenida del Libertador 750, entre Montevideo y Libertad, Recoleta (4814 7411/www.trosman.com). Bus 67, 92, 93, 130. **Open** 10am-9pm daily. **Credit** AmEx, DC, MC, V. **Map** p278 G7.
Jessica Trosman (formerly half of the celebrated Trosman-Churba label) is one of the international queens of new Argentinian fashion. Her mark is elaborate collections, using innovative materials like plastic and latex to create an edgy, chic look. Must-haves include filmy tops with heavy beading and flared skirts with licks of paint. Snap her up now. **Other locations**: Armenia 1998, Palermo Viejo (4833 3058).

Varanasi
Unit 29, Jorge Newbery 1651, entre Migueletes y Soldado de la Independencia, Las Cañitas (4771 8955/www.varanasi-online.com). Bus 15, 29, 55, 59, 64. **Open** 11am-2pm, 3pm-8pm Mon-Fri. **Credit** AmEx, MC, V. **Map** p279 L6.
Mario Buraglio and Victor Delgrosso (architects-turned-designers) combine sophistication and daring in equal doses, using overlayered materials, experimental shapes and pairings of natural and synthetic fabrics. From glam eveningwear to the denim casuals, you can recognise their background skills. **Other locations**: Libertad 1634, Recoleta (4813 5685).

Mid-range

Juana De Arco
El Salvador 4762, entre Armenia y Gurruchaga, Palermo Viejo (4833 1621/www.juanadearco.net). Bus 15, 39. **Open** 11am-8pm Mon-Sat. **Credit** AmEx, MC, V. **Map** p279 J4.

This shop offers cute undies and bathing suits, pyjama-like pants, funky skirts and apparel for children as well. T-shirts with wings go for AR$65.

Kosiuko
Avenida Santa Fe 1779, entre Callao y Rodríguez Peña, Recoleta (4815 2555/www.kosiuko.com.ar). Bus 10, 37, 39, 152. **Open** 9.30am-8.30pm Mon-Sat. **Credit** AmEx, DC, MC, V. **Map** p278 G6.
The pioneer of hipster jeans poses only one question – how low can you go? Bold and bright, figure-hugging clothes for people with pop aspirations. **Other locations**: throughout the city.

Maria Vazquez
Libertad 1632, entre Posadas y Libertador, Recoleta (4815 6333/www.mvzmariavazquez.com.ar). Bus 67, 92, 93, 130. **Open** 10am-8pm Mon-Fri; 10am-6pm Sat. **Credit** AmEx, DC, MC, V. **Map** p278 G8.
MV experiments with textures and colour, creating revealing and sexy clothes. Latin American singer Shakira shops for her gold silk-screened jeans here. **Other locations**: throughout the city.

Ona Saez
Avenida Santa Fe 1651, entre Montevideo y Rodríguez Peña, Recoleta (4813 2834/www.onasaez.com). Bus 10, 37, 39, 152. **Open** 10am-9pm Mon-Fri; 10am-8pm Sat. **Credit** AmEx, DC, MC, V. **Map** p278 G6.
A trendsetting, seductive and provocative clothing store for him and her, famed for their 'nice ass' jeans. Its creator, Santiago Saez, also directs valuable local charitable schemes through the brand. **Other locations**: throughout the city.

Paula Cahen d'Anvers
Avenida Santa Fe 1619, entre Montevideo y Rodríguez Peña, Recoleta (4811 3176). Bus 10, 37, 39, 152. **Open** 10am-8pm Mon-Sat. **Credit** AmEx, DC, MC, V. **Map** p278 G6.
Vibrant colours, prints and oh-so-soft fabrics make this women's clothing line the closet favourite, and the logo, a pretty embroidered crown, is in high demand. Great kiddies' range, too. **Other locations**: throughout the city.

Las Pepas
Avenida Santa Fe 1631, entre Montevideo y Rodríguez Peña, Recoleta (4811 7887/www.laspepas.com.ar). Bus 10, 37, 39, 152. **Open** 9.30am-9pm Mon-Fri; 9.30am-8pm Sat. **Credit** AmEx, DC, MC, V. **Map** p278 G6.
Vintage-inspired clothes fill this busy, on-the-button boutique. There are handbags, satchels and pointy shoes in bright colours and cool designs, and a kaleidoscope of leather jackets, coats and skirts. **Other locations**: Paseo Alcorta shopping centre (5777 6553).

Rapsodia
Arguibel 2899, y Báez, Las Cañitas (4772 2716/www.rapsodia.com.ar). Bus 15, 29, 59, 60, 64. **Open** 10am-midnight Mon-Sat; noon-midnight Sun. **Credit** AmEx, DC, MC, V. **Map** p279 K6.

Eat, Drink, Shop

Tremendous **Tramando** – where to find Martín Churba's original creations. *See p147.*

Model Sol Acuña and partner play with bright colours to achieve a cowgirl-visits-the-crib look. The jeans are current must-haves.
Other locations: Libertad 1673, Recoleta(4816 1610); Paseo Alcorta shopping centre (5777 6500).

Vicki Otero

Fitz Roy 1714, y Honduras (4771 2373). Bus 39, 93, 111. **Open** 11am-8.30pm Mon-Sat. **Credit** AmEx, DC, MC, V. **Map** p278 K4.
The clothes in this beautiful house are uniquely Vicki's. Hers is an Asian-inspired look, slightly boxy yet ultra-feminine, with dresses and blazers crafted in innovative ways to really dress you up.

Multi-brand boutiques

Aristocracia

Rodríguez Peña 1815, entre Quintana y Alvear, Recoleta (4813 7112). Bus 17, 67, 92, 93, 130. **Open** 10.30am-8pm Mon-Fri; 10.30am-2pm Sat. **Credit** AmEx, DC, MC, V. **Map** p278 G7.
Top designers, including Lesley George and Lucrecia Gamundi – British and Argentinian respectively – hang their party threads in this locale. The clientele? It's not called Aristocracy for nothing.

La Aurora

Honduras 4838, entre Armenia y Gurruchaga, Palermo Viejo (4833 4965). Bus 39, 55. **Open** *Jan, Feb* 11am-1.30pm, 3.30-8.30pm Mon-Sat. *Mar-Dec* 11am-8.30pm Mon-Sat. **Credit** AmEx, DC, MC, V. **Map** p279 J4.
Rubén Perlmutter turned the front of his house into a multi-brand boutique, selling Varanasi's conceptual designs, artistic T-shirts from Ana Fuchs and Dolores Elortondo and, of course, Birkin – the casual line designed by Perlmutter himself.

Cat Ballou

Avenida Alvear 1702, y Rodríguez Peña, Recoleta (4811 9792). Bus 17, 67, 92, 93, 130. **Open** 11am-8pm Mon-Fri; 11am-5pm Sat. **Credit** AmEx, MC, V. **Map** p278 G7.
Hand-crafted objects and clothes at Cat Ballou go together as if curated. Look for hand-painted stones by Argentinian sculptor Renata Shussheim (from AR$120), as well as rugs, shawls and decorations with a ranch house aesthetic. The clothes, designed by Alicia Goñi and Florencia Pieres, the dynamic duo behind the store, are airy and ultra-romantic.
Other locations: Costa Rica 4522, Palermo Viejo (4833 1035).

Retro

Malabia 1583, entre Honduras y El Salvador, Palermo Viejo (4831 4141/www.retro.com.ar). Bus 39, 55, 111. **Open** 11am-8.30pm Mon-Sat. **Credit** AmEx, DC, MC, V. **Map** p279 J4.
Womenswear from a select handful of emerging designers line the hangers of this boutique. Prêt-à-porter casualwear from Lupe Posse, Kukla and Ay Not Dead, as well as some Adidas trainers that you won't find in the sports shops.

Salsipuedes

Honduras 4814, entre Armenia y Gurruchaga, Palermo Viejo (4831 8467). Bus 39, 55, 168. **Open** *Jan, Feb* noon-8pm Mon-Fri; 10.30am-1pm, 3-8pm Sat. *Mar-Dec* 10.30am Mon-Fri; 10.30am-1pm, 3-8pm Sat. **Credit** AmEx, MC, V. **Map** p279 J4.
Some 30 designers sell their unique designs at owner Mariana's Salsipuedes (meaning 'get out if you can'). In particular, look for Mariano Toledo's experiments with suspenders and Pablo Ramírez denimwear. A sure bet to find something original. Check out also Salsidpuedes Condimentos for accessories. *See p151.*

Street & clubwear

Galería Bond Street
Avenida Santa Fe 1670, entre Montevideo y Rodríguez Peña, Recoleta . Subte D, Callao/37, 39, 111, 152 bus. **Open** 10am-10pm Mon-Sat. **Credit** varies. **Map** p278 G6.
Underground teens and students (punks, metalheads and skaters) buy their look at this arcade; great for funky local T-shirt designs. If you smell burning flesh, don't worry – needle artists are working hard drawing blood in the many tattoo parlours.

Galería Larreta
Florida 971 or San Martín 954, entre Paraguay y Marcelo T de Alvear, Retiro (4311 9112). Subte C, San Martín/6, 26, 93, 130, 152 bus. **Open** *Arcade* 8am-10pm Mon-Sat. **Credit** varies. **Map** p277 E8.
This arcade is a mixed bag: collectibles (Te Acordás Hermano, *see p141*), customised leatherwear from Zoo (Unit 12-13) and an ever-changing roster of young designers who set up shop on the second floor. Some fashion stars got their start in this gallery, like Nadine Zlotogora (*see p147*).

Red Store
El Salvador 4801, y Gurruchaga, Palermo Viejo (4833 4839). Bus 39, 55, 168. **Open** 11am-8pm Mon-Sat. **Credit** AmEx, MC, V. **Map** p279 J4.
Mostly imported (and therefore more expensive) street designs, like Diesel and Levi's (including the Engineered Jeans line) and, occasionally, some groovy Italian watches. There's also a good selection of the latest international trainers.

Menswear specialists

It took a while for fashion for the boys to catch up in Buenos Aires, but Palermo Viejo has become a top place for men to shop. On Gurruchaga street alone, as well as **Felix** (*see below*), **Kristobelga** at No.1677 (4831 6677, www.kristobelga.com) does great jeans and military-inspired clubwear. Try **Sixseet** at No.1653 (4833 6202) for preppie checked or striped shirts or **Antique Denim** at No.1692 (4834 6829) for a more rock 'n' roll look. **El Cid** at No.1732 (4832 3339) has an impressive range of bags and luggage, starting at AR$1,000, as well as motor-sport-inspired leather jackets. The shoes here are worth a look too.

Bensimon
Avenida Quintana 492-4, y Ayacucho, Recoleta (4807 5218). Bus 17, 101, 102. **Open** 10am-8.30pm Mon-Sat. **Credit** AmEx, DC, MC, V. **Map** p278 G7.
Put together a great casual look, in bold colours and soft cotton. Bensimon kits out staff at some of the city's funkiest bars and restaurants. As a tribute to its success, there are Bensimon copies around.
Other locations: Paseo Alcorta & Abasto shopping centres.

Etiqueta Negra
Dardo Rocha 1366, y Pringles, Martínez (4792 7373). Bus 60. **Open** 10am-8pm Mon-Sat. **Credit** AmEx, DC, MC, V.
After years of moving and shaking in BA's fashion scene, Federico Alvarez Castillo has opened this bold and beautiful shop in the northern suburbs to sell his super-chic but highly wearable menswear line. It's also worth the trip to drool over his collection of vintage sports cars and bikes, parked in store.

Félix
Gurruchaga 1670, entre El Salvador y Pasaje Santa Rosa, Palermo Viejo (4832 2994/www.felixba. com.ar) Bus 15, 39, 55. **Open** noon-8pm Mon; 11am-8pm Tue-Sat. **Credit** AmEx, MC, V. **Map** p279 J4.
If you like Paul Smith and Pringle, you'll love Félix. Details stand out but the price doesn't. Buenos Aires Ts make great gifts at AR$60. Jeans, shirts, boxers, wallets, belts and scarves – the stock is all cool.

Giesso
Avenida Santa Fe 1557, entre Montevideo y Paraná, Recoleta (4811 3717). Subte D, Callao/ 10, 17, 39, 132, 152 bus. **Open** 9am-8.30pm Mon-Fri; 9am-2pm Sat. **Credit** AmEx, DC, MC, V. **Map** p278 G7.
Classic tailoring and over 80 years in the business make this Argentinian brand credible to executives of all ages; now with a new women's line too.
Other locations: throughout the city.

Hermanos Estebecorena
El Salvador 5960, entre Ravignani y Arévalo, Palermo Viejo (4772 2145/www.hermanosestebecorena.com). Bus 39, 93, 111. **Open** 11am-9pm Mon-Sat. **Credit** AmEx, DC, MC, V. **Map** p279 K4.
These brothers are on the cutting edge of style, applying all the principles of industrial design to hip, comfy and functional items, from underwear and socks to all-weather coats. Their original approach is applied to stylish shoes, shirts and trousers too – deck yourself out top to toe.

Vintage & used clothing

Second-hand used to be for the lower ranks, but now in every barrio there is a consignment/second-hand shop. Keep eyes peeled for vintage Italian handbags. **Juan Perez** (Marcelo T de Alvear 1439, 4815 8442) is a great pit stop if you are headed out and forgot to pack elegant shoes. Here you'll find perfect save-my-night heels.

Galeria 5ta Avenida
Avenida Santa Fe 1270, entre Libertad y Talcahuano, Recoleta (4816 0451/www.galeria 5taavenida.com.ar). Bus 10, 39, 59, 152. **Open** 10am-9pm Mon-Sat. **Credit** varies. **Map** p277 F7.
This L-shaped arcade is lined with used clothing shops and tattoo parlours. For vintage eyewear, visit Hernán Vazquez at Optica Nahuel (4811 2837).

Las Pepas

FASHION BOUTIQUE

LEATHER WOMENSWEAR
SHOES
BAGS
TROUSERS
SKIRTS

Las Pepas

Av. Santa Fe 1631
& Paseo Alcorta,
Buenos Aires
Argentina

The kids are at **Galería Bond Street** (*p149*).

Salamanca Warehouse

Pasaje Santa Rosa 5038, entre Thames y Serrano, Palermo Viejo (4832 3666/www.salamanca.com.ar). Bus 39, 55, 168. **Open** 2.30-9.30pm Mon-Thur; 3-10pm Fri, Sat. **Credit** AmEx, MC, V. **Map** p279 J4.
A fantastic selection of second-hand threads, many with first-hand prices, crowd this warehouse.

Children & maternity

Cheeky

Avenida Santa Fe 1499, y Paraná, Recoleta (4813 1875/www.cheeky.com.ar). Bus 10, 59, 102, 152. **Open** 9.30am-8pm Mon-Sat. **Credit** AmEx, DC, MC, V. **Map** p278 G7.
One of Argentina's most successful – and loveable – purveyors of adorable baby and kiddie wear. **Other locations**: throughout the city.

Gimo's

Avenida Santa Fe 1250, entre Talcahuano y Libertad, Recoleta (4814 2466/www.gimos.com.ar). Bus 10, 39, 59, 152. **Open** 9.30am-8pm Mon-Fri; 10am-2pm Sat. **Credit** AmEx, DC, MC, V. **Map** p277 F7.
Colourful and playful wear for children and now with a new line – Venga Madre – for mums-to-be, also with its own store at Paraná 1052 (4813 0662). **Other locations**: throughout the city.

JopaJapa

Gurruchaga 1660, entre Santa Rosa y El Salvador (4831 6570/www.jopajapa.com.ar). Bus 15, 39, 55. **Open** *Jan, Feb* 2-8.30pm Mon-Fri; Sat noon-8.30pm; Sun 3-8pm. *Mar-Dec* 11am-8pm Mon-Sat; 2-7.30pm Sun. **Credit** AmEx, MC, V. **Map** p279 J4.
Hand-made toys here – like the kitty cat rucksacks – will make you want to procreate. And if you already have, bring them to weekend performances of song and dance shows; call for exact times.

Fashion accessories

For groovy sunglasses, the best local boutique is **Infinit**; *see p156.*

Fahoma

Libertad 1169, entre Santa Fe y Arenales, Recoleta (4813 5103). Bus 10, 17, 39,102, 152. **Open** 10am-8pm Mon-Fri; 10am-1.30pm Sat. **Credit** AmEx, DC, MC, V. **Map** p277 F7.
Women who know how to accessorise aspirationally buy their bold jewellery and elegant handbags here. This shop is always busy, maybe thanks to designer Julio Toledo's exclusive line of handbags.

Salsipuedes Condimentos

Honduras 4874, entre Armenia y Gurruchaga, Palermo Viejo (4833 9403.) Bus 39, 55. **Open** 10.30am-9pm Mon-Fri; 10.30am-8pm Sat. **Credit** AmEx, MC, V. **Map** p279 J4.
Designers Mariana Szwarc and Luna Garzon opened this boutique in a converted garage, selling a come-hither range of hand-crafted and designer accessories. Don't miss Mishal Katz's retro bags or those printed with Argentinian maps from SIMA and the silver jewellery by Mineralia.

Jewellery

Plata Nativa

Unit 41, Galería del Sol, Florida 860, entre Córdoba y Paraguay, Retiro (4312 1398/www.platanativa. com). Subte C, San Martín/6, 26, 93, 132, 152 bus. **Open** 10am-7pm Mon-Fri; 10am-2pm Sat. **Credit** AmEx, MC, V. **Map** p277 E7.
This small, hidden gallery of indigenous and Latin American art also sells antique silver and contemporary ethnic accessories. The necklaces woven in agate and turquoise, inspired by Mapuche jewellery, are in a class of their own. If it's good enough for Pedro Almodóvar, Sharon Stone and Liv Ullmann…

Siempre

Ayacucho 1883, entre Quintana y Guido, Recoleta (4806 9240). Bus 17, 101, 102. **Open** 10.30am-8pm Mon-Fri; 10.30am-2pm Sat. **Credit** AmEx, MC, V. **Map** p278 G7.
Statement-making jewellery from María Fernanda Sibilia. Her chosen material is silver, either on its own or with polished stones.

Leather goods

Thanks to Argentina's cheap and plentiful leather, bag hags will be thrilled to know that, like shoes, they are sold nearly everywhere – on and around Florida street has become the main leather zone, though you'll have to contend with an overly zealous sales approach. Or check out Murillo street in Villa Crespo, where the leather wholesalers' are gathered – most sell direct to the public. Also check out the funky bags and coats at **Las Pepas** (*see p147*) and **Materia** (a

Eat, Drink, Shop

chain store in all the shopping centres), as well as *cueros de vaca* (cowhide rugs) and leather furniture at **Calma Chicha** and leather homewares at **Puro Diseño** (*for both, see p142*).

Casa López

Marcelo T de Alvear 640 and 658, entre Florida y Maipú, Retiro (4311 3044/3045/www.casalopez. com.ar). Subte C, San Martín/7, 10, 17, 152 bus. **Open** 9am-8pm Mon-Fri; 9.30am-7pm Sat; 11am-6pm Sun. **Credit** AmEx, DC, MC, V. **Map** p277 F8.

Old-lady leather at first glance, but look closer. Pocketbooks, wallets, bags and briefcases designed with decadence and a seductive modern edge. Be warned, this shop also carries an extensive collection of animal fur coats, blankets and accessories. **Other locations**: Galerías Pacífico (5555 5241) & Patio Bullrich (4814 7477) shopping centres.

EU Cueros

Florida 948, entre Marcelo T de Alvear y Paraguay, Retiro (4312 6766). Subte C, San Martín/7, 10, 17, 152 bus. **Open** 9.30am-8pm Mon-Sat. **Credit** AmEx, DC, MC, V. **Map** p277 E8.

Customised fitting and tailoring in two working days. Pick the exact colour and type of leather along with styling and expect to pay upwards of AR$400.

Prüne

Florida 963, entre Marcelo T de Alvear y Paraguay, Retiro (4893 2634/www.pruneweb.com). Subte C, San Martín/ 7, 10, 17, 152 bus. **Open** 10am-8.30pm Mon-Fri; 10am-8pm Sat; 11am-6.30pm Sun. **Credit** AmEx, DC, MC, V. **Map** p277 E8.

Formerly a wholesaler, now smartened up to unleash numerous styles and colours to the general public. Design, colours and options are excellent, priced from as little as AR$110. Look for the great leather-jacket line and shoes at the Florida branch. **Other locations**: throughout the city.

Santesteban

Promenade Gallery, Alvear 1883, entre Callao y Ayacucho, Recoleta (4800 1174/www.santesteban disegno.com). Bus 17, 67, 92, 93,130. **Open** 10.30am-1pm, 2pm-8pm Mon-Fri; 10.30am-2pm Sat. **Credit** AmEx, DC, MC, V. **Map** p278 G7.

Exquisitely sculptured bags and boots from Verónica Santesteban. Look for handbags decorated with polished cowhorn or Louis XV-style shoes, bordered with Czech glass, or hand painted pieces from local artists such as Carlos Gorriarena.

Uma

Honduras 5225, entre Uriarte y Godoy Cruz, Palermo Viejo (4832 2122/www.umacuero.com). Bus 39, 55. **Open** 11am-8pm Mon-Sat. **Credit** AmEx, DC, MC, V. **Map** p279 J4.

Uma is where to head for the youngest and freshest of looks in leather – from clothes to shoes and bags – in a striking range of colours, styles and finishes. Check out the striking little dresses, for cutting a dash in the office, as seen in *Vogue*. **Other locations**: Galerías Pacífico, Alto Palermo, Patio Bullrich & Paseo Alcorta shopping centres.

Lingerie & swimwear

Swimwear (though mostly bikinis) and undies can be found almost everywhere – Argentina has one of the highest spends per capita on lingerie. In shopping malls look for the sexy but comfortable **Caro Cuore** or visit **Juana De Arco** (*see p147*) for fun and bright panties, and **Jadda** (Bonpland 1524, Palermo Viejo, 4772 7720, www.jadda.com.ar) has some cute items too – check out the bra and pants with leather trims (AR$35 each). At **Salsipuedes** (*see p148*), look for the owner's swimwear brand – Al Ver Veras. If you want a sports swimsuit, go to **Speedo**'s large store at Avenida Santa Fe 1570, Recoleta (4816 2169).

Amor Latino, Lingerie & Corseterie

Gorriti 4925, entre Serrano y Gurruchaga, Palermo Viejo (4831 6787/www.amor-latino.com.ar). Bus 39, 55. **Open** 11am-8pm Mon-Sat. **Credit** AmEx, MC, V. **Map** p279 J4.

The lounge wear is the right combination of fluffy and feminine here. The matching undies and bras are a bit less 'practical', but very pretty.

Studio A

Unit 7B, Avenida Alvear 1883, entre Callao y Rodríguez Peña, Promenade Gallery, Recoleta (4806 7587). Bus 17, 67, 92, 93, 130. **Open** 11am-8pm Mon-Fri; 10am-1pm Sat. **No credit cards**. **Map** p278 G7.

Maybe these great bathing costumes are expensive (starting at AR$300) because they're created as much for out of the water as in it.

Zoel

Paseo Alcorta, Salguero 3172, y Figueroa Alcorta, Palermo (5777 6026). Bus 67, 102, 130. **Open** 10am-10pm daily. **Credit** AmEx, DC, MC, V. **Map** p278 I7.

Loads of itsy-bitsy-teeny-weeny bikinis in a range of colours and styles, plus some cute Ts.

Shoes

If you need shoe repairs, **Fix Shoe** in Recoleta (Vicente López 1668, 4811 0226) can get most jobs finished in a day, and they deliver. You'll find shoe shinemen on street corners in the centre; expect to pay AR$3 for a job well done.

Check out also **Hermanos Estebecorena** and **Etiqueta Negra** (*for both, see p149*) for a selection of stylish men's shoes.

De María

Libertad 1655, entre Libertador y Posadas, Recoleta (4815 5001). Bus 62, 67, 92, 130. **Open** *Jan, Feb* 10.30am-7.30pm Mon-Fri; 10.30am-6pm Sat. *Mar-Dec* 10am-9pm Mon-Sat. **Credit** AmEx, DC, MC, V. **Map** p278 G8.

One for the boys: **Etiqueta Negra**. *See p149*.

Multiespacios

When is a shop not a shop? When it's also a restaurant, bar or performance space. Spaces that double-up food, drink, retail and art are not necessarily a new concept. The Centros Culturales throughout the city are the ultimate *multiespacios* (literally, multispaces). At **Centro Cultural Recoleta** (*p180*) or **Centro Cultural Konex** (*p212*) you can see a show or talk, buy books or peruse art – among other activities.

Now private ventures are getting in on the act. Whether the inspiration comes from a commercial necessity to squeeze the biggest return out of a single place or the owner's own more-the-merrier sensibility is not always clear. For restaurants hanging art, try **Lomo** (*p111*), **Filo** (*p117*), **Bar Uriarte** (*p108*), or the ultimate bar/art hangout, **Sonoridad Amarilla** (*p135*). Sculptor Renata Shussheim has even turned her Palermo Viejo home into a multispace. At **Espacio Renata** (Flat B, Malabia 1835, 4831 1440; call first), while surrounded by her hilarious sculptures, you can also eat or hear music (Renata's son is prodigious on the piano and his musician mates often join in).

Traditional cafés **Clasica y Moderna** (*p131*) and **Café Tortoni** (*p125*) have music and tango performances, and while **Milión** (*p130*) is mostly a bar and restaurant, it also hangs art, projects films and hosts music performances and DJ nights. Another musical mixed media space is **Notorious** (*p195*) – a café, restaurant, CD shop and live music venue.

La Corte restaurant (*p109*) doubles up as a shop selling designer homewares, while Martín Churba's latest venture **Tramando** (*p147*) has concerts in its yard to listen to while you shop. **Milagros** (*p143*) offers interior design, women's clothing and a small bar. For tango, ethnic music, film, food and a bookstore, visit **Un Gallo Para Esculapio** (Uriarte 1795, Palermo Viejo, 4831 7666). Other spaces promoted as multi- this or that, like **Soldba** (Costa Rica 4645, Palermo Viejo, 4833 7990), have strengths (rare CDs and a bar) and weaknesses (the clothes). You can even have a cocktail with your haircut at **Club Creativo** in Recoleta (Montevideo 1161, 4811 2202). BA – a city of multifaceted people – is truly multimedia.

De María's hand-made shoes are exquisitely crafted and affordable. The slick, feminine styles reflect a 1920s influence, but in the soul there's rock 'n' roll. Ring the bell to be let in to the minimalist, yet distinctly luxurious showroom.

Josefina Ferroni

Armenia 1471, entre Gorriti y Cabrera, Palermo Viejo (4831 4033). Bus 39, 55, 106, 109. **Open** 3-8pm Mon; 11am-8pm Tue-Sat. **Credit** DC, MC, V. **Map** p275 J4.

Josefina's boot range makes her the queen of shoes. All hand-crafted and immaculately executed, each pair is extraordinary. Her handbags, belts and flats are also startlingly fresh.

Mandarine

Honduras 4940, entre Borges y Gurruchaga, Palermo Viejo (4833 0094). Bus 39, 55, 151, 168. **Open** 10.30am-8pm Mon-Sat. **No credit cards**. **Map** p275 J4.

This small, simple shop has a cute collection of classic women's shoes – sweet details and great value.

Mishka

El Salvador 4673, entre Armenia y Malabia (4833 6566). Bus 39, 55. **Open** 11am-8.30pm Mon-Sat. **Credit** AmEx, DC, MC, V. **Map** p275 J4..

Every season Mishka launches a couple of new models of boots and shoes, with sophisticated lines and excellent finishing. Be warned – they're chiefly designed for slender models with dainty feet.

Rallys

Avenida Santa Fe 1401, y Uruguay, Recoleta (4811 6266/www.rallysonline.com). Bus 10, 39, 59, 102, 152. **Open** 9.30am-8.30pm Mon-Fri; 9.30am-5pm Sat. **Credit** AmEx, DC, MC, V. **Map** p277 F7.

From this large selection of women's shoes, there are always one or two cute designs to pick out – the Ballerina line has some fun flats.

Other locations: Posadas 1171, Recoleta (4815 8761); Arenales 1362, Recoleta (4812 9499); Avenida Cabildo 1610, Belgrano (4781 5629); Federico Lacroze 2433, Belgrano (4771 1123).

Food & drink

Supermarkets are stocked with all the basic edibles, as well as kitchen supplies, bathroom products and household goods. Three large chains have plenty of branches in the centre: **Coto** (Tribunales branch – Viamonte 1571, 4812 9178), **Disco** (Recoleta branch – Talcahuano 1055, 4813 3090) and **Norte** (Microcentro branch – Avenida Rivadavia 999, freephone 0800 888 6678). In Palermo, **Carrefour** (Salguero 3212, 4809 2700) and **Jumbo** (Avenida Bullrich 345, 4778 8000) are both hypermarkets.

While you're shopping, it's worth noting that every supermarket, and almost every food store and restaurant in town, offers free delivery.

(vertical tab) **Eat, Drink, Shop**

Bakeries, delis & healthfood

There are *panaderías* (bakeries) in every neighbourhood selling takeaway *sandwiches de miga* (paper-thin filled sandwiches), bread, *facturas* (pastries) and cakes. **Haus Brot** (Rodríguez Peña 1591, Recoleta, 4816 8003) is a natural bakery, specialising in German seeds. *Dietéticas* (health food shops) also crop up across the city. Look out for **100% Natural Dietética** in Barrio Norte (Bulnes 2042, 4821 1674). As Argentinian regional produce grows in popularity too, delis are becoming more common. Two established names, with good selections of cold meats and cheeses and many locations, are **La Casa del Queso** (Corrientes 3587, Abasto, 4862 4794) and **Al Queso, Queso** (Uruguay 1276, Recoleta, 4811 7113).

Taura

Republica Arabe de Siria 3073, entre Gutierrez y Cabello, Palermo (4804 2080/2044/www.tauraencasa.com.ar). Subte D, Plaza Italia/10, 37, 59, 60, 67. **Open** 9am-9pm Mon-Sat. **Credit** AmEx, MC, V. **Map** p279 J6.
The owners of La Corte restaurant (*see p109*) created this designer deli and butcher in 2003. Beautifully designed, and less expensive than many supermarkets, with free-range meats you can order straight from the farm with 48 hours' notice – and everyone is raving about their *dulce de leche* (AR$8).

Valenti Especialidades

Patio Bullrich, Avenida del Libertador 750, entre Montevideo y Libertad, Recoleta (4815 3090/3080). Bus 67, 92, 93, 130. **Open** 10am-9pm daily. **Credit** AmEx, DC, MC, V. **Map** p278 G8.
The best-quality cold cuts and cheeses from the Valenti family: salmon from Scotland, true Greek feta or Spanish *jamón ibérico de bellota*. It's a pleasure to shop at this top-notch deli or to succumb to the delicious sandwiches they prepare on their home-made bread.
Other locations: Soldado de la Independencia 1185, Belgrano (4775 2711); Vuelta de Obligado 1820, Belgrano (4783 0324); Feria de Belgrano, Juramento y Ciudad de la Paz, Belgrano (4782 1305).

Speciality

Look out for *alfajores* – *dulce de leche* between two cookies, dipped in chocolate. **Havanna** (Avenida Santa Fe 3150, Barrio Norte, 4822 1482) is one of the most famous makers with shops and coffee bars across town. Or pick up a box from the airport. **Un Altra Volta** ice-cream parlour does great choccies too; *see p168*.

Asia Oriental Shopping

Arribeños 2233, entre Mendoza y Olazábal, Belgrano (4784 6628). Subte D, Juramento/15, 60, 130 bus. **Open** 10am-9pm daily. **No credit cards.** **Map** p281 N5.

Salsipuedes Condimentos. *See p151.*

You'll find ginger tea, seaweed snacks, noodle chips and even live eels in this Chinatown market. Very crammed, very varied and very refreshing when you get tired of beef-centricity.

Dos Escudos

Montevideo 1690, entre Quintana y Guido, Recoleta (4812 2517/www.dosescudos.com.ar). Bus 17, 102. **Open** 7am-9pm daily. **Credit** AmEx, MC, V. **Map** p278 G7.
If you want to make an impression when invited to someone's house, buy a cake from Dos Escudos – an institution among old-school patisseries.
Other locations: Juncal 905, Retiro (4327 0135); Las Heras 3014, Barrio Norte (4805 4329).

El Gato Negro

Avenida Corrientes 1669, entre Rodríguez Peña y Montevideo, Tribunales (4374 1730). Subte B, Callao/12, 24, 37, 60 bus. **Open** 9am-11pm Mon-Fri; 9am-midnight Sat; 3-11pm Sun. **Credit** AmEx, MC, V. **Map** p277 F6.
A favourite of any cook keen on flavouring: the top-quality selection of herbs, spices, and aromatic seeds is unsurpassed in the city. The best way to appreciate the ambience is by taking tea at the in-house café. The building's original 1928 architecture and old-world feel has resulted in El Gato Negro being named a heritage site.

Tikal Chocolates

Honduras 4890, entre Gurruchaga y Armenia, Palermo Viejo (4831 2242/freephone 0800 444 8454). Bus 39, 55. **Open** 9am-9pm Mon-Sat. **Credit** AmEx, DC, MC, V. **Map** p275 J4.
This lovely chocolate shop uses Venezuelan cacao. The chocolate bonbons are faintingly delectable. Eat in or take it away in charming little packages.

Wine & spirits

Mendozan wine specialist **La Finca** (*see p134*) is also recommended.

Grand Cru

Avenida Alvear 1718, entre Callao y Rodríguez Pena, Recoleta (4816 3975/www.grandcru.com.ar). Bus 17, 67, 92, 93, 130. **Open** 10am-8pm Mon-Fri; 10am-2pm Sat. **Credit** AmEx, MC, V. **Map** p278 G7.
Sophisticated wine shop with an incredible cellar harbouring some of the world's finest wines.

Eat, Drink, Shop

Winery is well-stacked.

Ligier

Avenida Santa Fe 800, y Esmeralda, Retiro (4515 0126/www.ligier.com.ar). Subte C, San Martín/10, 111, 152 bus. **Open** 9.30am-9pm Mon-Sat. **Credit** AmEx, MC, V. **Map** p277 F7.

Catering to tourists with personalised attention, delivery, travel packaging and their strategically located branches close to many of the major hotels in Buenos Aires. They stock the big name wineries and some aged wines that date back to 1970.

Other locations: throughout the city

Winery

Corrientes 302, y 25 de Mayo, Centro (4394 2200/www.winery.com.ar). Subte B, Alem/26, 93, 99, 152 bus. **Open** 9am-8pm Mon-Fri; 9am-2pm Sat. **Credit** AmEx, MC, V. **Map** p277 E7.

A fast-growing chain that has a modern look and an excellent selection of Argentinian wines and accessories, as well as an attractive on-premises wine bar.

Other locations: Avenida LN Alem 880, Retiro (4311 6607); Avenida del Libertador 5100, Belgrano (4774 1190); Avenida del Libertador 500, Retiro (325 3400).

Health & beauty

All the shopping centres have beauty outlets, including **Verónica Zuberbuhler** with a cute range for bath and body, including confetti gels. Patio Bullrich (*see p139*) has the **Beauty Shop**, a whole floor of make-up and pampering.

MB Centro de Belleza

4th Floor, Flat H, Avenida Santa Fe 1592, entre Montevideo y Parana, Recoleta (4816 7755). Bus 10, 37, 39, 59, 152. **Open** 9am-8pm Mon-Sat. **Credit** MC, V. **Map** p278 G7.

This no-frills beauty salon is efficient and excellent value. The 'all you can wax' promotion (Monday to Wednesday, AR$15) is a godsend if you need smoothing off for the good weather. Manicures and pedicures too, and pleasant staff.

Nail Designers

Juncal 1615, entre Montevideo y Rodríguez Peña, Recoleta (4813 1892/www.naildesigners.com). Bus 10, 37, 59, 152. **Open** 10am-8pm Mon-Fri; 10am-4pm Sat. **Credit** AmEx, MC, V. **Map** p278 G7.

Go for the simultaneous manicure and pedicure treatments (AR$54) – lie back in a comfy leather armchair, let them do the work and walk out with beautiful hands and feet 50 minutes later.

Other locations: Cabello 3440, Barrio Norte (4800 1695); Coronel Díaz 1691, Barrio Norte (4821 8858).

Valeria Mazza Beauty

Avenida Santa Fe 1815, entre Callao y Riobamba, Recoleta (4812 7295/www.vmbeauty.com). Bus 10, 37, 39, 152. **Open** 9am-8.30pm Mon-Sat. **Credit** AmEx, DC, MC, V. **Map** p278 G6.

Blonde bombshell supermodel and TV presenter has her own line of beauty products and makeup – lip lacquer and shimmer body powder are the best buys.

Hairdressers

Glam

Quintana 218, entre Montevideo y Rodríguez Peña, Recoleta (4812 4578). Bus 17, 102. **Open** 9am-9pm Mon-Sat. **Credit** AmEx, DC, MC, V. **Map** p278 G7.

Slick semi-exec/semi-punk salon where cool cuts start at AR$25 and the new look is edgy.

Staff Cerini

Marcelo T de Alvear 1471, entre Paraná y Uruguay, Recoleta (4811 1652/www.cerini.net). Bus 39, 102, 111, 152. **Open** 8am-10pm Mon-Sat. **Credit** AmEx, DC, MC, V. **Map** p277 F7.

Staff Cerini is a super-modern and incessantly bustling salon. Appointments are not essential, but if you come in the hectic after-work period, you'll have to wait. Cuts start at AR$25.

Other locations: Sucre 2245, Belgrano (4783 4231).

Opticians

International opticians chain **Vision Express** (freephone 0800 555 0182, www.visionexpress. com.ar) offers no-nonsense service in one hour; there's a branch in the Microcentro (Florida 713, 4314 4155) and in Alto Palermo and Abasto shopping centres.

Infinit Boutique

Thames 1602, y Honduras, Palermo Viejo (4831 7070/www.infinitnet.com). Bus 39, 55. **Open** noon-8pm Mon; 11am-8pm Tue-Sat. **Credit** AmEx, DC, MC, V. **Map** p279 J4.

This is the first sunglass brand, wholly designed and made in Argentina, to open up a shop to the public. There's a great range of styles and fine craftsmanship; regular eyewear made to prescription too.

Pfortner Cornealant

Avenida Pueyrredón 1706, y Juncal, Barrio Norte (4827 8600). Subte D, Pueyrredón/41, 60, 62, 118 bus. **Open** 9am-6.30pm Mon-Fri; 8am-noon Sat. **Credit** AmEx, DC, MC, V. **Map** p278 H6.

Excellence in lenses as far as the eye can see. This optician has been in business for nearly 60 years and is considered the best in town.

Other locations: throughout the city.

Pharmacies

Farmacia Magister
Parera 57, entre Guido y Quintana, Recoleta (4814 4815). Bus 59, 67, 102. **Open** 9am-7.30pm Mon-Fri; 9am-3pm Sat. **Credit** AmEx, MC, V. **Map** p278 G7.
When you need medicine, style doesn't matter, but this is a singularly elegant pharmacy. A lone desk stands at the front, while out the back chemists in lab coats concoct made-to-order remedies.

FarmaCity
Florida 474, entre Corrientes y Lavalle, Microcentro (4322 6559/www.farmacity.com). Subte B, Florida/ 10, 59, 111 bus. **Open** 24hrs daily. **Credit** AmEx, DC, MC, V. **Map** p277 E7.
A mega-chain with 35 well-stocked stores across the city – and growing. There's a good range of imported products and the pharmacists are skilled professionals, but remember some prescriptions cannot be filled outside your home country. Most branches are open 24 hours, and all deliver.
Other locations: throughout the city.

Spas

Most of the city's five-star hotels (*see chapter* **Where to stay**) open their spa facilities to non-guests for a fee: AR$40-$95 per day for use of facilities, while one-hour massages cost an extra AR$45-$70.

Aqua Vita Medical Spa
Arenales 1965, entre Riobamba y Ayacucho, Barrio Norte (4812 5989). Bus 29, 39, 152. **Open** 9am-8pm Mon-Sat; 10am-6pm Sun. **Credit** AmEx, DC, MC, V. **Map** p278 G6.
Indulge in a range of delicious treatments – facial purification, aromatherapy massage or half-day head-to-toe programmes – in this aesthetically calming treatment centre. Prices start at AR$50.

Buenos Aires Spa
Avenida Medrano 1047, entre Córdoba y Cabrera, Palermo Viejo (4863 1574/www.spabuenosaires. com.ar). Bus 26, 92, 109, 151. **Open** 11.30am-10pm daily. **No credit cards.** **Map** p278 I4.
There's a touch of Asian influence at this affordable spa charging AR$15 per day. Separate men's and women's amenities include Turkish baths, sauna, jacuzzis and chill-out rooms. Kimonos and sandals are included in the price; treatments are extra.

Evian Agua Club & Spa
Cerviño 3626, entre Scalabrini Ortiz y Ugarteche, Palermo (4807 4688/www.aguaclubspa.com). Bus 10, 37, 59, 60, 93. **Open** 7.30am-10.30pm Mon-Fri; 10am-9pm Sat; 6-9pm Sun. **Credit** AmEx, DC, MC, V. **Map** p278 I6.
Get away from the city while you're still in it starting at AR$140 a day. This spa has a fitness centre, solarium, spa services, massage pool, a naturally lit reading and relaxation room, a doctor and a bistro.

Laundry & dry-cleaning

5 à Sec
Avenida Las Heras 2420, entre Laprida y Agüero, Recoleta (4803 9218/www.5asec.com). Bus 10, 59, 60, 92, 102. **Open** 8.30am-8pm Mon-Sat. **No credit cards.** **Map** p278 H7.
Drop off your suit for the advertised one-hour dry clean at this French chain – but expect it to take a few more. Still, a great deal at AR$4-$11 per item, within the day; AR$5 to have a load of laundry washed, extra to get it picked up and delivered.
Other locations: throughout the city.

Lave Rap
Arenales 1280, entre Libertad y Talcahuano, Recoleta (4814 3392). Bus 10, 21, 39, 152. **Open** 8am-9pm Mon-Sat; 10am-3pm, 5-7pm Sun. **No credit cards.** **Map** p277 F7.
For AR$6, these guys will pick up your dirty laundry and drop it off clean the following day.
Other locations: throughout the city.

Music

Miles
Honduras 4912, y Gurruchaga, Palermo Viejo (4832 0466). Bus 39, 55, 151, 168. **Open** 10am-10pm Mon-Sat; 1-9pm Sun. **Credit** AmEx, DC, MC, V. **Map** p279 J4.
Interesting and credible jazz and world music sections organised by categories (voice, piano, country of origin, horns and so on). There are also books, magazines and a patio to hang out on.

Musimundo
Avenida Santa Fe 1844, entre Callao y Riobamba, Barrio Norte (4814 0393/www.musimundo.com.ar). Bus 10, 37, 39, 152. **Open** 10am-10pm daily. **Credit** AmEx, DC, MC, V. **Map** p278 G6.
Argentina's own, Musimundo has a good, mainstream selection of music from around the world and stocks plenty of Argentinian rock and *folklore* music. Some branches also sell audio and computer equipment and have ticket sales outlets.
Other locations: throughout the city.

Make like the name at **Glam**. *See p156.*

See p156.

Eat, Drink, Shop

Shopping & f**king

Buenos Aires drips with humidity and positively buckles under the weight of its own languorous sexuality. Its plazas are an orgy of glad eyes, frantically kissing couples, crossdressing coke dealers and strutting machos with the mindset (and, they dream, the twinset) of prize bulls. Girlie bars and pick-up joints line *calle* Reconquista, where loveless sailors bought their Polish women 100 years ago, and libertine sociologists write books on the *porteño* penchant for anal sex. However you choose to look at it, there's definitely something horny in the air.

Buy it

For sexiness with class, look out for pieces from top Argentinian designers, **Laura Valenzuela** (her store will open in Palermo Viejo early 2004; call 4800 1752 to check location). Though famed for her wedding garments, her Percanta collection has a temptingly titillating air. Test the lace-up corsets and skirts created with hooks, leather binding, lace and suggestive statements. For something more explicitly goth-cum-fetishist, check out Noemi Maldavsky's clothes at **Mundo Aparte** (Fitz Roy 1879, Palermo Viejo, 4777 4340, www.mundoaparte.2ya.com; pictured): handcuffs and chains, collars and push-up corsets, whips and gloves, mostly in black PVC or leather. She can accommodate special requests for tailor-made goodies. If it's what's underneath that counts, then for the girls, try sexy undie sets from **Amor Latino** (*see p152*) or cute knickers from **Juana De Arco** (*see p147*) and, for men, ergonomic boxers from **Hermanos Estebecorena** (*see p149*). For some super-silly, OTT dressing up, there are eco-leather outfits for him and her to order from www.clandestine.com.ar – including matching sub-dom 'butler and housemaid' sets and a nun's costume to suit ultra-catholic tastes.

For *chicos* who really want to make a statement, **Monde Rituel** (Cabrera 5315, Palermo Viejo, 4831 9199, www.monde rituel.com) has throngs of thongs, from frontal feathers to buttless varieties – the outlet's outre gay clientele die for these pared down designs. For toys, gizmos and gadgets of every conceivable description, there's **SexShop** (13th Floor/G, Avenida Corrientes 1628 , Tribunales, 4373 8540, www.jugueteseroticos.com.ar) – you can shop online, by phone or in person.

Try it

If you're tired from shopping and sightseeing, but don't want your romantic holiday to blur into sightseeing and steaks, then do two hours at one of BA's many 'assignation hotels' (or *telos* as they are called in backslang). A *telo* is a love motel: with rooms to rent for a few hours to have sex. You can take a *turno* (turn) – two to three hours – or turn up after 10pm and *pernoctar* (stay the night). *Telos* were conceived for pre- and extra-marital escapades, but today are often used by couples who want a session without the kids shouting for a story or who just need a break from their usual bedrooms.

The centre is full of *telos* (look for a tell-tale red light and the words *albergue transitorio*), but two extra fun options lie beyond the city limits. For the ultimate kitsch experience – visually somewhere between the *Wizard of Oz* and *Scarface* – take the Nebuchadnezzar suite (pictured below right) at **Jardines de Babilonia** (www.jardinesde babilonia.com.ar), 40 minutes from town in Don Torcuato. It contains, for your pleasure, two life-size models of horses pulling a red velvet bordered carriage containing a waterbed, a huge jacuzzi, sunbed, sauna, mini pool under a glass roof and terrace.

At the other extreme is **Torres del Lago** (www.torresdellago.com.ar), opened in 2000, about 15 minutes from Ezeiza airport, and often used as an overnight stop before or after travelling. It bills itself as a couples' hotel, rather than a *telo*, and aims to play a subtler card, though arriving via the towered entrance and lit up gardens, it's intense enough. Here, instead of being hard sold vibrators, you can buy perfume or lacy underwear from your room (sex toys can also be ordered). A chef prepares quality meals, mirrors are less obvious and the emphasis is on a wider range of diversions – the duplex (go for water-themed room 24) and triplex suites (try the Spanish styling of room 22) have non-sexual diversions such as a pool or table football, as well as small terraces.

Swap it

Finally, BA boasts the largest swingers' centre in South America. The seven-floor **Anchorena SW Club** (Anchorena 1119-23, Barrio Norte, 4961 8548, www.anchorenasw. com) has a club, pool, restaurant, bar and hotel and hosts an annual 'marathon'.

Zival's

Avenida Callao 395, y Corrientes, Tribunales (4371 7500/www.zivals.com). Subte B, Callao/12, 24, 37, 60 bus. **Open** 9.30am-10pm Mon-Sat. **Credit** AmEx, DC, MC, V. **Map** p277 F6.

Claiming to stock the widest selection of music in South America, Zival's (also a bookshop) has all genres, but specialises in classical, jazz, folk, tango and independent local recordings.

Photography

In every barrio there's a fast colour processing lab. For more specific or professional needs use **Buenos Aires Color** (Piedras 980, San Telmo, 4361 4831, www.buenosairescolor.com.ar), with a wide range of services, from larger formats to black-and-white processing to digital imaging. For professional equipment go to **Cosentino** (Bartolomé Mitre 845, 4328 3290, www.optica cosentino.com.ar) where big-name Argentinian snappers shop. It's an exclusive stockist of Mamiya and Hasselblad, alongside a wide selection of Canon, Nikon and Leica goods. For slide film, visit **Centro Mayorista** (Office 1, Libertad 434, Tribunales, 4382 6566).

Sports & outdoor gear

On Santa Fe between Callao and Rodríguez Peña you'll find international name brand shops like **Adidas** at No.1774 (4815 4253), **Puma** at No.1766 (4815 6420) and **Nike** at No.1665 (4811 5223) – Puma and Nike also have outlets along Florida street. Prices locally are great value. Also at Rodríguez Peña and Santa Fe there is the best selection of skate/surf/snowboarding gear, try **Cristóbal Colón** (Rodríguez Peña 1127, 4813 6614). Also, in every shopping centre there's a general sporting goods store.

Alternativa

Corrientes 324, entre Reconquista y 25 de Mayo, Centro (4328 0090/www.tennisya.com). Subte B, LN Alem/26, 93, 130, 152 bus. **Open** 9am-8.30pm Mon-Fri; 10am-2pm Sat. **Credit** AmEx, DC, MC, V. **Map** p277 E7.

Tennis, golf, swimming, fishing, camping: all the best gear at this makes-you-wanna-play shop, with a super-helpful sales force.

Other locations: Avenida de Mayo 1424, Monserrat (4381 6390); Las Heras 3000, Barrio Norte (4806 9499).

Código Fútbol

Juncal 2002, y Libertad, Recoleta (4815 0459/www. codigofutbol.com.ar). Bus 17, 101. **Open** 10am-8pm Mon-Fri; 10am-1pm Sat. **Credit** AmEx, DC, MC ,V. **Map** p277 F7.

Specialising in football paraphernalia, this chain is frequented by home and away football fans. Pick up your favourite team's shirt from around the world; the official Argentinian top costs AR$99.

Eat, Drink, Shop

Other locations: Shop 10, Retiro Bus Station (4315 1461); Estadio Monumental, Figueroa Alcorta 7597, Núñez (4896 0019).

La Martina
Paraguay 661, entre Florida y Maipú, Retiro (4576 7998/www.lamartina com). Subte C, San Martín/ 7, 10, 17, 152 bus. **Open** 10am-8pm Mon-Fri; 10am-2pm Sat. **Credit** AmEx, DC, MC, V. **Map** p277 E7.
La Martina has a polo team, a polo training camp and a brand of polo clothing and equipment. It's been said that Sting, Sophia Loren and Ali MacGraw all shop here. This branch sells clothes, boots, helmets and saddles (all made in Argentina). The official Argentinian polo team shirt costs AR$170.
Other locations: Galerías Pacifico (5555 5234) & Patio Bullrich shopping centres.

Wildlife
Hipólito Yrigoyen 1133, entre Salta y LIma, Congreso (4381 1040). Subte A, Lima/29, 59, 64, 67, 86 bus. **Open** 10am-8pm Mon-Fri; 10am-1pm Sat. **Credit** AmEx, DC, MC, V. **Map** p277 E6.
Camping, outdoor and extreme sports gear – new and second hand – for climbers, anglers, campers, parachutists and more, with expert staff. Also a great source of information on where to practise.

Traditional crafts

Silver and leather are Argentina's greatest natural resources with which artisans make clothes, bags, rugs, belts, decorative objects and jewellery. They make good souvenirs. The most popular craft items include:
● *Boleadoras* Similar to a lasso, with heavy leather-covered balls on one end, which loop around the leg of a horse, cow or rhea.
● *Bombacha* Baggy pants worn by gauchos.
● *Mate* The custom of drinking this bitter herb was inherited from the native Guaraní Indians, and it is now an inherent part of everyday *porteño* life. The herb and the cup-shaped gourd that it's drunk from are both called *mate* (pronounced *ma-tay*).
● *Poncho* A shawl worn over clothes, Clint-style. The quality and colour of the threads determine the region of origin.

Kelly's
Paraguay 431, entre Reconquista y San Martín, Retiro (4311 5712). Subte C, San Martín/10, 93, 111, 132, 152 bus. **Open** 9.30am-7.30pm Mon-Fri; 9.30am-4pm Sat. **Credit** AmEx, MC, V. **Map** p277 E8.
This double-fronted shop contains a diverse range of quality crafts – pottery, silver, traditional weavings, *mates* – as well as a range of cheaper souvenirs.

El Nochero
Patio Bullrich, Avenida del Libertador 750, entre Montevideo y Libertad, Recoleta (4814 7400/www. elnochero.com). Bus 67, 92, 93, 130. **Open** 10am-9pm daily. **Credit** AmEx, DC, MC, V. **Map** p278 G8.

Kelly's.

A finely crafted selection of leather and suede jackets and silver *mates*, plus fashionable gaucho-inspired womenswear.

Platería Parodi
Avenida de Mayo 720, entre Piedras y Chacabuco, Monserrat (4342 2207). Subte A, Piedras/10, 17, 64, 86 bus. **Open** 9am-7.30pm Mon-Fri; 10am-1pm Sat. **Credit** AmEx, DC, MC, V. **Map** p277 D6.
Even the Pampean cowboys are known to frequent this souvenir shop, at least in part because the goods are so authentic. It's crammed from top to bottom with *mates*, belt buckles, silver jewellery and leather products, including tanned hides, all at fair prices. Ask Norberto for assistance, as he'll amiably share his knowledge on skilled workmanship and throw in an interesting anecdote or two.

Tierra Adentro
Arroyo 946, entre Suipacha y Carlos Pellegrini, Retiro (4393 8552/www.tierraadentro.info). Bus 61, 67, 93, 130. **Open** 10am-8pm Mon-Fri; 10am-6pm Sat. **Credit** AmEx, DC, MC, V. **Map** p277 F8.
Beautifully crafted, colourful indigenous crafts from Argentina and across South America – weavings, pottery, furniture and musical instruments. Tierra Adentro supports indigenous cultures and tribes and products are made using traditional techniques.

Travel

Equinoxe
3rd Floor, Avenida Callao 384, y Corrientes, Tribunales (4371 5050/www.equinoxe.com.ar). Subte B, Callao/12, 24, 37, 60 bus. **Open** 9am-7pm Mon-Fri. **Credit** AmEx, DC, MC, V. **Map** p277 F6.
Multilingual staff can arrange onward travel in Argentina, packages to destinations such as Iguazú, Mendoza or Patagonia, as well as *estancia* (ranch) trips, plus international flights.

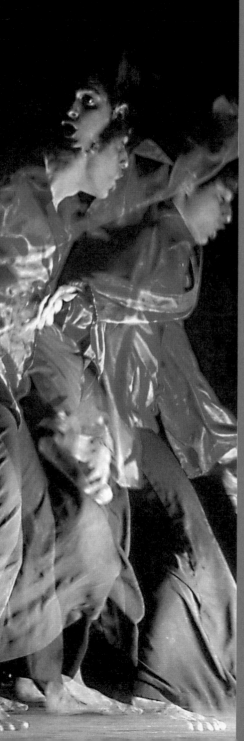

Arts & Entertainment

Festivals & Events

Musicians, tango dancers, animals, virgins and saints crowd the calendar.

For such a temperate climate, Buenos Aires suffers extreme seasonal mood swings. Winters are mild by European standards, but *porteños* spend them shielded behind long coats and longer faces. It's a time for hanging around cafés and galleries and taking in cultural events. The chilly spell is brief and its end is marked on or around 30 August – Santa Rosa Day – when the storm of that name blows in, flooding the streets and felling trees. Come the first hint of spring – when the jacaranda trees carpet plazas with blue-violet blossom – bikini-clad sunbathers clog the parks and the city experiences one big sneeze of activity. Schools and colleges close from Christmas to March, and in the scorching heat of summer those who can hit the coast, leaving a deserted metropolis. As tanned travellers return in the autumn, BA cranks up for the new academic year, theatres and concert halls kick off their new seasons and competitive football begins again.

Two annual rituals are the major agricultural fair, **La Rural** when the cows come to town, and the **Feria del Libro** (Book Fair; *for both see p165*). It seems like a new tango festival is organised every month to cash in on growing interest both in the dance and in Argentina as a tourist destination. However, none can compete with the international **Festival Buenos Aires Tango** (*see p164*). There's a similar proliferation of wine fairs, but any of the ones sponsored by gourmet magazine *Joy* (www.revistajoy.com) are bound to be high spirited.

Argentinians can find excuses to celebrate anything and everything – there's a day for all sorts of bizarre occupations (*see p165* **Name the day**). Festive days include Día del Amigo – celebrated with a night out with friends – on 20 July and Día del Niño (Children's Day) on the first Sunday in August. Other events are largely commercial in nature, among them Casa FOA (dates vary) and November's Feria de las Naciones – expos dedicated to interior design and international commerce, respectively.

Event organisation can be haphazard, so check websites for the latest information. Otherwise, newspapers (especially on Fridays) or tourist information points are your best sources. Government supported events are detailed on its website: www.buenosaires. gov.ar (then look for *cultura*, *agenda* or *expos*) or call 0800 3-FESTIVAL (3378 4825).

Spring

Festival Martha Argerich

Teatro Colón, Libertad 621, entre Tucumán y Viamonte, Tribunales (4378 7300/www.teatrocolon. org.ar). Subte D, Tribunales/29, 39, 59, 67, 100, 109 bus. **Map** p277 F7. **Date** varies in spring.
Renowned Argentinian pianist Martha Argerich delights crowds with solo performances, or accompanied by guest musicians and an orchestra, during this ten-day celebration of classical music.

Fiesta del Inmigrante

Museo de la Inmigración, Avenida Antártida Argentina 1355, y de los Inmigrantes, Puerto Madero (4317 0285/www.fiestadelinmigrante). Bus 6, 20. **Map** p277 E8. **Date** wkend closest to 4 Sept.
Ethnic groups celebrate the flavourful food, music, dance and sacrifices of their immigrant ancestors.

Festival Internacional de Buenos Aires

Teatro San Martín & other theatres (festivaldeteatro ba.com.ar). **Date** every 2yrs in Sept; next Sept 2005.
BA's major performing arts festival, this is a fortnight of mainly Latin American theatre, dance and musical performances, with some big-name guests such as Peter Brook and Robert Wilson.

Festival Guitarras del Mundo

Centro Cultural San Martín and across Argentina (www.festivaldeguitarras.com.ar). **Date** Oct.
Two-week gathering of more than 100 top national and international strummers in genres from jazz and tango through folk and classical.

Marcha del Orgullo Gay

Plaza de Mayo (www.marchadelorgullo.org.ar). Subte A, Plaza de Mayo or D, Catedral or E, Bolívar/24, 64, 86, 152 bus. **Map** p277 D7. **Date** 1st Sat in Nov.
BA's growing Gay Pride March gathers gays, lesbians, trannies and heteros for serious protest combined with a colourful *fiesta*.

Maratón de Buenos Aires

Information *www.maratondebuenosaires.com.* **Date** 1st Sun in Nov.
Roadrunners clog Avenida 9 de Julio in this annual marathon whose start and finish line is the Obelisco.

Alvear Fashion & Arts

Along Avenida Alvear, Recoleta (4807 0545). Bus 17, 67, 93, 124, 130. **Map** p278 G7. **Date** early Nov.
A one-week, red-carpet exhibition of local painters, sculptors and photographers held at the top-flight boutiques on BA's Fifth Avenue.

Arts & Entertainment

Día de la Tradición

Feria de Mataderos, Lisandro de la Torre y Avenida de Los Corrales (4687 5602). Bus 55, 80, 92, 126. Also San Antonio de Areco, BA province (Tourist Office 02326 453165). **Date** wkend nearest 12 Nov.
The annual gaucho day has regional food and music and brave shows of horsemanship, with events during the preceding 'Tradition Week'. San Antonio de Areco (*see p228*), 113 km (70 miles) north-west of the capital or BA's Feria de Mataderos are where to be.

Festival Internacional de Cine y Video de Derechos Humanos

Various cinemas (4322 9191/www.derhumalc.org.ar). **Date** Nov.
This annual gathering of documentary filmmakers and their activist public focuses on human rights issues in Latin America and beyond.

Feria Internacional de Turismo

Predio La Rural, Avenida Santa Fe 4201, y Avenida Sarmiento, Palermo (4322 2585/www.fit.org.ar). Subte D, Plaza Italia/10, 29, 39, 60, 152 bus. **Map** p279 J6. **Date** end Nov.
Get travel info from all of Argentina's provinces, plus Latin American and other countries, in a four-day event for the tourism sector and general public.

Abierto Argentino de Polo

Campo Argentino de Polo, Avenida del Libertador 4000 y Dorrego, Palermo (Asociación Argentina de Polo 4343 0972/www.aapolo.com). Bus 10, 64, 130, 160. **Map** p279 K6/L6. **Date** mid Nov/mid Dec.
Two- and four-legged competitors get together to wow the smart set in the country's biggest polo event, in its most impressive stadium. There's lots to keep you amused if chukkas aren't your thing.

Waiting for a miracle

Desperate Argentinians just don't hunt for work – they pray for it. In what's, sadly, an increasingly popular kind of folk ritual, on the 7th of every month, peaking on national saints' day in August, desperate pilgrims flock to the the church of San Cayetano in the gritty suburb of Liniers. They go to beg the patron saint of bread and work for relief in the coming year. The procession is but one of several cult-making exercises throughout the year.

How is holiness bestowed? On foot usually. Every year on 5 October, thousands of worshippers march – or crawl – the 68 kilometres (42 miles) west of the capital to Luján Cathedral, to pay homage to the Virgin of Luján, Argentina's most important saint. The last Sunday in September is a chance to see a different sort of believer, when 6,000 gauchos from all over the country make their own pilgrimage to see the virgin.

Competing with this traditional ritual are new saint-making sacraments. One of the strangest takes places every 8 December when some 50,000 people line up outside a church in the northern suburb of El Talar to plead with the Virgen Desatanudos (literally the Virgin of Knot Untying) for help in unravelling life's inevitable knots.

But more than virgins and saints, it's dead, pop-music icons and former barrio bigwigs

that garner the bulk of devotion. In the southern suburb of Quilmes, fans of tropical music star Rodrigo have erected a roadside shrine the size of a football pitch next to where he suffered a fatal accident in 2000. Every 24 June, an impromptu, 24-hour dance festival takes places on the site as crying fans pay tribute to El Potro (The Stud). Superstitious *porteños* can't overlook the 'divine' coincidence that Rodrigo died 65 years to the day after Carlos Gardel's life ended in a tragic plane crash. Every anniversary devout fans head to Gardel's tomb in Chacarita cemetery, where at a beaming statue of the famed tango crooner they keep vigil making sure that a cigarette placed between his bronze fingers stays lit.

Perhaps the least likely candidate for canonisation is Victor 'Frente' (forehead) Vital, a Robin Hood-like thug who used to heist trucks and share the stolen goods among his poor neighbours before being shot dead by police, aged 17, during a raid. Disenchanted slum dwellers and delinquents have converted his tomb in the northern suburb of San Fernando into a shrine where they leave offerings of beer cans and joints, especially leading up to his birthday on 6 February. Unless looking for an unadvisable dose of urban adventure tourism, this is one place that most foreigners will avoid.

Arts & Entertainment

There'll be dancing, dancing in the streets at the **Festival Buenos Aires Tango**.

Summer

Festival Buen Día
Plaza Palermo Viejo, Costa Rica y Armenia (www. festivalbuendia.com). Bus 15, 39, 55. **Map** p279 J4/5. **Date** late Dec.
Fashion, shopping, electronica dance music and cocktail mixing are fused in this low-culture, youth-oriented open-air party from noon to midnight.

Festival Buenos Aires Danza Contemporánea
Teatro San Martín & other theatres. (www.buenos airesdanza.com.ar). **Date** every 2yrs in Dec; next in Dec 2004.
For two weeks BA's overlooked modern dance scene is centre stage at theatres presenting the best local as well as international talent.

Christmas
The main celebration is the night of 24 December – Nochebuena, as it's known locally – usually spent *en famille* launching fireworks. Christmas Day itself is a public holiday. There is little build-up.

Chinese New Year
Along Arribeños 2000-2200 blocks, Belgrano (Chinese Embassy 4541 5085). Bus 15, 29, 60, 64. **Date** Jan or Feb. **Map** p281 M5/N5.
This small-scale festival is an explosion of colour and clamour in Belgrano's tiny Chinatown.

Festival Buenos Aires Tango
Various theatres & Centros Culturales (www.festivaldetango.com.ar). **Date** late Feb-Mar.
This is the big one: it's the city's – and the world's – most important tango festival, a nine-day extravaganza of concerts, shows, free classes, exhibitions, open-air *milongas* (Avenida Corrientes is closed for an evening) and other tango-associated festivities. In 2003, around 220,000 people took part in the festivities. If you're in town, don't miss it. If you're a fan of tango, you should plan your trip around it. Serious dancers will return in August for the Tango Dance World Championship.

Carnaval
Plazas & social clubs throughout Buenos Aires (tourist information 4313 0187). **Date** Feb.
Don't expect Rio or New Orleans – here, it's small scale, with teams of *murga* drummers and dancers performing on some plazas. The best carnivals in the region are in the Uruguayan capital, Montevideo (*see p238*), while in Argentina the main action is in Gualeguaychú in Entre Ríos province.

Autumn

Opera Season
Teatro Colón, Libertad 621, entre Tucumán y Viamonte, Tribunales (box office 4378 7300/4378 7301/www.teatrocolon.org.ar). Subte D, Tribunales/ 29, 39, 59, 109 bus. **Map** p277 F7. **Date** Mar-Dec.
The Colón (*see p189*) officially opens its curtains in early March, with ballet, opera and classical concerts.

Fashion Buenos Aires
Predio La Rural, Avenida Santa Fe 4201, y Avenida Sarmiento, Palermo (4784 3205/www.grupopampa. com). Subte D, Plaza Italia/10, 29, 39, 60, 152 bus. **Map** p279 J6. **Date** Mar & Sept.
The latest fashions from local designers grace the catwalk in Buenos Aires' twice-yearly, four-day fashion week: the winter collection is presented in March, the summer one in September.

Easter
Easter sees large attendance at churches, but little in the way of other visible celebration. The city is emptier as many people go away for a long weekend or spend the time with family.

Festival Internacional de Cine Independiente
Hoyts Abasto & other cinemas (www.bafilmfest.com). **Date** Mid-late Apr.
Highly popular 10-day showcase for non-Hollywood films from all over the world, including the work of local directors. It attracts one or two name directors and actors usually seen only at the likes of the Cannes or Venice film fests.

Feria del Libro

Predio La Rural, Avenida Santa Fe 4201, y Avenida Sarmiento, Palermo (Fundación El Libro 4374 3288/ www.el-libro.com.ar). Subte D, Plaza Italia/ 10, 29, 39, 60, 152 bus. **Map** p279 J6. **Date** mid Apr-May.

The three-week long P.A Book Fair is a monster event. It's geared more towards the readers than publishers, and attracts hundreds of thousands of *porteño* bookworms. Readings, performances, signings and debates and stands from all over the world.

ArteBA

Predio La Rural, Avenida Santa Fe 4201, y Avenida Sarmiento, Palermo (Fundación ArteBA 4816 8704/ www.arteba.com). Subte D, Plaza Italia/10, 29, 39, 60, 152 bus. **Date** mid May. **Map** p279 J6.

National and international galleries, joined by specialist publishers and artists, group together for the city's biggest, week-long contemporary art fair.

Aniversario de la Revolución de Mayo

Plaza de Mayo (Museo del Cabildo 4334 1782). Subte A, Plaza de Mayo or D, Catedral or E, Bolívar/24, 29, 64, 86, 152 bus. **Map** p277 D7. **Date** 25 May.

The humble celebration of the day of the 1810 revolution begins the midnight before when people gather in front of the Cabildo to sing the national anthem. At 8pm on the 25th visitors are invited again to the Cabildo's patio to join a patriotic choir.

Winter

Día de la Independencia

Across Argentina. **Date** 9 July.

Although the main events are held in freedom's birthplace in Tucumán, cafés along Avenida de Mayo partake in the festivities serving up traditional *chocolate con churros* for breakfast. A solemn Mass – and tongue-lashing homily – at the Cathedral is attended by the President, who arrives on foot from the Casa Rosada when the political situation permits.

Marcha del 26 de Julio

City centre streets & plazas. **Date** 26 July.

To mark the anniversary of the death of Evita, their spiritual leader, loyal Peronists stage torchlight marches through the city centre and hold graveside vigils in Recoleta Cemetery.

La Rural

Predio La Rural, Avenida Santa Fe 4201, y Avenida Sarmiento, Palermo (4324 4700 ext 780/www.rural arg.org.ar). Subte D, Plaza Italia/10, 29, 39, 60, 152 bus. **Map** p279 J6. **Date** end July-Aug.

The Exposición de Ganadería, Agricultura e Industria Internacional – known as La Rural – is the nation's supremely important two-week agro fair. Lambs, rams, pigs and other farm animals get a look-in, but it's the bulls who are most respected. The best events are the madly macho gaucho stunts.

Feria del Libro Infantil y Juvenil

Centro de Exposiciones, Avenida Figueroa Alcorta y Avenida Pueyrredón, Recoleta (Fundación El Libro 4374 3288/www.el-libro.com.ar). Bus 67, 92, 93, 124, 130. **Map** p278 H8. **Date** mid July-Aug.

This hugely popular children and teenagers' book fair is a spin-off of the big Feria del Libro.

Encuentros Abiertos de Fotografía – Festival de la Luz

Centro Cultural Recoleta & other venues (www. encuentrosabiertos.com.ar). **Date** Every 2yrs in Aug; next in Aug 2004.

BA's main photography event is the local segment of the worldwide Festival of Light photo expo.

Name the day

At school, Argentinians have to stand in line and sing anthems about their national heroes on days called *feriados*. Every important historical figure gets a day – San Martín, Sarmiento, Belgrano – usually on the anniversary of their death. More bizarre are the days dedicated to jobs you never knew existed or days for inanimate objects or abstract ideas. Below are just a few of the 365 examples. Whatever your occupation, there'll be a day in the year when people say ¡*Feliz Día!*

7 April Día del Acoplado y Semirremolque (Trailer and Breakdown Trucks Day).
8 May Día Nacional de la Prevención Sísmica (National Day for Preventing Earthquakes).
22 May Día del Obrero Fideero (Day of the Noodle Maker).
25 May Día del Agente de Propaganda Médica (Day of the Medical Advertising Agent).
9 June Día del Banquero (Bankers' Day).
18 July Día del Riel (Day of the Rails – yes, as in train tracks).
2 August Día del Empleado Mensual de la Dirección de Hipódromos (Day of the Salaried Employee in Racecourse Administration).
21 September Día del Porteño (Porteño Day).
5 October Día del Turista (Tourist Day).
26 October Día de los Cafés de Buenos Aires (Day of BA's Cafés).
14 November Día del Amor (Love Day).
11 December Día Nacional del Tango – Nacimiento de Julio De Caro y Carlos Gardel (National Tango Day – Birthday of Julio De Caro and Carlos Gardel).

Arts & Entertainment

Children

Kids get a whole lotta love in Buenos Aires.

Your parental pride will be reinforced by endless smiles and murmurs of approval from all-comers as you stroll the city with your children. Out and about in BA with kids is enjoyable, but there are hazards. Sidewalks lack ramps, so pack a sturdy pushchair and good luck negotiating the pot-holed pavements and kerbs. Also be prepared to change your routine; evening meal times, in particular, are much later than you may be accustomed to.

Still, there are dozens of child-friendly restaurants to sample. Among them **Cumaná** (*see p103*) where kids can scribble on the table cloths and **Pizza Banana** (Avenida Costanera Rafael Obligado y La Pampa, 4314 9500) where they can work up an appetite on the bouncy castle. Many eateries have special menus and free sweets for little ones too.

Most hotels are also family-oriented, and there are many apartment hotels with large living spaces and kitchenettes. There are no babysitting agencies, but most major hotels can find a trustworthy child-minder (*see chapter* **Where to stay**), or ask a local to put you in touch with a reliable babysitter.

BA has excellent markets, fairs, museums, cinemas and theatres for families. To find out where and when, consult newspaper supplements or *Planetario*, a free monthly magazine available from Recoleta and San Martín cultural centres. Look out for musical group **Los Musiqueros**, an impressive trio which uses use traditional and home-made instruments. **Al Tun Tun** and **Caracahumba** combine inventive musical sets with puppet shows, while theatre company **Groupo Alas** is also worth investigation.

Outdoors

Built-up though the city is, there are still plenty of green areas where kids can safely burn off excess energy. Most parks, recreation areas and plazas have playgrounds for children although some may not be in the best state of repair.

For a family day out with a range of sporting facilities, pools and outdoor space, try the all-inclusive sports clubs (*see p202*). Recoleta with its open-air market, though not exclusively aimed at youngsters, has such diverting attractions as street performers, fire-eaters, living statues, puppeteers and jugglers.

The biggest expanse of greenery is Palermo's **Parque Tres de Febrero** (*see p84*). Here, kids will run out of puff before they run out of park and it's one of few places largely free of dog mess. Hire a bike with child seats (AR$5 per hour) or rollerblades (AR$8 per hour) and discover the area at your own pace. Or float out on the lake in a pedalo or rowing boat (AR$12 per hour). At weekends, there are rides in *mateos*, horse-drawn carriages found dotted around the park; AR$30 for 30 minutes.

Nestled within this area is the lovely **Jardín Japonés** (*see p84*), which hosts puppet shows on weekends from 4-5pm, as well as a series of recycling workshops, and you can also feed the shoals of insatiable koi carp. Palermo park is also home to the city's **Jardín Zoológico** (*listings below*) and the planetarium (*see p168*).

Another escape from the crowded streets is the **Reserva Ecológica** (*see p91*). The circuit around the reserve is quite long on foot, especially for under-fives, but you can hire bicycles at the entrance. The reward at the end of the walk is a spectacular view of the River Plate. The tram ride in the barrio of Caballito (*see p88*) is also a family favourite.

For wannabe cowboys or cowgirls, a visit to the gaucho themed **Feria de Mataderos** (*see p94*) in the far west of the city is a must. Look out also for street theatre from **Grupo Catalinas Sur** in La Boca (*see p73*) and **Las Calandracas** in Barracas.

Jardín Zoológico de Buenos Aires

Avenidas Las Heras y Sarmiento, Palermo (4806 7412). Subte D, Plaza Italia/15, 36, 37, 60, 152 bus. **Open** *Jan, Feb* 10am-6pm daily. *Mar-Dec* 10am-5.30pm Tue-Sun. **Admission** AR$4-$8.50, free under-12s, concessions. **Credit** V. **Map** p279 J6. This city zoo houses over 350 species, plus aquariums and an educational farm, where kids are taught to bake, milk cows and recycle paper. Indigenous animals include the llama, vicuña and guanaco (don't get too close – they spit). The zoo also runs a breeding programme for condors, and in late 2003 Bengal tiger sextuplets were born. *See also p83*.

Indoors

On cold or wet days, museums, cinemas, cultural centres, theatres and shopping centres are great ways to keep the kids entertained. The **Abasto** mall (*see p139*) is tailor-made for

Arts & Entertainment

Animal magic

For captive creatures – and kids – it doesn't get much better than Parque Temaikèn (a native Tehuelche word meaning Land of Life) in Buenos Aires province. Taking an unhurried stroll around this wonderful wildlife park, it's hard to believe that any of the 200 species that inhabit the open plan spaces are anything other than comfortable.

An interesting selection of land mammals, including tigers and pumas roam the vast expanses, while river and marine creatures can be viewed in huge water tanks. There's also an exotic array of reptiles and 1,500 species of birds (including pelicans, penguins and flamingos) in and around the outdoor pools and artificial lakes. Bird lovers get an extra bonus: Temaikèn was created beside the Granja Heladería Munchi's (Route 25 y Miguel Cané, Belén de Escobar, 03488 4436 800) – a bird sanctuary set up on the farm belonging to an ice-cream manufacturer – and

Temaikèn's entrance fee includes admission to both attractions (but not vice versa).

The park is thoughtfully planned and designed. Sturdy wooden, rope and bamboo walkways and platforms connect the exhibits. They blend in naturally with the environment and allow elevated views of the wildlife. Hippopotamus pools permit these loveable creatures to be seen frolicking above and below the water's surface, while in the aquarium the designers have gone one better and built sections of the tank in the ceiling so that sharks and stingrays can be observed gliding effortlessly above your head. In the cinema, educational films are projected on a 56-metre-wide (184-foot) screen completely surrounding the audience.

Just 30 minutes away (around AR$50 by cab) from downtown Buenos Aires, Temaikèn is an excellent family day out. Equipped with indoor and outdoor play spaces, interactive centres and a gift shop, kids are spoilt for choice. As is normal with theme parks, you can't take your own food, but there's plenty inside the park from fast-food shacks and ice-cream parlours to reasonably priced cafés and restaurants. Choike Aike serves up pasta and El Cañadon, bizarrely perhaps, offers many cuts of barbecued meat and a surprisingly good wine selection.

Parque Temaikèn
Ruta Provincial 25, Km 1, Escobar (03488 436900/www.temaiken.com.ar). **Open** 10am-7pm daily. **Admission** *Mon-Fri* AR$10; AR$5 3-10s, concessions. *Sat, Sun* AR$15; AR$10 3-10s, concessions. **Credit** AmEx, DC, MC, V.

children. As well as the excellent **Museo de los Niños** (*see p168*), restaurants, games arcades and play areas, there is a fully functional indoor amusement park equipped with roller coaster, swinging pirate ship and even a Ferris wheel. Well worth a whirl.

The Sala Alberdi in the Teatro San Martín (*see p217*) offers a choice of shows and events for children, while **Cine Los Angeles** (Corrientes 1770, Tribunales, 4372 2405) specialises in children's movies, although they are shown dubbed in Spanish. Most cinemas, however, do show English versions of the latest animated movies, but check before purchasing a ticket. **Village Recoleta** (*see p176*) has child-minding facilities where young children are entertained while parents take a two-hour break to watch a

film. You must take photo ID and your movie ticket. Outside the cinema complex, pick up flyers for musical and theatrical shows for kids.

La Calle de los Títeres
Centro Cultural del Sur, Avenida Caseros 1750, y Baigorri, Constitución (4305 6653/4306 0301). Bus 45, 59, 67. **Open** Puppet shows *Mar-Dec* 3pm Sat; 3pm, 4pm Sun. **Closed** Jan, Feb. **Map** p276 C4.
'The puppet street' presents free shows and puppet-making in the picturesque patio of an old mansion.

Museo Argentino de Ciencias Naturales Bernardino Rivadavia
Avenida Angel Gallardo 470, entre Warnes y Marechal, Caballito (4982 1154/4494/www.macn. gov.ar). Subte B, Angel Gallardo/55, 65, 112, 105, 124 bus. **Open** 2-7pm daily. **Admission** AR$2. **No credit cards. Map** p274 F2.

Arts & Entertainment

This old-fashioned natural history museum thrills kids who are dotty about dinosaurs, with a skeleton of a carnotaurus – the 'bad guy' in Disney's *Dinosaur* movie – and a megaterio; 3m (10ft) tall and 6m (20ft) long, dating from 10-15,000 years ago. Also on show, a meteorite and skeletons of a boa constrictor and an Indian elephant. *See also p88.*

Museo de los Niños

Level 2, Corrientes 3247, entre Agüero y Anchorena, Abasto (4861 2325/www.museoabasto.org.ar). Subte B, Carlos Gardel/24, 26, 124, 146, 168 bus. **Open** 1-8pm Tue-Sun. **Admission** AR$5; AR$12-$18 family ticket; free under-3s. **Credit** AmEx, DC, MC, V. **Map** p278 G4.

This mini adult world is perfect for curious youngsters. They can run a fast-food restaurant or operate a crane on a building site. If their aspirations are higher they can test their medical skills in the hospital, extract teeth in the dental surgery or run a TV studio. Also on offer are science, art and cooking workshops, and under-3s have two playrooms.

Museo Participativo de Ciencias

1st Floor, Centro Cultural Recoleta, Junín 1930, y Quintana, Recoleta (4807 3260/4806 3456/www. mpc.org.ar). Bus 10, 17, 60, 67, 92, 110. **Open** *Jan, Feb* 3.30-7.30pm Tue-Sun. *Mar-Dec* 10am-5pm Tue-Fri; 3.30-7.30pm Sat, Sun. **Admission** AR$6; free under-4s. **No credit cards. Map** p278 H7.

'Prohibido no tocar' (it's forbidden not to touch) is the motto of this science museum in the Recoleta cultural centre, where kids can explore the mysteries of physics and have fun at the same time – enjoying the distorting mirrors and experimenting with lenses and lights. It's best for children over seven.

Planetario de la Ciudad de Buenos Aires Galileo Galilei

Parque Tres de Febrero, Belisario Roldán y Avenida Sarmiento, Palermo (4772 9265/4771 6629/www. planetario.gov.ar). Subte D, Plaza Italia/37, 67, 130, 160 bus. **Open** *Museum* 10am-6pm Mon-Fri; 1-7.30pm Sat, Sun. *Shows* 3pm, 4.30pm, 6pm Sat, Sun. **Admission** *Museum* free. *Shows* AR$4; free under-5s, concessions. **No credit cards. Map** p279 J7.

The spaceship-shaped planetarium is in the middle of Palermo's main park. Shows (best for age seven and up) are in Spanish, but visually stunning, so worth it for non-Spanish speakers. They include a view of the cosmos from the earth and far-reaching images from the Hubble space telescope.

Outside Buenos Aires

Outside BA there are child-friendly attractions that can be visited in a day trip. The best is **Temaikèn** (*see p167* **Animal Magic**); other options include the República de los Niños in La Plata and, if visiting the Atlantic coast (*see p233*), Mundo Marino. A visit to an *estancia* (ranch – *see p230*) or to Tigre (*see p223*) is also a good family option. Also try the following:

I scream...

Using traditions brought over by Italian immigrants, Buenos Aires boasts some of the best artisan ice-cream (*helados artesanales*) in the world.

Freddo (Avenida Callao 1410, Recoleta, 0800 3337 3336) was once the number-one choice, but it lost a certain something when the family who created it sold the chain. It's still worth licking flavours like Lemon Pie, however, or slurping on the fruity ice shakes. Part of the Freddo family took their serious approach to ice-cream and started **Un Altra Volta** (Avenida del Libertador 3060, Palermo, 4805 1818), a designer ice house. Delicious scoops such as Mascarpone as well as delicate chocolates are up for grabs. The other side of the family created **Persicco** (on the corner of Salguero and Cabello, Palermo, 4808 0888), another perfect parlour. Try Dulce de Leche with Brownie flavour and their classic cakes.

The creamy taste of **Munchi's** (Larrea 1541, Recoleta, 0800 555 5050) ice-cream comes from the milk of Jersey cows – and it's also a great place to pick up a jar of *dulce de leche* or jam. Finally, **Bris** is a hidden gem at Costa Rica 4592 in Palermo Viejo (4833 6776). Their Dulce de Leche is arguably the best around, and original flavours include Borgoña Pears and Mousse de Café Cognac.

Parque de la Costa

Vivanco 1509, y Mitre, Tigre (4002 6000/www. parquedelacosta.com.ar). Tren de la Costa to Delta/ 60 bus. **Open** 11am-8pm Thur-Sun. **Admission** *Park* free. *Shows & rides* AR$18; AR$9 3-12s; AR$6 concessions; free under-3s. **Credit** AmEx, DC, MC, V.

This attractive amusement park – the only major one near BA – is beside the Delta station in Tigre, the terminus on the Tren de la Costa (*see below*). There are fairground and boat rides, roller coasters, theme restaurants and a lake with a dancing fountain show. There's something for all ages and sizes.

Tren de la Costa

Avenida Maipú 2305, Olivos (4002 6000/www.trende lacosta.com.ar). From Retiro, Ramal 2 train on Mitre line to Olivos/59, 60, 71, 152 bus. **Open** 6.30am-11pm Mon-Fri; 8am-midnight Sat, Sun. **Return ticket** AR$3; free under-3s. **Credit** AmEx, DC, MC, V.

On this delightful 25-minute train ride from Olivos to Tigre, you can get on and off at stations along the route, where there are games, cinemas, restaurants and shops. San Isidro station has the most options.

Arts & Entertainment

Clubs

Dance the night – and half the next day – away in BA's kicking clubland.

Buenos Aires' club scene has boomed – this is Latin America's leading dance destination. Regular visits from foreign DJs, complemented by the talents of local mixmasters, feed a growing appetite for beats. Names to look out for include Javier Zuker, Cristóbal Paz, Carlos Alfonsín and Argentina's most successful DJ export, globe-trotting Hernán Cattáneo (*see p172* **Mi Buenos Aires Querido**).

In addition to regular club nights, festivals, outdoor events – including sporadic full moon parties and raves in the city's parklands or along the river – and one-offs cater to the increasingly exacting demands of clubbers who only a few years ago were still clinging to a middle-of-the-road musical diet. Look out in particular for **Moon Park** events attracting international DJ superstars of the status of Sasha, Carl Cox and John Digweed, organised by clubbing supremo Martín Gontad (five dates are planned for 2004), as well as **Creamfields**, the hugely popular Argentinian version of the UK's classic festival (*see p192*).

Disco (shortened from *discoteca*) is equivalent to the generic word 'club'. Of course, it's not all western-style rock and *electrónica*, either – there is also a lively Latin scene. Some salsa clubs are recommended in this chapter, but you can also shake your thing to some *son* and cha-cha-cha at **Rey Castro** (Perú 342, Monserrat, 4342 9998), a Cuban restaurant, which has weekend dance nights. Home-grown tropical rhythms focus on cumbia; the vital venue is **Metropolis** (Avenida Santa Fe 4389, Palermo, 4773 3030), but it's only advisable to go if you're with a local who knows the score.

When planning a night out, pace yourself, and be prepared to travel. Venues are split between central locations and the Costanera Norte along the river. Clubs get lively late (after 3am) and go on until they run out of people. Popular places, especially those with outside terraces, such as **Pachá** (whose Saturday nights were traditionally one of the city's main events; *see p173*) and **Big One** (*see p171*), rumble on until 11am the next day; after-hours, like **Caix** (*see p171*), keep the party going until 3pm (remember shades in summer months as that afternoon sun is cruel).

Though there is rarely a strict dress code in any club, *porteños'* slavery to fashion makes them militant about following style

commandments. Yet this enthusiasm for all that is hip reaps handsome visual rewards – BA's clubbers are a good-looking and flirtatious lot. The places that succeed are invariably stylishly packed with chatty people who never tire of foreign visitors. It's a friendly, non-agressive vibe, perhaps partly thanks to how little the locals drink, and trouble is mercifully rare.

During weekdays clubbing traffic decreases, though some bars host top mid-week grooves (Voodoo Lounge, La Cigale, Asia de Cuba). There's even a straight-from-work club – on Wednesday from 8pm-2am – for the after-office

The best Club nights

Monday
You gotta sleep sometime, don't you?

Tuesday
El Dorado's (*see p171*) drum 'n' bass stomper or **La Cigale** for *electrónica* and a Gallic vibe (*see p125*).

Wednesday
Voodoo Lounge (*see p135*) has a stellar DJ roster and **Asia de Cuba** (*see p170*) ups the urban bpm.

Thursday
The weekend unofficially starts here. Go to **Club 69** at Niceto (*see p173*) for BA's most original mid-weeker or groove down to the **Basement** (*see p170*) for serious sounds.

Friday
TGIF. Palermo's **Podestá** (*see p173*) heaves with an alternative crowd, while upriver, **Mint** (*see p173*) is the freshest option.

Saturday
It's the big one – and **Big One**'s (*see p171*) is huge. Look for **Moon Park** parties too or drop in on the starry crowd at **Tequila** (*see p173*) before checking who's spinning at **Pachá** (*see p173*). Keep on going till...

Sunday
... to dance by day at **Caix**'s (*see p171*) after-hours. Or save energy for the Brazilian beats at **Maluco Beleza** (*see p173*).

Arts & Entertainment

Fashion and funksters at **Mint**. *See p173.*

crowd at San Telmo's **Museum** (Perú 535),
a space otherwise used for private corporate
events. The biggest nights take place at
weekends, but there's enough variety
to create a week-long clubbing calendar;
see p169 **The best club nights**.

Some clubs have survived through the years –
El Living, Buenos Aires News and Pachá – but
in general the scene is volatile. There are one-
off parties and short-run events, and even
the long-standing venues listed below change
their weekly schedules regularly. As well as
established club nights, look out for: **Fiesta
Garage** (www.fiestagarage.com.ar) downtown,
where you can rave and salve your conscience
too – the entrance fee is a donation of a non-
perishable food item; **Club 69** at Niceto Club
(*see p173*), one of the most popular long-running
club nights in town; **Brandon Gay Day** (*see
p185*), a hip gathering of modern hybrids that
tours the city. Some clubs, like Niceto, have live
bands before the dancing starts.

PRICES AND INFORMATION

Door policy isn't very strict and a foreign accent
pretty much gets you in anywhere. Admission
in smaller venues ranges from AR$5 to AR$12
(women usually pay less then men), with larger
clubs charging AR$20-$30. As a rule, credit
cards are not accepted for admission. If there's
a restaurant you may be able to use plastic (and
sometimes, too, to pay your bar tab). A drink is
normally included with the cost of entrance:
listen out for *'con consumición'* or *'con trago'*.
Many bars work on an annoying double queue
system; pay for your drink at the cashier and
get your receipt before grabbing a barman.

The best source of information is website
www.buenosaliens.com – check the site once
in town for the week's schedule. Also, harvest
flyers (which sometimes offer discounted
admission) from Galería Bond Street (*see p149*),
boutiques in Palermo or downtown bars such as
Dadá (*see p125*). Tour agency **Curiocity** (4803
1112/1113) offers a useful personalised service –
they can take you out, get access to the city's
best clubs and secure tables in the VIP sectors.

Venues

Asia de Cuba

*Pierina Dealesi 750 y Macacha Güemes, Madero
Este (4894 1328/www.asiadecuba.com.ar). Bus 2,
130, 152.* **Open** *Restaurant* 12.30pm-1am daily.
Club 1-5am Tue-Sat. **Map** p277 D8.
At this flashy dockside spot (open all day as a
bar/restaurant) you can dine on sushi, sweat it out
on the dancefloor, or just enjoy the slightly mob-
scented scenery while relishing a decent drink. The
public bridges the generation gap and though the
beats aren't the hippest, there are nights (currently
Wednesdays) when 'tribal house' takes hold. The
best part is the end, when you heroically slide past
security, a Martini and companion in hand to stroll
by the river. For taxis, or a room, head to the nearby Hilton (*see p35*).

Azúcar

*Avenida Corrientes 3330, entre Agüero y Gallo,
Abasto (4865 3103/4866 4439/www.azucarsalsa.
com). Bus 24, 26, 124, 146, 168.* **Open** from
midnight Fri, Sat. **Map** p278 G4.
This small first-floor salsa venue verges on the
tacky, with one wall painted with cartoon-like
images of salsa's famous names, but it has energy
to spare and an enthusiastic crowd. The dancefloor
is small, but there are plenty of places to sit and sup.
There are daily dance classes in a variety of styles;
check the website for schedule.

The Basement Club

*The Shamrock, Rodríguez Peña 1220, entre Juncal y
Arenales, Recoleta (4812 3584, www.theshamrock
bar.com). Bus 10, 37, 39, 101, 124, 152.* **Open** from
1am Thur-Sat. **Map** p278 G6.

Beyond the curtains to the basement of this ever popular bar awaits another world – fresh sounds, a giant glitter ball and disco floor lights. An energetic vibe emanates from the residents Waltie, Lucas Ferro and DJ Boro, with Cristóbal Paz making regular appearances on Thursday nights. Underground house radiates from the DJ booth, while the enthusiastic crowd raises the temperatures on the intimate dancefloor below. On two Sundays per month, a rock 'n' roll party offers up some good old fashioned fun.

Big One
Adolfo Alsina 940, entre Bernardo de Irygoyen y Tacuari, Monserrat (4331 1277/www.palaciobuenos aires.com). Bus 10, 17, 59, 64, 86. **Open** from 1.30am Fri, Sat. **Map** p277 E6.

Weekends in a building known as Palacio Alsina are BA's most hardcore electronic club nights, called Big One. The architecture and spirit mimic a cathedral-turned-clubbers' paradise. The vaulted structure provides a crisp acoustic backdrop for sounds that emanate from long DJ sets encompassing progressive, house, trip hop and dark, deep grooves. International DJ sets are common on Saturdays, while Fridays are gay nights (*see p186*).

Buenos Aires News
Paseo de la Infanta, Avenida del Libertador 3883, y Avenida Infanta Isabel, Palermo (4778 1500/www. buenosairesnews.com). Bus 10, 34, 36. **Open** from 9.30pm Thur-Sat. **Map** p279 K6.

Famous to different people for different reasons, but famous nonetheless, the News stopped making any a long time ago. This huge space has one massive dancefloor mixing up party classics, cumbia and rock/rap, surrounded by assorted drinking and dining areas. Despite loftier pretensions, the door policy isn't that strict. The emphasis is more on chatting than dancing; boy-meets-girl is the guiding motive.

Caix
Centro Costa Salguero, Avenida Rafael Obligado, y Salguero, Costanera Norte (4806 9749). Bus 33, 37, 45, 130. **Open** 9am-3pm Sun. **Map** p278 I8.

For the energetic, the after-hours at Caix – situated close to a putting green, evangelist temple, city airport and the river's most polluted waters – is as surreal as clubbing gets. The place is at its busiest while the rest of the city is sleeping. At 9am on Sunday morning, hundreds of charged up clubbers descend into a world of unrepentant hedonism. The action takes place upstairs where a mix of high-octane build-ups and releases keep the dripping crowd in raptures. If, as is bound to happen in summer, it gets too hot, an airier second dance room looks out across the heads of a few bewildered fishermen.

Club 24
Aráoz 2424, entre Güemes y Santa Fe, Palermo (4833 7775). Subte D, Scalabrini Ortiz/12, 39, 152 bus. **Open** 10pm-3am Wed-Sun. **Map** p278 I5.

Members of the 'salsa scene' flock here on Wednesday nights, though there are classes and club nights from Thursday to Sunday too. The standard of dancing is high, and the crowd easily fills the large floor.

CODO (Club Ocioso del Oso)
Guardia Vieja 4085, entre Acuña de Figueroa y Medrano, Almagro (4867 0268). Subte B, Medrano/ 99, 124, 151, 160, 168 bus. **Open** from 12.30am Fri, Sat. **Map** p274 E4.

One of Palermo's oldest, and least flashy, clubs, CODO is spread over two floors. The first plays light-hearted commercial dance, while upstairs is more stylish and a bit more serious. On both floors the atmosphere is friendly and not too predatory.

El Dorado
Hipólito Yrigoyen 947, entre Bernardo de Irigoyen y Tacuarí, Monserrat (4334 2155). Subte C, Avenida de Mayo or A, Lima/10, 17, 59, 64 bus. **Open** from 12.30am Tue, Sat. **Map** p277 E6.

It may be past its golden years, but El Dorado strives on, now housing a niche underground dance scene, featuring eclectic sets in which new DJs mix it up next to established names. The night with the hottest reputation is Tuesday's live drum 'n' bass set; Saturdays are for alternative parties and artists.

The buzzing **Basement Club** at the Shamrock. *See p170.*

Mi Buenos Aires Querido
Hernán Cattáneo

My beloved Buenos Aires

I like the part of Palermo where I live because of the wide open spaces, the greenery and the chance to see the horizon. It's less hemmed in here than in many cities. **No matter how much I travel, I'm still a real barrio kid at heart.** I love local things, people and places. I'm international because of my work, but BA is the place I love.

That mix of Latin American joy and rioplatense [River Plate region] suffering that is unique to Buenos Aires is what I miss when I'm away.

If friends come to visit, I take them on a drive around the city – especially the areas around Recoleta and Palermo and out to Zona Norte – just to take it all in on a beautiful day.

La Boca inspires me – as a football fan and historically.

If I'm not working I love long dinners with friends. For meat I go to El Trapiche *parrilla* or to Cabaña Las Lilas if I'm with visitors. The food at Sucre is great too, and I like eating at Morelia when I fancy having pizza.

The film *The Son of the Bride* reflects the reality of Argentinian society. I suspect that people are overly optimistic right now about the future – something bad is usually around the corner. But then for many people, the only thing they have is hope.

It's hard for kids to start DJing here – imported records cost a lot in local terms since the peso devalued, and the pay is low – and yet there are loads of people who want to do it, and a lot of competition.

The internet is how people here stay in touch with the scene. Two great local websites are www.buenosaliens.com and www.dancenet.com.

Metrodance FM95.1 (on which I have my show) is the best dance radio station – it manages a great balance between daytime and night-time programming for people who are into *electrónica*.

***Porteños* have a special enthusiasm for clubbing,** and they really show it. It's a great crowd to play to – especially for international DJs who come over. They get a fantastically warm reception.

Clubbing fulfils a need in Buenos Aires. People really live for letting go and having fun at the weekend, though maybe too much so.

Some tunes are guaranteed to get the crowd going in Buenos Aires: Sander Kleinenberg's *My Lexicon, Dark and Long* by Underworld, Sasha's *Xpander* and any track by Deep Dish – though I tend to play all new stuff.

Argentina has some excellent DJs: I really respect Martín García, Javier Zuker, Carlos Alfonsín and Cristóbal Paz. Good clubs or nights are the Basement Club, Club 69 at Niceto, Batonga (with DJ Rama at Voodoo) and the Moon Park parties.

● Hernán Cattáneo, South America's most popular DJ, plays across five continents. He has a weekly radio show on Metrodance and, as well as being signed to Paul Oakenfold's Perfecto label, was chosen for the relaunch of the Renaissance *Masters Series*.

Kika

Honduras 5339, entre Godoy Cruz y Juan B Justo, Palermo Viejo (4831 1081). Bus 39, 93, 111, 140. **Open** 1.30am-7am Fri, Sat. **Map** p279 J4.

Opened in late 2003, it remains to be seen how Kika will fare. It's a low-profile choice, away from the hysteria of the Costanera Norte, with two dancefloors featuring a potpourri of past pop decades. The first is a spacious corridor next to a stage, the second a raving techno ballroom that only opens at 3am. There's a sniff of '70s soul in the style of the place and the laid-back crowd. The star DJ is techno-punk Romina Cohn, at time of writing the resident queen.

El Living

Marcelo T de Alvear 1540, entre Montevideo y Paraná, Tribunales (4811 4730/4815 3379/www. living.com.ar). Bus 39, 152. **Open** from 10pm Thur-Sat. **Map** p277 F7.

El Living is an attractive, compact and relaxed bar and club. Although the dance area is pretty small, the music, a mix of 1970s and modern funk and rap, has enough life to keep you bopping. Don't expect a wild crowd or the beautiful set, but for a little drink and a chance to move your feet, it's perfect. Get there before 12.30am (when the club starts), and you can tuck into a decent dinner.

Arts & Entertainment

Maluco Beleza

Sarmiento 1728, entre Rodríguez Peña y Callao,
Tribunales (4372 1737/www.malucobeleza.com.ar).
Bus 12, 24, 26, 60, 146. **Open** from 10pm Wed,
Fri-Sun. **Map** p277 F6.

Maluco Beleza is a little slice of Brazil in the centre
of town. The music shows a typically Brazilian disregard for genre (mixing Dire Straits into samba),
and the people an equally typical desire to have a
good time. Sunday nights gather a great crowd, but
you're guaranteed some fun whenever you show up.
The disco gets going after 1am, before then, it's lambada or, on Wednesday, a supper-show.

Mint

Avenida Costanera Rafael Obligado, y Sarmiento,
Costanera Norte (4771 5870). Bus 37, 160. **Open**
Feb-Dec 9pm-3am Thur; 1.30-8am Fri; 1.30-7am Sat.
Closed Jan. **Map** p279 J8.

One of the top new high-maintenance dancefloors
on the Costanera Norte, Mint fills out with a colourful fauna of college kids, rich young things and
tourists, while providing a stage for local and international guest DJs, spinning techno to progressive
house. Before you melt on the dancefloor, escape to
the riverside terrace and kick back on the beds set
out for the occasion. Groups can rent a cosy muslin-
screened box for up to AR$250, no extras included.
Even mintier inside is ExtraMint: a VIP sector where
champagne is the main commodity.

Niceto Club

Niceto Vega 5510, entre Humboldt y Fitz Roy,
Palermo Viejo (4779 9396/www.nicetoclub.com).
Bus 39, 93, 151, 168. **Open** From 1.30am Thur,
Fri; from 11pm Sat. **Map** p279 K4.

This is the home of Thursday's Club 69, a stylish,
independently run event, long-established as one
BA's essential nights. At 3am, a Rocky Horror-style
stage show, replete with scantily clad dancers,
marks the transition from 1970s funk and disco to
energetic house music. The floor is usually packed,
but there's also a spacious and beautifully lit chill-
out room where DJ Dellamonica's groovy sets spir-
itualise the back bar. Saturday's are less established:
sometimes it's a night called Magic – though the
visual display is not as magical as Club 69's. Before
1.30am, this venue offers a range of live music shows
from local and international artists; styles range
from Jamaican ska to flamenco, electropop and jazz.

Pachá

La Pampa, y Avenida Costanera Rafael Obligado,
Costanera Norte (4788 4280/www.pacha-ba.com).
Bus 37, 160. **Open** Mid Feb-Dec from midnight Fri;
from 2am Sat. **Closed** Jan. **Map** p281 M7.

It was Saturday night's Clubland@Pachá that put
Buenos Aires on the global clubbing map. Clubland
is heading out, however, leaving the future Saturday
night schedule for this 3,000-capacity riverside
superclub up in the air. Friday's Club Pachá,
remains a reliable regular event, however, attracting a youngish, more mainstream crowd.

Podestá Súper Club de Copas

Armenia 1740, entre El Salvador y Costa Rica,
Palermo Viejo (4832 2776/www.elpodesta.com.ar).
Bus 15, 39, 110, 140. **Open** from 11pm Thur-Sat.
Map p279 J4.

Podestá retains a resolutely underground feel, while
attracting a loyal crowd of regulars. The atmosphere
comes mainly from the combined beat of alternative
rock in the lively, cheap, ground-floor bar and
upbeat techno in the lofty converted upstairs studio.
The grittiness of the building and the art student
crowd give the place a slightly illegal feel at 7am.

Requiem

Avenida de Mayo 948, entre Tacuarí y Bernardo de
Irigoyen, Monserrat (4331 5870/www.requiemgothic.
com). Bus 10, 17, 59, 64. **Open** from 1.30am Wed-
Sun. **Map** p277 E6.

Meet the creatures of the night at this ghoulish goth
hideout. Founded a decade ago, Requiem resists
change, gathering Robert Smiths of all ages and sweet
sixteens discovering the joys of lipstick. Friday's
sounds are dark pop '80s classics, live bands play on
Wednesdays, while Sundays are for industrial music.

Tequila

La Pampa, y Avenida Costanera Rafael Obligada,
Costanera Norte (4781 6555). Bus 37, 160. **Open**
11pm-3.30am Wed-Sun. **Map** p281 M7.

More of a pre-club than a club – ideal for pre-Pachá
drinks – this posh spot maintains its exclusivity
through a mailing-list policy: you have to be invited,
entrance is free and no unknowns make it in.
However, first time visitors can gain access with a
dinner reservation (Med/Argentinian combos). Study
the beautiful people's mating rituals from a table or
a comfy booth. The circular dancefloor is designed
for maximum voyeuristic opportunities. Don't expect
radical sounds – this is a see-and-be-seen scene.

Niceto Club always packs 'em in.

Film

A new generation of local directors are winning over international audiences with gritty, no-frills productions.

A handful of box-office hits and the occasional art-house fest in the 1980s and early '90s weren't enough to return Argentinian cinema to its former glory. But the post-dictatorship period did see Argentina win an Oscar – for Luis Puenzo's drama *La historia oficial* (1985), about the 'disappeared' – and the reappearance of two influential directors: Fernando Solanas, whose *El exilio de Gardel* (1986) and *Sur* (1987) explore exile, love, politics, memory and the darker side of tango; and Leonardo Favio with *Gatica el mono* (1993), a fictionalised account of the life of an Argentinian boxing icon, a metaphor for the rise and fall of Peronism.

NEW ARGENTINIAN CINEMA

From the mid-1990s, film schools flourished and talented graduates began exploring Argentinian reality from a variety of new angles. They were influenced by Italian-style neo-realism, but had a gift for measured surrealism and powerful drama. Many dealt directly with the vicissitudes of contemporary life, thus appealing to a new generation of film-goers.

The Universidad del Cine played a leading role as the only school in Argentina teaching the art of filmmaking while also financing student works. Made on shoestring budgets, these independent films gave an invigorating twist to a trite and agonising narrative.

Among the new talents is Martín Rejtman, the movement's spiritual father, whose *Rapado* (1992) is a mordant exploration of the torpor affecting Argentinian youth and their families. Released locally in 1996, *Rapado* gained a small following and some critical acclaim. Also in 1996, Alejandro Agresti premiered *Buenos Aires Viceversa*, which tells several interwoven stories about Argentina's unsettling present. Its success opened a much-needed door to the commercial circuit for low-budget independent productions, such as *Pizza, birra, faso* (1997), the impressive debut of Bruno Stagnaro and Adrián Caetano, which depicts the everyday life of young outcasts in a hostile Buenos Aires.

In 1999, Pablo Trapero broke on to the scene, with his award-winning *Mundo grúa*. His second film, *El bonaerense* (2002), about corruption in the Buenos Aires provincial police, established Trapero's reputation as a talented and resourceful filmmaker.

Further international acclaim met Lucrecia Martel's stirring *La Ciénaga* (2001), judged best film at the Berlin festival. Martel is one of several young women directors coming to the fore. Her tale of two families sunk in emotional and physical paralysis amid a stagnant, menacing environment, creates an oppressive atmosphere that mirrors Argentina's social disintegration. In 2002, Caetano's *Bolivia* (Cannes Young Critics' Award) used ordinary people in place of professional actors, while his second feature that year, *Un oso rojo* picked up the Special Jury Prize at Havana.

The 2003 Buenos Aires International Festival of Independent Cinema (BAFICI) spotlighted Argentina's latest talents: Albertina Carri, Sergio Wolf and Lorena Muñoz, Celina Murga and Ezequiel Acuña. Carri's *Los rubios* (New Cinema Award) attempts to fill the void left by the disappearance of the director's parents by the army in 1977, when she was only four. Her moving documentary calls for the reconstruction of haunting memories that many in Argentina would rather ignore. Memory is also a guiding theme in the heartfelt docu-drama *Yo no sé qué me han hecho tus ojos* (Best Latin American Film Award). Co-directed by Sergio Wolf and Lorena Muñoz, it deals with the turbulent love life of the late tango singer Ada Falcón, one of the great divas of the 1920s and '30s.

For 2004, both Martín Rejtman and Pablo Trapero return to the spotlight. Rejtman's film, *Los guantes mágicos*, is a story about confronting loss, crisis, and separation. It melds the cut-and-dried tone of *Rapado* with the infectious humour of *Silvia Prieto* (1999), his second feature. Trapero's new work, *Familia rodante*, is a contemporary road movie set in the northern river provinces. First-rate indie cinema is still alive and well in Argentina.

THE MODERN MAINSTREAM

Fabián Bielinsky, Marcelo Piñeyro, Juan José Campanella and Damián Szifrón fall into the category of quality mainstream – which in Buenos Aires is more like a dried-up trickle. Bielinsky's stunning *Nueve Reinas* (*Nine Queens*, 2000) is about two grifters waiting for their big break, and a powerful metaphor for living conditions in Argentina – three years after its release it was big news in European capitals. Piñeyro's latest film *Kamchatka* (2002), a sober exploration of a family trying to survive the last military dictatorship, stars two leading figures of the Argentinian screen: Ricardo Darín and Cecilia Roth (*see p178* **Mi Buenos Aires Querido**). Darín was also the star of Campanella's Oscar-nominated dramatic comedy *El hijo de la novia* (*The Son of the Bride*, 2001) – an enormous success locally and abroad. It followed his inspired 1999 feature, the bittersweet romantic comedy *El mismo amor, la misma lluvia*. Finally, Damián Szifrón's – who is best known for his TV work – made his feature film debut with the stylish thriller *El fondo del mar* (2003).

LOOKING IN FROM THE OUTSIDE

For a foreigner's cinematic perspective, it's worth checking out some of the films starring Buenos Aires. One of the first celluloid images of the city comes from the campy 1940s musical *Down Argentine Way*. In 2002 Robert Duvall showcased his tango steps – and stunning, Argentinian wife – in the box office bomb *Assassination Tango*. Spaniard Carlos Saura's *Tango* (1998) is a far better homage to the dance. Perhaps the most soulful elegy to the city is Wong Kar Wai's *Happy Together* (1997), about a gay Chinese couple drifting apart in the dark entrails of San Telmo and La Boca.

Cinemas

Buenos Aires always had two types of cinema: city-centre ones – around Avenidas Santa Fe, Corrientes, Callao and on the pedestrianised stretch of Lavalle – and neighbourhood screens. These days, new multiplexes offering state-of-the-art technology and US-style facilities draw the audiences. Smaller cinemas are fading at an alarming rate, though a handful of art house venues and amateur *cine clubs* still thrive.

INFO, TIMINGS AND TICKETS

Nearly all films are shown in their original version with Spanish subtitles. Children's films are the only exception, and even then dubbed and original-language versions will be released. Some cinemas have late-night showings (*trasnoches*) beginning around 1am on Fridays and Saturdays. Tickets cost almost half-price on Wednesdays and at many early showings. Wednesdays and weekends are busiest.

For information on films at several major cinemas, contact Hola Cine (4000 2463/www.holacine.com.ar) and book tickets with your credit card, but only for films shown at the Hoyts multiplex in the Abasto shopping centre. There is a surcharge of AR$1 per ticket. You can buy tickets in advance at Village Recoleta multiplex by phoning the cinema directly.

Check the *Espectáculos* sections of local papers for cinema listings. As English-language film titles are often translated and end up bearing no resemblance to the original, it helps to buy the *Buenos Aires Herald*, which publishes English-language listings. The Friday edition includes capsule reviews of recommended films. Celluloid lovers who can read Spanish should pick up long-running film magazine *El Amante*. The website www.cinenacional.com is an excellent Spanish-language resource on Argentinian cinema, with an exhaustive, searchable database. If you are staying somewhere with cable TV, tune in to Volver channel, with its classic reruns. I-SAT channel also shows hard-to-find classics and indies.

The film rating system in Argentina has four categories: ATP suitable for all ages; SAM13 under-13s only if accompanied by an adult; SAM16 no under-16s; and SAM18 no under-18s.

Top to bottom: **El bonaerense**, **Yo no sé...** and **Los guantes mágicos**.

Arts & Entertainment

City centre

These are the best of the city-centre cinemas – others are old with poor facilities. New releases include Hollywood blockbusters, European artfare and Latin American cinema.

Atlas Lavalle

Lavalle 869, entre Suipacha y Esmeralda, Microcentro (4328 6643/www.atlascines.com.ar). Subte C, Lavalle/10, 17, 70 bus. **Open** from noon daily. **Tickets** AR$6 Thur-Sun; AR$4.50 Mon-Wed. **No credit cards. Map** p277 E7.

This once-historical cinema has been split up into five smaller screens, but is still a bit of a relic. Though it mostly features Hollywood new releases, it serves as a reminder of the golden days when Lavalle was 'the street of cinemas'.

Atlas Santa Fe

Avenida Santa Fe 2015, entre Ayacucho y Junín, Barrio Norte (4823 7878/www.atlascines.com.ar). Subte D, Callao/39, 60, 111, 124, 152 bus. **Open** from noon daily. **Tickets** AR$8 Thur-Sun; AR$4.50 Mon-Wed, before 4pm Thur-Sun. **Credit** AmEx, V. **Map** p278 G6.

An ordinary two-screen cinema, last renovated in the 1980s, showing new releases.

Espacio INCAA KM 0 – Gaumont Rivadavia

Rivadavia 1635, entre Rodríguez Peña y Montevideo, Congreso (4371 3050). Subte A, Congreso/12, 37, 64, 86 bus. **Open** from 12.30pm daily. **Tickets** AR$4; AR$2.50 concessions. **No credit cards. Map** p277 E5.

The **Metro**: one serious marquee.

This three-screen cinema, and the Complejo Tita Merello at Suipacha 442 (4322 1195), are supported by INCAA (the National Film Board). They only show new Argentinian releases (no English subtitles). The Gaumont is the better equipped of the two and is home to Cine Club Núcleo, the distinguished film club run by renowned critic Salvador Sammaritano.

Lorca

Avenida Corrientes 1428, entre Paraná y Uruguay, Tribunales (4371 5017). Subte B, Uruguay/24, 26, 102 bus. **Open** from 2pm daily. **Tickets** AR$6 Thur-Sun; AR$4.50 Mon-Wed. **No credit cards. Map** p277 F6.

One of the most traditional cinemas on Corrientes, showing an excellent pick of local and foreign non-mainstream movies on its two screens. Some films are shown in video-projected versions.

Metro

Cerrito 570, entre Tucumán y Lavalle, Tribunales (4382 4219). Subte D, Tribunales/29, 39, 59, 109 bus. **Open** from 12.30pm daily. **Tickets** AR$6.50 Thur-Sun; AR$4.50 Mon-Wed. **No credit cards. Map** p277 E7.

Conveniently close to the Obelisco, the Metro was last renovated in the 1980s; it remains a very decent, though not the most high-tech cinema. It has three screens and shows new releases.

Multiplexes

Buenos Aires' shopping centres (*see p139*) are home to many of the multiplexes. They usually screen a wide variety of new releases, including Hollywood mainstream, children's features, but also international independent productions. The **Abasto** centre has a 16-screen cinema and is the main venue for the annual Festival Internacional de Cine Independiente de Buenos Aires (*see p178* **Festivals**). **Paseo Alcorta** has two screens, **Galerías Pacifico** has four and **Patio Bullrich** has three.

Cinemark 8

Alicia Moreau de Justo 1920, y San Juan, Puerto Madero (4315 5522/www.cinemark.com.ar). Bus 4, 64, 130, 152. **Open** from noon daily. **Tickets** AR$9; AR$5.75 Mon-Wed, before 4pm Thur-Sun, under-12s, concessions. **Credit** AmEx, MC, V. **Map** p276 C6.

This modern complex down in the docklands features eight screens and a restaurant. A 10-screen branch, conveniently located near the Alto Palermo shopping centre, opened in 2001.

Other locations: Cinemark 10, Beruti 3399, Palermo (4827 5700/4827 9500 information).

Village Recoleta

Vicente López 2050, y Junín, Recoleta (0810 444 66843/4800 0000 credit card booking/www.village cines.com). Bus 10, 130. **Open** from 11am daily. **Tickets** AR$10.90; AR$6.50 11.30am-1pm and all day Wed, under-12, concessions; **Credit** AmEx, DC, MC, V. **Map** p278 G7.

This huge complex near Recoleta Cemetery includes bars, restaurants, a food court, games arcade, bookshop, Tower Records and a 16-screen cinema on three floors. The childcare facility at weekends for 2- to 12-year-olds is a big draw for cinephile parents.

Repertory & art-house

Malba (*see p85*) hosts excellent cinema events: new indie releases, outstanding retrospectives with restored 35mm prints and lectures by prominent filmmakers. The Museo del Cine (*see p71*) also features film cycles, and the British Arts Centre (*see p66*) shows films focused on British culture. Opening hours vary according to the screenings – call or check webs for details.

Alianza Francesa de Buenos Aires

Avenida Córdoba 946, entre Suipacha y Carlos Pellegrini, Microcentro (4322 0068/01/www.alianza francesa.org.ar). Subte C, Lavalle/59, 99, 106, 109, 132. **Open** from 7pm daily. **Closed** Jan, Feb. **Tickets** free. **Map** p277 F7.

Breakthrough film: **Mundo grúa**. *See p174.*

The French-language institution is also a prestigious cultural centre offering riveting cycles of international cinema in its refined, comfortable auditorium.

Centro Cultural Ricardo Rojas

Avenida Corrientes 2038, entre Junín y Ayacucho, Once (4952 5879/www.rojas.uba.ar). Subte B, Callao/24, 26, 60, 124 bus. **Tickets** AR$2-$5. **No credit cards. Map** p277 F5.
This lively cultural centre shows interesting art house and experimental fare in its one cinema.

Take ten

Well before the recent boom, Argentinian directors laid the foundations of a national film industry – the following is a chronology of selected key works.

Tango (José Luis Moglia Barth, 1933). First film of the 1930s, Argentinian cinema's golden age, and the first to use sound.

La vuelta al nido (Leopoldo Torres Ríos, 1937). A sensitive, heartfelt evocation of family life under the keen eye of Argentina's historical director from the silent era who continued to work through the late 1950s.

Dios se lo pague (Luis César Amadori, 1948). A classic melodrama starring the legendary Zully Moreno and Arturo de Córdova by one of Argentina's most imaginative directors.

Las aguas bajan turbias (Hugo del Carril, 1952). A feature about the exploitation of workers on the *yerba* tea plantations in Misiones province in the 1920s. A perfect blend of western, social realism and melodrama pulled off by a charismatic tango singer-cum-actor-cum-filmmaker.

La mano en la trampa (Leopoldo Torre Nilson, 1961). The decadence and despair of the upper classes under ruthless scrutiny in a claustrophobic thriller with a twist. It earned the critics' award at Cannes, and its director – the son of Torre Ríos – was nominated for the Palme d'Or.

Crónica de un niño solo (Leonardo Favio, 1965). Dedicated to his mentor, Leopoldo Torre Nilson, Favio's powerful directorial debut movingly explores the misfortune of a young street kid standing alone. Austere and bleakly beautiful, it's an unalloyed masterpiece.

La hora de los hornos (Fernando 'Pino' Solanas/Octavio Gettino, 1968). The ideas behind revolutionary Peronism are explored in this classic of militant documentary filmmaking. Secret screenings were deliberately interrupted in order to force viewers out of their passivity and into debates on history and politics.

La tregua (Sergio Renán, 1974). A lonely middle-aged man finds solace in a love affair with a younger woman. It's an unflinching view of everyday alienation. Oscar-nominated for Best Foreign-language Film.

Camila (María Luisa Bemberg, 1985). The first local feature released under democratic rule tells the story of a Jesuit priest and a young Catholic socialite who fall in love in 19th-century provincial Argentina. Oscar nominated for Best Foreign-language Film.

La historia oficial (Luis Puenzo, 1985). The only Argentinian production to win the Oscar for Best Foreign Language Film focused on the fate of the children of disappeared Argentinians during the dictatorship. But for a less oblique version of events, see Marco Becchis' *Garage Olimpo* (1999), which looks at the relationship that develops between torturer and prisoner.

Arts & Entertainment

Mi Buenos Aires Querido
Cecilia Roth

My beloved Buenos Aires

Living and working abroad has given me an additional outsider's angle on Buenos Aires – when I was 17, we went to live in Spain because of the military dictatorship.

Now I notice the city's paradoxes. It's amazing how, following a crisis, hundreds of bars and restaurants suddenly open.

I live in the Botánico district – it's still very beautiful and feels like a real neighbourhood.

In the '70s, young people were into politics – it was all less frivolous. As a teenager, I'd go to parties and hang out with my friends, but we'd also see art house films and talk politics.

Buenos Aires is about extremes. *Porteños* like to do things in excess, whether that's love, suffering or drinking.

I used to go to the cinema four times a week. I liked the Italian and French directors, as well Brits like Ken Russell. I'd sneak into adult films, like Russell's *Women in Love*. Our great films were *La Tregua* and the works of Leonardo Favio and Torre Nilsson.

Argentinian cinema has always been good – especially outside the mainstream. We have a strong sense of identity in our films.

Our cinema is rooted in daily life; it's all about our reality.

***La Cienaga* is a world-class film**, and I also like the work of Adrián Caetano and Pablo Trapero. Of the new generation I rate Luis Ortega, who is only 23.

I don't go out as often as I did, but there are places I like: El Obrero in La Boca for a meal, a walk along the river to Fundación Proa, the terrace of Milión and also Bar 6 for drinks.

***Porteños* are very open and sociable.** We're generous by nature; we like to share.

***Porteños* are more insecure than Europeans**, especially women, though men here are also on heat all the time. Sex is very important. I guess I take these traits into my work because I seduce the camera when I act.

We still like to meet foreigners – especially now when we can't travel much ourselves.

Culture is a space where we find freedom.

● Cecilia Roth has acted in dozens of theatre, TV and film productions. She won Spain's Best Actress award for her performance in Adolfo Aristarain's *Martin Hache* (1997) and is regularly cast in Almodóvar films, most recently as Manuela in *All About My Mother* (1999).

Cosmos

Avenida Corrientes 2046, entre Ayacucho y Junín, Once (4953 5405/www.cinecosmos.com). Subte B, Callao/24, 26, 60 bus. **Tickets** AR$6 Thur-Sun; AR$4.50 Mon-Wed, before 4pm Thur-Sun. **No credit cards. Map** p277 F5.

This film buff's paradise features new Argentinian releases, retrospectives and auteur films from all over the word.

Leopoldo Lugones

10th Floor, Teatro San Martín, Avenida Corrientes 1530, entre Paraná y Montevideo, Tribunales (freephone 0800 333 5254/www.teatrosanmartin. com.ar). Subte B, Uruguay/24, 26, 60, 102 bus. **Tickets** AR$3. **No credit cards. Map** p304 F11.

Located within the San Martín theatre complex, this historical auditorium offers screenings of first-rate art house movies from all over the world, including films that never have been, and never will be, released commercially.

Festivals

Started in 1999, the booming **Festival Internacional de Cine Independiente** (*see p164*) takes place in mid-April. From mid-morning to midnight, for ten days of cinematic frenzy, the state-of-the-art Hoyts Abasto multiplex and other city cinemas screen more than 180 films from the most diverse sectors of the international indie scene. There's a fierce official competition as well as several parallel sections and late night screenings of bizarre cinema. It's become the designated spot for the brightest discoveries in New Argentinian Cinema. Every March, another festival – the **Festival Internacional de Cine de Mar del Plata** – is held on the Atlantic coast, though it's a mediocre event by world standards, with poor programming.

Galleries

New spaces, open evenings and urban initiatives – it's a fine time for art in BA.

In Buenos Aires, artists manage to express their inner voice, no matter how tough the times. As art has become less expensive (for foreigners), innovative galleries and alternative spaces have proliferated, and today the Argentinian masters, such as Antonio Berni (a sort of Don Quixote of social conscience), Quinquela Martín (*see p74*) and Xul Solar (*see p81*), share ground with the city's upcoming artists.

Geographically, Palermo Viejo, San Telmo and Abasto now compete with traditional art zones Recoleta and Barrio Norte. The alternative circuit is flourishing: **Belleza y Felicidad** (Acuña de Figueroa 900, 4867 0073) is a hip art space, hangout and organiser of art happenings in Almagro; **Elespacio** (Niceto Vega 5635, 4774 9222), **Sonoridad Amarilla** (*see p135*) and **Pabellón IV Multiespacio** (Uriarte 1332, 4772 8745, www.pabellon4.net) are all multi-functional gallery/restaurant/lounge spaces in Palermo Viejo; and the walls of **Boquitas Pintadas** 'pop hotel' near San Telmo (*see p41*) are rehung every two months with fresh works.

Alongside a growth in non-traditional spaces, there is an increasing interest in other means of expression, such as video art and photography. Outstanding local artists in these fields include Anne-Marie Heinrich, Aldo Sessa and Sara Facio, the latter celebrated for her feminist viewpoint and exquisite portraits. To sample the work of photographers and video artists, **Arte x Arte** gallery (*see p180*) is unmissable.

Look out for the collective groups too. Work by conceptual artists Juliana Lafitte, Agustina Picasso and Manuel Mendanha – known as **Arte Mondongo** – alludes to painter Guiseppe Arcimboldo. They portrayed the Spanish royal family using fragments of coloured glass and painter Lucian Freud with meat and salmon.

Urban initiatives have aided Buenos Aires' artistic renovation. **Gallery Nights** (4805 7257, www.artealdia.com) organises open galleries events on the last Friday of the month (April to November). These evenings take in 41 of the more traditional downtown venues including Galería Zurbarán (Cerrito 1522, 4815 7703), Principium (Esmeralda 1357, 4327 0664), El Socorro (Suipacha 1331, 4327 0746) and Van Riel (Talcahuano 1257, 4811 8359).

In Barracas, Marino Santa María's urban art project involves painting the façade of 36 houses (*see p76*), while prolific *porteña* artist

Nora Iniesta has opened her San Telmo studio at Perú 715 to curious visitors. Furthermore, the city government organises hugely popular and expertly guided open studios weekends (**Estudio Abierto**; see www.buenosaires. gov.ar). The key annual art event is the two-week **ArteBA** fair (*see p165*), which pulled over 100,000 buyers and enthusiasts in 2003. The city's cultural centres, in particular **Centro Cultural Recoleta** (*see p180*), also play a crucial role in the art scene.

Sharp-eyed entrepreneurs and corporate sponsors give an additional boost. Businessman and philanthropist Eduardo Costantini's venture, **Museo de Arte Latinoamericano de Buenos Aires** (Malba; *see p85*), has become one of most exciting art spaces in the city, challenging the hegemony of major institutions such as the Museo Nacional de Bellas Artes (*see p79*), the Museo de Arte Moderno (*see p71*) and the Palais de Glace (*see p79*). Argentina's international art superstar, Guillermo Kuitca (*see p182* **Mi Buenos Aires Querido**), after a long absence, held a major retrospective in Malba in 2003. Glass mosaic company Murvi, opened the **Espacio de Arte Musivo** (*see p181*) in spring 2003. It's the only space in South America dedicated to the Venetian mosaic. **Espacio** (*see p181*) is a striking contemporary space created by the arts foundation of Spanish phone operator Telefónica, which opened in November 2003.

INFORMATION

Websites www.ramona.org.ar and www.arte baires.com.ar provide listings for most gallery spaces. Look for an *inauguración* (opening) or *muestra* (show). Newspapers also highlight major events. For less mainstream happenings, flyers and invitations are often available in places as diverse as downtown bars or Palermo boutiques. Or head for specialist bookshops such as Asunto Impreso (*see p142*) or Libros de Arte (Libertad 1384, Recoleta, 4812 0023), or try shops within the major museums.

Galleries

Galleries do not charge admission or take credit cards, unless otherwise stated. Many are closed in summer (January and February). The **Teatro San Martín** (*see p217*) also has a small photo gallery and sculpture courtyard.

Fundación Proa (*see p181*).

Dabbah Torrejón.

180° – Arte Contemporáneo

*Basement, San Martín 975, entre Paraguay
y Marcelo T de Alvear, Retiro (4312 9211/www.
180gradosarte.com.ar). Subte C, San Martín/10, 93,
130, 152 bus.* **Open** noon-midnight Mon-Fri; 1-5pm,
9pm-midnight Sat. **Map** p277 E8.
The basement gallery beneath Filo restaurant (*see
p117*) has undergone a complete transformation.
Directed by Pelusa Borthwick and Eduardo Miretti,
this well-lit, intelligently put together space is now
geared towards photography, video and digital art.

Arroyo

*Arroyo 830/834, entre Suipacha y Esmeralda, Retiro
(4325 3485/0947/www.galarroyo.com). Subte C, San
Martín/17, 59, 61, 67, 92 bus.* **Open** 11am-8pm
Mon-Fri; for auctions Sat, Sun. **Map** 277 F8x.
Arroyo's real strength is its monthly auctions. They
offer a wide range of works by renowned artists, at
relatively affordable prices.
Other locations: Caesar Park Hotel, Posadas 1232,
Recoleta (4819 1194).

Arte x Arte

*Lavalleja 1062, entre Córdoba y Lerma, Villa Crespo
(4772 6754/4773 2738/www.artea.com.ar/artex
arte). Bus 15, 92, 106, 109, 168.* **Open** Apr-Dec
1-7pm Mon-Sat. **Closed** Jan-Mar. **Map** p274 F4.
Arte x Arte claims to be the largest South American
gallery – 1,800sq m (19,355sq ft) – dedicated to photography, video and digital art. It boasts five show
rooms, a library, laboratories and an auditorium.

Braga Menéndez Schuster

*1st Floor, Studio C, Darwin 1154, entre Castillo
y Loyola, Villa Crespo (4857 0075/www.braga
menendezschuster.com). Bus 151, 168.* **Open**
10am-4pm Mon-Fri; 4-8pm Sat. **Closed** 1st 2wks
Jan. **Map** p275 K3.
Artist Florencia Braga Menéndez and Marcelo
Schuster's spaces are a huge white loft in Palermo
Viejo and an attractive, small Recoleta gallery. Both
favour works exploring original inner worlds from
artists such as Marcia Schvartz and Tomás Fracchia.
Other locations: Quintana 229, Recoleta (4813 4272).

Centro Cultural de España

*Basement, Florida 943, entre Paraguay y Marcelo
T de Alvear, Retiro (4312 3214/5850/www.icibaires.
org.ar). Subte C, San Martín/10, 17, 152 bus.* **Open**
Jan, Feb 10.30am-4.30pm Mon-Fri. *Mar-Dec* 10.30am-
6pm Mon-Fri. **Map** p277 E8.
This centre promotes visual arts and media by both
Argentinian and Spanish artists. There are also music
and theatre events, poetry readings and a library.

Centro Cultural Recoleta

*Junín 1930, y Quintana, Recoleta (4803 1041/www.
centroculturalrecoleta.org). Bus 10, 17, 60, 67, 92,
110.* **Open** 2-9pm Mon-Fri, 10am-9pm Sat, Sun.
Admission free; AR$1 suggested contribution.
Map p278 H7.
The darling of BA's art scene, the scope of CCR's 21
showrooms ranges from children's drawings through
work produced by both psychiatric patients and well-
established artists. Its largest space, Cronopio, is used
for major retrospectives or group shows (as diverse
as Yoko Ono, Liliana Porter and Russian icons).

Dabbah Torrejón

*Sánchez de Bustamante 1187, entre Córdoba y
Cabrera, Barrio Norte (4963 2581/www.dabbah
torrejon.com.ar). Bus 99, 109.* **Open** 3-8pm Tue-Fri;
11am-2pm Sat. **Closed** Sat in Jan, Feb. **Map** p278 H5.
Since September 2000, this cutting-edge gallery,
created in a gorgeously converted house near Abasto,
has pledged to be 'a bridge between creativity and the
public' – and has kept its word. Its shows of work by
a stable of promising young artists – including
Fabián Burgos, Alejandra Seeber, Sergio Avello and
Manuel Esnoz – receive excellent reviews.

Del Infinito Arte

*Ground Floor, Quintana 352, entre Rodríguez Peña
y Callao, Recoleta (4813 8828). Bus 17, 67.* **Open**
Feb-Dec 11am-8pm Mon-Fri, 11am-1pm Sat. **Closed**
Jan. **Credit** AmEx. **Map** p278 G7.
This gallery's well-curated shows, concentrate on
both the new generation (Juan Andrés Videla, Analía
Zalazar and Carlos Masoch) as well as established
artists (Clorindo Testa, Raul Lozza and Enio Iommi).

Arts & Entertainment

Galleries

Daniel Maman Fine Arts
Avenida del Libertador 2475, entre Salguero y San Martín de Tours, Palermo (4804 3700/3800/www. danielmaman.com). Bus 10, 37, 59, 60, 102. **Open** 11am-8pm Mon-Fri; 11am-7pm Sat. **Map** p278 I7.
Openings at Daniel Maman's chic and excellently equipped gallery has the crowd literally queuing to get in. With an uncanny flair for selecting talented and charismatic figures, such as Rómulo Maccio, Alicia Penalba, Nicolás García Uriburu and Karina El Azem, Maman's shows create serious impact.

Dharma Fine Art
1st Floor, Door 1, Rue des Artisans, Arenales 1239, entre Libertad y Talcahuano, Recoleta (4814 4700/ www.dharmafinearts.com). Bus 17, 102. **Open** noon-8pm Mon-Fri. **Credit** AmEx, MC, V. **Map** p277 F7.
A first-rate gallery and interactive meeting place, where artists and sponsors get together to create new projects. Excellent shows of Argentinian masters.

Elsi del Río
Arévalo 1748, entre Honduras y El Salvador, Palermo Viejo (4899 0171/www.elsidelrio.com.ar). Bus 39, 55. **Open** Feb-Dec 3-8pm Tue-Fri; 11am-2pm Sat. **Closed** Jan. **Map** p279 K4.
This former grocer's shop shows artists who display forceful social commitment. The exhibitions always distill a sense of play, no matter how serious the message. The private views are much loved by art fans.

Espacio Fundación Telefónica
Arenales 1540, entre Montevideo y Paraná, Recoleta (4816 3183/www.fundacion.telefonica.com.ar/ espacio). Bus 10, 37, 59, 102. **Open** 2-8.30pm Tue-Sun. **Map** p278 G7.
Opened in late 2003, this two-floor contemporary centre has both artistic and educational ambitions. Sophisticated multi-media technology is applied to the visual arts, social projects and research. There are media labs and educational activities on-site, alongside the striking exhibition space.

Fundación Alberto Elía/Mario Robirosa
Ground Floor, Studio A, Azcuénaga 1739, entre Pacheco de Melo y Las Heras, Recoleta (4803 0496). Bus 10, 37, 41, 101, 102 . **Open** Mar-Dec 2-8.30pm Mon-Fri. **Closed** Jan, Feb. **Map** p278 H7.
This small, smart space has a mind of its own, staging coherent exhibitions by contemporary artists, such as painter Carlos Gorriarena or film-maker Jorge Polaco. The guest list at openings reads like a who's who of the BA art circuit.

Fundación Federico Jorge Klemm
Basement, Marcelo T de Alvear 626/628, entre Maipú y Florida, Retiro (4312 5553). Subte C, San Martín/10, 17, 70, 152 bus. **Open** Feb-Dec 11am-8pm Mon-Fri. **Closed** Jan. **Map** p277 F8.
This important downtown gallery, once run by mega-personality/TV presenter/art patron/artist, the late Federico Klemm (now by the National Fine Arts Academy), houses many key Argentinian works

(including some Bernis) and an impressive international collection (Picasso, Dali, Warhol, Maplethorpe). It also presents shows by upcoming Argentinian artists. At the back, Klemm's own creations and his collection of personal objects – costumes worn by Nureyev and dresses owned by Evita – are exhibited. The foundation also stages art competitions.

Fundación Proa
Pedro de Mendoza 1929, y Del Valle Iberlucea, La Boca (4303 0909/www.proa.org). Bus 29, 64, 152. **Open** 11am-7pm Tue-Sun. **Admission** AR$3; AR$1-$2 concessions. **Credit** MC, V. **Map** p276 A5.
Since landing in a recylced building in La Boca in 1996, Proa has presented some of the most stimulating and insightfully curated shows in town. Six major annual exhibitions and other cultural events keep the premises busy, while the gorgeous roof terrace offers great views of the Riachuelo. Some memorable shows have included Sol Lewitt, Diego Rivera, Sebastião Salgado, Metropolitan Icons, Scenes of the '80s and Art in La Boca.

Murvi Espacio de Arte Musivo
Darwin 1038, entre Loyola y Aguirre, Villa Crespo (4854 8091). Bus 151, 168. **Open** noon-8pm Mon-Fri; noon-5pm Sat. **Map** p275 K3.
Murvi is the first space dedicated to the Venetian mosaic. Its first show, 'Los Precursores', convened a group of renowned artists, including Luis Benedit and Clorindo Testa, working in this medium for the first time, assisted by expert craftsmen.

Palatina
Arroyo 821, entre Suipacha y Esmeralda, Retiro (4327 0620). Bus 59, 61, 93, 130, 152. **Open** 10.30am-8pm Mon-Fri; 10am-1pm Sat. **Map** p277 F8.
In operation for 29 years, Palatina is one of the busiest galleries in town, promoting mainly well-established names such as painters Jorge Diciervo and Eduardo Faradje and sculptor Vivianne Duchini.

Praxis
Arenales 1311, y Talcahuano, Recoleta (4815 4986/ 4812 6254/www.praxis-art.com). Bus 10, 39, 152. **Open** 10.30am-8pm Mon-Fri; 10.30am-2pm Sat. **Credit** AmEx, DC, MC, V. **Map** p277 F7.
Praxis is one of few galleries with international reach, with spaces in BA, the US and Brazil. Dedicated to contemporary figurative art, it's a driving force in promoting Argentinian art. It also launched the career of Uruguayan painter Ignacio Iturria.
Other locations: Arroyo 858, Recoleta (4393 0803).

RO Art
Paraná 1158, entre Santa Fe y Arenales, Recoleta (4815 6467/www.roart.com.ar). Bus 10, 39, 59, 102. **Open** Feb-Dec 11am-8pm Mon-Fri; 10.30am-1pm Sat. **Closed** Jan. **Map** p278 G7.
Roxana Oliver's gallery is principally committed to the work of painter Carlos Alonso, whom she believes to be 'the greatest living Argentinian artist'. Different facets of his work are displayed together with pieces from other local or international artists.

Arts & Entertainment

Mi Buenos Aires Querido
Guillermo Kuitca

My beloved Buenos Aires

Belgrano is completely unbohemian. As a residential neighbourhood it has no artistic tradition, and that's what attracted me to living and working here.

Going to the corner of Florida and Paraguay streets was a big deal for me and my family in my youth. We made a real outing of it.

The first place I'd take a visitor is to the south of the city: San Telmo or La Boca. It's an area I need to discover more myself. I don't subscribe to the Borgesian concept of El Sur, but I think the area has some real attractions.

Palermo's recent development is impressive – and the area still has more potential. Yet real life goes on there: that's what makes it so interesting. Palermo harbours surprises too – you always discover something new.

The Teatro Colón is a cultural heavyweight. When the programme is good, it's the most important institution of its type in this city. But I also have a strong affinity with Malba – it does a formidable job with its shows, conferences, cinema and tours. It's light years ahead of the Museo Nacional de Bellas Artes. The Museo de Arte Moderno in San Telmo also hosts very good exhibits, even though the building itself is ugly.

Eduardo Catalano's flower sculpture (Floralis Genérica) delights me every time I see it. I adore the fact that this city, which hasn't produced great public works of art of late (and of which I'm not a fan anyway), can put something so wonderful and so otherworldly in such a prominent place.

To appreciate some of the most popular places in Palermo, eat dinner early. I love Central at 8.30pm – you get the best of everything. I like restaurants that combine being the place to be with really good food and drinks, such as Olsen or Green Bamboo or Sudestada.

When it comes to eating meat, I'm a fan of the most ordinary *parillas*.

The visual noise in Buenos Aires is overwhelming. There's no planned aesthetic in this city. I'm all for the bright lights and advertising of big cities, but here it reaches a level of madness.

The best side you'll see of a *porteño*'s character is if you need help or information on the street. The worst – most agressive – side you'll see is when he or she is behind the wheel of a car.

We need to change the city's icons. Gardel, Maradona, Evita, Borges, Piazzola and the like, should be left aside to make room for more eccentric personalities – [musician] Charly García is a perfect example.

Three adjectives that I would use to describe Buenos Aires are complex, sweet and secretive. Compared to cities like São Paulo, it's paradise.

Buenos Aires has it all. Just because I don't always know where to find it, doesn't mean that it doesn't exist.

● Guillermo Kuitca is Argentina's most internationally successful contemporary painter. Madrid's Reina Sofía and Buenos Aires' Malba recently staged a retrospective of 20 years of his work. He also directs an arts scholarship programme.

Arts & Entertainment

Rubbers

Alvear 1595, y Montevideo, Recoleta (4816 1864/ 1869/www.rubbers.com.ar). Bus 17, 61, 67, 92, 93. **Open** 11am-8pm Mon-Sat. **Map** p278 G7.

Directed by Natalio Povarché, the name of this gallery has always been a synonym of solidity in art. The Alvear gallery opened in 2003 with a spectacular Berni exhibit; the other location is in the stunning Ateneo bookshop (*see p142*). Both possess Povarché's unmistakable seal: quality and depth. **Other locations**: 3rd Floor, Santa Fe 1860, Barrio Norte (4816 1782).

Ruth Benzacar

Florida 1000, y Marcelo T de Alvear, Retiro (4313 8480/www.ruthbenzacar.com). Subte C, San Martín/7, 10, 17, 132, 152 bus. **Open** 11.30am-8pm Mon-Fri. **Map** p277 E8.

Founded in 1965 by the late Ruth Benzacar – and now run by her daughter, Orly – this well-located gallery at the end of Florida Street was the jewel in the crown of swinging 1960s BA. Young artists are enthusiastically received and this forceful gallery remains one of the leaders of the pack. Also opens Saturday mornings in March only (10.30am-1.30pm).

Gay & Lesbian

Move over Brazil – welcome to South America's number one gay destination.

Gay visibility in Argentina resurfaced with the long-awaited advent of democracy in 1983 and the re-emergence of numerous civil rights organisations. Correspondingly, the scene flourished as new venues opened to cater to an eager clientele (almost all gay venues had closed down during the dictatorship). By the '90s, gays, lesbians and transvestites had attracted the attention of the media at large and queer was suddenly chic; Argentina had finally broken free from its ominous past into a brighter present.

Of late – in line with the upsurge in tourism and a scene that continues to blossom – Buenos Aires has become South America's top gay destination. While devaluation has made it ideal for budget travellers, that's not the sole reason for its success. More important is the diversity of the non-stop social scene, plus Argentinian society's open-minded – if not outright friendly – attitude towards its citizens' sexual orientation.

The queer community in Argentina has gained an important position as the first Latin American country to approve the civil union of same sex couples (*see p187* **Happy ever after**). As expected, on the marketing side, gays and lesbians now have all kinds of services to meet their demands, from travel agencies such as **Pride Travel** (2nd floor, Office E, Paraguay 523, 5218 6556, www.pride-travel.com) and gay city tour guides, to tango teachers at bars like **Goddess** (*see p185*). There's even a gay map backed by the tourist office of the city government, available from

many gay bars, tourist information points and the Tangol tourist agency office on the first floor of **Galería Larreta** (*see p19*). And for the first time there are two small, gay-owned hotels (*see p184*), with more bound to follow. The community's major annual event is the **Marcha del Orgullo Gay** (Gay Pride – *see p162*), first staged in 1992.

On a more frivolous note, the legendary sex appeal of the locals (equalled only by the size of their ego) adds that extra something to this alluring scenario. Gay New York or London may still outshine Buenos Aires, but if you know where to go, you'll find good times aplenty.

FINDING A PIECE OF THE ACTION

For daytime, sunshine cruising, head to Plaza Las Heras and the Jardín Botánico, or get active with roller skating and other sports around the Rosedal in Palermo. Although defining specific queer areas is tricky, the neighbourhoods of Palermo and Barrio Norte form part of a notional 'Gayland'. Historic San Telmo is also gay-friendly and the Sunday Antiques Market is as busy as it is cruisey. For a change of scene, take a stroll along the docks at Puerto Madero down to the popular Reserva Ecológica at Costanera Sur where there's plenty going on. For more information on all these, *see pp53-96* **Sightseeing**.

If you're an indoors person, head for the shopping malls, especially Alto Palermo, Galerías Pacifico and El Abasto (*see pp137-60*

Add some **Glam** to your life. See p185.

Shopping). Or stop at any of the cafés along the 20 blocks of Avenida Santa Fe between Scalabrini Ortiz and Callao, particularly **El Trébol** (Santa Fe 2128, 4822 6417), and **Babieca** (Santa Fe 1898, 4813 4914).

By night, the heart of Gayland is best represented by the bar/café **El Olmo**, at Santa Fe and Pueyrredón (*see p185*). On weekends between midnight and around 2.30am at this intersection you can get flyers and discount passes for the main clubs and pubs in town, as well as info on events such as the meetings of the Bears' Club (Club de los Osos). For those into leather, check www.fierroleather.com.ar.

There are also male-only adult cinemas, open daily, with non-stop screenings. **Box** (Laprida 1423) in Palermo is best from Mondays to Wednesdays and Sundays from 7pm to 3am. Downtown, **Ideal** (Suipacha 378) and **Cine ABC** (Esmeralda 506) are busiest during the weekday lunch hour around 1pm, or after work at 5pm. There's not much action downtown at the weekends. For a one-night stand or just a couple of intimate hours, feel free to go to any *telo* (short stay 'love hotel'). The law states same sex couples have the same rights as heterosexual couples. For recommendations, *see p158* **Shopping & f**king**.

SAFETY & INFORMATION

Though the general guidelines on safety while being in BA apply to the queer scene (*see p255* **Staying safe**), there are a few specifics. The one simple rule is that sex with anyone under the age of 18 is illegal (gay or straight). Street prostitution is also illegal, so picking up a hustler could lead to arrest (be careful around the red light transvestite zone in Palermo Viejo). Few venues supply condoms, so always carry them with you. If you need information about health, safety or resources in Buenos Aires, contact the organisations listed below. Most have someone who speaks some English. For up-to-the-minute information on BA's queer scene, check out *La Otra Guía* and *Queer* (free in pubs and clubs), or buy *ImperioG*, the best gay magazine of late.

Resources

As well as the important gay and lesbian organisations listed below, **Lugar Gay de Buenos Aires** (*listings below*) is another useful information point.

Comunidad Homosexual Argentina (CHA)

Tomás Liberti 1080, y Irala, La Boca (4361 6382/ www.cha.org.ar). Bus 10, 24, 39, 70, 93. **Open** phone advice 1.30-8pm Mon-Fri; otherwise, call first. **Map** p276 B5.

Argentina's oldest and most politically influential queer organisation. Advice, information and an exhaustive library of books, videos, films, newsreels and press clippings.

La Fulana

Avenida Rivadavia 3410, entre Sánchez de Bustamante y Billinghurst, Almagro (4941 7640/ mobile 24hrs 15 4046 2007/http://groups.msn.com/ fulanas). Subte A, Loria/52, 86, 132, 151 bus. **Open** 11am-10pm Mon-Fri. **Map** p274 D3.

The most useful and efficient community centre for lesbians and bisexual women in Argentina.

Sociedad de Integración Gay-Lésbica Argentina (SIGLA)

Pasaje del Progreso 949, y Salas, Parque Chacabuco (4362 8261/www.sigla.org.ar). Train to E Mitre/26, 86 bus. **Open** 3-6pm Mon, Wed, Fri; 5-10pm Sat.

Legal advice, health information, workshops and recreational activities for gays and lesbians.

Where to stay

Some hotels are referred to as (or market themselves as) gay-friendly – and while they may be welcoming to gay visitors, they often lack close contact with the community. Try these gay-owned and run bed and breakfasts.

Bayres B&B

Córdoba 5842, entre Carranza y Ravignani, Palermo Viejo (4772 3877/www.bayresbnb.com). Bus 39, 93, 111, 151, 168. **Rates** US$25-$50 single/double. **No credit cards. Map** p275 K3.

Close to Amerika, Sitges, Bach and Goddess, this cosy B&B is as good as it gets. Breakfast anytime you want, free net access, plus air con and cable TV in all five rooms. The likeable owners' knowledge is another big plus. A comfortable lounge doubles up as a meeting point for tourists and locals.

Lugar Gay de Buenos Aires

Defensa 1120, entre Humberto 1º y San Juan, San Telmo (4300 4747/www.lugargay.org). Bus 24, 29, 126. **Rates** US$10 per person dorm; US$25-$50 single/double. **No credit cards. Map** p276 C6.

In the heart of picturesque San Telmo, the place is best known as a meeting point, with workshops on literature, gay issues, film, and music. Now there's bed and breakfast too; seven simple but functional rooms with cable TV. In summer ask for one of the three with air conditioning. Free Internet access.

Bars & clubs

The action in most bars doesn't start until past 1am and clubs get frisky even later around 2.30-3am. Many bars feature singers, strippers, karaoke and games, while drag queens preside over much of the city's gay nightlife. There's usually a cover charge or minimum spend in bars (AR$2-$10) and an admission charge in clubs of up to AR$20. One drink is included, but ask at bars for club discount passes. None of these venues accepts credit cards.

As venues open and close overnight, places recommended here are the most representative of gay BA today. Gay men enjoy greater visibility than lesbians – except at **Boicot** (*listings below*), **Unna** and **Sitges** (for both, *see p186*), three hot spots for lesbian nightlife.

A number of special nights move from venue to venue. Look out for **Brandon Gay Day** (two Saturday nights per month), when a funky young crowd gathers to drink, dance to electronic music or just chill. Go to their website (www.brandongayday.com.ar) and click on 'Próxima fiesta'. Other mainstream clubs also attract large gay crowds, particularly **Pachá** (*see p173*) and **Buenos Aires News** (*see p171*).

Amerika

Gascón 1040, entre Rocamora y Córdoba, Almagro (4865 4416/www.ameri-k.com.ar). Bus 26, 106, 109, 140, 168. **Open** from 1am Fri-Sat. **Map** p278 I4.

It used to be BA's gay mega-disco, but these days it's more straight than gay, so forget about scoring – unless, that is, you head to the darkroom after hours of drinking at the free beer bar. In fact, there are three bars by three equally crowded dancefloors, offering techno, house and Latin tunes. Not as much fun as before it got confused about its identity.

Angels

Viamonte 2158, entre Junín y Uriburu, Once (no phone). Bus 29, 68, 99, 109. **Open** from 1am Fri-Sat. **Map** p278 G6.

A laid-back alternative to the trendier venues on the scene. Transvestites, transgenders, friendly gays and even friendlier heterosexuals happily mingle in

Babieca on Santa Fe's cruising strip. *See p184.*

this loud, dive-club. The spacious bar on the middle floor faces a chill-out area and one of the two dancefloors plays Latin sounds only. Occasionally opens on Thursdays too.

Boicot

Bulnes 1250, entre Cabrera y Córdoba, Palermo Viejo (4861 7492). Bus 26, 106, 109, 140. **Open** 10pm-3am Fri-Sun. **Map** p278 H4.

Another venue from the good folk behind Sitges, Glam and Unna, this large space opened in November 2003 as an exclusively lesbian space – an ideal pre-clubbing spot. Booth seating, pool tables, a friendly vibe and enjoyable pop tunes make this a fun option and a welcome addition to the scene.

Buenos Aires Mix

Anchorena 1119, y Paraguay, Barrio Norte (4964 4095). Bus 12, 39, 111, 152. **Open** 11pm-5am Tue, Thur-Sun. **Map** p278 H5.

One of a number of less attractive venues that never really made it into the limelight, this small bar's saving grace is its breathtaking strippers.

Contramano

Rodríguez Peña 1082, entre Marcelo T de Alvear y Santa Fe, Recoleta (no phone). Bus 12, 37, 39, 124, 152. **Open** from midnight Wed-Sun. **Map** p278 G6.

BA's most relaxed club for gay men is also the pioneer of the scene: it has survived since opening in 1984, keeping its regular clients. For your musical delight, there's cheesy pop, golden oldies and Latin beats. The chill-out area upstairs has two further bars.

Glam

Cabrera 3046, entre Laprida y Agüero, Barrio Norte (4963 2521/www.glambsas.com.ar). Bus 29, 109, 111. **Open** from 1am Thur, Sat. **Map** p278 H5.

This spacious, colonial-style house has been transformed into one of BA's most vibrant good-time discos, with three bar areas plus a patio. Hip, sexy boys (lesbians are also welcome) gyrate till late to great tunes. It's the place to be on Thursday nights – Saturdays can be unbearably crowded.

Goddess

Córdoba 4185, y Pringles, Palermo Viejo (4861 2961/www.goddessdiscopub.com.ar). Bus 26, 106, 109, 140, 168. **Open** 10pm-3am Wed, Thur; 10pm-7am Fri, Sat; 10.30pm-3am Sun. **Map** p278 I4.

Kitsch is an understatement here, but luckily the decor is funny enough not to be hideously tacky. Classic tracks and pop tunes keep the young crowd happy. If your footwork is fancy, join the *milonga* nights on Wednesdays; if you need help, tango lessons are included. Sunday is karaoke night.

El Olmo

Santa Fe 2502, y Pueyrredón, Barrio Norte (4821 5828). Subte B, Pueyrredón/39, 41, 61, 118, 152 bus. **Open** 7am-2am Mon-Thur, Sun; 24hrs Fri, Sat. **Map** p278 H6.

El Olmo is a classic BA *confitería* by day that mutates into a meeting spot for gay men by night. The atmosphere is relaxed and friendly, and the joint gets positively lively by midnight at weekends when people come looking for their club discount passes on the opposite street corner.

Palacio Buenos Aires

Adolfo Alsina 940, entre Bernardo de Irigoyen y Tacuari, Monserrat (4331 1277/3231/www.palacio buenosaires.com). Open from 1.30am Fri, Sat; 8pm-1.30am Sun. Map p277 E6.
Hot, clean-cut guys gather in this huge, stylish venue to swing their well-built bodies to dance and house. Saturdays are a straighter affair, called Big One (*see p171*). Friday nights and Sunday's tea dance are gay only. Check the website for occasional parties at partner venue Vip Club (Bulnes 2772, Palermo).

Search

Azcuénaga 1007, entre Santa Fe y Marcelo T de Alvear, Barrio Norte (4824 0932). Subte D, Pueyrredón/12, 39, 64, 152 bus. Open from 11pm daily. Map p278 G6.
Limited in size and appeal, this venue has had a hard time building a regular clientele. However, sporadic first-rate shows from some of the best female impersonators in town are a compensation.

Sitges

Córdoba 4119, entre Palestina y Pringles, Palermo Viejo (4861 3763/www.sitgesonline.com.ar). Bus 26, 106, 109, 168. Open from 10.30pm Wed-Sun. Map p278 I4.
Three spaces interconnect at this big, modern venue: a cosy front room, circular middle bar and a covered patio. It's a great spot for making new friends among the mixed gay and lesbian clientele before going clubbing. Live drag shows too.

Titanic Club

Callao 1156, entre Santa Fe y Arenales, Recoleta (4816 1333/www.the-titanic-club.com.ar). Bus 10, 37, 39, 101, 124, 152. Open from 7pm Mon-Sat. Map p278 G6.

Gay Pride: fight for your rights. *See p183.*

Opened in late 2003, this kitschy, cutesy pub caters to a mixed, mostly male, crowd of from twenty- to fifty-somethings. Go-go dancers, a huge bar and friendly bartenders heighten the pleasure.

Unna

Suipacha 927, entre Paraguay y Marcelo T de Alvear, Retiro (no phone). Bus 10, 17, 59, 152. Open from 1am Sat. Map p277 F7.
Close to the Obelisco, Unna is the city's only lesbian disco. It's split between a front bar and a dark 'n' lively dancefloor with ample space to get intimate, and a busy bar. Music ranges from pop to techno.

Dining out is a gay-friendly experience throughout the city (especially in the chic gastrozone of Palermo Viejo), though a few places in particular pull the crowd: try **Filo** (*see p117*) and **Empire Thai** (*see p120*) and downtown, **La Farmacia** (*see p127*) in San Telmo, Recoleta's **Piola** pizzeria (*see p107*), self-styled aphrosidiac eaterie **Te Mataré Ramirez** (Paraguay 4062, 4831 9156 – and also with a branch in San Isidro at Primera Junta 702) and colourful **Rave** in Palermo Viejo (Gorriti 592, 4833 7832). There are also these two gay-owned restaurants cooking up a storm:

Chueca Resto-Bar

Soler 3283, entre Agüero y Gallo, Barrio Norte (4963 3430). Bus 29, 99, 106, 109. Open 9pm-3am Thur-Sat. Closed 1-10 Jan. Main course AR$16-$19. No credit cards. Map p278 H5.
Chueca is located in an eye-catching old house, with tables facing the stage where drag acts perform. The service is good and the fusion flavours even better. The menu changes weekly, but desserts such as the fresh fruit brochette or chocolate cake are always exquisite. Book in advance.

Tacla

Charcas 2626, entre Ecuador y Anchorena, Barrio Norte (4966 1909). Bus 29, 39, 41, 61, 118, 152. Open 8pm-4am Tue-Sun. Main course AR$10-$13. Set menu AR$10 weekdays; $18 weekend. No credit cards. Map p278 H6.
Tacla's eclectic, modern cuisine is worth checking out for dishes like a creamy chicken curry with spicy potatoes or the succulent steak. Too bad that service can be slow. Then again, there's usually a cruisey crowd sinking some drinks at the bar, plus strip shows on Wednesdays to Sundays to stimulate the appetite while you wait.

American Hot Gym

Ayacucho 449, entre Corrientes y Lavalle, Once (4951 7679). Subte B, Callao/12, 60 bus. Open 8am-midnight Mon-Fri; 9am-9pm Sat. Admission AR$10 per day; AR$36 per mth. No credit cards. Map p277 F5.

Happy ever after

Sexually tolerant Río may have South America's wildest scene, but all those sun worshippers will have to come to BA if they want to get hitched. In December 2002 the BA city legislature approved a civil union law that in effect recognised gay and lesbian couples, allowing them, as well an unwed straight couples, to enjoy the same legal rights and social benefits as married folk.

Light years ahead of puritanical state legislatures in the US and the rest of Latin America, the landmark decision was also a major coup for its biggest backers, the CHA (Comunidad Homosexual Argentina). For two decades, BA's most important gay-rights organisation worked in relative obscurity to challenge a culture of official homophobia. Among its achievements, it was the first gay rights organisation to win legal recognition from the government and helped pressure the cities of BA and Rosario to add sexual orientation to their non-discrimination laws.

Thanks to the CHA's efforts, social welfare plans and public healthcare benefits are now available to gay and lesbian couples joined by civil union. Furthermore, municipal employees are granted a pension if their partner dies, and same sex partners also won the right to visit one another if admitted into intensive care; access was previously restricted to only the direct relatives of the patient.

The CHA's current president, university professor César Cigliutti and its secretary, Marcelo Suntheim (both pictured) were the first happy gay couple to be joined in civil union on 19 July 2003, followed by many more in BA. Months after the law came into effect in Argentina's capital, the province of Río Negro approved its own civil union law; projects for a similar law have been presented in other provinces. As of December 2003, some 100 couples (around 15 per cent of whom are heterosexual) had been through the obligatory ceremony in order to be joined in civil union today.

According to Cigliutti and Suntheim: 'The civil union law was approved because most people recognise that it is part of the solution to our problems. In fact, the positive change in the media towards gays and lesbians mirrors a cultural shift seen in everyday life in today's more tolerant Argentinian society.'

Pressure for change doesn't stop here, however. The CHA latest proposals include adoption rights for gays and lesbians, life pension for all workers in case of death of their partners, and inheritance rights for the queer community (as yet unapproved).

While much has been accomplished for gays and lesbians, police harassment of transvestites and transgenders still continues, though to a lesser extent. Not all traces of discrimination have vanished, but an irreversible change has been set in motion.

Arts & Entertainment

This fully equipped gym, caters to a mainly gay clientele, offering aerobics, kick-boxing, Capoeira and personal trainers.

Buenos Aires A Full

Viamonte 1770, entre Callao y Rodríguez Peña, Tribunales (4371 7263/www.afullspa.com). Subte D, Callao/12, 29, 37, 60 bus. **Open** noon-1am Mon-Thur; 24hrs Fri-Sun. **Admission** AR$25. **No credit cards**. **Map** p277 F6.

This spacious sauna pulls a good-looking crowd, and has a bar, jacuzzi, steam rooms and gym.

Tom's

Basement, Viamonte 638, entre Maipú y Florida, Microcentro (4322 4404/www.buenosairestoms.com). Subte C, Lavalle/10, 17, 26, 99, 109, 132 bus. **Open** noon-3am Mon-Thur, Sun; 24hrs Fri-Sat. **Admission** AR$7-$8. **No credit cards**. **Map** p277 E7.

Tom's isn't strictly speaking a sauna, but it is a steamy place for easy scoring. Dimly lit hallways with private cabins and peep holes lead to two labyrinthine, busy darkrooms. There's also a comfortable chill out area, video booths and a conveniently located bar.

Music

Drums from the plains, River Plate rock, slum cumbia and classical at the Colón.

Classical & Opera

Thanks to a flourishing post-independence arts scene, by 1900 Buenos Aires had no less than five opera houses. Two of those opera houses still stand: the **Teatro Colón** and the **Teatro Coliseo** (Marcelo T de Alvear 1125, Tribunales, 4816 3789), though only the former maintains a regular opera season. The Colón is a world-class opera venue and also stages ballets, concert cycles and intimate recitals and experimental workshops; *see p189* **Opera magnifica**.

Given its status as the key classical music centre in South America, it's surprising that BA does not have a venue devoted to symphonic concerts. Instead these are performed across the city, in places like the **Teatro Avenida** (*see p219*), **Museo Isaac Fernández Blanco** (*see p66*), the University's **Facultad de Derecho** at Avenida Figueroa Alcorta and Pueyrredón in Recoleta, **Auditorio San Rafael** (Ramallo 2606, Nuñez) and **Teatro Margarita Xirgú** (*listings below*), among others.

There is a year-round music scene (the Colón's season runs April to December, but some programming continues in summer, including opera). Much is in the hands of private professional and amateur groups, including important associations such as Mozarteum Argentino (www.mozarteum argentino.org), Festivales Musicales (www.festivalesmusicales.org.ar) and Harmonia (www.fundacioncoliseum.com.ar, who perform at the Coliseo). The Buenos Aires Philharmonic holds a sell-out season of around 20 concerts at the Colón. There are also more modest, unsubsidised institutions – like **La Scala de San Telmo** (Pasaje Giuffra 371, 4362 1187, www.lascala.com.ar) – which open their doors to talented performers, many of them young virtuosi from local conservatories.

Classical music's status has been bolstered by keen critics, especially Marcelo Arce, whose lectures are attended by thousands of fans, plus classical radio stations such as Radio Cultura Musical (100.3FM), Radio Cultura (97.9FM) and Radio Nacional Clásica (96.7FM). Social clubs, libraries and cultural centres also occasionally screen ballet and opera videos: try the **Círculo Italiano** (Libertad 1264, Recoleta, 4815 9693) and **Centro Cultural Konex** (*see p212*).

If gala nights at the Colón are still occasions for tiaras and tuxes, interest in opera extends beyond BA's aristocracy. Performances take place not only at the Colón, but also at Margarita Xirgú and even in the **Manufactura Papelera** (*listings below*) – a former paper factory where several groups stage rarely performed works.

Outside the capital, the most impressive venue is the **Teatro Argentino** (Calle 51, 0221 429 1746) in La Plata (56 kilometres/35 miles from BA; free buses from Callao 237, Tribunales, 4373 2636). It seats 2,300 in the main Alberto Ginastera auditorium, and the smaller Astor Piazzolla Auditorium accommodates 500 more. The **Teatro Roma** (Sarmiento 109, 4205 9646) in Avellaneda – ten minutes from downtown – is a small opera house with good acoustics and an offbeat repertoire, featuring the likes of Verdi's *Corsario*, or Bellini's *Capulets and Montagues*. Finally, in Zona Norte, try the first-rate Sacred Music series on Sunday afternoons at the **Catedral de San Isidro** (*listings below*).

These are all places where opera fans can sate their appetite thanks to the efforts of Juventus Lyrica, Buenos Aires Lírica, Casa de la Opera, Peco o Peco, and Opera del Buen Ayre. There are many locally trained, talented performers, directors and designers, including conductor/pianist Daniel Barenboim (now an Israeli citizen) and pianist Marta Argerich (a festival named after her is held at the Colón; *see p162*). Tenors José Cura and Marcelo Alvarez are also acclaimed at home and abroad.

Catedral de San Isidro

Avenida del Libertador 16199, y 9 de Julio, San Isidro (4743 0291). Train Mitre or de la Costa to San Isidro/60, 168 bus. **Open** 8am-8pm Mon, Fri; 8am-10pm Sun. **Admission** free.
Performances are usually at 4pm, from April to December; arrive early to secure a good seat.

La Manufactura Papelera

Bolívar 1582, entre Brasil y Caseros, San Telmo (4307 9167/www.papeleracultural.8m.com). Bus 24, 29, 39. **Shows** 6pm or 8.30pm Thur-Sun. **Closed** Jan. **Tickets** AR$7-$40. **No credit cards.** **Map** p276 C5.

Teatro Margarita Xirgú

Chacabuco 875, y Estados Unidos (4300 8817, www.mxirgu.com.ar). Bus 10, 17, 29, 59, 156. **Open** *Box office* 2-8pm Tue-Sun. **Tickets** AR$5-$40. **Credit** AmEx, DC, MC, V. **Map** p276 D6.

Opera magnifica

As a *porteño* cultural icon, almost nothing beats the Teatro Colón. BA's renowned opera house (named after Christopher Columbus) was inaugurated in 1908 with a performance of Verdi's *Aïda*, and its perfect acoustics are unbeatable, according to experts. It's also one of the most beautiful theatres in the world.

The tapping of the conductor's baton and the dimming of the 702 lights of the theatre's chandelier is always a magical moment. The Colón has welcomed some of the world's greatest international performers: Arturo Toscanini, Herbert von Karajan, Rudolf Nureyev, Enrico Caruso, Rita Rufo, Maria Callas, Montserrat Caballé, Maurice Béjart and Daniel Barenboim, to name just a few.

The stunning interior comfortably seats 2,500 people. Add in the layers of spacious public galleries set above the boxes – the *gallinero* (chicken coop), *paraíso* (gods) and *infierno* (hell), in ascending order of height and descending price – and the total capacity rises to more than 3,000.

Originally conceived as a lyric theatre or opera house, the Colón presents ten full operas or operatic productions a year, with at least five performances of each. There are also some 20 individual concerts and symphonic cycles performed by the resident 98-piece Orquesta Estable del Teatro Colón or the 103 musicians of the Filarmónica de Buenos Aires. Visiting international ensembles have included the Chicago Symphony Orchestra, the Orchestra of Munich and the Vienna Philharmonic.

The Colón's policy is to make opera more accessible to the general public. Most operas have surtitles in Spanish, and the theatre usually programmes a series called 'El Colón x $2', which offers access to a first-rate concert or chamber opera for the price of a *cortado* coffee. Almost all the season's productions also have one dress rehearsal open to the public, with tickets from just AR$2-$10. On many Sunday mornings, the Colón stages quality productions of operas adapted for children – such as *The Magic Flute* or *Hansel and Gretel* – sung in Spanish.

The theatre's artistic direction even leans to embrace more popular musical forms – rock, electronic and world music rhythms rang out in this esteemed venue in 2003.

It's worth a visit even if just to take in the splendour of the building. The mysteries of the theatre's basement and labyrinthine passages that house the wardrobe and set workshops have been dispelled, thanks to daily guided tours (book in advance). An ambitious multi-million dollar renovation plan, due for completion in 2008, includes installing air-conditioning and extensive renovation of the interior and exterior.

Teatro Colón

Cerrito, entre Tucumán y Viamonte, Tribunales (box office 4378 7344/7316/tours 4378 7132/www.teatrocolon.org.ar). Subte D, Tribunales/29, 39, 59, 109 bus. **Open** *Box office* Feb-Dec 10am-8pm Tue-Sat; 10am-5pm Sun. **Guided tours** *Spanish* on the hr 11am-4pm Mon-Sat; 11am, 1pm, 3pm Sun. *English* 11am, 3pm Mon-Sat; 11am, 1pm, 3pm Sun. **Tickets** *Ballet* AR$25-$30. *Concerts* AR$3-$15. *Opera* $15-$150. *Tours* AR$7; AR$2 under-17s; concessions. **Credit** varies (not for tours). **Map** p277 F7.

Arts & Entertainment

The **Babasónicos** rock out.

Rock, Folk & Jazz

Buenos Aires may mean tango to the rest of the world, but rock is far more prolific, with 60 to 80 gigs each week, and a popular local variant. Trad rock, folk and jazz all coexist with more avant-garde musical expressions, as well as bands performing music spiced with influences from native folk to hardcore to Caribbean beats.

ROCK ON THE RIVER PLATE
Brazilians and Mexicans might beg to differ, but local legend tells that Latin American rock was born in BA – and Argentina's Spanish-language *rock nacional* is preferred by many to the imported version. Since the mid 1960s, more than 1,000 bands have released albums under this genre. Influential early groups include Los Gatos, Manal, Luis Spinetta's Almendra – Spinetta is many Argentinian rockers' poet – and the definitive *rock nacional* artist, Charly Garcia and his band Sui Generis.

Initially, there was conservative opposition to a local rock culture and it took the return of democracy to free up the genre and the local gig scene. By the end of the '80s, Argentinian rock had spread across Latin America, aided by Rock & Pop (95.9FM) radio station. Tours of up-and-coming groups, such as Los Enanitos Verdes and the now-disbanded Soda Stereo caused mass hysteria wherever they played.

Today *rock nacional* is accepted as a bulwark in the international music industry – the first Grammy awarded to a Latin rock artist was given to BA band Los Fabulosos Cadillacs, whose mega-hit, 'Matador', is a classic across South America. The most successful bands of recent years have been Catepecu Machu, Ratones Paranóicos and Babasónicos.

Despite this passion for Argentinian rock, most local hipsters still consider the Rolling Stones to be the definitive band. 'Los Stones' generated a fashion cult in Argentina, with musicians copying the Ronnie Wood hairdo and Mick Jagger skinny T-shirts of the '70s, and music fans christening their own lifestyle 'Rolling'. And that lips logo is ubiquitous in the city. An opposing fan group is (almost) equally as passionate about Los Beatles.

This love of the Stones has influenced local bands such as La 25, Intoxicados (formerly Viejas Locas) and La Mancha de Rolando. Others, such as Expulsados, were influenced by US proto-punk outfit the Ramones – punk and metal are still popular in BA, and ska, swing and even oi! music have small, devoted followings.

Many bands inspire the same fanaticism as local football teams, and audiences display an alarming degree of loyalty, with self-styled 'tribes' who bellow slogans and insults at followers of rival bands. This is particularly the case at concerts by Patricio Rey y Los Redonditos de Ricota, a band that openly rejects

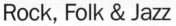

the music industry, enjoying iconic status in a market where the lines between protest and a clan-like need to belong get blurred.

Other bands like Los Piojos, whose rock is tinged with nuances of *murga* (carnival street music) and Uruguayan *candombe*, or La Renga, who stick to pure rock, also ignite fervour in their fans. They pull huge audiences: in 2003, La Renga filled River Plate stadium with more than 50,000 fans, while Los Piojos packed in 70,000 – the sort of numbers that Los Redonditos used to attract.

THE SOUND OF THE COUNTRY

With roots in the rural communities of the northern provinces and outlying pampas, *folklore* (pronounced folk-LAW-ray) was until recently viewed as the old-fashioned music of country bumpkins and a fetish for ageing hippies. But it now attracts a large number of followers, partly for the social and political force of the lyrics, but also because *folklore* lends itself to a good knees-up and hoe-down.

There are hundreds of different styles. Many are based on dances – the *chacarera, zamba* or *chamamé* – which are now played by young megastars like Soledad and Luciano Pereyra. Legendary folk figures such as the late, great Atahualpa Yupanqui and Cuchi Leguizamon, and Eduardo Falú (who still occasionally performs) transformed and enriched these traditional rhythms, providing *folklore* with a new virtuoso dimension.

Mercedes Sosa, one of the grandes dames of classic *folklore*, performs in Europe, and occasionally in Argentina – often at charity and solidarity gigs. Nonetheless, she has ventured into other genres with multifaceted rock stars such as León Gieco, Fito Páez and Charly García.

Among the best known traditional groups are Los Chalchaleros, Los Fronterizos and Los Trovadores, while Victor Heredia and Antonio Tarragó Ros have explored new folk idioms departing from traditional rhythms. Raúl Barboza (accordion), Jaime Torres (perhaps the world's best *charango* player), and Juanjo Dominguez (guitar) along with Chango Spasiuk (accordion) are among the most talented contemporary folk players.

La Folklórica (98.7FM) radio can be received almost anywhere in the country. It airs *folklore* round-the-clock and attracts a wide audience. But to catch these earthy sounds live, the best places are the *peñas* (see *p196*), or venues such as **La Trastienda** (see *p193*), **Clásica y Moderna** (see *p131*) or **ND/Ateneo** (see *p194*), which have regular folk cycles. The traditional Sunday fair, **Feria de Mataderos** (see *p94*), is an open-air alternative if you're willing to head out to the capital's western limits.

DANCE, LATIN & JAZZ

At the end of the 1990s, dance music hit town. Big-name DJs from Buenos Aires, such as Javier Zuker, Carlos Alfonsín and transatlantic star Hernán Cattáneo (see *p172* **Mi Buenos Aires Querido**), all make regular appearances on the club circuit and at dance festivals. Rock bands have also embraced *electrónica*. Daniel Melero and ex-Soda Stereo leader Gustavo Cerati were the first to take it on; Leo García is another well-liked exponent of experimental *electrónica*, whose style has a loungey vibe.

Simultaneously, local popular dance music – or *música tropical* – is gaining wider acceptance. This music was originally confined to *bailantas* (clubs where two or three different groups play live), but has now broken class barriers to become one of the most profitable sectors of the Argentinian music industry. The premature deaths of star performers Gilda in 1996, Rodrigo in 2000 and Walter Olmos in 2002 have only served to boost the phenomenon. The spots where they died have been turned into shrines by mourning fans (see *p163* **Waiting for a miracle**). Another awesomely popular phenomenon is *cumbia villera*, which sprung from the slums and a culture of drugs, crime and despair (see *p194* **Tropical gangstas**).

Jazz is also enjoying a boom; every day a wide variety of jazz musicians play styles from Bebop to Dixieland. The local jazz scene contains some outstanding artists, such as

Rock/folk crossover icon **León Gieco**.

guitarists Valentino and Luis Salinas – BB King's protégé – bass player Javier Malosetti, trumpeter Fats Fernandez, pianist Adrian Iaies and bass quintet leader Alejandro Herrera. There's even a government initiative to promote live jazz, known as the Jazz Route (*see p194*).

GIGS & FESTIVALS

Despite the financial (exchange-rate) challenge of bringing major foreign stars to the city, BA is slowly regaining its place on the international circuit. In 2003, alternative artists (US punk-vixen Peaches) and DJs (John Digweed) made appearances in Buenos Aires, while the Latin superstars, such as Luis Miguel, continue to make regular visits, selling tickets to tens of thousands of (mostly female) fans. Major rock acts are thin on the ground, though the 2004/05 agenda looks more promising.

The festival scene is also kicking. In 2003, Cosquin Rock (in the province of Córdoba) attracted 60,000 people and the seven-night Quilmes Rock Festival in Buenos Aires pulled in an enthusiastic 100,000-strong crowd. The 2003 BA edition of Creamfields dance festival (www.creamfieldsba.com) attracted a roster of foreign artists include Layo & Bushwacka!, Audio Bullys, Sander Kleinenberg and Josh Wink, pulling a crowd of 38,000 party people. Barring unforeseen circumstances, these events are regular fixtures. In summer, the city government (www.buenosaires.gov.ar) often subsidises free concerts, while over the water, Uruguay hosts a first-class jazz festival in Punta del Este (*see p241*). Keep an eye out also for posters advertising smaller, impromptu festivals throughout the year

Buenos Aires boasts a huge number of live music venues. In this chapter we list places that have at least two shows a month. As with so many city spaces, music venues are often multifunctional – a place listed under 'Jazz' might have a folk evening on Tuesday, tango classes on Thursday and an occasional art exhibition. The quickest way to find out what's on is to check specialised weekly supplements in the newspapers or free publications like *Wipe*. It is often possible to buy tickets on the night from the venue itself, although big-name concerts often sell out in advance.

Many venues, especially clubs, are unlikely to accept credit cards. However, you can buy tickets using major credit cards at these two agencies; the booking fee is ten per cent of ticket price, and both work principally with Visa and MasterCard, though it varies according to the promoter. **Ticketek** (5327 7200, www.ticketek.com.ar, nine locations) and **Ticketmaster** (4321 9700, two locations). For record shops, *see p157*.

Major venues

Mega stars – these days more likely to be local bands than international groups – play the city's football stadiums. The main locations for live concerts are River Plate, Velez Sarsfield and Ferro Carril Oeste. Other sports grounds, such as the Palermo polo field and the Club Hipico are also periodically transformed into music venues. It's best to get a ticket down in the main ground – *el campo* – not up in the stands, as the number of large screens is often limited. On windy evenings, the sound quality can be appalling, unless you get up close to the speakers. For details of sports stadiums, *see chapter* **Sport & Fitness**. Below is a list of other major venues, less monumental, but each with its own pros and cons. Look out also for jazz concerts at the **Teatro Coliseo** (*see p188*).

Estadio Obras Sanitarias

Avenida del Libertador 7395, entre Núñez y Manuela Pedraza, Núñez (4702 3223/www.estadioobras.com. ar). Bus 15, 29, 130. **Open** Box office Feb-Dec noon-8pm Mon-Fri. **Closed** Jan. **Tickets** AR\$15-\$40. **No credit cards. Map** p281 O6.
The so-called Temple of Rock, and a favourite with Argentinian rock fans, can hold 5,000 souls, packed in like sardines. Eric Clapton, James Brown, Roxy Music, Kiss, the Ramones, David Byrne, Megadeath and Manu Chao, along with BA's hottest bands,

The **Gran Rex**: sure is grand.

have all played here. Recently renovated toilets and a new air-conditioning system have relieved the place of some of its traditional drawbacks.

Luna Park
Bouchard 465, entre Corrientes y Lavalle, Centro (4311 1990/4312 2135/www.lunapark.com.ar). Subte B, LN Alem/26, 93, 99, 152 bus. **Open** *Box office* 10am-8pm Mon-Sat; varies Sun. **Tickets** AR$10-$100. **Credit** AmEx, DC, MC, V. **Map** p277 E8.

Ray Charles, Jeff Beck, BB King and Ricky Martin have all graced the dressing rooms of this boxing stadium, and it has also hosted Moon Park DJ events. It's a good space for enthusiastic audiences, but there are some drawbacks: thick columns can obscure the view and as for the sound... Oasis sounded like they were playing underwater.

Teatro Gran Rex
Avenida Corrientes 857, entre Suipacha y Esmeralda, Centro (4322 8000). Subte B, Carlos Pellegrini or C, Diagonal Norte or D, 9 de Julio/10, 17, 24, 29, 70 bus. **Open** *Box office* 10am-10pm daily. **Tickets** AR$15-$60. **No credit cards. Map** p277 E7.

Ideal for artists who require the attention of a comfortably seated audience; past performers include Brazilian Caetano Veloso and Boy George. It holds 3,500 people who can choose between the stalls (*platea*), the mezzanine (*super pullman*) or the dress circle (*pullman* – cheap seats, but the worst sound). The Gran Rex is also a venue for musicals, and has its own car park and coffee shop.

Teatro Opera
Avenida Corrientes 860, entre Suipacha y Esmeralda, Centro (4326 1335). Subte B, Carlos Pellegrini or C, Diagonal Norte or D, 9 de Julio/10, 17, 24, 29, 70 bus. **Open** *Box office* 10am-8pm daily. **Tickets** AR$15-$55. **Credit** varies. **Map** p277 E7.

Opposite the Gran Rex, this is one of BA's classic Deco- and Nouveau-style auditoriums. Since it opened in 1872, many great local artists have performed here, including tango stars Hugo del Carril and Edmundo Rivero, as well as international greats such as Louis Armstrong and Ella Fitzgerald.

La Trastienda
Balcarce 460, entre Belgrano y Venezuela, San Telmo (4342 7650/www.latrastienda.com). Subte A, Plaza de Mayo or D, Catedral, or E, Bolivar/24, 29, 126, 130 bus. **Open** *Box office* Jan 4-8pm daily. *Feb-Dec* noon-8pm Mon-Sat. Sun 3pm-8pm. **Tickets** AR$8-$60. **Credit** DC, MC, V. **Map** p277 D7.

In the ruins of an old mansion dating from 1895, the Trastienda holds 400 people seated at small tables and another 1,000 standing. It has hosted the likes of ex-Weather Report member Joe Zawinul and groovers Medeski, Martin and Wood. For younger audiences, there are concerts by the likes of Stereolab or Café Tacuba, plus occasional free events. Dance, theatre and other performing arts get their turn in this likeable venue too. Decent sound and a cool small foyer bar (with pavement tables as well), dishing out beers and pizza.

The best Venues

Cemento
A good old down and dirty house of rock.

Club del Vino
Fine wines and great grooves across the genres. *See p194.*

ND/Ateneo
Celebrating the urban and folk sounds of Argentina. *See p194.*

Notorious
Daily shows from the best selection of musicians in town. Tasty food and drinks too. *See p195.*

Teatro Colón
Peerless accoustics and splendid aesthetics in one of the world's great opera houses. *See p189.*

Thelonious Bar
This bar honouring Sr Monk doubles up as a jiving, jamming jazz joint. *See p196.*

La Trastienda
Big names, new acts and avant-garde experiments in a cool warehouse space in San Telmo.

Rock & folk

Cemento
Estados Unidos 1234, entre Santiago del Estero y Salta, Constitución (4304 6228). Subte E, Independencia/39, 59, 60, 102, 168 bus. **Open** from 10pm usually Wed-Sun. **Tickets** AR$3-12. **No credit cards. Map** p277 D5.

One of the seedier underground joints that have survived from the 1980s, it has finally done up its bathrooms and installed air conditioning. Originally a disco, it soon became a centre for rock, punk and Goth concerts. Rock legends – Stiff Little Fingers, Virus and Los Redondos as well as Brazilian band Ratos de Porão – have played here and nowadays the place hosts trendy groups like Intoxicados, Almafuerte, Expulsados and Quebraditos.

Club del Vino
Cabrera 4737, entre Armenia y Malabia, Palermo Viejo (4833 8330). Bus 15, 39, 110, 141, 168. **Open** *Shows* from 9.30pm Tue-Sun. *Restaurant* noon-3pm, 8pm-1am Mon-Sat. **Tickets** AR$8-$30; free jazz Tue, tango Wed. **Credit** AmEx, MC, V. **Map** p279 J4.

A statue of Bacchus dominates the patio and sets the tone. With its restaurant, wine museum, wine shop and 200-seat theatre, this is one of the best

Arts & Entertainment

spots in the city for lovers of good grape and classy music. Past performers include Cesárea Evora, Chavela Vargas, James Brown and Mercedes Sosa. During the show, you can order cold cuts and cheeses, along with outstanding wines by the bottle or glass. A special US$45 package for tourists includes transport to and from your hotel, dinner, the show and a bottle of wine to take home with you.

Mitos Argentinos

Humberto 1° 489, entre Bolívar y Defensa, San Telmo (4362 7810/www.mitosargentinos.com.ar). Bus 24, 29, 126, 130, 152. **Open** from 9.30pm Fri, Sat; from 12.30pm Sun. **Tickets** AR$5 women Fri, Sat, all Sun; AR$8 men Fri; AR$10 men Sat. Free before 11pm. **Credit** AmEx, DC, MC, V. **Map** p276 C6.

Local rock and blues bands play in this old San Telmo house, and though most are barely known they're wisely selected, so it's worth the experience. Dinner is available here on Fridays and Saturdays (10.30pm), while on Sundays lunch is served while tango shows and classes take place.

ND/Ateneo

Paraguay 918, y Suipacha, Retiro (4328 2888). Subte C, San Martín/10, 59, 109, 152 bus. **Open** Box office Feb-Dec noon-8pm Mon-Sat. **Closed** Jan. **Tickets** AR$10-$30. **No credit cards**. **Map** p277 F7.

This traditional theatre was reopened in 2002 with hugely improved acoustics, and is now a key venue for all musical genres, from *folklore* and tango to rock and jazz. There are concerts most Thursdays to Sundays, mainly from Argentinian or other Latin American artists – Adriana Varela and Fito Páez played in late 2003. There are also occasional film screenings, theatre performances and poetry recitals.

Templum

Ayacucho 318, entre Sarmiento y Corrientes, Once (4953 1513). Subte B, Callao/24, 37, 60, 124 bus. **Open** *Feb-Dec* from 9pm Sat, Sun. **Closed** Jan. **Tickets** AR$5-$8. **No credit cards**. **Map** p277 F5.

This early 20th-century house hides a cultural centre inside. It's principally devoted to theatre but, on Saturday nights at 11pm, there are carefully chosen ethnic, jazz or world music gigs. One spacious room, seating 60 people, is used as the concert hall.

Jazz & blues

Buenos Aires's jazz scene is gaining momentum, both in terms of musicians and venues, while outside the capital, events like the La Plata Jazz Festival or Bariloche Jazz Festival attract ever-increasing audiences.

More and more places are dedicated to jazz and blues, and as a result the city of Buenos Aires has organised and is promoting a jazz circuit called **La Ruta del Jazz** (the Jazz Route). It's an attempt to bring together dozens of formal and informal joints – often bars and restaurants – where some kind of jazz, fusion, ethnic, R&B or Caribbean/Latin jazz takes

Tropical gangstas

'Suck it little baby', 'I'm going to kill a snob (*cheto*)' and 'Now I only do coke,' are the singalong lyrics of Buenos Aires' latest musical phenomenon, *cumbia villera*. A provocative offspring of a tinny, tacky, bastardised sub-genre of Colombia's noble cumbia sound, this new music is a tropical fusion of Latin beats, punky attitudes and gangsta rap morality.

Replacing the usual cumbia themes of love, betrayal, love, dancing and yet more love with raw, everyday stories of life on the margins (*villera* comes from *villa miseria* – shanty town), the scene first emerged in the late '90s in rundown outlying suburbs such as San Fernando and La Matanza, where large gangs of teens and 20-somethings gather in vast hangars to dance and flirt to a tropical beat. It soon gained a following, generated a whole look (pictured) and spread to all social classes, appearing as the soundtrack of prime time TV series *Tumberos* (about life in prison) and the cutting-edge feature film *El Bonaerense* (*see p174*). Consecrating the lowlife dance music as high art, a stage adaptation of *Romeo and Juliet* adopted *cumbia villera* as a soundtrack to the dissing dialogues of the Montagues and Capulets.

While swearing they are anti-establishment, all the main bands compete to be the biggest and to get on lucrative TV shows. Pioneers Rafaga and Guachín present the softer side, with stories of noble destitution and anti-heroic suffering at the hands of the police and evil politicians. Yerba Brava, Damas Gratis and Pibes Chorros are more likely to sing about *lolas*, *lapices* and *leche* – that is, tits, cocks and spunk, with syringes, murder, football and lots of lairy lads' stuff in between. But these unreconstructed *chicos* have met their match in La Piba, a female cumbia star from the infamous Fuerte Apache area who likes to sing about flashing her '*cucaracha*' to fit football players – much to the chagrin of her dad, who's a cop.

Banned by COMFER, Argentina's national radio broadcasting authority, for its crime-oriented apologetics, and much discussed by

Music

place at least once a week. As well as places listed in this chapter, other venues on the Ruta in Palermo Viejo include **Cavas y Cuevas** (*see p133*), **Bar Abierto** (Borges 1613, 4833 7640), **Binaural-Fragrance Bar** (Soler 4202, 4865 3839, www.binauralbar.com.ar), **Cala Bistro** (Soler 4065, 4823 0413) and **El Gorriti** (Gorriti 3780, 4862 8031, www.elgorriti.com). If you're in the San Telmo area, try **Perro Andaluz** (Defensa 1066, 4362 5562).

Some traditional cafés also host jazz events. At **Café Tortoni** (*see p125*) on Fridays the Creole Jazz Band play, while on Saturdays the Fenix Jazz Band takes over. At **Clásica y Moderna** (*see p131*) there are all kinds of musical happenings, including jazz, bolero and tango, plus other cultural events.

A fun alternative is **Paladar Orestes**, inspired by the Cuban 'paladar' restaurants. It's a sort of open house, serving a variety of tasty tapas, *ceviches* and stews, accompanied every Friday and Saturday by a good jazz show. It costs AR$35 all in, but you must to call to reserve and be given directions (4301 8526).

Blues Special Club

Avenida Almirante Brown 102, y Pilcomayo, La Boca (4854 2338). Bus 29, 53, 64, 93, 168. **Open** from 10pm Fri-Sun. **Tickets** AR$5; international shows AR$15 (1wk in advance), AR$20 (on the door). **No credit cards. Map** p276 B6.

academics and left-wing journalists for its stereotyping of the underclass, *cumbia villera*, like tango before it, is nonetheless a fascinating folk music from the often ignored urban fringes. Though with a couple of big money labels managing what they consider 'the product' and powerful promoters working their artists till they drop, slum cumbia is unlikely to join tango, *folklore* and *rock nacional* and other rebellious genres in the annals of Argentinian musical heritage.

This soulful establishment is a classic for *porteño* blues fans. Affable owner Adrián regularly brings new artists over from the US. 'It doesn't matter who's playing, but what he's playing' is the ethos here. On Fridays, there are lawless *zapadas* (jam sessions).

No Avestruz

Humboldt 1857, entre El Salvador y Costa Rica, Palermo Viejo (4771 1141/www.noavestruz.com.ar). Bus 39, 93, 111. **Open** *Shows* Jan, Feb 10pm Fri, Sat. Mar-Dec 8pm-1am Thur-Sat, 7-11pm Sun. **Tickets** AR$6-$10 **No credit cards. Map** p279 K4.

Jazz is played once or twice a week in this spacious warehouse. The scattered couches and chairs make for an informal atmosphere, but be prepared to sweat as the place gets hot. For snacking, the empanadas are acceptable. It attracts trendy tourists looking for an unconventional vibe.

Notorious

Avenida Callao 966, entre Marcelo T de Alvear y Paraguay, Barrio Norte (4815 8473/www.notorious bar.com.ar). Subte D, Callao/12, 39, 60, 111 bus. **Open** 8am-midnight Mon, Tue; 8am-1am Wed, Thur; 8am-3am Fri; 10am-3am Sat; 6pm-midnight Sun. **Tickets** AR$7-$15. **Credit cards** (restaurant only) AmEx, DC, MC, V. **Map** p278 G6.

Notorious has daily live shows by respected local jazzers such as Fats Fernandez and Adrian Iaies, as well as occasional new folk and world music acts. The stage is close to the tables, so you can catch every groan and moan during the improvs – but reserve ahead to be as near to the front as possible. The space also holds a café-cum-music-shop, with touchscreen consoles for sampling the latest sounds. The new branch – above classic bookstore Ghandi – offers a similarly eclectic live programme and simple, decent food, but sound and view from the very back tables are poor.

Other locations: First Floor, Gandhi, Corrientes 1743, Tribunales (4371 0370).

La Revuelta

Avenida Alvarez Thomas 1368, entre Elcano y 14 de Julio, Chacarita (4553 5530/www.larevueltabar.com.ar). Bus 19, 93, 140. **Open** from 9.30pm Tue-Sun. **Tickets** AR$5-$15. **Credit** AmEx, MC, V.

Hear top local performers like Walter Malosetti or the Ricardo Nole Trio, while chowing down on fine food. Music ranges from jazz standards and improv sessions through Brazilian bossa nova to tango.

El Samovar de Rasputín

Del Valle Iberlucea 1251, entre Lamadrid y Magallanes, La Boca (4302 3190). Bus 29, 53, 64, 152. **Open** *Shows* from midnight Fri-Sat; from 6pm Sun. **Tickets** free, minimum spend. **No credit cards. Map** p276 A5.

This mythic joint, in the heart of La Boca, is managed by Napo, a blues enthusiastic who often hangs around until dawn telling tales from his hippie glory days. A huge painting of Gardel, holding a *criollo*-style guitar, dominates the room, and the walls are covered with photos of Boca and Che. Taj Majal,

Arts & Entertainment

The name says it all at La Boca's **Blues Special Club**. *See p195.*

James Cotton and BB King's band have all played here. There are tango classes on Sunday afternoons (2-9pm), and good barbecued meats are available.

Splendid

Gorriti 5099 ,y Thames, Palermo Viejo (4833 4477/3535/www.splendidrestaurant.com). Bus 34, 39, 55. **Open** 8am-3am daily. *Shows* 9pm Thur-Sat. **Tickets** included with dinner. **Credit** AmEx, DC, MC, V. **Map** p279 J4.

The laid-back atmosphere with black-and-white portraits of Louis Armstrong attract creative types from the art world. Enjoy the wonderful bebop sounds of the Splendid Jazz Band and Marcelo Barragán Trío.

Thelonious Bar

Salguero 1884, entre Güemes y Charcas, Palermo (4829 1562). Subte D, Bulnes/29, 39, 111, 152 bus. **Open** 9.30pm-4am Tue-Sat. *Shows* 10.30pm Tue-Sat. **Tickets** AR$8. **No credit cards. Map** p278 I5.

If you're after the best local jazz, this is the place. Every night, you can hear some of the most talented musicians in the country, while nibbling on tapas or Mediterranean platters. Sound quality is excellent; less so the seating comfort levels.

Other venues

Pubs & bars

If music makes you thirsty, BA offers a myriad of opportunities to enjoy music to suit every taste and style while sipping excellent cocktails or enjoying a cold beer. In the city centre, **La Cigale** (*see p125*; free live shows on Thursdays) is the place to enjoy well-prepared drinks while listening to the latest in electronic music, pop and retro rock. **Bartolomeo** in Congreso (Bartolomé Mitre 1525, 4372 2843) has local music (tango, jazz, blues and latino) from Thursdays through Saturdays, and theatre performances in the underground room on Thursdays. Tickets cost AR$3-$5. **Milión** (*see p130*) in Recoleta uses a small part of its large mansion to provide an intimate setting

for live music on Wednesday nights, while **Imaginario** (www.imaginariocultural.com.ar) at Bulnes and Guardia Vieja in the heart of Abasto, has a basement where funk and rock bands play through a permanent fog of cigarette smoke.

Clubs

Some of BA's discos incorporate live bands before and during dance sessions. **Niceto Club** in Palermo Viejo is a cutting-edge place for techno-pop, funk and performance art. Another Palermo club, **Podestá Super Club de Copas**, acts as a venue for new pop bands. For both, *see chapter* **Clubs**.

Peñas

Peñas are where you can experience the typical *folklore* sounds and taste the regional cuisines of Argentina's interior provinces.

Del Colorado

Güemes 3657, entre Salguero y Vidt, Palermo (4822 1038/www.delcolorado.com.ar). Subte D, Bulnes/29, 39, 92, 111, 152 bus. **Opens** from 8pm daily. *Shows* 10pm Fri, Sat. **Tickets** AR$5-$7. **No credit cards. Map** p279 I5.

Between sips of *mate*, customers strum and sing their own traditional sounds within the brick walls of this welcoming, warm (too much so in summer) venue.

La Peña del Abasto

Anchorena 571, entre Lavalle y Pasaje Carlos Gardel, Abasto (5076 0148). Subte B, Gardel/24, 26, 124, 168 bus. **Open** *Shows* 10pm Fri-Sun. **Tickets** AR$7-$10. **No credit cards. Map** p278 G4.

At this *folklore* centre in the heart of the tango district, you may be lucky enough to hear guitar player Luis Salinas and other virtuosi pushing the trad envelope. If the music moves you, there's dancing to be done. It also hosts spontaneous *peñas libres*, where members of the public bring in their own instruments and jam on stage – though with more respect for tradition than for improvisation.

Arts & Entertainment

Sport & Fitness

An essential stop for any football pilgrim, Buenos Aires has plenty to delight fans and practitioners of other sporting disciplines, too.

Spectator sports

Argentina's sporting history is studded with greats – formidable athletes who combine natural ability, determination and pragmatism. What's more, teams can rely on a special kind of support; whatever the event, Argentinian fans turn up en masse ready to cheer and sing.

Sport is a life-affecting endeavour; the economic upturn predicted to follow the longed-for victory of the national football squad in the 2002 World Cup never came about when they were promptly knocked out in the first round (though it could justly be argued that economic recovery relied on weightier factors).

Although most of the plaudits usually revolve around football, excellence is not just a footy thing; Argentina boasts the number one women's hockey team (Las Leonas, 'the lionesses'), the world's best polo players, a respected rugby team (called – keeping up the big cats theme – Los Pumas), NBA star Emanuel 'Manu' Ginóbili and a group of brilliant young tennis players known as 'la legión argentina'. In fact, the only real sporting disappointment is that so many top atheletes perform outside the country.

Despite today's glut of talent, there's an overwhelming sense of nostalgia. Walk down Lavalle Street on any given day and you'll find scores of men gesticulating excitedly at televised replays of sporting events from years ago. Visually, the city is plastered with sports memorabilia – on newsstands and in bars, collectors' emporia and the stadiums themselves. Investment has also been made in two new sports museums, one dedicated to Boca Juniors football team (see p73) and a rugby museum in San Isidro (see p96). River Plate football team also plan to open their own museum (currently scheduled for 2005).

Football is the main event for spectators (see p198), though basketball continues to grow in popularity (see below). Any week in Buenos Aires (except in January) offers a huge choice of footy matches and venues. On the other side of the tracks, both geographically and socially, is polo (see p200). Equestrian sports, in general, are popular, and there is an in-town race track, plus a grass track in San Isidro (see p199).

For shops selling sporting goods, see p159.

Basketball

In the 2002 World Basketball Championships, the Argentinian national team became the first foreign squad to beat the US Dream Team in international competition. The victory, resulted in two Argentinians, Pepe Sánchez and Manu Ginóbili, being picked to play in the NBA, the latter becoming an integral figure in the San Antonio Spurs 2003 championship run.

On the local scene, the phenomenon is more pronounced in the interior than in BA, which has only three important teams: best to watch being Boca Juniors (whose home court is La Bombonerita) and Obras Sanitarias. La Liga Nacional de Básquetbol (the national league) runs from October to June; matches are usually on Friday and Sunday evenings at 8 or 9pm.

Estadio Luis Conde (La Bombonerita)
Arzobispo Espinoza 600, y Palos, La Boca (4309 4748/www.bocajuniors.com.ar). Bus 10, 24, 29, 53, 64, 152. **Tickets** AR$2-$10. **No credit cards.** **Map** p276 A5.

Club Atlético Obras Sanitarias de la Nación
Avenida del Libertador 7395, entre Crisólogo Larralde y Campos Salles, Núñez (4702 4655/4702 9467/www.clubosn.com.ar). Bus 15, 29, 130. **Tickets** AR$8-$12; free under-12s. **No credit cards.** **Map** p281 O6.

Boxing

Boxing was very much part of the local sporting calendar until the mid 1980s. **Luna Park** (see p193), BA's version of Madison Square Garden, used to attract enormous crowds. Today, it's mostly used as a cultural venue, though since early 2003, the red carpet is rolled out every month or so for the glamorous ritual of the Saturday night fight. Smaller bouts are staged at the stadium of the Federación Argentina de Box (capacity 3,000).

Federación Argentina de Box
Castro Barros 75, y Rivadavia, Almagro (4981 8615). Subte A, Castro Barros/86, 128, 160 bus. **Closed** mid Dec-mid Jan. **Tickets** AR$10-$25. **No credit cards.** **Map** p274 D3.
Can also recommend boxing instructors for lessons.

Local heroes

In Buenos Aires, football is not just a macho thing. When prompted, women, teens and toddlers will all be able to tell you who is their favourite team. The city's two most famous sides, locally and internationally, are Boca Juniors and River Plate. Both have die-hard fan bases and their fiercely fought derby matches (*superclásicos*) are the stuff of legend.

Boca's stadium, La Bombonera, remains the heart and soul of the barrio of La Boca and is worth a visit, even if you don't see a game, while their erstwhile superstar player Diego Maradona is still a national icon.

But Boca is not the only team. In order correctly to answer the one question you are certain to be asked during your stay in Buenos Aires – '*¿sos hincha de quién?*' (who are you a fan of?) – best get acquainted fast with the city's number one passion.

This bluffer's guide will help you pick your local team – and decide what football shirt or souvenir to go home with. Note: *barra brava* is the name of the team's toughest hardcore fan group (ie, the hooligan faction).

Boca Juniors

Stadium: La Bombonera, La Boca (capacity 60,245).
Nickname: Fans – Xeneizes (Genovese, for the Italian immigrant population; River fans call them Bosteros, or dung men); *barra brava* – La Doce (12, the country's most vociferous thugs, so loud, they are said to be a worth a twelfth player).
Biggest stars: Diego Maradona, Gabriel Batistuta, Carlos Tevez.
Finest hour: December 2003, Tokyo: Intercontinental champions for the third time, beating AC Milan in a penalty shoot-out.
Biggest downer: Boca wait eleven long years (1981-92) for a league championship title.
Titles: Intercontinental x 3, Copa Libertadores x 5, Campeonatos Nacionales x 20.

Football

Each club has its own stadium – 30 within a comparatively small area – and there are at least five top-flight matches at weekends; hardcore fans can easily get worn out. The league is split into Primera A, equivalent to England's premier league, and Primera B, a second division which breaks down regionally (Metropolitana, Nacional, and so on). Once you go down to Primera C level, the standard is more akin to a schoolyard kick-about. There are two annual championships on the football calendar – Apertura (August-December) and Clausura (February-July).

Seeing a match, especially at La Bombonera stadium, is one of the ultimate BA experiences. Come kick-off time, a cacophonous cocktail of fireworks and abuse greets players and ref alike. Buy your ticket in advance, and get a seat in the *platea* (the seated area). Down in the standing-room-only *popular*, it's more tribal. Note that the better a team is doing, the higher the *platea* price; standard ticket prices are AR$10-$40, rising to AR$100 if a team is heading for a title win.

Dress down, don't carry valuables or potentially dangerous implements and take care when leaving the stadium at night. You can buy tickets for Boca or River through **Ticketek** (5237 7200, MasterCard only), or for any team at their ground (cash only). Go with a local fan or one of the companies that escort tourists to matches (they guarantee good seats and transport, for a premium price of US$35-$50). **Argensud** (4326 6604, www.buenosaires. com, then search for football promotions) and **Go Football** (4816 2681, www.gofootball. com.ar) are recommendable options.

Estadio Alberto J Armando (La Bombonera)

Brandsen 805, y la Vía, La Boca (4309 4700/ www.bocajuniors.com.ar). Bus 10, 24, 29, 53, 64. **Map** p276 A5.
Watching a game here is a unique and vertiginous experience: the concrete stands vibrate and at the higher levels you feel like a wrong move will tip you out onto the pitch itself. The *platea baja* in the stands area is your recommended vantage point. There's also a museum, plus guided tours of the grounds; *see p72.*

Estadio José Amalfitani

Avenida Juan B Justo 9200, y Jonte, Liniers (4641 5663/5763/www.velezsarsfield.com). Train from Once to Liniers/2, 52, 86, 106 bus.
Renovated for when Argentina hosted the 1978 World Cup and well maintained ever since, this comfortable stadium is the home ground of Vélez

River Plate

Stadium: El Monumental, Núñez (capacity 66,449).
Nickname: Fans – most River fans are known as Los Milionarios, an alusion to their superior financial status (the stadium is in the city's wealthy northern area). But Boca fans call them Las Gallinas, or chickens; *barra brava* – Los Borrachos del Tablón (*borrachos* means drunks, *tablón* is stands; enough said).
Biggest stars: Alfredo Di Stéfano, Enzo Francescoli, Pablo Aimar, Hernán Crespo.
Finest hour: 1986: River Plate win the league, Intercontinental and Libertador trophies.

Biggest downer: The 1966 final of the Copa Libertadores; River lose a 2-0 lead against Uruguay's Penarol.
Titles: Intercontinental x 1, Copa Libertadores x 2, Campeonatos Nacionales x 31.

Independiente

Stadium: Doble Visera de Cemento, Avellaneda (capacity 57,901)
Nicknames: Fans – Los Diablos Rojos (the Red Devils); *barra brava* – 4 de Julio (named after a rough area of tower blocks in Avellaneda).
Biggest stars: Ricardo 'El Bocha' Bochini, Jorge Burruchaga.
Finest hour: 1972, fourth time lucky: Independiente 1, Juventus 0 – Independiente finally conquer the world.
Biggest downer: 1928, construction finishes on their stadium, a happy fact if it weren't one of the ugliest in the world.
Titles: Intercontinental x 2, Copa Libertadores x 7, Campeonatos Nacionales x 13. ▶

Sarfield who beat Milan in 1994 to become World Club Champions. It also hosts matches between smaller clubs and bigger, more popular teams.

Estadio Monumental

Avenida Figueroa Alcorta 7597, y Udaondo, Nuñez (4788 1210/1200/www.cariverplate.com.ar). Bus 12, 29, 42, 107, 130. **Map** p281 O6.
The Monumental – home to Club Atlético River Plate, eternal rivals of Boca Juniors – was the setting for the opening and the final of the 1978 World Cup. It's the largest stadium in the country and, thanks to its location, probably the safest. It's also the only all-seater stadium in Buenos Aires that meets FIFA standards.

Horse racing

Introduced by the British, horse racing – called here by the English word turf – is one of the city's oldest sports. Turf's main venue, the elegant Hipódromo Argentino (which can accommodate 100,000 spectators) is in Palermo. The palatial building housing the main stands and *confitería* was designed by French architect Faure Dujarric and opened in 1908. Even if you don't end up backing the winner, you'll enjoy the eccentric cast of characters who gather here on race days. The biggest day on the racing calendar is the Gran Premio Nacional, held in November, although there are around ten regular meetings per month, usually Mondays, Saturdays and Sundays. The other major race on the calendar is the Gran Premio Carlos Pellegrini, run in December at the smart, family oriented Hipódromo de San Isidro in Zona Norte – the only grass track in Argentina – with flat races on Wednesdays, Saturdays and some Sundays.

Hipódromo Argentino de Palermo

Avenida del Libertador 4101, y Dorrego, Palermo (4778 2800/www.palermo.com.ar). Bus 10, 37, 160. **Tickets** AR$1-$10; free under-12s. **No credit cards. Map** p279 K6/L6.
Under-18s must be accompanied by an adult. For guided tours of the Villa Hipica, telephone 4778 2820.

Hipódromo de San Isidro

Avenida Márquez 504, y Santa Fe, San Isidro (4743 4010/4743 4011/www.hipodromosanisidro.com.ar). Train from Retiro to San Isidro. **Tickets** AR$1-$5. **No credit cards.**

Motor racing

Though you can no longer hear the roar of Formula 1 racing at the Autódromo, the layout is exactly the same as it was in the days of Juan Manuel Fangio, five-times world champion in

Local heroes (continued)

Racing Club

Stadium: Presidente Perón, Avellaneda (capacity 55,000).

Nicknames: Fans – La Academia; *barra brava* – La Guardia Imperial (who claim to be toughest, though other *barras bravas*, such as Los 95s and La Racing Stone, after the Rolling Stones, would disagree). Racing was also Perón's favourite team and President Kirchner is a fan, though this hasn't yet produced any new nicknames.

Biggest stars: Claudio 'El Piojo' López, Rubén Paz.

Finest hour: Coach 'Mostaza' Merlo leads Racing to victory in the Apertura in 2001...

Biggest downer: ...they had been waiting for 35 years.

Titles: Intercontinental x 1, Copa Libertador x 1, Campeonatos Nacionales x 7.

San Lorenzo

Stadium: Nuevo Gasómetro, Bajo Flores (capacity 42,000).

Nicknames: Fans – Los Cuervos (crows); *barra brava* – La Buteler (an area of Bajo Flores).

Biggest stars: Nestor Gorosito, Oscar Ruggeri.

Finest hour: Arch-rivals Huracán are demoted to the Primera B in 2002.

Biggest downer: In 2001, Huracán fans steal San Lorenzo's 2,800-square-metre (30,108-square-foot) flag.

Titles: Campeonatos Nacionales x 9.

---

the 1950s, and a national sporting idol. Argentinian motor racing (*automóvilismo*) today lacks any really outstanding drivers on the international scene but still maintains an attractive local calendar, with two main categories: Turismo Carretera (with very powerful cars that must be more than 25 years old) and the TC 2000, for souped-up saloon cars.

Autódromo de la Ciudad de Buenos Aires Oscar Gálvez

Avenida Roca y General Paz, Villa Lugano (4605 3333). Bus 21, 28, 114, 141. **Tickets** AR$10-$100. **No credit cards**.

Races are held most Fridays, Saturdays and Sundays, and there is stock car racing some Fridays at 8.30pm.

Pato

Although *pato* holds the title of Argentina's national sport, most people in Buenos Aires have never seen it, let alone played it. The game is a bizarre cross between polo and a previously popular, but now extinct sport, *pelota al cesto*. Originally played with a dead duck wrapped in leather straps, a ball has now replaced the unfortunate fowl. If you can catch a match, it's a unique spectacle; the main tournament runs in November/December. The ground is 50 minutes outside town – entrance is usually free.

Campo Argentino de Pato

Ruta 8, at km 30, Campo de Mayo, San Miguel (information 4331 0222/www.fedpato.com.ar). Train from Chacarita to Sargento Cabral. **Games** Sat, Sun.

Polo

Polo is played in Buenos Aires from September to November, which is the golden month when the venerable Abierto Argentino de Palermo (Argentinian Open – *see p163*) is contested. Top teams include La Aguada, Ellerstina, Indios Chapaleufú I and II and La Dolfina. The latter has the added, if rather incongruous support of football team Nuevo Chicago's most vocal fans.

Beginners and experienced players can have polo lessons at several *estancias* in Buenos Aires province: **La Martina** (*see p231*) is top notch.

Campo Argentino de Polo de Palermo

Avenida del Libertador 4000, y Dorrego, Palermo (information Asociación Argentina de Polo 4342 8321/www.aapolo.com). Bus 15, 29, 55, 60, 64. **Tickets** AR$12-$55; Argentinian Open AR$14-$160. **Map** p279 K6/L6.

A wonderful polo field, in the heart of the city, with capacity for 45,000. The Argentinian Open tournament is over 100 years old. Tickets for all tournaments are available from Ticketek (5237 7200).

Arts & Entertainment

Rugby

The national team, Los Pumas – which takes its name from the native Argentinian big cat – had a difficult decade after the retirement of Hugo Porta (the best Argentinian rugby player of all time), but has resurfaced in recent years. Now players like Agustin Pichot with his legendary pack are rated among the world's best.

Major rugby internationals are played at Estadio Monumental (*see p199*). In the normally respectful world of international rugby, watching Los Pumas is a unique experience; fans boo during the opposing team's national anthems and blow cow horns as the enemy attempts a conversion.

On the domestic scene, two teams from the northern suburb of San Isidro dominate; Club Atlético de San Isidro (CASI) and the San Isidro Club (SIC). Their match is the apex of the season (known as '*el superclásico del rugby*') that runs from April to October. Because Argentinian rugby is still an amateur sport, the clubs do not have huge stadiums, so spectators enjoy a close view of the game.

Club Atlético de San Isidro
Roque Sáenz Peña 499, y 25 de Mayo, San Isidro (4373 4242). Train from Retiro to San Isidro. **Tickets** AR$7; AR$3 13-18s; free under-13s. **No credit cards**.

San Isidro Club
Blanco Encalada 404, entre Sucre y Darregueira, San Isidro (4763 6374/www.sanisidroclub.com.ar). Bus 60 (Panamericana line). **Tickets** AR$5; AR$2.50 7-15s; free under-7s. **No credit cards**.

Tennis

Guillermo Villas had a wicked backhand and Gabriella Sabatini was appreciated for more than just her playing talent, but these days fans are talking about young tennis stars Guillermo 'El Mago' Coria and David Nabaldián. They have raced their way up the Association of Tennis Professionals (ATP) ratings and they are not alone; take a look down the ATP top 50 players and you should see at least a couple of other Argentinians. The only annual international event in Buenos Aires which spectators can enjoy is the Copa AT&T, which takes place in mid February. The major local tournament is the Copa Argentina in December. Both are played at Buenos Aires Lawn Tenis Club.

Buenos Aires Lawn Tenis Club
Olleros 1510, y Libertador, Palermo (4772 0983/9227). Train to Lisandro de la Torre/ 15, 29, 59, 60 bus. **Tickets** AR$18-$100. **No credit cards**. **Map** p281 M6.

Participation sports

Buenos Aires is paradise for budding Beckhams. On any open space, you'll find children, teenagers and adults playing on improvised pitches, shouting '*golazo*' ('gooooaaaaaal') every time the ball slips through the posts. At weekends, the parks are full of people playing *picados*, as informal games are called. If you want to play, just ask – *porteños* are often more than happy to welcome

La Aguada and La Dolfina battle it out in the 2003 Argentinian Open final at the **Campo de Polo**. *See p200.*

Arts & Entertainment

a stranger into the game. Alternatively, turn up to one of the city's many *canchas* (five- or seven-a-side football pitches) and you should be able to get a game going.

Apart from football, Buenos Aires has no great leisure sporting culture and little development in amateur sports. However, the city government supports various free activities (from volleyball to aerobics classes) in some public parks. Those that are the most accessible and in the best condition are the Parque 3 de Febrero in Palermo (*see p84*) and the Costanera Sur (*see p91*), which serves as the gateway to the Reserva Ecológica.

Otherwise, there are a host of multi-sport venues (*centros deportivos*). Two recommended for their location and facilities are: **Punta Carrasco** (Avenida Costanera Rafael Obligado y Sarmiento, 4807 1010, www.puntacarrasco. com.ar) in Costanera Norte or, closer to the centre, **Club de Amigos** (Avenida Figueroa Alcorta 3885, Palermo, 4801 1213, www.clubdeamigos.org.ar). Both have outdoor swimming pools (open in summer months – December to February – only), tennis courts and football pitches. The former also offers beach volleyball, and the latter has a covered pool, Astroturf hockey pitches and a gym.

Not surprisingly, with a huge river lapping at its edges, Buenos Aires boasts lots of water-related sports – kite-surfing, kayaking, windsurfing, sailing, parasailing – though you'll need to head out to the less polluted waters of Zona Norte. **Perú Beach** (Elcano 794, Acassuso, 4798 2759/4793 5986 climbing wall, www.peru-beach.com.ar) is one of the best. As well as kite surfing and windsurfing, it offers climbing, roller hockey, skateboarding, football and plenty of chill out space – a bar, DJs, and a riverside lawn.

Cycling

Buenos Aires is not very bike-friendly. Even though the government has built many *bicisendas* (cycle paths shared with pedestrians) and *ciclovías* (shared with cars), the general lack of respect shown by drivers means that cycling as a method of transport is not recommended.

Nevertheless, there are decent guided bike tours with a choice of circuits (*see p55* **Guided tours**; these companies also offer bike hire). Or use the cycle paths in Palermo's Parque Tres de Febrero. Bike hire is available close by at **Bicicleterías Saúl** (Salguero y Cabello or San Benito y Libertad, 15 4916 5645) for AR$4 per hour (take ID). The **Reserva Ecológica** (*see p91*) is a great spot too, but you'll need your own wheels. Or use the **Circuito KDT** (Avenida Castillo y Salguero, Costanera Norte,

4807 7700), which belongs to the Club Federación Ciclista Argentina. Admission costs a modest AR$2; cycle hire is AR$2.50-$4.50 per hour and there are also *parrillas* and a bar.

Fishing

There's stunning fly-fishing far from the city, in Patagonia and other regions, but fishing in the Rio de la Plata is a dirty (and unpredictable) business. Although you will see some locals throwing out a line on the Costanera Norte – and there is a fishing club for members only, you should head upriver, or deeper into the basin, for any action. Your best option is San Pedro, 150 kilometres (93 miles) up the coast where you can fish for two feisty local species – *dorados* and *surubíes*. Daniel Beilinson (4311 1222, dbeilinson@flyfishingcaribe.com) is an experienced guide who can take you there on a day trip (US$400 for two adults, tackle, transport and lunch included).

Football

If you want more than a kick around in the park look for the words *cancha de fútbol* (football pitch); there are hundreds of them. They generally have long opening hours, and pitch hire will set you back around AR$60-$80 per hour (depending on the time of day). Two of the bigger five-a-side centres are **Catalinas Fútbol y Paddle** (Avenida Eduardo Madero 1220, 4315 1138) and **Claudio Marangoni** (Coronel Díaz y French, 4805 4210, www. claudiomarangoni.com.ar) with artificial grass.

Golf

Campo de Golf de la Ciudad de Buenos Aires

Avenida Torquinst 6397, entre Olleros y Alsisa, Palermo (4772 7261/7576). Bus 42, 107, 130. **Open** 7am-5pm daily. **Rates** AR$10-$30; AR$8-$10 under-18s. **No credit cards. Map** p281 M6.
This well located, popular 18-holer is challenging in terms of length (6,585 yards) and bunker placements. Club hire costs AR$30 extra, carts are AR$5-$10, and you'll have to buy balls from the shop (AR$12 for 6). Information on other golf courses further afield in Argentina is available at www.aag.com.ar.

Costa Salguero Golf Center

Avenida Costanera Rafael Obligado, y Salguero, Costanera Norte (4805 4734/4732/www.costasalguero golf.com.ar). Bus 33, 45. **Open** noon-10.30pm Mon; 8am-10.30pm Tue-Fri; 8am-9.30pm Sat, Sun. **Rates** AR$6-$10.50. **Credit** AmEx, MC. **Map** p279 J8.
Located on the Costanera Norte, with a spectacular view of the rarely seen River Plate. Ball rental is AR$5 for 50 balls, while clubs are AR$2-$4.50 each.

Horse riding

Argentina is renowned for its horsemanship, but city options are limited – head to a ranch (*see p230* **Estancias**) or try these two centres.

Club Alemán de Equitación

Avenida Dorrego 4045, y Lugones, Palermo (4778 7060/www.robertotagle.com). Bus 37, 130, 160. **Open** 9am-1pm, 3-8pm Tue-Sun. **Rates** AR$50 per class for 45 mins. **No credit cards. Map** p279 K7.
This club offers instruction for all standards (including showjumping). Once you've taken your test, you'll be allocated a suitable level, and offered the choice between individual or group lesson.

Club Hípico Buenos Aires

Avenida Figueroa Alcorta 4800, entre Roldán y Dorrego, Palermo (4778 1982/4777 8777/www. escuelahipocampo.org). Bus 37, 130, 160. **Open** 8am-8pm Tue-Sun. **Rates** AR$35-$45 per class for 45 mins. **No credit cards. Map** p279 K7.
An expertly run school offering classes, showjumping training, a pony club and, once a month, a full-day or night-time ride for AR$75 – call for details.

Karting

Kartódromo Argentino

Avenida Roca, y General Paz, Villa Lugano (4605 1383/www.kartodromoargentino.com). Bus 21, 28, 114, 141. **Open** 6pm-midnight Thur-Sun. **Rates** AR$20-$30. **No credit cards.**
Sharing premises with the Autódromo (*see p200*), drivers can compete in a ten-lap race, once the pecking order is established. The price includes all the extras (racing overalls with elbow and knee pads, gloves and helmet), and the use of the mini-pits, but there is no ambulance or medical team on-site.

Pool/billiards

You won't have to hunt too hard for a game of pool. There are numerous specialist pool bars; **Deep Blue** (*see p126*) has the best atmosphere, or try **Tazz** (Serrano 4835, Palermo Viejo, 4808 9545). Other bars, like friendly **Gibraltar** (*see*

p129) in San Telmo, have the odd table stuck out the back, and even the esteemed old **Café Tortoni** (*see p125*) has a pool room. Rules may vary from what you are used to back home, so double check before you challenge a local.

36 Billares

Avenida de Mayo 1265, entre Salta y Santiago del Estero, Congreso (4381 5696). Subte A, Saénz Peña/ 39, 56, 64, 86 bus. **Open** 8am-2am Mon-Thur; 8am-6am Fri, Sat; 3pm-midnight Sun. **Rates** AR$6 per hr. **No credit cards. Map** p277 E6.
A historical café and billiard/pool hall – it's over 100 years old – where poet Federico García Lorca used to have coffee. The tables are in the basement.

Racquet sports

The *centros deportivos* (*see p202*) also have tennis and squash courts.

Catedral Squash

1st floor, Defensa 267, entre Alsina y Moreno, Monserrat (4345 5511/www.catedralsquash. com.ar). Subte A, Plaza de Mayo or D, Catedral or E, Bolívar/29, 130, 152 bus. **Open** 8am-10pm Mon-Fri; 11am-7pm Sat. **Rates** AR$16-$22. **No credit cards. Map** p277 D7.
There are five courts on the first floor, rackets available to rent (AR$2) but rather manky balls. We advise you to buy your own ball beforehand. Day use of the gym facilities costs just AR$10.

Salguero Tenis

Salguero 3350, y Figueroa Alcorta, Palermo (4805 5144). Bus 37, 67, 102, 130. **Open** 8am-midnight Mon-Sat; 8am-9pm Sun. **Rates** Tennis AR$22-$27; squash AR$14-$18; paddle AR$15-$18. **No credit cards. Map** p278 I7.
Tennis (open-air clay courts), squash and paddle (a cross between the two) are on offer, plus free parking.

Running

The Palermo Parque Tres de Febrero and Parque Thays (for both, *see chapter* **North of the Centre**) are popular with joggers and runners. However, there are no clay tracks, so you have to

The storming **Campo de Golf de la Ciudad**. *See p202.*

alternate between grass and pavement. Around the Palermo lakes, there are marked paths for runners and cyclists, but they are not much respected by other users. If you are downtown, the best bets are the flat promenades along Puerto Madero, down into the lovely, red-earth Reserva Ecológica (*see p91*).

Swimming

Whatever you do, don't swim in the River Plate anywhere near the city centre – it's too polluted (though once away from town, there are places where you can bathe, if you don't mind the brown water). Most gym chains have at least some premises with pools too – **Megatlón** (*listings below*) has several. Hotel pools generally open to non-guests for a daily or monthly fee. The loveliest outdoor pool is at the **Hilton** (*see p35*; day use pool and spa AR$65-$95); for undercover swimming, head to the stunning Le Mirage pool and spa on the 23rd floor of the **Crowne Plaza Panamericano** (*see p35*; day use pool only AR$80) – it has a small outside sun deck too. A cheaper bet for a summer dip is one of the multi-purpose sports clubs (*see p202*). You will usually have to submit yourself to a brief medical inspection before swimming.

Watersports

Most of the aquatic and nautical activities on the River Plate are concentrated in Zona Norte, 45 minutes from the city centre. In addition to **Perú Beach** (*see p202*), at **Wakeboard** in San Fernando (Avenida del Libertador 1999, 4725 0260, www.wake-board.com.ar), you can take lessons in waterskiing and wakeboarding. A 25-minute class, using one of the school's boats, costs AR$45. Add AR$35 to cover ski hire, lifejackets and ropes and handles. At **El Molino** in Acassuso (El Cano 888, 4742 5428) a single lesson costs $30 for windsurfing, $50 for kitesurfing; longer courses come cheaper. Of course, with BA's gentle waters, sailing is big. With a recognised helmsman's certificate, you can charter a boat for a reasonable AR$300-$500 per day, or, for upwards of AR$1,000 per day, rent out a motorboat complete with crew and picnic. The second day's rental is half price for both. Contact skipper **John Wright**, who operates out of Puerto Madero (4361 5403/15 5108 1584). If you are still learning, you can take sailing lessons out of Dársena Norte. Call the Yacht Club Argentino (4314 0505, www. yca.org.ar); they will direct you to the best qualified instructor for your needs.

Punta Carrasco's pool. *See p202.*

Fitness

Gyms & spas

Buenos Aires gyms are generally well-equipped and fashion conscious; skin-hugging Lycra, make-up and a healthy tan are the standard accessories. For a day's work-out or a quick swim, it's cheapest to go to one of the multi-sport complexes (*see p202*). Most posh hotels allow non-guests to use their gym/spa for a daily fee of AR$50 upwards (*see chapter* **Where to stay**). Or try these health clubs:

Megatlon

Rodríguez Peña 1062, entre Marcelo T de Alvear y Santa Fe, Recoleta (4816 7009/www.megatlon.com). Subte D, Callao/37, 39, 111, 152 bus. **Open** 24hrs from 7am Mon-8pm Sat; 10am-6pm Sun. **Rates** AR$15 per day; AR$80-$90 per mth. **Credit** AmEx, DC, MC, V. **Map** p278 G6.
Slick, clean and busy, the Megatlon chain has all the latest gadgets and a wide range of classes, as well as day access. Membership entitles you to use their 10 branches around the city. The Recoleta branch also offers tango classes for an additional fee.
Other locations: Throughout the city

Le Parc Gym & Spa

San Martín 645, entre Tucumán y Viamonte, Microcentro (4311 9191/www.leparc.com). Subte B, Florida/6, 26, 93, 130, 152 bus. **Open** 7am-11pm Mon-Fri; 10am-8pm Sat. **Rates** AR$20 per day; AR$175 per mth. **Credit** AmEx, DC, MC, V. **Map** p277 E7.
One of the city's most exclusive health clubs, with computerised exercise machines, swimming pool, squash courts, sauna and beauty treatments.

Pilates

Tamara Di Tella Pilates

Araoz y Juncal, Palermo (4833 0603/www.cuerpo diet.com). Subte D, Scalabrini Ortiz/37, 41, 60, 102 bus. **Open** 8am-9pm Mon-Fri; 9am-1pm Sat. **Rates** AR$30 group class, AR$40 private. **Credit** AmEx, DC, MC, V. **Map** p278 I6.
Tamara Di Tella is Latin America's queen of pilates; there are ten high-tech, pristine locations (and more opening all the time) for you to stretch and tone.
Other locations: Throughout the city.

Yoga

All the city's main gyms offer yoga classes (*see above*). Alternatively go to major specialist centre **Fundación Hastinapura** (Venezuela 818, Monserrat, 4342 4250, www.hastinapura. org.ar). It teaches all levels, with variants of Hatha yoga, such as Karma and Raja, among others, on offer. Single classes cost AR$5, and there are locations throughout the city.

Arts & Entertainment

Tango

The city's tragically sensual dance is alive and kicking, supported by an exciting musical revival, and the tango spirit – for better or worse – is everywhere.

Remember 'Everybody Salsa'? Well, be warned – some misguided crossover pop outfit is probably busy recording 'Everybody Tango' right now. Yep, the old, cold, dusty, nostalgic, passionate (and other well-worn clichés) dance of downtown Buenos Aires is booming and assorted Latino crooners with an eye for fashion (and hard cash) – from Julio Iglesias to Shakira – are giving tango a whirl. Old rockers are testing their tonsils on tango tunes, cafés and clubs are giving dance classes round the clock and there are new cabaret-style shows opening every month.

The upside of this commercial boom is a hatful of offbeat but inspired takes on a sometimes tired vernacular. This includes slick tango *electrónica* from Paris-based trendsetters Gotan Project or the Buenos Aires-based Bajofondo Tango Club collective, downbeat dub tango in a Tom Waits style by Argentinian ex-rocker Daniel Melingo and carnivalesque *milonga*-style tangos from Juan Carlos Caceres, also local. The drawback is you have to be on guard to quickstep past the crasser, overacted tango shows invading Buenos Aires' barrios and bizarre ventures such as *Gardelias, femmes flambés*, the 'first ever erotic tango show'. The theatres – once closely linked to tango through the *sainete* (music hall) culture of the '20s and '30s – are returning to the theme too, whether through dramas about tango greats like *Discepolín y yo* or in cannily themed extravaganzas such as the *Tango: Love & Sex* at the Teatro Avenida (*see p219*).

Whatever the excesses, the homegrown, amateur dance scene is thriving at the *milongas* (dance halls). Traditional tango music is very much alive too. In any one week, there will be concerts by local heroes like Julio Pane, who plays the *bandoneón* (the button accordion essential to tango) or singer Adriana Varela (*see p214* **Mi Buenos Aires Querido**) and several orchestras playing live (usually free) at municipal theatres, cultural centres or even on the streets of San Telmo for Sundays market in Plaza Dorrego. There are also live quintets and small bands at the Torquato Tasso, Club Del Vino or Canning clubs, and, if you're really lucky, some superstar act like Daniel Barenboim or the Sexteto Mayor doing grand tangos at the Colón theatre.

For all this, some think tango has had its day and is an anodyne fixation for a culture too slothful to enter a new, more relevant phase. But few would deny that Buenos Aires and tango are inextricably linked. That tango should be exploited by private and public sectors looking for the tourist buck is unsurprising, so to avoid a cheesy or merely dull night out, check the listings in this chapter before booking a show, searching for artists to see, or looking for your first lessons. Even if you're not moved to get into tango – and it's not the easiest of world music genres to penetrate – do gen up on the history and the broader culture of tango for a better understanding of *porteños* and their rich cultural heritage.

HISTORY FOR BEGINNERS

First appearing around 1880, the dance had its debut in Buenos Aires' outlying immigrant quarters, where Italians, Spaniards, blacks and urban gaucho *criollos* uprooted from the pampas brought together elements of *habanera*, polka, Spanish *contradanza* and Argentinian *milonga* (country songs) to create a new beat.

Responding to this hybrid sound, the local *compadritos* (small-time hoods) forged a lively, leg-twitching bop, which simulated the violent knife fights that characterised life in the *arrabales* (slums). Some tango historians believe

Abasto's walls proclaim its tango heritage.

the early dances were a send-up of those performed by black Africans, and links have been traced to 500-year-old dances in Angola.

It was in this context that *lunfardo* – BA's unique street slang – evolved, as the semi-literate *compadritos* modified the Spanish language, mixing in Italian and Genovese words and, occasionally, the names of products or local businesses. Like young guns everywhere, they wanted to show that they belonged to a group and a particularly cool one, at that; at the same time, the slang helped them to communicate without the authorities – police, jailers, even their parents – understanding what they were saying.

In the city's southern barrios of Pompeya, La Boca and Barracas, life moved to the rhythm of tango and the romance of *el Sur* was given its first impulse. From humble beginnings in social and football clubs, tango moved to more central *boites* (salons) and the richer residents of Recoleta and Palermo began to take an interest in this new fashion. Between 1870 and 1910, the dance was transformed from a morally dubious jig of the underclasses into the latest craze of the *niños bien* (rich kids).

To become truly acceptable to the upper classes, though, tango had to be shown worthy of European culture. As early as 1906, tango scores had travelled to France and by 1910 the dance was consecrated as the preferred dance of the Parisian bourgeoisie. London and New York were quick to follow suit. This excursion overseas sealed it for Buenos Aires, and tango was no longer a scandalous, proletarian affair. By the time the brothels were banned in 1919, tango was already as respectable as the waltz, but far more exciting.

Tango took a new musical turn with *tango canción* (tango song) when Carlos Gardel recorded 'Mi Noche Triste' in 1917. Though tango-like songs had been set to music before, this is recognised as the first true sung tango in terms of its structure and Gardel's vocal style. Of obscure roots, Gardel incarnates the *porteño* model of the working-class immigrant made good (a myth that often obscures his musical achievements), but for audiences in the 1920s it was his emotive tenor voice that made him a star. After establishing a name for himself as a *payador*, singing country songs to guitar accompaniment, he gradually moved to tango, becoming its leading exponent and ambassador. His life, musical career and the films he made in the US exemplify the social metamorphosis of tango from impromptu suburban bop to cross-cultural classless art form.

At the same time, the musical form moved on, trios becoming sextets to provide a richer sound for the dance halls. By the late 1930s, *orquestas típicas* – four *bandoneóns*, four

The best Tango spots

La Catedral
Catch cool new *tangueros* and avant-garde artistes. *See p211.*

Centro Cultural Torquato Tasso
Where to see great live shows and lively dancing. *See p211.*

La Esquina de Carlos Gardel
For razzamatazz and high kicks. *See p214.*

Salon Canning
For traditional dancing in suits and split skirts. *See p211.*

San Juan and Boedo
Hang out on this street corner to feel like a tango-loving hood.

San Telmo barrio
Nowhere else evokes the turn of the century tangopolis so well. *See p69.*

violins, piano and double bass – were the darlings of the salon and dozens of them played the circuit. Conservatory-trained Italians, such as Juan de Dios Filiberto and Julio De Caro, made tango more sophisticated, Filiberto in a traditional vein and De Caro exploring tango's potential as an evolving, experimental form. Just as the adoption of tango by the middle classes conveniently ignored its origins, so the importance of the dance's black roots was forgotten as tango shed its folky origins and took on classical airs; even in contemporary histories, tango is presented as a very white, European affair.

From the 1920s on, tango was the 'in' thing in Buenos Aires and the artists of this period – all those named above as well as conductor Osvaldo Fresedo, lyricist Enrique Santos Discépolo and Francisco Canaro – make up the bulk of its most famous exponents. Booms in film, radio and the recording industry helped its success. In the late 1930s and '40s, new talents emerged, among them two giants: composer and *bandoneón* player extraordinaire Anibal Troilo and composer Osvaldo Pugliese. Troilo's orchestra was widely considered the best in town and Pugliese shone as a key innovator, his ear-pleasing onomatopoeic compositions and staccato rhythm adored by dancers. Inspired by Gardel, Ada Falcón, Nelly Omar and Ignacio Orsini kept up the songs of *tango canción* for adoring audiences in BA and overseas.

It takes two

In 1934, two tango greats – one man at the peak of his talents, the other unaware of the groundbreaking career that awaited him – met on a film set. The star, Carlos Gardel (pictured above), in his 30s, was an accomplished singer and songwriter and a hugely popular, if somewhat stiff, actor. It was this production at Paramount's New York studios, *El día que me quieras*, that would further establish his status as a Latin American legend.

Despite his fame, Gardel's liking for fellow Argentinians allowed a 12-year-old errand boy, Astor Piazzolla (right), to take on a tiny role in the movie. Days later, the two friends would peform a tango, 'Arrabal amargo', together. It was all good fun for amiable wag Gardel, but for little Astor it was the inspiration for embarking on a career that would advance tango's international appeal – thus furthering Gardel's cause while also taking the genre in new, iconoclastic directions.

In some ways, Gardel and Piazzolla represent opposite ends of tango. The former appeared as tango reached its first period of maturity and, decked out in gaucho gear or the cocked *funyi* (fedora-type hat) and tailored suit, Gardel sang songs of pained

passion, nostalgia, migration and mothers. His best recordings – whether numbers he penned himself such as 'Volver' (a sublime ode to exile and the yearning for homeland) and 'Mi Buenos Aires Querido' or covers of 'Yira, yira' and 'A media luz' – can be compared to Frank Sinatra's legendary songs in the US, both for the lush musicality of Gardel's powerful baritone and for the importance of the songs for his compatriots. If there is a touch of the Italian *canzonetta* and Caruso in there, and even a hint of *chanson* (Gardel was of French extraction), it's all subdued by the macho warbling and the melodramatic, tortured timbre of tango.

Gardel was there at the right time – an immigrant star who could please the middle classes and dazzle the workers. His dreams, sorrows, travels and tribulations were theirs, and as the man who created *tango canción*, he gave words to define the muddled identity of the modern, non-creole Argentinian. Films, radio and new recording technologies, and his likeably laddish personality helped no end, but Gardel had genuine gifts and he helped tango to evolve and expand as a genre.

Evolution was also to become Piazzolla's raison d'être. After a classical education with Nadia Boulanger and Albert Ginastera, followed by a stint as lead *bandoneón* for Troilo's magnificent band of the 1940s, he explored symphonic composition, jazz and *electrónica* and fused his influences to blow apart the constrictions of the official tango canon. Early pieces like 'Tres minutos con la realidad' (1957) suggest an audacious spirit, but it was landmark recordings like the *Suite Troileana* in 1975 that upset traditionalists (some even threatened to kill him) and forced

The young *bandoneón* player Astor Piazzolla worked with Troilo, but wanted to take tango even further – in a direction that would leave dancers cold, but thrill music-lovers. Exploring tango's affinity with jazz, he successfully fused the two forms and created Nuevo Tango. With poet Horacio Ferrer, he took tango into the modern world, attracting a new international audience and leaving traditionalists in BA to debate whether his highly lyrical, often frantic and explosive sound was tango at all.

In the 1970s and '80s, Piazzolla spent time in Italy and toured the US and Japan, moving increasingly towards jazz fusion. *Milongas* continued to draw the tango faithful and since

young professional dancers still sought a challenge, an era of exportable shows set in. Dancer-choreographer Juan Carlos Copes' bestselling show *Tango Argentino*, which boomed in Buenos Aires, before repeating its success on Broadway in the 1980s, created a new international fashion in tango shows that has been re-imported into the capital by the burgeoning tourist industry.

If it is through the great composers and lyricists that tango's history can be traced, then it is the dance that offers an opportunity to explore the roots of the *porteño* psyche. Many commentators cite memorable, pithy expressions for tango – 'the vertical expression

Arts & Entertainment

THE TANGOPOLIS

As well as being a visible, audible, danceable cultural expression, tango is also a set of myths, values, traditions and aspirations. Poet, librettist and songwriter Horacio Ferrer has coined the term 'tangopolis', alluding to an essential tango soul in BA and its residents. At the obvious level, this would include the iconography of the songs – street lamps, corners, old bars, dancers in split skirts and suits strutting their stuff on the cobbled streets – but Ferrer believes tango is wired into the Argentinian psyche and embedded in the hidden archaeology of the city.

You can't avoid tango. Gardel's mug smiles from murals, shop windows, posters, CD covers and magazines. In the Chacarita cemetery, there's a bronze of his body and another one in Abasto – Gardel's 'hood – as well as Gardel chemists, a Gardel Subte station and sections of the shopping mall named after his songs. Even the language is infected by icons – a great person is called 'Gardel'.

It's not all the main man though. Street corners, plazas and streets are dedicated to Enrique Santos Discépolo, Homero Manzi and, since late 2003, Astor Piazzolla. In barrios that have adopted tango – La Boca, San Telmo and Boedo all claim a key role in its genesis – there are bars and cafés named after tango stars. Dusty, off-the-beaten-track holes and themed bars are now part of tango mythology. Even when there are no shows, concerts or lone strummers, there's a *tanguero* nostalgia hanging in the air like French tobacco.

You can study for a degree in tango at the **Academia Nacional del Tango** (*see p212*). Radio shows, including a tango-only service at Radio de la Ciudad (92.7 FM), and the Solo Tango cable TV channel allow non-dancing fans to live and breathe the rhythms of the old port town while they drive taxis, do the ironing or get togged up for a night out. All major record shops have tango sections, and specialists such as **Zival's** (*see p159*) and **Casa Piscatelli** (San Martín 459, Microcentro, 4394 1992) have an amazing range. There are numerous tango tack shops, with enough kitsch paraphernalia to keep any fan happy – check out the market stalls on Plaza Dorrego and the shops around the square or the wacky tango diaries in city bookshops. There's even a newsstand dedicated to tango at the corner of Avenida Corrientes and Paraná, with books and pamphlets on tango's history, lyrics and heroes, as well as CDs. If you want scores or obscure memorabilia, visit **Club de Tango** (*see p141*).

For the more serious tangophile, specialist shops such as **Chamuyo** (Sarmiento 1562, Tribunales, 4381 1777) and **Fattomano**

Piazzolla to seek open-minded audiences in Italy, France and his beloved New York. But even Argentinians couldn't resist the emotive tribute to Piazzolla's father 'Adios Nonino' and the genre-busting song 'Balada para un loco' (with lyrics by Horacio Ferrer) and the tango revolutionary was soon a hit at home too.

By the time he recorded three superb CDs for the American Clave label – *Zero Hour* and *La Camorra* are must-haves for any fan – in the mid 1980s, Piazzolla was a global star. His back catalogue includes sonatas, film soundtracks and even a 'little opera' called *María de Buenos Aires*.

When Gardel died tragically in a plane crash in 1935, there was a massive public outpouring of grief. The passing of Gardel marked the beginning of the end of the belle époque, the golden age of tango. Piazzolla's death in 1992 left a similar gap in the contemporary tango world which musicians have been trying to fill ever since – whoever takes on the mantle and muse of Carlos Gardel and Astor Piazzolla will be the tango equivalent of Maradona.

of a horizontal desire' – or wax excitedly about the dance's sensuality. But it has many shades, which can be read as an index of social, emotional and sexual traits: the playful suggestiveness, the decorous codes, the repressed hysteria, the absence of frivolity and let-it-all-go sexuality – in tango, there is nothing of the explosive, orgasmic energy of Brazilian rhythms. Moreover, the obvious machismo in the dance – it is the male who gives the nod to dance, who approaches, who leads – is reflected in the tango scene of mainly male composers, male singers and male DJs on the radio. Women are certainly great metaphors in tango, but the solid core is stiffly male.

Arts & Entertainment

(Guatemala 4464, Palermo Viejo, 4823 3156) supply dancers with stilettos and belle époque accoutrements. There are even tango hotels, with all-inclusive packages of lessons, *milongas* and shows – check out the **Mansion Dandi Royal** (*see p38*), opened late 2003, for a live-in monument to kitsch nostalgia.

If you want to see tango exhibits, there are a few places to check out. The Academia Nacional (*see p212*) has a well put together **Museo Mundial del Tango**, the **Casa del Teatro** (Avenida Santa Fe 1243, 4813 5906) has a small Gardel room, open Tuesday and Thursday afternoons from 4-6.30pm, and **Bótica del Angel** (Luis Sáenz Peña 541, Congreso, 4384 9396) is a 'living museum' of tango and folklore, but can only be visited via prearranged guided tours. **Piazzolla Tango** (*see p214*) downtown has a small museum and photo gallery, and the revamped **Museo Casa Carlos Gardel** (*see p87*), where the star was born is worth visiting. Round the corner from this last, on Zelaya, are murals venerating the Gardelian image. Accompanying Gardel in Chacarita cemetery (*see p88*) is a whole pantheon dedicated to other *tangueros* including Pugliese, Goyeneche and Troilo.

After all the tombs and artefacts, you might even feel like dancing. The annual **Festival Buenos Aires Tango** (*see p164*) in February is the city's main tango extravaganza. Free classes build up to the week-long event, which involves hundreds of shows and tango-inspired events, when the whole city jives to the rhythm of its native sound. It takes place just after the Rio carnival, meaning lovers of spectacle and sexy thighs can do both in a single trip – this is what the canny BA culture mandarins would like you to do, anyway.

But it's not all memorabilia and museums. Ferrer – a tangosopher and tanganalyst to his core – also hints at a more subtle tango play being performed on the city streets. What about the way *porteña* women walk? The way the sexes look each other up and down in the streets? Is not that imperious gaze the icy legacy of forebears reared on tango? That macho pose an attempt to look like a *compadre*? Tangopolitans also include lonely bachelors, taxi drivers and caretakers, with radios as their only company, arguably the true bearers of the tango heritage – modern-day versions of those immigrants who came up with the first tangos. Nationalist writer Raúl Scalabrini Ortiz wrote a novel infused with the tango spirit called *El hombre que está solo y espera* – the man who is alone and waits… you don't necessarily need music, fancy clothes or even a partner to feel the rhythms and resonances of tango in Buenos Aires.

INFORMATION

Finding your way round such a thriving scene isn't easy. A seasonal foldout leaflet called Tango Map, found in San Telmo bars, is packed with *milonga* info and the map makes navigating easy. Targeting younger readers and with a selection of articles in English, free monthly *El Tangauta* contains the *Lo que vendrá* supplement, with info on classes and *milongas*. Both are available in tourist information offices, hotels, some downtown kiosks and the Academia Nacional del Tango. *Guia Trimestral* (quarterly, AR$2 from kiosks) includes just about everything related to tango. It's also worth checking the listings guides in the main newspapers, particularly *La Nación*'s Friday entertainment supplement, *Via Libre*. Government sponsored website www.tango data.com.ar has useful listings and www.todo tango.com.ar is a bilingual site with news, profiles and essays, plus listings.

Where to dance tango

Milongas

Traditional *milongas* – dance nights which at best combine the neighbourliness of a social club with the faded elegance of a 1930s ballroom – mostly attract an older generation who prefer to dance *al suelo*; that is, feet pegged to the floor, legs discreetly doing tricks as couples shuffle through steps called backward-eights, little sandwiches and sit-downs with ghostly subtlety. **Niño Bien** (Humberto Primo 1462, 15 4147 8687, Constitución) is an elegantly old-fashioned *milonga* at 9pm on Thursdays, where couples get dressed up for the occasion. By contrast, other clubs such as underground bar **La Catedral**

and **La Viruta** (*listings below*) are more casual and attract a mixed crowd (aged 18 to 70), some of whom perform flicks and fancy figures. Some venues, such as the excellent **Salon Canning** (Scalabrini Ortiz 1331, Palermo Viejo, 4832 6753) are taken over by a variety of different *milongas*. At the Canning, they range from trad, orchestral gigs to Catedral-style events with Omar Viola as the MC. Classes are often held prior to *milongas* so even beginners can feel part of the action.

Any *milonga* worthy of the name plays tangos according to the following ritual code: three sets (*tandas*) separated into straight tangos, more playful *milongas* (country songs) and waltzes. Nods and signals are used to find a partner – the man leading the way, as he does in the dance. While the couple waits for the first few bars to be over before moving, they locate each other's hands as they look into each other's eyes – anything more obvious is considered amateur and unrefined. The music is usually piped in – which might sound cheesy, but it can add to the nostalgic, scratched-record atmosphere. *Milongas* go on late – like bars and clubs, generally until the last dancers leave (5-6am at weekends, earlier in the week).

La Catedral

Sarmiento 4006, y Medrano, Almagro (mobile 15 5325 1630). Subte B, Medrano/24, 26, 168 bus. **Open** from 8.30pm Mon-Fri. *Milonga* 11pm Mon, Tue, Fri. *Classes* 8.30pm Mon-Fri. **Admission** *Milonga* AR$5. Free with class. *Classes* AR$5 Mon, Wed-Fri; AR$7 Tue. **No credit cards. Map** p274 E4.
The atmosphere at this underground venue is pitched between post-punk/neo-goth and circus/music hall. Omar Viola, the brains behind BA's legendary Parakultural organisation, is an MC with edge and enthusiasm. Go for a drink if you don't fancy a dance – it's as cool as the tangopolis gets.

Centro Cultural Torquato Tasso

Defensa 1575, entre Caseros y Brasil, San Telmo (4307 6506/www.tangotasso.com). Bus 24, 29, 39, 93, 130. **Open** from 4pm daily. *Milonga* 10pm Fri-Sun. *Classes* 8pm daily. **Admission** AR$5-$15. **No credit cards. Map** p276 C5.
This is a serious tango venue, with respected artists performing regularly. It's getting more popular all the time, so arrive early to bag a table close to the dancefloor. Friday and Saturday's events have live music, including renowned orchestras such as Sexteto Mayor, rare in the *milonga* scene. Check out the *fileteado* (traditional decorative lettering) outside the venue. Food and drink are available.

Club Gricel

La Rioja 1180, entre Humberto 1° y San Juan, San Cristóbal (4957 7157/8398/www.clubgricel.com). Subte E, Urquiza/41, 53, 101 bus. **Open** 10am-10pm Mon-Thur; 10am-5pm Fri, Sat; 6.30pm-2am Sun. *Milonga* from 11pm Fri-Sat; from 9pm Sun. *Classes* 6pm, 8.30pm Mon; 7pm, 9pm Tue, Thur, Sun; 8pm Fri, Sat. **Admission** *Milonga* AR$5 Fri; AR$3 Sat, Sun. *Classes* AR$4-$7. **No credit cards**.
On Friday night, Club Gricel is packed and lots of fun, with regulars coming back again and again with fixed table reservations. Classes are available throughout the week.

Nuevo Salón La Argentina

Bartolomé Mitre 1759, entre Callao y Rodriguez Peña, Congreso (4371 6767). Subte A, Congreso/5, 7, 12, 37, 60 bus. **Open** *Milonga* after classes Tue, Thur; 10.30pm Fri; after class & 10.30pm Sat; 8pm Sun. *Classes* 4pm Tue, Thur, Sat. **Admission** *Milonga* AR$5 men, AR$3 women. *Classes* AR$6. **No credit cards. Map** p277 F5.
Plenty of young dancers and good music in an attractive 1930s building. It can pull in more than 300 dancers and the floor is small, so you need some cunning floorcraft to dance. There's a live orchestra on Saturdays. Great home-cooked food.

Moody *milonga* moments at **Torquato Tasso** with Juanjo Dominguez (left).

Carlos Gardel smiles beside Abasto mall.

Sin Rumbo

Tamborini 6157, y Constituyentes, Villa Urquiza (4574 0972). Bus 110, 111, 112, 117, 140. **Open** from 8pm daily. *Milonga* 10pm Tue, Wed, Fri-Sun. *Classes* 8pm Tue, Wed, Fri-Sun. **Admission** *Milonga* AR$3 Fri. *Classes* AR$5. **No credit cards.**

It's worth a trip to the edge of town to Villa Urquiza to get the feel of a genuine neighbourhood *milonga*. Small, friendly and welcomes foreigners. Private classes are available for AR$15-$30.

La Viruta

Armenia 1366, entre Cabrera y Niceto Vega, Palermo Viejo (4774 6357/www.lavirutatango.com). Bus 15, 55, 168. **Open** from 8pm Wed-Sun. *Milonga* midnight Fri-Sun. *Classes* varies; check web. **Admission** AR$5-$6. **No credit cards.** Map p279 J4.

Milonga nights in a homely community centre. Lots of ages happily come together for tango, with a sprinkling of salsa and even rock 'n' roll dancing, as well as classes in all styles. A live orchestra plays four times a month.

Classes and information

All of the above *milongas* have resident teachers, and hundreds of couples offer classes (look for adverts in the specialised magazines). **Estudio La Esquina** (1st Floor, Avenida de Mayo 784, Monserrat, 4343 6440) offers personalised two-hour classes for all levels, with experienced teachers. On Sundays, at **Mitos Argentinos** in San Telmo (*see p194*), a live orchestra show and classes pull in punters from the nearby flea market. The **Confitería Ideal** (Suipacha 384, Microcentro,

5265 8078), a gorgeous – though scandalously dilapidated – old café, holds afternoon tango classes for beginners in rooms on the first floor, and the **Mansion Dandi Royal** hotel (*see p38*) does daily classes. **Piazzolla Tango** (*see p214*) and **Torquato Tasso** (*see p211*) run programmes of dance classes too. Many neighbourhood cultural centres teach tango too, though check to make sure someone speaks English if you don't have enough *castellano* to keep up. Below are some recommended options.

La Academia

First Floor, Riobamba 416, entre Corrientes y Lavalle, Once (4953 2794). Subte B, Callao/24, 26, 37, 60, 124 bus. **Open** *Classes* 8.30pm Mon, Wed, Fri; 8pm Sun. *Milonga* 11pm Tue, Wed, Sat, Sun. **Admission** *Classes* AR$10 per class; AR$48 for 8 classes. *Milonga* AR$5. **No credit cards.** Map p277 F6.

This is the name of a respected venue run by Susanna Miller, who also teaches in the US. Her own schedule is complicated so call for information – and expect the style to be Salon tango, close and free of showy tics. All the group classes are great, and have a personal element.

Academia Nacional del Tango

1st Floor, Avenida de Mayo 833, entre Piedras y Tacuarí, Monserrat (4345 6968/6967). Subte A, Piedras/10, 17, 70, 86 bus. **Open** 2-9pm Mon-Fri. *Classes* from 6pm Mon-Fri. **Admission** free. *Classes* AR$5. **No credit cards.** Map p277 E6.

As well as running classes, this is Argentina's very own 'university of tango' and an excellent source of information. A research library is open Tuesday and Thursday from 5-7pm, and the World Tango Museum is open daily from 2-6pm (AR$3); entry to the museum is via Rivadavia 830.

Centro Cultural Konex

Avenida Córdoba 1235, entre Libertad y Talcahuano, Tribunales (4813 1100/www.centro culturalkonex.org). Subte D, Tribunales/29, 39, 109 bus. **Open** *Jan-Feb* 2-9pm Mon-Fri. *Mar-Dec* 10am-10pm Mon-Fri; 4-9pm Sat. *Classes* 4pm, 5.30pm, 7pm. **Admission** free. *Classes* AR$10; AR$5 Wed. **Credit** AmEx, DC, MC, V. Map p277 F7.

This cultural complex offers 90-minute tango classes with teachers who all speak English, as well as courses on the history and culture of tango.

Where to hear tango

For the wooden-legged, there is, of course, tango music and not all of it is made for dancing. There is a classical tradition, which goes back to early composers such as Juan de Dios Filiberto, and is kept up tpday by Piazzolla disciple *bandoneón*-player Rodolfo Mederos and virtuoso pianists Pablo Ziegler and Sonia Possetti. Also look out for Julio Pane and Rubén Juárez on *bandoneón*, and guitarist Juanjo Dominguez. For top female vocals, Adriana Varela's strong, sensual shows

Arts & Entertainment

are exceptional while Lidia Borda can pack a punch with her moody singing with a strong French lilt. Both **La Trastienda** (*see p193*) and **ND/Ateneo** (*see p194*) are serious venues for folk and tango and they tend to attract these big names. The planned **Ciudad Cultural Konex** complex in Abasto (*see p87*) is also destined to be a major hub for all things tango.

At **Club del Vino** (*see p193*), sardonic Néstor Marconi and his Trio join veteran pianist Horacio Salgán and guitarist Ubaldo del Lio at 10pm most Fridays and Saturdays for an hour or more of virtuoso tango (tickets AR$10-$30). Trad Argentinian restaurant **Miramar** (*see p105*) is recommended for hearty food, and *bandoneón* player Julio Pane's appearance on Sunday nights makes it a hot spot for fine tango. There's also **Café Homero** in Palermo Viejo (Cabrera 4946, 4701 7357). One of the city's most respected venues for quality performances, both vocal and musical, it has sessions from Wednesday thorough to Sunday evenings (Friday and Saturday only in January and February).

Outside the ever-evolving mainstream, there's a new scene led by Daniel Melingo, grumpy-voiced Omar Mollo (linked to the rock band Los Piojos) and Latino fusioneers La Chicana. Several orchestras and smaller outfits keep the spirit of salon tango alive; among the best are Sexteto Mayor, Quinteto Piazzolla, Atilio Stampone Quinteto, El Arranque and Orquesta del Tango de la Ciudad.

Finally **Bar El Chino** (Beazley 3566, Nueva Pompeya, 4911 0215) and **Lo de Roberto**, on the corner of Bulnes and Perón in Abasto, are off-the-beaten-track bars with an informal atmosphere suggestive of how neighbourhood tango used to be. Both featured in the successful documentary *Subtango*. Another film, *Bar El Chino*, caught the last years of owner El Chino as he served and sung to his faithful clientele.

Where to watch tango

These are the city's best dinner shows. **Bar Sur** and **El Viejo Almacén** are more intimate venues and **Piazzolla Tango** and **La Esquina de Carlos Gardel** can't be faulted for ambition – these are listed in full. But for a highly stylised, razzmatazz intro to the dance – that locals deprecatingly call 'tango for export' – you can go along to the likes of: **La Esquina Homero Manzi** (Avenida San Juan 3601, Boedo, 4957 8488, www.esquina homeromanzi.com.ar), **El Querandí** (Perú 302, Monserrat, www.querandi.com.ar), **Sabor a Tango** (Perón 2535, Abasto, 4953 8700, www.saboratango.com.ar) and the most spectacular spectacular of all, **Señor Tango** (Vieytes 1653, Barracas, 4303 0231, www. senortango.com.ar). Just to give you an idea of the kind of business these joints are doing, consider that Señor Tango regularly fills to capacity – 1,500 people – with customers paying from AR$85 to AR$135 per head.

Even tourists tango.
Take classes at
**Academia
Nacional**.
See p212.

Arts & Entertainment

Mi Buenos Aires Querido
Adriana Varela

My beloved Buenos Aires

I was born in Avellaneda, but came to live in Barrio Norte when I was 19. Since then, I've always lived in Barrio Norte or Palermo, and I like the area because it's where I fell in love, seperated, all the usual stuff.

I first heard tango in my early thirties, when I saw Roberto Goyeneche singing in the film *Sur*. It was a revelation – I'd found the rock 'n' roll of Buenos Aires.

I used to visit Goyeneche and Enrique Cadícamo. I learnt *lunfardo*, our street slang, which was the language Cadícamo wrote in.

Tango allows us to explore our own identity.

I realised we lived with our backs to the river, so I looked outwards and found the music of the River Plate and, in Uruguay, made contact with African culture through *candombe* music. Here in Argentina we killed all the blacks.

Tango comes from the margins – which isn't communicated by the big, kitschy tango shows. They're OK for foreigners or business people. Anyone who really wants to get into tango should go to a *milonga* – La Viruta is great.

In 2003 I performed at ND/Ateneo, Teatro Opera and at La Plata's Teatro Argentino – in my opinion, the finest theatre in Latin America. At these venues and also at the Club del Vino – where Horacio Salgán and the Nuevo Quinteto Real play – you can find good tango music.

I'm involved with the Bajofondo electro-tango project, which I think is far truer to the essence of tango than Gotan Project. It also uses good musicians. What Omar Mollo does with tango is interesting and Daniel Melingo's tangos are great, too.

There is no such thing as new tango. Tango is not a thing you buy, it's in constant evolution. There are tangos of yesterday, today and for eternity.

The market is our only enemy, as it forces music on us. I like world music, because it is not imposed on us by anyone – you have to go out and find it for yourself.

● Adriana Varela is Argentina's best-known tango diva. Her albums include *Tangos de Lengue* (1995) and *Cuando el río suena* (1999), and her music was used in Carlos Saura's Oscar-winning film *Tango*.

Bar Sur

Estados Unidos 299, y Balcarce, San Telmo (4362 6086/www.bar-sur.com.ar). Bus 29, 93, 130. **Open** 8pm-3am daily. *Show every 2hrs.* **Tickets** AR$65-$135. **Credit** AmEx, DC, MC, V. **Map** p276 C6.

The show is fairly fancy, but the intimate bar and emphasis on participation makes this a fun and friendly little joint. Used in films, the setting – both inside and out on the street – evokes the Buenos Aires of cobbled streets and streetcorner men.

La Esquina de Carlos Gardel

Pasaje Carlos Gardel 3200, y Anchorena, Abasto (4867 6363/www.esquinacarlosgardel.com.ar). Subte B, Carlos Gardel/24, 26, 124, 168 bus. **Open** 8.30pm-12.30am daily. **Tickets** AR$100-$150; AR$200-$300 superior. **Credit** AmEx, DC, MC, V. **Map** p278 G4.

Okay, so it's a show. But the venue is grand, the dancers sexy and showbizzy, and the food is big steaks and blood red wine. Leave your cynicism hanging in the cloakroom and enjoy – at least until they offer you a Gardel T-shirt.

Piazzolla Tango

Florida 165, entre Mitre y Perón, Microcentro (0810 333 82646/www.piazzollatango.com). Subte D, Catedral/10, 29, 64, 111 bus. **Open** noon-midnight Mon-Sat; varies Sun. *Classes* 5pm, 8pm Mon-Sat. *Dinner* 8.30pm, *show* 10.15pm Mon-Sat. **Admission** AR$5. *Classes* AR$10. *Show* AR$150 stalls; AR$300 box. **Credit** AmEx, DC, MC, V. **Map** p277 E7.

Theatre, gallery and museum, this dashing new venue in one of the city's most gorgeous buildings – the Galería Güemes – is also a place to take classes and see a posh, pricey show featuring top dancers.

El Viejo Almacén

Avenida Independencia 300, y Balcarce, San Telmo (4307 7388/4300 3388/www.viejoalmacen.com). Bus 29, 93, 130, 152. **Open** 2pm-2am daily. *Dinner* 8pm, *show* 10pm daily. **Tickets** AR$95-$135. **Credit** AmEx, DC, MC, V. **Map** p276 C6.

A charming colonial venue and a long-established tourist favourite. In 1968, singer Edmundo Rivero took over the building as a refuge for musicians, dancers and, as a plaque in the doorway states, 'those who have lost their faith'.

Theatre & Dance

Eclectic and experimental performing arts thrill the *porteño* public.

Theatre

Watch out London and New York – judging from the number of weekly premières, Buenos Aires is muscling in as a world theatre capital. On any given weekend *porteños* flock to more than 150 productions. Given such a mass following, choice ranges from over-the-top, Broadway-style musicals to sparse, independent productions by local playwrights. Spanish-language Shakespeare and an experimental troupe reciting local classics in complete darkness are among BA's eclectic offering.

Porteño obsession with theatre goes back to the end of colonial times, when picaresque satires were a barely tolerated forum by which creole elites poked fun at incompetent Spanish rulers. Over time, new genres developed, with each subsequent crisis giving birth to a new generation of innovative thespians. The latest is no different. Reflecting Argentina's peso-poor economy, the fringe theatre scene, in part thanks to government subsidies to small playhouses and companies, is thriving, with an explosion of new venues and productions.

The traditional spotlight, though, shines on Avenida Corrientes. The 'street that never sleeps' was for many years Buenos Aires' answer to Broadway, though at some point the glittering neon billboards began to fade and several magnificent playhouses were pulled down to make room for car parks and other more profitable businesses.

For the old-time theatres that escaped the bulldozers, the big attraction is the *revista porteña*, a type of cabaret revue show, currently staging a big comeback. Starring scantily clad showgirls known as *vedettes* and slapstick comedians, or *capo cómicos*, they draw huge crowds. Between monologues, sketches and dance routines, *capo cómicos* pull off mordant satires of local politics – neither the feathers nor the beautiful girls can dilute the vitriol that is aimed at the country's political leadership. Tired of mimicking presidents from the stage, comedian Nito Artaza, the genre's number one showman, flirted with running for the top job himself under the banner of his fledgling 'Swindled Argentinian Savers' movement.

Thanks to the success of home-grown and imported musicals, *porteños* have warmed to a genre that was previously unknown to them. The mega-show *El Diez*, a musical version of idol Diego Maradona's tumultuous life, is scheduled to premiere in 2004. Although devaluation means that expensive imports like Bob Fosse's *Chicago* (which was given a dazzling local production) are no longer affordable, the musical is still very much alive thanks to a new, energetic generation of writers, directors and singer-dancers.

Reflecting the popularity of independent theatre, a number of smaller, multi-purpose spaces featuring experimental, crossover fare have also cropped up on Corrientes and elsewhere to compete with mainstream or state-run theatres. Many of these new venues, in lieu of charging a small entrance let viewers in for

He's behind you! Dance and theatre group **El Descueve** perform *Hermosura*. See p218.

Mi Buenos Aires Querido
Diqui James

My beloved Buenos Aires

The '80s – with the return of democracy – were really important. They were interesting times in Buenos Aires.

San Telmo in the '80s was like Palermo today – that's where it was all going on. Those days are my fondest memories of the city. There was a genuine, young underground movement.

Today Palermo manages to be the home of alternative subcultures, while retaining its neighbourhood vibe.

There's always something going on until late there, even on weekdays. At Unico bar any night, there's always a scene – but it's best early in the week, when it's not complete madness.

For clubbing, both Pachá and Big One have real personality. The best bet is to arrive early and get into it before the crowds arrive.

Independent theatre today can exist without being totally dependent on media coverage, unlike in the 1990s, when everything had to be huge, expensive and media friendly.

There's a new public for theatre now – people who are prepared to go and take in offbeat productions. Tourists should definitely check out the alternative theatre circuit.

There still aren't enough people taking a ballsy, whole-hearted approach to theatre here, but then theatre is in crisis everywhere.

I hope that the current trend of valuing all things Argentinian is genuine, and that it's not all just because we have no choice as we can't afford access to anything else.

Argentinian actors and dancers have no need to envy their European counterparts: their level of skill is incredible.

There's a vast choice of performance spaces in the city, from rooms for 20 people, to huge open spaces like La Rural.

Buenos Aires is really easy – all you have to do is go to a bar, hang out, ask around, and you'll find out about (and probably get taken to) cool parties and underground events. It's also a great city to walk in, and most things

free and then pass the hat around when the curtains close. It's not only a sign of Argentina's economic reality, but also of the actors and playwrights' confidence in the quality and impact of their works. Even living rooms, plazas and old factories – just about every space imaginable – are used as alternative performance venues.

It's this non mainstream scene – known as Off-Corrientes and Off-Off-Corrientes – that is expanding from Abasto to other barrios such as Almagro, Villa Crespo and even trendy Palermo Hollywood. Independent productions are keeping alive Buenos Aires' passion for theatre – that and an abundance of instinctual talent (a result of confronting so much drama in their everyday lives), which *porteños* have learned to channel on to the stage through Method acting and other techniques.

FESTIVALS

Theatre and dance festivals are usually of the highest quality in terms of performance and, sadly, also in their level of disorganisation. The most important theatre and dance event is the biannual **Festival Internacional de Buenos Aires** (*see p162*). An alternative yearly event, helping to keep alive the memory of Argentina's 'Dirty War' past, **Teatro x la Identidad** (Theatre for Identity – www.teatroxlaidentidad. net) usually takes place in August, with works touching on the identity of children abducted from their disappeared parents.

TICKETS

You can buy tickets at the *boletería* (box office) of the venue itself (often cash only) or by phone for major productions or venues using credit cards through Ticketek and Ticketmaster; *see p192*, booking fees apply. Discounted tickets – 30 to 50 per cent off – for plays, musicals, supper shows and films are available at: **Cartelera Lavalle** (Lavalle 742, Microcentro, 4322 1559, www.123info.com.ar); **Cartelera Baires** (Unit 24, Avenida Corrientes 1382, Tribunales, 4372 5058); and also **Unica Cartelera** (Unit 27, Lavalle 835, Microcentro, 4370 5319, www.unica-cartelera.com.ar). You can reserve seats by phone, but must pay cash when you go to collect the tickets.

of interest are in a manageable area along the coast from La Boca to Palermo. **The river is undervalued.** From the Costaneras Norte and Sur to Tigre and the Delta, which is amazing – especially the El Dorado and San Antonio arteries, where there are hidden restaurants, *fiestas*, bars, tiny beaches and lovely people. **To really blow someone's mind, I'd take them to see** *murga* [carnival dance/drum troupes], ideally Los Amantes de la Boca. *Murga* is really important in barrio life. It's completely amateur – nobody lives off it – but it's also very official and highly organised at a local level. The energy is amazing, the dance is fascinating. *Murga,* **football and cumbia music are all about real BA life** – tourists should make friends with a local to enjoy these scenes. ● Diqui James is at the centre of the street and underground theatre scene in Buenos Aires. After founding experimental theatre group Organización Negra, he co-created De La Guarda with Pichón Baldinú. They have taken the show *Villa Villa* to cities across the world.

Venues

State-run theatres

There are two main theatre centres funded by the national government. The 80-year-old **Teatro Cervantes**, a work of art in its own right, seats 1,000 people in two auditoriums and shows Latin American and Spanish theatre and some dance. Grouped together as the **Complejo Teatral de Buenos Aires** is a complex of five separate venues, which stage principally, but not exclusively, contemporary works and universal classics. The complex includes the centrally located Alvear, Regio and Sarmiento theatres, and the picturesque Teatro de la Ribera in La Boca, but the flagship is the **Teatro San Martín** on Avenida Corrientes. Famous for the quality and variety of its productions, ranging from the most classic of classics to avant-garde experiments, it houses three separate auditoriums, with a combined capacity of around 1,700, as well as a cinema – the Sala Leopoldo Lugones – showing art-house films and established classics (*see p178*).

At the Teatro San Martín you can pick up a copy of the programme for all five theatres in the complex. You can buy tickets in person or online at www.teatrosanmartin.com.ar.

Teatro Cervantes

Libertad 815, entre Córdoba y Paraguay, Tribunales (4815 8880/8884 ext 121 box office/www.teatro cervantes.gov.ar). Subte D, Tribunales/29, 39, 109, bus. **Open** *Box office* Feb-Dec 10am-8pm Tue-Sun. **Closed** Jan. **Tickets** AR$5-$10. **No credit cards.** **Map** p277 F7.

Teatro San Martín

Avenida Corrientes 1550, entre Paraná y Montevideo, Tribunales (freephone 0800 3335254/www.teatrosan martin.com.ar). Subte B, Uruguay/24, 26, 60, 102 bus. **Open** 10am-10pm daily. **Tickets** AR$2.50-$8 children's shows; from AR$5 adult shows. Half-price Wed. **Credit** AmEx, MC, V. **Map** p277 F6.

Corrientes

Also on Avenida Corrientes are the venerable **Teatro Opera** and **Gran Rex** (for both, *see p193*), used mostly for concerts. The **Teatro Nacional** at No.960 (4326 4218), was restored and reopened in March 2000. Like its sister playhouse, the **Broadway** at No.1155 (4382 2345), as well as the **Teatro Astros** at No.746 (4325 5541), it's famed for big-budget musicals.

Belisario

Corrientes 1624, entre Rodríguez Peña y Monevideo, Tribunales (4373 3465/www.belisarioteatro.com.ar) Subte B, Callao/24, 26, 60, 102 bus. **Open** *Box office* Jan, Feb Wed-Sat. Mar-Dec 4-9pm Thur-Sun. *Shows* Jan, Feb Fri, Sat. Mar-Dec Thur-Sun. **Tickets** AR$6-$10. **No credit cards.** **Map** p277 F6.
Home to the best experimental theatre around, including improv shows where actors take their cue from audience requests.

Complejo La Plaza

Avenida Corrientes 1660, entre Montevideo y Rodríguez Peña, Tribunales (6320 5350/Sala Colette 6320 5346). Subte B, Callao/12, 24, 37, 60 bus. **Open** *Box office* 10am-9pm Mon-Sat; 1-9pm Sun. *Complex* 10am-2am Mon-Thur, Sun; 10am-4am Fri, Sat. **Tickets** AR$15-$35; AR$5 children. **No credit cards.** **Map** p277 F6.
La Plaza is the most commercial complex in the area, with two theatres presenting classic works and contemporary productions, and several bars and cafés.

Multiteatro

Corrientes 1283, y Talcahuano, Tribunales (4382 9140). Subte B, Uruguay/24, 26, 60, 102 bus. **Open** *Box office* 10am-10pm daily. *Shows* 9pm Wed-Sun. **Tickets** AR$20-$25. **No credit cards.** **Map** p277 F6.
Renovated into three comfortable though smallish auditoriums, Multiteatro regularly stages provocative one-person shows as well as local adaptations of contemporary classics.

Arts & Entertainment

Teatro Astral

Avenida Corrientes 1639, entre Montevideo y Rodríguez Peña, Tribunales (4374 5707/9964). Subte B, Callao/12, 24, 37, 60 bus. **Open** *Box office* 10am-10pm daily. **Tickets** AR$20-$30. **Credit** AmEx, DC, MC, V. **Map** p277 F6.

Argentina's most famous feather-clad *vedettes* have swayed their hips on the stage of Astral, the main revue theatre on Corrientes (along with the Maipo – Esmeralda 443-9, 4322 8238, www.maipo.com.ar). Colourful and noisy light entertainment.

Teatro del Pueblo

Avenida Roque Sáenz Peña 943, entre Carlos Pellegrini y Suipacha (4326 3606/www.teatrodel pueblo.org.ar). Subte B, Carlos Pellegrini or C, Diagonal Norte or D, 9 de Julio/17, 24, 59, 67 bus. **Open** *Box office* 3.30-8pm Wed-Sun. *Shows* from 8.30pm Fri-Sun. **Tickets** AR$10; AR$5 concessions. **No credit cards. Map** p277 E7.

Founded in 1930, this was one of the first independent theatres in Latin America. Located on the basement level of a beautiful French-style building, it's dedicated to socially minded works by Argentinian playwrights, both classic and contemporary.

Teatro Liceo

Avenida Rivadavia 1494, y Paraná, Congreso (4381 4291/box office 4381 5745). Subte A, Sáenz Peña/ 60, 64, 86, 102, 168 bus. **Open** *Box office* 10am-8pm Mon; 10am-11pm Tue-Sun. **Tickets** AR$10-$35. **No credit cards. Map** p277 E6.

This 140-year-old venue is the oldest in the city and still going strong as the stage for numerous theatre productions, everything from Spanish music concerts to classic works.

Teatro Lola Membrives

Avenida Corrientes 1280, y Talcahuano, Tribunales (4381 0076). Subte B, Uruguay/24, 26, 29, 39 bus. **Open** *Box office* 10am-8pm daily. *Tickets* AR$15-$30. **Credit** AmEx, DC, MC, V. **Map** p277 F6.

Opened in 1927, this classic Corrientes theatre is also one of the largest, seating 1,100. It was renovated a few years ago, but maintains its original colonial style. A recent tango tribute wouldn't have been amiss on Broadway.

Off-Corrientes

There are some companies, playwrights and performers whose work you should look out for. Spearheading the renaissance are such playwright/directors as Rafael Spregelburd, Javier Daúlte, Federico León and Alejandro Tantanián. Most of their works have a realist bent in the Arthur Miller tradition and take fresh look at corrupted, Argentinian social mores.

Argentina's most successful troupe abroad, crossover dance performers De La Guarda – cofounded by Diqui James (*see p216* **Mi Buenos Aires Querido**) – are more likely to be seen performing their high-energy rave *Villa Villa* in

Tokyo, Tel Aviv or New York then they are in Buenos Aires. When they do make rare home appearances, it's at their Sala Villa Villa auditorium in the Centro Cultural Recoleta (*see p78*). De La Guarda collaborators, dance/theatre group El Descueve, and young challengers Los Susodichos draw inspiration from Barcelona's Fura dels Baus and New York's Blue Man Group, combining action theatre with biting satire of everyday life. Daniel Veronese's company El Periférico de Objetos explores human rights issues, focusing on the poetics of cruelty through a theatrical language that dispenses with the spoken word. For comic relief, Los Macocos' circus-like brand of intelligent humour is another Off-Corrientes fixture. Also good for a laugh is the musical comedy *Fulgor Argentino*, performed by La Boca's grassroots Grupo de Teatro Catalinas Sur (*see p73*).

Most Off-Corrientes venues (including those listed here) are in and around the Abasto neighbourhood, although the scene is expanding geographically. The **Actors Studio** is on Avenida Corrientes itself, but way up at No.3565/71 (4867 6622, www.actors-studio.org) in an old house converted into a restaurant-cum-theatre. It features new versions of classics and an eclectic selection of outrageous new works and performers. **El Camarín de las Musas** (Mario Bravo 960, 4862 0655) is a hip, comfortable multipurpose space that gets rave reviews for its highbrow productions. You can catch a meal or drink before descending to the basement theatre. **Espacio Callejón** (Humahuaca 3759, 4862 1167) is one of the gutsiest showplaces for new talent in BA, including modern dance, and it also offers evening classes in singing and theatre for amateurs. An old factory with room for 110 has been converted into **El Portón de Sánchez** (Sánchez de Bustamante 1034, 4863 2848). This is where to drops in for a taste of the city's most innovative, controversial works. Tickets at all these venues cost AR$5-$10.

Teatro Cervantes.
See p217.

Arts & Entertainment

Check out neighbourhood *murga* dance/
drum groups, especially pre-Carnival.

Dance

Most people associate BA with tango. But the waves of immigrants who settled in Argentina also forged with their native dances and deep-rooted customs *milongas*, *zambas* and *chacareras*, all popular in the interior. Spanish dance enjoyed a following until the middle of the 19th century, and the first academic classical ballet company in South America started in the school of the Teatro Colón in the 1920s, just a few years after the Argentinian elite had been bowled over by visits from Anna Pavlova and Isadora Duncan.

Ballet remained the preserve of a few connoisseurs until Julio Bocca arrived on the scene in 1985. With his dance partner Eleonora Cassano, Bocca succeeded in bringing classical ballet to the masses with hugely successful, open-air performances in such non-conventional stages as Avenida 9 de Julio and Boca Juniors stadium. His choreography to Astor Piazzolla's tango music was equally audacious. In 1990, Bocca founded his own company, the Ballet Argentino, which tours the world, and together with the school of the Teatro Colón, churns out new ballet dancers. Nowadays, Argentinian dancers – such as Paloma Herrera, Maximiliano Guerra, Iñaki Urlezaga and Herman Cornejo – have become, in their field, as internationally famous as football stars.

Although modern dance isn't yet as popular as classical, the leading company is the Teatro San Martín's resident ensemble, Ballet Contemporáneo. Directed by Mauricio Wainrot, the troupe has been remarkably successful in attracting new audiences with such social-minded productions as a version of Anne Frank's diary. Their haunting production of Carl Orff's *Carmina Burana*

gets reruns upon popular request whenever the theatre's schedule permits.

The Resident Ballet of the **Teatro Argentino** in La Plata (*see p188*), under the aegis of choreographer Oscar Aráiz, formerly with the Ballet Contemporáneo, dabbles with both classical and contemporary dance. When you're in town, keep an eye out for the work of Tangokinesis and Roxana Grinstein's El Escote, two avant-garde companies renowned for their absurd, surreal take on tango.

Venues

Argentina's best contemporary dance troupes perform at the **Teatro San Martín** (*see p217*). Other venues worth checking out for modern dance are the **Alvear** (part of the Complejo Teatral de Buenos Aires), the **Centro de Arte y Cultura** (Guardia Vieja 3783, y Bulnes, 4866 2671), home to Maximiliano Guerra's Ballet del Mercosur. Among the Centros Culturales staging dance performance are **Recoleta** (*see p78*), **Borges** (*see p62*) and **De la Cooperación** (*see p62*). Alternative venues include **Espacio Callejón** and **El Portón de Sánchez** (*see p218*), and also the **Teatro del Sur** (Venezuela 2255, San Cristóbal, 4941 1951) and **El Ombligo de la Luna** (Anchorena 364, Abasto, 4867 6578). Flamenco and Spanish dance fans should check the listings for the **Teatro Astral** (*see p218*), the **Teatro Avenida** (Avenida de Mayo 1222, Congreso, 4381 0662), and look for *tablaos* at Spanish restaurants like **Avila** (*see p120*).

Lessons & dance schools

Dance classes are very popular and there are plenty of schools. The cultural centres are the most accessible (you can usually take a free trial lesson), particularly the **Ricardo Rojas** (Avenida Corrientes 2038, Once, 4954 5521, www.rojas.uba.ar), which offers flamenco, *folklore* and jazz dance among many others.

At **Danzario Americano** (Guardia Vieja 3559, Abasto, 4863 8401, www.danzario.com), instructors from all over Latin America teach native dances and customs. Classes include salsa, lambada, Arabic, modern, flamenco, jazz and classical. For modern and classical dance, from flamenco to hip-hop, try the school run by Noemí Coelho and Rodolfo Olguín (First Floor, Montevideo 787, Tribunales, 4812 5483 and Blanco Encalada 2126, Belgrano 4781 0130). The **Centro Cultural Konex** (*see p87*), moving to a megaspace called Ciudad Cultural Konex in Abasto in 2005, runs tango classes for locals and foreigners, and also teaches a variety of other types of traditional dances.

Arts & Entertainment

ARGENTINA
at your fingertips

Bus & Air Tickets
Accommodation
Excursions
Buenos Aires
Iguazú Falls
Patagonia
Perito Moreno Glacier
Península Valdés
Salta & Jujuy
Chilean Fiords
Brazil
Adventures
Ecotourism

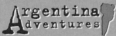
Argentina Adventures

Travel Designers
Buenos Aires Tel: (0054) 11- 4326 6907
www.aaye.com.ar   info@aaye.com.ar

Argentina
OUTDOORS

Your next adventure

- *RANCHES*
- *EXCURSIONS & TOURS*
- *HOTELS*
- *OUTDOORS ACTIVITIES*
- *DESTINATION INFO*

*Florida 868   14 H, Buenos Aires,
Argentina.   Tel.   54-11-4312-2355
info@argentinaoutdoors.com*

www.argentinaoutdoors.com

CURIOCITY
DESTINATION MANAGEMENT COMPANY

make it easy

WWW.CURIOCITY.COM.AR
EVT LEG. # 11752 DISP. # 0253

Gay & Lesbian Travel

Gay & Lesbian
Information Center

**General Information
Air Bookings
Tours & Packages
Adventure Travel**

IGLTA

PrideTravel
Paraguay 523 2° E
C1057AAL - Bs. As. - Argentina
Tel.: 5218-6556 Fax: 5218-6554
e-mail: info@pride-travel.com

www.pride-travel.com

Pride Travel S.R.L., Legajo Nro. 11735, Expediente Nro. 162/03

Trips Out of Town

Getting Started

Argentina is too big to cover all at once, but there are some choice adventures within easy reach of BA – and you can even cross a border on a day trip.

Porteños are fond of saying that Buenos Aires is located in *'el culo del mundo'* (the rear end of the world) – a characteristic description of their apparent southern hemisphere isolation. Indeed, big distances separate it from the glaciers, wineries and everything else Argentina has to offer. Still, within a day trip from the capital – and certainly a weekend – lie a host of contrasting destinations and experiences.

Depending on the season and your interests, BA serves as a great hub for seeking out sun, sand, history and horses. We've divided Argentinian trips thematically, into different physical environments – river destinations, countryside retreats and beaches on the Atlantic Coast in southern Buenos Aires province. You can even visit another country for the day or longer – as a separate chapter, we have grouped together a handful of top destinations in neighbouring Uruguay.

The first section – **Upriver** – is centred around the continuation of a very *porteño* presence: the brown waters of the Río de la Plata. North of BA beyond the city limits, riverside **Tigre** – itself an ideal destination for a lazy lunch or sightseeing – is a gateway to another world: the islands and waterways that make up the **Delta**. Rivers also provide one of South America's most spectacular experiences. Further than the typical short-trip destination, but eminently accessible from Buenos Aires, is the superlative-inducing **Cataratas de Iguazú**, stunning waterfalls in the jungle border region of Argentina, Brazil and Paraguay.

If you prefer to head inland to enjoy the wide open spaces of the **Country**, picturesque **San Antonio de Areco**, just a couple of hours from BA, is where you can pick up the trail of Argentina's legendary gauchos. Throughout Buenos Aires province you can explore the pampas on horseback, or just kick back and let someone do the hard work of stoking the barbecue at one of the region's beautiful, historical *estancias*, as farms are known.

Of course, looking at a map, and at BA's proximity to the ocean, you may want to hit the **Beach**. If you are visiting between November and April, the chances are you'll get a bit of sunshine that warms you enough to make you yearn for some sand between your toes. If you can't be bothered with border crossings, you

need to go south to the Atlantic coast for the sound of the surf and all the fun of resort life. **Mar del Plata**, **Pinamar** or **Mar de las Pampas** and **Mar Azul**, all offer varying degrees of sun-soaked action among the crowds or peaceful, soporific summer solitude.

Just a short one-hour ferry across the puddle, as the River Plate is affectionately known, and you can be in **Uruguay**. Popular **Colonia de Sacramento** is a World Heritage Site that marries time travel with tranquillity, and further north is the even more secluded tiny town of **Carmelo**. Uruguay feels like an oversized *pueblo* and even its capital, **Montevideo**, exudes a small-town feel. Once you slip into its easygoing groove though, you'll be pleasantly surprised by how urban it is too. Throughout Uruguay, small beaches line the river shore from Colonia to Montevideo and beyond, but the country's contender for queen of the beach scene is **Punta del Este**, summer home of South America's fashionistas.

Information

The local tourist office for each destination is provided at the end of each relevant section.

Administración de Parques Nacionales
Avenida Santa Fe 690, entre Maipú y Marcelo T de Alvear, Retiro (4312 0820/www.apn.gov.ar). Subte C, San Martín/10, 17, 59, 152 bus. **Open** 10am-5pm Mon-Fri. **Map** p277 F7.

Provincia de Buenos Aires
Casa de la Provincia de Buenos Aires, Avenida Callao 237, entre Perón y Sarmiento, Tribunales (4371 7045/3587/www.vivalaspampas.com). Subte B, Callao/12, 24, 26, 60 bus. **Open** 9.30am-7pm Mon-Fri. **Map** p277 F6.

Provincia de Misiones
Casa de la Provincia de Misiones, Avenida Santa Fe 989, entre Carlos Pellegrini y Suipacha, Retiro (4312 0686/1097/0677). Subte C, San Martín/10, 17, 59, 152 bus. **Open** *Jan, Feb* 9am-6pm Mon-Fri. *Mar-Dec* 9am-5pm Mon-Fri. **Map** p277 F7.

Uruguay Tourist Information
Embajada de Uruguay, Ayacucho 1616, entre Las Heras y Vicente López, Recoleta (4807 3040, ext 1). Bus 10, 37, 59, 60, 101. **Open** 9.30am-4.30pm Mon-Fri. **Map** p278 G7.

Upriver

Water, water everywhere – so don't miss the islands, falls, fish and birdsong.

Tigre & the Delta

On the southern bank of the Río Luján, some 30 kilometres (19 miles) from downtown, is BA's easiest and most popular day-trip destination: Tigre. Appealing to both locals and foreigners alike, the colonial edifices and bloody sunsets give Tigre a somewhat exotic reputation, but it distracts from the fact this is as much a working town as a spot for recreation.

With 10,000 square kilometres (3,860 square miles) of islands in a network of waterways and channels surrounding it, Tigre acts both as a port and gateway to the surrounding delta. One English wag joked that if you crossed the Norfolk broads with *Apocalypse Now*, you'd end up with the Delta. While no one can deny the muddy waters and jutting reeds bear certain similarities to both, there are far too many exclusive homes and private jetties and hidden gems to pigeonhole it so neatly.

Though it was first colonised in 1520, its waters providing a calm spot for loading and unloading ships, the town of Pago de las Conchas – as it was called then – emerged in part due to the bootleggers who used the surrounding maze of ducts to avoid duties imposed by Spain. However, by the late 19th century flooding was a permanent threat to the town, and further construction was prohibited. Subsequently, shipping activities drifted to a new location, and Tigre was established.

By the end of the 19th century, Tigre was enjoying its belle époque – BA's high society used it as a summer playground, hosting extravagant galas and balls. The constructions of the magnificent **Buenos Aires Rowing Club** and the **Club Canottieri Italiani**, the Italian rowing club – its intricate façade built with materials shipped from Italy – recall this remarkable era of ostentatious development. But, no sooner had the party begun than it was over. With improved transport and the prospects of white sand the aristocrats abandoned their summer homes for the coastal city of Mar de Plata. In the past decade, Tigre has witnessed a mini-renaissance, having been rediscovered as a perfect bolt hole by *porteños* (around 80,000 visit each weekend) and due to the construction of the **Parque de la Costa** amusement park and the **Tren de la Costa** (*see p168*).

On arrival, visit the tourist office to pick up a map, then head to the **Mercado de Frutos** where incense and flowers perfume the air and stalls stacked high with fruits and wicker furniture trade from dawn to dusk. If thirsty, grab a *licuado* (milkshake) from the juice bar in front of the catamarans. A peaceful stroll is rather spoilt by the cacophony of dock drilling and the wild screams emanating from the amusement park – though there are great views from the Big Wheel. Next to the park sits the huge, incongruous **Nuevo Trilenium Casino de Tigre**, with slots, roulette tables and shows.

Heading past the **Estación Fluvial** – starting point for boat trips into the Delta – you'll come to the bridge that crosses to the delightful Paseo Victorica, a leafy promenade where people come to to eat, stroll and smooch. Facing the green verges are Italian restaurants, *parrillas*, ice-cream parlours, and even the odd corner bar, and in the backdrop, the splendid sight of the **Club de la Marina**, built in 1876.

At the far end of the strip is the interesting **Museo Naval de la Armada Argentina** (*see p225*), displaying models, paintings, manuscripts and fighter planes, tracing the highs and lows of the armed forces. From here, head to the Río de la Reconquista. In 1806, troops led by Santiago de Liniers retreated to the river's banks after a foiled attack on the English at the Bay of Olivos. The **Museo de la Reconquista** (*see p225*), displaying captured English weapons, is where Liniers and his officials successfully plotted the reconquest of Buenos Aires.

Delta Queen: Tigre's **Club de la Marina**.

Water world

Waterside restaurants, uninhabited islands, hotels lost in thick vegetation, rare flora and fauna; the Delta del Paraná has it all. You just need is a good mosquito repellent and time – the Primera Sección (first section) alone comprises 220 square kilometres (85 square miles), cross into the Segunda Sección and you're two hours from Tigre.

Departing on a *lancha colectiva* (riverbus) from the Estación Fluvial (fares AR$5-$10), the shortest excursions branch off the Río Luján and head down Río Sarmiento, a congested channel bordered by gardens and private jetties. The most interesting feature is former president Sarmiento's summerhouse (built 1855) – today the **Museo Sarmiento** (4728 0570, closed Mon, Tue), encased in glass. As the river bears right it is met by two others, Río San Antonio and the Río Capitán. This confluence is locally known as **Tres Bocas**, with a posse of restaurants, mid range *hosterías*, and even a wakeboard school (4728 0031, www.wakeschool. com.ar). Here, you can either disembark, head home via the San Antonio or continue into the further reaches of the Delta via the Capitán. Both rivers Capitán and Carapachay yield to the Río Paraná de las Palmas – named after the palm trees lining its banks. Deep and wide – one kilometre (0.5 miles) across, the river is shared by old cargo ships heading in and out of the River Plate.

For a different way of doing the delta, **Bonanza Deltaventura** (4798 2254, www.deltaventura.com) organise kayaking and trekking with bilingual guides to explain the flora and fauna, or check out **Nautical Escapes** for a similar deal (4731 6917, www.nauticalescapes.com).

But you don't have to just make a passing visit, you can eat or even stay in the delta – the starry, silent nights are truly relaxing. On Río Sarmiento at Muelle Masmor, **El Remanso** (4728 0575, main courses AR$8-$17, closed dinner Mon-Thur, Sun) is signposted by an imposing pine tree and bamboo pergola. Enjoy juicy steaks and the house speciality – home-made pasta. **La Riviera** (Río Sarmiento 356, 4728 0177) is a river classic, just 30 minutes from Tigre, serving trad Argentinian dishes on the terrace, AR$15 for a three-course meal.

A comfortable and cute accommodation option on the Rama Negra is the **Hostería**

Alpenhaus (4728 0422, www.alpenhaus. com.ar). Resembling an Alpine chalet, the charming complex includes bungalows with a jacuzzi, and there's a gym and sauna and games for kids. Weekend specials (two days, one night) start from AR$290 for two. Just across the river, on the tip of the confluence is the rather eerie **El Tropézon** (Río Paraná de las Palmas, y Canal de la Serna, 4728 1012, from AR$35-$80 per person). Rooms are basic and the bar area surreal, especially when a tanker slips behind the waterfront reeds – it's also where writer Leopoldo Lugones committed suicide in 1938. A little further up is the delightful **La Pascuala Delta Lodge** (Arroyo Las Canas, 4728 1253, www.lapascuala.com.ar, US$195 per person for two days and one night, all inclusive; pictured), undoubtedly the Delta's most luxurious digs and chosen location for TV reality show *Confianza Ciega*. Hidden under thick foliage, the Pascuala – entirely built from wood on its own island – includes 15 luxury cabins, a pool, haute-cuisine, and a self-service cocktail bar. The prices may look a little expensive, but the deal includes food, booze and a fantastic service (transport not included – it's beyond where the riverbuses will take you – and no children allowed).

Museo Naval de la Armada Argentina

Paseo Victorica 602 (4749 0608). **Open**
8.30am-5.30pm Mon-Fri; 10.30am-6.30pm Sat,
Sun. **Admission** AR$2; AR$1 concessions.
No credit cards.

Museo de la Reconquista

Liniers 818, y Padre Castañeda (4512 4496).
Open *Feb-Dec* 10am-6pm Wed-Sun. **Closed** Jan.
Admission free.

Where to stay & eat

The most interesting options for food and
lodging are out in the Delta del Paraná (*see
p224* **Water world**), though in Tigre itself,
Casona La Ruchi (Lavalle 557, 4749 2499,
www.casonalaruchi.com.ar, doubles AR$84),
built in 1893, is a sublime small hotel. Its
exquisite rustic decor, large bedrooms and back
garden with swimming pool make it a must if
you're staying in Tigre. The **Villa Akapana**
(Paseo Victorica 800, 4749 0642, www.aka
pana.org, doubles US$130), opening March
2004, is a beautiful old colonial house being
converted into hotel. It's part of a project
to promote and protect aboriginal Argentinian
art and culture. The eight rooms vary in
size – pick the one facing the Delta with a
huge balcony. There are regular concerts,
exhibitions and a fine pool.

For food, the riverside terrace, towering trees
and waiters in white jackets at **María Luján**
(Paseo Victorica 611, y Vito Dumas, 4731 9613,
main courses AR$13-$25) give this seafood
restaurant an elegantly old-fashioned feel.
It's a shade more expensive than the rest, but
well worth it. For something quick, closer to the
port, try **La Vaca Atigrada** (the Tigered Cow
– Lavalle 369, 4749 0698); for AR$10 (AR$12 at
the weekend), you get a self-service salad bar,
soft drinks, two mini empanadas and unlimited
servings of barbecued meat.

Tourist information

Ente Municipal de Turismo de Tigre

*Estación Fluvial de Tigre, Mitre 305 (4512 4497/
www.tigre.gov.ar)*. **Open** 9am-5pm daily.

Getting there

By bus

The omnipresent *colectivo* No.60 from Buenos
Aires takes between 1hr 15mins and 1hr 45mins,
depending on traffic, and costs AR$1.35 one way.

By train

Tigre is a 50-min train ride from Retiro (return
AR$1.90). Trains run every 15mins from 4am-1.30am.

Cataratas de Iguazú

Having got everything else out of the way,
God must have spent the eighth day creating
the dazzlingly beautiful Cataratas de Iguazú –
the Iguazú Falls. At just over an hour and a
half's plane ride from Buenos Aires, this jewel
of the jungle tops the list of weekend breaks
to be had outside the capital.

One of the true wonders of the natural
world, the 23 kilometres (14 miles) of foaming
waterfalls dropping into a 70-metre (230-foot)
high river canyon are everything you could ever
hope to see in the way of an eco-spectacular.
Whether it's the jungle setting, the primordial
soupy look of the iron-rich water or the
remoteness of the area, the Iguazú Falls make
the likes of Niagara (which has a greater
volume) and Venezuela's Angel Falls (many
times higher) appear mere taps by comparison.
After a fling in BA's urban mayhem, this is a
salutary lesson that nature is more awesome
than anything that humankind can rustle up.

Numerous travel agencies in Buenos Aires
offer package tours to Iguazú, including flights,
accommodation and excursions; it's a case of
shopping around. As a guideline expect to pay
AR$700-$1,200 for a three-day/two-night deal,
depending on the standard of accommodation.

The falls lie in the glorious setting of the
Parque Nacional Iguazú, at the northern
tip of the province of Misiones, on Argentina's
frontier with Brazil and Paraguay (the three
countries' tripartite border is at the confluence
of the Iguazú and Paraná Rivers). Puerto
Iguazú, the small town on the Argentinian side
where planes and buses from BA arrive, is the
best place to stay for a two- or three-day visit.
There are bus services every half hour (AR$4
return trip) to the park gates, 15 minutes away,
where you pay AR$30 admission per day
(AR$12 Argentinian nationals).

Arriving by plane or overland, you'll see
what looks like a cloud of steam rising from
the broccoli of subtropical rainforest. It's the
water vapour and spray rising from over 250
separate falls, including the stunning **Salto
San Martín** and the even vaster **Garganta
del Diablo**, the horseshoe-shaped 'Devil's
Throat' cataract, which receives around 70
per cent of the tumbling Río Iguazú.

As you approach the falls on *tierra firma*,
imagine the impact made on Don Alvar Núñez
Cabeza de Vaca when, in 1541, while searching
for a waterway linking Brazil with the River
Plate, he became the first European to cast
eyes upon the falls. He might have understood
the animistic awe of the local Guaraní, who
lived in caves by what they called the 'great
waters', from which comes the name Iguazú.

The falls are truly superlative, leaving visitors thrashing around for adjectives. Nor is this a static, short-lived emotion. Every turn opens up a new vista and the mood of the water changes constantly. Between the main falls, it streams, trickles and drops all day from great bottle-green leaves, lianas and grasses that hug the cliffs, and the back-to-nature blast will have you wanting to escape into the verdure like Tarzan or scramble up the vertical rocks like De Niro in *The Mission* to shed your city sins.

Vencejos (grey-rumped swifts) dart in and out of the cascades and butterflies flutter at peril around the vapour clouds, while on rocks jutting out of the frothing maelstrom below, larger birds build their nests. From the first shy flap of the Toco toucans at dawn, the national park is a treasure for bird-lovers. Plush-crested jays, night herons, snowy egrets, vultures and cowbirds are common sights, and you might see a snail kite searching for prey in the shallows.

Lemur-like coatis abound throughout the park. Higher up, capuchin monkeys and squirrels inhabit the forest's canopy. Caimans feed on snails, fish and toads in some sections of the Iguazú, but you're more likely to see lizards like the large *tegu*. At night, jaguars stalk the undergrowth and when the moon is full, park rangers run night walks (organised via the tourist office; AR$15-$35). By day, a walk down the **Sendero Macuco** trail is a chance to escape humanity: look for birds and mammals and, at the very least, listen to the jungle. The pool at the end of the trail is technically not for bathing, but most walkers use it to cool off, showering beneath the Salto Arrechea Fall.

Visits to this jaw-dropper of a national park begin at its reception area and information centre, just beyond the entrance, from where excursions can be organised. The centre is worth a visit for an overview of the area's flora and fauna. From here, head by eco-train or by foot – car access is prohibited – to one of the three main trails offering views of the falls.

The propane-fuelled train which transports visitors from the reception area to the falls runs every 30 minutes, stopping at the Cataratas Station before going on to the Garganta del Diablo Station. Most tour parties take the first train at 8.30am, so arrive early or wait until 'rush hour' is over. Those who just miss a train might try the short walk via the **Sendero Verde** (Green Trail) from the train terminus in the reception area to Cataratas Station. From here, a further short trek leads to the park's two main trails: the Superior and the Inferior. As these names suggest, the choice is between straddling the falls from above or coming up close to where the water cannons into rocks below – both wonderful viewpoints. The lower

trail is a more arduous, but neither is really tricky and the chance to get soaked metres away from the pounding waters is unmissable.

For a view of the most powerful part of the falls, take the train on to Garganta station. From here a catwalk that stretches for just over a kilometre traverses the Río Iguazu to the breathtaking Garganta del Diablo, shared by Argentina and Brazil.

BOAT TRIPS & DAY TRIPS

To get up close to the falls, visit the *cabaña* (office) of **Iguazú Jungle Explorer** – the company that runs various excursions and boat trips (AR$30 per person) – in the information centre. The longest trip, the Gran Aventura (AR$70), takes you through the jungle by open-top truck, after which you pick up a motorboat and speed towards the falls. You'll be drenched by the spray, but it's a rush. The quieter Paseo Ecológico takes you on the Iguazú Superior from the jetty near the Garganta del Diablo back to the main park; it's serene, even though the falls are just a few hundred metres away. Take lots of suncream as it's very exposed.

For happy snappers, the Safari Fotográfico, offered by **Explorador Expediciones** (03757 421632) from the information centre, takes you on a two-hour overland photo safari (AR$35) or a four-hour birdwatching trip (US$60). Both companies can be contacted via the Sheraton Hotel inside the park on 03757 421600.

Iguazú Falls: and you will too.

You can also walk from Puerto Iguazú to the Hito frontier post, marking Argentina's borders with both Brazil and Paraguay. Though there's little to see, it's worth doing: there's something very Graham Greene-ish about these wild frontiers and it seems astonishing that such jungly regions were colonised at all. A small crafts fair functions at the Hito.

Many visitors to the falls also take day trips to the city of Foz do Iguazú in Brazil or the massive Itaipú dam in Paraguay – but not the ugly, dangerous Paraguayan city, Ciudad del Este. Your hotel will organise a trip to the dam if a man-made waterfall is really what you want to see. A visit to Foz is a chance to eat more tropical food and slug a Caipirinha, while a trip into the Brazilian side of the park – worth doing, and offered as a day trip by numerous tour operators on the Argentinian side – offers stunning panoramic views of all the falls. The Brazilian visitors' centre and gift shop is informative and well organised. Buses to the city of Foz depart from the Puerto Iguazú terminal every hour. Staying in Foz (though cheaper) is not recommended, however, as the city has a reputation for dangerous crime.

Where to eat

For daytime in the park, there are three restaurants and various snack stands. Back in Puerto Iguazú for the evening, try **Charo** (Avenida Córdoba 1186, 03757 421529, main course AR$8-$26), for a grilled *surubí* river fish. For outdoor eats and live music, **Tío Querido**, next to the Libertador Hotel on Bompland, is the nicest-looking, though there are several basic beer-and-pizza places with terraces on Avenida Victoria Aguirre near the plaza.

Where to stay

All hotels can organise tours and excursions. Inside the park, the **Sheraton International Iguazú** (03757 421600, www.sheraton.com) has five-star comforts and rooms with a view, but is expensive (US$218-$278, depending on view) and allows for zero contact with the local people. Better to stay in Puerto Iguazú, where the best three-star hotel is the **Hotel Saint George** (Avenida Córdoba 148, 03757 420633, www.hotelsaintgeorge.com, doubles AR$120). It's only a couple of minutes from the bus terminal, with pool, air-con and breakfast.

Budget travellers should seek out the attractive, Swiss-owned **Hostería Los Helechos** (Calle Paulino Amarante 76, 03757 420829, www.hosterialoshelechos.com.ar, doubles AR$45-$50), which has patios and a pool. For hostel accommodation, the **Hostel-Inn Iguazú Falls** (Ruta 12, Km 5, 03757 421823, www.hostel-inn.com), five minutes from the bus terminal, has a pool and dorm accommodation for AR$15-$20.

If you do want to spend a night on the Brazilian side of the falls, make sure you get a room at the delightful, colonial-style, pink-hued **Hotel Tropical das Cataratas** (00 55 45 521 7000, www.tropicalhotel.com.br), safely tucked inside the national park. Rooms start at US$116 for a double. Guests can do breakfast on the hotel's veranda, from where views of the falls, just a short stroll away, are spectacular.

For serious nature enthusiasts, 60 kilometres (37 miles) from the falls in the middle of a jungle reserve is the stunning **Yacutinga Ecolodge**. Check the website for information on packages: www.yacutinga.com.

When to go

The mean temperature in Iguazú is a pleasant 23°C (73°F), although extremes can range from zero in July to a skin-lacerating 40°C (103°F) in January. Most Argentinians visit the falls on Easter weekend or during the winter school holidays (late July), when prices rise and the park has queues on the catwalks. It rains all year, with peaks in April/May and October/November, the latter coming in the unwelcome company of 90 per cent humidity. Still, you'll get wet anyway if you hop in a boat or approach the falls, so make sure you take a plastic bag for your camera.

Tourist information

Secretaria de Turismo

Avenida Victoria Aguirre 311, y Brañas, Puerto Iguazú (03757 420800). **Open** 8am-midnight daily.

Getting there

By air

Flying is the wisest option, with several direct daily flights with **Aerolineas Argentinas, Austral, American Falcon** and **Southern Winds** to Puerto Iguazú from BA's Jorge Newbery city airport. The flight takes 1hr 30mins and costs about AR$595 return; Argentinians pay approximately half-price.

By road

Buses leaving Retiro bus station take a whopping 16hrs to get to Puerto Iguazú. Operators include **Crucero del Norte** (4315 0478, four buses a day, AR$80-$90 one way) and **Vía Bariloche** (4663 3219, three buses a day, AR$80-$95 one way). If you drive, allow at least 20hrs depending how often you rest – but even if you want to visit the San Ignacio ruins in southern Misiones, a car is a costly inconvenience: buses run regularly from Puerto Iguazú

Country

Ride out to the pampas and round up the world's best beef.

San Antonio de Areco

San Antonio de Areco (population 20,000), about 113 kilometres (70 miles) north-west of the capital in the province of Buenos Aires, is smack dab in the middle of gaucho country.

With its cobblestone streets of one-storey, century-old buildings surrounded by seemingly limitless expanses of flat, grassy plains, the sleepy town looks straight out of the movies. No surprise then, that during 2002, it was used as the location for the box-office flop *Imagining Argentina*, starring Antonio Banderas and Emma Thompson.

A popular weekend destination with few traffic lights or signs of urban blight, prior to its discovery by Hollywood San Antonio was the backdrop for the classic Argentinian gaucho novel, *Don Segundo Sombra*, written by the town's famous son Ricardo Güiraldes and published in 1926. More an aristocratic *bon vivant* than real cowboy, Güiraldes wrote the book as a tribute to his gaucho farmhand-turned-mentor at **La Porteña**, a now famous *estancia* (ranch) outside town; *see p231*.

Named after the Areco River that flows to its north, the town dates from a chapel built in 1728 in honour of San Antonio de Padua on the estate of an early settler, José Ruiz de Arellano. Settlers prayed to the saint to protect them from the indigenous tribes that populated the area. Now called **Iglesia Parroquial**, the chapel

was converted into a parish in 1730, and the town and its tropical-looking central plaza (later named after Ruiz de Arellano), mushroomed around it. Across the plaza is the pink and white **Municipalidad** (town hall) and the **Casa de los Martínez**, considered to be the site of Ruiz de Arellano's ranch house. A block north, on Alsina, between Lavalle and Matheu, is the **Centro Cultural Usina**, which exhibits work by mostly local artisans.

The main drag is Alsina, which runs through the town centre to Plaza Ruiz de Arellano and the river beyond. **Parque Criollo** and the **Museo Gauchesco Ricardo Güiraldes** (*see p229*) are located on the north side of the river, on Ricardo Güiraldes, a short distance from the pink **Puente Viejo**, one of the country's first toll bridges and the town's unofficial symbol. The park contains Pulpería La Blanqueada, a tavern/general store that Güiraldes wrote about in *Don Segundo*. The museum, which opened in 1938, is a replica of an 18th-century ranch, with a cactus in front and a bridge of tree branches over the small gully that surrounds it. Its eight rooms exhibit saddles, silver knives and other assorted gaucho gear collected by the writer, whose work has been translated into 17 languages, including Croatian, Ukranian and Tagalog.

San Antonio is known for its crafts – silver, leather products, woven rugs and jackets and a variety of typical gaucho articles, such as *facones* (large knives). Visitors can watch

Trips Out of Town

Go gaucho at **El Ombú** *estancia* in San Antonio de Areco. *See p231*.

artists ply their craft in the 40 or so workshops scattered around the town (the tourist centre can provide a map). At the top end of the scale, Cristina Giordano (Sarmiento 112, 02326 452829) weaves custom-made ponchos, blankets and *fajas* (cloth belts worn by gauchos) in the workshop attached to her home (ring the bell if you don't see her). Raul Draghi makes silver and gold jewellery at a workshop in his house at Guido 391 (02326 455499; by appointment). José Draghi is San Antonio's best-known *platero* (silversmith) and his workshop on Lavalle 387 (02326 454219; 10.30am-1pm, 4-8pm daily) doubles as a museum housing his large collection of 19th-century gaucho articles.

If this quiet town has a high season, it's throughout November, when there's a buzz of rural activities in preparation for the spirited gaucho parade and festivities on the annual **Día de la Tradición**.

The town is small enough to be covered on foot though locals get around on bicycles, which you can rent at Zerboni 315, between Alsina and Belgrano. Taxis are rare, except for the ones that await new arrivals at the bus station on the edge of town. If you want to save time or are heading directly to an *estancia*, your best bet is a car service. Remis Zerboni (02326 453288/455800) at Alsina and Alem operates 24 hours a day. If San Antonio's small, weekend tourist rush is too much for you, then **Capilla del Señor** is an even less crowded, bucolic prairie town, located about 40 kilometres (25 miles) east. To get there, take any bus heading towards BA, get off in El Pilar, and take a city bus to the end of the line.

Parque Criollo & Museo Gauchesco Ricardo Güiraldes

Camino al Ricardo Güiraldes, y Camino al Parque (02326 455839). **Open** 11am-5pm Mon, Wed-Sun. **Admission** AR$2; free under-12s. **No credit cards.**

Where to eat

For a taste of the local scene, **Confitería Jockey Club** (Alsina 226, no phone), is a basic hamburger joint but with pool tables and enough chairs and tables to make it look like a bingo hall. It's open on weekends, from 7pm. **Pizzeria Dell'Olmo** (Alsina 365, 02326 452506, closed lunch) is bright, slick and air-conditioned pizzeria, which also serves up empanadas and ice-cream.

Don't miss **El Bessonart** (no phone), a classic gaucho *pulpería* at Segundo Sombra and Zapiola. It closed in 2004 after the death of the long-time owner, but now his children sporadically reopen and a city subsidy could see hours extended. Whether open or not, its

barely-standing heap of whitewashed bricks is worth admiring from the outside.

Meat-lovers can easily find a decent *parrilla* alongside the river. For a more memorable meal, walk across the Puente Viejo to **Arte y Oficio de la Pampa** (no phone) on the corner of Güiraldes and Ciriaco Díaz, which has quiet, terrace dining and sells home-made jams and chesses as well as handicrafts. It's open from 9am Wednesday to Sunday. A few blocks off the tourist circuit, family-run **La Filomena** (Vieytes 395, 02326 453507, www.lafilomenadeareco.com.ar, open after 7pm at weekends only) is San Antonio's only gourmet hangout, specialising in modern fusion cuisine with a country kick and live music.

Where to stay

If you don't return to BA the same day, there's a handful of simple hotels to crash in, though most overnight travellers will prefer to stay at an *estancia* in the surrounding countryside (*see p230*). Prices go up on weekends and holidays, and reservations are recommended. **Hotel San Carlos** (Zapiola y Zervoni, 02326 453106, www.hotelsancarlos.com.ar, doubles AR$35-$45) has small rooms with a ceiling fan, TV and tiny bathrooms, as well as two six-person apartments with air-con. There's a tiny pool and bicycles that guests can use. Across the street, **Hotel Los Abuelos** (02326 456390, doubles AR$50) has a slightly larger pool and better rooms; the price includes breakfast.

Tourist information

Dirección de Turismo de la Municipalidad

Boulevard Zervoni, y Arellano (02326 453165/www.arecoturismo.com.ar/www.arecogaucho.com.ar). **Open** 8.30am-7pm Mon-Fri, 8am-8pm Sat-Sun. English is spoken. Provides brochures and maps pointing out the town's historic sites. Can organise a 3-hour tour of the town in English for AR$50.

Getting there

By bus

Chevallier (4314 3639) offers the most frequent daily service, about once an hour, AR$12 each way, from Retiro bus terminal. The journey takes about 2hrs. Upon arrival in San Antonio, ask at the station for the departure schedule; at weekends, if you want a seat on the way back, come at least 30mins early, though drivers will allow a certain number of passengers to stand.

By car

San Antonio de Areco is 1hr 30mins from BA on Ruta 8. A *remise* from BA will cost around AR$170.

Holy cow

Leave it to meat-eaters in the UK and US to worry about mad cow or foot and mouth. In Argentina carnivores face a more primal dilemma: rump or tenderloin?

As the sacred cow of Argentina's national diet, meat is cheap, tasty and, above all, macho. In the 17th and 18th centuries, when gauchos roamed the pampas, they were allowed to kill cows and eat whatever was left over after their valuable hides were delivered to their owner. A culinary custom inherited from the gauchos is the *asador* technique, still used at traditional restaurants, where meat is hung on cross-poles and cooked round an open fire of glowing embers. Even today, at *estancias*, meat is prepared as *carne con cuero*: half a cow barbecued with the hide on, the modern-day gauchos eating hairy slabs straight off their knives.

The macho-gaucho folklore also explains the manly girth of some steaks – so thick is a true *bife de chorizo* that it can be deep brown on the outside, but remain so rare inside that you can almost feel a pulse. Those bountiful pampas, not hormones or special feeds, are why steaks are bigger, more tender and tastier in Argentina.

The *asado* (barbecue) is a supremely important ritual, ranking above football as a source of carefree camaraderie and family values. It's an unforgettable, if marathon-like, experience. As wine flows, a sweetish aroma rises from the grill and everyone tucks into a *choripán* (sausage sandwich). Just be sure to leave your squeamishness aside – among the entrails Argentinians feast on are blood sausage, intestines, kidneys, even the occasional brain and testicle. And don't forget to clap keenly when, at meal's end, someone calls for an *aplauso para el asador* (a round of applause for the pit master).

The Atkins diet may be a North American creation, but its most devout followers, albeit unintentionally, are in Argentina. Per person beef consumption is, with Uruguay, the highest in the world and triple that of the UK. In the provinces, it is still customary to eat meat twice a day and in downtown Buenos Aires, construction workers and other labourers often set up a small, primitive grill at the side of the road for their lunchtime repast.

Estancias

In the 19th century, European immigrants flocked to Argentina to take advantage of a vast, fertile, untapped territory, building *estancias* throughout the countryside. Many ranches have been in the same family for generations and still raise cattle and crops. In the past decade, more and more of these homes opened to the public as agro industry replaced the family farm and owners faced the choice of shuttering large homes that were too expensive to run or opening them as upmarket B&Bs.

Buenos Aires province has the highest concentration of these ranches, ranging in style from Tudor castles to Italian villas. Choose from a one-day Día de Campo package – often including all-you-can-eat *asado* (barbecue), horse riding and a folk music or gaucho show – to a weekend or longer stay. Many *estancias* host corporate events or weddings, so enquire first to avoid your tranqillity being breached by smiling salesmen or drunken relatives. It may look expensive at first, but horse riding and all your food (which is usually excellent) are included – though some drinks and activities may be extra – and children generally pay half-price. Many also offer rides in horse-drawn carriages and some have pools. They will cater for vegetarians, but tell them in advance. Bring insect repellent in summer to ward off the area's voracious bugs and mosquitos.

With the rise in rural tourism some *estancias*, like **San Ceferino** (02323 441500, www.estancia sanceferino.com.ar, AR$220 per person), are broadening their reach and incorporating traditional hotel-like services such as spas. Upscale resorts offering a relaxing rural retreat but with more modern conveniences and none of the gaucho lore have also sprung up. Near the capital is **Elevage General Rodríguez Resort** (4891 8022, www.elevage.com.ar, doubles AR$180). Among the best, further south near hilly Tandil, is delightful **Posada de los Pajaros** hotel and spa (in BA 4811 5662, 02293 432013, www.posadapajaros-spa.com, AR$295-$365 per person).

Owing to its popularity as a tourist destination, several *estancias* are located near San Antonio – we've listed the best below – but almost all *estancias* are within 125 kilometres (78 miles) of Buenos Aires. Reservations are a must: call the *estancia* direct or book through knowledgeable BA-based travel agent **José de Santís** (Office 313, Avenida Roque Sáenz Peña 616, Microcentro, 4343 2366, www.estancias argentinas.com) or **Lan & Kramer Travel** (14th Floor, Florida 868, Retiro, 4748 4440, www.estanciastravel.com). If driving, ask for directions when you book.

Santa Rita and **La Candelaria** – the ultimate in rural elegance.

La Bamba

San Antonio de Areco (in BA 4732 1269/02326 456293/www.la-bamba.com.ar). **Rates** US$180 double; AR$40 Día de Campo. **Credit** AmEx, MC V.

La Bamba is one of the San Antonio region's most traditional *estancias* offering an authentic window into the country's *criollo* past. An 1830s main house, painted bloody red, was the backdrop for the legendary Argentinian film *Camila*. Comfortable rooms are furnished in the same colonial style, the most romantic being the main one with an open fireplace. The food is also top notch.

La Candelaria

Lobos (02227 424404/www.lacandelaria.com.ar). **Rates per person** AR$110-$170; AR$75 Día de Campo. **Credit** MC V.

When travelling 19th-century aristocrats Rebeca Piñeiro and Manuel de Fraga fell in love with a castle in France, they tracked down the architect and brought him back – along with plenty of French, German and English furniture – to the pampas. The result, after nine years of construction, is the most regal, if out of place, of Argentinian *estancias*. Landscape architect Carlos Thays' vast gardens are equally magnificent, but the rather worn bedrooms don't quite match up to the awesome first impressions created from the exterior.

La Cinacina

San Antonio de Areco (02326 452773/02326 452045/www.lacinacina.com.ar). **Rates** AR$34 Día de Campo. **No credit cards.**

Located about eight blocks from Plaza Ruiz de Arellano in San Antonio, La Cinacina is more of a gaucho theme park than a country estate, but its Día de Campo packages are among the most affordable. Always busy at the weekends.

La Encantada

Capilla del Señor (02323 492063/www.posada laencantada.com.ar). **Rates per person** AR$80-$100; AR$40 Día de Campo. **No credit cards.**

The small, but picturesque, country house was built in 1856. If it's not too windy or raining you can take a 50-minute hot-air balloon ride for AR$210 and there's also a swimming pool and horse riding (which costs AR$10). La Encantada is probably best for a day trip, since it doesn't offer many other attractions and is relatively close to Buenos Aires. During summer months, there is a programme of teatime classical music concerts in the garden.

La Martina

Vicente Casares (02226 430777/www.lamartinapolo. com). **Rates per person** US$300 for polo-playing guests; US$150 for non-polo-playing guests. US$50-$70 Día de campo. **No credit cards.**

Adolfo Cambiaso – one of the world's leading players – runs a top-flight polo school for foreigners out of this century-old *estancia* 45 minutes from downtown BA. Cambiaso breeds all the ponies and he can often be found playing an exhibition match on one of the ranch's four full-size polo fields. Rooms are simple but elegant. There's also a swimming pool, tennis courts and all-important massages after a day of strenuous chukkas.

El Ombú de Areco

San Antonio de Areco (4710 2795/02326 492080/ www.estanciaelombu.com). **Rates per person** US$75; US$35 Día de Campo. **Credit** V.

About 6km (4 miles) from San Antonio, El Ombú was built in 1880 in the style of an Italian villa for Indian-slayer General Juan Pablo Ricchieri, but in the ensuing century has taken on a more *criollo* look. It's the ultimate stress reliever with an unpretentious working ranch feel. Walls are covered in ivy and its sizeable acreage of soya bean fields and cattle pasture border the Areco River. There's a games room with a pool table, backgammon and a TV, and a small pool, and the delicious home-made eats include unforgettable empanadas. The owner speaks English and German.

La Porteña

San Antonio de Areco (02326 453770/452513/www. estancialaportenia.com.ar). **Rates** US$150 double; US$35 per person Día de Campo. **No credit cards.**

All you'll hear across the enormous expanses of manicured lawns and stately trees is the wind and a few birds chirping. The first owner, a railroad magnate, named the estate after Argentina's first steam locomotive. The four spacious rooms, all in the main house, have hardwood floors and large windows. Ricardo Güiraldes wrote in the single second-floor room. Perfect for couples.

El Rosario de Areco

San Antonio de Areco (02326 451000/www.rosario deareco.com.ar). **Rates per person** US$110 double; US$50 Día de Campo. **No credit cards.**

Former stables house the bedrooms, and the dining room and lounge are in an old barn. The owners raise polo horses and have an official polo field; the

A bird's eye view

Whether on foot or, even better still, on horseback, birdwatching out on the pampas is a glorious way to get to know the province and its abundant wildlife. The reasons are simple: the treeless pampas are an endless spread of wetlands, marshes and rush-filled lagoons which attract large wading birds as well as a variety of coots, grebes and ducks. And the fact that the pampas are dead flat means you can spy on birds for miles as they go about their daily chores.

Following in the furtive footsteps of 19th-century ornithologist extraordinaire William Henry Hudson, Argentina-bound birdwatchers flock to **Punta Rasa** and the huge spaces of **Campos del Tuyú** reserve near San Clemente del Tuyú on the South Atlantic coast, about 300 kilometres (186 miles) south of the capital. Even birders en route to the exotic southern wilderness of Patagonia or the Argentinian North-west make sure they spend a day or two at this much-loved site, where it's possible to see more than 200 species on any given day. The proximity of the coast and the bay of the Samborombón river means you can also see buff-breasted sandpipers, oystercatchers, red shovelers and a variety of gulls. Beautiful migrants such as the scissor-tailed flycatcher pass through in summer.

Born to British parents in Quilmes in 1841, now a built-up suburb in southern Buenos Aires, but then a handful of ranches, Hudson learned to spot the common species without binoculars. Whether or not you take along his eloquent field notes or his famed tribute to gaucho life and feathered friends, *Far Away and Long Ago*, you'll have little trouble clocking the two common carrion hawks – the *chimango* and *carancho* – as well as the three sizes of white egret, the black-necked swan, the tiny, attractively-coloured musical *chingolo* sparrow, the raucous *kiskadee* and Argentina's national bird, the rufous *hornero* (ovenbird, after its clay oven-style nests). A constant companion is the southern lapwing, which calls out its onomatopoeic local name *tero tero* all day.

Impressive common species include the roseate spoonbill, the even pinker Chilean flamingo, the tall *maguari* stork, the night and white-necked herons and foraging packs of emu-sized flightless greater rheas, known locally as *ñandues*. Hawks, such as the snail kite, can frequently be seen hovering above ditches looking for juicy shells.

Birds of Argentina & Uruguay: A Field Guide, by T Narosky and D Yzurieta (Vazquez Mazzini Editores) has useful sketches and notes, with names in Latin and Spanish, the latter useful if you need to ask a passing gaucho what you are looking at. Between enjoying the birdlife, look out also for skunks, *coipus*, foxes, hares, and, er, cows. **Fundación Vida Silvestre Argentina** (www.vidasilvestre.org.ar) administers Campos del Tuyú reserve and has information about visiting. A good website for background information is www.avesargentinas.org.ar.

Polo Week package is offered during Argentina's Polo Open tournament in November, for US$250 per night. Anyone can participate and they teach you how to play. El Rosario is on the small side and a bit pricey, but there's a 10% discount for online bookings. English, French and Italian spoken.

Santa Rita

Antonio Carboni, Lobos (4804 6341/02227 495026/ www.santa-rita.com.ar). **Rates per person** AR$145 double; AR$70 Día de Campo. **No credit cards**.
This mini, magical estate's first construction, a chapel for converting the local native population, dates from the colonial era – the main house was built in 1790. All the rooms have their charm, but the front-facing one on the first floor has an incredible panoramic view of the leafy grounds. Horseback rides across the property to a quiet rivulet are a must. There's also the chance to see farm activities being carried out, and a swimming pool can be used during summer months.

Villa María

Máximo Paz (4322 7785/02274 450909/www. estanciavmaria.com.ar). **Rates per person** US$120; US$50 Día de Campo. **No credit cards**.
Celebrity Argentinian architect Alejandro Bustillo, also responsible for Buenos Aires' Banco Nación, built this monumental Tudor mansion in 1925 for beef baron Celedonio Pereda. Sixteen bright, elegant rooms look over an impressive artificial lake and immaculate grounds designed by Carlos Thays. There's a swimming pool and cosy billiard hall, as well as horse riding and carriage rides. The high prices reflect its popularity with a jet-set clientele.

▶ For more information on **polo** and the **Polo Open** tournament, *see p200.*
▶ For where to go **horse riding** in Buenos Aires, *see p203.*
▶ For the **Día de la Tradición**, *see p163.*

Beach

It's not Brazil, but Argentina's Atlantic seaboard is great for family fun, partying or an escape into peaceful pine forests and sand dunes.

Mar del Plata

For many Argentinians, holidays are synonymous with the coastal resort of Mar del Plata. It's a big seaside city in all its tack and glory, and people come in droves year after year. A huge chunk of Buenos Aires life – cultural events, football matches, even TV productions – decamps to the coast for summer.

The town – 400 kilometres (250 miles) south of Buenos Aires, with a year-round population of 650,000, swelling to over a million in summer – was founded in 1874. It became a refuge for the *porteño* aristocracy and more recently, the Argentinian middle-class tourist destination par excellence, though it has lost much of its former splendour. Whatever its fortunes, the town has always enjoyed the beauty of undulating hills, 47 kilometres (30 miles) of beaches and to the north, the woodlands of **Parque Camet**, which are great for every kind of outing and sport.

To the south, 20 kilometres (12 miles) beyond the lighthouse, lie the most exclusive beaches: **La Reserva**, **Del Balcón** and **La Caseta**. Continuing on Ruta 11 brings you to **Miramar**, with magnificent views, woodland and 20-metre (65-foot) high cliffs running down to the ocean. This is the best spot for surfing; for more information, see www.elsurfero.com.

Out of season there's a chance to enjoy the life, rhythm and attractions of the city away from the midsummer madness. Mardel (as it is affectionately known) does what it can to entice visitors once summer closes, the major draw being the city's international film festival, held every March (though outstripped in popularity by BA's own independent film fest).

The seafront boardwalk, **La Rambla** – constructed in 1940 by architect Alejandro Bustillo, who also built the casino – and the San Martín pedestrian area are the most popular walkways. The *puerto* (port) is full of pervasive odours from the fishmeal factories and old, rusting yellow boats. In the south docks, there's a large colony of sea lions (the symbol of Mar del Plata), and you can take a one-hour boat trip to view the main beaches from the sea. At night, the port fills with people visiting the dozen or so local restaurants serving seafood specialities.

For a blast of Mardel's past, walk through the barrios of Stella Maris, Playa Grande, Los Troncos and Divino Rostro. There you'll find the **Centro Cultural Victoria Ocampo** (Matheu 1851, 0223 492 0569), open from 3-9pm daily. Also known as Villa Victoria, it's an English-style mansion that was once the home of the writer Victoria Ocampo. Art-lovers should check out the **Museo Municipal de Arte Juan Carlos Castagnino & Villa Ortiz Basualdo** (Avenida Colón 1189, 0223 486 1636). If it rains, or you have kids to entertain, there's a large aquarium, nature reserve, zoo and interactive children's park (ask the tourist office for details). For fresher air, head for the hills on Ruta 226 to the **Laguna de los Padres** forest nature reserve; among the attractions are a zoo and a museum dedicated to the author of *Martín Fierro*.

Where to eat

During the high season, the all you can eat *tenedor libres* concentrated in the San Martín area, are extremely cheap and usually have queues outside the door. **Montecatini Alpe** (Belgrano 2350, 0223 494 3446/6894) has decent, cheap nosh, while **La Fontanella** (Rawson 2302, 0223 494 0533) has more serious haute cuisine – the seafood pastas are splendid. If you're heading for the port, seek out **Chichillo**, where the *mejillones a la provenzal* (mussels with garlic sauce) are highly recommended.

Where to stay

Mar del Plata has multiple accommodation options, including thosands of apartments to rent, and great deals can be found with most BA travel agents. Opposite Playa Grande is the five-star **Hotel Costa Galana** (Boulevard Patricio Peralta Ramos 5725, 0223 486 0000, www.hotelcostagalana.com.ar, doubles AR\$281-\$336). With similar sea views and luxurious amenities, the **Sheraton Mar de Plata** (Avenida Alem 4221, 0223 499 9000, www.mardelplata360.com, doubles AR\$320-\$479) has the added boon of being just opposite a golf course. For something cheaper, try the lovely sea-facing **Hotel Guerrero** (Diagonal Juan B Alberdi 2288, 0223 495 8851, www. hotelguerrero.com.ar, doubles AR\$68–\$119); out of season promotions are fantastic value.

Spot the sand: midsummer **Mar del Plata**.

Getting there

By air
Aerolineas Argentinas and **Southern Winds** offer several flights daily from Jorge Newbery domestic airport: 45mins, AR$180-$336 return.

By bus
Numerous hourly services from Retiro station make the 5hr journey – AR$75-$85 round trip. Try **Condor y la Estrella** (4313 1700) or **Flecha** (4315 2781).

By car
The drive on Ruta 2 takes 4hrs. Up to 4 people can take a *remise* for around AR$300 one way.

By train
If you have time on your hands (the journey is at least 6hrs), there are trains from Constitución; *see p246*.

Tourist information

Centro Informacion Turistica
Boulevard Maritima Jose Peralta Ramos 2270 (0223 495 1777/www.mardelplata.com). **Open** 8am-8pm daily.

Pinamar, Cariló & Ostende

Pinamar – located 340 kilometres (211 miles) south of BA – is surrounded by dunes and fragrant pine forests. It clings to a reputation as the most exclusive beach resort in Argentina, but don't expect peace: the resident population of 22,000 explodes to 600,000 during the summer months of January and February.

It was founded in 1944 by Jorge Bunge, a Munich-born architect. It's one of the few towns in Argentina designed and built in accordance with urban planning regulations. It has large, clean beaches and the water temperature is 4°C (8°F) warmer than in Mar del Plata. Pinamar is also well known for its nightlife, although the 'in' places vary from year to year. They're not hard to find, however – just follow the cars.

Seven kilometres (five miles) to the north is the **Estación Maritima**. It dovetails as a centre for scientific research and a recovery area for distressed marine creatures. The huge **Reserva Dunícola** is also worth visiting; the

sand dunes are up to 30 metres (100 feet) high and fun for sandboarding. Quad bikes, another entertaining way of tackling the dunes, can be rented for AR$90 per hour (in Playa Cozumel, 02254 47 0109). Some cultural diversion is provided by **Altera Galería de Arte** (Martín Pescador 1485, 02254 48 9000). In addition to modern art exhibitions, the building itself is worth seeing, having been designed by the artist and architect Clorindo Testa.

A couple of kilometres from Pinamar is the exclusive resort of **Cariló**. It's a separate, and far more peaceful world of red brick houses set among the forest reserve of pines, cypresses, acacias and poplars. Eight kilometres (five miles) from Pinamar is **Ostende**, a small resort with one of the best beaches in the area. It was founded at the beginning of the 20th century by a group of Belgians who wanted to duplicate the resorts of the North Sea. They built a 200-metre (650-feet) long jetty and a promenade, only recently found beneath the dunes and now a local attraction.

The resort's first hotel was the Thermas Hotel (built in 1913), which lodged Argentinian writers Silviña Ocampo and Adolfo Bioy Casares, as well as Antoine de Saint-Exupéry, author of *The Little Prince*. Now called the Viejo Hotel Ostende (*see p235*), it's been modernised, but still maintains its original spirit.

Where to eat

For snacks or a beer in Pinamar, there are lots of stop-offs around the beaches. For something sexier, try **Dry** in Hotel Las Calas (Bunge 560, 02254 482447, main courses AR$19-$23), where Tato, BA's star barman, otherwise seen at Sucre (*see p113*), shakes and stirs the best cocktails on the coast; food is an inventive modern Argentinian mix. It's open at the weekend only once the summer season is over. **Green Mango** (Quintana 56, 02254 407990, main courses AR$30, open in summer only) is also a good bet for classy drinks and delicacies plucked from the coast. Pinamar is renowned for good fish; local classic **El Viejo Lobo** (Avenida del Mar y Bunge, 02254 48 3218, main courses AR$25) offers a good wine selection and decent seafood.

Where to stay

Cariló Village (Carpintero y Divisadero, Cariló, 02254 47 0244, www.carilovillage.com, doubles AR$230-$360 all-inclusive) is a large hotel complex with 59 bungalows spread through the woods. In the centre of Pinamar is the coolest accommodation option: **Hotel Las Calas** (Bunge 560, 02254 40 5999, doubles AR$180-$275). The 16 fully-equipped boutique suites sleep up to four. **Viejo Hotel Ostende** (Biarritz y El Cairo, Ostende, 02254 48 6801, www.hotelostende.com.ar, AR$50-$67 per person) opens January to March, Easter week and long weekends. Rates include breakfast and dinner. There are also apartments.

Tourist information

Secretaría de Turismo

Avenida Bunge 654, entre Marco Polo y Libertador, Pinamar (02254 49 1680/www.pinamar.gov.ar). **Open** *Jan, Feb* 8am-10pm daily. *Mar, Dec* 8am-8pm daily. *Apr-Nov* 8am-8pm Mon-Sat; 10am-6pm Sun.

Getting there

To reach Cariló and Ostende, most people take a taxi or a minicab from Pinamar.

By bus

Buses for Pinamar depart daily from Retiro (AR$23-$30 one-way, AR$46-$60 return); companies include **Río de la Plata** (4305 1405) and **Plusmar** (4287 2000). The trip takes 5hrs. You can also take the *colectivo intercostero* (coastal bus) from Mar del Plata.

By car

For Pinamar, take Ruta 2 to Dolores, Ruta 63 to Esquina de Croto, Ruta 11 to General Conesa, Ruta 56 to Madariaga, then Ruta 74 to Pinamar. A *remise* for up to four people costs around AR$190 one-way.

Villa Gesell, Mar de las Pampas & Mar Azul

Founded by Carlos Gesell, the resort of **Villa Gesell** had its moment of glory in the 1960s, when it became the summer headquarters for psychoanalysts, rock groups and 'made in Argentina' beatniks. Today, it's the place for the children of that generation; on summer nights, thousands of youngsters pack the strip of bars, pubs and nightclubs on Avenida 3,

Puerto de Palos in Mar Azul. *See p236.*

parallel to the beach. It's the number one destination for groups of teens taking their first holidays free from prying parental eyes.

It's not an attractive destination in itself any more, but Villa Gesell serves as the arrival point for two tiny villages, 12 kilometres (7.5 miles) to its south, which are currently the loveliest – and for now, the most unspoilt – places on the Atlantic coast for sun, sea and relaxation.

Emerging out of the thick pine forests bordering the coast, **Mar de las Pampas** is how Pinamar was 25 years ago: quiet and beautiful. The village has been built to avoid another seaside catastrophe; cul-de-sacs and sandy roads limit the speed of passing vehicles and stringent building laws keep the town predominantly populated by pine trees. Nevertheless, it's booming; there are small commercial centres and hundreds of cabins under construction and property prices have jumped five-fold in the last few years.

The village is neatly split into three zones: commercial, residential and hotels. Most of the apartments and *cabañas* (wood cabins) for rent and restaurants are found in and around the main thoroughfare, Cruz del Sur. Many businesses are run by escapees from Argentina's banking restrictions who have invested in tourism rather than the country's financial institutions, and they look relieved for it. As a result, the vibe is friendly.

On the beach, the *balneario* **El Soleado** is where people come to buy refreshments, relax and shelter from the strong winds. The sands are golden and the water is considerably cleaner than in the major resorts up the coast.

Mar Azul is even smaller, even quieter and equally paradaisical. The village is little more than a clutch of sandy roads centred around cabin-style lodgings, a hotel and a supermarket. The maximum action during the day is a boy hosing down the main crossroads to keep the sand in check. At the yellow **Las Carabelas** hut on the beach, you can rent sun loungers, umbrellas and chairs (AR$15 per day). Just by the beach there are horses to rent by the hour (AR$10). Ride across the dunes or along the silent roads that fan out into the forest.

Both Mar Azul and Mar de la Pampas have all you need for self-catering if staying in cabins, and *remises* will come from Villa Gesell if you don't have your own transport.

Where to eat

Amorinda Tutto Pasta (Avenida Cerchunoff, 02255 479750, main courses AR$10-$23) opened in Mar de las Pampas in 1999, and is already a village classic – try the chef's macaroni special. **Cabaña Huinca** (Avenida Lucero y El Ceibo,

Trips Out of Town

The delightfully deserted beaches of **Mar Azul**.

02255 479718, main courses AR$15, open weekends only in winter) serves up treats like shrimp hotcakes with asparagus and rich chocolate brownies in ice-cream, but Osvaldo, the owner, is proudest of his home-made beer. Hidden down Cuyo, a little cul-de-sac, the ever-smiling Verónica runs cute **Casa del Sol** (02255 453311, main courses AR$6-$25). Choose between cosy inside tables or the deck terrace and enjoy cocktails and mod-Argentinian dishes with a tasty twist.

Tiny, Mar Azul has less dining options, but it somehow boasts an excellent sushi restaurant; **Apart Heiwa** by the beach on Calle 34 (02255 453674). The owners, a Japanese/Argentinian couple, have a special salmon delivery from BA to roll up fresh nigiri and maki rolls – they also have accommodation. Treat yourself to a platter on their seafront deck. Alternatively, for decent Patagonian lamb or beef ribs *al asador*, modern **El Rodeo** (Calle 35 y Mar Azul) slow roasts them over embers in the front of this large, brightly lit cabin-style restaurant.

Where to stay

In the summer, many places offer lodging for a one-week minimum. Outside January and February, it's cheaper and more flexible.

In Mar de las Pampas, metres from the beach are the cottages (capacity 4-7 people) of **Rincón del Duende** (Virazón y Roca, 02255 479866, www.rincondelduende.com, rental per week AR$2,100-$2,800). As well as a fine restaurant, the complex boasts a swimming pool and tennis court. The white **Miradores del Bosque** (JA Roca y Hudson, 02255 452147, www.miradores delbosque.com) doesn't quite blend into the woody style of the village, but the apartments with individual terraces are luxurious and there is a spa. Rates are AR$1,800-$3,200 per week for 2-6 people; 40 per cent less out of season.

Just off the crossroads in Mar Azul, are the **Puerto de Palos** *cabañas* (Calle 35 y Mar del Plata, 02255 470311, www.puertodepalos.rtu. com.ar, AR$100-$260 per day). It's a mini complex of well-run and well-appointed wood cabins, set in the woods, with a pool. For a seafront location, check out the modern, cool apartments at **Rincón del Mar** (Calle 30 y La Playa, 02255 456 003, www.rincondelmar. com.ar). A two-person studio costs AR$2,030 per week. For more money you can get a loft or suite with jacuzzi, white linen and immaculate views stretching across the South Atlantic.

Tourist information

Información Turística

In Villa Gesell: Camino de los Pioneros, y Avenida 3 (02255 458596, www.villagesell.com.ar). **Open** 8am-9pm daily. **In Mar de las Pampas**: Avenida 3, y Rotunda (02255 470324). **Open** Jan-Mar, Dec 10am-6pm. See also www.mardelaspampas.info.

Getting there

From Villa Gesell to Mar de las Pampas it's 10km (6 miles) or AR$10-$12 by taxi. Add another AR$5 by taxi to Mar Azul, 5km (3 miles) further on. There's a regular bus service running from Villa Gesell to Mar de las Pampas and Mar Azul (AR$1.80 one-way).

By air

There are flights to Villa Gesell (Jan, Feb only) with **Aerolineas Argentinas** for AR$132-$165 one-way.

By bus

Expreso Alberino (4576 7940) or Plusmar (4315 6085/3424) have regular daily services to Villa Gesell from Retiro; AR$33-$43 one-way. It's a 5hr trip.

By car

It's 415km (258 miles) to Villa Gesell. Take Ruta 2 to Dolores, then Ruta 63 approximately 30km (19 miles) to Ruta 11, which takes you all the way to Gesell.

Uruguay

South America's best-kept secret is a short hop over the Plate.

Colonia del Sacramento

The closest place from BA across the River Plate is also the loveliest: Colonia del Sacramento. This tiny town with a huge history – it was declared a UNESCO World Heritage Site in 1996 – is ideal for an escape from urban chaos. Exploring its cobbled streets, lined with colourful, picture-perfect, colonial houses, surrounded on three sides by water, is like travelling back in time.

You'll arrive at the port, just blocks from the heart of the **Barrio Histórico** (old town). It's easy to cover Colonia on foot, but there are also bicycles, mopeds, cars and even golf carts for rent at the port's entrance. English guides can be arranged at the tourist office, but exploring on your own is also easy.

The history of Colonia – founded in 1680 – is a dizzying tale of territorial struggle between the Spanish and Portuguese crowns for most of the 17th and 18th centuries. Peace finally descended in 1778, when Portugal acquiesced. For a physical sense of the town's early days, walk through the **Puerta de Campo**, the restored city gate dating from 1745. Enter from **Plaza 1811**, next to a tourist information stand. On the **Plaza de Armas Manuel Lobo**, wooden walkways with plaques showing early

Bewitching **Colonia**.

plans guide you around the ruins of the earliest foundations. Off the plaza are the simple white walls of the **Iglesia Matriz**, the oldest church in Uruguay. Though much damaged and reconstructed, traces of the original edifice are still visible, and the cool interior contains colonial-era religious art.

The museum circuit is another option. For US$1, buy a pass (available at the Municipal or Portuguese museums) gaining access to the seven small museums in the old town. You can hit them all in one day – they're open 11.30am-5.30pm. Often, the real interest is the buildings themselves – all (except the Museo Indígena) are restored 18th-century Portuguese houses. Part of the **Museo Portugués** on the Plaza Mayor dates from 1720, and its collection is one of the more interesting.

But the real pleasure of Colonia is just walking. Explore the **Calle de los Suspiros** (Street of Sighs) with its huge cobbles and typical colonial houses; the active lighthouse, amid the ruins of the 17th-century **Convento de San Francisco**; and around the limits of the Barrio Histórico along the river, past the disused railway station and on to the **Bastión del Carmen**, the old town fortification. As you go, look out for the reproduction of a 1740 French map on the wall of the Argentinian consulate (General Flores 209) or the exquisite tiles on the wall of Calle del Comercio 186.

For a little more action, the main street, **General Flores**, is lined with souvenir shops and cheap eateries preferred by locals. There is also a daily **Feria de la Ciudad Artesanal** (craft fair) two blocks off Flores, next to the sportsground on Daniel Fosalba.

Once you're all walked out, throw yourself down in a plaza or head to the beach on the Rambla Costanera, which is clean enough for bathing. Colonia can become relentlessly hot in midsummer, so any watery relief offers respite (bring plenty of mosquito repellent with your sunscreen). If you prefer sanitised submersion, there's a pool at **El Mirador** hotel-casino (Avenida Roosevelt 381, 00 598 52 22552); day use costs US$10, including buffet lunch.

Finally, if time allows, try **Real de San Carlos** for something truly... well, strange. Located five kilometres (three miles) out of town along the coast road (go by bike or hop on one of the city buses) are the 100-year-old remains of an

Argentinian playboy's dreams of a leisure complex. You can see the ruins of the Moorish-style bull ring (where just eight fights were held from 1910 to 1912, before the sport was outlawed) and *pelota* court, also used as a theatre. The racetrack, which opened later, in 1942, still functions. Next door, a new luxury resort is being built by Sheraton, to open in 2005.

Where to eat

Colonia is full of very average places to eat, and it's hard to escape *parrilla* (Uruguayans eat even more meat than Argentinians) and pizza. A local favourite is *chivito*: in BA, this is baby goat, but in Colonia, it's strips of beef with mounds of potatoes, cheese, eggs and more. To try it, head for the *cantinas* on General Flores.

In the old town take a table on the terrace of colourful **El Drugstore** (Portugal 174, 00 598 52 25241, main courses US$5) for a variety of tapas, salads and sandwiches. For pizza, **La Bodeguita** (Del Comercio 167, 00 598 52 25329, main courses US$4) has tasty varieties and a lively deck on the water. It opens for dinner and, from April to November, for weekend lunches. The restaurant of the discreet **Club de Yachting y Pesca** (Puerto de Yates, 00 598 52 22197, main courses US$11, closed Wed) offers fresh seafood for lunch and dinner.

Where to stay

In the Barrio Histórico, **Posada Casa de los Naranjos** (18 de Julio 219, 00 598 52 24630, doubles US$25-$40) is an attractive colonial house, with a garden and the rare luxury of a swimming pool. The finest lodging in the old town is at the **Plaza Mayor** (Calle del Comercio 111, 00 598 52 23193, www.hotel plazamayor.com.uy, doubles US$76-$130), a historic house with well appointed rooms, a lovely flower-filled patio and a small back garden near the river. Another classy option is the **Hostal del Sol** (Solís 31, 00 598 52 23349, doubles US$50), which has spacious rooms decked out with antiques. Outside the Barrio Histórico, **Hotel Beltrán** (General Flores 311, 00 598 52 22955, doubles US$20-$35) offers individually designed rooms around a central courtyard. There's also a campsite at the end of the Rambla Costanera and a youth hostel on General Flores 440 (00 598 52 30347). Note that some hotel rates are hiked at weekends.

Tourist information

Oficina de Turismo General

General Flores y Rivera (00 598 52 23700). **Open** 8am-8pm daily.

Carmelo

Just 40 kilometres (25 miles) north-east of Buenos Aires and 77 kilometres (48 miles) along the coast from Colonia, the sleepy backwater town of Carmelo is situated where the Uruguay river broadens to become the River Plate.

In this oasis of tranquillity, and nestled in a pine forest outside town on Ruta 21, is the stunning **Four Seasons Carmelo Resort** (in BA 4321 1711, 00 598 542 9000, www.four seasons.com/carmelo, doubles US$290-$480), Carmelo's budget-busting, big draw. With 20 Zen-inspired bungalows around a gigantic pool, plus deluxe spa and golf course, it's the nearest thing to Bali on the River Plate. For something less flash, stay in town at the **Hotel-Casino Carmelo** on Rodó street (00 598 542 2314/2333, US$40 double). From there, it's a short walk across the swing bridge – built in 1912 – to the golden beaches that are Carmelo's fame.

Close by, a few minutes towards Nueva Palmira, is delightful **Finca Narbona** (Ruta 21, km 267, 00 598 540 4778; www.fincaygranja narbona.com), a restaurant, cheese factory and bakery in a converted 1909 general store. For about US$15, feast on a cheese and meat spread followed by lamb cooked in an adobe oven.

Carmelo is in the heart of Uruguay's little explored wine country. Among the handful of wineries receiving tourists – by appointment – is **Los Cerros de San Juan** (00 598 481 7200, www.loscerrosdesanjuan.com.uy), the country's oldest, on Ruta 21 between Colonia and Carmelo. Founded in 1854, it still stores its wines in a century-old stone warehouse. After a visit, there's a sampling of local delicacies served with a glass of Tannat, Uruguay's answer to Argentina's Malbec.

Tourist information

Dirección de Turismo

Casa de Cultura, 19 de Abril, y Rodríguez (00 598 542 2001). **Open** *Jan, Feb* 10am-noon, 5-9pm Mon-Thu; 9am-9pm Fri-Sun. *Mar-Dec* 8am-6pm Mon-Thur; 9am-3pm Fri-Sun.

Montevideo

At first sight, the Uruguayan capital appears every bit the spitting image of Buenos Aires, from which it's separated by only a 40-minute flight or short ferry ride. But the similarities are barely skin deep. Unlike BA, where temptation abounds, mellow Montevideo's main attraction is its absence of frenzied activity, undoubtedly helped by its 23 kilometres (14 miles) of sandy beaches. Another secret of its enigmatic way of life may be *mate*. Uruguayans are the region's

Markets maketh man in **Montevideo**.

most voracious suppers of the *yerba* drink and do just about everything with a *mate* in one hand and a thermos flask in the other.

Montevideo is the seat of the Mercosur trading block (the Southern Cone equivalent of the Common Market), but, despite this role, has not lost its colonial spirit. Indeed, its historic fortifications seem to have protected it from the assault of the 21st century. The oldest left standing, the **Fortaleza del Cerro** (José Valle y Ordóñez, 00 598 2 313 6716), was strategically built on the city's highest point during the first decade of the 19th century, after the English Invasions of the River Plate. From the battlements, there are stunning views of the city stretching around the bay.

Although tagged as a cruise liner stopover, Montevideo was, until the 1930s, every bit BA's rival and the architectural richness of its **Ciudad Vieja** (Old City) is even more notable. Economic stagnation has left much of the city's grandeur, like its many vintage cars, in a dilapidated state reminiscent of old Havana. At its apex, though, Montevideo was the world's largest importer of French tiles. More than 2,000, belonging to architect Alejandro Artucio Urioste, are housed in the impressive **Museo del Azulejo** (Calle Cavia, Pocitos, 00 598 2 709 6352).

Palacio Salvo, built in 1928 on Avenida 18 de Julio and Convención, is the non-official symbol of the capital and for decades was the highest structure in South America. Owing to Montevideo's low skyline, the office building appears even more majestic than its elder twin, the Palacio Barolo in Buenos Aires (*see p58* **Divine inspiration**).

Another belle époque showpiece is the **Teatro Solís** (Buenos Aires 652, y Juncal). It was built in 1841 with red pine from Russia, gold from Genoa and marble from across the world. Puccini, Caruso, Vittorio Gassman, Sarah Bernhardt and Isadora Duncan have all graced its stage. Currently being renovated, it's due to reopen for regular performances and guided tours in August 2004.

Try also to catch one of the many tango and *murga* (a type of carnival dance) shows that move from venue to venue around the city. For details of these and other events, check *El País*, the daily newspaper, or *Pimba!*, a free monthly cultural guide. In February, the African-inspired *candombe* music moves to the street for what is South America's longest carnival.

If you're in Montevideo on a Sunday, don't miss the **Feria Tristán Narvaja** (Tristán Narvaja, y 18 de Julio), up there with the world's great outdoor markets such as London's Portobello Road. Every Sunday from 9am to 2pm seven blocks of Tristán Narvaja Street are lined with antique dealers. Market-lovers should also visit the bustling **Mercado del Puerto** (Piedras y Yacaré, 00 598 2 915 4178) in the port. Under the old cast-iron roof, dominated by an English clock, fruit and vegetable stalls, antique vendors, *parrillas*, musicians and street entertainers provide an authentic marketplace vibe. It's open every day from 10.30am to 5pm and 9pm until 1am.

Montevideo-born painter Joaquin Torres García's modernist 'school of the south' was an early attempt to challenge US and European hegemony in politics and art. His best-known image, an upside-down map of South America from 1936 with Tierra del Fuego located where 'north-centric' maps place the equator, is displayed alongside Cubist-inspired work at the **Museo Torres García** (Sarandi 683, 00 598 2 62663), located one block from **Plaza Independencia**, the city's main square.

Fitting for a country so out of sync with global corporate capitalism, Uruguayan handicrafts are top notch. With five locations in Montevideo, including its showroom in a colonial house at Reconquista 587 (00 598 2 915 1338), artisan co-op **Manos del Uruguay** (www.manos.com.uy) sells wool sweaters, homespun yarn and other quality handicrafts.

Where to eat & drink

One of Montevideo's attractions is the many photogenic bars and cafés. In the Ciudad Vieja, look for art nouveau **Café Brasilero** (Ituzaingó 1447) and **Baar Fun Fun** (Ciudadela 1229), whose house shot, the sugary sweet Uvita, was praised in a tango by patron

Trips Out of Town

NH Columbia hotel on Montevideo's Rambla.

Carlos Gardel. It fills up Wednesday through Saturday, when there is live music.

If you like a bit of action while you eat, head to the Mercado del Puerto. Among the many *parrillas*, **La Posada Don Tiburón** (00 598 2 915 4278, main courses US$3) on *calle* Piedras is comfy with terrace tables, while **El Palenque** (Pérez de Castellano 1550, 00 598 2 915 4704 main courses US$9) pulls international celebs and local politicians. For upscale but still relaxed dining, there's a growing bar and restaurant scene surrounding the one-block pedestrianised street of Bacacay in the Ciudad Vieja. *Parrilla* **El Abasto** (00 598 2 916 9026)

and Italian trattoria **Roma Amor** (00 598 2 917 0974) are two lively options. A few blocks away, **Love** (Mercedes 753, 00 598 2 901 5843) is a late-night hipster hangout. From Thursday to Sunday, bars like **Don Trigo** (00 598 2 711 5952) and the five dance floors of **W Lounge** (00 598 2 712 5287) surrounding Parque Rodó rival those of Buenos Aires for fun and fashion.

Where to stay

A few blocks from the Ciudad Vieja, friendly and functional **Hostel de Montevideo** (Canelones 935, 00 598 2 908 1324, www.hostel uruguay.org, US$6 per person) is the city's only youth hostel. Also good value, the refurbished **Hotel Lafayette** downtown (Soriano 1172, 00 598 2 902 4646, www.lafayette.com.uy) charges just US$35 for a double.

The **NH Columbia** (Rambla Gran Bretaña 473, 00 598 2 916 0001, www.nh-hoteles.es, doubles US$60), part of a stylish Spanish hotel chain, is in a strikingly refurbished building with attractive rooms and river views. For luxury, **Belmont House** (00 598 2 600 0430, www.belmonthouse.com.uy, doubles US$130), in the stylish Carrasco barrio, is an elegant B&B full of antiques and near the beach.

Here comes the sun

It's not all frivolous materialism in Punta. Thankfully, there's journeyman painter and philanthropist Carlos Páez Vilaró, and his beloved **Casapueblo**, to provide some much-needed nourishment for the soul amid so much money-love and body-worshipping.

Inspired by the *hornero* (ovenbird) – Uruguay's national bird – and by white, turreted Moorish architecture, Casapueblo is a hotel-cum-museum that tumbles down the rocky cliff face of Punta Ballena, 14.5 kilometres (nine miles) west of Punta del Este. Over the decades that its construction lasted, Páez Vilaró came and went, travelling, painting, mingling with artists like Picasso, Dalí and Warhol – even helping out in an African leper colony. No task is too great for this man. In 1972, he led a search party in the Andes for a downed plane carrying his son and fellow Uruguayan rugby players, an episode recounted in the Hollywood film *Alive*.

Casapueblo expanded from a live-in workshop and place to entertain friends into a world-famous icon of fantasy architecture visited by 60,000 people each year. Páez

Vilaró apologises for not respecting the angles and lines of traditional architecture – he shouldn't. Walking through the endless, eight-floor labyrinth of curves each room is more unique than the last. The museum exhibits and sells Páez Vilaró's African-inspired, colourful paintings and books and there's a touching biographical film.

But the real point to Casapueblo, and indeed to Páez Vilaró's life, is the sun. It appears on his paintings. Alternately smiling and laughing, it pops up behind the walls, and when the real fireball dips into the sea each night a silent, ritual tribute is performed. For less spiritual folk, a gin and tonic will suffice. Either way, the sight of the sun dropping dramatically into the stunning blue bay of Portozuelo makes for one of the world's greatest sunsets.

Casapueblo

Ruta Panorámica, Punta Ballena (00 598 42 578 611/041/www.carlospaezvilaro.com). **Open** *Museum* 9am-sunset. **Rates** US$60-$132 double. *Museum* US$3. **Credit** AmEx, DC, MC, V.

Tourist information

Centro de Información Turística

Explanada Palacio Municipal, Avenida 18 de Julio, y Ejido (00 598 2 1950 1830). **Open** 10am-6pm Mon-Fri; 9am-5pm Sat, Sun.

Punta del Este

Located 140 kilometres (87 miles) from Montevideo, and light years from the capital's original colonial style, is the town of Punta del Este. A cross between California and Ibiza, the narrow peninsula straddling the Atlantic Ocean and Rio de la Plata is a world-famous resort and bustling bathing hole for the rich and famous.

In the past decade, massive overdevelopment has swamped the town centre and stripped it of much of its exclusive sheen. Fleeing the concrete jungle, the international fashion set has now set up camp further north along the coast, at the upscale beach and dining strip **La Barra** and the exclusive **José Ignacio** resort.

On maps, at least though, the peninsula remains the central reference point. It's divided into two zones: **Playa Mansa**, to the west, lapped by the still waters of the River Plate, and

Playa Brava, to the north, extending up the Atlantic coast. Along both beaches, summer *paradores* (Marangatú at Parada 7, Playa Mansa is one of the best) offer services ranging from sun-loungers and beach games to lunch – and all with a sea view. The less crowded beaches on La Mansa are more family-oriented, while the waves along Playa Brava attract a younger, more playful crowd. Peaceful by day, as the sun sets, mobs of hungry tourists and hitchhiking 'Argenteenagers' storm the main street, Avenida Gorlero, for a pizza or a *parrilla*.

As you travel north out of the peninsula the beaches become progressively less populated and the high rises are replaced by mansions and exclusive resorts. After about ten kilometres (six miles), the panorama abruptly changes at Punta's most happening patch: La Barra. The main strip is an architectural mismatch of clubs, restaurants and five-star complexes but no one cares as the only beauty that counts are the model-like figures on the beach. **Bikini Beach**, in the hub of La Barra, resembles the Cannes Film Festival – proof, if any were lacking, that people are Punta's main attraction.

If La Barra is for the brash, José Ignacio, some 40 kilometres (25 miles) north of Punta, is more discreet. This tiny, former pirates' hideaway is a must-visit for its white sands, dusty roads and internationally acclaimed restaurants. To get there you need a car – though there is sporadic bus service. It gets over-run in summer by sunbathers, ravers and hundreds of pick-ups parked around the hotspot, **Las Huellas** (*see p242*), but there are more tranquil comforts like the lighthouse, the plaza and the fisherman going about their business. Like Punta, the populace hibernates from March to December, but several restaurants stay open throughout the year making a trip worthwhile out of season.

Where to eat & drink

In the woods, far from the hysteria, is the delightful **L'Auberge Hotel** (Barrio Parque de Golf, 00 598 42 48 2601, www.laubergehotel. com). This 36-room hotel (doubles US$110-$182), with its landmark water tower, has a wonderful salon dedicated to tea and waffles, with home-made *dulce de leche*, chocolate or raspberry. In La Barra, three established places on the main strip (Ruta 10) are **Baby Gouda** (00 598 42 771874, main courses US$4-$8), an original restaurant with a Moroccan/Asian menu, the Punta branch of **Novecento** (*see p111*; open summer only) and, just half a block off this road towards the beach, **Le Club** (00 598 42 770246), a swish hotel-cum-bar-cum-restaurant great for a cocktail from its gorgeous

Trips Out of Town

deck. Every summer famed Argentinian chef Francis Mallman – the visionary who put José Ignacio on the map back in the '70s – returns from NYC, to preside over his sublime **Los Negros** (Faro de José Ignacio, 00 598 48 62091, main courses US$40). **Las Huellas** (Playa Brava, José Ignacio, 000 598 48 62279, main courses US$7) is a fish/sushi restaurant that's also a magnet for cocktail cruisers. Everyone brags about where the best nightlife is, but look out for **Tequila** and **Mint** clubs in La Barra and José Ignacio's **Cream del Mar** (00 59848 62027) sunset bar, where white-robed revellers share stories over Clérico (white wine sangria).

Where to stay

Lodging in Punta is expensive, but becomes considerably cheaper, even at top-bracket hotels or classic spots like **Casapueblo** (*see p240* **Here comes the sun**), if you buy a package through ferry operator Buquebus (*see listings below*). **Hotel Conrad** (Parada 4, Playa Mansa, Rambla Claudio Williman, 00 598 42 49 1111, www.conrad.com.uy, doubles US$180-$300), best known for its bikini fashion shows and casino, is the peninsula's most expensive option. To some, the spiral shaped tower is an eyesore – but no one can deny it's classic Punta. **La Posta del Cangrejo** (La Barra, 00 598 42 770021, www.netgate.com.uy/laposta, doubles US$80-$150) has a respected kitchen, fine sea view and country-style rooms where George and Barbara Bush and Julio Iglesias have slept. La Barra's charming **Villa de Mar** (Calle Las Estrellas, 00 598 42 772147, www.villa demar.com.ar, US$80-$200) is a four-star hotel

of Italian colonial design, steps from the beach. If cash is running thin, take refuge in four-room **La Ballenera** (Ruta 10, Km 162, 00 598 42 771079, www.vivapunta.com/laballenera, doubles US$25-$120), a *Little House on the Prairie* wooden abode near the beach. José Ignacio's most scenic hotel is **La Posada del Faro** (Calle de la Bahía, 00 598 48 62110, www.posadadelfaro.com, doubles US$140-$190), with ten individually designed rooms. Real high-rollers stay at **Cipriani Punta del Este Hotel y Casino** (www.cipriani.com), opened late 2003, or Miami-styled **Esturion de Montoya** (www.esturiondemontoya.com.uy).

Tourist information

Centro Información Turistica
Parada 1, Calle 31, La Mansa (00 598 42 440514). **Open** *Dec-Feb* 8am-10pm daily. *Mar-Nov* 10am-6pm daily.

Getting there

By air

To Montevideo **Aerolineas Argentinas**, **American Falcon**, **Aerovip** and Uruguayan airline **Pluna** run several direct flights a day; also to Punta del Este (over a dozen in summer). Flights leave from Jorge Newbery. To Montevideo 40mins, US$120-$340 return; to Punta, 45mins, US$140-$300 return. For airline phone numbers and BA's domestic airport information, *see chapter* **Getting Around**.

By boat & bus

The easiest way to Uruguay is by boat, with **Buquebus** (www.buquebus.com), whose excellent packages include lodging. To Colonia, at least two fast crossings (1hr, AR$154 return) daily on a comfy hydrofoil and two slow ferries (3hrs, AR$92 return), both with room for cars. Also at least two boats a day to Montevideo (2hrs 35mins, AR$290 return). Buses connect Colonia and Montevideo and go on to Carmelo (1hr from Colonia) or Punta del Este (2hrs 30mins from Montevideo). Boat and bus round trip to Punta del Este costs AR$222-$336 via Colonia or Montevideo. Tickets can be purchased by phone (4316 6500) or in person at Patio Bullrich (*see p139*), at Avenida Córdoba 879 or at the Puerto Madero terminal (Avenida Córdoba y Madero) from where boats leave. For direct service to Carmelo **La Cacciola** (4393 6100, www.cacciolaviajes.com) has boats daily from Tigre (3hrs, AR$56 return).

By car

Buquebus charges AR$218 or AR$318 extra for putting a car on a boat to Colonia and Montevideo respectively. Otherwise, its 235km (146 miles) from BA to Gualeguaychú in Entre Rios province – the closest border crossing to Fray Bentos in Uruguay.

Party on **Punta** style.

Directory

Directory

Getting Around

To & from Ezeiza

Ezeiza (Aeropuerto Ministro Pistarini)

Ezeiza, Buenos Aires, 35km (22 miles) from city centre. Recorded flight information or operator, plus listings of airline telephone numbers 5480 6111 (English & Spanish)/www.aa2000.com.ar.
The official name of Buenos Aires' international airport is Aeropuerto Ministro Pistarini, although it is more commonly known by the name of the area in which it is located, Ezeiza. All international flights arrive and depart from here, except those between Buenos Aires and Uruguay (*see below* **Aeroparque Jorge Newbery**). The airport has two interlinked terminals: A and B, in close proximity. Aerolíneas Argentinas uses Terminal B, while all other airlines operate out of the remodelled and improved Terminal A.
During rush hour allow 1 hour 20 minutes to travel between downtown BA and Ezeiza Airport. At all other times, plan for 30-40 minutes.

By shuttle bus

Manuel Tienda León

Avenida Santa Fe 790, y Esmeralda, Retiro (4314 3636/www.tiendaleon. com.ar).
Operates from the airport – with a stand in the arrivals hall and also outside the terminals – and its city centre office (above). Buses leave every 30 minutes from the city centre, from 5am to 8.30pm, with three additional services leaving at 4am, 9.30pm and 11.15pm. From the airport, there is a 24-hour service, with buses every 30 minutes. Fares per person: AR$19 one way, AR$34 return. There's free pick-up and drop-off at hotels, offices or homes in a defined area of the city centre; otherwise, journeys start and finish at the firm's office on Avenida Santa Fe. English-speaking operators.

By *remise* or taxi

On entering the airport's arrival area, you are likely to be approached by any number of drivers offering you *remise* (minicab) or taxi services.

These are best avoided. Instead, use one of the approved companies that operate from the airport, or call and arrange your own transport with a company of your choice.
Manuel Tienda León (4314 3636, AR$51), **Transfer Express** (0800 4444 872/4852 6776, AR$49) and **Universo** (4776 1117/4776 2229, AR$49) all operate from the airport and offer *remise* services. Fares are one-way to the centre and include road tolls. Several other *remise* companies accept advance calls on airport pick-ups and drop-offs. Alternatively, call on arrival, once you have cleared customs, and they will send a driver within about 15 minutes. Try **Le Coq** (4964 2000/4963 9155, AR$24), **Recoleta Vip** (4801 6655, AR$30) or **Blue** (4777 8888, AR$30). These fares exclude road tolls (AR$5.40 one-way).
Radio taxi companies include **Mi Taxi** (4931 1200, AR$25), **Pidalo** (4956 1200, AR$28) and **Siglo XXI** (4633 4000, AR$25).

By city bus

If you have plenty of time but desperately little cash, you can take a *colectivo* (city bus) for just AR$1.35, but allow at least two hours. Bus 86 (make sure you take one that says Aeropuerto Ezeiza) runs to/from La Boca and Avenida de Mayo.

To & from Aeroparque

Aeroparque Jorge Newbery

Avenida Costanera Rafael Obligado, entre La Pampa y Sarmiento, Costanera Norte. Recorded flight information or operator, plus listings of airline telephone numbers 5480 6111 (English & Spanish)/ www.aa2000.com.ar. **Map** p279 K8.
Aeroparque Jorge Newbery, more commonly known simply as Aeroparque, is the arrival and departure point for all domestic flights, as well as those to and from Montevideo and Punta del Este, Uruguay. It's conveniently – if scarily – located on the Costanera Norte, beside Palermo park, just 10 minutes from the city centre.

Manuel Tienda León, (4314 3636/4315 5115, AR$6 one way, AR$16 return) has a shuttle bus service to/from Aeroparque every 30 minutes, as well as *remise* services. **Transfer Express** (0800 4444 872/4852 6776) and **Universo** (4776 1117/4776 2229), operating from the airport, also have *remise* services to the city centre. *Remises* cost AR$14-$16. Several *colectivos* (city buses) also serve the airport; the fare is AR80¢. The 37C (make sure it says Aeroparque on the front) and 160 buses run from Plaza Italia, the 45 from the centre and the 33 from Plaza de Mayo. There is also a taxi rank at the airport entrance. A taxi to a city-centre hotel will cost you AR$9-$11.

Airlines

International

In addition to these airlines, all the major Latin American airlines have services to Buenos Aires.
Aerolíneas Argentinas
0810 222 86527/4139 3000/
www.aerolineas.com
Air Canada
4327 3640/www.aircanada.ca
Air France
0800 222 2600/4317 4700/
www.airfrance.com.ar
Alitalia
4310 9999/www.alitalia.com.ar
American Airlines
4318 1111/www.aa.com
British Airways
4320 6600/www.britishairways.com
Iberia
4131 1000/01/www.iberia.com
KLM
4326 8422/www.klm.com
Lufthansa
4319 0600/www.lufthansa.com
Swiss
4319 0000/www.swiss.com
United Airlines
4316 0777/www.united.com.ar

Domestic

Several of these airlines also offer international routes to neighbouring countries, particularly to Uruguay. Note that non-Argentinian residents pay significantly higher prices for internal flights in Argentina.
Aerolíneas Argentinas
0810 222 86527/4139 3000/
www.aerolineas.com

Aerovip
0810 444 2376/4312 6954
American Falcon
0810 222 3252/4393 5700/
www.americanfalcon.com.ar
Austral
0810 222 86527/4340 7800/
www.austral.com.ar
Lade
0810 810 5233/5129 9000/
www.lade.com.ar
Pluna
4329 9211/www.pluna.com
Southern Winds
0810 777 7979/0351 426 6626/
www.sw.com.ar

Arriving by other methods

By bus

Estación Terminal de Omnibus

Avenida Ramos Mejía 1680, Retiro.
Passenger information 4310 0700.
Buenos Aires' bus station is in Retiro,
next to the train station. It is on the
Subte C line and is served by many
colectivos (city buses) including the
93, 106, 130 and 152. In the station,
left-luggage lockers cost AR$2.50,
but are not completely secure. Also,
be wary of pickpockets in and
around the terminal.

More than 80 long-distance buses
operate from Retiro. Don't panic: they
are grouped together by region (i.e.
North-west or Patagonia), so it's easy
to compare prices and times. There
are services to every province in
Argentina, and also to Uruguay,
Paraguay, Brazil, Chile, Peru and
Bolivia. There are two levels of
service to many destinations known
respectively as *común* and *diferencial*
or *ejecutiva* (which has hosts or
hostesses and includes food), and
also different types of seat – comfiest
is the *coche cama*, larger, almost fully
reclining 'bed seats'. Tickets to all
destinations must be purchased at
the bus station. In high season
(Decemeber to February, Easter week
and July) it is worth buying your
ticket in advance.

By sea

Unless you are arriving from
Uruguay, across the River Plate, or
stopping off on a cruise, it is unlikely
that you will arrive in Buenos Aires
by boat. Boats from Uruguay arrive
at the passenger port in **Dársena
Norte**, a few blocks from the city
centre at Avenida Córdoba y
Avenida Alicia Moreau de Justo.
Regular boat services run between
BA and Colonia (*see p237*) and

Montevideo (*see p238*) in Uruguay.
Cruise ships dock at the new
**Terminal Benito Quinquela
Martín** (4317 0671) at Avenida de
los Inmigrantes and Castillo.

Public transport

Getting around Buenos Aires
is relatively easy and cheap.
Colectivos (city buses) run
frequently, cover the whole
capital and offer 24-hour
service, while the Subte –
the small but reliable subway
network – is a fast alternative
branching out from the
city centre. Taxis are also
numerous and affordable,
especially outside peak hours.
If you're heading out to the
suburbs use the train service,
although you may wish to hire
a car if you want to explore the
surrounding countryside or
venture further afield.

Buses

City buses are called *colectivos*, or
sometimes *bondis* in slang. There are
140 bus lines, many of which run
along a variety of routes (*ramales*)
through every city barrio. Each line
has its own number and bus colours.
If there are different *ramales* on the
same line, a board on the right-hand
side of the front window will indicate
this. The service is very frequent –
you will rarely have to wait more
than five minutes during the day –
and companies are obliged to provide
all-night service, with at least one
bus every half hour, although not
every line complies.

With so many routes it can be hard
to work out which one you need. For
AR$5-$10, you can buy one of the
bus guides on sale at newspaper
kioscos – Guia T, Filcar or *Lumi* –
although working out the guide itself
is another matter. First, look up
the page and grid reference of your
departure and destination street
in the street index. The grid is
replicated on the page facing or
above each map, and each square
is filled with bus numbers. See if
any of the numbers in the square
corresponding to your departure and
destination points match. If so, that's
the bus for you. You can then look up
the route that the bus takes in the
listing at the back of the guide, so
that you know which roads it runs
along. Simple, right? In reality, the
easiest thing to do is ask. With even
basic Spanish you'll should easily

find someone to help, and *porteños*
tend to know the system well.

Bus fares are AR75¢ or AR80¢ for
journeys within the capital, paid
directly into the machine behind
the driver – coins only, no notes.
Some bus lines operate a *servicio
diferencial*, with air-conditioning
and reclining seats. They are faster,
stopping less frequently. Tickets
cost a minimum of AR$1.50.

Be warned that bus drivers have
frustrated Formula 1 ambitions, and
often don't even like to come to a
complete stop to let passangers on
and off. You need to be agile, hold on
tight while on board, and be ready to
shout at the driver if he tries to leave
while you're hanging out the door.

For complaints or information,
call freephone 0800 333 0300.

Subte

Buenos Aires' underground train
network, operating since 1912, is
called the Subte. It is the quickest,
easiest and cheapest way to get
around the city during the day,
though it can be very crowded
during morning and evening peak
hours. The service runs from 5am
to 10pm (8am to 10pm on Sundays)
– so it won't help you get around the
city's nightspots. Large parts of the
city are not served by the network
either, including some important
tourist areas such as Recoleta and
Palermo Viejo. A single journey to
anywhere on the network costs just
AR70¢. Magnetic card tickets, for
anywhere between one and thirty
Subte journeys, can be bought at the
boleterías (ticket offices), located
inside the stations.

There are four parallel lines – A, B,
D and E – that link the centre with
barrios to the north and west, and
one line – C – that runs north-south,
connecting these lines and the
mainline train stations of Retiro
and Constitución. Every train line
runs along a main avenue: A along
Avenida Rivadavia; B along Avenida
Corrientes; C along Avenida 9 de
Julio; D along Avenidas Santa Fe
and Cabildo; and E along Avenida
San Juan. Crossing from one outlying
barrio to another is problematic as
you have to come into the centre in
order to transfer to another line,
though the new line H will help; a
bus is probably the better option.

Work on the first new line for half
a century – H – which will connect
Retiro with Nueva Pompeya, is
ongoing. Every station on the new
line will have both lifts and
escalators to improve access for
people with mobility problems.
Currently only four stations on Line
D have lift access. It is scheduled to
start running in 2005.

Directory

For complaints or suggestions, call Metrovías on 0800 555 1616. The website www.metrovias.com.ar also has updates about the service.

Trains

Trains connecting the northern suburbs with the city centre are modern and air-conditioned, while those serving the south are more run-down. Trains linking the capital with destinations in Buenos Aires province, such as Mar del Plata or Tandil, are not in great nick either, but they do have three classes: *turista* (wooden seats); *primera* (soft seats); and *pullman* (even better seats and air-conditioning).

There are several different private companies running the trains, which can make it difficult to get the times, prices and information you need. These are the main stations:

Constitución

General Hornos 11, Constitución. **Map** p276 C4.
Trains from Constitución go south. **Metropolitano** (passenger information freephone 0800 122 358736/4018 0719) runs services on the Roca line to Buenos Aires province, to La Plata, Glew, Ezeiza (20 minutes from the airport by a connecting bus) and Temperley. **Ferrobaires** (passenger information 4305 5577/4306 7919) runs a long-distance service to the coastal destinations of Mar del Plata, Tandil and Bahía Blanca.

Federico Lacroze

Lacroze 4181, Chacarita. **Map** p275 L2.
Metrovías (passenger information freephone 0800 555 1616/4555 1616) runs trains along the Urquiza line to General Lemos in BA province.

Once de Septiembre

Avenida Pueyrredón, y Bartolomé Mitre, Once. **Map** p278 G4.
Known just as Once station. The Sarmiento line, run by **Trenes de Buenos Aires** (TBA – passenger information freephone 0800 333 3822/4317 4400) serves Moreno, with connections to Mercedes, and Merlo, with connections to Lobos. **Ferrobaires** (passenger information 4861 0043) serves Bragado and Santa Rosa in the province of La Pampa.

Retiro

Ramos Mejía 1508, Retiro. **Map** p277 F8.
Trains run north and west from Retiro, actually three stations in one, known by their old names: Mitre, Belgrano and San Martín.

From **Mitre**, **Trenes de Buenos Aires** (TBA – passenger information

4317 4407/4445) runs services to Tigre, with connections to Capilla del Señor, José León Suárez and Bartolomé Mitre (in Olivos). There is a weekly service to Rosario in Santa Fe province. From **Belgrano**, **Ferrovías** (passenger information 4511 8833) runs trains to Villa Rosa. From **San Martín**, **Transportes Metropolitanos** (passenger information 4011 5826) has a service to Pilar.

Taxis & remises

Taxis in Buenos Aires are reasonably priced and plentiful (except in rainy rush hours). Travelling by taxi, however, has some risks and visitors need to be wary of being taken for a long ride, or worst of all, being robbed by an unlicensed driver. For this reason, it is recommended that you use only a radio taxi or a *remise* (licensed minicab). Both will come to any destination in the city to collect a passenger. You will need at least a few words of Spanish to call a radio taxi or remise company, though staff in hotels and restaurants will usually be happy to help. If you're in a rush and need to hail a cab in the street, you should still try to stop a radio cab. Look for 'radio taxi' and the name and telephone number of the company written on the back passenger doors.

Taxis run on meters: the initial fare is AR$1.28, plus AR16¢ for every 200 metres or one minute of waiting time. You are not expected to tip taxi drivers and they should give you change to the nearest AR10¢. Change is the perennial problem with taxis. Anything larger than a AR$10 bill is guaranteed to produce a sigh, a AR$20 note may provoke a verbal complaint and you are unlikely to find a driver if you only have a AR$50. Needless to say, AR$100 bills are out of the question. Many radio taxis have a minimum charge of AR$3, and a few charge an extra fee for making a pick-up (*adicionales*). Check first.

Taxis are black and yellow (radio cabs included), with a red *libre* (free) light in the front window. *Remises* look like other private cars and do not run on meters. You should agree a price before setting off. Also, bear in mind that *remises* are often less punctual than radio taxis. It's a good idea to make a second call, ten minutes before pick-up time, to check the *remise* is on its way.

Radio taxis

Mi Taxi 4931 1200. AR$3 minimum, no extra charges.
Pidalo 4956 1200. AR$1.40 call-out.
Siglo XXI 4633 4000. AR$3 minimum, no extra charges.

Remises

Remises Blue 4777 8888.
Remises Le Coq 49641 2000.
Remises Recoleta Vip 4801 6655.

Driving

Driving in Buenos Aires is neither easy nor relaxing. Chaos rules as buses, taxis and private cars fight it out on the roads. Driving is seen as a macho pursuit, although women have also taken aggressive driving to heart. People drive at very high speeds, change lanes with dizzying frequency, and generally get worked up into a feverish state while behind the wheel. If your masochistic tendencies are strong enough to tempt you to give it a go, there are a few basic rules:

● You have to be 17 to drive (16 with a parent or guardian's permission).
● Front seatbelts are compulsory.
● Under-10s must sit in the back.
● Priority is given to cars crossing other streets from the right. Cars fly out of nowhere on cross streets, so be warned.
● Overtake on the left – that's the principle, anyway. No one respects this rule, and even the law bends a little to say that if the left-hand lane is moving slower than the right-hand one, you can overtake on the right instead.
● There are minimum and maximum speeds, punishable by a fine if you break them. On streets (*calles*), the maximum speed is 40kmh, minimum 20kmh. On avenues (*avenidas*), maximum 60kmh, minimum 30kmh. On semi-motorways (*semiautopistas*), maximum 80kmh, minimum 40kmh (contrary to what most *porteños* believe, Avenidas General Paz and Lugones are semi-motorways, not motorways). On motorways (*autopistas*), maximum 100kmh, minimum 50kmh. On main national roads (*rutas nacionales*), signs on different stretches of road indicate minimum and maximum speeds, but the max is never over 130kmh.
● Private cars are prohibited from accessing the *microcentro* part of downtown between 11am and 4pm, Monday to Friday.
● The government recently introduced an unpopular system of speed cameras and fines. But, as they say in Buenos Aires, laws are

made to be broken, and an internet site quickly appeared, revealing the location of all the cameras. In any case, it is not unusual for the officer handing out the fine to ask: '¿Y cómo podemos arreglar esto?' ('How are we going to sort this out?'), to which is up to each individual to decide which is the best answer out of 'Hágame la boleta' ('Write me out the ticket') or 'Ehh… ¿cuánto quiere, oficial?' ('Ummm, how much do you want, officer?').

Breakdown services

Only members of automobile associations or touring clubs with reciprocal agreements with other regions (FiA in Europe and FITAC in the Americas) can use the breakdown services of the Automóvil Club Argentino (ACA, www.aca.org.ar). This includes members of the British AA and RAC. You can use this facility in Argentina for up to 30 days. You will have to present the membership credentials of your local club, showing the FITAC or FiA logo, to the mechanic.

Various companies offer emergency assistance to drivers. The basic call-out price is AR$35-$45. Try **ABA** (4572 6802), **Estrella** (4922 9095) or **Mecánica Móvil** (4925 6000).

Automóvil Club Argentino (ACA)
Information 4808 6200/breakdown service 4803 3333.
FITAC members also get special deals on hotels and car rental.

Fuel stations

There are numerous 24-hour service stations in Buenos Aires, especially on the main avenues, such as del Libertador, Figueroa Alcorta and Córdoba. Try these:
● **YPF** Avenida del Libertador 1850, entre Tagle y Perrera Lucena, Palermo; Avenida Córdoba 101, y Madero, Retiro; Avenida Corrientes 3351, entre Agüero y Gallo, Abasto.
● **Shell** Lima 899, e Independencia, Constitución; Cerrito, y Libertador, Retiro; Avenida Figueroa Alcorta 3099, y Castilla, Palermo.

Parking

Parking restrictions are indicated on street signs, but in general there is no parking in the Microcentro area downtown during working hours (and on some streets, there's no parking at any time). Parking is prohibited in the left lane on streets and avenues throughout the city, unless otherwise indicated.

The easiest option is a private garage (*estacionamiento privado* or *garaje*), signalled by a large blue sign with a white letter 'E' in the middle, costing around AR$3 per hour. There are also some pay-and-display machines and a few parking meters (buy tokens at a nearby *kiosco*). In some areas, you can buy tickets straight from a uniformed parking attendant. Some barrios (such as Palermo Viejo) still have free on-street parking, though you'll probably be approached by an unofficial *guardacoche* (car-keeper, possibly a child), offering to look after your car while you're gone. You will be expected to pay a couple of pesos on your return. If you're not happy with this arrangement, find somewhere else to park. Always take all valuables out of your car (stereo included, if possible), close windows and lock all doors.

Vehicle hire

You need to be over 21, with a driver's licence, passport and credit card to hire a car in Buenos Aires. There are no fixed prices; every agency has its own rates and special deals – but a rough guide is AR$120-$160 per day, depending on required mileage. Extra mileage costs AR37¢ per km. Major car rental companies will allow you to take the car out of the country (to Uruguay or Chile, for example) if you sign a contract in front of a public notary, which will set you back around AR$150. You can often return the car to a different office within Argentina. You must have at least third party insurance (*seguro de responsabilidad civil*), but it sensible to take out fully comprehensive insurance.

Dollar Rent a Car
Marcelo T de Alvear 449, entre Reconquista y San Martín, Retiro (4315 8800/www.dollar.com.ar). Subte C, San Martín/93, 130, 132, 152 bus. **Open** 9am-7pm Mon-Fri; 9am-1pm Sat. **Credit** AmEx, DC, MC, V. **Map** p277 E8.

Hertz Annie Millet
Paraguay 1138, entre Cerrito y Libertad, Tribunales (4816 8001/www.milletrentacar.com.ar). Subte D, Tribunales/10, 17, 59, 132, 152 bus. **Open** 8am-8pm daily. **Credit** AmEx, DC, MC, V. **Map** p277 F7.

UniRent
Avenida Leandro Alem 699, y Viamonte, Microcentro (4315 0777). Subte B, LN Alem/62, 93, 115, 130, 152 bus. **Open** 9am-8pm Mon-Fri; 9am-1pm Sat. **Credit** AmEx, DC, MC, V. **Map** p277 E8.

Cycling

Cycling in Buenos Aires can be a hazardous undertaking, thanks to numerous potholes, inconsiderate drivers, pollution and a lack of respect for the few cycle lanes that exist. However, there are pleasant cycling areas in Palermo, the Reserva Ecológica and the riverside neighbourhoods.

There are bicycle hire stands (open at weekends during daylight hours, and on some weekdays) around the entrance to major parks, including Parque Tres de Febrero and the Reserva Ecológica, the most cycle-friendly areas. In the south of the city, you can hire a bike in Parque Lezama. For information on circuits and bike hire, *see p202*.

Walking

Walking in Buenos Aires is a pleasure, despite certain factors that are stacked against it. Some of the streets in the city centre are extremely narrow, while broken pavements, potholes and ongoing street repairs add to the challenge.

Don't give up though. Green spaces in Palermo and Recoleta make these ideal barrios for a stroll; in the latter a number of major sights are close enough to easily walk from one to another. San Telmo is also a delightful area to explore on foot; on Sundays, it is partly closed to traffic for Plaza Dorrego's antiques market. Buenos Aires is also a safe city for walking – provided you aren't flashing jewellery, cameras or cash. That said, in most parts of La Boca, Constitución and away from the most centrally located tourist zones you should exercise more than the normal caution, especially at night or if you're on your own. Our street maps start on p269.

Directory

Resources A-Z

Age restrictions

The law says that to buy alcohol or have sex you must be 18 years old; to buy cigarettes you need to be 16; and you have to be 17 (16 with parental consent) to drive. The law, in general (or, at least, in the first three of those four cases), is broken.

Attitude & etiquette

Meeting people

Argentinians are gregarious and friendly, usually interested in meeting foreigners. Tactile and physically demonstrative, most exchange kisses (usually a single cheek-to-cheek kiss) on first meeting – men as well as women, although if you're meeting a more senior person it's safer to shake hands.

Personal contacts and introductions are highly valued. In business, if someone is proving difficult to contact, a quick name-drop can help, or, better still, use a third party for an introduction. When selling, it does no harm to lean on the foreign side of your business background.

It's best to start most conversations with a *buen día* (before noon) or *buenas tardes* (afternoon) and a brief exchange of pleasantries, if your Spanish is up to it. You will find that most business people speak – and are happy to use – at least some English, although this is not true in other environments. Any kind of attempt to speak in Spanish will always be appreciated, in every situation.

Don't sweat if you are delayed on your way to an appointment; punctuality is a phenomenon that barely exists. Most people always turn up late. Out of politeness, as the foreigner, it is better if you are on time, but expect to be kept waiting, always.

Dress & manners

Argentinians are always well presented. Best classified as casual but smart, the dress code is applicable from the pub to the boardroom.

Argentina's contradictory quality is never more apparent than in the behaviour of its citizens. On the one hand, they are champions of door-opening, friendly salutations and good manners; on the other, they are among the world's greatest perpetrators of shoulder-barging and shameless queue jumping.

Business

When considering doing business in Argentina, you should first contact the commercial department of your embassy. It's also worth contacting the Cámara Argentina de Comercio (Argentinian Chamber of Commerce, 5300 9000).

Conventions & conferences

Many of Buenos Aires' major hotels offer comprehensive convention and conference facilities. The **Sheraton** in Retiro (*see p33*) is a well-located and established convention venue that can hold events for up to 1,800 people in its 20 conference rooms. Smack next to the Obelisco, the **Crowne Plaza Panamericano** (*see p35*) has 16 event rooms for between six and 1,000 participants, while the newer **Hilton** in Puerto Madero (*see p35*) has extensive convention facilities for up to 2,000 attendees.

For smaller meetings, lunches or dinners, many restaurants – particularly those in Puerto Madero – offer a private room for business functions. Most do not charge for room hire if you are hosting a meal on their premises.

Couriers & shippers

DHL

Avenida Córdoba 783, entre Esmeralda y Maipú, Microcentro (4314 2996/freephone 0800 222 2345). Subte B, Florida/6, 26, 93, 130, 152 bus. **Open** 9am-7pm Mon-Fri; 9am-noon Sat. **Credit** AmEx, DC, MC, V. **Map** p277 E7.
Call two hours ahead to arrange pick-up from your premises at no extra charge, between 9am and 6pm.

FedEx

Maipú 753, entre Córdoba y Viamonte, Microcentro (4393 6139/ customer service 4630 0300). Subte B, Florida/6, 26, 93, 130, 152 bus. **Open** 9am-7pm Mon-Fri. **Credit** AmEx, MC, V. **Map** p277 E7.
International door-to-door express delivery. Home, office or hotel pick-ups costs US$3 extra.

UPS

Bernardo de Irigoyen 974, entre Estados Unidos y Carlos Calvo, San Telmo (freephone 0800 222 2877). Subte E, Independencia/17, 59, 67, 100, 126 bus. **Open** 9am-7pm Mon-Fri. **Credit** AmEx, DC, MC, V. **Map** p277 D5.
International delivery for packages from 0.5-50kg. Free home pick-up.

Office hire & business centres

If you need use of a telephone, fax or internet, your best bet is one of the many *locutorios* (call centres) situated all across town (*see p257* **Telephones**). Charges are usually AR$1 per page for sending or receiving faxes and around AR$1.50 for half an hour's internet usage.

If you need something more permanent (or to give that impression), there are several choices for temporary office hire. Options range from the

Directory

excellent, upmarket and very expensive international companies, such as Regus (4590 2200/www.regus.com), to these local choices:

Cerrito Rent an Office

2nd Floor, Cerrito 1070, entre Santa Fe y Marcelo T de Alvear, Recoleta (4811 4000/www.rent-an-office. com.ar). Bus 10, 59, 101, 152. **Open** 8am-8pm Mon-Fri. **Credit** AmEx, V. **Map** p277 F7.
Temporary office hire by the day, week or month. Monthly rates from AR$700-$1800. Translators, lawyers, accountants and architects available at extra charge.

SG Oficinas

6th Floor, Maipú 267, entre Sarmiento y Perón, Microcentro (4328 3939/www.sgoficina.com.ar). Subte B, Florida/6, 10, 17, 24, 29 bus. **Open** 9am-7pm Mon-Fri. **No credit cards**. **Map** p277 E7.
Serviced offices from AR$750 per month, or from AR$75 per day.

Translators & interpreters

Centro Internacional de Conferencias

Juncal 695, entre Basavilbaso y Maipú, Retiro (4313 3299). Subte C, Retiro/61, 93, 100, 130, 152 bus. **Open** 9.30am-6pm Mon-Fri. **No credit cards**. **Map** p277 F8.
Includes audio-visual services.

Copy Luar

Lavalle 1374, y Uruguay, Tribunales (4371 6273). Subte B, Uruguay/29, 39, 102 bus. **Open** 8am-7pm Mon-Fri. **Credit** AmEx, DC, MC, V. **Map** p277 F6.
Commercial and technical translations in English, German, Italian, Portuguese and Arabic.

Interhotel

11th Floor, Office 112, Lavalle 357, entre 25 de Mayo y Reconquista, Centro (4311 1615). Subte B, LN Alem/26, 62, 93, 130, 152 bus. **Open** 9am-6pm Mon-Fri. **No credit cards**. **Map** p277 E7.
Scientific and public translations.

Laura Rosenwaig

3rd Floor, Apartment C, Billinghurst 2467, entre Las Heras y Pacheco de Melo, Recoleta (4801 4536). Subte D, Bulnes/10, 37, 59, 60, 102 bus. **Open** 9am-7pm Mon-Fri. **No credit cards**. **Map** p278 I6.
Simultaneous translation for conferences and written translation work via fax or e-mail.

Useful organisations

Ministerio de Relaciones Exteriores, Comercio, Internacional y Culto

Arenales 1212, entre Esmeralda y Suipacha, Retiro (4829 7504). Subte C, San Martín/10, 17, 152 bus. **Open** 9am-6pm Mon-Fri. **Map** p277 F7.
The public face of the government arm dealing with international business relations.

Dirección Nacional de Migraciones

Avenida Antártida Argentina 1355, Dársena Norte, Retiro (4317 0200). Subte C, Estación Retiro/6, 7, 9, 92, 100 bus. **Open** 8.30am-1.30pm Mon-Fri. **Map** p277 E8.
For entry visas, student permits and work permits. Three month business visas are also issued here.

Consumer

Dirección General de Defensa y Protección al Consumidor

Esmeralda 340, entre Corrientes y Sarmiento, Microcentro (5382 6200/ www.buenosaires.gov.ar). Subte B, Florida/6, 26, 93, 130, 152 bus. **Open** 9am-5pm Mon-Fri; 9am-1pm Sat. **Map** p277 E7.
Receives and investigates consumer complaints, and gives advice on what rights and actions are available to consumers (and tourists).

Customs

Entering Argentina from overseas you can bring in the following, without paying import duties: 2 litres of alcoholic drinks, 400 cigarettes, 5kg of foodstuffs, 100ml of perfume. If entering from a neighbouring country, these quantities are halved.

Disabled

Getting around

BA is not known for its efforts to make it easier for those with mobility problems to get around. Pavements are in bad condition and there are often no drop-kerbs – or if there are, people will have parked in

front of them. Using the Subte is practically impossible, as few stations have lift access. An increasing number of *colectivos* are *super-bajo* (ultra-low), and just about accessible for accompanied wheelchair users. Radio taxis and *remises* do what they can to help, but are not specially equipped and many do not have enough space to stash a wheelchair.

A couple of companies specialise in transport and trips for disabled passengers.

Movidisc

4328 6921/fax 4682 9953.
Specially adapted vans for wheelchair users. It costs around AR$45 for a single journey in or around the capital. City tours also available, book 48 hours ahead.

QRV – Transportes Especiales

4306 6635/15 4022 3000 mobile.
Adapted minibuses for wheelchair users, equipped with microphones and guides. AR$20 for a standard journey within the capital; call to check prices for city tours. Book 24 hours ahead.

Useful contacts

Red de Discapacidad (REDI)

4706 2769/redi@ddnet.com.ar.
Eduardo Joly, a sociologist who has also studied tourism, is a wheelchair user and director of this disabled persons' network, which can provide advice and information.

Electricity

Electricity in Argentina runs on 22 volts. Sockets take either two or three-pronged European-style plugs. To use US electrical appliances, you'll need a transformer (*transformador*) and an adaptor (*adaptador*); for UK appliances an adaptor only is required. Both can be purchased in hardware stores (*ferreterías*) all over town. Power cuts are occasional, though become more frequent when it rains heavily. Supplies are usually restored within three hours, but can be out for a day or longer.

Directory

Embassies & consulates

American Embassy & Consulate

Avenida Colombia 4300, entre Sarmiento y Cerviño, Palermo (5777 4533). Subte D, Plaza Italia/37, 67, 130 bus. **Open** *Visas 7.30am-12.30pm Mon-Fri by appointment only. Information 8am-noon Mon-Fri.* **Map** p279 J6.

Australian Consulate

Villanueva 1400, entre Zabala y Teodoro García, Palermo (4779 3550). Bus 59, 60. **Open** 8.30am-12.30pm, 1.30-5.30pm Mon-Thur; 8.30am-1.35pm Fri. **Map** p281 M5.

British Embassy & Consulate

Luis Agote 2412, entre Libertador y Las Hera, Recoleta (4808 2200). Bus 37, 60, 102. **Open** *Jan, Feb* 8.45am-2.30pm Mon-Thur; 8.45am-2pm Fri. *Mar-Dec* 8.45am-5.30pm Mon-Thur; 8.45am-2pm Fri. **Map** p278 H7.

Canadian Embassy & Consulate

Tagle 2828, entre Figueroa Alcorta y Juez Tedin, Recoleta (4808 1000). Bus 67, 130. **Open** 8.30am-12.30pm, 1.30-5.30pm Mon-Thur; 8.30am-2pm Fri. **Map** p278 I7.

Irish Consulate

2nd Floor, Suipacha 1380, entre Juncal y Arroyo, Retiro (4325 8588). Suhte C, Retiro/59, 130, 152 bus. **Open** 9.30am-1.30pm, 2-3.30pm Mon-Fri. **Map** p277 F8.

New Zealand Embassy & Consulate

Carlos Pellegrini 1427, entre Arroyo y Posadas, Retiro (4328 0747). Subte C, Retiro/10, 59, 130 bus. **Open** 9am-1pm, 2-5.45pm Mon-Thur; 9am-1pm Fri. **Map** p277 F8.

South African Embassy & Consulate

Marcelo T de Alvear 590, entre San Martín y Florida, Retiro (4317 2900). Subte C, San Martín/7, 9, 17, 92 bus. **Open** 8.15am-12.30pm, 1.15-5.15pm Mon-Thur; 8.15am-2.15pm Fri. **Map** p277 E8.

Emergencies

All available 24 hours daily.

Fire

100.
For the fire brigade you can also call 4383 2222, 4304 2222, 4381 2222.

Travel advice

For up-to-date information on travel to a specific country – including the latest news on safety and security, health issues, local laws and customs – contact your home country government's department of foreign affairs. Most have websites packed with useful advice for would-be travellers.

Australia
www.dfat.gov.au/travel

New Zealand
www.mft.govt.nz/travel

UK
www.fco.gov.uk/travel

Canada
www.voyage.gc.ca

Republic of Ireland
www.irlgov.ie/iveagh

USA
www.state.gov/travel

Police

101.
Also 4370 5911 in an emergency.

Defensa Civil

103 or 4956 2106.
For gas leaks, power cuts, floods and other major catastrophes.

Medical emergencies

107.
To call an ambulance.

Emergencias Médicas Náuticas

106.

Gay & lesbian

For more contacts, as well as gay hotel options, *see chapter* **Gay & Lesbian**. For HIV/AIDS advice and info, *see below* **Health**. The **Centro Cultural Ricardo Rojas** has a gay library and archive; *see p177*.

Grupo Nexo

4375 0359/www.nexo.org.
Another useful multifaceted cultural centre, offering counselling, information and help.

Health

No vaccinations are required for BA and the city's tap water is potable. Argentina, however, doesn't have any reciprocal healthcare agreements with any other countries, so you should take out your own medical insurance policy.

Accident & emergency

In case of poisoning, call the **Centro de Intoxicaciones del Hospital Ricardo Gutierrez** on 4962 6666.

Ambulance services are provided by **SAME** (Sistema de Atención Médica de Emergencia) – call 4923 1051 or 107. The specialist burns hospital, the **Hospital de Quemadas**, is at Avenida Pedro Goyena 369, Caballito (4923 3022 or emergencies 4923 4082).

For public and private hospitals, *see p251*.

Contraception & abortion

Public hospitals will supply the contraceptive pill after an appointment with a doctor. Alternatively, condom machines are found in the toilets of most bars, clubs and restaurants and are available in pharmacies. Abortion is illegal in Argentina.

Dentists

For emergency dental treatment, call the Servicio de Urgencias at the dental faculty (*see p251*).

Directory

Hospital Municipal de Odontología Infantil

Pedro de Mendoza 1795, entre Palos y M Rodríguez, La Boca (4301 4834). Bus 29, 53, 64, 152. **Map** p276 A5.
24-hour dental attention for children.

Dr José Zysmilich

1st Floor, Apt C, Salguero 1108, entre Córdoba y Cabrera, Palermo Viejo (4865 2322). Bus 26, 36, 92, 128. **Open** 3-7pm Mon, Wed, Fri. **Map** p278 H4.
English-speaking private dentist: a member of the American Dental Association.

Servicio de Urgencias

Marcelo T de Alvear 2146, entre Junín y Uriburu, Barrio Norte (4964 1259). Subte D, Facultad de Medicina/12, 39, 60, 111, 152 bus. **Map** p278 G6.
Treatment is free to Argentinians only at this university dental faculty; foreigners are welcome, but are usually asked to pay a small fee of between AR$5 and AR$10.

Hospitals & doctors

For emergency or general non-emergency medical needs, you can see a doctor at one of these hospitals. All will have staff who can get by in English. Alternatively, many hotels offer 24-hour medical call-outs to their guests.

Hospital Británico

Pedriel 74, entre Finnochietto y Caseros, Barracas (4309 6400/6500). Bus 59, 67, 100. **Map** p276 C4.
Your best bet as an English speaker is this private, well-equipped and modern hospital, in a somewhat out of way location. The Hospital Británico also has a number of clinics around the city where an appointment can be made to see an English-speaking doctor, at a cost of AR$36.30 per appointment. The most centrally located is in Barrio Norte at Marcelo T de Alvear 1573, (4812 0048/49).

Hospital de Clínicas José de San Martín

Avenida Córdoba 2351, entre Uriburu y Azcuénaga, Barrio Norte (5950 8000). Bus 29, 61, 101, 111. **Map** p278 G6.
Buenos Aires' largest, most centrally located public hospital. It has departments for all specialities and the city's main accident and emergency unit. If you don't have insurance, this is where to come.

Hospital de Niños Dr Ricardo Gutiérrez

Sánchez de Bustamante 1330, y Paraguay, Barrio Norte (4962 9232/9229). Bus 29, 92, 111, 128. **Map** p278 H5.
Public, paediatric hospital.

Pharmacies

There are always some pharmacies open all night. Go to the nearest; if it's not open, it will post details of the nearest *farmacia de turno*. Mega-pharmacy Farmacity has 24-hour branches across the city – for details, *see p157*.

STDs, HIV & AIDS

Gay information service **Nexo** (*see p250*) runs a phone line for people who are HIV-positive: Linea Positiva 4374 4484.

CEPAD

(Centro de Prevención Asesoramiento y Diagnóstico de VIH/Sida) *Hospital Ramos Mejía, Urquiza 609, entre Venezuela y México, San Cristóbal (4931 5252/4127 0276). Bus 53, 88, 103, 132.* **Open** 9.30am-3.30pm Mon-Fri.
Consultations, testing and treatment for people with HIV/AIDS.

Pregunte Sida

0800 3333 444. **Open** 9am-10pm Mon-Fri; 9am-4pm Sat-Sun.
Free HIV/AIDS helpline. Also advice on general sexual health issues and where to go for testing or treatment.

Helplines

Though no helplines have English-speaking staff, most will find someone with at least a few words – be ready with your phone number in Spanish in case they need to call back.

Alcohólicos Anónimos

4788 6646.

Centro de Atención a Víctimas de Violencia Sexual

4981 6882/4958 4291.
Support for victims of sex crimes.

Centro de Orientación a la Víctima

4801 4444/8146.
Victim support.

Jugadores Anónimos

4328 0019/15 4412 6745.
Gamblers Anonymous.

Servicio de Orientación en droga dependencia

4822 1030/4823 4827.
Support for the drug-dependent.

Teleamigo

4304 0061.
Phone support for people in crisis.

ID

By law, everyone must carry photo ID. Checks are rare, but if you do get pulled over, you would be expected to show at least a copy of your passport or (photo) driving licence.

Insurance

Argentina is not covered by any reciprocal health insurance schemes, so visitors from all countries are recommended to buy comprehensive private insurance before they travel.

Internet

The main concentration of online services is downtown, on Lavalle and Florida. Most cybercafés operate about 30 machines which surf at a reasonable speed for about AR$1.50 an hour. *Locutorios* (call centres) also provide internet services, though prices are higher than in cybercafés. Most hotels and hostels are hooked up; some throw in the service for free. Local service providers include NetEx (www.netex.com.ar) and Netizen (www.netizen.com.ar).

Callao Web

Avenida Callao 1160, entre Santa Fe y Arenales, Recoleta (5219 8080). Subte D, Callao/29, 60, 124, 152 bus. **Open** 8am-10pm Mon-Fri; 9am-9pm Sat. **Map** p278 G6.

Star Cyberbar

Avenida de Mayo 933, entre Tacuari y Irigoyen, Microcentro (4345 6767). Subte A, Piedras/10, 17, 64, 86 bus. **Open** 8am-2am Mon-Sat; 11am-2am Sun. **Map** p277 E6.

Directory

Legal help

For legal help, contact your consulate or embassy (*see p250*) in the first instance.

Libraries

Buenos Aires has no major English-language lending library, but the **Biblioteca Nacional** (National Library, *see p80*) has a reasonable reference section and the Hemeroteca in the basement is a good resource for newspapers and magazines.

Lost property

In general, if you've lost it, forget it. Your chance of recovering any stolen or lost property will depend on the good nature of the person who happens to find your belongings. If you've lost something on public transport, you can call the transport operator, which should hang on to lost property – but don't hold your breath.

This is another good reason to take radio taxis, as you can call the operating company if you leave something in a cab. Always make a mental note of your cab number for just such an eventuality.

Media

Magazines

El Amante del Cine
Reviews of international films and interviews with local filmmakers.

Gente
The bestselling weekly guide to models, TV stars, media types and any wannabes who hang out their wares at society parties.

Los Inrockuptibles
Funky monthly mag with the word on BA's music scene and gig listings.

Noticias
Popular news weekly, juxtaposing provocative investigative specials and society nonsense.

TXT
Prankster journalist Adolfo Castelo's weekly rag usually gets the inside scoop and if not, titillating photos keep you entertained.

Veintitres
Local loudmouth celeb journo Jorge Lanata's anti-establishment organ.

Newspapers

Buenos Aires Herald
English-language daily, read by ex-pats and Argentinians. Sunday edition includes articles from the *New York Times* and the *Guardian*.

Clarín
Mass-market daily that's fat with both local and international news. Somehow manages to be high-, middle- and low-brow at the same time and so sells loads.

La Nación
BA's grand old daily, beloved of the safe middle classes and conservative on culture, art and lifestyle.

Página 12
Here the word on every article is '*opina*' – as every leftie in the city gives his or her opinion on every subject, squeezing in a bit of news here and there. *Página* flies the flag for independent journalism. The Sunday cultural supplement *Rádar* is among the best.

Radio

FM de la Ciudad
92.7FM
Municipal service started in 1990 to ensure that tango, the essential soundtrack to Buenos Aires life, is available all day and all night.

FM La Folklórica
98.7FM
Get your fix of folky strumming and gaucho choirs to help you slow down in the big brash city.

Mega – Puro Rock Nacional
98.3FM
No chat, only music, and *rock nacional* at that. One of the most listened to stations by young people.

Metrodance
95.1FM
By day, hip variety shows and news; by night and on weekends, even hipper dance and electronic music.

Rock & Pop
95.9FM

Brought *rock nacional* and rock culture in general to the fore. Mario Pergolini's morning show is the soundtrack young office workers wake up to city-wide.

Television

This is just a smattering of what you'll find; most hotels and homes also have cable and satellite channels.

América TV
Plenty of sports coverage, plus general soaps, current affairs and entertainment.

Canal 7
The only state-run TV channel, and one that can afford not to play the ratings game. Programming is big on Argentinian culture and music.

Canal 9
Sex, scandals, sex, alien abductions and more sex are the hallmarks of BA's lowest of low-brow channels.

Canal 13
The most watched channel with the best series. Good nightly news.

Telefe – Canal 11
Big channel, fronted by big personalities like Susana Giménez and Marcelo Tinelli. Also soaps and imports such as *The Simpsons*.

Money

The Argentinian currency is the peso. After the old convertibility system which pegged the peso to the US dollar at 1:1 was abandoned in January 2002, the currency was allowed to float freely and consequently devalue. Its value has since remained largely stable, at AR$2.75-$3 to one US dollar, despite initial fears that it would plummet, sending Argentina back to the mad, bad old days of hyperinflation. This is Argentina, however, and, given the country's economic record, things could easily change.

The peso is divided into centavos. Coins are the silver and yellowy-gold one peso coin, 50, 25, ten and five centavos. Some 50 and 25 centavo coins are the same size

Stars of the small screen

La tele is a favourite topic for any *porteño*, and in a country that's a world leader in personality cults, it's often a question of not what, but who's on the box tonight?

Undisputed queen and darling of the small screen is aging diva Susana Giménez. The 59-year-old platinum blonde with the voluptuous curves holds court over an hour long, thrice weekly fest of family entertainment involving phone-ins, comedy sketches and chat (*Susana Giménez*, Telefe, 8pm Mon-Fri). Better known for her hilarious verbal blunders than for any rigorous or cerebral approach to interviewing, 'Su' has become a national treasure. Off screen, the ex-glamour girl's love life has proved equally entertaining. Her last husband, having had his nose broken by a flying ashtray, divorced the temperamental star in a vicious public battle, involving a custody tussle over the couple's pet Yorkshire terrier. Susana lost out to the tune of AR$10 million, but she got to keep the mutt.

'La Señora' of Argentinian TV is Mirtha Legrand, septuagenarian presenter of a daily, lunchtime chat show (*Almorzando con Mirtha Legrand*, América, 12.30pm). This venerable television matriarch has been getting high-profile guests to join her for lunch for the last thirty years. Famed for putting her guests to the sword, presidents included, with her acid questions, Legrand's interviews are respected as sharp and incisive.

King of prime time is Marcelo Tinelli, whose show, *VideoMatch* (Telefe, 11pm Mon-Fri), regularly tops the ratings, dishing up comedy sketches and practical pranks of the hidden camera variety. Entrepreneur Tinelli, who runs marathons for fun, also owns a successful production company, Ideas del Sur, two radio stations and a pro volleyball team.

The small screen's bad boy, and long-time rival to Tinelli (he even owns a competing volleyball team) is Mario Pergolini, creator and main host of stylish *Caiga Quien Caiga* (Canal 13, 11pm Mon), a weekly satirical show. Innovative and slickly produced – camera flips, rock soundtrack and near fit-inducing visual effects – *CQC*, and its outspoken creator, revel in exposing the hypocrisy of the country's elite. Exported to Europe, *CQC* represents the biggest success yet for Pergolini's production stable, Cuatro Cabezas, or Four Heads (there are only two partners, so take your guesses), whose other exports include the heartbreaking football reality show *El Camino a la Gloria* and the *Super M* model-search series.

Fellow player behind the camera is Adrián Suar, whose company Pol-ka churns out the formulaic – hero chases, wins, loses, then wins again the heart of the female lead – but psyche-tapping and massively successful soap operas that dominate Argentinian prime time. Suar has made recent forays into the world of film, producing and financing the Oscar-nominated *The Son of the Bride*.

Unlikely ever to be nominated for an Academy Award is Moria Casán, the publicity-hungry ex-go go girl and B-movie star, famed for owning Argentina's first nudist beach, which she opened in Mar del Plata in 1993 with a ceremonial snip of her bra. While this annual '*Corte de Corpiño*' is now shown live every January, Casán was also famous as host of a Jerry Springer-style show, likely to pop back up on the box soon.

and colour (yellow-gold) so hard to differentiate. Newer 25-centavo coins are silver. Notes come in denominations of 100 (purple), 50 (dark grey), 20 (red), ten (brown), five (green) and two (blue) pesos, and in every kind of condition.

Beware of fake money. There are many falsified notes and coins in circulation, so check your change, especially in cabs. False bills are generally quite detectable, as the colours tend to lack the precision of authentic notes and the texture has a plasticky feel. Fake coins (predominantly 50 centavos) are commonplace: they're lighter in both colour and weight than the legal tender, so easy to spot.

Also, avoid the illegal money changers lining Florida and its adjacent streets, known as *arbolitos*, or little trees. They are the ones who are most likely to sting you with fake pesos and give a low rate of exchange.

ATMs

Most banks have ATMs, signalled by a 'Banelco' or 'Link' sign. They distribute pesos only and usually charge a fee (US$1-$5). Some are only for clients of the bank in question, so look for a machine showing the symbol of your card company. If withdrawing large sums, do so discreetly and be careful taking a cab: either walk several blocks first or call a radio taxi.

Directory

Banks

It's extremely difficult to open an Argentinian bank account if you are a foreigner. Banks ask for endless paperwork, including wage slips and a local ID. To compound the situation, most banks won't accept a transfer unless you have an account. To receive money, use Forexcambio, who can also cash foreign cheques or bankers' drafts, or Western Union. Charges vary according to the state of the market. In early 2004, Forexcambio was charging a minimum of US$50 per transfer, while Western Union was charging US$16 for a US$50 transfer and US$56 for a US$1,000 transfer.

Forexcambio

Marcelo T de Alvear 540, entre Florida y San Martín, Retiro (4311 5543). Subte C, San Martín/26, 61, 93, 152 bus. **Open** 10am-3pm Mon-Fri. **Map** p277 E8.

Western Union

Córdoba 975, entre Suipacha y Carlos Pellegrini, Microcentro (freephone 0800 8003030). Subte C, Lavalle/10, 59, 111 bus. **Open** 8am-8pm Mon-Fri. **Map** p277 F7.

Travellers' cheques & bureaux de change

Travellers' cheques are often refused by business establishments and can be difficult and expensive to change in banks.

There are various bureaux de change in the city centre, which will change travellers' cheques. Commission is usually around 2%, with a minimum charge of US$5. Many are situated around the intersection of Sarmiento and Reconquista streets. Usual opening hours are 9am-6pm.

American Express

Arenales 707, y Maipú, Retiro (4310 3000). Subte C, San Martín/10, 17, 70, 152 bus. **Open** 10am-3pm Mon-Fri. **Map** p277 F8.
Will change AmEx travellers' cheques without charge.

Credit cards

Credit cards are accepted in most outlets. Visa (V), MasterCard (MC) and American Express (AmEx) are the most accepted cards. Diners Club (DC) is also valid in a number of places, but check first.

Lost & stolen cards

American Express 0810 555 2639, select option 2.
Diners Club 0810 444 2482.
MasterCard Call the card issuer in your home country.
Visa 4379 3333.

Tax

Local sales tax is called IVA, aka Impuestos a Valor Agregado. It's a whacking 21 per cent, though as a rule it's always added on the bill or pricetag. The exception is hotel rack rates that are generally listed without IVA in more expensive hotels. However, in our **Where to Stay** chapter we have quoted all prices with IVA included, so there's no nasty shock on the final bill.

Natural hazards

Apart from a volatile economy, Argentina is largely free of natural hazards. The only blip comes during when a strong wind from the south – La Sudestada – brings torrential rain and flash flooding to Palermo, Belgrano and La Boca. *Sudestadas* are more common from June to October.

Opening hours

Opening hours are extremely variable, but here are some general guidelines:

Banks

Generally open from 10am-3pm weekdays, although some branches open an hour earlier, and some close an hour later.

Bars

Many bars and cafés in Buenos Aires are open 24/7. Pubs, or evening bars, open around 6pm for happy hour, or 8pm out of the centre, and most stay open till the crowds thin out.

Business hours

Ordinary office hours are 9am-6pm, with lunchbreak from 1pm-2pm.

Post offices

The Correo Central (Central Post Office; *see p255*) is open 8am-8pm Mon-Fri and 8am-1pm Sat. Other branch post offices are open weekdays from 9am-6pm. Many telephone centres (*locutorios*) also have postal services and are often open until midnight.

Shops

Most malls open 10am-10pm, though there can be one hour's variation. The food court and cinemas stay open after the other shops. Shops on the street tend to open from 9am-10am and close at around 7pm.

Police stations

Public safety in the capital is the responsibility of the Policía Federal, divided into 53 *comisarías* (at least one per barrio), with a central police station. Tourists needing to report a crime should go to the **Comisaría del Turista**. Alternatively you can head to the station in the barrio in which the incident occurred. *See p250* for emergency telephone numbers.

Comisaría del Turista

Avenida Corrientes 436, entre San Martín y Reconquista, Microcentro (0800 999 5000). Subte B, Florida/10, 93, 99 bus. **Open** 24 hrs daily **Map** p277 E7.
English-speaking staff are on hand especially to help tourists needing to report a crime.

Staying safe

Over the last five years, BA's reputation as one of the world's safest capitals has taken a bruising. Outbreaks of lootings and violent protests in 2001-2002 did nothing for the city's image, and as poverty has increased, crime rates have risen. *La inseguridad* now ranks alongside unemployment as the topic of most concern for *porteños*.

Tourists should remember, however, that while opportunistic robberies continue on the up, they are by and large targeted at shops and households, not people. With a little common sense, visitors to Buenos Aires will avoid most crime. Don't display eye-catching jewellery, cameras or clothes synonymous with the typical tourist. Keep an eye on belongings on public transport and always use radio taxis (*see p246*). Remember that while most tourist areas remain safe, more care should be taken in the barrios of La Boca and Constitución, and to a slightly lesser extent in San Telmo and Palermo.

Anywhere in the city, it's best to avoid pulling out a wallet stacked with bills – and keep loose change handy, just in case you are approached by people asking for '*una moneda*' (a coin); don't feel obliged, but bear

in mind that a small coin means a lot to others. If you are actually threatened, whoever the assailant, hand over your goods calmly; BA has a gun problem.

Street aggression can be verbal. Local women have a dismissive shrug or hardened stare as a natural defence. At worst, it's usually plain crude; if he's really annoying, walk into a shop or lose him in the nearest ladies toilet. Note that Argentina's culture is inherently macho and friendly behaviour may be taken as a come-on. 'No' will not always be interpreted as 'no', so take care.

If you need to report a crime, head first to the city's centrally located **Comisaría del Turista** (*see p254*), where English-speaking staff are at hand. When dealing with local police on a street level, however, bear in mind that corruption in Argentina's police force is considered widespread. While officers can be approached for advice (but are unlikely to speak English), avoid confrontations on highways and in more remote areas. If approached by the police to assist in any way, insist on going to the station with a witness before handing over documents or information.

Departamento Central de Policía

Moreno 1550, entre Luis Sáenz Peña y Belgrano, Congreso (4370 5800 24hrs). Subte A, Sáenz Peña/39, 60, 64, 86 bus. Map p277 E5.

The police stations below are in central areas, but it's best to use the Comisaría del Turista:

Comisaría 1ª (Centro)

Lavalle 451, entre Reconquista y San Martín, Microcentro (4322 8033). Subte B, Florida/10, 93, 99 bus. Map p277 E7.

Comisaría 2ª (San Telmo)

Perú 1050, entre Carlos Calvo y Humberto 1°, San Telmo (4361 8054). Bus 24, 126, 30, 152. Map p276 C6.

Comisaría 17ª (Recoleta)

Avenida Las Heras 1861, entre Callao y Ayacucho, Recoleta (4801 3333). Bus 10, 59, 60, 124. Map p278 G7.

Postal services

Numerous competitors offer postal, courier and other express delivery services, though not all can provide international postal facilities. Nor does increased competition appear to have brought many price benefits as Correo Argentino is still the cheapest for domestic mail.

A letter weighing up to 20 grams costs AR$0.75, from 20 to 100 grams costs AR$2.75. To neighbouring countries, a letter of up to 20 grams costs AR$3.50, to other countries in the Americas and other, worldwide destinations, AR$4.

Registered post (essential for any document of value) costs a minimum of AR$7.50 for up to 20 grams nationally, and AR$10.25 for up to 20 grams internationally.

There are Correo Argentino branches throughout the city, and many larger *locutorios* offer their postal services.

If you want to receive post in Buenos Aires, get it sent directly to your hotel or to a private address if you have contacts here. There is a *poste restante* service at the Correo Central; it costs AR$4.50 to collect each piece of mail, which should be sent to:

Recipient's name,
Lista de Correos,
Correo Central,
Sarmiento 189,
(1003) Capital Federal,
Argentina.

Correo Central

Sarmiento 151, entre Leandro N Alem y Bouchard, Microcentro (4891 9191). Subte B, LN Alem/ 26, 93, 99, 152 bus. **Open** 8am-8pm Mon-Fri; 8am-1pm Sat. Map p277 D7.

Directory

Religion

Roman Catholicism is the official state religion, though only about 20 per cent attend church regularly. Other religions co-exist with Catholicism; there are many synagogues in Once, and many other evangelical gatherings which occur in converted stores around BA. Here are a few addresses of places of worship around the city. For a more complete listing, check the local *Yellow Pages*.

Anglican

Catedral Anglicana de San Juan Bautista *25 de Mayo 282, y Sarmiento, Microcentro (4342 4618). Bus 126, 130, 146, 152.* **Services** *English* 9.30am Sun. *Spanish* 11am Sun. **Map** p277 D7.

Buddhist

Templo Budista Honpa-Hongwanji *Sarandí 951, entre Carlos Calvo y Estados Unidos, San Cristobal (4941 0262). Subte E, Entre Ríos/12, 37, 126, 168 bus.* **Service** 5pm Sun. **Map** p277 E4.

Roman Catholic

Catedral Metropolitana *Avenida Rivadavia 412, y San Martin, Microcentro (4331 2845). Subte A, Plaza de Mayo or D, Catedral or E, Bolívar/24, 29, 64, 86 bus.* **Services** Spanish only 9am, 11am, 12.30pm, 6pm Mon-Fri; 11am, 6pm Sat; 11am, noon, 1pm, 6pm Sun. **Map** p277 D7.

Jewish

Gran Templo de la Asociación Comunidad Israelita Sefardí *Camargo 870, entre Gurruchaga y Serrano, Villa Crespo. Subte B, Malabia/15, 24, 57, 106 110 bus.* **Services** 7.10am, 6.45pm Mon-Fri; 9am, 5.30pm Sat; 8am, 6.30pm Sun. **Map** p275 J2.
See also **Templo Libertad,** *p60.*

Muslim

Centro Islámico Ray Fahd *Avenida Bullrich 55, y Libertador, Palermo (4899 0201). Subte D, Palermo/39, 60, 64, 130, 152 bus.* **Map** p279 K6.

Presbyterian

Presbyterian Scottish Church of Saint Andrew *Avenida Belgrano 579, entre Bolívar y Perú, Monserrat (4331 0308). Subte E, Piedras/24, 29, 86, 126 bus.* **Services** *English* 10am Sun. *Spanish* 11.30am Sun. **Map** p277 D6.

Smoking

Argentines love a fag, so don't expect many no-smoking places. Despite an ambitious effort to change public opinion, the bottom line remains the same, nicotine is in. With the exceptions of public transport, cinemas and some restaurant areas, smoking is permitted.

Study

Language classes

Every year new institutes open, offering Spanish for foreigners. There are huge ranges in price and quality.

To organise an *intercambio* or language exchange, check noticeboards in universities and student travel agencies. There are usually lots of willing partners. Check, too, the ads in the *Buenos Aires Herald*; most language institutes and private teachers advertise there. Or try:

Latin Immersion

Virrey Arredondo 2416, entre Cabildo y Ciudad de Paz, Colegiales (4789 0849/www.latinimmersion. com). Subte D, José Hernandez/41, 59, 60, 68, 152 bus. **Open** 8.30am-6pm Mon-Fri. **Rates** *Group classes* US$170 20hrs per wk. *Private classes* US$270 20 hrs per wk. **Credit** MC, V. **Map** p281 M4.

UBA – Laboratorio de Idiomas, Facultad de Filosofía y Letras

25 de Mayo 221, entre Perón y Sarmiento, Centro (4343 5981/ 1196/www.idiomas.filo.uba.ar). Bus 126, 130, 146, 152. **Open** 9am-9pm Mon-Fri. **Rates** *Group classes* AR$500 4hrs per wk for 17 wks or 8hrs per wk for 8 wks. **No credit cards.** **Map** p277 D7.

Students' unions

FUBA (Federación Universitaria de Buenos Aires)

3rd Floor, Azcuénaga 280, entre Sarmiento y Perón, Once (4952 8080/www.fuba.org.ar). Subte A, Alberti/24, 26, 101, 105 bus. **Open** 9am-8pm Mon-Fri.

Universities

There is state-run and private university education available in BA. The Universidad de Buenos Aires (or UBA, state run) is, in general, the most academically respected. Study at UBA is free. Private universities tend to have greater numbers of classes throughout the year, and better facilities, but the disadvantage, of course, is the fees.

UBA (Departamento de Títulos y Planes)

6th Floor, Office 602, Azcuénaga 280, entre Sarmiento y Perón, Once (4951 0634 ext 100 or 101). Subte A, Alberti/24, 26, 101, 105 bus. **Open** noon-4pm Mon, Thur.
If you want to study at UBA, contact this department or go in person to the Centro Cultural Ricardo Rojas (*see p177*), which has general information for the university.

Universidad Argentina de la Empresa

Lima 717, entre Independencia y Chile, San Telmo (4372 5454/ www. uade.edu.ar). Subte E, Independencia/ 17, 59, 67, 105 bus. **Open** 9am-8pm Mon-Fri. **Map** p277 D5.
A business school with agreements with universities in the US, Chile, Brazil and Germany, among others.

Universidad de Palermo

Avenida Córdoba 3501, entre Mario Bravo y Bulnes, Palermo Viejo (4964 4600/www.palermo.edu.ar). Bus 26, 36, 92, 128. **Open** 9am-8pm Mon-Fri. **Map** p278 H4.

Useful organisations

www.delestudiante. com

Listings of every university, degree and postgrad offered.

www.studyabroad.com

Information in English on studying around the world; includes Argentina.

Asatej

3rd Floor, Office 320, Florida 835, entre Córdoba y Paraguay, Microcentro (4511 8700/www.al mundo.com). Subte B, Florida/10, 26, 93, 130, 152 bus. **Open** 9am-7pm Mon-Fri. **Map** p277 E7.
Student travel agency, with locations across town. ISIC cards issued here.

Telephones

BA is geographically divided between **Telefónica** and **Telecom**. However, smaller companies offering discount international phone services are now popping up to shake the giants from their slumber.

Dialling & codes

All land-line numbers within BA begin with 4, 5 or 6 and consist of eight digits. To call a cellphone number, 15 must be added to the front of an eight-digit number, which will begin with 4 or 5. For land-lines and cellphones, when calling BA from outside the city, you need to add 011. From overseas, dial your country's international dialling code followed by 54 11 and the eight-digit number. To call cellphones from overseas, dial 54 9 11 and leave out the 15. To dial overseas from BA, dial 00 followed by the country code and number (Australia 61, Canada 1, Ireland 353, New Zealand 64, UK 44, USA 1).

Other useful numbers:

Directory information 110
International operator 000
National operator 19
Repair service 114
Talking clock 113
Telecom/Telefónica commercial services 112
Telelectura 121. This is a free, 24hr service, which tells you the call charges within a billing period.

Call centres

BA is awash with *locutorios* (call centres), generally run by Telefónica or Telecom. Calls cost a few *centavos* more than from a public phone, but for a seat, air-con and the guarantee that your last coin won't be gobbled, it's worth it. They offer fax services and often net access and post services.

Public phones are coin- or card-operated, sometimes both. Phonecards can be bought from kiosks.

Mobile phones

CDMA/TDMA is the predominant system, though it's cheaper to rent locally than bring your own phone. Most UK cellphones will not work.

Altel

1st Floor, Office 4, Avenida Córdoba 417, y Reconquista, Microcentro (4311 5000/15 4411 3333 mobile/ www.altel.com.ar). Subte C, San Martín/111, 132, 152 bus. **Open** 8.30am-8pm Mon-Fri. **Map** p277 E8 Free rental, air time charge of US$1 per min. Daily minimum, 10mins.

Phonerental

San Martín 945, entre Paraguay y Marcelo T de Alvear, Retiro (24hr hotline 4311 2933/www.phonerental. com.ar). Subte C, San Martín/10, 93, 30, 152 bus. **Open** 9am-6pm Mon-Fri. **Map** 277 E8.
Free phone rental, AR$1.25 per min air time charge, no minimum.

Time

The clocks have been known to go back and forward by an hour in a rather arbitrary manner, although in recent years, winter and summer time has remained the same. Thus, Argentina is three hours behind GMT during the southern hemisphere summer, and four hours behind GMT during the southern winter.

Tipping

Tips tend to be left in the same quantities as most developed countries. As a rule of thumb, leave 10 to 15 per cent in a bar, restaurant, or for any delivery service. In older cinemas, ushers expect a tip of 25 or 50 centavos; in a cab, just round off a fare. In hotels, bellboys expect AR$1 for helping with your bags. When checking out, it's normal to leave a small *propina* for the maids.

Toilets

Needles in haystacks have been found more easily than public toilets in BA. However, most bars and restaurants accept, with resignation, the role of offering evacuatory relief to the public. All shopping centres have clean public toilets. And, of course, bathroom use is one of the few advantages conferred on the world by fast-food outlets.

Tourist information

The tourist board website is www.buenosaires.gov/turismo. These are the official city tourist information points:
Abasto de Buenos Aires *Avenida Corrientes y Agüero, Abasto (4959 3507). Subte B, Carlos Gardel/bus 24, 26, 124, 168.* **Open** 11am-9pm daily. **Map** p278 G4.
Florida *Avenida Roque Sáenz Peña y Florida, Microcentro (no phone). Subte D, Catedral/bus 24, 130, 103, 152.* **Open** 9am-6pm Mon-Fri; 10am-3pm Sat. **Map** p277 E7.
Recoleta *Avenida Quintana y Ortiz (no phone). Bus 17, 67, 124, 130.* **Open** 10am-8pm daily. **Map** p278 G7.
Retiro *Terminal de Ómnibus, Avenida Antártida Argentina y Calle 10 (4311 0528). Subte C, Retiro/Bus 92, 130, 152.* **Open** 7.30am-1pm Mon-Sat.
Puerto Madero *Dique 4, AM de Justo al 200 (4313 0187). Bus 4, 130, 152.* **Open** noon-6pm Mon-Fri; 10am-8pm Sat, Sun. **Map** p277 E8.
San Telmo *Defensa 1250, entre San Juan y Cochabamba (no phone). Bus 29, 64, 86, 130, 152.* **Open** noon-6pm Mon-Fri; 10am-7pm Sat, Sun. **Map** p276 C6.
San Isidro Turístico *Ituzaingó 608, y Libertador, San Isidro (4512 3209). Train Mitre or de la Costa to San Isidro/660, 168 bus.* **Open** 8.30-5pm Mon-Fri; 10am-5pm Sat, Sun.
For national tourist info, go to:
Secretaría de Turismo de la Nación *Avenida Santa Fe 883, entre Suipacha y Esmeralda, Retiro (4312 5611/15). Subte C, San Martín/Bus 59, 111, 132, 152.* **Open** 9am-5pm Mon-Fri. **Map** p277 F7.
Freephone information line (8am-8pm Mon-Fri) 0800 555 0016.

Visas

Visas are not required by members of the European Community or citizens of the USA and Canada. Immigration grants a 90-day visa on entry that can be extended by a quick exit out of the country –

Directory

to Uruguay for example – or via the immigration service for AR$100. The fine for overstaying is AR$50; if you do overstay, arrive at the airport early so you can pay the fine.

More information about longer-stay visas for students or business travellers can be obtained from your nearest Argentinian Embassy.

Weights & measures

Argentina uses the metric system, though a few old measures still stand good in the countryside: horses are measured by *manos* (hands) and distances are sometimes measured by *leguas* (leagues).

When to go

Climate

Summer is December-March, and the winter season is July-October. The proximity to the River Plate and sea-level location make the city humid, so the summer heat and winter chill are felt more acutely.

You'll also hear plenty about a local obsession: *sensación térmica*. This isn't the real temperature, but how hot it feels; so prepare yourself for a midsummer day and being told that it is 44ºC (111ºF)!

Spring and autumn are ideal times to visit – gorgeous weather and lots going on. At any time of year, be prepared for rain; heavy storms or a day or so of solid downpour are common. The sun comes out again before long, but pack a raincoat and brolly.

For meteorological information within BA, phone 4514 4253.

Public holidays

The following *feriados*, or public holidays, are fixed from year to year:

1 January (New Year's Day); **Jueves Santo** (Thursday before Easter); **Viernes Santo** (Good Friday); **1 May** (Labour Day); **25 May** (May Revolution Day); **9 July** (Independence Day); **8 December** (Day of the Immaculate Conception); **25 December** (Christmas). For these, the day of the holiday moves to the Monday before if it falls on a Tuesday or Wednesday, or to the Monday following if it falls Thursday to Sunday: **2 April** (Falklands/Malvinas War Veterans Day); **20 June** (Flag Day); **17 August** (San Martín Memorial Day); **12 October** (Columbus Day).

Women

Argentinian men can be macho and flirtatious, but seldom behave agressively, making BA one of the safest cities for female travellers in Latin America.

0800 666 8537 is a 24-hour, city-run hotline to assist women in violent situations, with a network of organisations where they can seek counselling and legal advice. The **Dirección General de la Mujer** (7th Floor, Carlos Pellegrini 211, Microcentro, 4393 6466) is a city-run commission charged with promoting women's welfare – it's not a help desk.

Working in BA

Finding work as an English teacher is not difficult, but opportunities dry up from December to February when everyone goes on holiday. Pay averages AR$15-$25 an hour.

Apart from mixing cocktails or bussing tables, most other job opportunities are published in the *Buenos Aires Herald*, which also occasionally hires novice journalists.

Work permits

Most foreigners work on tourist visas, hopping to Uruguay and back every three months, though, strictly speaking, it's illegal.

To obtain a work permit, you need translated birth, police and medical certificates, sponsorship from an employer, bags of patience and about AR$400. To facilitate the procedure, *escribanos* (notaries) will act on your behalf for a fee of AR$300-$500. Once your papers are in order, you have to exit the country in order to make the official application. Permits are valid for a year; renewal costs another AR$200.

Weather report

Month	Average high	Average low
January	30.4°C (87°F)	20.4°C (69°F)
February	28.7°C (84°F)	19.4°C (67°F)
March	26.4°C (80°F)	17°C (63°F)
April	22.7°C (73°F)	13.7°C (57°F)
May	19°C (66°F)	10.3°C (51°F)
June	15.6°C (60°F)	7.6°C (46°F)
July	14.9°C (59°F)	7.4°C (45°F)
August	17.3°C (63°F)	8.9°C (48°F)
September	18.9°C (66°F)	9.9°C (50°F)
October	22.5°C (73°F)	13°C (55°F)
November	25.3°C (78°F)	15.9°C (61°F)
December	28.1°C (83°F)	18.4°C (65°F)

Average rainfall 124cm (49 inches) per year.
Average sunshine 213 days per year (124 clear, 89 partly cloudy).

Directory

Language & Vocabulary

Porteños living and working in tourist areas usually have some knowledge of English and generally welcome the opportunity to practise it with foreigners. However, a bit of Spanish goes a long way and making the effort to use even a few phrases and expressions will be greatly appreciated.

As in other Latin languages, there is more than one form of the second person (you) to be used according to the formality or informality of the situation. The most polite form is *usted*, and though not used among young people, it may be safer for a foreigner to err on the side of politeness. The local variant of the informal, the *voseo*, differs from the *tú* that you may know from European Spanish. Both forms are given here, *usted* first, then *vos*.

Pronunciation

Spanish is easier than some languages to get a basic grasp of, as pronunciation is largely phonetic. Look at the word and pronounce every letter, and the chances are you will be understood. As a rule, stress in a word falls on the penultimate syllable, otherwise an accent indicates stress. Accents are omitted on capital letters, though still pronounced. The key to learning Argentinian Spanish is to master the correct pronunciation of a few letters and vowels.

Vowels

Each vowel is pronounced separately and consistently, except in certain vowel combinations known as diphthongs, where they combine as a single syllable. There are strong vowels: a, e and o, and weak vowels: i and u. Two weak vowels, as in *ruido* (noise), or one strong and one weak, as in *piel* (skin), form a diphthong. Two strong vowels next to each other are pronounced as separate syllables (as in *poeta*, poet).

a is pronounced like the **a** in army.
e is pronounced like the **a** in say.
i is pronounced like the **ee** in beet.
o is pronounced like the **o** in top.
u is pronounced like the **oo** in mood.
y is usually a consonant, except when it is alone or at the end of the word, in which case it is pronounced like the Spanish **i**.

Consonants

Pronunciation of the letters **f, k, l, n, p, q, s** and **t** is similar to English. **y** and **ll** are generally pronounced like the French *'je'*, in contrast to the European Spanish pronunciation. **ch** and **ll** have separate dictionary entries. **ch** is pronounced as in the English **chair**.
b is pronounced like its English equivalent, and is not distinguishable from letter **v**. Both are referred to as **be** as in English **bet**. **b** is **long b** (called *b larga* in Spanish), **v** is known as **short b** (*b corta*).
c is pronounced like the **s** in sea when before **e** or **i** and like the English **k** in all others.
g is pronounced like a guttural English **h** like the **ch** in loch when before **e** and **i** and as a hard g like **g** in **g**oat otherwise.
h at the beginning of a word is silent.
j is also pronounced like a guttural English **h** and the letter is referred to as **jota** as in English **h**otter.
ñ is the letter **n** with a tilde accent and is pronounced like **ni** in English **oni**on.
r is pronounced like the English **r** but is rolled at the beginning of a word, and **rr** is pronounced like the English **r** but is strongly rolled.
x is pronounced like the **x** in ta**x**i in most cases, although in some it sounds like the Spanish **j**, for instance in Xavier.

Basics

hello *hola*
good morning *buenos días*
good afternoon *buenas tardes*
good evening/night *buenas noches*
OK *está bien*
yes *sí*
no *no*
maybe *tal vez/quizá(s)*
how are you? *¿cómo le va?* or *¿cómo te va?*

how's it going *¿cómo anda?* or *¿cómo andás?*
Sir/Mr *Señor*; **Madam/Mrs** *Señora*
please *por favor*
thanks *gracias*; **thank you very much** *muchas gracias*
you're welcome *de nada*
sorry *perdón*
excuse me *permiso*
do you speak English *¿habla inglés?* or *¿hablás inglés?*
I don't speak Spanish *no hablo castellano*
I don't understand *no entiendo*
speak more slowly, please *hable más despacio, por favor* or *habla más despacio, por favor*
leave me alone (quite forceful) *¡déjeme!* or *¡déjame!*
have you got change *¿tiene cambio?* or *¿tenés cambio?*
there is/there are *hay/no hay*
good/well *bien*
bad/badly */mal*
small *pequeño/chico*
big *grande*
beautiful *hermoso/lindo*
a bit *un poco*; **a lot/very** *mucho*
with *con*; **without** *sin*
also *también*
this *este*; **that** *ese*
and *y*; **or** *o*
because *porque*; **if** *si*
what? *¿qué?*, **who?** *¿quién?*, **when?** *¿cuándo?*, **which?** *¿cuál?*, **why?** *¿por qué?*, **how?** *¿cómo?*, **where?** *¿dónde?*, **where to?** *¿hacia dónde?*
where from? *¿de dónde?*
where are you from? *¿de dónde es?* or *¿de dónde sos?*
I am English *soy inglés* (man) or *inglesa* (woman), **Irish** *irlandés*; **American** *americano/ norteamericano/estadounidense*; **Canadian** *canadiense*; **Australian** *australiano*; **a New Zealander** *neocelandés*
at what time/when? *¿a qué hora?/¿cuándo?*
forbidden *prohibido*
out of order *no funciona*
bank *banco*
post office *correo*
stamp *estampilla*

Emergencies

Help! *¡auxilio! ¡ayuda!*
I'm sick *estoy enfermo*
I need a doctor/policeman/ hospital *necesito un médico/un policía/un hospital*
there's a fire! *¡hay un incendio!*

On the phone

hello *hola*
who's calling? *¿quién habla?*
hold the line *espere en línea*

Getting around

airport *aeropuerto*
station *estación*
train *tren*
ticket *boleto*
single *ida*
return *ida y vuelta*
platform *plataforma/andén*
bus/coach station *terminal de colectivos/omnibús/micros*
entrance *entrada*
exit *salida*
left *izquierda*
right *derecha*
straight on *derecho*
street *calle*; avenue *avenida*;
motorway *autopista*
street map *mapa callejero*;
road map *mapa carretero*
no parking *prohibido estacionar*
toll *peaje*
speed limit *límite de velocidad*
petrol *nafta*; unleaded *sin plomo*

Sightseeing

museum *museo*
church *iglesia*
exhibition *exhibición*
ticket *boleto*
open *abierto*
closed *cerrado*
free *gratis*
reduced *rebajado/con descuento*
except Sunday *excepto los domingos*

Accommodation

hotel *hotel*; bed & breakfast
pensión con desayuno
do you have a room (for this evening/for two people)? *¿tiene una habitación (para esta noche/para dos personas)?*
no vacancy *completo/no hay habitación libre*; vacancy *desocupado/vacante*
room *habitación*
bed *cama*; double bed *cama matrimonial*
a room with twin beds *una habitación con camas gemelas*
a room with a bathroom/shower *una habitación con baño/ducha*
breakfast *desayuno*; included *incluido*
lift *ascensor*
air-conditioned *con aire acondicionado*

Shopping

I would like... *me gustaría...*
Is there a/are there any?
¿hay/habrá?
how much? *¿cuánto?*
how many? *¿cuántos?*
expensive *caro*
cheap *barato*

with VAT *con IVA* (21 per cent valued added tax)
without VAT *sin IVA*
what size? *¿qué talle?*
can I try it on? *¿me lo puedo probar?*

Numbers

0 *cero*
1 *uno*
2 *dos*
3 *tres*
4 *cuatro*
5 *cinco*
6 *seis*
7 *siete*
8 *ocho*
9 *nueve*
10 *diez*
11 *once*; 12 *doce*; 13 *trece*; 14 *catorce*; 15 *quince*; 16 *dieciséis*; 17 *diecite*; 18 *dieciocho*; 19 *diecinueve*; 20 *veinte*; 21 *veintiuno*; 22 *veintidós*
30 *treinta*
40 *cuarenta*
50 *cincuenta*
60 *sesenta*
70 *setenta*
80 *ochenta*
90 *noventa*
100 *cien*
1,000 *mil*
1,000,000 *un millón*

Days, months & seasons

morning *la mañana*
noon *mediodía*;
afternoon/evening *la tarde*
night *la noche*
Monday *lunes*
Tuesday *martes*
Wednesday *miércoles*
Thursday *jueves*
Friday *viernes*
Saturday *sábado*
Sunday *domingo*
January *enero*; February *febrero*; March *marzo*; April *abril*; May *mayo*; June *junio*; July *julio*; August *agosto*; September *septiembre*; October *octubre*; November *noviembre*; December *diciembre*
spring *primavera*
summer *verano*
autumn/fall *otoño*
winter *invierno*

Others

Argentina is Spanish-speaking. But as anyone arriving from Spain or Mexico can attest, the expressive, Italian-laced street slang of Buenos Aires known as *lunfardo*, can, at times, make communicating a confusing if not comical experience.

Talking among friends, *porteños* will start every few sentences with 'che' ('hey, you' or 'mate') in the monotonous way Southern California skateboarders say 'dude'. Of course, the most famous 'che', and everybody's buddy, was Ernesto 'Che' Guevara.

The real fun begins, though, when you start sifting through the more than 1,000 *lunfardo* words and expressions with which *porteños* liven up even the most mundane conversation. Many of them have their origins in the tango underworld at the beginning of the 20th century, but now are used even by presidents to get messages across in a typically straight-shooting manner.

A few choice words or expressions you might hear only in Argentina (and Uruguay) include: *laburo* (work), *piola* (cool), *cana* (police, jail), *chabón* (man, guy), *mina* (girl/chick), *faso* or *pucho* (cigarette), *chamuyar* (sweet talk, bullshit), *chapita* (crazy), *limado* (incapacitated by drugs), *birra* (beer), *bocha* (large quantity, as in money). Although many of the words have a macho connotation, as in *boludo* or *pelotudo* (big balls, used as an insult or to kid a friend), they also, illogically, can take a feminine form as in *boluda* or *pelotuda*.

Some local terms are so out of whack with traditional Spanish that using them incorrectly runs a risk of public ridicule. For example, in Mexico when you ask for a *paja*, you'd be given a straw, whereas to do the same in Argentina would be to confess you want a wank. Meanwhile, the Spanish verb *coger* (to take, or catch, as in a bus) means to fuck in Buenos Aires, inappropriate no matter what you think of public transport. Better to *tomar* a bus instead.

Further Reference

Books

Non-fiction

Jimmy Burns *The Land That Lost Its Heroes: Argentina, the Falklands, and Alfonsin* The essential analysis of *that* conflict.
Jimmy Burns *Hand of God: The Life of Diego Maradona* Lively, intelligent deconstruction of an icon.
S Collier, A Cooper, MS Azzi and **R Martin** *¡Tango!* Currently the definitive guide to tango in English, lavishly illustrated and lovingly collated by the late Simon Collier.
Ronald Dworkin (introduction) *Nunca Más: The Report of the Argentine National Commission on the Disappeared* Still awful to read, the necessary accounts of torture and murder perpetrated by the 1976-83 dictatorship.
Miranda France *Bad Times in Buenos Aires: A Writer's Adventures in Argentina* Insightful travelogue that has fun with the big Argentinian myths: shrinks, sex, machismo and historical myopia.
Uki Goñi *The Real Odessa* How Perón helped his Nazi mates find homes in Argentina after the war.
Diego Armando Maradona *Yo soy el Diego* In Spanish – the best No.10 in his own inimitable words.
Germinal Nogués *Buenos Aires Ciudad Secreta* Psycho-geographer's treasure chest of historical anecdotes and architectural minutiae about BA's barrios and back streets.
Gabriela Nouzeille and **Graciela Montaldo** (eds) *The Argentina Reader* Great collection of primary texts from 16th-century journals to sociological analyses of soccer.
VS Naipaul *The Return of Eva Perón* Old-style travel writing, full of sharp political observations on Argentina in the '70s.
Richard W Slatta *Gauchos and the Vanishing Frontier* Puts the cowboys of the Argentinian countryside in their historical context.
Jason Wilson *Buenos Aires: A Cultural and Literary Companion* Open your eyes to the roots and remains of literary greats and their influence on the city.

Literature

Jorge Luis Borges *Selected Poems* Buenos Aires conjured up through the exquisitely crafted words of Argentina's literary hero.
Julio Cortázar *Hopscotch* The king of experiment's masterpiece jumps between BA and Paris.

Graham Greene *The Honorary Consul* Mainly set in northern Argentina in the 1970s, Greene's novel captures the conflicting currents of Argentinian society.
José Hernández *Martín Fierro* Epic 19th-century poem following the hoof prints of a persecuted gaucho.
Alejandro López *La asesina de Lady Di* If you can read Spanish, laugh out loud to this camp cocktail of superstars, sex and silly provincial girls let loose in big, bad BA.
Tomás Eloy Martínez *Santa Evita* A gripping tale of the afterlife of Eva Perón's corpse. Brilliantly revealing on the blurred boundaries between history and fiction in Argentina.
Tomás Eloy Martínez *The Perón Novel* A fiction-based-on-fact portrait of the general, recounting his return from exile in Madrid.
Manuel Vázquez Montalbán *The Buenos Aires Quintet* Detective Pepe Carvalho tries to find a relative in the city of the disappeared.
Ernesto Sábato *The Tunnel* The definitive existentialist portrait of Buenos Aires, with plenty of gloom and urban alienation.
Domingo Faustino Sarmiento *Facundo: Or, Civilization and Barbarism* A subjective assessment of the country during the era of Rosas and the provincial *caudillos*.

Film

Alejandro Agresti *Buenos Aires viceversa* Earthy, but plot-driven, Ken Loach-like work from one of the best young film directors around.
Adrián Caetano and **Bruno Stagnaro** *Pizza, Birra, Faso* Down and out in Buenos Aires with a gang of street urchins.
Juan Carlos Desanzo *Eva Perón* Esther Goris and Victor Laplace star in this local, no-frills biopic.
Lucrecia Martel *La ciénaga* Award-winning and moving metaphor for a paralysed society.
Alan Parker *Evita* Madonna, Jonathan Pryce, Antonio Banderas and Jimmy Nail... go on, you know you want to.
John Reinhardt *El día que me quieras* A 1935 black-and-white tango classic: Gardel goes to Hollywood.
Fernando 'Pino' Solanas *Sur* Surreal evocation of tango as the buried life of the southern barrios.
Eliseo Subiela *Hombre mirando al sudeste* Where a psychiatric patient challenges notions of reality.
Pablo Trapero *Mundo grúa* Dark humour on the not-so-funny subject of unemployment.

Music

Charly García *Piano Bar* A solo work, considered by many to be the *porteño* rock icon's best.
Carlos Gardel *20 Grandes Exitos* An absolute gem; the voice still comes through as the finest in tango and every track is a classic.
León Gieco *De Ushuaia a La Quiaca* A rocker's anthropological adventure in regional folk music.
Manal *Manal* The first, and perhaps, best blues disc in Spanish.
Daniel Melingo *Tangos Bajos* Tom Waits meets the tango traditions of Edmundo Rivero.
Astor Piazzolla *Buenos Aires: Zero Hour* Late, subtle, stirring tango from the postmodern maestro.
Ariel Ramirez and **Mercedes Sosa** *Misa Criolla* The diva of folk with an interpretation of this elevated folk masterpiece.
Soda Stereo *Canción Animal* Finest hour from the stadium-filling trio who conquered Latin America.
Mercedes Sosa *Mujeres argentinas* Music from pianist Ariel Ramirez, lyrics by historian Félix Luna and the young voice of 'la Sosa'. Songs like 'Juana Azurduy' made history.
Carlos Libedinsky *Narcotango* Sexier than the Gotan Project, *tango electrónica* for dancers, dark bars and horizontal coupling too.
Yerba Brava *Corriendo la coneja* One of the best *cumbia villera* albums – rude, lewd, crude and shrewd.
Atahualpa Yupanqui *El payador perseguido* Master work from the folk poet and guitarist.

On the web

www.argentinesoccer.com Everything you need to know about the national obsession.
www.buenosaires.gov.ar The city government's site, includes details of cultural events.
www.buenosairesherald.com Daily news, resources, and useful classifieds in English.
www.buenosaliens.com Dance music and clubbing in the city.
www.cinenacional.com Spanish-only Argentinian cinema site.
www.gardelweb.com Wonderful site paying homage to Carlos Gardel and the whole of tango culture.
www.piazzolla.com Serious resource for fans of Astor Piazzolla.
www.winesofargentina.com Official site for viticulture and the booming local wine scene.
http://argentina.indymedia.org/ Good for getting the lowdown on new politics and protest.

Directory

Index

Advertisers' Index

Please refer to the relevant sections for contact details.

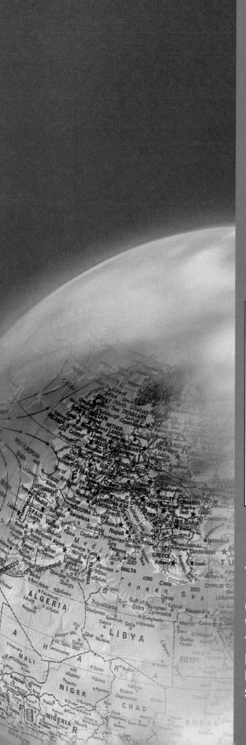

KEY TO MAPS

Place of interest and/ or entertainment	▮▮
Railway station	▮
Railway	▬
Park	▮
Church	✚
Synagogue	✡
Hospital	✚
Tourist information	ℹ
Subte	● ● ● ● ●
Line H (under construction)	- - - - - -
Area	NUÑEZ

Maps

Trips Out of Town

SANTA FE PROVINCE

Embalse Salto Grande

Santa Fe
Paraná

ENTRE RÍOS PROVINCE

Concordia • Salto

Santana do Livramento
Rivera

Colón • Paysandú

URUGUAY

Rosario

San Nicolás de los Arroyos

Gualeguaychú

14 Fray Bentos • Mercedes

San Pedro

12

Colón

Carmelo (p238) (Arg.)

Zárate

San Antonio de Areco (p228)

Campana

9 Belén de Escobar

Carmen de Areco

Capilla del Señor

Tigre (p223)

Colonia del Sacramento (p237)

Canelones • Minas • Rocha

San Andrés de Giles

Pilar

BUENOS AIRES See p272-3

RIO DE LA PLATA

La Paloma

Junín 7

Mercedes

Luján

LA PLATA

Piriápolis 1 Maldonado

Chivilcoy

MONTEVIDEO (p238)

Punta del Este (p241)

Lobos

San Miguel del Monte

Límite del lecho y subsuelo

Saladillo

3 Chascomús

Las Flores

11

BUENOS AIRES PROVINCE

Límite exterior del Río de la Plata

San Clemente del Tuyú

Límite lateral marítimo argentino-uruguayo

Azul

Olavarría

11

Pinamar (p234)

Tandil

Villa Gesell

Laprida

2 Mar Azul

Mar de las Pampas (p235)

Tres Arroyos

Mar del Plata (p233)

11 Miramar

3

Necochea

ATLANTIC OCEAN

Monte Hermoso

VENEZUELA
COLOMBIA
GUYANA
SURINAM
GUAYANA FRANCESA
ECUADOR
PERU
BRAZIL
BOLIVIA
PARAGUAY
Puerto Iguazú (p225)
URUGUAY
Buenos Aires
CHILE
ARGENTINA

0   100 miles
0   200 km

© Copyright Time Out Group 2004

1000 miles
1000 km

Tigre & Zona Norte

Parque de la Costa
TIGRE DELTA

CANAL SAN FERNANDO
Yacht Club Río de la Plata
Club Náutico Belgrano

TIGRE

AVENIDA J B JUSTO
CARUPA

ALVEAR

Club San Fernando
SAN FERNANDO
Yacht Club Argentino

SAN FERNANDO

AVENIDA HIPOLITO YRIGOYEN

CHACABUCO

Marina Norte
Puerto Chico
MARINA NUEVA

AVENIDA AVELLANEDA
VIRREYES

SAN FERNANDO

Cementerio de
San Fernando

Marina Punta Chica
PUNTA CHICA

MALVINAS ARGENTINAS

URUGUAY

RÍO DE LA PLATA

BECCAR

Club Náutico San Isidro

T.B.A. (EX MITRE)
AVENIDA CENTENARIO

AVENIDA ROLON

JOSE INGENIEROS

NEYER

Club Hípico
del Norte

INTENDENTE TOMKINSON

Museo Biblioteca y Archivo Histórico Municipal
SAN ISIDRO
Museo Histórico Municipal
Juan Martín de Pueyrredón
Reserva Ecológica Municipal
Perú Beach
LAS BARRANCAS

NICOLAS AVELLANEDA

SAN ISIDRO
Museo del Rugby

Catedral
de San
Isidro

SAN
ISIDRO

Lomas de
San Isidro

DON BOSCO

ACASSUSO

Hipódromo
de San Isidro

Golf Club
San Isidro

Jockey Club
de Buenos Aires

AVENIDA BERNABE MARQUEZ (CAMINO DE CINTURA)
Campo
de Golf

DARDO ROCHA

MARTINEZ

Parque Ecológico

AVENIDA DE LA UNION NACIONAL

CATAMARCA

DIAGONAL SALTA

ANCHORENA

TOMAS EDISON

DIAGONAL TUCUMAN

Unicenter

AVENIDA PARANA

DEBENEDETTI

LA LUCILA

AVENIDA USAL

SAN LORENZO

CASEROS

LIBERTADOR

BUENOS
AIRES
PROVINCE

Tigre

MARIANO PELLIZA

BORGES

Club Náutico
Puerto de Olivos

MAIPU
OLIVOS

GOBERNADOR UGARTE

MITRE

Residencia
Presidencial

Vicente López

BUENOS
AIRES
CITY

VICENTE LOPEZ

CETRANGOLO

ITALIA
HIPOLITO YRIGOYEN

AVENIDA SAN MARTIN

VICENTE LOPEZ

0   10 miles
0   10 km

© Copyright Time Out Group 2004

0   2.5 miles
0   5 km

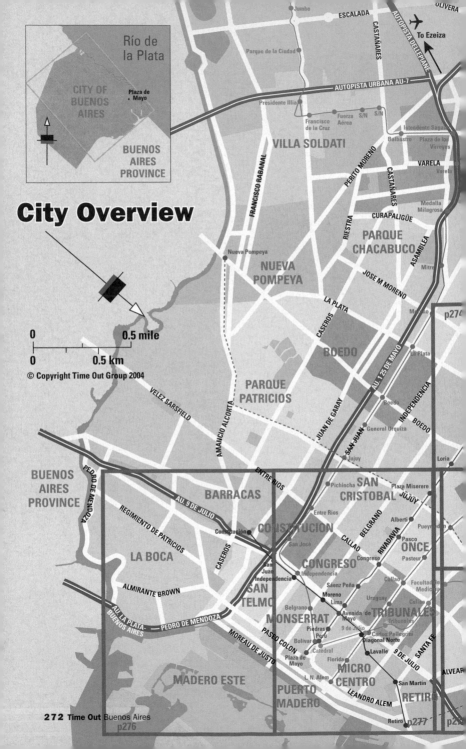

City Overview

Río de la Plata

CITY OF
BUENOS
AIRES

Plaza de
Mayo

BUENOS
AIRES
PROVINCE

0   0.5 mile
0   0.5 km
© Copyright Time Out Group 2004

OLIVERA
ESCALADA
AUTOPISTA DEL PLATA
To Ezeiza
Jumbo
CASTAÑARES
Parque de la Ciudad
AUTOPISTA URBANA AU-7
Presidente Illia
Fuerza   S/N   S/N
Aérea
Francisco
de la Cruz
Intendente Saguier
Balbastro   Plaza de los
Virreyes
VILLA SOLDATI
PERITO MORENO
CASTAÑARES
VARELA
Varela
Medalla
Milagrosa
FRANCISCO RABANAL
CURAPALIGÜE
RIESTRA
PARQUE
CHACABUCO
ASAMBLEA
Nueva Pompeya
JOSE M MORENO
Mitre
NUEVA
POMPEYA
LA PLATA
Moreno   p276
CASEROS
La Plata
BOEDO
AU 1 25 DE MAYO
PARQUE
PATRICIOS
JUAN DE GARAY
Boedo
INDEPENDENCIA
BOEDO
SAN-JUAN
General Orquiza
AMANCIO ALCORTA
Jujuy
Loria
VELEZ SARSFIELD
ENTRE RIOS
Pichincha   SAN
CRISTOBAL
Plaza Miserere
JUJUY
BUENOS
AIRES
PROVINCE
PEDRO DE MENDOZA
AU 9 DE JULIO
BARRACAS
Entre Rios
Alberti
BELGRANO
RIVADAVIA
Pueyrredón
REGIMIENTO DE PATRICIOS
Construcción
CONSTITUCION
CALLAO
Pasco
ONCE
San José
Pasteur
LA BOCA
CASEROS
Congreso
CONGRESO
Congreso
Callao
Facultad de
Medicina
San
Juan
Independencia
Independencia
Sáenz Peña
Moreno
Uruguay
ALMIRANTE BROWN
SAN
TELMO
Belgrano
Lima
Avenida de
Mayo
TRIBUNALES
Tribunales
AU LA PLATA-
BUENOS AIRES
PEDRO DE MENDOZA
MONSERRAT
Piedras
Perú
9 de Julio
Carlos Pellegrini
SANTA FE
PASEO COLON
Bolívar
Diagonal Norte
MOREAU DE JUSTO
Catedral
Lavalle
9 DE JULIO
Florida
MICRO
CENTRO
MADERO ESTE
Plaza de
Mayo
L. N. Alem
ALVEAR
San Martin
PUERTO
MADERO
LEANDRO ALEM
RETIRO
Retiro   p277   p28

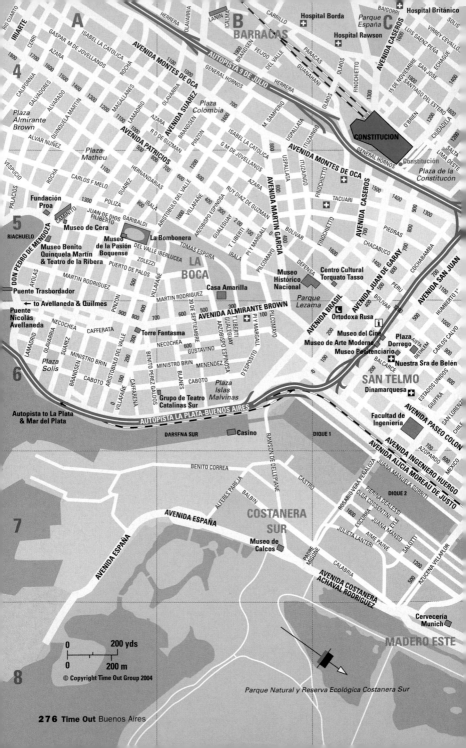

IRIARTE

A

B BARRACAS

Hospital Borda

Parque España

C

Hospital Británico

BAIGORRI

Hospital Rawson

4

Plaza
Almirante
Brown

AVENIDA MONTES DE OCA

AUTOPISTA 9 DE JULIO

Plaza
Colombia

AVENIDA SUAREZ

AVENIDA PATRICIOS

Plaza
Matheu

CONSTITUCIÓN

Constitución

Plaza de la
Constitucón

5

Fundación
Proa

Museo de Cera

RIACHUELO

CAMINITO

Museo Benito
Quinquela Martín
& Teatro de la Ribera

Museo
de la Pasión
Boquense

La Bombonera

AVENIDA MARTIN GARCIA

Museo
Histórico
Nacional

Centro Cultural
Torquato Tasso

AVENIDA JUAN DE GARAY

AVENIDA SAN JUAN

LA
BOCA

Casa Amarilla

Parque
Lezama

AVENIDA BRASIL

Puente Trasbordador

Ortodoxa Rusa

Puente
Nicolás
Avellaneda

to Avellaneda & Quilmes

Torre Fantasma

Museo del Cine

Plaza
Dorrego

Museo de Arte Moderno
Museo Penitenciario

Nuestra Sra de Belén

6

Plaza
Solís

Grupo de Teatro
Catalinas Sur

Plaza
Islas
Malvinas

SAN TELMO

Dinamarquesa

AVENIDA PASEO COLON

Autopista to La Plata
& Mar del Plata

AUTOPISTA LA PLATA-BUENOS AIRES

Facultad de
Ingeniería

AVENIDA INGENIERO HUERGO

DARSENA SUR

Casino

DIQUE 1

AVENIDA ALICIA MOREAU DE JUSTO

BENITO CORREA

DIQUE 2

7

COSTANERA
SUR

AVENIDA ESPAÑA

Museo de
Calcos

AVENIDA COSTANERA
ACHAVAL RODRIGUEZ

Cervecería
Munich

MADERO ESTE

0   200 yds
0   200 m

© Copyright Time Out Group 2004

Parque Natural y Reserva Ecológica Costanera Sur

8

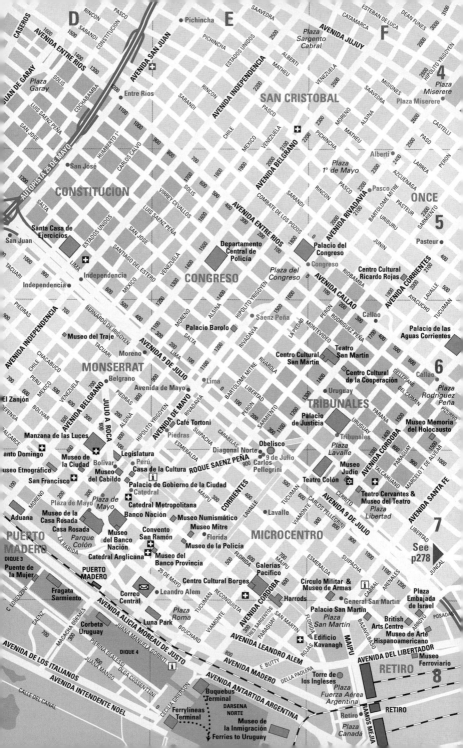

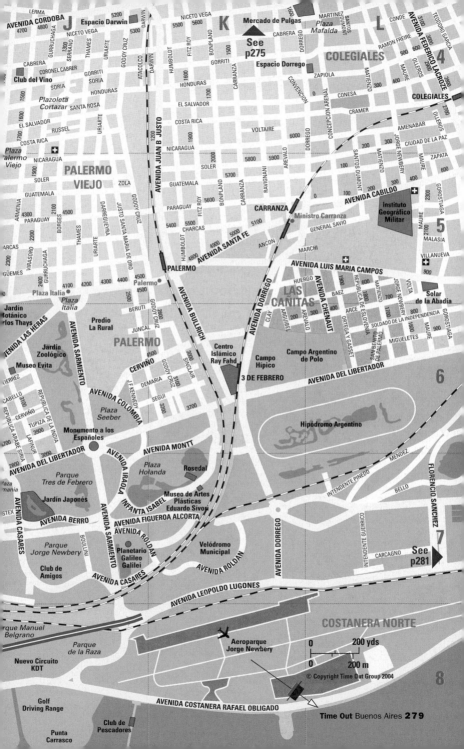

A taste of Time Out City Guides

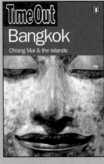

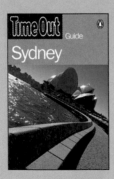

Available from all good bookshops
and at www.timeout.com/shop

www.penguin.com   www.timeout.com

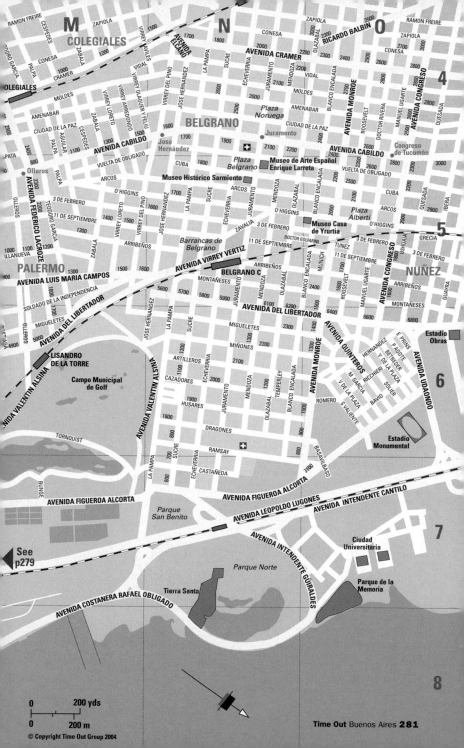

© Copyright Time Out Group 2004

Street Index